THOSE GLAMOROUS

GABORS

Bombshells from Budapest

"There are guilty pleasures. Then there is the master of guilty pleasures, Darwin Porter. There is nothing like reading him for passing the hours. He is the Nietzsche of Naughtiness, the Goethe of Gossip, the Proust of Pop Culture. Porter knows all the nasty buzz anyone has ever heard whispered in dark bars, dim alleys, and confessional booths. And lovingly, precisely, and in as straightforward a manner as an oncoming train, his prose whacks you between the eyes with the greatest gossip since Kenneth Anger. Some would say better than Anger."

—Alan W. Petrucelli
The Entertainment Report
Stage and Screen Examiner
Examiner.com

OTHER BOOKS BY DARWIN PORTER

Those Glamorous Gabors

Gabors

| *Jolie* | *Magda* | *Zsa Zsa* | *Eva* |

Bombshells from Budapest

Darwin Porter

THOSE GLAMOROUS GABORS
BOMBSHELLS FROM BUDAPEST

by Darwin Porter

Manufactured in the United States of America

ISBN 978-1-936003-35-8

Production management and design by Danforth Prince, with
special thanks to the Stanley Mills Haggart Collection, the Woody Parrish-Martin
Collection, the H. Lee Phillips Collection, the Polish National Archives,
and Elsa Maxwell Cafe Society.

Cover designs by Richard Leeds (Bigwigdesign.com)
Videography and Publicity Trailers by Piotr Kajstura

Distributed in North America and Australia
through National Book Network (www.NBNbooks.com)
and in the UK through Turnaround (www.turnaround-uk.com)

1 2 3 4 5 6 7 8 9 10

WITH RESPECT AND ADMIRATION FOR TWO HOT,
ARTICULATE, AND INTELLIGENT WOMEN,
THIS BOOK IS DEDICATED TO

JOLIE GABOR

The FEROCIOUSLY AMBITIOUS MATRIARCH AND SUSTAINER OF
THE GABOR CLAN,
AND TO THE GABOR FAMILY'S CLOSE FRIEND AND CONFIDANTE
(AND MY CLOSE FRIEND AND HOUSEMATE)
THE AUSTRIAN CABARET ENTERTAINER

GRETA KELLER

WITHOUT WHOSE INSIGHTS AND REVELATIONS
THIS BOOK WOULDN'T HAVE BEEN POSSIBLE.

DARWIN PORTER
JULY, 2013

| At a publicity photo shoot for her jewelry store in Manhattan, **Jolie Gabor** proclaimed, "I'm just as glamorous as my daughters." | The fabled Austrian chanteuse, **Greta Keller,** said, "Marlene Dietrich stole my singing style in the 1930s, and I kidnapped her look in the 40s." |

CONTENTS

PROLOGUE

Jolie

It was four o'clock on a dull gray February afternoon in the Hungarian capital of Budapest. The year was 1924. Behind the wheel of her Mercedes, painted a battleship gray, Jolie Gabor was rolling down Andrassy út, known as "The Fifth Avenue of Budapest."

In those days, only six ladies of Budapest owned and drove their own cars.

In the seat beside her sat her beloved daughters—nicknamed "Magdika," age 9; "Zsazsilka," 7; and "Evika," 5.

Suddenly the sun broke through for the first time that day, adding at extra sparkle to Jolie's diamonds. While getting dressed, she'd told her beautiful daughters, "These are my daytime diamonds. For the evening, I really dazzle. That's when a woman should bring out the king's ransom stones."

She wanted to make a spectacular appearance that afternoon at tea. Both Jolie and her daughters wore scarlet-colored dresses that matched the upholstery of the Mercedes. The clothing had been designed by Jeanne Lanvin, who also designed matching gray coats for each of the Gabors, which duplicated the exact color of the vehicle itself.

The fashion-conscious Jolie preferred the French designer because she was celebrated for her mother-and-daughter outfits and exquisite *robes de style,* as well as for her modern and global approach to fashion. Before heading out, Jolie had also doused her daughters in *Après l'Ondée* by Guerlain (1906). "It's a piece of art created from hellotrope, violette, and iris that gently touches our skin like a scent from heaven."

Arriving at the Café Gerbeaud, the Gabors were greeted by a doorman in a puce-colored uniform. Starched, gloved, and beribboned, the daughters emerged first onto the sidewalk.

Franz Lutsky was the manager of the Café Gerbeaud, on Vörösmarty tér, which had been founded in 1858 by Swiss confectioner Emile Gerbeaud. It was Jolie's favorite rendezvous. He always reserved the best table for her. Privately he referred to her as "This Magyar mother hen with her three beautiful spring chickens."

1

Although the café was bustling at that time of day, nearly all of the patrons stopped to take note of the new customers making such a glamorous entrance.

Later, Magda would recall, "Everything that mother did in those days was to teach us a lesson. That day at the café, the lesson involved how to make an entrance. Her forever advice was, 'When you arrive in town, don't keep it a secret.'"

The Gabors were about to embark on a life so glamorous Jolie often said in later years, "No one would believe it!"

As designer Donald F. Reuter put it: "The early lives of the Gabors is a fascinating tale that reads like a cross between *Doctor Zhivago* and *Gypsy,* with a generous sprinkling of *Fiddler on the Roof* and *Auntie Mame* thrown in for good measure."

With a grand flourish, the *maître d'hotel* guided Jolie, followed by her "three *vonderful wimmen*" down the long railroad-style layout of the café until they arrived at one of the sitting areas, decorated in a tone of scarlet that matched their dresses. The aging waiter, who had been born in 1854, knew what to bring to table. The aromatic coffee had been dispensed from a *cafetière* whose perimeter was sheathed in hand-painted panels of Herend porcelain—one of only three on Earth, and the confection he brought was the celebrated chocolate-and-marzipan royal torte. "It's positively sinful," Jolie told her daughters. "But a woman born into a man's world must be sinful to advance herself."

Away from her domineering husband, Vilmos Gabor, Jolie always seized the opportunity to lecture her daughters about the future roles they'd play.

"*Dahlinks,* each of you will grow up to become a fabled Hungarian beauty. But you must never become a delicate porcelain figure. The blood of Attila the Hun flows through your veins, the blood of Genghis Khan. You were meant to conquer as the daughters of a once-great empire. Your homeland is a nation of powerful warriors and passionate lovers. Each of you will grow up to marry a king...or at least a prince."

"A few months ago, in the lobby of the Ritz Hotel here in Budapest, I was stunned to encounter the handsome, charming, and very rich Prince of Wales—with his entourage—parading through. Last week, I sent him a letter acknowledging our meeting, along with that gorgeous photograph of you, Zsa Zsa. I told him that you were growing more beautiful every day, and that in just a few years, you'd be one of the most dazzling beauties of Europe, fit to sit on his throne as Queen of England when he becomes King."

Zsa Zsa wasn't embarrassed or intimated by Jolie's behavior and point of view. In fact, she amplified her mother's idea with: "I'd be a queen and rule over all the British colonies—and I'd also become the Empress of India."

CHAPTER ONE
Budapest—*"In Za Beginning"*

The mother of the three famous Gabor sisters was born in Budapest in 1896 to Josef and Francesca Tilleman, who named her Jancsi, which later evolved into "Jolie."

Along with her three sisters, Jolie grew up in a *belle époque* city, once the seat of a great empire. At the turn of the 20th Century, Budapest was a lighthearted city full of gaiety and *joie de vivre.* The bustling cafés were filled with gypsy music at night, and fashionable ladies promenaded through the parks in the latest *couture* creations from Paris.

That gaiety ended with the debut of World War I, in which Hungary suffered terribly, its luster dimmed for the rest of the century. Even so, the Tillemans still dressed well, ate well, and lived well, thanks to the family's successful costume jewelry business, "The Diamond House." It specialized in artificial pearls.

After an "ugly duckling" childhood—"I was all pimply-faced"—Jolie blossomed into an attractive teenager. At the age of seventeen, she was pursued by various suitors. One was her father's amorous partner. At a costume ball one night, he escorted her out onto a terrace. As music from an orchestra filtered into the Hungarian night, he glided her into a tango dip. With his right arm, he clasped her narrow waist and with this left hand, he cupped the nape of her swan neck as he passionately kissed her.

"As I looked up from my first real kiss, I didn't know it at the time, but I was staring into the face of my future husband, Vilmos Gabor," Jolie later recalled. "I found out later that he was a major in the Hungarian cavalry."

Freed from her suitor's embrace, she confronted (and appraised) Vilmos directly. The lamps cast light on his thick hair, the blondish color of sand. It was tousled into great scallops. His eyes were as black as the uniform he wore, which was decorated with gold braid and stripes from his regiment. His trousers were tight, showing off shapely legs, and he was a man of broad shoulders and imposing physique.

"As I met him, he snapped his highly polished black boots together as he kissed my hand," she said. "For him, it was love at first sight. For me, it was the love that never happened. In the days ahead, he wooed me."

"I didn't want to get married," Jolie said. "Even then, I was an independent woman in an era when wives were mere chattel to their husbands."

"I wanted to pursue a career in the theater, becoming Hungary's answer to Sarah Bernhardt or Eleonora Duse," Jolie said. Actually, her role model was closer to home. Jolie had never missed a performance of Sári Fedák, the great Hungarian actress and singer, one of the celebrated *prima donnas* of her time.

Fedák was already forty-five, and Jolie dreamed of replacing her. She fantasized about the older woman's romantic life. In 1922, she'd married the writer, Ferenc Molnár. Six years later, during their divorce proceedings, he accused his wife of having affairs with forty-two different men.

A **Hungarian Hussar,** between duels and horse maneuvers, finds romance on the Danube. When Vilmos married Jolie, his brutality spilled into her boudoir.

Of course, Jolie was committed to completely avoiding politics, which had led to Fedák's imprisonment after she agitated for Hungary to ally itself with the Russian Red [i.e., socialist] Army during World War I.

[Fedák,, who had publicly endorsed the virtues of Nazi Germany, went to prison again after World War II because she'd rallied Hungary to continue its fight against the Allied armies as spearheaded by the U.S..]

Dedicated to a career as an actress, Jolie found her plans derailed by Vilmos. With a feather in his cap and a closet full of dashing uniforms, he was the epitome of a Hussar. She remembered him as "Having the flash of Douglas Fairbanks (Senior)."

Sári (Zsa Zsa) Fedák, the tragic Hungarian diva and nationalist who inspired the name Jolie assigned to her second daugher.

"In just a short time, this older man proposed to this schoolgirl, namely me," Jolie said. "In spite of my better judgment, I said yes, although I knew that many, many lovers lay in my future, with perhaps another husband to come along the way, perhaps three, maybe even four or more."

"The only reason I married Vilmos was to escape the strict discipline of home," she claimed. "I was not physically attracted to him. His uniform

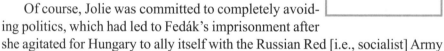

4

was far more dashing than he was. Yet I found myself accepting his proposal. The discipline from my parents, Francesa and Josef, was so strict I wanted to escape almost at any cost."

"I postponed falling in love by agreeing to marry Vilmos," she said. "I'm a romantic. I went to the silent movies once or at least twice a week. I wanted one of the lovers on the screen, my favorite being Rudolf Valentino. I dreamed of a Sheik capturing me, taking me in his arms, a real kidnapping. In his desert tent, I wanted him to rip off my clothes and devour me. Instead, even though I have a Gypsy spirit in my soul, I agreed to settle down with Vilmos. I could always dump him later."

Vilmos: Furious that his wife produced only girls.

"I had another secret reason for marrying him," Jolie recalled. "I was still a virgin. To play a sophisticated role on the stage, I knew I could not come out as a virgin. I had to know what it was like to have been made a woman by a man in bed."

As part of a bizarre request, she made Vilmos sign a contract, agreeing to stay married to him for just six months. Conceivably during this time, she would become pregnant with his infant son and future heir. "Vilmos did not want a girl. As our contract stated, even if I'd left him after six months before the boy was born, I was to turn the infant over to Vilmos. I agreed, figuring that with my stage career, I didn't want to be hampered by bringing up a baby."

On her wedding night, she found her military husband nervous and unsure of himself. To entice him to bed, so she could lose her virginity, she stripped off her clothing, except for an almost transparent veil.

A family portrait, circa 1925: **Jolie** and **Vilmos** hold their beautiful daughters *(left to right)*, **Zsa Zsa**, **Eva**, and the oldest, **Magda**.

"In the living room, I fancied myself dancing the notorious dance of Salomé with seven veils. Vilmos, I imagined, was King Herod, but I had only one veil, not seven."

"It seemed to work," she said. "He escorted me to the bedroom and cut off the light before disrobing. I'd never seen a man's *pimpi* before. I still didn't know what it looked like, so I felt it with my fingers. Nothing happened to it, so he finally rolled off me and went to sleep."

"It took until the second night for me to lose my virginity. I dreamed it would be like Ramon Novarro taking me in his arms and making mad, passionate love to me. It was nothing like that. It was all about jabbing pain, pain, and more pain. Not only that, but he bit my breasts so hard I was left with black and blue marks the next day."

He was so savage, she accused him of being a sex maniac. "He practically bit off my left nipple."

The following night, she infuriated him when she came into a hotel dining room in plunging *décolletage* which showed off her bruises. She exposed so much cleavage that he accused her of dressing like a *kurvas*. "You're so common," he said, practically spitting out his words. "You look like a low-rent prostitute from the street."

During their honeymoon in Italy, when he became embroiled in nine different fistfights because he claimed that men looked at his teenage bride "that way," she realized what a violent, jealous man she'd married.

Back in Budapest, she was almost suicidal after her tumultuous honeymoon, where Vilmos had to pay several fines to the police for attacking men who even smiled at her.

She endured life with him for only three months. One night, she emptied the money from his wallet and deposited all her jewelry into her mother's vault. Then she boarded the night train to Vienna, where she checked into a suite at the Grand Hotel, hoping to meet some rich, eligible bachelor.

In Budapest, Vilmos filed a report with the police, claiming his young wife had been kidnapped. Through informants, the police learned she'd taken a train to Vienna. They tracked her down to the Grand Hotel.

"With his pockets filled with diamonds," [Jolie's words], Vilmos traveled by train to Vienna to bring her back. His timing was right: That very afternoon, a doctor had informed Jolie that she was pregnant.

"At last, you're going to deliver me my son and heir," Vilmos told her when their train pulled into the main terminus in old Pest.

A taxi drove them to their *grand bourgeois* residence on the fifth floor of 31 Múzeum Körut.

Months later, on June 11, 1914, Vilmos got what he called "the disappointment of my life," when Magdolna (Magda) Gabor

Behind the wheel, **Vilmos Gabor** shows off his birthday present from **Jolie**, taking a rare back seat. Seated on the running board are future connoisseurs of expensive cars, **Eva** *(left)* and **Zsa Zsa** *(right)*.

was born. "You promised me a boy, you bitch!" Vilmos screamed at Jolie.

Whereas Vilmos was a sandy blond, he soon saw that the hairs growing on Magda were red. Immediately, he accused Jolie of having an affair with a red-haired man.

Jolie was horribly disappointed as well, viewing her daughter as "ugly and wrinkled. Not only that, but she cried day and night for her first two years. She drove me crazy. And to think I gave up a glittering career on the stage for this."

After the birth of Magda, with Jolie putting on weight, she agreed to extend her six-month contract with Vilmos and stay with him until she conceived another child. "This time, I promise you it will be a boy."

***

After two months, Jolie changed her mind, referring to her reversal as "a woman's privilege. I hear the siren call of the theater, and I must leave you," Jolie told Vilmos.

Impulsively, he went into the nursery and picked up baby Magda, who was wrapped in a pink blanket. He carried it to an open window, and, still holding the child, extended his arms, threatening to drop her five stories unless Jolie agreed to stay on with him.

Screaming and shouting that he was a madman, she finally broke down and, in tears, agreed to stay on until the birth of her next child, as she had originally promised.

"That night, the sex maniac attacked me again, biting and chewing at my flesh like some vampire from Transylvania."

Apparently, he also impregnated her that night. "You will deliver me a son this time, or else you may live to regret it."

"How dare you threaten me?" she shouted at him.

"Historically, Hussars and Turks beheaded their enemy. My sword is sharp. I'd hate to use it on you."

"You wouldn't dare!" she said.

"Don't test your luck," he answered. "A son...or else."

Three Hungarian Graces *(left to right)*—baby fat **Magda, Zsa Zsa**, and **"Little Eva."**

Jolie sparked early sibling rivalries by teaching them to fight each other "with your little fists."

Zsa Zsa was usually the winner.

As a means of defying him, Jolie dined out every night, often going to the theater, the opera, or the ballet with friends. Although her doctor advised her to stay home as she neared term, she refused to obey.

On the night of February 6, 1917, she attended Budapest's Orpheum Theater for a performance of a play by Shakespeare. At an *après-theater* dinner at one o'clock in the morning, Jolie told friends, "I should have been up there on stage tonight playing Lady Macbeth. The no-talent bovine who played her was eighty if she were a day. True, she got four standing ovations. But with me in the role, I'd have gotten twenty."

She'd consumed a large meal, beginning with love apple soup. She'd taken generous helpings from platters of jellied paprika fish, poached breasts of chicken in champagne, and roasted goose with apricot stuffing. She also "just had to sample" the Hussar steak and, of course, beef goulash with dumplings. Finally, she ate the queen of all pastries, the Dobos torte, before her final order of apricot *palcsinta* with fresh whipped cream.

In the middle of her favorite dessert, she began to groan. Her friends told her the pains were from all her food intake. "You must be feeding quintuplets," a friend suggested.

But Jolie believed it was labor pains. "That son that Vilmos demands can't wait to escape from my womb, so he can start chasing after all the beautiful girls in Budapest."

In a taxi, she was taken to her home, where she was placed on a pink silk canopied bed. The doctor was called, but couldn't get there on time. Fortunately, a woman on the Gabor household staff also doubled as a midwife. She delivered the baby.

Future coquettes in training: *(left to right)* **Eva**, **Zsa Zsa**, and **Magda**. Jolie took them to the theater every week "so they would get stardust in their eyes."

"Tell me it's a boy," Jolie called out. "*Please, oh god, a boy!*"

"It's a beautiful girl," the midwife said.

"My second child entered the world as a greedy little monster child," Jolie later recalled. "She attacked my breasts with all the savagery of Vilmos on the second night of my honeymoon. She was voracious, as if she were sucking the life's blood from me. She consumed so much milk she nearly choked to death."

The choking seizures continued for three days. Horrified at disappointing Vilmos a second time, Jolie became increasingly irrational. At one point, she confessed that she had considered feigning sleep during one of her daughter's choking seizures. "I know it was crazy, but I thought of let-

8

ting her choke to death. I would wake up later, scream for help, and define it all as an accident."

Jolie named her second daughter Sári after Sári Fedák, "whom I despised, envied, worshipped, and admired." *La Fedák,* as she was known in the theater, had been nicknamed "Zsa Zsa" by her own daughter. When Jolie learned about that, she decided to nickname her own daughter Zsa Zsa, too.

After a disappearance of five days, Vilmos returned home to learn that Jolie had given birth to yet another daughter. Nervous about receiving him, Jolie made herself as beautiful as possible, even weaving pink orchids into her hair. She wore a see-through black *négligée,* and also ordered the maid to place a silver bucket of champagne on ice by her bedside.

Taking her hand, Vilmos looked into her eyes. "You must not leave me yet. You owe it to me to try one more time to give me a son. Then I will stand aside and let you pursue a career on the stage."

The next morning, a summons arrived from the lawyer of a woman who claimed that Vilmos was the father of her newly born son. "It's ridiculous," he said. "I hardly know her. She's fat with a pachyderm ass. She was already pregnant when I met her."

Jolie was delighted to hear of his affair. At last, she'd found a good reason to divorce him. The next day, the summons was withdrawn—perhaps Vilmos had paid off the fat lady. He came home from his regimental headquarters the following night and entered Jolie's boudoir with two presents—a big green emerald and a blue fox stole. The question of adultery never came up again.

During the months ahead, Jolie and Vilmos virtually lived in separate worlds, though sharing the same apartment. Almost every night, she went out with friends.

Jolie was once again dining *après theater* when she experienced labor pains associated with the birth of Zsa Zsa.

She partied with friends until midnight of February 10, 1919, laughing, dancing, and gossiping, before heading for a late-night supper in a gypsy restaurant which was known for its old-fashioned Hungarian specialities.

She ordered jellied and highly seasoned pigs' feet with a zesty red horseradish sauce, followed by a huge slice of poppy seed cake with chocolate whipped cream. "I was always eating, eating, eating."

[*In 1962, as a by-product of her deep-seated interest in food and its preparation, she'd publish Jolie Gabor's Family Cookbook, featuring an assortment of her favorite Hungarian recipes.*]

At two o'clock, as the evening was winding down, Jolie was enjoying coffee and cognac when labor pains set in. It was a repeat of her same experience giving birth to Zsa Zsa. She was rushed home, where once again, the midwife on her household staff assisted her during childbirth, since the doctor who'd been summoned didn't make it on time.

When she opened her eyes and stared into the face of the stocky midwife, she asked, "Tell me at long last that it's a boy."

"Kislány," the woman said as Jolie's heart sank. That meant "little girl" in Hungarian.

"My spirits improved when I stared into the face of my baby," Jolie said. "If it were a girl, I had already decided to call her Eva. She was beautiful, far more beautiful than Magda or Zsa Zsa. Eva was blonde with blue eyes and had the most stunning pink skin."

"As I lay back in bed, I knew I had failed once again to deliver a boy," she recalled. "That meant I would never get rid of my bastard husband, who still ranted incessantly about my giving birth to a son and an heir. I decided there and then I would have no more children. Vilmos had spent his last night in my boudoir. Even though forced to abandon my dream of becoming an actress, I could reinvent myself and seek a new role in life—and I was determined to do just that."

With a steely reserve, she rose from bed on the second day. Even though the skies had been gloomy and cloudy for days, this February morning was

"Look what I produced!" **Jolie** proclaimed when this picture was taken **in the mid-1920s.** *(left to right)* **Eva, Zsa Zsa,** and **Magda.** "I want all of them to grow up to be the most beautiful, the most elegant, the most glamorous, and the most pursued by counts, princes, or kings."

Four bathing beauties on the beach at Lake Balaton in the mid-1920s: *(left to right)* **Eva, Zsa Zsa,** and **Magda,** with Mama **Jolie.**

Hungarian Hussars liked their women with extra poundage in those days, and bathing beauties wore high heels to the beach.

bright and sunny. Her appetite had returned, and she needed to fortify herself, to face Vilmos once again with her failure to deliver a boy.

She ordered the cook to prepare a dozen sour cream *palcsinta* (pancakes) with fresh strawberries and sour cream.

Athough she was only twenty-three, she lamented the loss of youth. "That was considered too old for a woman with a husband and three children to begin a career on the stage," she said.

"I was trapped in a loveless marriage, evoking a situation that would happen to each of my daughters," Jolie said. "In a case like that, my advice is for a woman to take a young lover. I'd met several handsome young men in Vilmos' regiment. I noticed they had a gleam in their eyes when they gazed upon me. I was still very attractive and desirable as a woman."

"Out of my womb and into my arms, god had delivered three beautiful daughters to me. And I knew just what to do with them. I would mold them into the three most famous daughters in the world—that's what. No small undertaking, I might add."

"Like I do with all my favorite dishes, I would sprinkle them with my fiery paprika and turn them loose to spice up a world that had grown dull."

"I wanted Magda, Zsa Zsa, and Eva to do *everything,* have all sorts of experiences, grand or small—lovers, rich husbands, diamonds, rubies, emeralds, mink coats, palaces. I wanted them to grow up and leave Hungary and conquer London, Paris, New York, Hollywood."

"If they did not manage to marry a king, then a prince might do, certainly a count, earl, or a duke if all else fails."

"I will teach them to climb to the top of the ladder and not to let anything stand in their way. If they break the hearts of men along the way, so be it. Hearts were made to be broken. The clever woman, however, does not allow her own heart to be broken."

"Men have used and abused women for centuries. I want my daughters to reverse that and use men the way women have been used. Like the black widow spider, they can discard their mate when he is of no more use to them. If they should lose a husband or lover, then find another. There are so many men in this world, and so little time."

Putting her thoughts aside, Jolie rose from the breakfast table after downing her last pancake. "Vilmos trained his men to become mighty Hussars. I will train my daughters with the same military discipline. How else can I turn them into the century's greatest courtesans?"

***

As her daughters grew older, Jolie demonstrated her policy of tough love.

11

Vilmos owned a summer cottage on the largest concentration of fresh water in Central Europe, Lake Balaton, where the fashionable people of Budapest went for the summer. *[Since Hungary has no seacoast, Lake Balaton, whose length of 50 miles and shoreline of 120 miles is surrounded by vineyards, was (and is) its "Riviera."]*

On the Pier at Lake Balaton, oil on canvas, circa 1937, by the influential modernist Hungarian painter **Béla Iványi-Grünwald** (1867-1940).

In an environment like the one evoked by this painting, the Gabor family spent summer holidays beside Hungary's inland sea.

One hot summer afternoon, when Vilmos was at his business headquarters in Budapest, Jolie took all three of her daughters out in the family rowboat, paddling to the center of this vast lake.

One by one, Jolie tossed her daughters overboard, even though they did not know how to swim. The girls screamed in terror, but Jolie shouted at them, "Swim! Baby puppies can do it. So can you."

As her mouth filled with water, Eva, the youngest of the trio, was frightened more than the others. The girls struggled to reach the side of the rowboat, but as they did, Jolie rowed farther away until the boat was out of reach of the little girls.

"Amazingly," as Magda later recalled, "we didn't drown. Floundering and choking on water at first, we managed to stay afloat until mama allowed us back in the boat. Still terrified, we climbed in. All three of us were filled with Lake Balaton cocktails. It felt like we'd swallowed gallons."

As her daughters were choking and spitting up lakewater, Jolie informed them. "Somehow you didn't drown. You've just learned one of life's most important lessons: How to survive."

***

As the girls became old enough to go to school, Jolie noticed that each of them had a completely different personality.

"I set high goals for each of my daughters," claimed Jolie. "I wanted each of them to play the piano as well as Arthur Rubinstein, especially when it came to Chopin. After all, he was one of the greatest pianists of the 20th Century. I wanted them to skate as well as that Olympic champion, Sonja Henie. I wanted them to sing like those great *chanteuse* artists Zara (aka Sara) Leander from Sweden or Vienna's own Greta Keller. And for ballet, who else but Anna Pavlova?"

"I demanded they take not only piano lessons, but ballet lessons, horseback riding lessons, tennis lessons. I wanted them to be the most glamorous, the most elegant, the most beautiful, the most pursued by men, the most talented. After all, I gave up my theatrical career for the little devils. They owed it to me to succeed."

Almost from the beginning, Jolie realized how different Magda was from Eva and Zsa Zsa. "To understand Magda is to understand the flower that closes its petals to the sun. She blooms in private with alluring timidity."

"Magda was the studious one," Jolie said. "We predicted she'd grow up to become the Madame Curie of Hungary. She always had her nose in a book when she wasn't at the piano. She was the most formal and reserved of my daughters. We nicknamed her the Duchess. Magda was the first of my daughters to learn French, German, and English. Each of my daughters would become proficient in four languages. Eva and Zsa Zsa would become celebrated as blondes—dye jobs, of course—but Magda had stunning Titian red hair that was natural. Her eyes were green like those of certain black cats."

"Magda was going to be the brain of the sisters," Jolie claimed. "I also thought she would be the most talented. When she was less than a year old, I brought her out on stage at a charity show."

"Magda was also the most snobbish and the best dresser," Jolie said. "When I'd take my daughters to tea, she would look at how Zsa Zsa and Eva were dressed. 'Oh, mother, must we have tea with these peasant girls from the field?' No wonder we called her Duchess."

In contrast to Magda, Zsa Zsa was a fat little girl who became a tomboy as she grew older. She was clearly the apple of Vilmos' eye. She remembered him as a man of passion, filled with jealousy and rage, usually directed at Jolie. But he doted on his second daughter, even though she had not been born a boy.

He set out to make her one, taking her with him to wrestling matches and prizefights, where at an early age, she learned to scream for blood.

He dressed her in gray leather Tyrolean pants

Jolie's Imperial mother, **Francesca Tilleman**, *the matriarch who inspired Zsa Zsa's appreciation for champange and diamonds:*

with a green felt hat with a feather in it.

Almost daily, he demanded that she take fencing lessons. Amazingly, at the age of fifteen, facing stiff competition, she became the Junior Fencing Champion of Hungary.

She was also the favorite of her maternal grandmother, Francesca Tilleman, the jeweler. Whenever Zsa Zsa came down with some illness, such as flu, her grandmother—"dripping in diamonds"—came to see her with a chilled bottle of champagne. "Even though I was only eight years old, Francesca claimed that champagne cured all sickness," Zsa Zsa later said. "It was because of Francesca that I became addicted to champagne and diamonds—not in that order, of course, *dahlink.*"

Vilmos called Zsa Zsa "my little soldier," and he lamented that women were barred from serving as soldiers in the Hungarian army. "Someday, perhaps not in my lifetime, women will be allowed to fight on the battlefields along with men. What authorities sometimes don't realize is that women are often the deadliest of the sexes."

The most beautiful of the Gabors, Eva decided at an early age that she wanted to become an actress, fulfilling a dream of Jolie's that was never realized. "One day, the entire world will take notice of me," she boasted to her parents.

Her earliest memories were of being taken to the National Theater or the National Opera. "Almost the first thing I recall was wearing this white organdy dress and being introduced to Grace Moore, the great blonde-haired opera diva, who became a movie star. She was from some place called Tennessee."

*Eva's role model: American opera diva, **Grace Moore**. So strong was Eva's attempt to emulate Miss Moore, that she became the first of the Gabors to emigrate to Hollywood.*

"I asked Miss Moore for her autograph, and she graciously obliged," Eva recalled. "From that night forth, Miss Moore became my role model. I wanted to grow up and become surrounded by adoring fans as the flashbulbs popped. My second meeting with her, however, was not so memorable."

"In Hollywood during the war, I met her again and reminded her of our first meeting in Budapest. She did not remember. She said, 'Surely you don't expect me to recall every fan who asked me for my autograph?' I was a bit insulted by that, because I considered myself very memorable. Even so, I was sorry to read of her early death in that plane crash in Copenhagen in 1947."

Even at the age of seven, Eva began to fear

the oncoming wrinkles of her future. At the National Theater, she'd seen "actresses who look like great-grandmothers playing roles for women in their twenties. Imagine a fifty-five year old Juliet," she said.

At home, Eva decided that Tuesday would be the day set regularly aside for her beauty sleep. She covered her face with her mother's cold cream and slept all day.

"My aim," she told Jolie, "is to stay young and beautiful forever."

Eva's fondest memories were of Josef Tilleman, her maternal grandpapa, who would take her on his knee. He predicted that she would marry a tall blonde-haired man who would take her to settle in the United States. He called her "my little honeydrop." She didn't realize until she grew older that many of his touches and fondlings of her were inappropriate.

"I predict, my little Eva, that you will live in a fishbowl, just like a guppy," he said. "You'll be surrounded by agents, publicity men, photographers, and fans. It is written in the goulash."

She recalled, "He actually said, 'written in the goulash.'"

"Grandpapa was right," she said, years later. "What he didn't tell me was that I would be called 'a bombshell,' 'dynamite,' 'blonde fission,' 'radioactive,' and 'the girl who broke the Geiger counter.' The press made me sound like a waste product of Oak Ridge."

"I feared my girls were growing up too fast in front of my eyes," Jolie said. "To my horror, I suspected they might become a flirt like me. It was in my nature: I was a natural born flirt, much to the outrage of Vilmos. Even at a family outing in a grand hotel dining room, waiters would discreetly slip me messages from possible suitors."

"My girls also began to flirt with boys, even though Vilmos warned them that the male sex was a menace," Jolie said. "To my knowledge, they had never seen a man in the nude. Vilmos has a natural modesty around the house, except in the boudoir."

"Magda was the first to notice a possible physical difference in boys and girls. A young Hussar dropped in for tea one afternoon. He was in Vilmos' regiment. As was the style, this handsome blonde wore tight black trousers."

"Magda kept noticing a large bulge in his pants when he sat down on the sofa. Later, after he'd gone, she asked me, "Do you think that charming young man has some unnatural growth down there? I don't bulge like that. Neither does Zsa Zsa, nor does Eva."

"I told Magda, 'No, no, my little dear. Boys are very different from girls. Haven't you noticed? I have breasts. Vilmos is flat-chested."

"Of course, I have noticed that," Magda said. "But I'm talking about a bulge down there. What was that Hussar hiding from us?"

"You see, men have this thing down there," Jolie said. "When they become

15

excited, the blood rushes to it and it grows large. You are far too young to be concerned with such matters. But in time, you will find out. It is nature's way. That thing the man has can plant a seed inside you, which will make a baby grow there. You surely don't want that to happen to you. So boys and their thing are to be avoided at all costs."

***

It was the custom of the day for rich Budapesters to send their teenage daughters to a finishing school in Switzerland. At the fashionable cafés, Jolie learned that the academy of choice was Madame Subilia's School for Young Ladies at Lausanne, which opened onto the beautiful waters of Lake Geneva.

Being the oldest, Magda was the first daughter sent to Switzerland. Although she did well at school, she was dreadfully homesick and wrote letters to Jolie almost every day.

When Zsa Zsa was sent there the following year, she turned out to be much more independent than Magda. Zsa Zsa stayed away for one and a half years, and didn't return home for holidays such as Christmas.

"Instead of going over those dull school books about history and mathematics, I read French novels," Zsa Zsa said. "Almost nightly, I dreamed of being kidnapped by some dashing knight on a white horse. In my dreams, I would become his sex slave and nightly have to give in to his outrageous demands. I had learned a lot by reading passages from the pornographic books of my father, which I accidentally found in his library one day. Several were illustrated. Unlike Magda, I knew what a young man looked like without his trousers."

Her favorite book, which she'd stolen from Vilmos, was entitled *The Diary of a Young Cadet of the Hungarian Hussars.* It was the story of his sexcapades, seducing a string of women in sumptuous *maisons de luxe,* his conquests ranging from waitresses to married women of the aristocracy.

Eventually, it became time for Zsa Zsa to return home. Her account and Jolie's account of her arrival at the Budapest train station differ remarkably.

As Zsa Zsa remembered it at the time, she was strikingly beautiful. "There was no street I could walk down without the boys hollering and whistling at me. I was no longer a chubby tomboy."

Jolie met her at the station and recalled her disappointment in seeing her daughter. "Pockets of fat hung off her, and she had red freckles, red pigtails, even red eyebrows. At school, my ugly duckling had majored in trouble. Beginning on her very next day back in Budapest, my beauty regime for her would begin, if I had to drag her in and out of every beauty salon in both Buda and Pest."

Unlike Magda and Zsa Zsa, Eva did not get to go to that finishing school. "I was born with a silver spoon in my mouth—a chauffeur to take me to school, servants living in their dark quarters downstairs, a closet full of pretty dresses."

"But when it was time for Vilmos to send me to Lausanne, he announced that it was not financially possible. The value of Hungarian currency had declined sharply against the Swiss franc, which had soared. The country was experiencing something akin to a recession. Patronage of the Gabor jewelry stores had dropped off."

The cost of living had gone up considerably for the Gabors. Thinking that business would continue to thrive, Vilmos had moved his family into an elegant villa on Stephanie út, an address otherwise surrounded by the private residences of Hungary's very wealthy, or by foreign embassies such as that of the United States.

The daughters loved their new home, especially their garden studded with acacia trees and walled in by a wrought-iron fence.

The Gabor villa stood immediately next door to the Romanian Embassy. Early one evening, Vilmos caught Zsa Zsa with her hand reaching through the fence to fondle a young man from the embassy. That night he threatened to cut his daughter's throat and called her "my little whore. Did that boy have his trousers unbuttoned and did you feel inside?"

"No, NO!" she screamed, running to her bedroom. Later, she admitted to Magda and Eva, "I have felt my first penis on a man. If you play with it, it becomes enlarged, three times its original size. Not only that, but there is a pouch that hangs below the penis containing what feels like two eggs."

"I don't know what happened to Zsa Zsa," Jolie said. "Almost overnight, she became a great beauty, the envy of her sisters. She was like a stunning butterfly emerging from its cocoon. But Eva was also beautiful, and Magda, although not the obvious beauty that Eva and Zsa Zsa were, had her own lovely looks and quiet charm. I had to be their guard dog."

From the Old World to the New World, Jolie carried this photograph of the interior of the **Gellért-Hegy Villa**, where she lived in bourgeois elegance with Vilmos and her three daughters.

When she left him, she came back with a truck to haul away her share of the building's antiques and Oriental carpets.

"Every time we went out the door, Mother warned us not to lose our virginity," Magda said. "But she never told us how a girl lost her virginity. I thought you might get pregnant by kissing a boy. "

"At one point, I caught Zsa Zsa flirting with the young man who delivered our coal," Jolie said. "I don't know what they did together, but her face was blackened and her white organdy dress had coal dust all over it."

One afternoon, Jolie confronted a sibling crisis. The bigger and taller Magda had entered a shop with the diminutive Eva. The store's owner had heard of the Gabors. To Magda's horror, he thought Eva was her daughter. Bursting into tears, Magda ran home sobbing and into her mother's arms.

Jolie not only had to confront sibling rivalry every day in the Gabor household, but had to put up with Vilmos' jealousy. In spite of his protests, she continued to be flirtatious.

One afternoon, when Jolie was driving back from the tennis courts, she spotted an old flame of hers, movie director André Zalábondy. She offered to give him a lift in her Mercedes.

Apparently, she was distracted by his striking presence, and old memories came flooding back. She was looking at him and not keeping her eye on the road when she rammed into another car. She urged Zalábondy to flee, but he refused to desert her in this crisis.

The police took both her and her suitor to the station. A reporter was present, and the next day, the incident was reported in the newspapers. Jolie's "mysterious suitor" was not named.

Vilmos, who learned about the incident over his morning coffee, exploded into a violent rage, threatening genocide. "First I'll kill you, then your mother, then your sisters, then your brothers-in-law, and later, all your nieces and nephews. I will behead them the way Hungarian generals did the invaders during the old Turkish Wars."

"As if I didn't have enough trouble of my own, the rivalry between Zsa Zsa and Eva grew more compeititve every day," Jolie said. "Although Zsa Zsa had the slight edge, Eva was almost equally as beautiful."

"Since Zsa Zsa and Magda had gone to finishing school in Switzerland, Zsa Zsa mocked Eva because she was not allowed to go, too. "You will remain our *un*finished sister," Zsa Zsa charged. "*un*couth, *un*attractive, *un*educated, and *un*kempt."

"From that day on, the race was on," Eva said. "Magda didn't enter the race. The competition was just between Zsa Zsa and me. Which one of us would be the most glamorous, the most seductive? Who would snare the handsomest lovers and the richest husband? Who would be the first to win world acclaim?"

"'*Kismet*!' I cried out loud in my fluent Magyar," Eva said. "My fate is decided. Destiny is on my side."

For years in her future, Zsa Zsa's press agents promoted her as Miss Hungary, although never defining the year. Actually, she was never Miss Hungary. The beauty contest in which she participated for the title is clouded in dispute. No one even agrees on the year, some writers claiming it was as late as 1938.

Since Zsa Zsa was disqualified because she was too young, that year doesn't make any sense. In 1938, Zsa Zsa turned twenty-one, far older than the minimum age (sixteen) defined as necessary to enter the pageant.

Records do not exist. When the communist rulers took over after World War II, they destroyed all "decadent and capitalistic" records associated with beauty pageants, defining them as an evil invention of the West.

It appears that Zsa Zsa entered the pageant during the late spring of 1932 when she was fifteen.

Picking up a copy of *Theatrical Life,* Jolie belatedly read that there was a beauty pageant being staged to select the new "Miss Hungary." Regrettably, the edition she read was old, and Jolie had missed the entrance deadline. Despite that "inconvenience," she nonetheless wanted to enter Zsa Zsa in the running, even though (technically) she wasn't old enough.

Jolie was distressed that the finals were scheduled for the very next day. That didn't give her much time. Like a Hungarian general slaying the invading Turkish heroes from the East, Jolie put her household staff on emergency alert.

Bursting into Zsa Zsa's bedroom, she virtually pulled her daughter from her bed. "We have only hours to convert you into the most beautiful girl in all of Hungary."

Within the hour, the teenager found herself in the most exclusive beauty parlor in Budapest. Jolie ordered that Zsa Zsa's hair be transformed into a stunning shade of reddish gold. In contrast, some reports claimed, inaccurately, that her hair was dyed in imitation of Jean Harlow in the film *Platinum Blonde* (1931), perhaps as a reaction to how "Harlow blondes" were pouring out of beauty parlors across America and Western Europe at the time.

A ferociously ambitious stage mother: **Jolie Gabor** in 1936, wearing couture by Jaques Fath, who later became her tenant in Manhattan.

"I ordered that Zsa Zsa get the full treatments—*everything*—mud packs, skin creams, eyebrow plucking, muscle toning," Jolie said. "My daughter insisted on this flashy green nail polish, which was advertised at the time as the color that Cleopatra wore to entrap Marc Antony and Julius Caesar."

Back home from the beauty parlor, Jolie discovered that Zsa Zsa had nothing to wear. However, in Magda's closet, Jolie found a long black rose print taffeta with a big skirt and an "hour glass waist." She immediately ordered that one of her staff, a talented seamstress, alter it for Zsa Zsa. As that was happening, Jolie discovered a pair of Magda's black satin high heels that fitted Zsa Zsa perfectly.

A newly repackaged Zsa Zsa emerged into the living room where Vilmos was reading a newspaper. He was horrified at the appearance of his daughter, claiming that Jolie had dressed her as a whore. He refused to allow her to enter the contest, but Jolie, with Zsa Zsa in tow, defiantly barged out the front door anyway. They were driven to the grand ballroom of Budapest's Hotel Royale, where the pageant was being staged.

Jolie became immediately engaged in a violent confrontation with the pageant's director, Incze Sandor, who told her that it was too late for Zsa Zsa to qualify.

Jolie denounced Sandor as a "fraud" and a "charlatan," and said she was entering Zsa Zsa in spite of his orders.

Zsa Zsa begged Jolie not to force her into the competition. "Oh, *Nuci, Nuci,* I can't do it. I would be too embarrassed."

When Sandor was called away to a dressing room, Jolie bribed the stage manager and pushed Zsa Zsa onto the stage in front of the judges anyway. "Walk sexy and keep smiling," was her final instruction.

When Sandor returned to his observation post in the wings, he immediately realized what Jolie had done, but it was too late to pull Zsa Zsa from the lineup. One by one, seventeen contestants were eliminated, leaving Zsa Zsa as one of three finalists.

All three of the male judges, each wearing purple sashes, went into a final huddle before announcing Sári

---

Zsa Zsa once admitted that during the course of her life, an entire Canadian forest had to be destroyed to produce the paper for the many printed articles and magazine covers she'd grace.

Her first of the hundreds that would follow appeared in a Viennese newspaper as part of an ad with an "apple-crunching Eve" promoting the apples of Austria.

Despite Jolie's frantic maneuvering behind the scenes, Zsa Zsa didn't win the "Miss Hungary" contest, unlike her future rival, Hedy Lamarr, who was designated as "Miss Austria."

Gábor as the winner. First prize included the equivalent of $1,000 in U.S. currency, plus ten exquisite dresses and an all-expense paid trip to Cannes on the French Riviera.

In spite of her earlier fears, Zsa Zsa was elated, basking in the enthusiastic applause. "I'm Miss Hungary!" she shouted.

As the applause died down, Sandor appeared on stage. As director of the pageant, he nullified the results, informing the audience that Zsa Zsa was not sixteen and therefore not eligible to wear the crown of Miss Hungary.

The First Prize then went to a seventeen-year-old named "Klarika." Jolie could never remember her last name. Her coronation was met with boos from the audience, its members clearly wanting Zsa Zsa.

Sandor allowed Zsa Zsa to be defined as runner-up, and awarded her with a bottle of perfume. In tears, Zsa Zsa exited from the stage, rushing to Jolie's arms.

When Sandor left the stage, Jolie was waiting for him in the wings. She pounded him in the face with her gloved hands until she was escorted out through the stage door by security guards.

In the early 1930s, after a well-known photographer (Manasse) took this picture of a teenage **Zsa Zsa** for the cover of *Excelsior,* an Italian fashion magazine, he dubbed her "the Blonde Daughter of the Danube."

Even at this early age, she demonstrated that lustrous beauty that would in time enchant kings and U.S. presidents.

There, she encountered Joe Pasternak entering the theater. "Your girl has absolutely no talent. Nothing. But she's pretty. My advice is to find some rich man and marry her off."

[Pasternak, of course, would go on to become one of Hollywood's best known directors. In time, his film, Three Smart Girls (1936), *starring Canadian singer Deanna Durbin, would save Universal Studios from bankruptcy. His biggest success came with* The Great Caruso (1951), *starring Mario Lanza, and he made musicals with everyone from Kathryn Grayson to Elvis Presley.*

Ironically, he would give Zsa Zsa her first movie role in Lovely to Look At *in 1952.]*

Zsa Zsa burst into tears at Pasternak's harsh appraisal. Jolie tugged at her coat, pulling her along the alleyway. "Okay, so you're not Marlene Dietrich. We'll have to think of some other way to make something out of you. You can't go through life being a nothing."

In tears, Zsa Zsa followed her mother up the alleyway onto the boulevard where she was instantly surrounded by dozens of admirers, mostly male. They did not know she had been disqualified. Her tears quickly evaporated with this adulation. "I was thrilled. Even though I was no longer Miss Hungary, I knew this was just the beginning of my public acclaim. Everyone in the audience knew I was the real winner."

Decades later, Jolie was still fuming over the results of the pageant. In Budapest, she told a reporter, "In 1985, I encountered this so-called winner, this Klarika. She was a fat sow weighing 220 pounds and had dumped six ugly brats. No doubt each one of them was illegitimate with a different father."

When Jolie had to enter Zsa Zsa into a talent contest, knowing that her daughter could neither sing nor act. she remembered a simple toy soldier routine that **Bessie Love** (upper photo) had performed in the hit film Broadway Melody of 1929.

She taught it to Zsa Zsa.

Jolie, indeed, nursed the grudge, even for a dispute that had occurred long before World War II.

***

Vilmos had opposed Zsa Zsa's entry into the beauty pageant, and he exploded in rage when he read the morning papers. Zsa Zsa's picture appeared alongside the "true winner."

"Zsa Zsa is the most beautiful!" he shouted. "Just look at their pictures side by side. This bitch who won looks like a broken-down streetwalker! One of my soldiers who had been deprived of a woman for months wouldn't even go to bed with her."

For once, Jolie shared her husband's rage. She lay on the sofa lamenting, "I should have won! I should have won!"

Obviously, Zsa Zsa had become an extension of herself and her own gaudy dreams of a theatrical career that had passed her by.

One afternoon, feeling depressed and defeated, Jolie went for a walk along Rakoczi út. She passed by the Urania cinema house, where she frequently visited with her daughters. The theater manager called out to her, and they chatted briefly, long enough for her to lean that the following evening, a talent contest was to be staged at the Urania. "If Zsa Zsa is as talented as she is beautiful, perhaps you'll enter her. The winner goes on to compete in the finals in Vienna."

Jolie retired to a café to think about the offer. Over her second cup of *fekete* (black coffee), she faced reality. Zsa Zsa could not sing, nor could she play the piano. She also couldn't dance. In Jolie's assessment, "Zsa Zsa on toes looked like a bowlegged poodle." Unlike Eva, Zsa Zsa showed no obvious talent for acting.

Before she left the café, Joie had come up with an idea. She remembered Bessie Love in the film *Broadway Melody of 1929,* in which she came out dressed as a toy soldier and performed a very simple but amusing number.

The movie had special significance for Jolie. It had won the Oscar for Best Picture of the year, and was Hollywood's first all-talking musical.

Jolie headed for a costume shop where she purchased a toy soldier uniform accessorized with bangles and gold braiding. Rushing home, she announced to Zsa Zsa that she was entering her in a talent contest at the Urania the following night.

"Put on this costume," Jolie ordered, opening the box from the shop. "If it takes all night, I'm going to teach you a song-and-dance number, even though you can't carry a tune. But this number is foolproof. Beside, you'll look so cute and charming, none of the judges will see you for the no-talent that you are."

"But *Nuci,*" Zsa Zsa protested. "I can't be humiliated again like I was at that beauty pageant."

"My dear girl, you must learn one basic lesson: Life is nothing but a series of humiliations. Now let's get to work."

***

Thirteen young girls competed in the talent contest at the Urania that evening. The winner had a beautiful operatic voice, which evoked that of Grace Moore, who had made such an impression on Eva. Zsa Zsa came in twelfth, beating out a chubby girl who sang off key in German.

In a taxi en route home, Zsa Zsa cried all the way. "Oh, *Nuci, Nuci,* I have failed again. I want to die."

"No, you will live, my dear, and go on to great triumph. In fact, right now, I'm plotting to take you to the finals in Vienna."

"But that little opera thing will represent Budapest," Zsa Zsa protested. "I'm not eligible."

"We'll see about that," Jolie said, as she directed the driver to take them to her dressmaker. Zsa Zsa needed to be outfitted with an entire wardrobe before her descent on Vienna.

Jolie's seamstresses usually required two or three weeks to make a dress, but Jolie warned them they had only seventy-two hours to turn out a wardrobe for her daughter. In Vienna, of course, she would have more time, and would order more clothing if someone spotted Zsa Zsa and wanted to make a star of her.

Years later, Jolie admitted that both Magda and Eva had long ago sensed that Zsa Zsa was her favorite daughter. "I don't think I concealed it very well. I love her the most, and I couldn't help myself. Call it mother's intuition, but I just knew that Zsa Zsa would become the most famous of my daughters, in spite of her lack of theatrical talent."

Although Vilmos accused Jolie of slipping away to meet a Viennese lover, a charge he'd leveled before, she packed up and bundled Zsa Zsa into Jolie's Mercedes. "I have a gut feeling that the Austrians will be far more sophisticated in recognizing talent than our native Hungarians. I'm sure we'll return to Budapest with her as a star."

Years later, Jolie remembered, "I know my dreams sounded foolish, but much of life is foolish," Jolie said. "I had this feeling that something wonderful was about to happen to Zsa Zsa in Vienna."

"And so it did."

***

Only a hundred or so miles from Budapest, Vienna was a dazzling city of music, cafés, waltzes, beautiful palaces, parks, pastries, and *Gemütlichkeit*. The capital of the Hapsburgs was a truly cosmopolitan city, a home to Mozart, Lehár, Schubert, Beethoven, the Strausses (all of them), Suppé, Gluck, Mahler, Brahms, Liszt, Lanner, Haydn, Weber, and Schoenberg. It was also the city of Sigmund Freud.

Erich von Stroheim came from Vienna, as did Josef von Sternberg, who created the "new" post-Berlin Marlene Dietrich. It was also the city of the great *chanteuse*, Greta Keller, who was destined to become a close friend of the Gabors.

The moment she arrived in Vienna in Jolie's Mercedes, Zsa Zsa proclaimed, "I should have been born Viennese!"

Summer had come to the city, and Vienna "between the wars" was a cultural hub. Checking into a suite at the Grand Hotel, Jolie immediately called room service to have Zsa Zsa's toy soldier outfit pressed.

Years later, Zsa Zsa almost refused to discuss how she managed to compete in the talent contest finals when she had not been eligible.

"All the women were talented, all except me," she said. "Even *Nuci* said I was awful. But I got a lot of applause. Everyone in the audience thought I was strikingly beautiful. Even so, of all the contestants, I placed last in the lineup."

That night, a party for the talent show participants was being thrown at a *Heurigen* (wine tavern) in Grinzig, on the outskirts of Vienna, at the edge of the romantic Vienna Woods. The setting was the Restaurant Mayer, a tavern where Beethoven had composed sections of his Ninth Symphony while living here in 1817.

For their entrance, Jolie had hired a gilded coach pulled by four white horses from the *Spanische Hofreitschule* (Spanish Riding School). Inside the lush golden coach, the seats were in polished red leather like the upholsteries of Jolie's red Mercedes. Crystal vases held purple Darwin tulips in the passenger compartment.

Emerging from the coach, Zsa Zsa created a dazzling appearance with pinkish champagne skin, a magenta gown, and plunging *décolletage*. Even at her age, her breasts were already fully developed. As she paraded through the bustling *Heurige,* she seemed to attract every male eye in the house. The fashionable women were jealous.

Jolie had told her that every major theatrical producer and director would be at Mayer that night.

At table, Jolie noticed that three men a short distance away kept eyeing Zsa Zsa and herself. Perhaps it was her vanity, but Jolie just assumed that the men were flirting with them, perhaps hoping to pick them up. A waiter approached Jolie. "*Gnädige Frau*, the distinguished gentleman at the table in the corner wishes to present himself to you."

She readily agreed. As the man approached her table, she immediately recognized him as Herr Klammersinger Richard Tauber, the famous operatic tenor and the matinée idol of Central Europe.

"I practically swooned," Jolie recalled.

At table, Zsa Zsa took in this stout, imposing stranger who had a monacle glistening in his right eye. She thought he looked like a general in the Prussian army, with his black hair brushed back to expose a widow's peak. "Forgive me, madame," he said to Jolie. "I think we have discovered our Violetta for my new operetta," he said. "I'm Richard Tauber."

After introductions and minor chit-chat, Tauber got to the point. "We've been looking for weeks for the right girl for the role, that of a sixteen-year-old *soubrette*, who will play the

Franz Lehár, one of the most revered composers in Hungarian history, was especially famous for operettas which included *The Merry Widow (Die lustige Witwe)*. In 1970, on the 100th anniversary of his birth, the Hungarian government issued a postage stamp in his honor.

role of an American *débutante*. She will have to sing and dance with the comedian Fritz Steiner, who's already cast as the second male lead."

Within five minutes, Tauber's friends, Franz Léhar and Hubert Marishka, the famous theatrical producer and director, had joined their table. *Der singende Traum (The Singing Dream),* was scheduled to open at the Theater an der Wien, where Léhar had premiered his operetta, *Die Lustige Witwe (The Merry Widow).*

Tauber and Léhar were already familiar names to Zsa Zsa. When she met Tauber, he had been assaulted in the streets of Berlin by Nazi Brownshirts because of his Jewish ancestry and had fled Germany for his native Austria, where he performed until the *Anschluss* in March of 1938.

She had read in the papers of Léhar's difficult relationship with the Third Reich. Although a Roman Catholic, he had married a Jewish wife. Nonetheless, Léhar was one of Hitler's favorite composers, so the Führer ordered Josef Goebbels to make Sophie Paschkis an *Ehrenarierin* (Honorary Aryan by marriage). The Nazis would later use Léhar's music for propaganda purposes.

During her talks with Tauber, Marishka, and Léhar, Jolie reveled in her role as an aggressive and well-connected stage mother.

In the middle of their talk, Joe Pasternak approached their table with a beautiful blonde-haired girl. He'd already given his opinion of Zsa Zsa's lack of talent in Budapest, so she ignored him. As it turned out, he was promoting the young singer for the role of Violetta.

"We've found her already," Tauber told Pasternak, "providing she passes the audition tomorrow."

Pasternak assured Tauber that Zsa Zsa would fail.

"By the way, my dear, what is your name?" Tauber asked.

"Zsa Zsa Gabor."

"I don't like it," he said.

"Her real name is Sári Gabor," Jolie piped in.

"I like that," Tauber said. "You'll be billed as Sári Gabor. He noticed that Pasternak and his presumed mistress left in a huff.

An audition was set for eleven the following morning.

Léhar, Marishka, and Tauber were very impressed when Jolie invited them to ride with her in her golden coach at the

Two views of the *Meistersinger* and matinee idol of Central Europe, **Richard Tauber.**

In the left photo, Tauber performs in front of huge crowds assembled in Berlin's *Zoologischer Garten* in 1932.

26

end of the evening.

Exiting from the coach in front of his hotel, Tauber paid Zsa Zsa a final compliment. "In that coach, you look like a fairy princess."

***

At eleven the following morning, Jolie showed up at the theater with Zsa Zsa dressed in her toy soldier uniform. In the front seat of the dark theater, Tauber sat silently through Zsa Zsa's audition, which included singing and dancing. "I stumbled and I giggled," she recalled. "Later, even *Nuci* told me how awful I was."

Amazingly, Tauber turned out to be very patient. He went backstage and told Jolie, "The girl looks the part, but she must rehearse, rehearse, and rehearse some more, for three solid weeks. Morning, noon, and night. She, of course, has no talent as a performer, but the role is easy to play because it calls for a silly little girl, a quality she demonstrated on stage this morning."

After leaving the theater, Jolie hired three instructors—one to teach Zsa Zsa how to dance, another how to sing, and yet another functioning as a drama coach. Tauber had given Jolie a copy of the script.

That night, she placed a call to Vilmos in Budapest, informing him that Zsa Zsa was going on the stage in Vienna. He attacked her for allowing that, claiming that "only painted whores went on the stage." After telling his wife that she was insane, he hung up the phone.

For the next three weeks, Zsa Zsa's coaches were stern taskmasters, especially Heinz Steiner, her singing teacher. She called him "a Prussian tyrant and a dictator, a short man with a hideous goatee." Steiner carried around the bow of a violin and hit Zsa Zsa on the head whenever she went off key, which was most of the time.

A legend in *Mitteleuropa*, **Mary Losseff** was the mistress and muse of Richard Tauber.

Zsa Zsa later claimed that Losseff inspired her to become "a modern woman."

"You can't sing a note," he shouted at her. "Tauber must have been drunk when he hired you."

The drama coach, Irene Knüpffer, was no better. "The part calls for you to blink your eyelashes and flirt. Surely you can be a coquette. Every sixteen-year-old girl on the streets of Vienna knows how to flirt. You Hungarian girls are just field hands."

The dancing master, Karl Werner, found Zsa Zsa hopeless as a pupil. "Miss Gabor, I'm not sure you could even make it in a chorus line in an all-night Bierstube. In my day, I danced in a troupe that featured the great ballerina, Anna Pavlova. Now I'm reduced to trying to teach a girl with two clubfeet."

One night, Tauber invited Jolie and Zsa Zsa to join him and Mary Losseff, the female star of *The Singing Dream,* to accompany them to a cabaret. Tauber and Losseff were conducting a torrid love affair on and off the stage at the time.

Zsa Zsa envied Losseff's grace. "She was a truly modern woman," Zsa Zsa said, "with her golden hair fashionably bobbed and a dress short enough to show off her legs. She was both lovely and talented. I envied her when Tauber on stage took her in his arms and sang, 'You Are the Entire World to Me.' I wanted some man to do that to me."

[Born in Vladivoskok, Russia, in 1907, Losseff was a singer and film actress, and was the screen and life partner of Tauber from 1929 until the mid-30s. When Tauber was forced to flee from Germany, Losseff went with him to Vienna, where she was both his muse and mistress. Her brilliant career, later in London, would be destroyed by acute alcoholism.]

The *grande dame* of *chanson,* **Greta Keller**, Jolie's close friend, became a kind of godmother to Zsa Zsa in Vienna and later, to both Eva and Magda in America.

She was Marlene Dietrich's lover, and Hitler's favorite singer.

At the cabaret, the featured *chanteuse* was Greta Keller, known as "The Great Lady of Chanson," having played to packed houses not only in Vienna, but in Berlin and Prague. She had the dubious distinction of being Adolf Hitler's favorite singer.

In 1927, she'd appeared on stage in *Broadway,* a play presented in Vienna, in which she'd starred with Marlene Dietrich. After their brief lesbian fling, Greta accused Dietrich of stealing "my singing style."

Both Jolie and Zsa Zsa found Greta a thrilling performer with her own distinctive singing style, and Tauber invited the *chanteuse* to join them at table after her show.

"Jolie and Greta were like two long lost sisters coming together, "Zsa Zsa recalled. "They bonded immediately, discovering that they liked Hungarian and Viennese food, handsome young men, and champagne in that exact order."

Greta later told the author of this book, "Jolie and I were also drawn together because we faced the same predicament. We'd both lost out on love. I had emerged from my disaster of a marriage to a musician, Joe Sergeant, and she was in a loveless marriage to Vilmos. In contrast, Zsa Zsa was on the dawn of dozens of international love affairs. In fact, in just two weeks I'd introduce this virgin to her first lover."

The following afternoon, Greta took Jolie and Zsa Zsa on a shopping tour of Vienna, stopping off at the singer's dressmaker, where Jolie ordered three evening gowns for Zsa Zsa, the most stylish and fashionable she'd ever owned.

That night, Greta invited Jolie and Zsa Zsa back to the cabaret to sit at the head table "with two of my dearest friends."

Those dear friends turned out to be a very young Hedy Lamarr, who at age nineteen in 1932, had been voted "Miss Austria" in a beauty pageant. She was with her lover, the notorious Austrian munitions king, Fritz Mandl, sometimes known as "The Merchant of Death" because of his lucrative armaments trade.

A friend of both Hitler and Mussolini, munitions king **Fritz Mandl** married Hedy Lamarr.

On their honeymoon, she discovered that he was a sadist.

He was a friend of Adolf Hitler, Josef Goebbels, and Benito Mussolini. Somehow, Hitler seemed to overlook the fact that Mandl was a Jew. He also had a close alliance with Gyula Gömbös von Jáfka, the general who was dictator of Zsa Zsa's native Hungary.

[Although a fascist, Mandl was attached to "Austrofascism" more than to German Nazism. At the time the Gabors met him, he was supplying weapons and ammunition to Prince Ernest Rüdiger Starhemberg, the commander of the Austrian fascist private army known as the Heimwehr (Home Defense Force).]

Both Jolie and Zsa Zsa were awed by Hedy's stunning beauty. "She was simply the most beautiful woman in the world," Zsa Zsa later said. "Her raven-black hair framed the most exquisite face, and she wore a shimmering gown the color of silver. Her lipstick was the brightest red I'd ever seen, and a diamond tiara crowned that magnificent head of hers."

Two nights before actually meeting her, Zsa Zsa and Jolie had seen her exit from the landmark Sacher Hotel. She'd worn a blue sequined dress

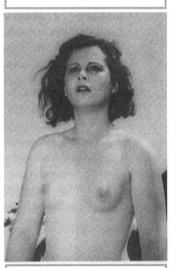

Hailed as "the most beautiful woman in Europe," **Hedy Kiesler (later Lamarr)** romped nude in the 1932 *Ekstase*, which was later released in America as *Ecstasy*.

Hedy developed a notoriety that remained with her for the rest of her life.

that mirrored her perfectly azure blue eyes. "She had on so many diamonds she sparkled in the night," Zsa Zsa said. She vowed that one day she would equal, if not surpass, Hedy in both glamor and sophistication.

[Years from that night at the Sacher, far away across the world in Hollywood, Zsa Zsa would find herself pitted against Hedy, competing not only for movie roles, but for some of the same men.

In Berlin, Hedy had worked with the great theatrical impresario, Max Reinhardt, who had called her "the most beautiful woman in Europe." She was a native Viennese, the child of as-

Transformed into **Hedy Lamarr** at MGM, the actress dazzled American audiences while seducing everyone from John F. Kennedy to Errol Flynn and Clark Gable.

She appears above with **James Stewart** in the 1941 film, *Come Live With Me.*

similated Jewish parents. Her mother, Gertrud Lichwitz, was a pianist and Budapest native, born into an haute bourgeoise family, and her father, Emil Kiesler, was a bank director.]

Mandl called Hedy "Hansi," meaning "little bunny."

The third richest man in Austria, he had an overwhelming presence.

"He was handsome in a terrifying way," Zsa Zsa said. "I was drawn to him. He was the first of an array of powerful men I'd meet in my life. He seemed to have power over women, a man used to giving orders and having them obeyed. He exuded a sexual allure. He wasn't a pretty boy, but he was utterly sexy. When he walked into a room, he seemed to dominate it."

"During the middle of Greta's concert, Mandl, under the table, put his hand on my knee," Zsa Zsa claimed. "When I did not object, that hand become more daring and traveled north on its inevitable course."

She later told Greta, "He was the first man who played with my vagina," she said. "He took control of it and before your parting song, he had practically masturbated me, while all the time seemingly paying all his attention to beautiful Hedy."

Later, after Hedy excused herself for a visit to the powder room, Mandl told Zsa Zsa, "Hedy may be the most beautiful woman in Austria, but you are the most beautiful woman in Hungary."

"I soon learned that Mandl had this obsession with actresses, but only if they were stunningly attractive," Zsa Zsa said.

***

Too much time had passed for Jolie in Vienna, and Vilmos demanded that she return at once to Budapest. She knew that Zsa Zsa needed a guardian, and she summoned "Cuki," one of her most faithful family retainers, to take the train to Vienna to act as a chaperone for Zsa Zsa during Jolie's absence. Greta Keller also promised "to take Zsa Zsa under my wing."

With her mother gone, Zsa Zsa quickly learned how to deal with Cuki. She noted that the maid drank nearly three cups of cocoa every night. At the druggist, Zsa Zsa purchased a sleeping potion. She began a ritual of putting the powder into Cuki's drink at night. "She never woke up until around nine o'clock the next morning, and she never got wise about what I was doing behind her back. She did say she'd slept better in Vienna than any place she'd ever been."

Greta called and invited Zsa Zsa to drop by her cabaret theater at one o'clock the following afternoon. From there, she planned to take her to lunch.

Ever since her arrival in Vienna, Zsa Zsa had paid more attention to her appearance than ever before. "I did my best to dress up and look sophisticated, like Hedy Lamarr. No more skirts and sweaters for me. A lot of makeup helped. *Décolletage* and high heels also did a lot for me. I could at last pass for eighteen, maybe nineteen, if not more."

Arriving at the night club where Greta had performed the previous evening, Zsa Zsa found her rehearsing on stage with a piano player. Standing near Greta was a tall, imposing figure of a man. Zsa Zsa would remember him as "looking like Beethoven, a wild, untamed Beethoven."

Greta introduced Zsa Zsa to Willi Schmidt-Kentner, who took her delicate hand and held it for at least two minutes, so it seemed. She knew who the German composer was, as he'd written some of her favorite songs. Only the night before, Greta had sung two of the songs he'd written for her fans.

In a memoir, Zsa Zsa claimed she'd been introduced to the man she soon called Willi by Richard Tauber himself. But Greta said she was the one who'd introduced Zsa Zsa to this imposing figure, who was known as a man of deep, dark moods.

When he wasn't in "one of my black periods," he was known for his continental charm, especially around beautiful women. Zsa Zsa suspected that Willi had been a former flame of Greta's before each of them had moved on to other lovers.

Willi had also heard of Sári Gabor, as Zsa Zsa was known at the time. He was a friend of Tauber's "Richard told me you are absolutely adorable in the role of Violetta, *Fräulein*. I am anxiously awaiting the premiere of your op-

31

eretta. I'm sure that after the opening, the entire city of Vienna will be at your feet, not to mention the lonely German composer you see before you."

"He had fierce dark eyes," Zsa Zsa recalled. "Right in front of Greta, he was undressing me piece by piece. I was terrified of him, but yet powerfully attracted to him. I was so overwhelmed by his presence, I could hardly speak. It was like he'd cast some spell over me."

Over lunch at Greta's favorite restaurant, the dining room at the Sacher Hotel, Zsa Zsa soon found her voice and was chatting pleasantly and flirtatiously with Willi.

"I was practically ignored," Greta recalled. "Fortunately, Madame Sacher came over to join us at table; otherwise, I'd have been a wallflower. Willi had once told me, 'I have eyes only for you,' but his vision had shifted to Zsa Zsa. His promises to me had gone the way of the Austro-Hungarian Empire."

After each of them had devoured a wedge of the famous Sacher torte, Willi asked Zsa Zsa if she were free to join him at his suite for a drink at eight o'clock that evening.

"I will count the minutes," she told him. By then, she'd learned to play the coquette that the role in *The Singing Dream* demanded.

As Zsa Zsa's recently appointed unofficial "godmother," Greta warned Willi, "She's very young, you know."

"Please," he said to Greta, "I don't need to be reminded of that from you, my dear. You, who started seducing the palace guardsmen when you were twelve." He turned to gaze into Zsa Zsa's eyes. "Sári here is the ripest fruit on the tree, eager for plucking before the birds devour her."

That night, Zsa Zsa dressed in a stunning emerald green gown designed by Greta's dressmaker and slipped out of their hotel without telling Cuki. She'd spend two hours getting dressed and making up. "As I looked at myself in a full-length mirror," she later said, "I was entranced. For the first time in my life, I'd become a *femme fatale.*"

At Willi's hotel, she was ushered into his suite and soon found herself sitting on his sofa, drinking white Austrian wine. Seated close to him, she studied his face more closely, later referring to it as lined and intelligent. "He looked like one of those wild Tartars of the Middle Ages who swept out of Asia to conquer Europe by fire and sword. I was desperately drawn to him."

"I was almost out of my mind, sitting so close to him on the sofa," she said. "This famous composer wanted me, desired me. Let Hedy keep Fritz Mandl. Willi was a man of the world, and I had captivated him. Boys had flirted with me but they were mere boys. Willi excited me as a man. There was a span in our ages, of course,. Perhaps he was forty, but what difference did that make? I preferred an older, experienced, sophisticated man, not some schoolboy with his tongue hanging out, lusting after me."

Over dinner that night, Willi described the real love story that had led to the creation of the plot for *The Singing Dream*. The leading lady, Mary Losseff, had fled from Russia during its Revolution and had escaped to Berlin, where she arrived penniless and unknown. Tauber met her one afternoon and had immediately fallen in love with her. Their subsequent affair inspired him to compose the operetta.

To impress him, Zsa Zsa told him outrageous stories of her life, presenting herself as the most emancipated woman in Hungary, a siren who had broken the hearts of army generals, actors, composers, dancers, and playwrights.

Finally, he'd heard enough. "Stop it with all these silly stories, entertaining though they may be. I want to deal in reality. I know you are a virgin. Your incarnation as a modern Helen of Troy will begin tonight, when I take you back to my suite and make a woman of you."

***

Over the years, Zsa Zsa seemingly contradicted herself, claiming at times that Willi Schmidt-Kentner was the first man to take her virginity, at other times the honor going to Mustafa Kemal Atatürk, dictator of Turkey.

Greta Keller relayed to the author of this book a possible motivation for this two-tiered claim.

"Willi was married and Zsa Zsa was very young," Greta said. "He heeded my warning and was careful. As Zsa Zsa confided to me, during their first date, he took her back to his hotel suite and made love to her, with lots of kissing and fondling. He claimed that instead of penetrating her, he enjoyed her 'between the legs.' At least that would not produce an unwanted pregnancy, of course. So, in a sense, Atatürk was the first man who actually penetrated her, if she is to be believed."

During the first week of their romance, Willi and Zsa Zsa were seen together at the chic Bristol Bar and often at Greta's night club. Sometimes they joined Hedy Lamarr and Fritz Mandl, who where planning their upcoming marriage.

With Zsa Zsa on his arm, Willi often took her to the Staatsoper (State Opera) or the Burgtheater (National Theater). His favorite theater was the Wiener Kammerspiele, where two-time Oscar winner, Luise Rainer, had gotten her start before her successes in Hollywoood.

Zsa Zsa was introduced to Zarah (aka Sara) Leander, the Swedish actress and singer. Over dinner at the Sacher after a performance, she told Willi and Zsa Zsa that she had been wooed by Josef Goebbels and that she was going to sign a contract with the then-Nazi-controlled film studio, UFA (*Universum Film AG*) to make films in Berlin.

The Swedish actress and singer **Zarah (aka Sara) Leander** suffered disgrace after World War II because of her associations with the Nazis.

Willi warned her about the potential dangers of linking her screen image to the German film industry, but Leander refused to listen. Later, she would become a leading film star in Berlin, making ten movies, each of which was very successful.

[After the war, Leander was shunned by most of the international public because she had been too extensively associated with Nazi propaganda. Her fellow citizens of Sweden boycotted her, though she continued to be very popular in Germany for many decades after World War II. Still in disgrace in many quarters, she retired from show business and died in Stockholm of a stroke in 1981.]

Willi also introduced Zsa Zsa to Tala Birell, a stage and film actress who had doubled for Marlene Dietrich in her German films in Berlin. Birell would later play minor roles in many famous American films, including *Bringing Up Baby (1938)* with Cary Grant and Katharine Hepburn and *The Song of Bernadette (1943)* for which Jennifer Jones won an Oscar.

During breaks from all this theater and cabaret viewing, it was inevitable that Zsa Zsa would eventually ascertain that Willi was already married. His wife had become an invalid and was in a sanitarium in Switzerland, "Taking the cure."

Zsa Zsa later confessed, "I had no guilt. In that time, men married for position or found a woman who would make a good wife and bring up his children. For love, men turned to a mistress on the side. Love in marriage was a luxury which only the very poor could afford."

After several nights, when Zsa Zsa's romance with Willi had blossomed into full flower, she received a call from Hedy Lamarr, inviting her to a special screening of a controversial movie she'd made in Czechoslovakia. Mandl was in Berlin, so she had the free run of his luxurious ten-room apartment at 15 Schwarzenbergplatz, at the southern end of the fabled Ringstrasse.

Greta, Willi, and Zsa Zsa arrived by limousine, hired by Hedy, to the lavish address, where they found Hedy presiding over an armada of servants.

In a stunning gown, the color of champagne, she appeared with diamonds.

After dinner, she invited them into a private screening room, where she ordered a male servant to begin showing a controversial movie, (entitled *Extaze* in Czech and *Ekstase* in German), she'd filmed at a woodsy location outside

Prague. In it, she was billed as Hedy Kreisler. It would eventually be released in the United States as *Ecstasy*.

In the film, Eva, as played by Hedy, goes for a swim in the lake. She takes off her clothes and puts them on the back of her horse, who later bolts, leaving her to run nude through the woods. In the film, she subsequently meets and falls in love with a man called Adam, a young engineer.

The film certainly didn't shock the worldly Greta or the sophisticated Willi. For Zsa Zsa, it inspired envy because she knew it would make Hedy notorious in both Europe and the United States. Zsa Zsa's hunch was correct. *Ecstasy*, in time, led to Louis B. Mayer offering Hedy a film contract at Metro-Goldwyn-Mayer.

At the end of the screening, Hedy claimed that the film's director, Gustav Machaty, wanted to show her face as she experienced orgasm. Not pleased with her first fifteen takes, he privately told her leading man to stick a safety pin into her butt at a crucial moment when she was close to a climax. "That was me, responding to a prick," Hedy told her guests, "but the prick of a pin."

That night cemented a friendship between Hedy and Zsa Zsa. At the end of the evening, Hedy's guests congratulated her on a groundbreaking film, the first A-list movie to depict sexual intercourse on screen, but not the first to show female nudity.

"I fear that when I marry Fritz, my short film career must come to an end," Hedy said. "That is, if he marries me. If Fritz sees this film, I think he'll break our engagement."

Zsa Zsa had plotted to go after Mandl herself if he ever dropped Hedy. But eventually, he married her in 1933, and tried to buy up every copy of *Ecstasy* that he could.

As predicted, Hedy's screen career was put on hold during her marriage to Mandl. Coincidentally, Zsa Zsa's stage career was almost sabotaged before it had begun.

When Richard Tauber became ill, the staff of *The Singing Dream* got time off. Willi asked Zsa Zsa to accompany him to the little village of Obenzl, high in the Austrian Alps. They rode to the plateau above the village by funicular. Once there, they checked into an old-fashioned bedroom opening onto a terrace with a panoramic view.

"It was the most romantic week of my life," Zsa Zsa later asserted to Greta, to whom she could confide. "I learned more about sex. Whenever I was a naughty girl, Willi spanked my bare butt until it was red. He became terribly excited during that and had to find his release. Through my entire week in Obenzl, I had one *derrière* that stayed lobster red. I practically couldn't do anything that Willi didn't interpret as naughty. Every night he took me in his arms and told me that I meant the entire world to him, that he could not live without me.

I believed him, of course."

"Willi Schmidt-Kentner was my first love, and, like all first loves, its memory remained bittersweet. For a while, I lived in a fantasy world—at least until I returned to Vienna, where I found another actress rehearsing for my role as Violetta in the operetta. I was devastated, and telephoned Jolie at once in Budapest."

Her daughter's voice was frantic, as she told her mother, "I fall out from the role [her exact words]."

Jolie was on the train to Vienna the next morning, where she confronted Marishka and Tauber. She quickly learned that the actress who had replaced Zsa Zsa was Joe Pasternak's young mistress. Jolie was infuriated, reminding Tauber and Marishka that they had signed a three-year contract with Zsa Zsa.

Jolie pleaded with Marishka at the Theater an der Wien. She even claimed that she had been "extra good to Fritz Steiner, the lousy comedian." *[He had been cast as the second male lead after Tauber.]* "I agreed to go to bed with him on the night of the premiere, and I also let him kiss and feel my breasts. I even gave him a two-karat diamond for his pinky."

"Being that gracious to one of our stars is not the point," Marishka said. "Sári has not grown into the role."

Jolie eventually reached a tense compromise with the producer, who agreed that the following night he would allow Zsa Zsa to perform a scene from the operetta preceded by the performance of an equivalent scene by Pasternak's favorite. "The winner of the audition will be our Violetta," Marishka promised.

That night, back at their hotel, Jolie launched a major assault on Zsa Zsa's performance skills and stage appearance. She was interrupted briefly by the appearance of Willi, thereby learning for the first time of her daughter's affair with the composer. Jolie quickly dismissed Zsa Zsa's fascination with Willi, saying, "It was just a teenager's first crush on an animalistic, very male-looking Asian with gray hair."

Ushering Willi out of their hotel suite, she turned her attention back to Zsa Zsa. She dressed her in a stunning white garden party dress with red polka dots and an organza picture hat. That night, she also lightened her hair with a blonde rinse.

During preparations for the following night's dress rehearsal, Jolie insisted on personally supervising her daughter's makeup. "I plan to make you look like a combined version of Marlene Dietrich and Jeanette MacDonald."

Zsa Zsa was trembling when it became her time to follow her competition. Pasternak's mistress (her name lost to history) had brilliantly interpreted the role of Violetta. Even Jolie had to admit that.

As an observer at the rehearsal/audition, Marishka had invited his wife, Lily Kartzog, a celebrated actress of the Vienna theater.

"Zsa Zsa in her scene was supposed to come out dragging Fritz Steiner—who had once felt me up—across the stage," Jolie said. "My poor darling tripped. I was horrified."

But Madame Kartzog laughed and told her husband and Tauber, "That was a charming bit. The girl is enchanting. She keeps the role."

"Obviously, in the Hubert Marishka household, his wife wore the pants," Jolie said. "I returned home to Vilmos, and Zsa Zsa rushed off to spend the night with Willi."

During the three month run of *Der singende Traum,* Zsa Zsa, as Sári Gabor, became "the toast of Vienna," according to the newspapers. Her picture appeared on the cover of magazines and was plastered on billboards around the city. She even filmed an advertisement—shown in movie theaters—promoting Austrian apples. "My first appearance on the screen and I was shown biting into the forbidden fruit, an apple that had tempted Eve in the Garden of Eden," Zsa Zsa said.

Even Vilmos, along with Jolie, showed up for opening night. "My jealous sisters did not attend," Zsa Zsa said, "but my aunts and cousins did."

Tauber invited the entire Gabor clan for dinner afterwards, where they awaited the morning reviews. Dr. Kurt Roger, in Vienna's *Neue Frei Presse,* recalled Sári Gabor as "extremely amusing and charming," and Dr. Rudolf Bolzedr in *Weiner Zeitung* stated that she showed "great promise for a future career in the theater."

During the run of the play, night after night, crowds formed on the street, shouting, "Sári, Sári!" They ignored the operetta's two stars, Tauber and Mary Losseff, when they emerged from the theater.

Eventually, the operetta's run came to an end, at which time, Willi told Zsa Zsa that he had a commitment to travel to Rome to write a musical for Marta Eggerth, the Budapest-born singer/actress noted at the time for her beauty. Zsa Zsa knew of her because she was one of the reigning queens from "The Silver Age of Operetta." Both Franz Lehár, Oscar Straus, and at least five other composers had each composed music especially for her. She had triumphed in 1935 as the coloratura star of

In Richard Tauber's operetta, *The Singing Dream,* **Sári (later, Zsa Zsa) Gabor** *(center)* was hailed as "the Toast of Vienna."

Crowds formed outside her stage door, and an aging German composer fell madly in love with her.

an Italian language film, *Casta diva*, a romantic musical drama based on the life of Bellini, noted as winner for Best Italian film of 1935 at the Venice Film Festival. Zsa Zsa feared that Eggert would steal Willi from her.

[In 2002, Eggerth sang at the 200ᵗʰ anniversary of Vienna's Theater an der Wien, and in April of 2013, she celebrated her 101th birthday.]

Willi begged Zsa Zsa to accompany him to Rome. Without telling Vilmos and Jolie, she agreed to run away with him. She traveled with him as far as the Austrian city of Klagenfurt, the last stop before crossing Austria's southern frontier into Italy.

Leaving Willi asleep in their compartment, she impulsively slipped off the train and rushed through the snow. In tears, she watched as the train pulled away from the station. Willi was apparently still asleep because he did not come looking for her.

In the railway station of Klagenfurt, she entered a tiny café and ordered a black coffee. It was three o'clock in the morning, and the next train headed for Vienna wasn't due for another two hours. She was in tears at the realization that her *grand amour* had come to an end, and she shocked herself at how abruptly she had finalized its demise, steeped in the belief that it was right for her to have run away.

***

When her train reached Vienna, she transferred to another headed for Budapest. She called Cuki and told her to pack her luggage and take the next train back to the Gabors.

From the compartment of her train, Zsa Zsa watched the rolling plains and villages pass in review before her. She'd decided against pursuing a career in the theater, even though the famous Hungarian-born producer, Alexander Korda, had wired her, informing her that he wanted her to take a screen test in London.

She wired Korda back, turning him down. Instead of a career, she decided she wanted to get married. But to whom? Willi was out of the question, as he already had a wife.

They were still very young, though not as young as their memoirs suggested, but each of the three Gabor sisters would marry before the beginning of World War II. None of their husbands would be a king or prince, as Jolie had hoped. But one would be a Polish count, another a Turkish ambassador.

"Only I would marry for love and for sheer male beauty, a Norse God directly descended from Valhalla!" Or so Eva would proclaim.

CHAPTER TWO
Goulash Lolitas Snare Their First Husbands

Arriving back home in Budapest, Zsa Zsa met a cold reception. In a pet shop on the Kärtnerstrasse in Vienna, Willi had purchased a cute little Scottie for her. She became enchanted with the dog at once, naming it Mishka.

When the Scottie encountered Vilmos, the dog barked every time Zsa Zsa's father entered the room. He ordered his daughter "to get rid of that mutt."

At that point in her life, Zsa Zsa loved her Scottie more than Vilmos. Determined no to give up her beloved pet, she plotted to leave her childhood home as soon as possible.

In the meantime, tragedy struck. Jolie's father, Josef Tilleman, became ill and was taken to the Payor Sanatorium, seven miles from Budapest, the site of extensive medical facilities. He was diagnosed as having "a bad stomach" and died within four days.

His widow, Francesca, the matriarch of the Gabor family, handled it bravely, but Jolie took to bed in her grief. She had been devoted to her father.

Bed-ridden, Jolie could no longer supervise the social life of her daughters. Each of them was pursuing a man. Romance was in the air, but not for Jolie, who almost daily grew increasingly disappointed by her life with Vilmos.

He spent more and more time away from their villa and sometimes was gone for three or four nights in a row. Both Jolie and her daughters just assumed Vilmos had a mistress, as most officers in the Hungarian army maintained one.

Jolie seemed relieved. "The sex maniac no longer comes to my bed to satisfy his lusts," she told her daughters.

Francesca recovered from her husband's death much more quickly than Jolie. After Josef's burial, his widow wore black and mourned him for less than two months.

In Budapest, Francesca was famed as a society hostess, entertaining foreign diplomats and generals. To one of her parties, she invited His Excellency, Burhan Belge, Press Director for the Foreign Ministry of Turkey.

He had just returned from a Turkish State visit to Berlin, where Adolf Hitler himself had arrived at the railway station to welcome him to the German capital. Belge was a personal friend of both Hitler and Joseph Goebbels, the Nazi propaganda minister.

Years later, Jolie claimed, "at the time, Zsa Zsa and I met Burhan, we didn't think Hitler was so bad. In fact, I was impressed that Belge was a friend of the Nazi leader. That was years before we became aware that Hitler's plan involved killing millions of us Jews."

At her grandmother's villa, Zsa Zsa was introduced to Belge.

Because of her emotional involvements with Willi, she had not thought of another man until her return to Budapest from Vienna. At the Gabor villa, because of Vilmos' increasingly tyrannical rule, she found conditions intolerable. At night, she dreamed of a possible suitor who would marry her and take her away with him.

She had attended her grandmother's party, hoping to meet the man of her dreams. Finding no one who met those qualifications, she focused on the Turkish minister. She'd heard that in Turkey, men often married women only half their age.

As she remembered him, Belge was "dour and sinister looking, and probably on the shady side of thirty. He appeared bored and world weary, but I caught his eye."

"We conversed in German," she recalled. "I was very aware that he was a Turk. Those warriors from the East had enslaved my country for a century and a half. I asked him about the Turkish dictator, Kemal Atatürk, and was it true that he had ordered Turkish women to abandon wearing the veil?"

"You are far too pretty to concern yourself with politics," he had told her. "If you and I were in Turkey, I would give your father three pounds of coffee, the standard purchase price, and establish you as the number one concubine in my harem. But first, I would measure the circumference of your head."

"Why would you do such a thing?" she asked.

"It was an ancient tradition with old Turkish pashas," he said. "The circumference of a young girl's head had to be no larger than her waist."

"Tonight I will go home and take my own measurements to see if I qualify," she had promised.

He studied her more carefully. "You're only fifteen yours old," he had said. "In some quarters even that is too old, but times are changing, and I'd better wait a little while longer until you've become more of a woman. Actually, I've changed my mind. A woman of your charm and beauty should not be a mere concubine, competing with other girls in my harem for my attention. I will return to Budapest at some point in the near future and marry you. I will take you back to Ankara as my wife."

In the months ahead, time hung heavy over Zsa Zsa's head. She had nothing to do, no career prospects. The boys she dated were pompous and silly, not at all to her liking. She was tired of school boys. She wanted to become either the wife or mistress of a man with great power. Obviously, that meant someone older.

One morning, she woke up and impulsively telephoned the Turkish Embassy, having read in the newspapers that Belge was due for a return visit to Budapest. It was now 1937.

She was told that His Excellency was in Vienna, and that he'd be in Budapest in less than ten days. She left a message to have him call her. "Tell him I measured my head and my waist, and my waist leaves me with an inch to spare. He'll understand."

Belge arrived in Budapest from Vienna in just two days, not ten, and on his first day back, he was seen window shopping along the Corso with Zsa Zsa.

That night, he invited her for dinner and dancing at the Ritz. Before heading out the door, she attired herself in an elegant, black, low-cut gown made for her in Vienna. Jolie rose from her bed and helped her with her hair and makeup, with each maneuver trying to make Zsa Zsa look older. At the conclusion of all their hard labor, Zsa Zsa gave her own verdict. "I look at least nineteen years old." Jolie agreed.

At the Ritz, she danced with Belge across the marble floor, attracting the attention of virtually every man in the room. "Burhan was a very serious man, not at all frivolous, but I supplied the gaiety."

At table, she showed him a series of provocative photographs taken by a well-known theatrical photographer in Budapest. One depicted her with her blouse partly open, revealing ample breasts. Another showed her with her head thrown back, dropping overripe cherries into her succulent mouth. The photographer had told her, "This will suggest to your man your willingness to perform fellatio on him."

As she recalled, "I could tell that Burhan was aroused while looking at those pictures. I decided to strike fast like the cobra."

"Excellency, will you marry me?" she asked.

"Did I hear that correctly?" he asked, almost choking on his drink.

"You promised to marry me when I grew up a bit," she said. "Look me over. Don't I look like I've matured?"

"Indeed you do," he said. "But I need some time to think it over. You will have my decision before I depart from Budapest."

"There is one condition," she said. "I must keep my Scottie dog. I'm very attached to him."

A look of extreme disapproval crossed his face before he softened his features. "If you wish."

That night on her doorstep, he kissed her long and passionately.

His call came in at five o'clock that very morning. A servant awakened her. When she picked up the receiver, he said, "Am I speaking to Mrs. Burhan Belge?"

"You are, indeed," she said as a feeling of joy overwhelmed her. "I am very happy, so many thanks to you. I will work very hard to make you a good wife. I will plan our wedding at once...in Budapest."

"The choice is yours," he said.

The time came when Zsa Zsa had to arrange for Belge's appearance at the Gabor villa for afternoon tea. Although polite to the ambassador, both Jolie and Vilmos had negative reactions.

Regardless of how hot it was, Zsa Zsa's first husband, **Burhan Belge**, the Turkish propaganda minister, never left the house without suit and tie.

Wearing her wide-brimmed hat to protect herself from the hot Turkish sun, **Zsa Zsa Gabor** was photographed in Ankara in 1940.

Jolie at once became involved with preparing a trousseau. As for Vilmos he almost had a stroke. "The daughter of a Hussar marrying a prominent member of the enemy? That's the equivalent of a rabbi's daughter announcing to her father that she is going to marry Hermann Göring! Don't tell me that within a year, I will have a little Turkish soldier marching through my house. It's God's revenge on me for killing so many Turks."

As part of Jolie's private appraisal of Belge, she said he was "so sad, so melancholy, so boringly serious...and a Turk. He was very disagreeable...and a Turk. He was ugly...and a Turk. But he was a very important man in Europe, although an infidel...and a Turk!"

The wedding at Grandmother Francesca's house was small and modest. Jolie cried. Zsa Zsa later said, "Eva and Magda were furious at me, so jealous, because I had snared a husband before they did. Not only that, but in the future, I'd be traveling on a diplomatic passport. Right after the wedding, I informed both Magda and Eva that in the future, they were to address me as 'Your Excellency.'"

As a parting gift, Zsa Zsa's grandmother, Francesca, presented her with a blood red ruby and diamond necklace. "You'll be the toast of Ankara, my dear, when you wear this adornment with a stunning gown." Vilmos gave her a ten-karat diamond, suggesting "My dear, dear daughter, in your future, you must not accept any diamond with lesser karats than this."

As Zsa Zsa headed for Turkey with her new husband, Jolie gave her some parting advice. "If it doesn't work out, you can always divorce him. When I get Eva and Magda married, I, too, will seek a divorce from Vilmos. You're still very young. By the time you're twenty-one, another shining knight might appear on a white horse."

As filtered through her interpretation of what Jolie had told her, men were to be used as long as they were useful, then discarded when boredom set in.

She would follow that advice for the rest of her life.

***

"Zsa Zsa isn't the only Gabor sister who could attract a man," Eva said to Jolie. "Everybody I met told me I was prettier than Zsa Zsa. Naturally, the opposite sex paid attention to me. I think if I really tried, I could have almost any man in Budapest I wanted."

Years later, Eva would recall her first love. She couldn't remember his full name, identifying him only as "Pista." She was fourteen and a half, and he was a mature lad of sixteen.

In winter, Budapest had an artificial lake for ice skating. One wintry afternoon, Eva spotted a young boy of such grace on the ice that she was enthralled. Even though she was freezing and longed for a warming fire, she could not tear herself away from looking at Pista., whose name she did not know at the time.

The romance was slow to develop. She followed him around for months, but he didn't seem interested. "I worshipped him, I adored him. He was my dream man. I longed for him to take me in his arms and kiss me. Even when ice skating gave way to summer grass hockey, I was standing on the field day after day watching him."

She was still his adoring fan by the time the bleakness of winter returned to Hungary once again. "At long last, Pista came to notice me. He'd always been pleasant. But one day, he asked me to meet him in secret near this cave in a park. Once I got there, he grabbed me and kissed me. I was in heaven. His lips tasted like cherries. His body was so firm and masculine."

"At twilight, he often scaled the walls to our villa to hold me and kiss me. We also discovered 'Lovers' Lane' near the artificial lake. It was a castle from the 13th century that was in ruins. Young couples came there to make love. One afternoon, Pista discovered that I was a woman all over. He made love to me with his hands. He also put my hand inside his trousers. I learned that cold afternoon that boys are made different from girls."

Pista faithfully attended her first involvement with acting on a stage. In a Christmas pageant, she played an angel singing a carol. "I was the only off-key angel in Heaven," as she remembered. "I was once a fairy with gossamer wings in another play. Once, Pista and I starred in a play together. All I recall was a king and queen who sat on a makeshift throne. I played a page boy in green tights, and Pista was a courtier."

Their romance ended that spring because of the involvement of Eva's best girlfriend, a fellow student named Kitty. Eva didn't recall her last name. "The three of us played hide-and-seek. When I was 'it,' I had to find Pista and Kitty. Regrettably, I found them."

She discovered Kitty in Pista's arms.He was kissing her passionately, his hand inside her blouse.

"They didn't see me," Eva said. "I ran away. Pista became the first of a long line of men who would break my heart. I decided then and there I would not place myself in such a position again."

"From that day forth, I would become a *femme fatale,* with a long cigarette holder. I would break hearts across the globe. No one would ever know that it was Pista who turned me into such a cold-hearted love goddess who enticed men to fall in love with her but who treated them with great cruelty."

***

 Magda, the oldest daughter of Vilmos and Jolie, would not be left out of the romance or marriage sweepstakes. She was soon to marry the 35-year-old so-called "Count of Warsaw," a union that would elevate her to the rank of "Countess of Warsaw."

At Madame Sublia's School in Lausanne, Magda had made a friend in Sylvia Barnes, an attractive and charming Londoner who was studying abroad.

At the end of the school term, Sylvia invited Magda to join her family in London for six months. Vilmos was skeptical, but Jolie thought it would be a good idea. "To move in international society, a young woman must know proper English," Jolie told Magda. "A few months in London, combined with what you already know of languages, will make you fluent in English. Taken with your knowledge of French and German, your opportunities for finding a rich husband will be multiplied."

During three weeks of exploring London with Sylvia, Magda fell in love with the city and its people. She would visit London frequently in the future, with each of her husbands-to-be.

One night, Hugh Barnes, Sylvia's father, announced that a friend of his, Count Jan de Bychowsky, would be their guest for dinner. "He has the title of

Count of Warsaw. Jan is also unmarried, in case either of you, Magda or Sylvia, want to become the Countess of Warsaw."

Magda would later write to Jolie in Budapest. "It took only two weeks, but I've fallen in love with the Count of Warsaw. He is a divine creature, so strong, so masculine, so handsome, so intelligent. He literally swept me off my feet. Can you imagine your Magda one day presiding as the Countess of Warsaw? Oh, I forgot to mention. He is the sole owner of the Bychowsky family castle outside Warsaw."

The count was the scion of one of the oldest and most prestigious families in all of Poland, his pedigree stretching back to the days of the Vikings.

Over the next few weeks, Magda's letters took a more serious turn. "Poor Jan is increasingly worried that Hitler has designs on Poland. But Mr. Barnes feels that Hitler will never invade Poland, because Britain has a mutual defense treaty. If Hitler invades Poland, England, because of its treaties and prior agreements, would be forced to declare war on Nazi Germany."

In her final letter before leaving London, Magda wrote to Jolie. "I hope you don't mind, but I've invited Jan to return to Budapest with me. You don't need to arrange a spare room for us. He can share my bedroom."

Vilmos didn't approve of his older daughter's sleeping arrangement, but since he had at least one mistress, he wasn't in a position to protest.

Jolie remembered going to the railway station to meet Magda and her Polish count. "He wasn't quite as handsome as Magda had suggested, but he was attractive—at least he was an aristocrat. I assumed at the time he was rich with vast holdings in Poland. In a taxi back to our villa, Count Bychowsky and Magda told me that they planned to be married in a civil ceremony at the Budapest City Hall. I was worried that she might already be pregnant, so I endorsed that idea. Vilmos also thought it would be the most discreet thing to do."

[In some news accounts, Magda was incorrectly reported to have married the

Hrabia (i.e., Count) **Jan de Bychowsky,** husband of *Hrabina* (Countess) Magda Bychowsky, prior to an aerial dogfight against the Nazis.

With delight, Magda, then a newlywed Polish countess, wrote Jolie in Budapest. "*Nuci,* you didn't tell me: men have such marvelous plumbing, and can do so much with it!"

similarly named Sgt. Jan Bychowski, who was a young Polish poet who died in England on May 22, 1944, at the age of twenty-two]

Jolie did not believe in lavish wedding receptions, thinking money could be better spent on life's necessities. After a brief ceremony in front of a civil judge, she invited about twenty family friends and relatives back to their villa for a reception.

For their wedding present, Vilmos treated them to a week's residency at Budapest's Hotel Gellert, an *art nouveau,* mosaic adorned historic monument, paying their dining tab as well. During their time there, Magda showed Jan the wonders of Budapest by day and by night.

The Gellert was a grand, 733-room palace constructed in 1918 on the Buda side of the Danube, with a restaurant that featured a gypsy orchestra that churned out dance music and nostalgic, sometimes tear-jerking *schmaltz.*

Before her departure with her husband for her new home in Warsaw, Magda assured Jolie that her count was "a *vonderful* lover, although I have no basis of comparison. But if all men are built like Jan, I extend my congratulations to every other woman on the planet."

Jolie hastened to warn Magda that all men were not built like her new husband. "When you and Jan stayed with us, and I passed by your bedroom door one night, I thought the Turks had invaded Hungary again. You really must not scream in ecstasy when he makes love to you. It is very unladylike."

When Jolie learned, to her disappointment, that the Bychowsky castle had been stripped of most of its art and furnishings, she sent her daughter and new son-in-law, as a wedding present, two truckloads of antique reproductions. "I've learned that the count has a prestigious title but no money. The family fortune and its treasures had disappeared at the end of World War I."

At Budapest's railway station, Jolie kissed Magda goodbye and promised to visit Warsaw within the year. "I had so desperately wanted her to marry a man with money," Jolie said. "At least she married a title—The Countess of Warsaw."

Before her departure, Magda urged Jolie to write to Zsa Zsa in Ankara. "Tell her for me that she is not the only one who is to be addressed in the future as Her Excellency," Magda said. "That leaves only poor Eva with no title and no husband."

"Have no fear for her," Jolie said. "She grows more beautiful by the day. I'm sure she'll find some dashing beau, hopefully one with both a title and riches. We cannot all be paupers."

Magda found Jolie's parting words insulting, but forgave her when the castle furnishings arrived from Budapest.

***

Zsa Zsa

As the Venice-Simplon Express roared eastward, Zsa Zsa cuddled her beloved Scottie, Mishka, in her arms, as if it would protect her. She didn't love her husband and was still in love with Willi Schmidt-Kentner, her long-ago composer. She dreaded her upcoming honeymoon night.

Burhan seemed engrossed in the newspapers, especially about the bombing of Barcelona by the armies of Spain's fascist dictator, Francisco Franco. Her husband told her he feared that this might be but a prelude to World War II, but the threat did not concern her.

Mishka did not approve of Zsa Zsa's new master. Every time Belge came near her, he barked ferociously at him.

Finally, the honeymoon night was at hand. Burhan went to the smoking car for a final cigar and glass of French brandy. He was a rich man with expensive European tastes.

Back in their sleeping compartment, Zsa Zsa put on a beige *négligée* and prepared for bed with Mishka sharing a pillow with her. When Burhan returned, he saw her with the dog. Instead of getting into her bed, he kissed her on the forehead. "Good night, my dear." Then he retired to an adjoining compartment, which he had booked just for his luggage and his documents. That is where he spent the night.

Weeks later, she learned that her husband, a devout Muslim, would not sleep where a dog had rested, regarding such an animal as unclean.

When the Venice-Simplon Express arrived in Istanbul, Burhan escorted Zsa Zsa, still clutching Mishka, off the train. There, they were greeted by Burhan's sister, Lehman Burhan Kadri, and her distinguished husband, Yakup Kadri Karaosmanoğlu, designated at the time as the Turkish ambassador to the strategically important neighboring nation of Albania.

Unlike many Turkish women, Lehman had a creamy white complexion, blue eyes, and blondish hair.

Yakup, her new brother-in-law, seemed the very opposite of Belge. With an imposing physique, he had a keen sense of humor and was outspoken and uninhibited. She later admitted to being attracted to "his sexy black mustache."

In the car carrying them to the Belge family's villa, the Belge siblings sat together in the vehicle's front seat, with Zsa Zsa and Yakup seated together in the back. "Welcome, welcome to Istanbul," he told her. "Burhan is one lucky man!"

According to Zsa Zsa's later retelling of her days in Turkey, "His shining black eyes—previously stolen from some impish devil," in her estimation— "virtually undressed me in the car. He even leaned over for a better look at my *décolletage.*"

When Zsa Zsa met her new brother-in-law with the impossible name *(see the two upper lines in the photo above)*, she claimed that he practically undressed her with his eyes on the way to the Belge family villa.

"I was attracted to him because of his sexy mustache," she recalled. "When a Turk wants a woman, he lets her know it."

The photo above depicts the cover of his novel, **Stranger,** which literary critics define as the most important testimonial to the plight of Turkish soldiers during World War I ever written.

This was the first man she'd met on Turkish soil, and she was shocked that he did not conceal his attraction for her. Fortunately, they were not being observed by her bridegroom. "Yakup was practically all over me, even putting his big hand on my leg, I felt he wanted to rape me right there in the limousine and was having trouble restraining himself. I would soon learn that when a Turkish man wanted a woman, he did not keep his intentions a secret, even if that woman was his sister-in-law. I think we were in love by the time we arrived at the home of my in-laws."

It took Zsa Zsa a week before she deciphered that Yakup was one of the most influential men in Turkey, a famous novelist, journalist, and diplomat. He was the favorite writer of Atatürk *[the revered dictator and modernizer of Turkey]*. Yakup's novel *Yaban (Stranger,* originally published in 1932), had depicted the bitter experiences of a Turkish intellectual after losing his arm in the Battle of Gallipoli. Critics compared both its theme and its influence to Erich Maria Remarque's *Im Westen nichts Neues (All Quiet on the Western Front)* originally published in 1929.

A decade older than Belge, Yakup, too, had descended from an old and prominent Ottoman family, the Kara Osmans of Manisa (a city near Izmir, on Turkey's Aegean coast), who had been collectively referenced in the poems of Lord Byron.

The Belge family's ancestral home in Istanbul, as she later related, was "an ivory-white mansion overlooking the Bosphorus. It loomed out at you like something in a fairytale."

At the entrance, a male servant bowed low before Zsa Zsa, removing her Viennese high heels and replacing them with intricately embroidered gold slippers. She and Belge were directed into a large parlor to meet her mother-in-law.

"Maria Ouspenskaya could have played Madame Belge in the movies," Zsa Zsa recalled. "She was a very tiny woman who sat on a silk sofa wrapped in a scarlet red Mohammedan *säl,* with a breast of rubies. She was almost enveloped in brocaded cushions in tones of cocoa brown and emerald green. She smoked a Turkish cigarette through a ten-inch tobacco-colored holder. Her long nails were painted blood red, and she had Bette Davis eyes set off by a thick black kohl. She was like the queen of some Pharoah who occupied the throne in ancient Egypt. I found her terrifying."

"Welcome to our modest home," she said to Zsa Zsa in Turkish, in phrases which had to be translated.

Seemingly from out of nowhere, her father-in-law appeared. He bowed and kissed both hands, welcoming her in French. "Our home is your home," he said.

As he talked to her, she decided that he would be the ideal stand-in for Adolphe Menjou in the movies. Both his manner and dress were impeccable. His mustache suggested a stage villain from the Victorian age. He could be both dashing and, alternately, wickedly sarcastic.

On the one hand, he seemed to be greeting her like an empress. In glaring and immediate contrast, he turned to his son and said, "I've just gotten off the phone with Atatürk. He wants you to call him at once. He seemed very distressed that you have taken a foreign woman as your bride."

Zsa Zsa was horrified to hear that. As she well knew, Mustafa Kemal Atatürk was not only her husband's boss, but the dictator of Turkey. From the moment of her arrival at Istanbul's railway station, she'd seen his photographic portrait everywhere. Reared in the military traditions of the Ottoman Empire, and acknowledged as the Patriarch of modern (i.e., secular) Turkey, he had led the movement for Turkish independence. As the nation's president, he had embarked on a then-radical program of political, economic, and social reforms, outlawing the Ottoman fashion of the fez (round-flat-topped headgear for men), and ordering Turkish women to remove their veils. He also officially ended the centuries-old Ottoman tradition of bigamy, outlawing, at least officially, the possibility of multiple wives for men.

Longtime character actress **Maria Ouspenskaya** (photo above), as remembered by Zsa Zsa, could have interpreted the role of Madame Belge, her new mother-in-law.

Fresh from the spotlights of Vienna, where she'd enjoyed success as a soubrette in a major-league operetta, Zsa Zsa was not amused by this imposing figure.

Neither was Madame Belge impressed with her son's foreign bride.

Leaving her new in-laws alone downstairs to chatter in Turkish, Zsa Zsa was directed upstairs by Lehman, who wanted to show her the bridal suite. She was told that the bedroom she would occupy was once the master suite of a harem that had, a generation ago, featured twenty beautiful young women and seven comely teenaged boys who had each been castrated and subsequently prized for their rectal skills.

The smell of incense assailed her nostrils as Zsa Zsa was ushered into the suite, which was lavishly decorated in regal tones of scarlet and gold.

"A large four-poster bed dominated the room, big enough for five couples," Zsa Zsa said. On each side of the bed was an ivory table laden with Turkish sweetmeats, including a platter of stuffed dates.

Lehman told her that these sweets were laboriously concocted by holy men according to an ancient tradition that insisted that their consumption would stimulate fertility in both a bride and her groom.

"I certainly didn't intend to feast on these sweetmeats," Zsa Zsa said. "There were enough there to rot a girl's teeth and make her gain thirty pounds."

The pillow cases were embroidered with blue pearls, which Lehman said would ward off the evil eye and ensure a happy marriage.

Zsa Zsa stayed alone in the suite for four hours until two servant girls came in to assist her in her bath and to help her get dressed. One of the young girls even washed Zsa Zsa's hair in rosewater to bring out its tones of reddish gold. That same girl turned out to be a supreme hairdresser.

After ablutions and massages equivalent to what she might have expected in a spa, Zsa Zsa made up her own face and donned a white satin gown that Jolie had ordered designed for her in Vienna. For the finishing touch, she adorned herself with the diamonds and rubies given to her by the Gabor family.

Despite her spectacular entrance, Zsa Zsa was later ignored at dinner, not understanding a word being said at table. "I felt I was Burhan's trinket, an amusement, not a wife." After dinner, the men retired to the library for cigars and brandy. Lehman told Zsa Zsa she should retire to the bridal suite and make herself ready for Belge. "He doesn't like to be kept waiting. His last two wives learned that rather painfully."

"That was the first time I learned that he'd been married before," Zsa Zsa said. "Before I climbed those long stairs, I tried to retrieve Mishka, but Lehman told me he'd been assigned to sleep in the kitchen, on direct orders from Belge."

For two hours, Zsa Zsa waited in the bridal bed, becoming almost intoxicated from all that incense. Candles had been placed around the bed. "Those servant girls had doused me with enough perfume to stock a boutique," she said. "I was given a beautiful robe of delicate red silk to wear for my deflowering."

She later wrote in a memoir that it had been with resignation that she had climbed those stairs. "I realized that the honeymoon had begun."

When Belge finally opened the door and entered the suite, she recalled "the lusty gleam in his Oriental eye."

At this point in her memoirs, the curtain is drawn. For years, based on her contradictory statements, Zsa Zsa seemed to deliberately confuse the picture as to which man took her virginity.

One afternoon at the Plaza Hotel in New York City, her friend, the chanteuse, Greta Keller, challenged Zsa Zsa to tell the truth.

"Was it Willi Schmidt-Kentner, whom I introduced you to, or was it your husband, Burhan Belge?" Greta asked. "Or perhaps it was Atatürk? If I remember correctly, in a second memoir, you wrote that as Madame Burhan Belge, you remained a virgin? The marriage, according to you, was never consummated."

"I can explain that," Zsa Zsa told Greta. "Burhan never penetrated me. He told me that since the age of six, a eunuch hired as his guardian had masturbated him sometimes three times daily until he was fourteen years old. After that, he could never ejaculate inside a woman. To achieve orgasm, he had to masturbate himself. Throughout our marriage, we indulged in what the Americans call 'heavy petting,' and he frequently went down on me. But in his bed, I remained as pure as the Virgin Mary…well, perhaps not that pure."

[In spite of Zsa Zsa's claim, Belge eventually fathered a child during the course of his fourth marriage, a son who evolved into the well-known Turkish intellectual, Murat Belge.]

***

The next morning, her father-in-law took her for a walk in a park. Along the way, he noticed and commented on every pretty girl. "I miss the old days. I used to have four wives until it was outlawed." Another lovely young girl passed by. "Zsa Zsa, wouldn't you like me to divorce my wife and marry that beautiful girl instead? A new mother-in-law for you."

Over lunch in the park, he warned Zsa Zsa that she was to remain faithful to her husband, even if she found out he had mistresses on the side. "That was the rule of the harem. A woman could only talk to her husband, one of the other wives, or a eunuch."

"I couldn't endure living in a harem, not even if I were the favorite," she told him. "Of course, I would be the favorite because I would have poisoned all the other girls."

Buxom, westernized, and with the distinct impression that she was universally viewed as a sexual trinket, Zsa Zsa received some early advice from her new father-in-law, who resembled **Adolphe Menjou** *(photo above)*. "It's the patriotic duty of every Turk to surrender his wife to the Turkish dictator."

Zsa Zsa listened carefully.

"There is only one time that you can cheat on your husband and commit adultery," he said.

"What would be the occasion for that?" she asked.

"If Atatürk should summon you to his palace bed, you must go and serve him as his maiden," he said. "It is the unwritten law in Turkey. Every Turk would surrender his wife to Atatürk. It is their patriotic duty."

"I will keep that in mind if I ever meet this Atatürk," she said, with a gleam in her eye.

***

 The arrival of 23-year-old Paul Yankovich, an army lieutenant into the life of Eva was literally a knight appearing in shining armor on a white horse. He was every Hungarian girl's dream of a dashing Hussar on horseback. "And that uniform of his…it was dazzling," Eva said.

[In her memoirs, Orchids and Salami, *Eva used the pseudonym "Ferenc" to identify this man—her first lover.]*

She was only seventeen when he came riding into her life "like a war-horse operetta," as she described it. Vilmos had more or less adopted Paul as his military side. In some ways, he had become the son that Jolie had never delivered to him.

To the ghost writer of her memoirs, Eva gave a detailed description of Yankovich, her Hussar lover, but fearing that he might still be alive, she removed most of the details from her final version.

Eva found "Paul's eyes bluer than Lake Balaton was in its pristine condition. He had raven-black hair, gorgeous skin, and it would take a Michelangelo to capture the contours of his well-developed body. You could see your face reflected in his shiny black Hessian boots. He wore tight black trousers with gold stripes down his studly legs. His broad chest was covered with medals, and what would a uniform be without epaulets on those broad shoulders? His tunic must have been made by the most expensive tailor in Budapest."

"His head rested under a bearskin helmet known within the ranks of the Hussars at the time as a *busby.* He also wore a *sabretache,* an ornate pouch hanging from his leather belt, and a *pelisse,* a short-waisted overjacket slung casually over one shoulder. Did I mention spurs, a jaunty cap with visor, a riding crop, black leather gloves, and marabou frills?"

"Right then and there, I decided it was father's aide who was *the one.* After all, Magda had been deflowered by her count, and Zsa Zsa by her ambassador (or so I assumed at the time). Little Eva was next, and she'd met the man upon whom she was going to bestow her favors."

[While living with Merv Griffin during the twilight of her life, Eva would confess that of all her many lovers, Paul was the most dashing, the most romantic, and the most adventurous. "Vilmos told me that any Hussar who is not dead by the age of thirty is a blackguard. By tradition, Hussars are swashbucklers like Errol Flynn in the movies. They are reckless and hard drinking, given to cursing and chasing women. Invariably, they are moustachioed."]

Although Vilmos seemed to dote on Paul, he warned Eva not to get involved with him. "He's charming all right," her father told her. "All the girls he meets succumb to his wit, grace, looks, and presence, but he's a notorious playboy. He's rumored to have fathered at least eight illegitimate children and even impregnated an officer's wife who, presumably, had passed the child-bearing age."

When Eva was first introduced to Paul after a parade, he leaned down to gaze into her eyes, using his riding crop to tickle her nose. "When he flashed those pearly white teeth at me, they outdazzled the sun. That day, I felt I'd captured the brass ring on the carousel. I knew he was attracted to me—just me—and I plotted to make him forget those other women he had known. They were mere trifles. I was the real thing."

HUSSAR (*def.*) A macho, dick-swinging, hell-raising, horse-riding, usually-dead-before-he-was-30 sex symbol of the Great Hungarian Plain.

Years after her affair with him, Eva remembered her lover, "Ferenc" (aka **Paul Yankovitch**) as having looked like this.

That very night when Paul dined at the Gabor villa, Eva's plan to capture him was made far easier when Vilmos announced that he would be joining them for a vacation at the family's summer cottage beside Lake Balaton.

"My romantic dream was coming true faster than I thought it would," Eva said. "I couldn't wait to see his naked body. I just hoped he would wear the skimpiest and most revealing bathing attire."

On their first afternoon at the Gabor's summer cottage, Eva spent most of the morning trying to find the most seductive bathing suit to wear. Paul had invited her for a swim and a picnic lunch along the lake. At eleven o'clock that morning, he appeared before her in a bathrobe and invited her for a late morning stroll. Along with a small bag, he carried the picnic basket.

The sun was high in the sky as they strolled along, taking in the beauty of the lake. "He had two subjects of conversation—my beauty and his military career," she said. "I found both topics fascinating."

Paul steered Eva toward a secluded spot set back from the lake. Under the shade of a tree, he spread out a blanket. She sat on the blanket, looking up at him as he dropped his robe.

She would later recall, "I have never seen such a beautiful male animal. Only his vital parts were covered. The rest of his olive-skinned body was on display, and it radiated power—long, lean, and muscular. As he moved, his legs, arms, and trunk were filled with a manly grace, almost ballet choreography. I took in every fiber of his bronze body. He could have posed for a statue of a Greek god. His luscious ruby-red lips were made for lovemaking."

"'Be still,' I cautioned my rapidly beating heart. "I know I sound like the romance writer of some bodice-ripper cheap paperback, but I'm recalling what I felt at the time. Schoolgirl or not, I wanted this man to take me, and, as was said at the time, make a woman of me. I also was aware that he had to be the aggressor. I knew he'd come to me the first chance we had to be alone. As for that afternoon, my only reward—and it was wonderful—was a deep, passionate kiss that aroused the fires within me."

The opportunity for Paul and Eva to be alone came about the very next afternoon. Vilmos announced that he and Jolie were driving to the nearest train station to meet another house guest he'd invited down for a two-week vacation. He would be occupying the second guest room.

When Jolie and Vilmos had been gone for fifteen minutes, Paul wasted no time. Eva was in her bedroom when she looked up at her open doorway. A completely nude Paul appeared in its frame.

During the years to come, she would dine out with friends, including Merv Griffin, telling him and others that "I lost it that afternoon in our summer cottage."

"I know that the first time can be traumatic to both men and women on occasion. But not with me. I wanted Paul to devour me, and he did so with great skill. That iron searing my insides reached the source of my needs, fulfilling them beyond my wildest dreams. He was the man I wanted and dreamed about. After that afternoon spent in his arms, it would be a downhill ride from then on, more valleys with an occasional peak. But no one ever measured up to my original seducer, no one, although a few came close."

After her deflowering that afternoon, complications arose when Vilmos and Jolie returned from the depot with their latest house guest. Count Joska Váler was one of Vilmos' fellow officers. He had just turned forty and was elegantly attired in full dress uniform. His speech, manner, and grace showed his breeding.

"The count was handsome in a traditional sort of way," Eva said, "but he didn't possess the show-stopping allure of my original seducer. He spent most of the early evening raving about what an enchanting beauty I was."

She later admitted that she had been flattered by the count's attention and did not feel in any way that "I was betraying the passion I felt for Paul."

On the second night, when Váler invited her for an evening stroll along the lake, Paul did not conceal his jealousy. He was furious. "The count hardly disguises his lust for you," he said. "It's characterized by flaring nostrils and asthmatic breathing."

Vilmos tried to be a mediator between Váler and Paul, but to no avail. The tension between the two men grew worse. They finally were reduced to the mutual exchange of biting insults.

The boiling point came one evening when Paul's rage exploded at the dinner table. Eva wrote that "He flung a magnum of sour cream into Count Joska's obliging face."

The count, an officer in the Hungarian Army, could not tolerate such insults from an enlisted man. He challenged Paul to a duel three days hence.

For the next three days, Eva admitted to being frantic, waiting for the sun to rise above a nearby park on the third day. Her two suitors would face each other in a duel with swords.

"All I could think about was what part of Paul that the count might lacerate," Eva said. "Perhaps his ear. Or perhaps Paul would cut off the sharp edge of the count's patrician nose."

"I had visions of six inches of steel protruding from the nether side of Paul, and I could hear him gasping, *'Eva! Eva!* as he died on the field of honor that chilly morning."

She also said she "had no desire to see the count skewered like so much shish kebab for his gallantry."

Before she retired to bed the night before the duel, she had visited each man in his bedroom and wished him luck. She also claimed that she was not terrified that either one would kill the other. "Perhaps a nick here or there, or a scar on the face. Dueling wasn't to the death the way it used to be. The joust was merely to cut off a piece of the opponent's face—a small slice, hardly enough for a cocktail canapé."

Eva could not bear to attend the duel. An hour later, word reached her that Paul "won me fair and square by cutting one cubic centimeter of the count's thin blue blood. A wound on the count's cheek left him with a scar for life, which he later claimed made him even more popular with the ladies."

Upon his return to Budapest, and having won Eva in a duel, Paul began to bestow lavish presents on her. During their evenings together, he proposed marriage to her and even told her that they would have six children. "I am fertile, very fertile, as my record shows."

Baskets of flowers arrived almost daily. She could not understand how he could afford such costly gifts on the meager pay of a Hussar. Weeks later, she learned that Vilmos was picking up the tab for all those gifts.

The affair came crashing to an end when Paul presented her with an expensive diamond ring. "The diamond was so very big and so very beautiful," she said.

Soon after, Vilmos learned that Paul had purchased the engagement ring at a well-known rival to the jewelry outlet operated by the Gabors. "He had the nerve to send me the bill from our competitor," Vilmos shouted at Eva, exploding in rage. "This is the final insult. You are forbidden to ever see this bastard again!"

"That was the end of my summer romance," Eva said. "For one entire week, I nursed a broken heart. But I soon got over it. One night at a party, I met the man of my dreams. If such a thing was possible, he was even more beautiful than Paul. It was love at first sight. I had to have him."

***

["When I lived in California in the years to come, Paul wrote me every season, including Christmas," Eva said in an interview. "He got married and had an array of children. In 1972, he sent me a family portrait of his wife and kids, none of whom had inherited his youthful beauty. It was obvious that the brood inherited the ugly genes of their mother. As for my darling Paul, time had taken a toll. That wife of his must have kept him on a diet of dumplings, pancakes, and goulash. He weighed 250 pounds...at least. The raven black hair had become a bald head. The luscious red lips that had explored every inch of my body were still intact, but they led to a triple chin. Alas, my dashing Hussar lived on only in my memories."]

***

Six months after Magda wed Count Jan Bychowsky, Jolie flew to Warsaw, the only time in her life she ever set foot on Polish soil.

Flying in a battered airplane, Jolie, attired in mink and diamonds, arrived there near the grisly dawn of World War II. "Before getting on the plane, I checked myself in a mirror. I looked like Greta Garbo."

At Warsaw's Airport, all the Bychowsky family had turned out to greet her—grandparents, brothers, sisters, nieces and nephews, distant cousins.

To her chagrin, as Jolie stepped off the plane onto its ramp, she was hit with hurricane-gust winds blasting across the great Polish plains. Her large hat and veil were blown to Siberia, she later claimed, as the winds lacerated her carefully coiffed hairdo. "After a few seconds, I looked like Elsa Lanchester in that 1933 movie, *The Bride of Frankenstein.*"

Her Excellency, the Countess of Warsaw, Magda herself, rushed to greet her windswept mother. Magda immediately chastised her, accusing her of looking like a bagwoman from the back streets of Budapest. She begged her mother to make emergency repairs.

"How could I?" Jolie later lamented. "I was on the tarmac only twelve feet from this bunch of Poles, most of whom looked rather unkempt themselves."

Arriving at the seedy, fast-decaying Bychowsky castle, whose heyday appeared to have peaked during the 14th Century, she asked the whereabouts of the Count of Warsaw. She was told that he'd gone hunting. As she surveyed the castle's interior, she decided that the only impressive elements were the furnishings she'd trucked in from Budapest.

"As I tried to restore my looks in the antiquated bathroom, I realized the rusty plumbing had been installed when dinosaurs roamed the earth. To add to my embarrassment, when I had to use the toilet and flushed it, its waters overflowed. When I went to take a bath, I saw, to my horror, that the tub had so much grime it looked like it had been used by the entire Polish army."

In the parlor, Jolie met with Magda for a long-delayed reunion. "Even though she was as poor as a pauper, she ruled the castle like she was Catherine the Great. The trouble was she had only two servants left—a maid and a cook. Obviously, one poor old maid could not be the housekeeper for an entire castle, so everything lay under a mountain of dust."

"Once, Jan and his father had a staff of twenty-eight," Magda told her. "They even had three gardeners. Now the grounds are overgrown."

"I could see that," Jolie said. "But before Jan gets back, I want to know how the marriage is going."

"Jan has two skills—one as king of the boudoir, the other as a military figure, great on a horse or piloting an airplane. Other than that, he is a horror at protecting his business interests. He is penniless. We haven't paid the grocery bill or our meager staff in weeks. But

When she arrived, disheveled, in Warsaw to meet the extended family of her oldest daughter's new husband, Jolie said she looked like the Bride of Frankenstein.

(Photo above: **Elsa Lanchester** *as The Bride of Frankenstein in 1953.)*

Later, after her close inspection of the Bychowsky family's crumbling castle and demolished fortune, a horrified Jolie said she felt, as well as looked like, the actress in the photo above.

we still have our titles: The Count and Countess of Warsaw."

"I don't give this marriage much chance," Jolie said bluntly. "Do you realize that Europe is awash with impoverished aristocrats? If war comes, kingdoms and aristocratic titles will mean nothing. A title without the money to back it up is meaningless. At least Zsa Zsa married a man of means, even if he is an infidel."

Even though Jan eventually made an appearance in military regalia, replete with boots and medals, she never really got to know her Polish son-in-law. She remembered him as a tall and austere man "devoted to hunting in the forests surrounding his castle. He spent most nights drinking with his men in his Polish Cavalry Regiment until the early hours of morning."

Over dinner, all he could talk about was his fear that an invasion of Poland by the forces of Nazi Germany was imminent. He did not seem to view Russia as a menace looming from the East.

Jan assured Jolie that he had great faith in the fighting spirit of Polish forces. "We will meet Hitler at the frontier and destroy his war machine," he boasted.

She angered him when she asked, "What are you prepared to do? Ride up on your horse and confront a German tank?"

The next morning, Jolie got up early and made her way to breakfast in the castle's kitchen while Jan and Magda were still asleep. At around midnight the night before, when she had passed by their bedroom, she had heard her daughter's screams of ecstasy, so loud that she was able to confirm that the count was at least good at something.

As she drank coffee which had "obviously been made with grounds left over from some army camp in World War I," the grocery boy arrived. He informed Jolie that he could not deliver the weekend groceries until Magda settled previous, still-unpaid bills. The tally came to about $600 in U.S. dollars. She retrieved her purse and paid the bill.

She also learned that neither the cook nor the maid had been paid for the past two months. She also settled their wage claims. "I felt like some Jewish banker," she later said.

Finding the conditions intolerable, Jolie cut short her visit.

On the day of her departure, the entire clan turned out to bid her *adieu* at the airport. "Even though it was daylight, I wore my nighttime diamonds and had never looked better," Jolie said. "I was hoping to erase the Bride of Frankenstein image I'd made on my arrival."

Jan kissed her hand and Magda embraced her. Jolie thanked each member of the clan, all of whom had collectively bestowed an enormous cluster of pink carnations upon her. "Actually, I was never a pink carnation woman. Orchids were my passion."

From the top of the ramp, before boarding the airplane, Jolie turned and waved to her in-laws. Except for Magda, she would never see any of them again, including her son-in-law.

The very airport at which she'd embarked would soon be bombed out of existence.

***

Ankara was still a work in progress when Zsa Zsa first arrived. Instead of the more obvious metropolis of Istanbul, Atatürk had defined this remote city on the high plains of Anatolia as his capital. "It was electrified by its mixture of exoticism and modernity," Zsa Zsa said.

Her new home was along the new capital's prestigious Embassy Row. As an ancient city, Ankara traced its lineage back to the Bronze Age. Over the centuries, it had seen a parade of conquerors—the Hittites, the Phrygians, the Lydians, the Persians, the Greeks, the Romans, and so many others.

She quickly learned that the city was known for its long-haired Angora goat, from whose lustrous fleece mohair is produced. "Its meat was so strong that even my Scottie, Mishka, turned up his nose." Ankara was also known for its Angora cats. Zsa Zsa preferred the city's pears, honey, and muscat grapes, and she soon identified her favorite Turkish dish as a regional version of tender chicken breasts beaten until they had the consistency of whipped cream.

She became accustomed to the eerie wail of the *muezzines,* whose call to prayer (*"Allah, illah, Allah!*) resounded regularly from the towers of the minarets. The sights, sounds, and smells of the endless bazaars lining the narrow, cobble-covered streets lured her into an exotic Eastern world. One time, she screamed in horror at the sight of a barrel of goat eyeballs. Her teenage houseboy, Ali, assured her, "In Ankara, this is a delicacy, Your Excellency!"

On the dawn of World War II, Ankara, functioning as a diplomatic bridge between the Soviet Union and the Western powers, had evolved into a centerpiece of intrigue and conspiracies. "Everyone seemed to be a spy for some country," she said. "Burhan warned me never to repeat anything I heard in our household, and he also warned me that our telephone was tapped."

A powerful man in Turkey, Belge was the leader of the staunchly nationalist movement known as "The Young Turks." Zsa Zsa defined them as "political zealots and hotheads."

These young men—sometimes thirty, forty, even fifty in all—met at Belge's villa on Embassy Row, a site which evolved more or less into their clubhouse and headquarters.

Embassy wife: **Zsa Zsa** in the gardens of her home on Embassy Row in Ankara.

As a means of keeping her figure, **Zsa Zsa** went riding on her horse, **Fatushka**, at a stable in a posh neighborhood of Ankara, nearly every day.

When she left her well-connected husband for a safer life in America, she feared that he would order that her horse be shot.

A rumor was circulating at the time about Atatürk's failing health, and that Belge might be his heir apparent. When Zsa Zsa heard this, she confronted her husband. "Does that mean I'll sit on the throne of Turkey as its queen? If so, I'd better learn Turkish and quick."

"Don't be a silly Hungarian goose," he told her. "Turkey has no queen. If I'm elected president, you'd become the First Lady of Turkey."

"Don't you be the silly one," she said. "As president, you could declare yourself king...or perhaps emperor. That way I could become the queen. You never thought of that, did you?" Then she stormed out of the room.

At that point in his career, Belge was a strong supporter of Hitler and the Nazi party. As Turkey's unofficial minister of propaganda, he often spoke on the phone with Josef Goebbels, Hitler's chief propagandist. Once, Zsa Zsa overheard her husband talking to Hermann Göring about the Nazi *Luftwaffe*.

As Jews, the Gabors, including all three sisters, were anti-Nazi. Belge warned his wife as she visited the various embassies, to suppress her opinions. At times, she did, although she could also be indiscreet.

Her first invitation was to the German Embassy, where her host was Franz von Papen, Hitler's ambassador to Turkey.

She devoured the fat goose he served, and told him, "It was so delicious and juicy, it could only have come from Hungary. You Germans buy up all the good food in Turkey and export it to your country, leaving us with leftovers."

Belge flushed with embarrassment, and Von Papen greeted her "with a sinister silence and the kind of smile a Nazi soldier gave a victim about to enter the gas chamber," according to Zsa Zsa.

The following week, she was the guest of the Russian ambassador, Lev Mikhailovich Karakhan, whom she remembered as a "giant of a man with a huge, oblong spade beard." He was married to a Russian ballerina."

In the Soviet Embassy, she feasted on pearls of Beluga caviar. "Here we are enjoying this succulent delight while millions of Russian peasants don't even have bread," she told him.

In spite of her impudence, Karakhan chose her as his bridge partner. During future bridge events, he chose her again, even though she'd lost every game for him. When asked why he continued to select her, he said, "I enjoy staring down into her delicious décolletage."

Soon after that, another ambassador would also stare at Zsa Zsa.

Belge had purchased a white Arabian mare for Zsa Zsa. She'd named it Fatushka, and had stabled her horse at the Ankara Riding Club, north of the city. Every day, she showed up wearing jodhpurs and carrying a riding crop.

One afternoon, as she prepared to go riding, she became aware of someone staring at her from behind. Her fellow rider was the British ambassador to Turkey, Sir Percy Loraine, 12th Baronet.

He later recalled, "I first saw Zsa Zsa on her horse, a perfect little figure in a riding habit with golden hair under a black velvet cap. I was afraid for her to turn around and face me, because I just knew I would be disappointed. When she turned around to look at me, I faced the most beautiful woman I had ever seen, and I was from London, which was awash with beautiful women. She literally bowled me over with her perfectly formed features. She was like a dreamy mask floating on a pink cloud."

She also took in Sir Percy's features, later describing his face as being "aflame with desire. He looked very dashing in his British khaki uniform. His blonde hair was graying, as he appeared to be a man in his early fifties. I was certain he was a hit with the ladies. A tall man with striking blue eyes, he had the compelling charm of an English aristocrat when they are at their very best and not snobbish."

He introduced himself to her and invited her to go riding with him, but only after telling her that he'd met Belge at a reception on Embassy Row three nights before. Later, when they stopped for a rest, she became aware of what an important diplomat he was, having served as the British ambassador to such

On the eve of war, sexy dalliances were commonplace among the very upper-crust along Ankara's Embassy Row :

Sir Percy Loraine, 12th Baronet, and British Ambassador to Turkey, found Zsa Zsa "the most beautiful woman I have ever seen."

61

cities as Teheran, Cairo, Athens, Beijing, Paris, and Madrid. Within months, he would become Britain's ambassador to Mussolini's Rome shortly before the explosive debut of World War II.

At the end of their ride, he invited her back to the British Embassy for tea with his wife, Lady Loraine. Over tea, both of them told her how disappointed they were to have been assigned to Ankara. Sir Percy referred to the "pathetic bleakness of Ankara," and Lady Loraine defined it as "the most Godforsaken hole I have ever been in." They referred to Ankara's Embassy Row, on which Belge and Zsa Zsa lived, as "a concentration camp for diplomats."

During the remainder of her stay in the Turkish capital, Zsa Zsa went horseback riding with Sir Percy every day. She quickly became aware of his physical attraction to her, and she flirted outrageously with him whenever Lady Loraine or Belge weren't around.

"I think Sir Percy fell madly in love with me," she would later tell her friends. "One afternoon, we got caught in a sandstorm blowing in from the desert. We sought shelter in a little cabin used for storing tools. We didn't go all the way—after all, Sir Percy was a gentleman and I was a lady—but he did smother me in kisses and became familiar with my breasts. We escaped from prying eyes whenever we could, and we had some rather torrid sessions, although he never invaded the prime target."

Sir Percy was not alone in his focus on Zsa Zsa. Yakup, her brother-in-law, continued to pursue her whenever they were alone. On occasion, he would grab her and kiss her passionately, feeling her ample breasts. "Burhan is just letting a beauty like you go to waste," he told her. "He is not man enough for you."

"I became familiar with Yakup's lusty tongue," she said. "He whispered in my ear all the naughty things he wanted to do to me. I suspected most of his sexual promises came from reading *Arabian Nights.*"

Some of Zsa Zsa's most ardent admirers in Ankara remained anonymous. Sometimes, after her daily horseback ride, she visited a shop run by six Circassian brothers, the eldest of whom was named Numad. In looks, she compared the brothers' dark eyes and long, slender faces to figures that might have been sketched by Modigliani.

She would visit the shop mainly as a distraction, having a Turkish coffee every afternoon and looking over the exquisite copperware and other handcrafts.

One afternoon, Numad showed her the most exquisite pearl she'd ever seen. He claimed that the Ambassador to Afghanistan would like to present her with the gem with his compliments.

"What does he want in return?" she asked.

"For you to be nice to him."

She turned from the pearl and stormed out of the shop. But instead of boycotting it, she returned a few days later, apologizing for the pearl incident. Then, despite the strong reaction his words had precipitated a few days before, Numad then presented her with a stunning gold bracelet studded with emeralds and rubies. This time, he said it was from an unknown admirer who wanted nothing in return, "perhaps a chance to visit the shop while you're wearing it, so he can enjoy it on your beautiful wrist."

Once again, she feigned more anger than she actually felt, feeling secretly flattered by the offer. Later, she said, "I was such a silly fool, and I regretted my foolish decision. I learned a valuable lesson for the rest of my life. In my future, I would no longer turn down jewelry from any source, anonymous or otherwise."

In time, she'd deliver a famous utterance: "I have never hated a man enough to give his diamonds back."

Whereas Zsa Zsa might have rejected some jewelry, she accepted any invitation from any embassy that was offered to Belge and her. One afternoon, Lady Loraine telephoned. Belge was away on another of his mysterious trips to Berlin. On the phone, Lady Loraine invited her to a dinner she was staging for Colonel Charles de Gaulle of France, a friend of Sir Percy. "I need a lady guest to sit next to him, and you would be perfect—not just for your beauty, but because you're fluent in French and can keep him amused."

"I never heard of De Gaulle, but I imagine him to look like Gary Cooper being chased through the desert by Marlene Dietrich in the film *Morocco,*" she said. She'd later recall, "I don't think General Eisenhower spent as much time preparing for the D-Day landings than I did making myself ready to meet this dashing French soldier. I was attired in diamonds, rubies, and red satin, my hair rinsed with a solution that turned it into a honey blonde."

As it turned out, De Gaulle didn't look like Gary Cooper at all. Nearing fifty years old when she met him, he was tall, hook-nosed, and austere. "I found him immensely patriotic, loving all things French. But he also had an eye for a beautiful woman of any nationality, even Hungarian. He towered over me. As we stood drinking a cocktail, he looked down frequently into my amply displayed bosom."

"Often, he was addressed in German, and I was surprised that he was fluent in that tongue as well. He told me that he'd been imprisoned by the Germans dur-

Zsa Zsa met **Charles de Gaulle** at an embassy dinner in Turkey. "He knew all things French except French kissing," she later said. "I taught him that."

"Jackie Kennedy went to Paris and enthralled him. But I enthralled him long before her."

ing the First World War, and that he had made five unsuccessful attempts to escape. 'I was eager to get back into the war,' he told me."

"I was so frustrated for being locked away in solitary confinement, away from the action on the front," he said. "I compared it to being cuckolded. No newspaper, no tobacco, what a shameful fortune. I was almost embarrassed to return to France when I was let out of prison."

He also told her, "Some misguided people refer to me as a writer instead of as a soldier. My latest book, *Vers l'Armée de Métier (Towards a Professional Army)*, sold only 700 copies in France, but 7000 copies in Germany. I heard that it was read by Hitler."

After the banquet, De Gaulle escorted Zsa Zsa back to her villa on Embassy Row. She invited him in for a nightcap of French brandy, and he accepted.

Over drinks, he told her that he might be a lowly colonel at present, but "one day I, not Adolf Hitler, will preside over a Free France."

"I had little desire to seduce him, and I don't know if he would have agreed had I tried, but I felt I was in the presence of a future world leader," she said. "Shortly before midnight, I stood on my tiptoes and kissed him passionately, which seemed to shock him. But his tongue responded. I guess that's called French kissing. Had I known that in the future, he would become one of the most important men in the world, I would have pursued him more aggressively. But at the time, I was still a technical virgin. I had not lost my cherry, as the Americans say. What a stupid expression to call the deflowering of a virgin."

"In the 1960s, I heard on the news that Jacqueline Kennedy had mesmerized De Gaulle, then the president of the French Republic, when she accompanied one of my lovers, John F. Kennedy, to Paris. What the First Lady might not have known was that I had enchanted De Gaulle and also had seduced JFK long before she ever met them."

***

Zsa Zsa's brother-in-law, Yakup, was soon to leave his post as the Turkish ambassador to Albania, with the understanding that he'd be reassigned to Prague.

He invited Belge and Zsa Zsa to fly with him to Tirana, where he was to gather up his possessions and bid an *adieu* to King Zog, who had ruled Albania since it had been molded into a kingdom in 1928.

Before arriving, Yakup tried to explain some of Albania's complicated political history to Zsa Zsa, with the understanding that she was about to be fêted at the highest levels of the Albanian government. After foreign occupation by the Serbs and the Italians in the aftermath of World War I, Albania had become an independent country. Zog had the powers of a dictator, although he faced constant interference from Italy. And although Zog resisted, Mussolini more or less wanted to bring Albania into Italy's expanding empire.

During their second night in Tirana, King Zog threw a lavish dinner in his palace, inviting Yakup, Zsa Zsa, and Belge as his guests of honor.

At the reception, the king had little to say to Belge, finding him "a sour and dour Turk." Instead, he devoted all of his time and attention to Zsa Zsa. Attired in diamonds and white satin, with plunging *décolletage,* she was clearly the most beautiful woman at the gala.

Zog was enchanted with her beauty, wit, and charm.

"We are still a bit primitive as a country, he told her. "Violence is not unknown. In 1923, I was shot and wounded in Parliament. Because of dangerous conditions, I've had to create a police state—no civil liberties, no free press. Of course, I've had my opponents. Often they are visited by the state police and never heard from again."

Instead of being appalled, Zsa Zsa, raised in an imperial family, found herself attracted to a king who had such power over his people.

As the evening progressed, he escorted her to a private room whose access and whose interior resembled a bank vault. In it, he displayed to her his treasure trove of gold coins and precious stones. He invited her to select a gem of her choice, and she rather greedily chose a large diamond ring.

She knew that Belge would interpret her acceptance of it as a personal insult, but for such a large stone, she was willing to risk her husband's displeasure.

At dinner, Zsa Zsa sat next to the king. He told her, "I share much in common with Atatürk. I, too, have abolished Islamic law, preferring a civil code based on Switzerland."

Zog looked over at Belge at the far end of the table with a disapproving eye. "An odd marriage," he said. "I understand you are a Jew married to a Muslim? Much of Europe, not to mention the Muslim

Géraldine of Albania, half Hungarian, half American, was hailed as the loveliest queen in Europe at the time of her ascension to the throne of Albania.

"The king himself told me I was more beautiful than his queen," Zsa Zsa alleged.

On a state visit with her ambassador husband, Zsa Zsa mesmerized **King Zog of Albania**, who claimed he'd divorce his queen for the chance of marrying her.

"I was King Zog's Cinderella, and he lusted after me. On those buggy rides in the park, he had roving hands."

world, is prejudiced against Jews," the king said. "That is not the case with Albania. Since 1938, I have opened the borders of my country to Jewish refugees fleeing from the Nazis in Germany."

That night over brandy, he told her that even though he was born an aristocrat, he had been more or less ignored by the other monarchs of Europe, including the King of England. "They are not impressed with my pedigree."

When she commented that he was heavily guarded, he told her it was necessary because he had survived fifty-five assassination attempts, "one of them in Vienna when I attended a performance of the opera."

"I noticed that your wife is not here tonight," Zsa Zsa said. She had been told that Zog had only recently married Countess Géraldine Apponyi di Nagyappony, a woman who was half-Hungarian, half-American. "I was looking forward to conversing with her in Hungarian."

"She is pregnant with my first child," he said. "She's experiencing some difficulties."

During the entire week Zsa Zsa spent in the Albanian capital, King Zog wooed her and made repeated passes at her. Ever flirtatious, she, nonetheless, managed to hold him off. "I should have met you before I married Burhan," she said. "My mother, Jolie Gabor, told my sisters and myself that we should marry kings, or at least princes."

Albania's Royal Family *(left to right)* **King Zog, Crown Prince Leka Zogu,** and **Queen Géraldine.**

In 1939, they fled into exile when Mussolini's army invaded Albania, putting an end to their kingdom.

"I can always divorce the countess," he told her, "and marry you, which is my desire. But I must await the birth of my son and heir."

[HRH Crown Prince Leka Zogu would be born in April of 1939.]

King Zog spent so much time with Zsa Zsa, including afternoon and evening buggy rides in public parks, that all of Tirana was buzzing with speculation about his new infatuation.

The local press was controlled and could not print the rumors, but an Austrian journalist filed a report. In Vienna, it ran under the headline *KING ZOG MEETS HIS CINDERELLA.*

On her final night in Tirana, Zsa Zsa was practically raped when she made a farewell visit to the palace, despite Belge's objections. His Majesty received her in his private suite. Later, she refused to comment on what happened between them, only to say, "I came away with my virginity intact but only narrowly, perhaps an inch or so." The comment was so enigmatic it gave way to all sorts of interpretations.

She later wrote Jolie in Budapest: "I turned down a chance to become the Queen of Albania."

[It was with a sense of horror that Zsa Zsa read that two days after the birth of King Zog's son and heir, Crown Prince Leka Zugo, on April 7, 1939, Mussolini's armies invaded Albania. King Zog, along with his wife and infant son, abandoned Tirana, fleeing for their lives. When Italian soldiers stormed Tirana Palace, they found a pile of linen stained with afterbirth in the Queen's suite. A wire was sent to Mussolini: "THE CUB HAS ESCAPED." In Rome, Mussolini declared Albania a protectorate under King Victor Emmanuel III.

When the Communists eventually took control after the war, the short-lived Kingdom of Albania dissolved, fading into history. The country became a full member of NATO in 2009.]

***

Back in Ankara, having flown there from Tirana, Belge staged a farewell dinner for Yakup and his wife, Lehman, before they left for their next diplomatic assignment in Prague.

In Ankara at that time, the choice of venues for late-night dancing and dining was very limited, confined mainly to the Ankara Palas Hotel and, around the corner, Karpiç's Restaurant. Founded by Ivan Karpiç, a Russian immigrant, this dining room (which featured a dance orchestra) stood near Ulus Square.

Writer Barry Rubin compared its interior to that of a "Kansas City railroad station lunch room." Its walls were adorned with portraits of Atatürk at various stages of his career. Sometimes, Atatürk himself held meetings of his cabinet ministers here.

The restaurant catered to embassy personnel from both the Allied and Axis powers. Sitting next to each other, along with a coven of spies from various countries, were tables filled with British, American, Russian, French, Italian, or German personnel.

Greeting the Belge party was bald, round-headed Karpiç himself. Always attired in an immaculately tailored white suit, he had a thick Russian accent.

"I sat at table with my boring husband, listening to his uptight sister, and fending off feels from under the table from my brother-in-law," Zsa Zsa recalled. "I felt marooned in this lonely outpost surrounded by an endless sea of sand. Within minutes, life was about to change."

Suddenly, there was a great deal of commotion at the entrance. Karpiç himself rushed out to greet the new arrivals. A dozen uniformed policemen, each of them heavily armed, entered the restaurant, followed by six beautiful women gowned in the latest *haute couture* from Paris fashion houses. They were followed by four Turkish men in tuxedos. Finally, Atatürk himself arrived at the entrance, as the entire group of diners rose in respect.

He paused briefly to survey the scene before him. He took out a gold case and removed a cigarette. A security guard rushed to light it for him.

As Karpiç led the progression of Atatürk's entourage, he passed the Belge party. His eyes seemed to lock on Zsa Zsa's. She agreed with the assessment of King Edward VIII during his visit to Istanbul. He remembered "those ice-blue eyes as the most penetrating I have ever seen."

Atatürk's somber eyes gazed into Zsa Zsa's long-lashed ones. "He looked at me as if he'd known me intimately for a millennium," she said. "Suddenly, I knew I would be his. All I had to do was wait for the summons to his palace."

At his banqueting table, no one sat down until the Turkish dictator was comfortably seated. Zsa Zsa had a clear view of him from her chair thirty feet away. She noticed that he kept glancing at her.

At long last, she had come face to face with this Turkish legend, who had once proclaimed himself as "King of the battlefield, King of the boudoir."

He'd made a striking appearance at the entrance, appearing in a tuxedo with a black cloak lined in red silk.

She didn't know what was accurate about his legend and what had been invented. He'd once boasted that, "I can outdrink, outfight, and outlove any man in Turkey." As a womanizer, he was known to have taken the virginity of some 2,000 young Turkish girls. He'd also seduced the wives of several foreign ambassadors, including Belge's first wife.

He was said to sleep only four hours a night and was a man of shifting, often terrifying moods. His followers called him "The Gray Wolf."

When he tired of a woman, he adopted her

Kemal Atatürk was the Father of Turkey, a warrior of great stamina and power who devoured beautiful young women. He is depicted above as a warrior *(on the left)* and as he looked *(right)* when Zsa Zsa enchanted him in Ankara.

The dictator and his Ambassador's wife met frequently at his secret hideaway in Ankara's Old City. "He taught me all the sexual secrets of the Sultans of the Ottoman Empire," she later claimed.

He also enlisted her as an unwitting spy within this government, gathering names of younger opponents who resisted him.

as his daughter. One of these former mistresses who became his daughter was Sabiha Gökçen, the first female pilot in Turkey and the first female fighter pilot in the world.

Atatürk was fifty-seven years old the night he met Zsa Zsa, and although he was a heavy drinker, he seemed to keep himself in excellent condition. Unknown to both Zsa Zsa and himself, he was entering the last months of a heroic and influential life.

At table, she kept looking at her husband, then sneaking glances at Atatürk. Belge emerged unfavorably from her on-the-spot comparison. "I was completely disenchanted with my marriage," she recalled. "Ready for some new and exciting adventure. Burhan left me alone every day and most every night. I had only the cook for company. My husband and I slept in different bedrooms."

Karpiç approached the Belge party. "His Excellency would like you gentlemen and your ladies to join him at table." Belge stood up and directed his sister, brother-in-law, and Zsa Zsa to Atatürk's table. Only Zsa Zsa needed to be introduced. From her position at the far end of the table, she curtsied to him, pronouncing the Turkish honorific greeting, *"Pasha Effendi."* Immediately, the other guests laughed at her. Later, Belge explained that she had said the equivalent of *"Excellency, Mister."*

From across the long length of the table, he asked her if she'd ever tasted the national drink of Turkey, *raki.*

She told him she had not, and he ordered the waiter to bring her a glass. After swallowing a mouthful of it, she coughed. The anise-infused *raki* was similar to Pernod and consisted of almost pure alcohol.

Then he asked her if she'd ever had a Turkish cigarette. When she again said she had not, he removed one from his gold case and sent it to her. The thin, flat-tipped cigarette was rimmed in gold, its scarlet letters proclaiming his initials of "K.A." After inhaling, she coughed again.

"Madame Belge will need some time before she becomes a true Turk," Atatürk called out to Belge, who nodded in agreement.

One of Ankara's most visible monuments is the *Anitkabir* (**Atatürk's Mausoleum**). It was built in 1944 in a monumental modernist style sometimes associated with the architectural tastes of Mussolini and Hitler, with an interior clad in gold leaf and intricate mosaics.

It's Turkey's most visited monument to the sweeping changes in Turkish society that where catalyzed by the visionary who's defined today as the Father of Modern Turkey.

Zsa Zsa said, "He was more than a man, more than a dictator. He was a God worshipped as deity by his people."

Circling around the dictator's table, Karpiç personally moved from guest to guest, dispensing large dollops of Beluga caviar, serving Atatürk first, then the others. At the place setting of each woman, he placed a flower. Later, he reappeared to supervise the serving of the shish-kebabs, the restaurant's specialty.

After the first two courses, when the Hungarian orchestra began the opening bars of a waltz, Atatürk asked each of his female guests if she knew how to waltz. Each told him they did not. Finally, he asked Zsa Zsa.

"Of course," she said. "I'm Hungarian, and born to waltz!"

In front of Belge's jealous eyes, she was escorted to the dance floor, where the other patrons formed a circle around them. He pressed his body so close to her, she later said, "I could hardly breathe he held me so tightly. I could feel a stirring in his trousers."

She later wrote, "I was dancing with a god." She only wished she'd worn a low-cut gown that night.

He whispered into her ear, "All the ladies at my table know how to waltz, but they deferred, so that I could dance with you."

Back at table, Atatürk ordered Zsa Zsa to sit on the chair next to his. Its female occupant quickly abandoned her seat and went to the far end of the table to sit in Zsa Zsa's chair next to Belge.

The dinner lasted for three hours. Atatürk hardly ate anything, but continued to consume *raki*. Finally, he rose, signaling that the banquet was over. When Belge came to retrieve Zsa Zsa, Atatürk announced, "I wish to drive Bayan *["Madam"]* Belge home."

The ambassador stood up to the dictator. "I prefer to drive my own wife home."

"But I will give you any of the ladies at my table to do with as you please," Atatürk responded.

Belge stood firmly, saying, "It is my own wife I prefer."

"A good choice," Atatürk said. "You are obviously a man who knows what he wants." Then he kissed Zsa Zsa's hand and shook that of Belge.

As he left the restaurant, the security guards preceded him, followed by his entourage.

En route back to the Belge villa, Yakup told him, "You were a very foolish man, my dear brother-in-law. In the past two years, Atatürk has had three husbands beheaded who did not immediately surrender their wives. Yakup then turned to Zsa Zsa. "You obviously have a new and not-so-secret admirer."

Belge drove the rest of the way in silence.

***

70

The following afternoon, after riding her white mare, Zsa Zsa paid her afternoon visit to the Circassians' antique shop, ordering her usual Turkish coffee. Numad appeared once again with a treasure for her, no doubt from another secret admirer.

The object was wrapped in tissue paper. He handed it to her and also gave her a magnifying glass. When she unwrapped it, she discovered an exquisite miniature Hand of Fátima. In gold, and holding a perfect diamond, it was one of the most beautiful *objets d'art* she'd ever seen. Weeks later, she learned that it was a precious relic removed from the fabled Topkapi Museum in Istanbul.

Numad told her that according to legend, the person who possessed this relic would have good luck forever. "Beauty with good fortune is a blessing, but beauty without good fortune is a curse."

"Who is my new secret admirer?" she asked. "Surely not that Afghan minister again."

"It is the gift of a very important man," Numad said. He reached into a drawer and removed a gold key. "I will give you the address in the Old Town. You are to go there tomorrow exactly at four o'clock and use this gold key to gain admittance. It will become your key to paradise."

Numad would tell her no more, and her curiosity was unleashed. She couldn't wait for the following afternoon.

She'd never been into the Old Town before, and for a single girl, the prospect was intimidating. She wandered along mazelike streets that had been created 2,000 years before. Rotting, fly-covered carcasses of sheep hung from some of the store rafters. Rug merchants tried to lure her inside. Many copper merchants hawked their wares as lusty men called out obscenities in Turkish.

As she maneuvered her way along the narrow, cobble-covered streets, she searched for the address. She'd never had such an adventure before, and all the images she could conjure came from the movies—*Ali Baba and the Forty Thieves*, *The Adventures of Sinbad, the Caliph of Baghdad*. Before reaching this secret hideaway of forbidden pleasures, she was pinched twice by merchants.

Finally, at the designated address, she stood in front of a huge oaken door, feeling a surge of fear as she inserted the gold key into its lock. It worked, and the door opened onto a courtyard paved with cobblestones. Six armed security guards invited her inside,

Over the decades, some of the most famous men in the world would present jewelry to Zsa Zsa. But her most cherished possession was a replica of the **Hand of Fátima** that Atatürk had given her when she was a young woman.

He ordered his staff to remove the precious relic from Turkey's most prestigious museum, the Topkapi.

71

the captain welcoming her, as white doves flew overhead. In the center of the courtyard was a gnarled and ancient olive tree, around which some of the city's famous blue-and-white Angora cats snoozed.

The captain of the guards motioned for her to climb a marble staircase lined with gilded iron banisters. The stately looking door at the top was half open, and she pushed it slightly to enter.

With his back to her, Atatürk said in a low, husky voice, "I knew you would come."

Without seeing his face, she sensed that the man whose back was turned to her was the ruler of all the Turks. Ever since she'd accepted the Hand of Fátima, she was aware of who had given it to her. The smoke from his *hookah* drifted over his head. He motioned for her to sit down amid the red and tobacco-colored cushions of the chair next to his.

She came face to face with the great demigod, "the Father of the Turks." It was said that eighty-five percent of the country's female population went to bed at night dreaming of being seduced by this great warrior.

The legacy of **Mustafa Kemal** is visible everywhere in Turkey. Most public monuments and the nation's currency (the Lira) all bear an image of the great leader.

"To me, Atatürk was no mere statue, but a powerhouse of a man who had seduced 2,000 virgins before he got to me, his final virgin, even though I was a married woman at the time," Zsa Zsa said.

He generously extended his water pipe to her, and she attempted to smoke it, coughing as she did. He also gave her a gold- and emerald-encrusted cup filled with *raki*. This time, she drank from it without coughing.

He clapped his hands and six dancing girls suddenly appeared, each wearing see-through veils in a rainbow of colors. At the end of their sensuous dance, the girls dropped their veils, standing nude before Zsa Zsa and Atatürk before disappearing behind a beaded curtain.

"When he dismissed the dancing girls," Zsa Zsa later said, "Atatürk stood before me and removed his robe. He was completely nude and erect. My clothes came off next. At long last, a man took my virginity, although many others had tried. Atatürk succeeded in doing what my husband never did. He made a woman of me on that hot afternoon of long ago."

In a memoir, she wrote, "He dazzled me with his sexual prowess and seduced me with his perversions. Atatürk was very wicked. He knew exactly how to please a young girl. He was a professional lover, a god, a king. I was thrilled to lose my virginity to him."

All other details of that hot afternoon had to be pieced together from slithers of impressions she told to friends over the years, and from a few indiscretions she'd revealed on talk shows with the likes of Jack Parr or Johnny Carson.

She described his nude body as being a rich and sensual brown. He was her fantasy image of a shiek as popularized in American movies starring Rudolph Valentino. He had long lashes over eyes that seemingly pierced her body. His thinning hair was coal black, his nose perhaps a bit too wide, his lips perhaps too thin. But his body was in excellent shape. He was strong and gracefully proportioned. His chest tapered to a slight V at the waist, with a perfectly flat stomach. He moved with an animal's ease. His sex was long, sleek, and heavy. In all, it was male beauty combined with savagery. "My Hungarian beauty," he told her. "We will begin by massaging every part of our bodies with our tongues."

He told her that after all the epic battles in which he'd engaged, life had become a bore. As related by Atatürk's biographer, Andrew Mango, Atatürk informed his private secretary, "I'm bored to tears. I am usually alone during the day. Everybody is at work, but my work hardly occupies an hour. Then I have the choice of sleeping, if I can, reading, or writing something. Life here is a prison, where I play billiards by myself as I wait for dinner. I face the same people, the same faces, the same talk."

"Your boredom is over," she reportedly told him. "I am the new girl in town. I never knew a man was capable of giving a woman such pleasure. But I fear I've begun with the best. After you, it will be a downhill ride for me."

"Your husband does not satisfy you?" he asked.

"The marriage has never been consummated," she said.

"What Burhan needs, perhaps, is this beautiful young boy from Damascus who has been imported to my palace," Atatürk said. "He is trained in all the exotic delights. I tried him myself. While Burhan is occupied with his comely buttocks, I will have you at four o'clock every afternoon. Do you agree to that, my fair lady?"

"I will live for the striking of the hour when I can insert that gold key into that oaken door out front," she said. "It is the key to such joy and ecstasy I never expected to experience in my lifetime."

***

After two failed romances, Eva, in Budapest, was ready for "the third ride on the carousel."

She'd been attending the Forsthner Girls Institute in Budapest, but had grown tired of it. More than ever, she wanted to pursue her ambition to become an actress on the stage.

For about six weeks, she became involved with a late middle-aged Pál Sztó-jay, a minor theater director. "The only role he wanted me to play was on the casting couch. Promises, promises, and awful sex. My dashing Hussar, Paul Yankovich, had spoiled me. When Sztójay cast a minor play with an ideal role in it for me, and gave it to some other actress, I dumped the pudgy dumpling."

"With no lover in sight, I had only one thing to look forward to, and that was Zsa Zsa flying in from Turkey."

From her base in Ankara, Zsa Zsa had announced that she intended to visit Budapest with her husband, Burhan, for the Hungarian regent's politically important "Flying Day Party."

"What is that?" Eva asked her mother.

"As Zsa Zsa explained it, Regent Horthy's three gorgeous sons are throwing a Flying Day Party, meaning that all sorts of important people will be flying into Budapest—princes, aristocrats, diplomats. Many will wing their way here in their private planes. The gala is being staged in the gardens of the King's Palace."

[The Regent who ruled Hungary in the 1930s was Miklós Horthy de Nagy-bánya, who had once been commander-in-chief of the Austro-Hungarian Navy.

Despite her status as a (persecuted) Jew, Zsa Zsa was politically naïve at the time. She seemed unaware that Horthy in 1938 had passed the first Hungarian anti-Jewish Law, limiting the numbers of Jews in any one profession to twenty percent and reducing their role in government. The Regent had proclaimed that "I have been an anti-Semite throughout my life. I have never had any contact with Jews. I found it intolerable they dominate factories, banks, hold large fortunes, even control much of the theater and other business enterprises."

Under pressure from Hitler, Horthy would eventually enact even more strident laws, reducing Jews to only five percent of Hungarian commerce, a decree that led to 250,000 Jews losing their jobs. A Third Jewish Law, passed in August of 1941, prohibited Jews from marrying non-Jews. A Jewish man who had non-marital sex with a non-Jewish woman faced three years in prison.

In time, of course, the Gabors were confronted with the enforced foreclosure of their jewelry stores.]

With her husband, Zsa Zsa arrived in Budapest as a guest of the powerful Horthy family. Eva met her at the airport, falling into her older sister's arms.

Belge seemed stunned by Eva's blossoming beauty. For a diplomat, he said something spontaneous and undiplomatic. "I see now that I married the wrong sister." When she heard that, Zsa Zsa did not speak to her husband for the rest of the day.

Back at the Gabor villa, Zsa Zsa reunited with Jolie. But within the hour, tension arose. Both Eva and Jolie just assumed they would be Zsa Zsa's guest at the Horthy gala. "I have no control over the guest list," Zsa Zsa protested. "Neither of you is invited."

On the following night, a spectacularly dressed Zsa Zsa entered the garden of the Regent's Palace, facing the jealous stares of the other female guests. "I was a vision in diamonds and shocking pink," she said. "Even Burhan said I had never looked more glamorous."

"By eleven o'clock that evening, I had been propositioned at least eighteen times, by everybody from the French ambassador to all three of the Horthy sons. The ambassador from Italy wanted to take me away to his estate in Tuscany."

"My most serious proposal came from Prince Fabrizio Pignatelli. When he learned that I was interested in titles, he told me the titles I would inherit if I married him: Prince of the Holy Roman Empire, 18th Duca di Terranova, 16th Principe di Noia, 16th Principe di Castelvetrano, Principe di Maida, Principe di Valle, Duca di Bellosguardo, Duca di Girifalco, Duca di Lacconia, Duca d'Orta, Marchese di Cerchiara, Marchese d'Avola, Marchese della Favara, Marchese di Caornia, Marchese di Borghetto, Barone di Casteltermini, Barone di Menfi, and Patrizio Napoletano."

Back at the Gabor villa, frustrated and fuming, Eva was still furious that she had not been invited. She'd retired to bed early with a platter of scallions and salami, which she consumed while listening to loud American music. Her face was covered with her mother's cold cream.

When the phone rang, Jolie picked it up to hear Zsa Zsa's eager voice. "Oh, *Nuci,* I have met the most beautiful man ever created on the planet Earth. He is absolutely divine, a Norse god, a Swedish prince. He towers over me at six feet, four. He has gorgeous honey blonde hair and eyes as blue as the sky. His suit, and of this I'm certain, hides a body that would have put Apollo to shame."

"That's *vonderful, dahlink,"* Jolie said. "You know I'm planning to leave Vilmos, and I have been wanting to find a new man to replace him."

"No, no, *Nuci,"* Zsa Zsa said. "This man is for Eva, not for you."

"How disappointing," Jolie said.

"The Horthy party is breaking up and going over to the Ritz for dancing all night. Tell Eva to make

After Eva divorced her first husband, **Erik Drimmer,** she said "he had the body of Apollo and the head of a Norse god," and destroyed all pictures of him.

He was a chiropractor whose most favored client was Greta Garbo.

herself gorgeous. In an hour, I want her standing in the lobby of the Ritz looking positively ravishing. I'll introduce her to body beautiful, although I really wanted him for myself, but…oh well. Since I'm such a devoted sister, and dour Burhan is my escort, I'm giving away this divine catch to my baby sister. Get her ready!"

In Eva's bedroom, Jolie confronted a daughter reeking of onions. Within the hour, Jolie had wiped the cream from Eva's face, made her up to look like Jean Harlow, and attired her in a long Biedermeier gown with a fetching bonnet. "She was a vision in emerald green crowned by golden blonde hair. I decorated her with some of my most precious rubies and diamonds, plus some high heels modeled after a pair worn by Mussolini's mistress."

Two days earlier, Jolie had purchased a Steyr, a small German car that locals called "The Bedbug." Without a license, Eva drove it to the entrance of the Ritz, where a doorman parked it for her. Adjusting her gown and checking her makeup one final time, Eva entered the lobby, where she immediately encountered Zsa Zsa and Burhan.

Within minutes, Zsa Zsa escorted her to the Ritz Bar where Erik Valdemar Drimmer was having a drink by himself.

"Your Excellency," Eva said, curtsying before him.

"I'm no royal," he said, holding her hand. Jolie had heard Zsa Zsa incorrectly. She had compared Drimmer to a prince, not meaning that he was actual royalty.

"Oh, I see," Eva said, covering her disappointment. "Prince or not, I was awed by his beauty. He told me he was awed by my beauty. Without being immodest, I could swear that we were the most beautiful couple ever to be seen together in Budapest."

As Eva chatted "with my new love," she learned he wasn't a doctor, as Zsa Zsa had said, but in training to be an osteopath. "Actually, right now I'm a chiropractor to the stars at MGM. I pound the flesh of some of the biggest stars in Hollywood. Greta Garbo is my best-known client, although the name of Clark Gable is not unknown to me. My clients on occasion include Mickey Rooney, Judy Garland, Jeanette MacDonald, Joan Crawford, Spencer Tracy, and Katharine Hepburn."

As Eva soon found out, one of Drimmer's wealthy clients had flown him to Budapest and had gotten him an invitation to the Horthy party.

Eva would later write, "Resisting Erik was useless. Surrender was the only course for me."

Years later, she admitted that she spent three days and three nights in Drimmer's room at the Ritz. "We didn't need to go out. There was always room service. He had only a short time before he had to fly back to Hollywood."

He'd been married before, and was in the process of getting a divorce in

Mexico.

"Two hours after meeting him at The Ritz, he was making love to me," Eva claimed. "It was an all-night event. He was perfect evidence that God did not create all men equal. He was more beautiful out of his clothes than in them. Fortunately, I had been broken in by my Hussar; otherwise, I could not have kept up with him. He was insatiable."

As the glow of a rosy dawn colored the early morning sky of pre-war Budapest, Erik proposed marriage to Eva.

Over breakfast, he promised to return to her in Budapest as soon as he could.

"At the airport, I clung to him and cried and then cried some more," Eva said years later. "Ingrid Bergman's pain on leaving Humphrey Bogart at the airport in *Casablanca* had nothing on me. My only hope was that he'd write me a love letter every day."

"As he flew away, I thought of him massaging all those nude movie stars. My future husband facing a naked Garbo. I'd heard she was a secret lesbian, so maybe my beautiful Erik would be safe. But he was also placing his manly hands on a nude Joan Crawford. I just knew that brazen hussy, who was known to have fucked every male star at MGM except Lassie, wouldn't keep her hands to herself."

"I looked up at the sky and prayed that my Norse god would soon descend on a chariot from Valhalla and rescue me from this dreary world."

***

Jolie

With all three of her daughters involved in a relationship of some sort, Jolie decided it was time to divorce Vilmos at long last. There was one major problem: She had no money.

She wanted to set up a business of her own, and a friend of hers proposed she invest $30,000 in a newly established film company based in Paris.

It took a lot of persuading, but she finally convinced Vilmos to sell one of the five houses he owned in Budapest and give her the investment money.

Within six weeks, the film studio had made no movies, but had accumulated a mountain of debts. She had to write off her venture into show business as a total failure.

"At forty, I was too old to become an actress, so I hoped to work behind the camera," she said. "Alas, it was not meant to be."

Jolie's mother, Francesca Tilleman, advised her to return to the family business, which was jewelry. Once again, she approached Vilmos, threatening to leave him if he didn't give her the seed money to open a jewelry store.

She finally persuaded him to finance her new venture. Naming her shop "Jolie," she opened it at Kigyó Utca, the most fashionable street in Budapest.

By Christmas of 1938, she had increased her staff to fifteen sales girls, each selected because of her beauty. "Of course, they weren't as pretty as my daughters."

Jolie had very good marketing skills, even producing costume jewelry copied after the old court jewels of the Kingdom of Hungary. "What Bulgari is to Rome, Jolie, my shop, was to Budapest," she said. Business was so good she opened another shop around the corner. With the profits, she bought five houses in Pest, which she rented to tenants.

As she later claimed, "My shops made me rich. It was time to divorce Vilmos, and after weeks of pleading, he finally consented."

For moral support she sent Magda an airplane ticket, flying her in from Warsaw to be with her parents on the day they were scheduled for an appearance in divorce court.

Even before the divorce, Jolie had rented an apartment, and divided up the antiques and Oriental rugs which had adorned the villa they had occupied, taking special care to retrieve her beloved crocheted Richelieu tablecloth. She made sure she retained the finest pieces for herself, which caused her relatively small apartment to overflow with possessions.

She told Vilmos that he was now free to carry on an open relationship with his secretary, a woman named Magda, the same as their oldest daughter.

Their daughter, Magda, went with them to court, and their chauffeur, Janos, drove them there. With a minimum of paper work, the divorce was granted. Magda waited in the family car, sitting up front with Janos.

When Jolie and Vilmos emerged from the courthouse, they got into the back seat together. Finally, Vilmos told the woman who had just become his ex-wife, "I will take you home, Jolie."

Five minutes later, as Magda reported in a letter to Zsa Zsa, she saw her parents "kissing madly like two lovebirds."

After dropping Magda off, Vilmos told her, "Jolie and I are going to dine. After that, we may spend the night together."

***

Back in Warsaw, Magda found that she and her count were growing increasingly estranged. She wanted to retain her title as the Countess of Warsaw, but Jan, for nights in a row, didn't come home. She suspected he had other women, although he kept telling her he was preparing his regiment for the imminent invasion of Hitler's forces from the West.

In her letters to Magda, Jolie said that she had lunch with Vilmos every day and that he came to her apartment almost every night to dine.

As the months went by, all of Jolie's daughters learned that she frequently spent the night in Vilmos' large apartment, where he'd moved after selling the Gabor villa.

Even after the war came, Jolie and Vilmos maintained conjugal visits. Then one day, Jolie journeyed to Györ, a small town lying between Budapest and Vienna to the west. She had arranged to open a shop there.

There, she met a young man who had never been married. His name was Paul Savosdy.

***

 Following the surrender of her virginity, Zsa Zsa became a frequent visitor to Atatürk's secret hideaway in Ankara's Old Town. If Belge knew about her affair, he never confronted her with it. After all, he was her husband in name only.

Nearly all their rendezvous time was conducted in private. Only once did they venture out of the city. He ordered his chauffeur to drive them to a scenic bend in the Sakarya River, thirty miles from Ankara. He wanted to look once again at the battleground where, in August of 1921, his army had fought back the invading Greeks in a great conflict called "the longest pitched battle in history." Within two months after the Battle of Sakarya, Atatürk had proclaimed establishment of the Republic of Turkey.

Almost without realizing it, Zsa Zsa became what she later labeled "the Mata Hari of Turkey."

After sex in the afternoon, Atatürk would quiz her about those long political meetings of the Young Turks at the Belge villa. As she later wrote, "He would question me ceaselessly about the secret meetings held in our house." He did more than that, ordering her to spy on the young men.

"Many of the Young Turks hated Atatürk and called him a despot," she said. "Three of the hotheads actually advocated the overthrow of Atatürk by assassination."

She reported all of this secret information to her lover, the dictator. At one point when she noticed that a trio of plotters never turned up again at any of the meetings in her villa, she asked her husband about them.

He looked at her very sternly, perhaps not aware that she may have indirectly led to their deaths. "Each of these young men, my friends and supporters, were found beheaded. It is not known who did it. I suspect fanatical supporters of Atatürk learned they were plotting against him. We will not speak of this matter again. Is that understood?"

"Yes, Your Excellency," she said.

In her second memoir, Zsa Zsa claimed that the secret information that she passed on to Atatürk "did not lead to the death of any of the men who had been guests in our house." That statement, of course, was blatantly false.

In exchange for her Mata Hari style services, Zsa Zsa stated that her lover gave her "lessons in love, in passion, and in intrigue."

Throughout the rest of her life, she continued to assert a familiar refrain: "Atatürk ruined for me every other man I would ever love, or try to love."

***

One night, Belge appeared depressed. He had learned that a Turkish mission from Ankara was being sent to Cairo for meetings with King Farouk of Egypt. He had wanted to lead that *corps,* but apparently was about to be passed over in favor of his brother-in-law, Yakup.

The following afternoon, Zsa Zsa informed Atatürk of her husband's secret desire to lead the Turkish delegation to Egypt.

Shortly thereafter, when Belge arrived back at their home, he seemed bursting to tell Zsa Zsa about a phone call he'd received from Atatürk. "I can't tell you what he said. You tell everybody everything you know."

After some arguments, she finally coerced him to reveal that Atatürk had asked him, instead of Yakup, to lead the diplomatic mission to Cairo.

She later confessed, "It was all I could do to refrain from telling him that I was the reason behind Atatürk's decision. She later wrote, "What have the great women of history—Pompadour, Du Barry, and Marie Antoinette—what have they on me?"

She was delighted when Belge informed her that she would accompany him on his diplomatic mission to Cairo. She immediately began readying a wardrobe. "I planned to create a sensation in Egypt."

A few weeks later, their Turkish airplane set down at the Cairo International Airport, where they were welcomed by dignitaries from the Egyptian government and driven by limousine to the Turkish Embassy, where they were installed in a lavish suite.

That night she and Belge had been designated as the guests of honor at Farouk's palace where he was presenting a lavish banquet for them. In its aftermath, comparisons to the debut of her adventure with King Zog became obvious.

The personnel at the Turkish embassy were dazzled by Zsa Zsa's beauty and assigned her a makeup artist—"the best in Cairo"—plus a talented hairdresser, both of them male. In addition, she was presented with two servant girls to assist her in her bath and to dress in her a sequined, Asian-inspired, lipstick red gown that fitted her like a glove. Trimmed in black, the gown came to a tapering V right below her ample cleavage. The scarlet-colored high heels she wore were already being defined in Hollywood as "Joan Crawford fuck-me shoes."

The embassy also provided her with an aide, Kálmán Bárdossy, to instruct her on details associated with King Farouk and Egyptian protocol. She found him delightful, a font of information about all aspects of the Egyptian regime. He was very effeminate, claiming that his boyfriend worked as a security guard at the palace— "and knows every time a cockroach crosses the floor over there."

Her dialogues with Bárdossy evolved into a good example of Zsa Zsa's easy going relationships, and in some cases, friendships, with homosexual men, many of whom she was to meet within the context of makeup, hairdressing, dress design, interior decoration, and as actors and support systems in the movie colony.

He told her that Farouk's formal title was, "His Majesty, Farouk I, by the Grace of God, King of Egypt and Sudan, Sovereign of Nubia, Sovereign of Kordofan, and Sovereign of Darfur."

He filled her in on the vital statistics associated with the king. Farouk had been born in 1920, which would make him thirty-eight years old. He was starting to put on weight as a result of his prodigious appetite—for example, he consumed 600 oysters a week.

Partly as a result of his education in

Portraits of **King Farouk of Egypt** in 1938 *(top photo)* and *(lower photo)* with U.S. President **Franklin Roosevelt** in 1945.

Middle photo: the brief Farouk dynasty's **heraldic coat of arms.**

Although the decadent Farouk was said to have "the tiniest penis in Egypt," Zsa Zsa always maintained that he raped her when she accompanied Burhan Belge on a diplomatic mission to Cairo.

Woolwich, England, she could converse with him in English.

His coronation as king occurred when he was sixteen years old. Since that time, he'd become a hedonist, obsessively pursuing glamour and diversion. "He doesn't even know the number of palaces he has," claimed Bárdossy. "His appetite for food is matched only by his appetite for sex. Although married, he dates many beautiful young women. He specifically prefers twelve-year-old virgins. He also owns the largest collection of pornography in the world."

As for his politics, Bárdossy told Zsa Zsa that Farouk planned to remain officially neutral if war was declared. "But he's partial to Hitler because he resents the British occupation of his country."

"What about his wife?" she asked. "I'm not so much interested in politics."

He has only recently married," Bárdossy said. "She is known as Queen Farida. Before that, she was a beautiful woman named Safinaz Zulficar, and she's only a year younger than the king. Both of them have a fondness for furnishings inspired by the court of Louis XV of France. The diplomatic corps mockingly calls these garish, overgilded reproductions 'Louis Farouk'"

At the sumptuous banquet Farouk staged for the Turkish mission, the king asked Zsa Zsa to sit next to him at the head table, relegating Belge to a seat at the far end of the dining room. During his feast, he paid special attention to her ample breasts on display.

She knew little about Egypt except for the legend of Cleopatra. Farouk amused her by telling her exploits of Egypt's final Pharoah, the last of the Ptolemaic dynasty.

He said that one notorious night, Cleopatra had ordered ninety-six of the palace guards to make love to her. Zsa Zsa immediately demanded that Farouk explain how that was physically possible. Apparently, he delivered a rather graphic answer, in which he said that the men had been ordered "to work themselves up until they were ready to explode right before penetration. They operated on a rapid, factory-style assembly line, unquestionably fulfilling their obligations to Her Majesty."

After the banquet, Belge retired to the library with the Egyptian ministers. Remaining behind, Farouk invited Zsa Zsa to see his coin collection, one of the rarest in the world. In his heavily guarded chamber, he also displayed some of his choice gemstones to her, especially when he heard that her family in Budapest were jewelers.

"My great dream is to purchase the pear-shaped, 94-karat 'Star of the East Diamond'" he told her. "If I can do that, perhaps I'll present it to you in honor of your beauty."

[In 1951, Farouk, through New York jeweler Harry Winston, would acquire the fabled diamond. Winston never got paid, and it would take years of litigation before Farouk actually came into full legal possession of the coveted gem.]

82

The only source for what happened that night at the palace was Bárdossy, who wrote a memoir, *The Secret Life of a Demented Pharoah: Farouk of Egypt.* He completed it in 1960, eight years after the overthrow of Farouk, Bárdossy submitted his tell-all manuscript to several publishers in both New York and London, each of whom turned it down.

Page after page revealed details about Farouk's sexual adventures and palace intrigue. Bárdossy's main source was a security guard at the palace, with whom he was having a sexual relationship.

In his book, Bárdossy devoted one entire chapter to the arrival of Belge and Zsa Zsa in Cairo. He claimed that Zsa Zsa had told him that the lecherous king had raped her after he'd shown her his gem collection.

The king had been accused of rape by other young women, so such an attack would not be out of character for him. Also, in the years to come, Zsa Zsa would also allege rape from other men, notably her second husband, Conrad Hilton, and her pursuer, Frank Sinatra.

Bárdossy maintained that Zsa Zsa never reported Farouk's attack on her to Belge. Even if she did, there was nothing the ambassador could do, as he was the guest of a dictator (Farouk) on his home territory.

William Stadiem, the biographer of King Farouk, wrote: "As a ladies' man, Farouk combined elements of Romeo and Buster Keaton, Don Juan and Daddy Warbucks, and Casanova and Caligula. He had a 'divine right' approach to the opposite sex. He saw no difference between seducing a woman and giving an order to one of his chambermaids; he expected both to jump to attention."

Stadiem also asked the question that could have brought death to anyone inquiring when Farouk was the ruler of Egypt: "How miniature was the penis the world loved to snicker and gossip about? Was it really so little? How could the 'sex king' have a tiny organ?"

As far as it is known, Zsa Zsa never provided Farouk's dimensions.

The only other mention of this alleged rape by Farouk appeared in a Paris newspaper in the 1960s when Zsa Zsa reportedly met Farouk's sister, Princess Fawzia Fuad. Shortly after Zsa Zsa's visit to Egypt, Fawzia had married Mohammed Reza Pahlavi (1939-1948), the Shah of Iran. Until her divorce, Farouk's sister had reigned as Queen of Iran.

At the party, it was alleged that Zsa Zsa confronted Farouk's sister, claiming that her brother raped her during her state visit to Cairo. This has never been proven one way or another, but by that time in her life, Zsa Zsa was audacious enough that she could have confronted her Highness with such an accusation.

There remains one nagging question in the wake of Zsa Zsa's blitz of Cairo, where she enchanted the *corps diplomatique.* Did she become impregnated during her short visit?

Back in Ankara, Atatürk just wanted to sit and talk to Zsa Zsa about Egypt. For the first time ever, he showed no sexual interest in her. He seemed sick and tired. When she asked about his health, he at first told her that he had eaten some bad food.

He admitted he suffered from a reoccurrence of malaria, which he had contracted in Egypt in 1911 when en route to the war against the Italians in Libya.

A strange man was present with him one day at his hideaway. Atatürk finally admitted it was his physician. He was under a doctor's care, suffering from cirrhosis of the liver, which had turned his skin a sickly jaundiced yellow. Not only that, but he had a bad heart; his kidneys were inflamed; and angina had evolved into a serious health issue.

His paunch had thickened considerably. He was also plagued with headaches, and he had frequent nosebleeds. Even so, he was still alert and searching for answers to his questions, but Zsa Zsa feared that more and more he was turning to bottles of *raki* for solace.

Shortly after her return to Ankara, Atatürk informed her that he was departing for Istanbul on business. He kissed her goodbye.

A few days later, on November 10, 1938, as she emerged from her riding club, she heard a large fat woman running, screaming, through the streets. In Turkish, she shouted, "El Ghazi, EL GHAZI! He's dead!"

Zsa Zsa rushed back into the office of the riding stable where she heard the news of Atatürk's death at the Marmora Palace in Istanbul.

Suddenly, a familiar voice was heard broadcasting from the radio. It was that of her husband, Burhan Belge, who announced to the world that Atatürk "entered immortality this morning."

She walked away from the stables, wandering alone across a field. She was shedding tears, not just for Atatürk, but for herself. She knew that with the passing of Atatürk, her life in Turkey was over.

During the weeks ahead, she had to figure out how to extricate herself from her role as Belge's wife.

With a war coming on, she told friends, "The lights are going out in Europe. They may not come on again for my generation."

There was still a beacon of hope for her:
AMERICA.

CHAPTER THREE

The Gabor Sisters as War Brides

Zsa Zsa had not yet figured out a way to extricate herself from her role as the wife of Burhan Belge. She hoped to find some solution when she agreed to accompany him on a diplomatic mission to pre-war London during late May of 1939.

As war clouds hung over Europe, and as guests of the British council, Zsa Zsa and Belge joined a party of five other Turkish diplomats and their wives. She had visited London before as a little girl.

Sir Percy Loraine, the British ambassador in Ankara, had made life in England sound intriguing to her. She cuddled a secret wish that she'd meet some influential Englishman in London, who would ask her to marry him. If so, she'd proceed rapidly with a divorce from Belge.

That trip to England would mark a turning point in Zsa Zsa's life. Almost overnight, she found herself a media sensation in London, marking a turning point in a career otherwise devoted to "being famous for being famous."

The British press idolized her, beginning with a headline in the *Daily Express:* ELEGANCE ARRIVES FROM TURKEY.

Within twenty-four hours, Zsa Zsa's arrival had become fodder for the tabloids. The press wrote about her *haute couture* wardrobe, her diamonds, her furs, but mostly they rhapsodized about her dazzling beauty.

Ivor Lambe, the leading society columnist of London, hailed her as "the most beautiful woman I have ever seen—most fair, with huge, lustrous eyes and a perfect mouth."

Her picture appeared on the front page of *The Star*, the paper praising her for her "Parisian sophistication."

At a reception, a photographer took a picture of Zsa Zsa with the Duchess of Norfolk, which appeared on the front page the next day. The article asked readers to "compare the beauty of these two women—one a duke's wife, the other a Turk's wife." Obviously, Zsa Zsa's beauty made her the undisputed winner.

"It seemed that all of London was waiting to see what I was going to wear,"

Zsa Zsa said. "Photographers even appeared at my hotel when I emerged on the street after breakfast. British men really seemed to go for me. I lost count of the propositions I received. Some of them—one in particular—was very famous, but I dare not reveal his name."

That famous man was obviously not Neville Chamberlain, the prime minister of Great Britain. At a formal gathering, he seemed to take no interest in her at all, directing all his attention to Belge.

She'd later write that she found him a "tiny, icy man who whistled through his mustache when he talked."

"I detested him, and he seemed to regard me as some cheap Budapest whore," she said. "Only the year before, he'd signed the Munich Agreement, conceding the Sudentenland in Czechoslovakia to Hitler. Vilmos was still ranting about that decision. Even Belge was beginning to get suspicious of Hitler, fearing he had designs on Turkey, and we were due soon to arrive in Berlin."

Chamberlain may have ignored Zsa Zsa, but not Anthony Eden. The handsome, dashing, debonair aristocrat, who became the First Earl of Avon, had formerly been Britain's Secretary of State for Foreign Affairs. When he had met Zsa Zsa, two weeks before, he had been named Secretary of State for Dominion Affairs.

DISGRACED: At the entrance to Hitler's Bavarian hideaway (The Berghof) **Neville Chamberlain** *(center figure in upper photo)* appeases **the *Führer*** a few months before the outbreak of World War II.

Lower photo: To the horror of many of his compatriots, including Churchill, **Chamberlain** waves a copy of Hitler's agreement in a moment of short-lived triumph after his return to London.

Enchanted by her charm and beauty, he would become the fourth man of influence and power with whom she would become intimately involved, the others being Atatürk, Zog, and Farouk.

She was devastated to learn that he was already married to his first wife, Beatrice Beckett, whom he eventually divorced in 1950. "The good ones are always grabbed up first."

Once Eden met Zsa Zsa, he monopolized all her attention at the party and wanted to throw his own reception for her. She thought that sounded wonderful and agreed to meet him for lunch at London's Ritz Hotel the next day to review the guest list, which eventually grew into an assembly that included many of the most important VIPs in London.

Before their luncheon, she spent time reading everything she could about this British conservative politician, who would eventually serve as England's Prime Minister from 1955 to 1957.

At the age of twenty-one, he had become the youngest brigade-major in the British Army. Known for his hot temper, he was also hailed as the most handsome man in British politics. Critic Rab Butler had defined him as "half mad baronet, half beautiful woman."

In fashion, Eden rivaled the immaculately dressed Duke of Windsor. He always wore a Homburg hat, a rigid version of a trilby, and it became his trademark. The press eventually labeled that style of hat as the "Anthony Eden."

He was known for wearing the most beautifully tailored men's clothing in London, an unofficial ambassador for Savile Row at its best. His enemy, Mussolini, referred to him as "the best dressed fool in Europe."

That following afternoon, Zsa Zsa appeared at the Ritz attired in "flamingo pink," from her high heels to her picture hat. The weather during that pivotal day in May of 1939 was gray and unseasonably chilly, and she wore a sable coat with a chocolate brown lining. As she entered the dining room, all heads turned.

Eden graciously kissed her hand, bowing slightly before her as if greeting Queen Elizabeth (a woman later identified as The Queen Mother).

They bonded at once and were soon engaged in animated conversation. "He was a ladies' man," she recalled, but not in her memoirs, where she saved him a lot of embarrassment by not going into their affair. "He didn't seem to worry that both of us were married. In fact, he told me, 'I never cared a good god damn, not even a tuppence, about protocol.' I had a suspicion that this attractive man, with such a roving eye, did not confine his sexual prowess just to his wife's boudoir."

[Zsa Zsa was right in her initial assessment. In fact, between 1946 and 1950, Eden would conduct an open affair with Dorothy, Countess Beatty, while she was still married to David, Earl Beatty, Admiral of the British Fleet. The adulterous affair became widely known throughout London.]

"Had I not married a British man, George Sanders, I would definitely have considered **Sir Anthony Eden** as marriage material," Zsa Zsa later said.

"Of course, it would be a constant competition between us as to who would be the best dressed."

Near the end of their luncheon, after having ironed out the details for his reception, he confessed, "I'm not really suited for politics. I hate public speaking. Churchill criticizes my speeches. He's always saying that I use every *cliché* except 'God is love.'"

Then he leaned over to her and whispered, "I'm known for behaving like a child and throwing a temper fit when I don't get my way. In fact, I've been called, at times, 'hysterical and pill-addicted.' Right here in this dining room, I'm liable to throw a fit if you turn down my offer to go upstairs with me to the suite I've reserved for us."

"Well, this lady does not want to contribute to a public scene, so my answer will have to be yes. What other choice do I have?"

She would later recall to friends how she spent the rest of the afternoon with Eden. "It was the most gentlemanly fuck I ever had. Even when he pulled off his suit, he spread it with precision across a chair. When he mounted me, he performed brilliantly, exiting only when he felt he'd satisfied me. Before heading to the shower, he even thanked me most graciously and kissed my hand."

"How so unlike Atatürk, who always slobbered all over me. When kissing me, Eden did not believe in exchanging body fluids. I adored him. If he weren't already taken, I would have agreed to divorce Belge and marry him at once."

The reception Eden threw for Zsa Zsa and Belge was so successful that one newspaper referred to her as THE NEW TOAST OF LONDON.

She was thrilled. "I love reading about myself in the papers."

When she learned of her daughter's reception in London, Jolie said, "She got the notion that she didn't have to actually do anything to become celebrated, like inventing a cure for cancer. All she had to do was look glamorous. Discounting her early press and social successes in Vienna, Zsa Zsa truly became aware of how important publicity would be. Let other stars win the Oscar. Zsa Zsa would walk away with the headlines."

Nicholas Eden was the ill-fated son of Sir Anthony Eden. Zsa Zsa befriended him, later claiming, "He never got over his deep love for his father, a love that could not be."

[During the years to come, Zsa Zsa would be involved in private rendezvous with Sir Anthony whenever she was in London. She would also befriend his son, Nicholas Eden. Born in 1930, he was to become the 2nd Earl of Avon.

Once, in London, Zsa Zsa threw a party for Nicholas and his gay friends. He showed up with the British actor, Laurence Harvey.

Like his father, Nicholas was an astute politician, and he became an Under-Secretary in the cabinet of Margaret Thatcher.

At Zsa Zsa's party, Nicholas confessed to her that "the love of my life has always been my father. But that love was never reciprocated, at least not in a sexual way."

She was greatly saddened to learn about Nicholas' death in August of 1985 at the age of 54. He'd died prematurely of AIDS.]

***

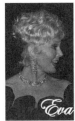

From her base in Budapest, Eva flew into London for a reunion with Zsa Zsa and, at long last, to marry her beau, Erik Drimmer. Their path to the altar had seen many setbacks.

When he returned to Hollywood after their brief but torrid hookup in Budapest, he had showered her with letters, which were so blatantly sexual that she claimed "they had to be kept in asbestos containers."

Three months later, he flew back to Budapest to marry Eva at City Hall. Jolie organized a small reception at the home of Sebastyen Tilleman, her brother, six miles outside Budapest.

At City Hall, some local official challenged Drimmer's papers, asserting that his Mexican divorce from his first wife was not valid: Until his papers were in order, he could not get married in Hungary.

Eva broke down and cried, and both Drimmer and Jolie tried to console her.

The reception was held anyway at the Sebastyen Tilleman's country home. Jolie later claimed that Eva lost her virginity that night, even though she was not married. Eva herself later admitted that she'd already lost her virginity long before the reception at the Tilleman house.

Several days later, Drimmer flew out of Budapest and returned to London, where he had a temporary position using his medical and rehabilitation skills to work with two paralyzed children belonging to a rich British couple. He lived as a boarder with this Jewish family and their handicapped children, pocketing $2,000 a month, with the understanding that room and board were provided as part of the arrangement.

Jolie felt that her daughter was going to expire of a broken heart, and suggested that travel would make her forget. She paid for Eva's trip to the Swiss Alps, but that didn't help. Eva later claimed she heard Erik's name "in every yodel." She even said, "I saw his face peeking at me over the crest of the Matterhorn."

When the Swiss Alps failed to provide emotional relief for the love-struck Eva, Joie shipped Eva off to visit old friends, Captain and Mrs. Ralph Seymour, who owned a townhouse in Monaco on the French Riviera. For a month, Eva was a guest of this elderly couple. Mrs. Seymour had spread pictures of Queen Mary of England throughout her living room, as they were close friends.

Eva admitted to spending a month there brooding on the beach and wishing the waves would wash Drimmer to the shore. At night, as she later admitted, he appeared to her in XXX-rated dreams.

Finally, when Drimmer could no longer endure the separation, he showed up in Monaco. Eva left the Seymour home and headed with him for a hotel in Nice.

"We made up for lost time," she admitted. "Love in the morning, love in the afternoon, love before dinner, and love *après* midnight."

While on the Riviera, Brimmer earned some money treating patients at the Sporting Club of Monte Carlo.

Six weeks later, he called her from London, telling her that the paperwork associated with his divorce was in order and that he was at last free to marry her. He wanted her to fly to London at once. By sheer coincidence, Zsa Zsa was in London at the same time as part of a diplomatic mission with Belge, so she could attend Eva's wedding to the handsome Swede.

Zsa Zsa renewed her acquaintance with her new brother-in-law. After seeing him again, she stated that "he could charm the dead."

In London, Eva and Drimmer checked into a suite at the Hyde Park Hotel as Zsa Zsa, through Belge's office, arranged for them to be married at the Registry Office in London.

At their civil ceremony, Zsa Zsa functioned as Eva's maid of honor. Belge was best man, although he'd just met Drimmer.

After the wedding, Drimmer rented a small flat in Paddington which was cheap, since their budget was limited. He had become a U.S. citizen, but a waiting period of three months was needed before Eva could get her entry permit into New York.

Before her departure from London, Zsa Zsa remembered saying goodbye to Drimmer and her little sister. "It was that rare sunny day in June in London. Standing bareheaded in the sun, Erik's hair was almost platinum like Jean Harlow's. In a lifetime of meeting stunning men, I'd have to rank him near the top."

"I have known many beautiful men who were cruel to women," Zsa Zsa said. "But Erik was kind. There was one thing wrong with the marriage. He was dirt poor. Even though I was still young, I knew you couldn't live on love."

"My parting words with Eva were perhaps inappropriate," Zsa Zsa said. "Blame it on the champagne." I told her, '*Dahlink,* I would gladly trade Belge for just one night of love with your Erik. Oh, to have been a woman long ago in England kidnapped by the invading Viking hordes.'"

Before kissing Zsa Zsa farewell, Eva confessed that she had a problem. "We're going to Hollywood, which is full of beautiful men—Clark Gable, Robert Taylor, Errol Flynn, Tyrone Power, to name only a handful. I want all of them. I fear I won't be able to remain faithful to my Norse god."

"Many women would love to have your problem," Zsa Zsa assured Eva, before her final *adieu.*

"Burhan and I left London, flying to Nazi Berlin," Zsa Zsa said. "We'd paid our respects to Neville Chamberlain. Adolf Hitler was next on the menu. Perhaps Burhan would broker peace between England and Germany. Poor Magda. In Poland, she was likely to be caught in the middle of it all. At least Eva would be safely in America. In Budapest, Jolie was carrying on a love affair and a social life like there was no tomorrow. As for me, I didn't have a clue what I was going to do."

Eva would later look back on those weeks with Drimmer in London "as the most idyllic in my life. We were madly in love. Nothing else seemed to matter, although the London papers suggested Britain and Germany might soon be at war."

"When my papers were in order, we packed our things and headed for Victoria Station to take the train to Southampton, where we boarded a Cunard liner, *The Queen Mary,* taking us to New York. We had almost no money after paying for our passage," she said. "I was a pauper in mink." Jolie had given her her cast-off mink coat.

Eva remembered the crossing as difficult. "We had the smallest cabin on *The Queen Mary.* Whereas it suited me at five feet, two inches, the bed could not contain Erik's long legs. My husband practically had to stick his feet out the porthole."

Sailing westward into the unknown, she held Drimmer in her arms for almost twenty-four hours a day. She later confessed, "He seemed to want to have his hands on me at all times—in bed, over drinks, at table, or even walking on deck. We made a funny pair dancing together. He was the Eiffel Tower. I was as tall as a mushroom in the forest."

When their ship entered New York Harbor, Eva stood on the deck with Drimmer, knowing that her former life in the Old Country had ended forever. There would be three days of frenzy in New York before taking the train to California.

As the train headed West, she told him, "All those Hollywood blondes out there had better move over to make way for the new girl in town."

***

In the wake of Jolie's divorce from Vilmos, a depressed Magda returned to Warsaw and to her titled husband, Jan de Bychowsky. She began to think more and more about obtaining a divorce herself. She and the count had grown farther apart, and he was away most of the time with the men in his regiment.

She also suspected he was having an affair with the young daughter of his cook, an eighteen-year-old of exceptional beauty, with both Russian and Polish blood.

Shortly after her return to the dank and crumbling interior of Bychowsky castle, she learned that the cook's daughter was pregnant. She suspected Jan was the father.

Like her husband, Magda, too, began to fear that war clouds were looming over Poland. She had learned to drive, and she volunteered to join the International Red Cross.

She also decided that she wanted to learn to fly, and although not unheard of at the time, it was still a daring ambition for a woman in Poland at the time. In preparation for that, she became a member of the Warsaw Flying Club.

There, she met a dashing aviator and fighter pilot, Zdzislaw Henneberg, who was only three years older than she was.

In 1937, he had represented Poland at the gliding championships at Rhön, Germany. Henneberg struck Magda "as the sexiest man I have ever met—not the handsomest, but the sexiest." Or at least that was what she claimed in a letter back to Jolie.

Henneberg agreed to teach Magda how to fly. Within a week, they were engaged in a passionate romance. As she wrote Jolie, "Before Zdzislaw, I thought Jan was a great lover. Now I know what a great lover really is."

Her lover spent most of his time as an instructor at the SPL, the initials for the Polish Air Force Cadet Officers' School, which had been formed in the 1920s. He was considered one of Poland's all time flying aces, and would perform heroic action in the upcoming war.

Privately, Henneberg and Magda plotted her divorce. He even introduced the "Countess of Warsaw" to his family.

A Polish national, he was devoted to his homeland and spoke endlessly about his fellow fighter pilots, calling them "the knights of the air."

"A lot of the Polish Army is on horseback, and both man and horse will be killed when

DAREDEVIL POLES: Probably the greatest flying aces in the Polish resistance: Magda's lover, **Zdzislaw Henneberg** *(left)*, shown here after a successful airborne mission with **Jan Daszewski**, his co-pilot facing the Nazi war machine," he told her. "But the fighter pilot can hurl himself at the enemy with all the strength of a thousand horses harnessed in his engine."

"On the ground, I'm a normal man in love with a great Hungarian beauty, a woman I cherish and worship. But in the air, I become a demon. I know that death can attack me at any minute with lightning speed. So I must attack first. A moment's hesitation, even a split second, can mean death."

As he became airborne with Magda, he told her that a change occurs in the pilot once he ascends. "I become one with my airplane—half man, half machine. My nerve ends extend to the very tips of my plane's wings. Instead of depending on my beating heart, the engine becomes my heart once I'm in the air. But when I'm on the ground, my heart beats only for you."

Magda was enthralled with that kind of talk, which she had really wanted to hear from Jan.

In her letters to Jolie, Magda claimed that "Zdzislaw has all the fighting spirit of the fiercest of the Hungarian Hussars. My great fear for him, and my fear for our love affair, is that he has such a grim determination to defend the borders of his homeland that he may sacrifice his life for Poland if war comes. Oh, pray for me, *Nuci.* I'm afraid for my life in the coming weeks."

Magda also claimed that on the surface, Zdzislaw appeared a gentle soul. "He has a shy smile, but that is misleading. At a military dance, a Polish army sergeant approached me and more or less forced me onto the floor when my true love was in the men's room. Upon Zdzislaw's return, he saw my distress. The soldier ended up with a broken jaw in a knock-out punch. That smile of my pilot is but a disguise for a man of iron muscles. I'm in love as I've never been before and never expect to be again. Knowing that my lover may sacrifice his life in a few weeks only intensifies our passion. Call it a kiss before dying."

Some three weeks before the Nazi invasion of Poland, Magda sent a letter of great distress. *"Nuci, Nuci,* I have just learned that when I divorce Jan, I will have to surrender my title as Countess of Warsaw. Zdzislaw is a common man. He has no title. But I will make the sacrifice to be with the man I will love through Eternity."

***

In London, Belge was invited to deliver a speech ("Turkey at the Crossroads") at Chatham House, the Royal Institute of International Affairs, although Zsa Zsa's chic appearance captured more attention than his lecture. Afterward, she and her husband were approached by H.G. Wells.

Acerbic and intellectual, and known as "the father of Science

Fiction," Wells was known throughout the world mainly for his novels such as *The War of the Worlds* and *The Time Machine*.

"George Bernard Shaw is very interested in Turkey, and I'm sure he would like to meet you," Wells said. Eyeing Zsa Zsa, he added, "Even at his age, he still has an eye for a pretty girl."

That Sunday afternoon, Zsa Zsa, with Belge, took a taxi across the Thames and arrived at Shaw's apartment on Adelphi Terrace. Wells, as agreed, met them there, introducing them to Shaw and his wife, Charlotte Payne-Townshend.

Thin, shy, and rather judgmental-looking, Mrs. Shaw obviously didn't approve of Zsa Zsa's glamorous look. But the great playwright obviously did, inspecting her carefully.

"You don't look Turkish to me," he said.

"I'm a wild Magyar from the Hungarian plains," she told him.

"In the latest Hungarian elections, the Nazis got the largest number of votes," Shaw said. "Do you agree with your countrymen?"

"I have Jewish blood," she said. "Jews don't cast ballots for Hitler."

"I can't stand the son of a bitch myself," Shaw said, "but Charlotte is crazy about him."

"Please don't say anything bad about Mr. Hitler," Charlotte said. "He's a wonderful man and has done marvelous things for Germany, which was falling apart until he took over."

When she left to check on lunch in the kitchen, Shaw whispered to Zsa Zsa. "When Marlene Dietrich came to see me, she fell on her knees and performed fellatio on me to honor me as a playwright. However, my dear lassie, I will not expect such tribute from you, although you're free to indulge, of course."

"Perhaps on our second meeting," Zsa Zsa said.

As they sat having a sherry before lunch, the talk quickly turned to a Turkish man's view of marriage as opposed to the views of Shaw and Wells.

"I was born in 1866, but I've always considered myself a mod-

Two brilliant and eccentric friends, **George Bernard Shaw** *(upper photo)* and **H.G. Wells** *(lower photo)*.

Each of them touched and petted Zsa Zsa inappropriately beneath the luncheon table during discussions with her diplomat husband about the state of affairs in Turkey.

ernist about marriage," Wells said. "I married my second wife *[Amy Catherine Robbins]* in 1895. We had an agreement at the very beginning that I was free to have love affairs with other women. I don't think that is the average view of a Turkish man." He looked over at Belge, who politely said nothing.

"My most celebrated affair was with that American birth control activist, Margaret Sanger," Wells said. "I managed the affair without impregnating her. She knew all about birth control. I have loved so many people, men and women, some very deeply, though I don't consider myself an amorist."

Zsa Zsa knew that the word obviously meant a devotee of love, but she'd never heard it used before.

"Today, even at my advanced age, it's more important to me to have good sex than a day spent writing some nonsense my brain conjured up that morning," Wells said.

Born in 1856, Shaw, the Irish-born playwright, was an ardent socialist. As Zsa Zsa remembered him, "He looked just like his pictures, with almost transparent skin."

Shaw surprised both Belge and Zsa Zsa when he said, "Charlotte and I have been married since 1898, but by mutual consent, the marriage was never consummated."

Without knowing it, the author was echoing the status of Zsa Zsa's marriage to Belge.

When Charlotte emerged to tell them lunch would be ready soon, Shaw warned them it would be an all-vegetarian meal. "I don't devour the blood of slain animals," he said. "Hopefully, it will be better than the hot dogs Franklin and Eleanor Roosevelt served George VI and Queen Elizabeth at Hyde Park in New York."

He recalled a party he'd once attended in Edinburgh. "This little harpie with a Scottish brogue cornered me and wouldn't stop talking. She became really annoying. After all, she was monopolizing the *great* George Bernard Shaw. To get rid of her, I reached over and felt her right breast. Without missing a beat, she said to me, 'Cup the other one and I'll follow you anywhere.' That annoying little vixen later became the Queen of England. Incidentally, I heard that to become pregnant with both of her daughters, she had to use a turkey baster. That doesn't say much for good old King George, does it?"

At lunch with its "overcooked Brussels sprouts and other atrocities" [Zsa Zsa's words], Shaw sat at the head of the table on her right, with Wells on her left.

Elizabeth Bowes-Lyon, later **Queen Elizabeth, the Queen Mother**

At a luncheon in London, G.B. Shaw made outrageous claims to Zsa Zsa about his first meeting with a future queen he defined as "a little harpie and an annoying vixen."

Shaw surprised both Belge and Zsa Zsa with his intricate knowledge of Atatürk. He asked Belge many questions and received enlightened, articulate answers. Shaw then turned to Zsa Zsa. "Did you ever meet Atatürk?"

"I once attended a dinner in his honor," she said. "I have never involved myself in politics, however."

"That certainly is not the case with my beloved friend here, Mr. Wells," Shaw said.

Wells then spoke of his political belief in World Government, a position he'd advocated as early as 1932 at the University of Oxford. He told students there that "the most progressive leaders will have to become liberal fascists or enlightened Nazis to implement such an idea."

[That policy didn't meet approval with the Nazis. After the war, an SS "Black Book" was discovered, documenting the Nazi intention that if Operation Sea Lion—the Invasion of England—had been successful, Wells was one of the persons that the Germans had singled out for extermination.]

At this point, Zsa Zsa's napkin slid off her lap. Both men ducked their heads under the table to retrieve it for her. "Each of these lecherous old men took advantage of tender, innocent me and used the opportunity to grab some quick feels," she later recalled.

The luncheon dialogue quickly shifted to Hitler again and his belief in creating "The Master Race."

"Both of you gentlemen have advocated the theory of Eugenics," Belge said. "Is that not true?"

Both Shaw and Wells said that his charge was accurate. Zsa Zsa had to be told that the theory of Eugenics dealt with the improvement—through forced control of human mating patterns—of hereditary qualities of a race or breed.

She was particularly alarmed to hear that throughout most of the 20th Century up to that point in time, Eugenics had enjoyed wide support in the United States. Theodore Roosevelt had advocated Eugenics, and courses on it were taught in various American universities. Booths were set up at state fairs promoting "fitter families." Even medals were awarded to "Eugenically sound" American families.

"The Nazis adopted American measures to selectively reduce the presence of those deemed to be socially inferior through involuntary sterilization," Wells said.

"My fear," Wells went on, "is that the Nordic race will vanish, or at least lose its dominance, to some degenerate and inferior human species."

Shaw also endorsed Eugenics. "Society needs a lethal chamber to solve the problem of the human race. We should find ourselves committed to killing a great many of the world's people we now leave living, and to leave living a great many people whom we at present kill. I believe in a deadly but humane gas for the purpose of killing many at a time, those unfit to live. For example, I should kill Hitler, but let Albert Einstein live."

Zsa Zsa could remember only some of the talk during her "historic" meeting with these two fabled authors.

"I do recall that at the end of our luncheon, the subject of their epitaphs came up. Wells said his tombstone should read: 'I TOLD YOU SO, YOU DAMNED FOOLS.'"

Shaw said that his should read—"I AM AN ATHEIST, ALBEIT AN INVOLUNTARY ONE."

"It was fortunate that a jealous Burhan was out in the hallway when both writers gave me sloppy wet ones as a farewell, while Charlotte stood nearby looking at me like I was the Whore of Babylon."

***

In her memoirs, Zsa Zsa wanted to bury any reference to her trip, with Belge, to Berlin on the eve of Hitler's invasion of Poland and the outbreak of World War II. In contrast, the Associated Press circulated a photograph of a smiling Zsa Zsa, in a crazy hat, arriving in the Nazi capital with a stern-looking Belge in June of 1939.

The "summit meeting" in Berlin, originally ordered by Atatürk, had been conceived as a means for Belge to determine what the Nazis planned for Turkey during the oncoming World War. Atatürk had insisted that Belge meet with Hitler, with Josef Goebbels, and with Hermann Göring of the Luftwaffe.

The big question to be addressed was whether Nazi Germany planned to invade Turkey. However, as Belge was to discover, the Third Reich's hierarchy was not disposed to laying out their upcoming military strategy as it concerned a small but strategically positioned "Third World" nation like Turkey.

In Berlin, Zsa Zsa did not get the adoring press coverage she received in London. Goebbels was aware of her Jewish heritage, and reportedly had told his colleagues, "Had Madame Belge been a German citizen, we might have sent her to Buchenwald by now."

Since her days in Vienna, Zsa Zsa had remained in touch with the *chanteuse,* Greta Keller, who had informed her that she'd fled from Berlin and was now in New York. The actor, Conrad Veidt, had warned her that Goebbels had learned of her Jewish heritage and was planning to arrest her.

Originally thinking Greta was an Aryan, Hitler had once said she was his favorite singer. "Goebbels wants me out of the picture, so the Führer wouldn't be embarrassed by praising a Jewish singer. Fortunately, I was able to get a flight out of Berlin, to Amsterdam, that very afternoon, but I had to leave my jewelry and furs behind. I'll arrive penniless in New York."

Despite that warning from Greta, and because she was traveling on a diplomatic passport, Zsa Zsa considered herself immune from any fear of the Nazis. She was aware, however, that she would lose her protected status once she filed for divorce from Belge. She had some long-range plan to escape to New York the way Eva had. There, she would file for divorce in a U.S. court.

Most of the meetings Belge arranged in Berlin were with Goebbels. Zsa Zsa herself got to meet the Nazi propaganda minister when she was invited to a reception in a *Schloss* (castle) on the outskirts of Berlin. An hour after the debut of the party, an aide summoned her to confer with Goebbels in the building's private library. He had just concluded a meeting alone with her husband.

She remembered how Goebbels resembled a timber wolf emerging from a recent kill but still hungry. He did not bother to get up, but flicked his hand limply toward a nearby chair. Except for his eyes, the rest of his face was expressionless, almost gnome-like.

"I've called you here to tell you that the Führer wants to meet you," he said. "He's convinced that our friend Burhan—your beloved husband—will be the future ruler of Turkey. You, Madame Belge, will be its First Lady. In such an important position, we trust that we can depend on your complete cooperation in any conflict we may have with the Western powers in the immediate future."

"My plans are uncertain," she said, tentatively. "As a loyal and devoted wife to my husband, my plans will depend on him, of course. My political positions will reflect his stance."

Arriving in Berlin, on the dawn of World War II, **Zsa Zsa** was photographed in a ridiculous hat, later claiming (falsely) that she was only seventeen years old at the time.

Accompanying her was her gloomy-looking husband, **Burhan Belge**, the Turkish minister of propaganda.

"That I understand," he said. "Fräu Belge, I trust we in Berlin can count on you and your support during the coming months. We trust that your husband will be our ally in any future conflicts. We are aware that you are Hungarian by birth. We hope your Fatherland will also be behind our cause, as I'm certain it will be."

"I'm sure you'll have not only my support, but the support of my husband." When she said that, she didn't believe her own words, but she had no intention of informing Goebbels of any of her plans.

***

As part of the logistics preceding their upcoming conversations with Hitler, Belge and Zsa Zsa were flown to the Berghof, Führer's lavish private retreat in the Bavarian Alps.

Within her bedroom there, Zsa Zsa decided to make her most glamorous appearance before the Führer. Before drinks and dinner, Belge met privately with Hitler to discuss the political situation in the wake of Atatürk's death.

She later recalled, "Even with Jewish blood flowing in my veins, I stared at my image in the mirror. I looked like a poster woman of the Aryan race."

Later, to the sounds of Wagner, she made her entrance into the Berghof's vast living room, holding onto Belge's arm. Goebbels was there, with his wife, Magda, who bore the same name as Zsa Zsa's sister. Hermann Göring looked fat and lascivious, and she was also introduced to Werner von Blomberg, Nazi Germany's Minister of War.

Among them circulated waiters— SS guards out of uniform, dressed in white vests and black trousers—carrying trays of drinks and canapés. Above the mantel, a bronze eagle on a large clock looked ferociously down upon the room as, against one wall, a bare-bosomed portrait by the Venetian Renaissance painter, Paris Bordone, surveyed the crowd, and on another, one of Titian's boudoir nudes reclined.

Seeing Zsa Zsa standing alone, Fräu Goebbels walked over and introduced herself before leading her over to Hitler, who stood in front of a large,

With their favorite pet dogs, **Eva Braun** and **Adolf Hitler** at the Berghof were ready to receive Burhan Belge and Zsa Zsa.

Hitler had been informed that they were the most likely candidates for the next President and First Lady of Turkey.

During her stay in the Berghof, Zsa Zsa expressed her admiration for one of the paintings it conspicuously displayed: **Paris Bordone's** masterpiece from the Venetian Renaissance, **_Venus and Amor._**

99

plate-glass window overlooking the Kehlstein.

Unlike his appearance on newsreel screens, his hair was completely black, with not one trace of gray, his face well-tanned, his figure trim.

He peered at her through eyes as clear and as blue as her own, then bowed from the waist and kissed her hand. "I'm a great admirer of your husband," he told her, "and now I must congratulate him on selecting the most beautiful woman in Hungary as his wife."

She told him how honored she was to meet him.

He invited her out onto the summer terrace.

"I used to rent a little place near here," he said. "*Haus Wachenfeld*, it was called. An old cleaning woman who worked for me then told me the legend of Untersberg. She claimed Barbarossa and all his knights lay sleeping in the limestone caves nearby. One day, they'd wake up and usher in Germany's golden age."

She wasn't exactly sure what he meant and was stumped for a reply. Before she could utter a word, a commotion sounded in another part of the huge room in back of them. Framed in the doorway with two barking dogs on a leash was a woman Zsa Zsa had heard about through Belge. It must be Eva Braun, Hitler's secret mistress.

He excused himself and went over to her, kissing her hand. *"Gnädige Fräulein!"*

Excited, the dogs jumped up on him, their tongues hanging,. Hitler hastily pulled back his hands and whipped out a handkerchief from his breast pocket, wiping them carefully.

Turning to Zsa Zsa, he laughed nervously and said. "These dogs are the biggest lickers I've ever seen. One of my relatives in Austria had a cow who did the same thing. No one could milk her. She kept licking all the time." He turned to Braun and introduced her to Zsa Zsa.

Other than a hello, Braun had nothing to say to Zsa Zsa, who suspected that Hitler's mistress might think she had designs on her lover.

To Zsa Zsa's surprise, she noticed that Braun was wearing a deep shade of lipstick, and a lot of it, in violation of Hitler's rules. He preferred German women to look more natural, without so much artifice.

Braun was immaculately groomed and had a good figure. Her blonde hair seemed tinted, and two diamond-studded clips accented her *décolleté*.

Whipping up hatred during one of his speeches, **Josef Goebbels**, with his "flytrap open mouth" was one of the "fun people" Zsa Zsa met at the Berghof.

She realized that he knew of her Jewish blood, but he was forced to treat her deferentially as the presumed future First Lady of Turkey.

100

At the lavish dinner table, Zsa Zsa was seated near Hitler. She ate off Meissen china with the initials "A.H." highlighted in gold in the center, on either side of a glazed swastika. Opposite her, Braun gave her a frosty nod.

"I know what people believe," Hitler told his guests. "That I'm a vegetarian and abhor alcohol. Actually, I'm fond of *Weisswürst*. I had a favorite little stall I used to visit in Munich early in the morning. That's the only time to eat them. Of course, I'd have a mug of beer as well." He turned to give a scolding look to Goebbels. "You make me too ascetic in the press," he informed his propaganda chief. "I'm actually very German."

After dinner, he showed Magda Goebbels, Belge, and and Zsa Zsa a watercolor he'd painted of the surrounding mountains. "I used to paint churches," he said, "but no more. I once did a watercolor of the Karlskirche in Vienna. I was very disappointed with it. The original, the real thing, was so much better. I had merely reproduced it badly, without my own interpretation. I went back and did it again, and this time I captured it in a golden pink light. I transcended my subject matter. I enlightened it! Unfortunately, I had very little money in those days. I did such a good job that my landlady took it from me for payment of back rent."

After brandy was served, a tapestry was suddenly pulled back to reveal a motion picture projector. Another tapestry was pulled back from the opposite wall to unveil a screen. Hitler's honored guests sat through a screening of Alice Faye in *Alexander's Ragtime Band*. The host informed his guests that the blonde musical actress at Fox was his favorite movie star.

***

Hitler was nowhere to be seen when Belge, with Zsa Zsa, were flown from the Berghof to Berlin as the first leg of their ongoing flight to Ankara.

En route back to Turkey, Zsa Zsa confided to Belge that Hitler seemed relaxed and very much at ease. "He didn't look to me like a man plotting war. Far from it. Perhaps I should write Magda that she is safe in Warsaw."

"Don't be a fool," he warned her. "I've met privately with both Hitler and Goebbels. I think they're deceiving me. I think they want Turkey as part of their ever-expanding Nazi empire. When I return to Ankara, I will begin to denounce them in my Saturday radio broadcasts."

"But the Nazis are killers," she protested. "As you know, they have agents in Ankara. You could be assassinated after your first broadcast."

"A chance I will have to take," he said.

***

[At a party in Hollywood years later, Zsa Zsa jokingly said, "I didn't be-come Hitler's mistress, although I'm certain I could have replaced Eva Braun in his life if I'd wanted to. However, I did become the mistress of Josef Stalin." She paused to allow the shock of her words to sink in, before adding, "But only on the screen."

She was referring to a 1957 espionage thriller she filmed with movie Tarzan Lex Barker entitled The Girl in the Kremlin.*]*

***

In Budapest, Jolie was concerned mainly with her new younger lover, Paul Savosdy, who worked for a local branch of Mendel Intercontinental Meat Packers. She had fallen madly in love with him, even though she admitted to friends that he was a sadist.

As a woman in her forties, she was taking more and more care to make herself glamorous, going to hairdressers and cosmeti-cians, and buying frilly, diaphanous nightgowns. She also sprayed herself with the most expensive perfumes "in the seven strategic zones."

Sometimes, Vilmos stalked her on the streets, even though they were di-vorced. Often, after she'd prepared a lavish meal for Savosdy, and was ready for him to take her to bed, he'd announced, "I'm so very sorry, but I must go over to the Countess Sasha's apartment. It's business, of course."

"Countess?" she'd yell at him. "She's nothing but a prostitute!"

Even though she threatened him with castration while he slept, he would still desert her for the night.

Sometimes, he'd deliberately leave love letters from other women lying around her apartment so she would discover them. "Even so, I was wild for him. We made love all over. The floor was the best. My jealousy was eating me alive. I suffered like a dog."

Savosdy was away on business for nine days at a time, returning to Bu-dapest every tenth day. He never told her what he did when he was away from her, but left tantalizing clues.

Her love affair was not Jolie's only concern. Magda's letters from Warsaw seemed to grow more and more desperate. "The oncoming war—that's all everybody talks about here," Magda wrote.

Jolie advised her that if she truly believed that Poland would be invaded, she should return to Budapest. "No harm will come to you here. Hungary will be safe. Life is still wonderful in Budapest. The violins still play at night. The goulash is better than ever. And Hungarian men are still the world's best lovers."

Magda was still deep into her affair with her pilot lover, Zdzislaw Henneberg. Like Magda's husband, Count Jan de Bychowsky, Zdzislaw believed that attacks on Poland were imminent from Germany in the West and from Soviet troops from the East. This became apparent to most Poles after the surprise signing of the Molotov-Ribbentrop Pact on August 23, 1939.

In his secret meetings with Magda, Zdzislaw told her that the Polish Air Force *(Lotnictwo Wojskowe)* had little chance against the Nazi Luftwaffe. "Our pilots are the best in the world, but we lack modern fighters."

Shortly before the debut of war, her dashing pilot had been instrumental in persuading the Polish Air Force to move their craft from dense clusters within air bases to a scattered series of small, camouflaged airfields. His own fighter plane was hidden on the outskirts of a small village in Western Poland.

Nine days later, at 4:45 on the morning of September 1, the Nazi invasion of Poland was launched when Nazi tanks rolled across the country's western frontier. It was an all-out *Blitzkrieg,* as Polish towns and villages were bombed. The German *Heer* (army) pushed forward with 2,400 tanks organized into six *Panzer* divisions.

During the first week of the war, Zdzislaw became a hero, shooting down eleven enemy aircraft before his own plane was hit. Miraculously, he parachuted to safety in a potato field, where he managed to hitch a ride in a truck back to Warsaw. Before checking on his own family, he visited Magda at Bychowsky Castle.

During his painful reunion with her, the pilot told her, "For the Nazis, it is like cutting the throat of an infant with a dagger. It's not a war. It's a massacre."

From the front, Jan had sent back thirteen wounded soldiers from the Polish Army. As a member of the International Red Cross, Magda tried to provide for them, although she was short of both food and medical supplies. In the Bychowsky Castle, Magda had opened a makeshift medical clinic.

Zdzislaw had learned from his superior officers that Soviet troops were preparing to invade from the East. "We'll be squashed. You must return to Budapest. When the Nazis take over Warsaw, they will make you wear a yellow star and will eventually send you to a concentration camp for extermination. You have no choice but to flee. We'll meet again after the war."

He kissed her goodbye, but she clung to his body, sensing she would never see him again. "It was the most painful goodbye of my life," she later recalled.

Within three days, her husband, Jan, with an injured leg, arrived back at his castle in a military truck. He still had not learned about her affair with Zdzislaw. When he saw her packing to flee from Warsaw, he refused to let her leave. "You're my wife. I need you. We have this battered old truck. There are five wounded men inside. I need you to drive us toward the Romanian border. That country, at least for the moment, is neutral."

"Once in Romania, we can somehow arrange to board a ship sailing west across the Mediterranean to either Spain or Portugal. From there, we'll go to England. Polish forces will be regrouping there to fight the Nazis."

It took several hours, but Jan finally convinced her to join in the war effort. When she notified Jolie of what she was doing, her mother commanded her to come home at once. "Otherwise, I will have you certified as insane."

"*Nuci,* I must do my part," Magda protested. "After all, I'm the Countess of Warsaw and I must be brave. No Jew will be safe in Poland."

In the uniform of the International Red Cross, Magda, in tears, left Warsaw for the final time, driving six wounded men southeast toward the Romanian border. Along the way, they had to pay "outrageous prices" for hard-to-find gasoline, but somehow, they managed.

At the border, they faced a delay of one entire day, but they were eventually allowed in, along with other Polish refugees. It would be weeks before they could arrange passage aboard a vessel heading west.

"It will be a long and hard journey to get to England," Jan told her. "But we will endure. I'll recover and will fly again in a plane to fight the Nazis over the English Channel."

He also told her, "By marriage, you are a Pole. You must do your share as the Countess of Warsaw. We will prevail in this war. It will take an awful toll, but one day, we'll return in triumph to our castle."

Magda was bathing him and preparing to dress his wound when he told her that. She listened politely, but in her heart, she knew there would be no triumphant return to Warsaw. That was a dream only to be dreamed, but right now, both of them needed not only a great deal of luck, but a lot of courage to carry on.

***

Jolie

Belge and Zsa Zsa arrived in Budapest to face an urgent meeting with Jolie. The next morning, while Belge was still asleep at his hotel, Zsa Zsa came by Jolie's apartment for a private talk.

She told her mother that with the death of Atatürk, Ankara was regressing to an increasing degree into a provincial country town. She revealed her closely guarded secret: She wanted to go to Hollywood and join Eva. Perhaps she, too, would become an actress, or else the wife of "some very rich American."

Jolie learned that Zsa Zsa's marriage had never been consummated. "Had I not fallen in love with Atatürk, I would have fled to America long ago. Once I get there, I plan to divorce Belge, although he has been a very patient, supportive husband to me. I know I've made it rough on him."

"The question is, why has he kept you on as a wife?" Jolie said. "You're not a wife to him."

"I think he wants me as eye candy," she said. "He's known for having the most beautiful wife in Turkey, and I think that does wonders for his ego."

Later, when Belge arrived at Jolie's apartment, his face was stern, the most severe look she'd ever seen. After coffee was served, he immediately came to the point. "You must flee from Hungary," he warned. "Not tomorrow or the next day, but today. Pack up your valuables and leave. Go to the United States, perhaps California with Eva, Even Mexico or Buenos Aires. But go."

"Aren't you being a bit melodramatic?" Jolie said. "I'm theatrical myself, but...the war will not come to Hungary."

"You're being a fool," Belge answered. "Hitler's armies will march through the streets of Budapest."

"I'm not political," she said. "I won't be rounded up like some dissident."

"You're a Jew," he said, raising his voice to her. "The Nazis are killing Jews. It's a massacre. How do you have such conceit to think you'll be spared? Zsa Zsa will be safe because I can give her diplomatic protection. Magda, however, is not safe."

"I don't even know where Magda is," she said.

I think she and my brother-in-law, Count de Bychowsky, are trying to make it to England," he said. "The long route. Obviously not by train through Germany. Please listen to me. I am political and can see what is coming. Within months, Europe will be burning. Millions are going to die. Even America will get involved at some point because that country and Japan are moving toward an inevitable war."

"Budapest is so gay," she said. "Including you and Zsa Zsa, I have invited fifteen guests to dinner tonight. We will drink Tokay wine with two succulent platters of roast goose with all the trimmings."

"Then stay here at your own peril," he said. "I am about to begin broadcasts in Turkey attacking the Nazis. I will be on their death list, so I will be of no help to you whatsoever."

"I could never leave Paul Savodsy," she protested. "I am madly in love with the bastard. I live to love him."

"Then take him with you," Belge answered. "Your lover is also in danger."

"But he is Catholic," she protested.

"Converted," he said. "Both of his parents are Jewish."

At the time, Jolie didn't take Belge seriously. But two weeks later, she had to travel to Germany for reasons associated with her jewelry business. In Berlin, swastikas were displayed more prominently and aggressively than ever, and Jews were being systematically attacked. Leaving Berlin, she arrived, as she had been doing at seasonal intervals for years, in Leipzig. One night, returning to her hotel from dinner, the city experienced a blackout. In the ominous darkness, she heard mobs of young Nazis storming through the streets shouting "DEATH TO THE JEWS! DEATH TO THE JEWS!"

Fearfully, she checked out of her hotel the following morning, concluding that Belge was right. Still, she could not seriously consider abandoning all that she had accumulated in Budapest—her antiques, her real-estate holdings, her lover, even Vilmos—to rush off to the uncertainty of America.

Even so, she decided to think seriously about leaving Hungary, with the intention of delaying her departure as long as possible.

On the train back to Budapest, she decided never to set foot in Germany again.

***

With her handsome Swedish husband, Erik Drimmer, Eva arrived in Hollywood during the closing months of 1939. The town had just experienced its apogee of filmmaking, releasing many of its greatest movies in just one year, including the blockbuster *Gone With the Wind.*

But with the outbreak of World War II in Europe and the closing of the profitable Continental market, those glory days, at least at the box office, were coming to an end. Currency restrictions also meant a drastic reduction in box office receipts from the United Kingdom and the Commonwealth. And with the onward march of invading soldiers from the Empire of Japan, the Far Eastern markets were on the verge of collapse as well.

As "the new girl in town," Eva soon learned that her arrival in Hollywood had occurred at a horrible time for an inexperienced actress who could barely make herself understood in English. Studios were tightening their purse strings and firing hundreds of their bloated staffs from the 1930s. All but the biggest stars, such as Clark Gable, were taking heavy pay cuts. Marlene Dietrich, Katharine Hepburn, and Joan Crawford, among others, had already been defined as "box office poison."

Hollywood was known at the time as The Dream Factory, but to her, it was more like a nightmare. She and Drimmer had very little money. At first, he rented a hotel room for her, which was damp, small, and noisy. Last decorated in 1917, it had peeling wallpaper, a bed with a soiled mattress, and a clientele of heavy all-night drinkers. Many of the female residents earned their living on their backs. After weeks, the newlyweds found a small apartment with battered furnishings.

Knowing only the Hollywood of legend, she discovered that the town was filled with people who drove trucks, waited on tables, carried out the garbage, and worked as clerks at five-and-dime stores. "I had expected to see Loretta Young or Errol Flynn walking along the streets. Perhaps Claudette Colbert with her maid shopping for fresh vegetables at the Farmers Market."

After Drimmer left every day for work, Eva spent most of her mornings sobbing, as she later confessed. She was desperately homesick, longing for the nostalgia of the good life back in Budapest.

She wrote to Jolie: "Erik is as beautiful as ever, but he is broke most of the time. You can't live on beauty alone, I have learned. He makes ten dollars for treating a patient,. But that quickly disappears on rent, car fare, an occasional pair of underwear, and food. There is no money left over for wine, much less champagne. I have forgotten what champagne tastes like."

Often, Drimmer did not come home until way past midnight. That usually led to screaming matches between them, as she accused him of sleeping with his patients. He was seeing a lot of Greta Garbo, his number one client.

In Europe, at the debut of their relationship, he had wanted to make love to Eva day and night. But in Hollywood, he was indifferent to her charms and often spurned her advances, claiming he was tired.

She found her own feelings for him growing dimmer day by day. She'd decided that she had married him only for his looks, and she didn't really know him at all. Unlike her dashing Hussar in Hungary, "Erik is a dull Swede," as she claimed in a letter to Jolie. "Swedes, as I'm learning, are as cold and icy as their country. I will never go there."

For her first Hollywood party, Eva put on her best dress and the mink coat Jolie had given her in Budapest. The invitation was from one of Drimmer's clients, Myrna Loy. Because of her witty portrayal of Nora Charles in *The Thin Man* series of the 1930s, she was temporarily voted the Queen of Hollywood by millions of fans. The host was Loy's husband, Arthur Hornblower, Jr. who was Samuel Goldwyn's production supervisor.

A mysterious and icy Swede, **Greta Garbo** was the number one patient of Eva's new husband, Erik Drimmer, also a Swede. "We speak Swedish to each other," Garbo said. "We do so as he mauls me."

She quickly told associates, "He is my chiropractor. Otherwise, I would never let a man manhandle me. Never!"

Eva was disappointed to discover that her hostess did not

evoke the warm, languorous, come-hither image she portrayed on the screen. She virtually ignored Eva. "I felt the Arctic wind blowing when I met her, although she doted on Erik. To add to the frigid cold, she wore smoked glasses. When you're greeted by a hostess in foggy glasses, you know storm clouds are on the way."

Daughter of a Montana rancher, Loy had made a career of playing exotic vamps on screen until she'd hit it big. When Eva met her, she'd just completed *The Rains Came* (1939), with Tyrone Power. Ironically, Power was slated to become "my greatest love," according to Eva.

Loy talked only briefly with Eva, telling her that if America entered the war, she'd abandon her screen career to focus on the war effort, working with the Red Cross.

"Myrna spent most of her party attacking Adolf Hitler to anyone wanting to listen," Eva said. "I heard her say, 'When the *Führer* in his mind conquers California, I, along with Clark Gable and others, am on his blacklist and slated for extermination.'"

At long last, Eva—at Loy's home—began to meet some of Hollywood's A-list stars. The English actor, Charles Laughton, was ugly but amusing. He called Loy "Venus de Milo at the intersection of Hollywood and Vine." Eva wished she could say something clever like that, but could hardly manage a few words in English.

Myrna Loy was the "Queen of Hollywood" when Eva was invited to her home.

"She was warm and kind on the screen, but rather icy to me," Eva claimed. "At her party, I also got to meet the King of Hollywood, Clark Gable, "and would later meet him in a more intimate setting."

Late arrivals at the party included Clark Gable and Carole Lombard. Lombard was glamorous in white satin, but she ignored Eva, except to say, "Just what this town needs—another blonde." Gable was warmer and called her "Baby."

William Powell, Loy's co-star in *The Thin Man* series, also showed up with his pencil mustache and slicked-back hair. Dapper and debonair, Powell chatted with her briefly before moving on. She realized that she wasn't going to replace that other blonde in his life, the late Jean Harlow. A rather stocky, average-looking guy, Spencer Tracy, came on to her, but she turned him down because he was drunk.

Hearing that her daughter might not have enough food, Jolie had sent Eva a "care" package containing twenty Hungarian delicacies, including both caviar and salami.

To celebrate its arrival, Eva decided to throw her own party. Since she had no friends in town, she asked Drimmer to invite six of his patients. "Make it a point that they can't bring spouses or escorts because our dining area is so small, we can only seat eight, including us."

The main guest Eva wanted to check out for herself was Drimmer's fellow Swede, Signe Hasso, who was being hailed as "the next Garbo." She was married to the German film director, Harry Hasso, but rumor had it that their marriage was unraveling. Drimmer had known her in Stockholm, and now, she'd moved to the United States and signed with RKO Studios.

"At least Hasso and Erik speak the same language," Eva wrote to her Jolie. "From her pictures, I'd say she is a beautiful woman but hardly in my league, *Nuci.*"

At Eva's dinner party, Hasso was polite but reserved to Eva, talking for most of the evening in Swedish to Drimmer. Prior to their arrival in her home, his two other female guests—Lynn Bari and Carole Landis—had each been unknown to Eva.

Eva would later learn who they were. A cool brunette, Bari was a second-tier actress appearing in such lackluster fare as *The Gay Deception* (1938) and *Bottoms Up* (1934), titles not as suggestive in the 30s as they would be today.

Of the female guests, Eva was the most suspicious of Bari, who specialized in the portrayal of sultry, statuesque man-killers on the screen. She was quoted as saying, "I seem to be a woman always with a gun in her purse, even though I'm terrified of guns. I go from one set to the other shooting people and stealing husbands."

Landis, on the other hand, was also the survivor of many a mediocre film, including *Gold Diggers in Paris* (1938) and *Moon Over Miami* (1941). She'd go on to become a pinup blonde of World War II and a suicide in 1948, de-

At the first dinner party she hosted in Hollywood, Eva got to meet some of the competition for Erik Drimmer's affections. In addition to Greta Garbo, his clients included **Signe Hasso** *(left)*, **Lynn Bari** *(center)*, and **Carole Landis** *(right)*.

"All these sultry women were man-eaters, and it was clear to me why Erik had almost ceased to make love to me anymore," Eva said.

spondent over her failed affair with Rex Harrison.

Eva was less suspicious of Landis, who, according to Hollywood gossip, got a 20th Century Fox contract by sleeping with producer Darryl F. Zanuck. Drimmer had told Eva that Landis was bisexual—"Better watch yourself around her."

The least good-looking of all the guests was the Cleveland-born actor, Burgess Meredith. He had a raspy voice and was a feisty, controversial guest. He spent most of the evening attacking Charlie Chaplin. Apparently, both of them viewed Paulette Goddard as marriage material. "God knows I was not a dashing swain," he told his fellow guests. "But a kind of mongrel dog chasing the foxes."

At the time Eva met Meredith, she wasn't attracted to him at all, even though they would become lovers in the future.

Suddenly, with no warning, Meredith broke into a rage, threatening to kill Chaplin.

[Later in life, it was revealed that he suffered from violent mood swings, a condition caused by cyclothymia, *a form of bipolar disorder.]*

Eva was unfamiliar with another male guest, Brian Aherne. Eva found out the British actor was married to Joan Fontaine at the time, but carrying on a "Back Street affair" with Marlene Dietrich.

A British actor of stage and screen, Aherne was finding success in Hollywood. Although he was married to Joan Fontaine at the time, the press was filled with news of his romantic liaisons with Ruth Chatterton, Merle Oberon, and even tobacco heiress Doris Duke.

"I'm not certain why European men marry American women," Aherne said. "For all their lively charm and beauty, they are so often spoiled and unhappy. It took me a while to go out with a woman. When I was a young man, whenever I saw a beautiful woman like Eva, I'd faint at the sight of her. I was well into my twenties before I worked up enough courage to actually be with a woman."

At her dinner party, the only male guest Eva knew anything about prior to his arrival was Fredric March, another of Drimmer's patients. She had seen him in the 1932 film version of *Dr. Jekyll and Mr. Hyde,*

At Eva's dinner party, **Burgess Meredith** *(left)* spent most of the evening making threats against **Charlie Chaplin** *(right)*. Both were contenders for the love of Paulette Goddard.

In time, of course, both men would marry Goddard.

Ironically, Meredith would become one of Eva's future lovers, with Chaplin crawling into bed with Zsa Zsa.

and as an actor, she was very impressed, having read he earned half a million dollars a year, making him the fifth highest paid person in America. But as an individual, she found him most unappealing, especially the way he kept licking his lips. He came on to her strong in the kitchen, but she eluded his advances.

"I fear my days as a romantic lead are beginning to wane just a bit, so I must prove myself an attraction with every beautiful woman I meet," March told her. "I got my come-uppance when

Dinner guest **Fredric March** seemed more interested in having Eva for his main course than in anything on the table. "March was a great actor, but not my idea of a good time," Eva said.

Famously married to Joan Fontaine, **Brian Aherne** told Eva that he was well into his twenties before he had sexual relations with a woman. "But now I'm making up for lost time. But I'm tired of dating women more famous than I am."

I reached up Katharine Hepburn's dress. I withdrew in horror, thinking she was a man in women's clothing. Later, I found she'd put a banana in her drawers, a very large banana."

In anticipation of her party, when Eva opened Jolie's package of Hungarian delicacies, she found that all its contents were rotten, even though everything had been preserved in tins. "I saved the night by serving bacon and eggs. As for all that witty talk at my dinner table, I really didn't understand most of the references. I knew who Chaplin was—and that was about it. I felt like such a failure."

Waking up one morning, Eva found herself with a dreadful toothache. She called a woman dentist who was a patient of Drimmer's. She agreed to take her as a patient that afternoon.

At the dentist's office, it was discovered that Eva had a rotting tooth. It would have to be drilled and a filling put in.

She remembered her mouth being stuffed with cotton, followed with enough drilling "to carve out New York City's Holland Tunnel."

When she opened her eyes, a fat, balding man was staring down her throat. "I thought he was checking out my tonsils," she later said. As it turned out, another of the dentist's patients had walked into her cubicle and observed her having her tooth drilled. He asked her, "Would you like to become a movie star?"

"It's my greatest dream," she said. In her memoirs, she never identified who this man was, but referred to him as "the first flesh peddler I ever met in

Tinseltown."

Actually, he was Burt Feingold, a theatrical agent so low on the totem pole he was virtually buried underground. Although he came and went very quickly from Eva's life, he played a role in launching her screen career.

"If he were on the level, he might help me reach my goal," Eva recalled. "Ever since I'd seen the actress, Gizi Bajor, at the National Theater in Hungary, I had wanted to be an actress."

[One of Hungary's most famous and influential actors, Budapest-born Gizi Bajor had been Eva's role model for years.

Eva was in awe of Bajor, watching her appear as Shakespeare's Juliet and in others of the Bard's plays. Bajor had played Titania in A Midsummer Night's Dream, *and Cleopatra in* Antony and Cleopatra.*]*

During World War II, Bajor hid Hungarian soldiers in her home when they deserted and didn't want to return to the Eastern Front.

Her third husband, Professor Tibor Germán, was mentally ill and feared that his wife was threatened by various diseases. In 1951, during the darkest and most ominous years of Hungary's occupation by the Soviets, he killed her before committing suicide.]

At the dentist's office, Feingold told Eva, "I can get a screen test for you, But you've got to take off ten pounds. You must have been stuffing yourself with hamburgers topped with fried bacon and cheese."

After leaving the dentist's office, she said, "I thought I'd never hear from him again. But when I called him the next day, he agreed to arrange a screen test for me at Paramount. He gave me a final warning: 'Don't eat a god damn thing for the next few days. Baby, that Hungarian salami and goulash fat has got to go.'"

Over the next five days, she survived on tea and lemon slices, with a lettuce leaf on the side. "I had to look fabulous. Instead of Gizi Bajor, I began to picture myself as a short and blonde Greta Garbo."

On a Tuesday morning, she rose early; the

Two views of Hungarian stage and film star **Gizi Bajor**

As a young girl, Eva attended any performance at Hungary's National Theater that starred the formidable actress **Gizi Bajor**. She later became a heroine during World War II, hiding Hungarian soldiers who didn't want to join the Nazis fighting on the Eastern Front.

She later met a tragic fate herself.

screen test had been scheduled for that afternoon. Even though it was a scorcher of a day, she put on her mink coat and headed for Baggerty's Department Store. "In spite of the weather, I wore the mink because that's how I remembered Joan Crawford and Barbara Stanwyck looked in the movies. My dress was awful, but the mink covered it."

At the store, she selected what she called "this Mata Hari" outfit, all slinky and black with the requisite froufrou of bangles, beads, and sequins.

She didn't have the money to pay for it, but asked the clerk if she could open a charge account. "Perhaps it was the mink, but the clerk agreed to it. I walked out of the store with no money, but with a mink coat and a chic dress."

Back at the house at around noon, she piled her hair on top of her head. "I looked like the meringue on top of a gooey lemon meringue pie. I was ready to face Paramount. Move over, Marlene!"

At the studio gate, she discovered that her name wasn't on the list. The security guard had to place three calls before she could be admitted to Studio Four.

Eva's future friend, Tallulah Bankhead, once proclaimed, "Coop discovered that he could do two things very well...ride a horse and fuck."

After being introduced to **Gary Cooper** on her first day at the studio, Eva soon learned that Tallulah's statement was accurate.

"What a dream boat," Eva proclaimed.

There, she met a photographer who said, "Before your test, I've been asked to take some stills of you. Would you come with me?"

She followed him down a long corridor, where she encountered what she'd later call "a beanpole of a man. I practically came up to the leather belt of this tall, rangy, cowboy."

The photographer knew him and asked him if he would stand next to Eva. "I want to take her picture to judge her comparative size."

"I don't mind being a tape measure," he said. "But most people want to measure another part of my anatomy."

She wasn't sure she understood what he meant.

"Eva, this is Gary Cooper. Gary, one of our new budding starlets, or at least a wannabe, from Hungary."

"Glad to meet you, ma'am," he said. "Maybe you'd like to be the leading lady in my next picture?"

***

113

Magda

After a long, difficult, and circuitous route, Count Jan de Bychowsky and Magda finally made it to the U.K. There, she rented a small country cottage for them in the southwest of England. Under its thatched roof, it had neither hot water nor indoor plumbing, but because of a severe housing shortage, she felt lucky to get it.

At the nearby air base, Jan joined the Polish fighter pilots of 303 Squadron. Each of these brave men had fled to England after the "rape" of Poland by Hitler and Stalin.

England was bracing for the upcoming Battle of Britain in which the country's officials expected to be attacked by the *Luftwaffe* as a prelude to a full-scale Nazi invasion from across the English Channel.

Discreetly, Magda tried to find out if Zdzislaw Henneberg had escaped from Poland, but she could learn nothing. She couldn't ask Jan for help in her search because he would want to know why she was interested. So far, she'd managed to keep knowledge of her affair a secret from her husband.

At a vodka party at the air base, Magda was introduced to General Wladyslaw Sikorski, the head of the Polish Armed Forces in Britain. He was very deferential to her, treating her—based on her status as Countess of Warsaw—like royalty. He brought news from Poland, informing her that the entire country had fallen to the simultaneous onslaught of the German and Soviet invaders, and that the Jews, especially those in Warsaw, were in great peril. He also told her that Hitler had predicted that by the time the autumn (of 1940) leaves had started to fall, the British Empire would also have blown away in the winds.

She asked the general if a man named Zdzislaw Henneberg had made it from Poland to join the Polish squadron in England. She was told that he had indeed escaped and was being debriefed in London and that he was scheduled to arrive the following week at the airbase. "He was the boyfriend of my house maid in Warsaw," she said to explain her curiosity about his welfare.

Because the pilots of 303 squadron were such a closely knit unit, Magda knew that Jan and Zdzislaw would eventually meet each other. What she didn't count on was that Zdzislaw, in an attempt to reunite with Madga, would befriend Jan. As she wrote Jolie, "Life is nothing but a series of coincidences. Jan and Zdzislaw have become friends. They even bunk together at the barracks."

Both of the adulterous lovers knew that they'd have to wait for the right moment to be in each other's arms again. That chance arose one afternoon when Jan called, telling her that he was bringing home five pilots for dinner. "I know our cupboard is pretty bare, but you can always add more water to the goulash," he told her. "I'll bring the beer."

She hoped, she prayed, that one of those pilots would be her lover. When twilight arrived, she stood in her doorway to welcome them. Her wish came true. One of the pilots was indeed Zdzislaw. Jan introduced him to Magda. As she later wrote, "I shook his hand. The only way we could communicate our love for each other was through our eyes."

"God was shining down on me when Jan was called back to the base after dinner. The rest of the pilots stayed late drinking my vodka. Fortunately, Zdzislaw and I managed to slip away to the garage, where we made passionate love. It was the greatest night of my life. I am madly in love with him. We are going to sneak around like criminals and meet for private rendezvous every chance we get."

The Battle of Britain was launched on August 8, 1940. As Jan told her, "Swarms of Nazi war birds blew over Southern England, dropping their explosives."

By the final count, at least 300 *Luftwaffe* planes bombarded England in one day. Within five days, that number had doubled. Göring's Cornier bombers were engaging English Hurricanes in to-the-death dogfights.

At her cottage, Magda was terrified, listening to any and every BBC news broadcast. She feared she'd lose both men in the air, but miraculously, they both survived.

Squadron 303, especially during the Battle of Britain, would distinguish itself as having the best fighter pilots in the world. In 1940 alone, the Poles downed three times as many enemy aircraft as the average RAF aircraft scored, while incurring only one-third of the casualties.

Three crucial scenes from the Battle of Britain:

Top photo: **London air watch** on the alert over St. Paul's Cathedral in London.

Middle photo: Laden with bombs, with the intention of destroying British morale, **German Heinkel He 111 Bombers** fly over the English Channel in 1940;

Lower photo: **Polish airmen** scramble into fighter planes prepped to carry them aloft into battle.

Jan's leg injury was still bothering him, but he was pronounced as able to fly. However, his friendship with Zdzislaw was tested during the weeks ahead. It wasn't jealousy over Magda, because Jan did not know his fellow pilot was a threat to his marriage. It was because Zdzislaw turned out to be a superior fighter pilot.

As early as September of 1940, he had been designated as commander of the "A-Team" flight crew, holding the post until February 22, 1941, when he was appointed commander of the entire 303 Squadron. Despite his status as the unit's commander, he flew on combat missions anyway.

Many Poles in the squadron considered Zdzislaw the best pilot in the regiment. Hailed as a hero, he distinguished himself during the Battle of Britain. In one battle alone, the Poles in their Hurricanes dueled the pilots of the Nazi Messerschmitts, mortally wounding dozens of them, sending them in crashing spirals into the English landscape, engulfed in billows of black smoke and flames.

In a notable battle on the final day of August, 1940, Zdzislaw witnessed the destruction of three Messerschmitts as they plunged, in flames, to earth. On the same day, in mortal danger, he was unaware that his wingmen had diverted their course. He signaled to his backup crew to follow him in their planes. But when he turned around, he realized that his fellow pilots had broken their formation.

Suddenly, he found himself directly in the center of four Nazi aircraft. On a fast impulse, he abruptly raised the nose of his Hurricane and, increasing his altitude, managed "to get in back of these little Adolfs. I followed them like a wolf after a fat sheep," he'd later tell Magda.

Three of the Messerschmitts quickly fled across the English Channel to the safety of Nazi-occupied France. Zdzislaw fired on the remaining Nazi pilot and watched as his plane burst into flames, plunging into the Channel, creating a giant waterspout as it crashed into the deep.

Time and time again, in equivalent ways, he averted deathtraps in the air. Magda praised his bravery, but he had grave doubts. "How long can a man's luck hold out?"

April 12, 1941, was one of the saddest days in Magda's life. She woke up that morning with a great apprehension. The night before, she'd held Zdzislaw in her arms before he set out on a dangerous mission over France. He was to fly his Spitfire II across the Channel to bomb a target in France.

After taking off from Dungeness, Kent, he steered his craft above the water. Seemingly from out of nowhere, a Nazi Messerschmitt appeared through the clouds and bombarded his plane.

His luck had run out. His plane nosedived into the English Channel. Neither his body nor his Spitfire were ever recovered.

Magda was devastated to hear the news of her lover's death, but she was forced to conceal her grief from Jan. He was very cavalier about his comrade/competitor's death. "He was a daredevil. It was inevitable that his number would come up sooner than later."

During the upcoming week, "lighting didn't strike me twice, but three times," as she wrote to Jolie. First, from Ankara, Belge sent her an urgent communication that the lives of Jolie and even Vilmos were in grave danger. He had learned that if they stubbornly stayed any longer in Hungary, the Nazis might arrest them and send them off to a concentration camp. "Jolie, particularly, would die here. She is a hothouse flower. She would be unable to withstand the rigors of such a camp."

Magda began to prepare to leave England, and with the help of a Polish officer in the British Army, she plotted a circuitous route to get her back to Budapest.

Her decision to leave Jan was made easier "when the third bolt of lightning struck me." More and more, Jan had been staying on the base and not coming home. After he'd been away for a week, he announced by telephone that he'd be arriving at the cottage that evening for dinner. She prepared his favorite dish, stuffed cabbage. After dinner, and over a bottle of vodka, he informed her that he had news to tell her "even though I know it is going to hurt you."

For the rest of her life, she'd remember his words: "I want to divorce you." Seemingly without any emotion, he asserted, "I've fallen in love with a ruddy-cheeked Devonshire girl. I call her my English Rose. She works as a nurse on the base. I won't change my mind. I want a divorce so I can marry her."

Apparently, he had been expecting a violent eruption from his wife. But Magda seemed detached. She spoke softly. "You will have your divorce," she said. "I will not stand in your way. I can only wish that you and your new bride will have the love and happiness I have known with you." She got up and walked away, shutting the bedroom door behind her.

After packing a few possessions, he left the cottage. She never saw him again.

When he returned a week later to the cottage, he found the front door unlocked. All her possessions were gone, and she'd departed without a note.

In her 1975 memoir, Jolie wrote that Magda returned to Budapest and she never learned what happened to Count Bychowsky. Actually, he died in 1944 when his Hurricane was shot down over the English Channel.

His fiery death evoked the fatal plane crash of Zdzislaw three years earlier. Neither Jan's plane nor his body were ever recovered from the cold waters of the Channel.

A year after the war's end, in California in 1946, Magda was granted a divorce from Jan by a judge in Santa Monica. In essence, she divorced a husband who had been dead for two years.

***

 In her letters to Zsa Zsa in Ankara, Eva constantly complained of her unhappiness in Hollywood. "Erik sems to be sleeping in every woman's bed but my own. We really have very little money to live on. He also needs money for further education if he is ever going to become a doctor. I'm going to take a screen test. Maybe I can become a famous actress. Please, please, come to Hollywood and be with me. I desperately need my sister."

When Zsa Zsa asked Belge if she could travel to California, he adamantly refused. "If you go to America, it will be only with me, and I have no intention of doing that right now, with Turkey facing such peril."

Privately, she plotted a trip to California without his permission. Her journey needed some careful planning. Belge had grown more and more strident in his radio broadcasts attacking the Axis and Hitler personally. He had completely reversed his position about Hitler, whom he'd previously referred to as "my dear friend."

Under normal circumstances, she would have traveled across Europe to Lisbon where she would have flown the Clipper to New York. But because she was Belge's wife, she feared she'd be arrested if she crossed Axis-occupied Western Europe. Ironically, her status as the wife of a Turkish diplomat was no longer a luxury—during the context of a World War, it would be dangerous.

Consequently, she'd have to travel via the Eastern, rather than by the Western route, to reach America. Without alerting Belge of her true intentions, she packed her most valuable possessions, mainly her jewelry, and told her husband that she was flying to Budapest because Jolie was desperately ill.

Reunited with her mother at her apartment, Zsa Zsa only picked at the Beluga caviar that Jolie had spread out.

She was jealous and upset that Eva had gone to Hollywood before her. "As my appearance on the stage in Vienna proved, *I* am the actress in the Gabor family, not Eva."

"You're going to Hollywood," Jolie—ever the stage mother—said. "I just know it. It's all over between you and Belge."

"I never loved him," she said. "We were never lovers. He deserves a woman who could be a real wife to him."

"What will you do for money?" Jolie, the practical one, asked.

"I have a few thousand dollars in diamonds and rubies, and I have saved most of the allowance Burhan gave me. If I avoid Axis Europe, I can travel safely on a diplomatic passport to the East, which should get me across any

118

border not controlled by the SS."

The next day, Zsa Zsa had lunch with Vilmos, not knowing if she'd ever see him again. Her father's greatest concern involved her transit through Chicago. He had learned that she planned to travel from New York to California by rail, with a change of trains in Chicago.

"The gangsters there might kidnap you or shoot you, perhaps something even worse. A fate worse than death! You are a beautiful woman. Al Capone will probably kidnap you and force you into unspeakable acts."

During her final night with Jolie, she urged her mother to travel with her and escape from war-torn Europe.

"I cannot, *Zsika*," Jolie said. "I have my roots here."

"You can't because of Paul Savosdy, isn't that true?" Zsa Zsa asked.

"He's in my blood. Even though he's not a good man, I absolutely adore him. I don't think I could survive without him. He told me he will never go to America, so I must stay behind with him and take my chance with the Nazis."

"I hope you don't regret that decision," Zsa Zsa said, "when Hitler's armies are marching through the streets of Budapest."

Jolie did not try to talk Zsa Zsa out of her elaborately circuitous upcoming journey to America. "Once there, you can divorce Belge and marry a rich Texan oil millionaire."

The next morning at the rail terminus, Jolie bid a tearful farewell to Zsa Zsa as she boarded the Orient Express. She recorded the date (February 15, 1941) as the day she departed from Budapest with two dozen pieces of luggage.

It would be a long, dusty, tedious trip, involving many forms of transportation—train, horse-drawn cart, ship, and even, at one point in India, a donkey and mule caravan. It would take an astonishing four months to reach New York via this route.

Her first stop was in Belgrade, Yugoslavia, where she consumed bad oysters which made her sick.

Most of the passengers aboard the train were sad-eyed Jewish refugees fleeing the Nazis and headed for Palestine. Most of them would discover that their entrance into "The Promised Land" would be barred. At almost every national boundary, these refugees would be turned back by various border guards.

"Poor souls," Zsa Zsa wrote in her diary. "I feel heartsick for them. No one wants them. I hear even the United States is closing its doors to them."

The Orient Express roared eastward toward Bulgaria. After a stopover in Sofia for the unloading and pickup of passengers, the train made it out of the Bulgarian capital only twelve hours before Nazi soldiers invaded and took control.

Zsa Zsa dreaded her stopover in Ankara, fearing that Belge would learn of her arrival and that he'd send policemen to remove her from the train and drag her back to the home they'd (unhappily) shared on Embassy Row.

When she arrived there, she noticed British flags flying over the railway terminus. The conductor told her that Sir Anthony Eden had arrived in Turkey. She recalled their brief affair when she'd been hailed in the British press as "The Toast of London."

She had a momentary regret that she didn't get off the train right then and resume her role as the belle of the *corps diplomatique*. She pictured herself dancing in the arms of Sir Anthony in the ballroom of Ankara's British Embassy.

More than Belge, she regretted having to leave her beloved horse, Fatushka, and she wondered what would happen to the beast after her departure. She feared that Belge would shoot Fatushka in the head as a revenge on her.

Finally, after what seemed for her an interminable wait, the train pulled out of the station. With musical backup from a pocket harmonica, two young Britishers sang, "It's a Long Way to Tipperary."

"To me, Tipperary was Hollywood," she later said. "At that moment, it seemed on the other side of the moon."

Crossing the Turkish border into Iraq, the train arrived in Baghdad. Here, the story of Zsa Zsa becomes blurred. In a memoir, she asserted that local authorities would not accept her diplomatic passport, suspecting that she was engaged in espionage for Turkey. According to her, she had to spend one month in Baghdad before the authorities would grant her permission to leave.

That she stayed for one month in the capital is not disputed. What is unclear involves the reason for which she was detained.

Rumors still persist that she was pregnant with Atatürk's child when she boarded the Orient Express in Budapest. It is alleged that she had a miscarriage in Baghdad and other complications, and that she was hospitalized in the city hospital, where she remained for several days. It was said that she hired a nurse who helped her recover her health so she could board the train again.

She has denied all these rumors, but the legend still persists.

Eventually, she was able to buy a ticket aboard a train rolling from Baghdad to Basra, the port city in the south of Iraq. From there, she journeyed to Karachi and from there to Bombay.

In Bombay, and for the first time, she met someone she knew. She renewed her acquaintance with Princess Uma Chatterjee of India, whom she'd known at Madame Subilia's finishing school at Lausanne.

The princess was also taking the ship, the *S.S. U.S. Grant*, to New York, a rough trip over turbulent seas that would last six entire weeks.

"The highlight of me afloat was when I danced one night in the ship's ballroom," Zsa Zsa recalled. "The sari I had purchased in Bombay unraveled. I was completely nude in front of everybody. I ran from the ballroom. There were several American missionaries aboard, returning to America because of the war. After my disgraceful performance, they prayed for my eternal soul, hoping that I would not be assigned to the hottest ovens in hell."

She thought it would never happen, but, finally, the *S.S. U.S. Grant* sailed into New York Harbor. "I stood on deck looking at the Statue of Liberty. For the first time in my life, I felt like my own woman. No husband, no parents to tell me what to do. I recorded the date in my diary as June 1, 1941. America still had not entered World War II."

In later years, she recalled, "I'd lived a life of luxury and now I was herded onto Ellis Island with the lowest ladder of refugees. I, too, was a refugee. I had been living like a rat making that four-month journey. Before that, I had lived a life of luxury,"

"I knew America was a big place, but I set out that very day to conquer it. I planned to spend the rest of my life in luxury with some man paying my bills."

"I knew myself very well. There would be a lot of bills to pay. I'm a woman who requires expensive maintenance. I don't want a box of chocolates or a teddy bear. I want diamonds, rubies, a few emeralds, gold, satin gowns, real estate, stocks, and a closet of only the most elegant of furs."

***

In a hideaway apartment in West Hollywood, where Gary Cooper conducted off-the-record trysts, Eva placed an urgent call to Feingold, her "flesh peddler agent."

Her voice sounded desperate. "I don't know what to do. I'm in this apartment with Gary Cooper. He's pulled off his shirt and shoes. It's obvious he wants to seduce me. Should I give in?"

"Don't be a silly little fool," the agent said. "Of course, you submit. Cooper is one of the biggest stars in Hollywood. He got his start on the casting couch by fucking big stars like Clara Bow. Years from now, it will be said that Eva Gabor got her start on a fabulous screen career by screwing around with Coop."

"If this is the road to stardom, then count me in as a traveler on that road," she told Feingold. She made herself look more glamorous in the bathroom before coming back into the living room to confront Cooper.

Although married to Veronica ("Rocky") Balfe, he played the field on both sides of the fence. His seductions included Tallulah Bankhead, Marlene Dietrich, photographer Cecil Beaton, Cary Grant, tobacco heir Anderson Lawler, Barbara Stanwyck, Merle Oberon, Randolph Scott, Mae West, Lupe Velez, and Carole Lombard.

"The men seemed more interested in him than the women," said Loretta

121

Young. "They wouldn't leave him alone."

Cecil Beaton claimed that the bisexual director, Edmund Goulding, "worshipped" Cooper twice a day. Clara Bow revealed why. "Coop's hung like a horse and can go all night." Later, Ava Gardner confirmed that.

Eva recalled, "I'd never met a man like Gary before, a cowpoke from Montana with English parents," she said. "He was such a gentleman, but he had this funny little habit. He took a tube of my lipstick and drew a face on my left breast, using my nipple as its nose. Isn't that adorable?"

After a night with Cooper, Eva proclaimed, "Now I know why he's called 'The Montana Mule' in Hollywood. I wish he were my husband instead of Erik Drimmer. Gary's a great lover, and certainly has the equipment for lovemaking, but he's also a kind and generous man. Every woman should have a Gary Cooper in her life—if not as a husband, then as a lover. I'm crazy about him."

She told her agent, "You know he originally set out to become a salesman of electric signs and theatrical curtains."

She later confessed to both Jolie and Zsa Zsa that she knew right from the beginning that Cooper never had any intention of leaving his elegant socialite wife. "I had no rights to him. Nor would I ever. After that initial encounter, which thrilled me, we saw each other five more times, always in that same apartment."

"The place had a small kitchen, and I prepared at least two meals for him. He loved Sauerkraut, claiming he ate it every day because it kept him regular."

"I prepared simple meals, often steak, but he insisted on making the guacamole dip, a taste treat I'd never had before."

"Comedians ridiculed his 'yups' and 'nopes,' but with me, he was highly articulate. He mocked people who said he was a great actor."

"It was all the director or the boys in the cutting room," he said. "I got my start in Montana hog calling."

"After saying that, he let out a high-pitched '*sooie-sooie.*'"

"I've had other lovers with blue eyes, but Gary's had the most amazing shade of blue. Behind his long eyelashes, those eyes sparkled when he looked at me. Everything about him was long, and I don't mean the obvious—long hands that nonetheless were graceful when moving across a woman's body. Long legs, long arms."

"Sometimes, he spoke of growing up in Helena, which at the end of America's Civil War was called Last Chance Gulch, a mining town. He searched the creek for flakes of gold so he could feed his addiction, which was licorice."

"How did I learn to stand up against the formidable stars like Bankhead and Dietrich, especially that crazy nut, Lupe Velez?" he asked. "I was toughened by the chinook which blows into Montana in the early spring. It melts the snow east of the Continental Divide."

"It would sweep our ranch down to bedrock. A chinook is the most treacherous woman I ever encountered. It prepared me for Hollywood. The only thing I wasn't prepared for was that the town is riddled with cocksuckers, even Howard Hughes."

When she constantly praised his penis, he modestly said, "God was good to me. A good-looking guy with a big penis and pretense at acting can go far in this nutty place."

Halfway into her brief affair with Cooper, Eva, as she confessed in her memoirs, came to realize that "I was not going to be Gary Cooper's leading lady. The demand for cowgirls with Hungarian accents was then at a low ebb."

"And then, he was gone from my life," Eva lamented. "Just as when I had fallen completely out of love with Erik and completely in love with Gary. He'd foolishly turned down the role of Rhett Butler in *Gone With the Wind.* And now he'd truly *Gone With the Wind*, like those chinooks in Old Montana."

***

At Paramount Studio's Soundstage Five, the cameras were on during the filming of Eva's screen test. She was instructed to walk onto the stage holding a tattered box containing a dress. She was to open it and exclaim how beautiful it was. Appearing in a slip, she was told to try on the dress before admiring herself in the mirror. Next, she was ordered to cry bitter tears before laughing, as if she were hysterically overjoyed at something.

"I cried because I was nervous," she said. "My laughter did not come, however, and the cackle that came from my throat belonged more in a henhouse."

Depressed, she left the studio knowing that she would be no competition for Dietrich, much less for Garbo. However, the next week, her agent, Feingold, called, telling her that Paramount was willing to give her a contract at $75 a week.

The Paramount executive had actually been very skeptical of her appearance. She wasn't really fat, but on film, she appeared in need of weight loss. Even so, she was signed. One executive said, "If she doesn't work out, we can drop her in eight months."

When she was summoned to Paramount three weeks later, she met drama coach Florence Enright, who told her she had to undergo a second screen test. "You look at least ten pounds lighter," the coach told her.

"After that and for the next eight months, I withered on the vine," Eva lamented. "The apartment grew smaller, and Erik seemed to always be in the opposite corner. Carole Landis, Lynn Bari, and god knows who, took care of him sexually."

"Because I was so isolated, I had no chance to improve my English. I spent my afternoons in the movie houses along Hollywood Boulevard. That's how I learned English. One day, I came back to the apartment talking like Joan Crawford, the next day I sounded more like Joel McCrea."

Eva's English was also improved through work sessions with drama coaches Florence Enright and Margaret Webster.

At Paramount, Eva met other young starlets hoping to become big stars. She developed a particularly close friendship with a fiery redhead from Brooklyn named Susan Hayward.

Born into poverty as Edythe Marrenner, she'd survived an automobile accident at the age of seven that might have left her handicapped for life. After years of rehabilitation, and after working as a fashion model, she'd traveled to Hollywood, hoping to be cast as Scarlett O'Hara in *Gone With the Wind.*

"When I first met her, she, too, was recovering from an affair with Gary Cooper. She had appeared with him in his movie *Beau Gest* in 1939," Eva said. "She was also getting over her love affair with this second rate bit actor, Ronald Reagan, who had dumped her for Jane Wyman."

Susan gave Eva some advice. "You have to slug your way to the top in this town, where people like to trample you to death. You can never relax around here. Life is too short for gals like us to relax."

At the time Eva befriended the sexy redhead from Brooklyn, both **Susan Hayward** and Eva had been dumped by Gary Cooper. Hayward had also been tossed aside by Ronald Reagan, who preferred Jane Wyman.

Hayward quickly became Eva's *confidante* in all matters concerning love affairs and Hollywood studs.

When Susan died of brain cancer in 1975, Eva remembered her with love. "To speak like an American, or at least like Frank Sinatra, I'd call Susan one gutsy broad. Like all of us, she had a disastrous marriage and suffered a lot of pain climbing that ladder to the top. She came to hate Hollywood. As for men, she once told me, 'I'd like to fry 'em all in deep fat.'"

"Susan's career was beginning to take off, but I felt I was going nowhere except to oblivion," Eva said.

Paramount called Eva to test her for a role in *My Life with Caroline* (1941), a comedy starring the English actor, Ronald Colman. John Van Druten had adapted the script from a frivolous French farce.

Eva was introduced to Colman and was intimidated by his cultured English accent. During her screen test, he watched her skeptically from the sidelines.

On camera, Eva appeared with another English actor, Reginald Gardiner, who played her husband returning from the war. For her big scene, she was supposed to burst into hysterical tears when he tells her he is leaving her.

At the end of the test, Gardiner told her, "You were smashing, my dear girl." She then had to face the director, Lewis Milestone, one of the best in Hollywood. He'd helmed the classic 1930 *All Quiet on the Western Front*. He thought she'd handled the role of the jilted wife perfectly.

Gardiner invited her to lunch and spoke about his recent appearance in *The Great Dictator* (1940) with Charlie Chaplin. "For mocking Hitler so devastatingly on the screen, the Nazis, if they ever capture the Little Tramp, will assign him to the hottest room in Dante's Inferno."

Elated, Eva returned to her little apartment to wait for the final judgment from Paramount. Feingold called her a week later. "You're off the picture. You photographed too young. But I'll get something even bigger for you, and that's a promise."

"For the first and last time in my Hollywood career, I wanted to photograph older," Eva said. "Someone at Paramount thought I looked like a sixteen-year-old on the screen, and that it would make Gardiner look like a child molester."

"If I hadn't photographed so young, I would have become a big star. Even so, plans for my career moved along. There was talk of grooming me as a replacement for Madeleine Carroll."

[When the reviews for My Life with Caroline *were posted, Eva may have been glad that she hadn't been cast. Miriam Hopkins, Paulette Goddard, and Jean Arthur were each considered before the film's director, Milestone, foolishly cast newcomer Anna Lee. Reviewers wrote that her lackluster performance sabotaged the picture.]*

Eva wondered why Madeleine Carroll needed to be replaced. At the peak of her career in 1938, she was earning $250,000 a year, making her the highest paid actress in the world. She'd become a household name after starring in Alfred Hitchcock's *The 39 Steps* (1935).

[Carroll was limiting her appearances on the screen to help her native England fight the war. She worked in field hospitals as a Red Cross

"I was hired to replace **Madeleine Carroll**, who was devoting her time to the war effort," Eva said.

"What a tough act to follow. This British-born beauty was one of the most elegantly beautiful leading ladies of the screen, and talented, too."

"In one film, *Lloyd's of London*, the character she played was unhappily married to George Sanders. Zsa Zsa should have seen that movie."

nurse. In 1944, after she became a naturalized U.S. citizen in 1943, she worked with the American Army Air Forces's 61st Station Hospital in Foggia, Italy, caring for wounded airmen. During the war, she donated her château outside Paris for the housing of more than 150 orphans.]

At long last, Eva got a small role in a forgettable movie with Mary Martin. A frothy romantic comedy entitled *New York Town* (1941), it co-starred Fred MacMurray and Robert Preston. Director Charles Vidor cast Eva as a nurse, and she made a glamorous appearance on the set wearing a uniform designed by Edith Head.

"When I appeared, Vidor yelled at me, 'You don't look like a nurse. You look so young you need a nurse.' Then he called to his casting director, 'Get me a Florence Nightingale type.'"

It was Eva's second chance to appear in a movie, and she was once again faulted for being too young. "I didn't cry. Right in front of Vidor, I bawled and then I bawled and bawled some more. My mascara was running, my grease paint melting, and I looked like a clown. Vidor felt sorry for me and agreed to give me another role, a very small one, in fact."

Pulling herself together, Eva appeared on the set the next day and was instructed to pitch a horseshoe and miss, and also "to lean flirtatiously into Mr. Preston's body."

Eva had never pitched horseshoes before. "I found Robert irresistible, and I guess that instead of leaning, I rubbed by body against his. He was very virile in those days, and he got an erection. I then tossed the horseshoe and scored a ringer."

Vidor yelled at me. "I told you to miss the god damn horseshoe. I said lean into Preston—not to give him a hard-on. We'll shoot it again. This time, I want you to score a ringer."

"I noticed in Robert's trousers his thing had deflated," Eva said. "I tossed the horseshoe and missed by four feet. The director called, "cut!" By telling me to score a ringer, I did just the opposite and missed it, which is what he wanted all along."

"Robert, I learned, had been married the year before, but he still had an eye for a beautiful woman," Eva said. "He called me to his dressing room that afternoon. I knew what was coming, and I welcomed it."

[Preston had married the actress Catherine Craig in 1940, the union lasting until his death in 1987.]

Eva's agent had instructed her to sleep with her leading men. Cast opposite **Robert Preston,** she took his advice.

"I was told to lean into Robert's body. That produced a reaction that did not make the final cut."

"My agent, Feingold, had more or less instructed me to sleep with my leading men to get ahead," Eva said. "But in Robert's case, I didn't have to be told. Unlike Gary Cooper, Robert was instrumental in getting me cast as the female lead in his next movie, *Pacific Blackout*."

"I knew he was still very much in love with his wife, but what red-blooded male could resist a blonde Hungarian bombshell? We were about the same age."

"As a lover, he was very gentle, very kind, perhaps too much so," she said. "He could have been more forceful, like my Hussar. But I found him adorable, definitely marriage material. He was also quite handsome back then in a wholesome American kind of way."

"I continued to see him on and off even when he joined the Army Air Force in the war. He looked great in and out of uniform. He was the first New Englander to seduce me. Now I know how women on those snowy nights in the Northeast stay warm."

***

Zsa Zsa did not immediately conquer New York the way she'd dazzled London. However, she had an immediate *entrée* into the cream of New York society.

As she disembarked from the *S.S. U.S. Grant* in New York harbor, an American industrialist, John King, was waiting to greet her. He was a friend of Belge, the husband she'd abandoned. Zsa Zsa had entertained King in Ankara, and he wanted to return the favor.

Thinking she was traveling with Belge's approval and on his money, King sent her luggage to a suite at the Plaza Hotel, which was really more than she could afford. In a memoir, she said, "When I checked into this grand American hotel, I never dreamed that one day I would own it."

[She never owned the Plaza Hotel. What she was referring to was the financial interest her second husband, Conrad Hilton, once had in the hotel.]

A multimillionaire, King seemed to know everybody in New York when he took her for a power luncheon at "21."

Within a luxury restaurant familiar with celebrities, she made a dazzling appearance. Before the night had ended, she'd been photographed several times as King escorted her to hotspots throughout the city.

When she retrieved a copy of her first American newspapers the next morning, she found herself featured in *The New York Herald-Tribune, The Daily Mirror,* and *The Journal-American,* the latter headlining her arrival as TURKISH BEAUTY ARRIVES.

Almost overnight, she had become a social success. Café society wanted her to "adorn" their chic gatherings. At "21," she and King had sat adjacent to the table where the celebrated author, W. Somerset Maugham, was lunching with his lover, Gerald Haxton.

Both men seemed dazzled by Zsa Zsa's appearance. "You should be in the movies, dear girl," Maugham told her.

She had never read anything by Maugham, but had seen the 1934 film adaptation of his novel, *Of Human Bondage,* starring Bette Davis and Leslie Howard. She'd also seen the 1932 film version of *Rain,* with Joan Crawford cast as the prostitute, Sadie Thompson. When Greta Garbo had starred in Maugham's *The Painted Veil* (1934), Zsa Zsa and Magda had gone to see it twice. And when she'd arrived in New York, Bette Davis was creating a sensation on screen in Maugham's *The Letter.* (1940).

At the end of that luncheon, Haxton invited Zsa Zsa and King to a small cocktail party they were having in their suite at the Ritz-Carlton.

The next afternoon, Zsa Zsa spent nearly two hours selecting the right dress and applying the most flattering makeup. "I was stunningly lovely," she later wrote Jolie.

Maugham and Haxton were Zsa Zsa's first introduction to a pair of internationally famous homosexual lovers. The British playwright and novelist was spending most of World War II in America, mainly in Hollywood.

At the cocktail party, Zsa Zsa sat with Maugham on a satin sofa. He gave her advice on matters of love. "You'll find many American men willing to marry you. Of course, it's always wise to sample them in bed. In England and America, too many women insist on remaining virgins until their wedding night."

"I did even better," she said. "I lived through my entire marriage and never let my husband enjoy the privilege."

"An amazing accomplishment," he said. "This could be seriously debated, but America per square foot has the most beautiful men who have ever lived. Walk down any block on Hollywood Boulevard, and you'll probably meet a dozen you'll want to take home."

"But will I ever find love?" she

When the celebrated novelist **W. Somerset Maugham** *(left)* met the handsome rogue **Gerald Haxton** *(right),* it was love at first sight. They met in 1914, and Haxton, a young American, would be the novelist's lover until Haxton's death in 1944.

He had always excited Maugham's gay friends at his Villa Mauresque on the Côte d'Azur by walking around nude all day.

asked.

"I'm not a fortune teller," he said. "Chances are a woman as glamorous as you will want to share her beauty with many men. You will not have time to fall in love. It won't be smooth. My own love life wasn't. I have mostly loved people who cared little or nothing for me. When someone has loved me, I have been embarrassed. So as not to hurt a man's feelings, I have often pretended a passion I did not feel. Perhaps you'll find yourself doing the same."

In contrast to the more somber Maugham, Haxton was a flamboyant character who had become involved with Maugham when they worked together for the Red Cross Ambulance Corps in Flanders during World War II.

An American, he explained to her that Maugham was living with him in the United States "because I was deported from England and told never to return. I'm viewed there as an undesirable alien. One night in London, two military policemen barged into my hotel room and caught me in *flagrante delicto* with a very virile young hustler. Shades of Oscar Wilde, I was arrested and charged with gross indecency. Willie and I went to live in his villa on the Côte d'Azur until the advancing Nazis forced us to escape to America."

Haxton was the first of literally hundreds of men who would be completely open with Zsa Zsa about their homosexuality. In an age of intolerance, she was very accepting. She once said, "I understand the homosexual. Who on God's earth wouldn't like men?"

In another chat with Maugham, he told her, "I have often used Gerald as the inspiration for one of my devil-may-care characters. He's a liar, a gambler, an idler, and a spendthrift, but he loves me. He doesn't even own his own soul, and he's completely dependent on me. He's unscrupulous but so charming you forgive him. He's an amusing companion, full of high spirits and an unfailing gaiety, and he has incredible sex appeal. He handles the guest lists for our parties, sorting out the wits from the bores."

"I find him an utter delight," she said.

Seeing the entrance of a late-arriving guest, Maugham rose slowly to his feet to introduce Zsa Zsa to Emerald Cunard, one of the most visible members of the fabled shipping family. She was known in the press as "Lady Cunard, a hostess *extraordinaire*."

One invitation led to another. Lady Cunard found Zsa Zsa "utterly charming," and invited her for the following evening to her suite at the Ritz-Carlton.

It has been said that Zsa Zsa learned to be outspoken, even outrageous, in public because of the example set by Lady Cunard.

Party giver, author, and professional hostess Elsa Maxwell once said, "Lady Cunard loved to gather her lions together, lash them with the whip of her tongue, and watch them fight to the blood. By pitting them one against another, she sought to make her guests more interesting to herself, to each other, and, not at all, accidentally, to exploit her own acid wit."

She had a waspist and cruel tongue and was a source of fascination to her guests, who tolerated her insults and usually came back for more.

Before introducing Zsa Zsa, Lady Cunard told her, "Darling, to be a success here in America, and especially in England and on the Continent, you must follow the dictum of old Rasputin himself—'Sin and obtain forgiveness.' One more thing, wherever you go, create an aura of excitement, especially when entering rooms. Being provocative will stand you in better stead than all the statelier rules of deportment combined."

After Maugham's introduction, Lady Cunard and Zsa Zsa became fast friends.

"I adore musicians—in fact, I'm in love with Sir Thomas Beecham," Lady Cunard confessed. "I keep him hidden away in the suite next door. In the future, when you check into a hotel with your lover, always request two suites with connecting doors. Let me introduce you to Sir Thomas."

Zsa Zsa talked briefly with Beecham, telling him about her emotional involvement in Vienna with Richard Tauber and Willi Schmidt-Kentner, both of whom were known to Sir Thomas.

[Sir Thomas Beecham, 2ⁿᵈ Baronet (1879-1961) was Britain's first international conductor and, in 1946, the founder of the London Philharmonic. Using funds from his industrialist family,

An American born but London based heiress, **Maud ("Emerald") Cunard**, *[later known as Lady Cunard]*, married Sir Bache Cunard, grandson of the founder of the Cunard shipping line in 1895 *(see portrait on the left)*.

On the right is a 1928 pencil-and-watercolor caricature of Lady Cunard who by then was infamous as the most lavish and provocative hostess in London.

Executed by Anthony Wysard, it's part of the permanent collection of the National Portrait Gallery in London.

GRAND OPERA

Sir Thomas Beecham, who eventually founded the London Philharmonic, was stunned by Zsa Zsa's beauty.

Lady Cunard had already staked him out for herself, however, in part by persuading many of her wealthy friends to support Beecham's extravagant operatic ventures.

he financed major productions of works never before presented in Britain, including Elektra, Salome, and Der Rosenkavalier (all by Richard Strauss) and a trio of operas by Delius. One of the famous musicians of the 20th century, he was frequently associated with Schubert, Sibelius, Berlioz, Haydn, and above all, Mozart.]

"You are a beautiful woman," he told Zsa Zsa. "I'll make a commitment to you. When Britain has beaten the Nazis to a pulp, I plan to found the Royal Philharmonic in London. I will dedicate the first concert to you and your beauty. It will be an all-Mozart concert, the composer I most revere."

"I'm flabbergasted," she answered. "I am a nobody. I have done nothing to deserve such an honor."

"Beauty deserves its own rewards," he said.

When he was free, Lady Cunard directed Zsa Zsa over to meet Cole Porter, who sat in a wheelchair in a corner of the suite's living room. Even though incapacitated, she found him elegantly groomed, sporting a *boutonnière* in the lapel of his Savile Row suit. His speech was cultured like Ronald Colman's and was rather reserved, almost clipped.

"I simply adore your music," Zsa Zsa gushed to him. "I'm a romanticist myself, and no one writes songs more romantic than yours. My favorites are 'What Is This Thing Called Love,' 'Night and Day,' 'Love for Sale,' and 'Begin the Beguine.'"

"I've composed some of my best songs at dinner parties sitting between two bores," he said. "I can feign listening to them while I compose beautiful music in my head."

"Your secret is safe with me," she said.

"I can see you're startled to find me in a wheelchair," he said. "I was horseback riding in 1937. The horse slipped and toppled me. The beast fell on top of me, breaking both my legs and damaging my spinal column. I'm in constant pain. It just goes to show you that fifty million Frenchmen can't be wrong. They eat horses instead of riding them."

Wheelchair-bound composer **Cole Porter** was enchanted with Zsa Zsa, predicting at one point that in the future, they were likely to share some of the same boyfriends.

"Hollywood? It's rather like living on the moon, isn't it?" he asked Zsa Zsa.

When she told him that she wanted to go to Hollywood to become an actress, he shocked her by telling her how little starlets got paid, sometimes as little as $50 a week, perhaps $75, which was what Eva was drawing. "Occasionally, some starlet will rise above the crowd like a big wage earner such as Barbara Stanwyck, but that is rare."

"I have no skills," she said. "What will I do?"

"Marry a rich man," he said. "There are at least six women at this party who did that, including three pretty boys over there who did the same. You're stunning. I'm sure that within six months, you will have nabbed a rich Texas millionaire."

Porter turned out to be a prophet.

When Zsa Zsa kissed Porter goodbye, he promised he'd send over two seats for his Broadway musical, *Panama Hattie,* starring Ethel Merman, Arthur Treacher, and Betty Hutton.

"But I'll need an escort," she protested.

"Would you consider a nineteen-year-old French millionaire who, in addition to being filthy rich, is also devastatingly handsome?"

"I would, indeed," she said, beaming.

"You amuse me," he said. "I'm flying to Hollywood. Let's see each other on the West Coast."

"It will be an honor." She bent over and kissed him on both cheeks.

At the door, she air-kissed Lady Cunard, thanking her for the invitation. The hostess whispered to her, "One more thing, my dear. Don't believe those hideous rumors that I'm a drug addict and was once the lesbian lover of the Duchess of Windsor."

***

Elsie de Wolfe, also known as Lady Mendl, was also visiting New York, lodged in a suite at the St. Regis. Through Cole Porter, Zsa Zsa received an invitation to attend one of Lady Mendl's exclusive cocktail parties. Porter assured Zsa Zsa that "everybody who is important will be there."

Lady Mendl was so famous at the time that Porter had even written her into his lyrics. She was mentioned in his song, "That Black and White Baby of Mine," and in the musical *Let's Face It.* In his lyrics about mod-

Elsie de Wolfe, more famously known as **Lady Mendl**, was already legendary the night Zsa Zsa met her. Famous for her lesbian associations in New York and London, she was the epitome of feminine chic.

Introduced at that same party to the Duke and Duchess of Windsor, Zsa Zsa told His Highness: "When I was a little girl, my mother wanted for you to wait for me to grow up so you could marry me."

ern scandals, *Anything Goes,* he observes: "When you hear that Lady Mendl, standing up/Now turns a handspring landing up/On her toes/Anything goes."

Lady Mendl was an American actress, interior decorator, and author of the influential 1913 book *The House in Good Taste.* She was a society *duenna* presiding over parties in Paris, London, and New York.

Before meeting Lady Mendl, Zsa Zsa had read in *American Decades* that "she was probably the first woman to dye her hair blue, to perform handstands to impress her friends, and to cover 18th-century footstools in leopard-skin chintzes."

Porter was always indebted to her because she had been one of the original backers of his first musical, *See America First,* in 1916.

She'd decorated homes for royalty, aristocrats, and the gilded heiresses of her day, including the Duke and Duchess of Windsor, the philanthropist Elizabeth Milbank Anderson, Adelaide and Henry Clay Frick, Anne Vanderbilt, and Anne Morgan.

For years, Lady Mendl was the lover of the celebrated theatrical and literary agent, Elizabeth Marbury, born in 1856. In New York society, they were known as "The Bachelors." Marbury's clients had included Oscar Wilde and George Bernard Shaw. Lady Mendl had been in mourning ever since her beloved "Bessy" had died in 1933.

Zsa Zsa later said, "Lady Mendl and I were charmed by each other. Secretly, I think she wants to adopt me as her *protégée,* but I don't go that route. I was not ready to become another 'Bessy' in her lonely life. You know you can be lonely even though surrounded by some of the most famous people in the world, including the Duke and Duchess of Windsor, who were in her suite the night of her party."

Lady Mendl did give Zsa Zsa some advice. "The only way to get married to a man is to live in separate quarters. When I married Sir Charles Mendl, the British diplomat, we kept separate apartments but appeared together as a loving couple at social functions. Of course, in your own apartment, you don't want your husband dropping in at inopportune moments. Perhaps when you're entertaining a young lover. Always insist that your spouse make an appointment before visiting."

At the end of Lady Mendl's party, Zsa Zsa returned to her hotel to find two invitations waiting. One was for a party the following evening at the apartment of Syrie Maugham at the Dakota; and the other for the subsequent evening, for a night on Broadway with an escort as arranged by Cole Porter. The composer had added, as a footnote, "You'll love your escort. All of us have had him—he's divine in bed. Enjoy!"

***

The New York Times defined **Syrie Maugham** as "a domestic-arts arbiter of adventurous originality. Possessed of a lavish Molyneux wardrobe, a quick temper, an appetite for a good scuffle, and a choppy verbal style rapped out in high birdlike notes, Syrie was something of a protofeminist."

The next morning, Zsa Zsa learned that a great deal of her popularity was based not just on her beauty and charm, but on some *faux* public relations generated by Porter. No one seemed well versed in Turkish politics, but everybody had heard of Atatürk.

Porter spread word that Zsa Zsa had been the First Lady of Turkey and that upon Atatürk's sudden death, she had fled that country "with practically the entire Treasury, most of it dating from the days of the Ottoman Empire."

When Zsa Zsa called Porter to tell him that she was never married to Atatürk, and that she was practically broke, he told her, "Not to worry, my darling. In high society, image is everything. Truth has nothing to do with it. It's called keeping up appearances. You don't have to confirm anything…Just nod in agreement."

When Zsa Zsa, wearing royal blue, arrived at the Dakota, Syrie Maugham herself answered the door. Her first words were startling to the point of bluntness. "I hear that old sod former husband of mine, Willie Maugham, and his male whore, that Gerald Haxton, have already entertained you."

"Yes, and they did it exceedingly well," she said.

"When I married the son of a bitch in 1917 in New Jersey, of all places, he told me he was only one quarter queer. Now he's one-hundred percent queer."

"Men are so attractive that even on occasion men themselves can't resist their fellow man," Zsa Zsa quipped.

"That's one way of looking at it," Syrie said. "I also heard you were entertained by that bitch, Lady Mendl. I knew her way back when she was Elsie de Wolfe. Once, she and I journeyed to India to paint the Black Hole of Calcutta white. Elsie's mad at me now because I rejected her lesbian advances. Watch that she doesn't try to entrap you. Now you must come over and meet my adorable guests, each of whom has so many secrets to hide that only the Black Hole of Calcutta could contain them!"

DeWitt Wallace did not hold particular interest for Zsa Zsa but yet was influential in her life. Along with his wife, Lila Wallace, he had co-founded *Reader's Digest* in 1922.

Learning that he was not only well read, but politically astute, Zsa Zsa asked Wallace, "Which political party should I belong to now that I'm an American?"

"There is no doubt," he told her. "Become a Republican. Democrats are communists, trying to overthrow this country. Franklin Roosevelt is a Jew working overtime at the White House to try to lure America into the war. He has only one intent, and that is to save the Jews in Europe."

Zsa Zsa followed Wallace's advice and became a Republican. Not only that, but thanks to Wallace, she developed an intimate relationship with a future Republican president, Richard M. Nixon.

Zsa Zsa was introduced to Alfred Lunt and Lyn Fontanne, the most famous English-speaking acting team of the 20th Century. When Zsa Zsa first met them, they had been touring America in the production of *There Shall Be No Night*.

This was the play in which Lunt cast a very handsome, nineteen-year-old actor, Montgomery Clift, with whom he had a "hot sheets affair," as Tallulah Bankhead called it.

Over the years, Zsa Zsa became a lifelong fan of the Lunts, sometimes flying to whatever city they were appearing in, including Phoenix, Arizona, on September 12, 1952, for a performance of Noël Coward's *Quadrille*.

The Phoenix newspapers carried reports of Zsa Zsa showing up "looking dazzling" along with Douglas Fairbanks, Jr. (her old flame), Hermione Gingold, Syrie Maugham, Rex Harrison, (with Lilli Palmer), and Constance Collier, who always lusted for Zsa Zsa. The press accused Coward himself of looking "like a Mongolian ghost in evening dress."

The reigning King and Queen of the American Theater, **Alfred Lunt and Lynn Fontanne** *(above)* joined Laurence Olivier and Vivien Leigh at Noël Coward's vacation home in Jamaica.

Zsa Zsa wrote Jolie, "Here I am, lying around the pool with these theatre greats...and all of us are naked."

[Weeks later, Coward invited some distinguished guests, including Zsa Zsa, to his vacation retreat, Blue Harbour, on the north coast (near Oracabessa) of Jamaica. Fontanne warned Zsa Zsa in advance, "The awful food he serves is always covered with pickled walnuts, and the desserts look like they'd been made in toilet seat moulds."

Nonetheless, Zsa Zsa showed up. On the day she arrived at Blue Harbour, she met her fellow guests, all of them naked beside Coward's pool. "Vivien Leigh was there, a naked Scarlett O'Hara, draped over Heathcliff's cock," Zsa Zsa recalled. Her reference, of course, was to Laurence Olivier and his film role in Wuthering Heights. Zsa

Zsa was astonished to see the distinguished Lunts, also "naked as the day they were born."

"We get beautifully tanned," Lunt told her. "When we return to New York, people find us ravishing to behold."

With some reluctance, Zsa Zsa stripped naked too. Those keen, jaded stars of stage and screen likened her nude figure to that of Venus de Milo.]

On the guest list at Syrie's party was Elsa Schiaparelli, the Italian fashion designer who was the rival of Coco Chanel. One of the world's leading fashion experts "between the wars," she had been heavily inspired by the Surrealists, including Salvador Dalí and Alberto Giacometti.

When she was presented to Zsa Zsa, Elsa said, "You must let me dress you. You have the perfect figure. I'd like to adorn it with my designs."

"My *dahlink*, even in Budapest, we saw your Lobster Dress, that silk charmer with a large lobster, compliments of Dalí, printed on the skirt," Zsa Zsa said. "It made the front page in Budapest when Wallis Simpson was photographed in it before her marriage to Edward VIII."

"Speak of the devil," Elsa said. "The King is here tonight."

"I really must go and introduce myself to him, although I don't want to make the Duchess jealous," Zsa Zsa said. "Perhaps I'm too voluptuous for him, assuming he's attracted to someone as slim as Wallis."

"The more boyish the figure, the more alluring it will be to His Highness," Elsa said, shocking Zsa Zsa. "If you don't believe me, ask any of the guards at Buckingham Palace."

Zsa Zsa and the Italian fashion designer **Elsa Schiaparelli** not only became close friends, but on occasion Zsa Zsa wore her designs.

"She often wanted to turn me into a vegetable garden on parade, but I went along with it." Zsa Zsa claimed.

Zsa Zsa never got to talk very much with the Duke and Duchess of Windsor, who were surrounded with a slavishly admiring entourage of Britishers.

"I did get to tell the Duke that my mother sent him a picture of me when I was but a girl. She suggested that you hold off on marriage until I grew up."

"A lovely offer," he said. "You must forgive me for not accepting. I've always been accused of being too impatient to get on with life."

Zsa Zsa would get to know the Duke and Duchess far better a few weeks later when she encountered them at a chic Hollywood party.

The next day she walked along Fifth Avenue and purchased a flacon of *Shocking,*

136

Elsa Schiaparelli's best-known perfume. She was amused by the shape of the bottle, sculpted by Leonor Fini in the shape of a woman's torso. The night before, Zsa Zsa had learned from Elsa that the bottle had been inspired by a mannequin from the Mae West film, *Every Day's a Holiday (1937)*. "We used Mae's measurements to shape the bottle," Elsa said.

[Long after the party, and over the years, Zsa Zsa and Elsa formed a casual friendship, often involving the exchange of gifts. Elsa once gave her a jacket she'd designed with silk-covered carrots and cauliflowers. Zsa Zsa wore it only once before selling it in a second-hand store hawking high fashion. She also became friendly with Elsa's daughter, Countess Maria Luisa Yvone Radha de Wendt de Kierlor, who had married the shipping executive, Robert Berenson. Zsa Zsa called her "Gogo."

She once gave a party for Gogo's two daughters, each of whom were featured in Vogue *during the 1970s. Marisa Berenson became a well-known model and actress, and Berry Berenson was a photographer. Zsa Zsa sent a wedding present to Marisa on the occasion of her marriage to gay actor, Anthony ("Psycho") Perkins, who died of AIDS in 1992.*

Berry perished in American Airlines flight 11 when it crashed into the North Tower of the World Trade Center on September 11, 2001.]

At Syrie's party, Zsa Zsa met American socialite and fashion icon, Barbara Cushing Mortimer, whom her friends called "Babe." She had recently married Stanley Grafton Mortimer, Jr., the heir to an oil fortune. Only weeks before Zsa Zsa was introduced to her, Babe had been designated as the second best-dressed woman in the world.

The number one best-dressed woman in the world was defined as the Duchess of Windsor, who was also at the party. Babe and the Duchess stood only ten feet apart, but didn't make any effort, it seemed, to address each other. Zsa Zsa noted, however, that both women kept glancing furtively at her competition to size up who was wearing what.

Zsa Zsa later said, "I realized I was going to have to marry very, very rich men to compete with these fashion icons. I was not

Barbara Cushing Mortimer as she appeared in VOGUE in 1947. For years, she was hailed as the best dressed woman in the world.

Years later, Zsa Zsa said, "Would you believe that she was so unfair to me just because I had an affair with her husband? Some women!"

Zsa Zsa's reference was to William S. Paley of CBS.

137

Bunny and Paul Mellon were caught on camera attending a gala together in 1967.

Zsa Zsa would always be grateful to Bunny for introducing her to a charismatic politician from Massachusetts, a young John F. Kennedy. "Later, when Jackie found out, Bunny iced me out," Zsa Zsa claimed.

impressed with Babe, however. On the one hand, she was the epitome of style and elegance, except that she insisted on lighting up constantly. She was no sooner finished with one cigarette, blowing smoke in your face, than she lit up another. I think this habit seriously detracted from her chic image."

[After divorcing Mortimer, Babe married William S. Paley, the founder of CBS, who cheated on her at least twice a week, sometimes with Zsa Zsa. She became one of Truman Capote's "swans" until Capote revealed scandalous details of her private life in his uncompleted novel, Answered Prayers. *Babe never spoke to Truman again. As Zsa Zsa more or less had predicted, Babe Paley died of lung cancer in 1978.]*

When Rachel Lambert Mellon was introduced to Zsa Zsa, she said, "You can call me Bunny." Her father was Gerard Barnes Lambert, Sr., President of the Gillette Safety Razor Company.

Throughout her life, Zsa Zsa would remain in awe of Bunny Mellon—an American horticulturalist, philanthropist, art collector, and thoroughbred racehorse owner. She was married to banking heir Paul Mellon from 1948 until his death in 1999.

Zsa Zsa always envied Bunny for getting on those International Best-Dressed Lists.

"I adored Bunny, but I never followed her advice," Zsa Zsa later said. "After all, she was known for her maximum discretion and minimum exposure. She once proclaimed, 'Nothing should be noticed.' Obviously, I didn't heed that advice."

[Bunny Mellon turned 103 in 2013.]

Zsa Zsa later claimed, "I will always be grateful to Bunny for introducing me to one of the most exciting men I've ever met—John F. Kennedy. Unfortunately, she liked Jackie more than me. In 1961, Jackie let Bunny design the White House Rose Garden. In fact, Bunny was designing the White House's East Garden when my beloved Jack was assassinated by some monster (or monsters) in Dallas."

Beginning what evolved into a long association, Zsa Zsa met the English-born designer, Cecil Beaton, fashion and portrait photographer, diarist, painter, interior designer, and an Oscar-winning stage and costume designer for films and theater. He was also one of the world best-dressed men, competing with the

Duke of Windsor.

"I've seen your photographs in *Vanity Fair* and *Vogue*," Zsa Zsa said. "Maybe you'll photograph me. I'd love to appear in *Vogue.*"

"Actually, my dear, you're too late. In an indiscreet moment, I inserted a tiny but still legible word, 'kike,' in an illustration for *Vogue.* I was fired. However, I'm still in favor with the Royal Family. In fact, I did the wedding photographs for the Duke and Duchess of Windsor, dear friends of mine who are here tonight."

Beaton loved Zsa Zsa's style, and they became friends. "I was making friends left and right that night," she said.

Over the years, she attended premieres of plays and films for which he'd designed the costumes, including both the Broadway and film versions of *My Fair Lady* (1956 and 1964, respectively), and such screen musicals as *Gigi* (1958).

"Cecil divided his love life between men and women," Zsa Zsa said. "His greatest love was Peter Watson, the art connoisseur. But he also screwed around with Greta Garbo, among other dames, including Adele Astaire, Fred's sister. He never made it with me, although we discussed the possibility one time."

At the party was Clare Booth Luce, the wife of Henry Luce, the Publisher of *Time, Life,* and *Fortune.* Her 1936 hit Broadway play, *The Women,* had been adapted into one of Zsa Zsa's favorite films, starring Norma Shearer and Joan Crawford, with an all-star, all-female cast.

After only ten minutes of talk, Zsa Zsa concluded that Clare's deceptively fragile blonde beauty was a façade covering the surface of a highly intelligent and fiercely ambitious Iron Lady.

At this point, Zsa Zsa was looking up to iconic American women to see what examples she might follow. Gossips told her that Clare had found her husband, Henry Luce, sexually incompatible, so she had turned to other men for satisfaction. According to rumor, they had included an early flirtation with Franklin D. Roosevelt before she became a staunch Republican for the rest of her life.

She was also known for having a dalliance with Wendell Willkie, who ran against FDR for president in 1940.

On the night he met Zsa Zsa, the fabled photographer, **Cecil Beaton**, who had seduced everyone from Marlene Dietrich to Gary Cooper, told her: "My attitude to women is this--I adore dancing with them and taking them to theaters and private views and talking about dresses and plays and other women. But I'm really much more fond of men."

Roald Dahl, an air attaché at the British Embassy in Washington, boasted that, "I screwed her from one end of the room to the other for three straight nights."

During the course of her chat with Zsa Zsa at Syrie's party, Clare told her, "With your beauty, you will not be able to attend any party or gathering without having to fend off would-be suitors. I've had that trouble, too. For example, in Princeton, New Jersey, I opened my play, *Margin for Error,* in which I mocked Nazism. Otto Preminger both directed and starred in it. On opening night, both Albert Einstein and Thomas Mann showed up. At different times, all three of these geniuses propositioned me."

"I hope you said yes to all of them," Zsa Zsa said. "Instead of Einstein's body, you could enjoy getting seduced by his brain power."

"I fear I don't know you well enough to reveal that indiscretion of mine," she said. "I have a highly developed intuition. Like myself, I think you have an obsessive rage for fame. The way I observed you conquering this room tonight, I think you'll get there, if not on talent, then on sheer Hapsburgdian allure. I bet in Hungary you could charm the trousers off any Hussar."

Later in the evening, Syrie approached Zsa Zsa again. "When you purchase your first mansion in Beverly Hills, you must let me decorate it. I became famous for doing all rooms in white, but now I've fallen in love with color. I'm inspired by that divine Spaniard, Picasso, who has such a lovely uncut penis. Today I'm likely to decorate with emerald wallpaper, magenta cushions, and Schiaparelli shocking pink satin for the upholsteries."

Syrie joined Zsa Zsa in the bathroom for emergency repairs to their faces.

Clare Booth Luce, wife of *Time and Life* magazine publisher Henry Luce, was caught on camera interviewing a U.S. soldier amid the ruins of Berlin in 1945.

She confided in Zsa Zsa that she'd been pursued by men such as Albert Einstein and Franklin D. Roosevelt.

As Zsa Zsa was applying more lipstick, Syrie looked at her image in the mirror. "If only I had looked like you, I could have gone so much farther in this world. I'm still holding up, but I'll let you in on a secret: I was born in 1879. Of course, I didn't do too badly. At least I survived. I had seven brothers and sisters, only four of whom lived. One of my siblings was a mentally retarded dwarf. Do you have brothers and sisters?"

"I have two beautiful sisters, Eva and Magda," Zsa Zsa said. "Like yours, or like mine, their first marriages were not successful. But both of them have assured me they're going to check the bank accounts of their next husbands before walking down the aisle."

"Smart thinking, girl," Syrie said. "I always married rich men. My first husband was Henry Wellcome, the British industrialist. He made millions in pharmaceuticals. I was just twenty-two when I married him. He was forty-eight. Marry an older and very rich man and take young lovers on the side. That's what I did."

"You dear, dear woman," Zsa Zsa said. "You will be a guiding light for me in my own career. I think ours is going to be the beginning of a beautiful friendship."

After Syrie's party, Zsa Zsa would become a fixture in international society, a position she would maintain for the rest of her life.

***

The night following Syrie's party, Zsa Zsa was dazzled by the young man who showed up to escort her to Cole Porter's Broadway musical, *Panama Hattie.* "He was only nineteen, but looked more like sixteen, and he was gorgeous. I was also stunned when he addressed me in fluent Hungarian. I decided that Alexis von Rosenberg was going to become my next husband, even though he was five years younger than me...*and rich.*"

[Alexis (born 1922, died 2004), who became the 3rd Baron von Rosenberg-Rédé (a title he held from 1942-2004), was the son of Oskar Adolf von Rosenberg-Rédé, a banker from the last days of the Austro-Hungarian empire. Alexis's grandmother was Hungarian. His mother was Edith von Kaulla, a member of

Alexis Rosenberg-Rédé at the Grand Prix de Paris in 1968,

a noble German-Jewish family which had been part owner of the Bank of Württemberg.]

Porter had arranged for the most desirable seats in the house for them. Alexis artfully delayed their entrance into the theater until two minutes before curtain. For the occasion, Zsa Zsa had chosen a satin gown in Schiaparelli's shocking pink. As an usher guided them down the aisle, there arose a buzz in the theater. "As a couple, we were stunning—forgive me, *dahlink,* for being immodest. As my escort, Alexis was incredibly handsome with an incredible sex appeal."

After the show, over supper at Sardi's, they also dazzled show-biz diners. "We had the world wondering just who in hell we were," Zsa Zsa said. "Obviously, a god and goddess who had fallen to Earth."

When Alexis became confidential over their second bottle of champagne, he told her that his lover was ar-

141

riving in New York the following evening. He was Arturo Lopez-Willshaw, a married multi-millionaire from Chile. "He has a wife, but he's settling a million dollars on me at the beginning of our affair. I'm not in love with him, but I need the security he can provide. He's promised to take me on a shopping trip to Tiffany's, where he suggests I bring a basket to hold our purchases. He's going to give me real estate, including a ranch in Chile, a town house in Paris, a chalet in Switzerland, and an apartment in New York. All I have to do is surrender my beautiful body to him at night to satisfy his perverted pleasures."

Instead of a lover and husband, Zsa Zsa became a close friend of Alexis. She even read author Christian Megret's novel *Danaé*, a *roman à clef* based on the love affair of Alexis and Lopez-Willshaw.

[When the Chilean millionaire Arturo Lopez-Willshaw died in 1962, Alexis inherited half of his vast fortune, allowing him to take partial control of the banks of Leopold Joseph & Sons. In that capacity, he was closely involved in managing the money of The Rolling Stones.

Beginning with their Broadway date, Alexis von Rosenberg (the Baron de Rédé) and Zsa Zsa Gabor became known as "male and female Eugène de Rastignacs."

In France, today, to refer to someone as a 'de Rastignac' defines them as an ambitious 'arriviste' (social climber). No description ever fit two people better than Alexis and Zsa Zsa.

The name is derived from a fictional, socially ambitious character who makes ongoing appearances within a series of mid-19th century novels (La Comédie Humaine) by Honoré de Balzac.

***

Before checking out of the Plaza in New York, Zsa Zsa wired Eva that she was on her way to Hollywood.

"My darling sister, I've conquered London and New York. Next goal: Hollywood. I hear the ruling gentry of the place were formerly Jewish tailors, prostitutes, chorus girls, cowboys, and bootleggers. Surely, I will appear like royalty to them. Within three months, I will be the town's new Queen.

CHAPTER FOUR
Sisters #2 and #3 (Zsa Zsa & Eva)
Invade the New World

In Hollywood, Eva's marriage to Erik Drimmer continued to deteriorate. With the arrival of Zsa Zsa in Hollywood, Eva hoped that her spirits, at least, would improve. Like her marriage, and even though she was booked as the female lead in a "B" film, *Forced Landing* (1941), her film career continued its downward spiral.

Directed by Gordon Wiles, it had a cast of "past their prime" (in Eva's summation) actors—Richard Arlen, Nils Asther, and Evelyn Brent. "The only one in the cast with a bright future in films was a character actor, J. Carrol Naish," Eva said.

The plot, in a nutshell, revolved around a Pacific Islands dictator who must compete with a military pilot for a woman's affection. The ruler underhandedly dispatches the pilot on what he knows (but the pilot doesn't know) is a suicide mission.

"The only thing I liked about my role was the name of my character, Johanna Van Deuren," Eva said. "The director (Wiles) told me that I should fall in love with my leading man for greater chemistry on the screen. But Arlen gave off no sign of passion whatsoever. In spite of my acclaimed beauty, he shook my hand and treated me like an overused dishrag."

A former pilot in the Royal Canadian Flying Corps, he was slick-haired, rugged, and solidly built, even though he had entered middle age at the time he met Eva. She'd seen him as a pilot in the Oscar-winning *Wings* (1927), in which he'd co-starred with Gary Cooper. As Eva admitted, "I was still coming down from my fling with Gary, but Arlen provided no insights into my Montana cowboy."

"Arlen was a very desirable man when I met him and still married to the actress, Jobyna Ralston, who had also been in the cast of *Wings*. But I think our other co-star, Nils Asther, was panting after him more than I was."

A Danish-born citizen of Sweden, the homosexual Asther had been called "the male Greta Garbo" when he'd co-starred with her in the 1929 *Wild Orchids* and in the same year *The Single Standard*. The year before, he'd played a socialite opposite Joan Crawford in that flapper epic, *Our Dancing Daughters*. He had also co-starred with Marion Davies and Pola Negri.

Garbo didn't like playing love scenes opposite him, claiming loudly, "I don't know where his mouth has been the night before."

Asther told Eva that he'd been working in England during the previous six years because of an alleged breach of contract that had gotten him blacklisted by most Hollywood studios. Although he was hoping for a comeback, he would never regain his box office appeal.

[In 1958, Asther turned his back on Hollywood—"or rather, it turned its back on me"—and returned to Sweden nearly destitute. He died in 1981. His autobiography Narrens väg *("The Road of the Jester")* wasn't published until 1988.]

In *Forced Landing,* Evelyn Brent, a legend of the Silent Screen, was cast in the fifth lead. She'd made her screen debut in 1915 and had become a WAMPAS Baby Star.

"She'd had a torrid affair with Douglas Fairbanks, Sr., losing out to Mary Pickford," Eva said. "She had also worked with that Nazi actor, Emil Jannings, and she'd been directed by Josef von Sternberg before he'd succumbed to the charms of Marlene Dietrich."

"When I met her, Brent was too mature for *ingénue* roles and was no longer desired by directors except in small parts: In time, she had three husbands, but was mainly known in Hollywood as a fixture in the lesbian colony. She came on strong to me when we shared a dressing room, and I soon learned not to take off my clothes in front of her."

After helming her, Wiles accused Eva of having "the talent of a plate of goulash." She accused him of "being an art director, not a real director." He had won an Oscar in 1931 for *Transatlantic.*

As Eva relayed later in an interview, "Both *Forced Landing* and Mr. Wiles faded into oblivion, which was where I was going unless I got a break. I also thought the picture should have been called *Crash Landing,* which described most of the actors in it."

"I had two strikes against me when I co-stared in *Forced Landing* (1942)," Eva claimed. Both of my male co-stars, **Richard Arlen** *(left)* and **Nils Asther** *(right)* were has-beens.

Nils was hot for Richard, and no one was hot for me."

***

Paramount didn't get rich on the 1941 movie, *Pacific Blackout*. In the middle photo are three of the movie's stars, **Martha O'Driscoll** *(left)*, **Robert Preston** *(center)*, and **Eva Gabor** *(right)*.

"It was an espionage potboiler, and I was supposed to be a spy. I was delighted to be back in Bob's arms," Eva said.

Except for a cameo appearance, Eva's last film at Paramount was the highly forgettable B-picture, *Pacific Blackout* (1941), which reunited her with her former lover, Robert Preston, who interpreted its title role—that of an inventor and engineer who is unjustly declared guilty for the murder of his partner. Eva was cast as the spy, Marie Duval. "I was no Mata Hari," she recalled. "Greta Garbo didn't have to lie awake at night worrying about my besting her in her famous spy role."

The second male lead was Philip Marivale, an English movie and stage actor born in India. He'd launched his career in silent films. At the time Eva met him, he was married to the famous English actress, Gladys George. On the set, he befriended Eva, telling her, "Whereas you're making this movie in an attempt to launch a film career, I'm appearing in this bloody awful disaster just to earn a paycheck."

Eva actually nabbed the part of the second female lead. The lead was played by Martha O'Driscoll, who had trained to become a singer and dancer. She'd just appeared as Daisy Mae in the first screen version of Al Capp's comic strip, *Li'l Abner* (1940). When not in front of a camera, O'Driscoll appeared in radio and print commercials. She's credited with introducing Eva, as a consumer of beauty products, to Max Factor Hollywood Face Powder.

By now, Eva had decided that Drimmer was cheating on her with increasing frequency. One day, he went to Palm Springs and stayed there for four nights with no explanation. "Two can play that game," she wrote to both Jolie and Zsa Zsa.

One night when Preston opted to spend time at home, alone with his wife, Eva turned her attention to an extra on the film. He was Rod Cameron, who was playing a small role as a pilot.

As Eva confessed to Susan Hayward, "Perhaps I was still dreaming of Gary Cooper, but I found Rod very attractive. His name, Rod, was certainly appropriate for him."

Born in Alberta, Canada, Cameron had drifted south to Hollywood, where he became a stuntman and a bit player at Paramount. Later, he became a household name throughout America for his roles in Westerns.

He was very tall, very rugged, and looked a bit like Fred MacMurray, with whom Eva had worked. In fact, Cameron was often the stand-in for Mac-Murray. "Rod was very virile both on and off the screen," Eva said. "It was just a mild romp. We weren't really serious."

[Cameron later became notorious when he divorced his wife of ten years and married his mother-in-law. For doing that, his former director, William Witney, publicly acclaimed Cameron as "the bravest man I've ever seen."]

There was one final attempt to turn Eva into a singing star. She rehearsed with a vocal coach for three days before making her singing debut in front of a director. "I knew I was no Jenny Lind, the

"I won't pretend that **Rod Cameron** *(pictured above)* was my first seduction by a cowboy," Eva said. "I had already rolled in the sagebrush with Gary Cooper. But Rod was appropriately named."

Swedish Nightingale, but I thought I might do a good imitation of Helen Morgan. I draped myself seductively on the piano and warbled. After two minutes, the director got up and walked out the door without a word. End of singing career."

Before Eva's contract with Paramount ended, she appeared in a cameo role in *Star Spangled Rhythm* (1943). Filmed with an all-star cast, it was a musical film made during World War II as a morale booster.

She appeared in the film with an array of stars, the finest on Paramount's lot. They included Betty Hutton, Bob Hope, Bing Crosby, Fred MacMurray, Ray Milland, Dorothy Lamour, Paulette Goddard, Veronica Lake, Mary Martin, and Dick Powell.

"Two of my on-again, off-again lovers, Robert Preston and Rod Cameron, also appeared in the movie, as did my gal pal, Susan Hayward," Eva said.

"Benito Mussolini," "Hirohito," and "Adolf Hitler" were also listed as characters in the film.

"If you blink, you'll miss me," Eva said. "The film cost $1,127,989. My $75 came out of that $89 tag end part."

"My contract was over—no job, no husband. I entered one of the unhappiest periods of my life. I wanted to become a star, but my efforts were futile. I was awful on my appearances on the screen. I was also too immature when I married Erik. The marriage was all but over except for the divorce. Both of us had moved on to others."

"As soon as Zsa Zsa arrived in Hollywood—well, maybe not immediately—I planned to file for divorce. I didn't know who my next husband would be. But I knew one thing: He would be rich. Jolie was right: None of her daughters were meant to live as paupers. I planned to start dating aggressively. Within one week, I received seven phone calls from possible suitors, including one from David Niven. He'd met Zsa Zsa at a party, and she'd given him my phone number.

***

Born in the twilight of the Austro-Hungarian Empire, with fresh memories of the destruction of Europe permeating her brain, Zsa Zsa arrived in Hollywood. After her horrific four-month trip, she fell into Eva's arms, sobbing and babbling in Hungarian.

Before taking her to her (temporary) new home—the apartment she still nominally shared with Drimmer—Eva, in her rusty car, took her on a tour of the strange new world she'd just entered. It was unlike anything Zsa Zsa had ever seen before.

It was a land of palm trees, in which all the women seemed to wear slacks and high heels. Restaurants were shaped like derby hats, and advertisements as big as railways cars hawked the great American hot dog. Instead of goulash, the natives ate hamburgers, some preferring a pineapple slice on top. She spotted at least three gingerbread-trimmed thatched cottages, looking as if Hansel and Gretel inhabited them. Some villas appeared to have been removed intact from Andalusia.

Zsa Zsa was shocked by Eva's new look. Apparently, Hollywood directors liked their women pencil thin. As Zsa Zsa wrote, "I saw a girl so thin as to look emaciated. Her cheeks were hollow, her eyebrows plucked, her hair bleached platinum blonde, wearing a black satin dress, black patent-leather shoes, with red spike heels, a huge brimmed black hat trailing a long black veil."

All the people she met spoke of only two topics—the latest fad diet and how to break into the movies.

Eva was still working for Paramount, a studio Mae West had saved from bankruptcy. Mae had immodestly told the press, "More people have seen me than saw Napoléon, Lincoln, and Cleopatra. I was better known than Einstein, Shaw, or Picasso."

"Okies" from the Dust Bowl had flocked to California, "the land of plenty," and the population there had vastly increased.

To Zsa Zsa, Los Angeles was obviously a city in transition. In just a few months, it would become a wartime center of West Coast defense plants.

As author Dudley C. Gordon aptly put it: "Having survived a long, leisurely pioneering infancy, and an uncouth adolescence characterized by intensive ex-

ploitation, Los Angeles had now blossomed into one of the major cities of the nation.

For Eva, or even for herself, Zsa Zsa knew that surfacing near the top as a movie star would be a formidable challenge.

The 1930s had given birth to some of the biggest female stars in history—Bette Davis, Joan Crawford, Kay Francis, Loretta Young, Marlene Dietrich, Barbara Stanwyck, Katharine Hepburn, and Claudette Colbert.

Arriving at Eva's small apartment, Zsa Zsa was shocked at how dismal it was. There wasn't even enough room for her luggage.

Eva invited her to sleep with her in her bed, claiming that Drimmer could take the sofa—"that is, if he should ever decide to spend a night at home."

Zsa Zsa found the cupboard so bare, she invited Eva to go with her to the market to stock up on food supplies.

Eva virtually demanded that Zsa Zsa use henna to make her hair more auburn in its tone. "One Gabor blonde is all Hollywood can digest," she said.

Obviously, breaking into the elite society of Hollywood was going to be much tougher than it had been in New York. Then, she remembered a promise made to her by Lawrence Copley Thaw, a wealthy writer-photographer she'd met in Ankara, who was touring at the time with his wife, Peggy. As a personal adventure, and for a series of articles which later appeared about it in newspapers and magazines, they'd been following the ancient overland route to India taken by the silk caravans, traveling in a fifty-foot motorized "Land Yacht," accompanied by a retinue of trucks and servants carrying their supplies. Despite the dangers of imminent war, their trip had begun in northern France in the summer of 1939, several months prior to their arrival in Turkey.

Belge and Zsa Zsa had accompanied them on a two-week expedition through the Taurus Mountains and had become friends. She enjoyed the warm-hearted, impulsive nature of the Thaws. By the end of the trip, she had promised to become "your friend for life."

She suggested she might come to Hollywood some day. "After meeting you people, I think I would like Americans very much."

148

He said she'd be most welcome, and he wrote down the name and address and Basil and Ouida Rathbone. "They are the ruling Duke and Duchess of Hollywood. An invitation to one of their parties is the most sought-after in Hollywood. I'll write them to receive you when you come."

Remembering Thaw's promise, Zsa Zsa late one morning summoned her courage and put through a call, not knowing if Thaw had kept his promise of writing that letter after all.

A maid summoned Ouida to the phone. A warm, lovely, inviting voice greeted Zsa Zsa. "That darling Larry wrote me all about you. I'm so anxious to meet you, and so is Basil. In fact, I'm having some people over tonight. I'm giving a party for Vivien Leigh and Larry Olivier before they go back to war-torn London."

"Cary Grant will be here. He's dating Barbara Hutton...you know, the five-and-dime Woolworth heiress. And oh, David Niven is also dropping in. If you wish, I'll let Douglas Fairbanks, Jr., be your escort for the night."

After the arrangements were made, Zsa Zsa hung up the phone in a state of elation. She was enthralled, but didn't want to give Eva the details out of fear of making her envious.

She'd spent the afternoon making herself look more glamorous. Fortunately, she'd brought wardrobe and diamonds from the Old World to flash before the New World.

"The town is filled with great beauties, with more stunning women than anywhere else on the planet," she'd been told.

"Somehow, someway, I've got to make Zsa Zsa Gabor stand out as a princess in a field of Cinderellas."

***

"To say that I was the belle of the ball would be a vast understatement." So said Zsa Zsa Gabor, summing up her appearance of the night before at the home of Basil and Ouida Rathbone on Bellagio Road in Bel Air.

The dashing, handsome actor, Douglas Fairbanks, Jr., picked her up in his sleek new car at Eva's modest apartment and drove her up a winding mountain road.

Debonair and beautifully tailored, he was the epitome of charm and elegance, although he spoke very frankly. She was not used to men saying what they thought, having become ac-

Actor **Basil Rathbone** and his wife **Ouida** were the King and Queen of A-List Hollywood.

It was they who introduced Zsa Zsa to the movie colony..."and to all the hot men," in Zsa Zsa's estimation.

customed to the diplomatic climate of Ankara, where no man ever said what he meant.

En route to the Rathbone's, Zsa Zsa expressed her sympathy about the death of his screen icon father, Douglas Fairbanks, Sr., who had died in 1939, two years before the party.

"Dad told me that one swashbuckler in the family was enough," Douglas said. "He didn't want me to become an actor and trade on his name. When I was a kid, I didn't play baseball. Dad called me 'foppish' and feared he was raising a homosexual until I started having affairs with all sorts of women. That led to my getting hooked up with Billie. Billie, I could tolerate, but when she became Joan Crawford around the house, it was a bit much. I told Joan that her ideal man would be a skilled butler during the day and a stud with a twelve-inch dick after midnight."

Two years before his date with Zsa Zsa, Douglas had married Mary Lee Hartford, the former wife of Huntington Hartford, the A&P supermarket heir. But he often cheated on her. Before bedding Zsa Zsa later that night, he had seduced some of the biggest stars in Hollywood and New York, including Tallulah Bankhead, Marlene Dietrich, Gertrude Lawrence, Lupe Velez, and Loretta young. Composer-playwright Noël Coward had a life-long crush on him and composed his hit song, "Mad About the Boy," in his honor. In the 1930s, Douglas had a torrid romance with Laurence Olivier when he was married to his first wife, the lesbian actress, Jill Esmond.

When they arrived at the Rathbone's party, after a butler let them in, "a handsome, plump woman" (Zsa Zsa's words) walked across the foyer to welcome them. It was their hostess, Ouida Rathbone.

After kissing Douglas, Ouida complimented Zsa Zsa on her coloring—"a perfect peach complexion, hair a tawny red, hazel brown eyes that positively glow in the dark. I think I'll name you 'my pretty,' the way the Wicked Witch of the West, Margaret Hamilton, referred to Judy Garland in *The Wizard of Oz.*"

Ouida was right. In a crowd of "tennis court tans," Zsa Zsa's skin stood out as luminous.

The host, Basil Rathbone, was right behind Ouida. Born in South Africa to a father who was a British mining engineer, he was suave, imperious, and grandly self-satisfied. He spoke with a precise, confident speech pattern. When Zsa Zsa complimented him on his *persona,* he said, "It's all a mask. After turning down the role of Rhett Butler in *Gone With the Wind,* I have no more faith in my judgment. I told David O. Selznick, 'Who would want to see a movie about the Civil War'?"

"To me, you are the eternal Sherlock Holmes," she said. "No one makes a better detective than you."

"It looks like I'll be stuck with that character for the duration of the War," he said. "There's even a script coming up called *Sherlock Holmes and the Spider Woman.*"

"I'm sure I'd make a divine Spider Woman, especially if the species were the Black Widow."

"We'll worry about future casting tomorrow," he said. "Now Ouida and I must share your beauty with my guests."

Within a large room filled with A-list stars, Ouida escorted Zsa Zsa to Ethel Barrymore, the First Lady of the American Theater. Barrymore carried herself with dignity while seated in a large wing-backed chair. With a skeptical eye, she looked Zsa Zsa up and down. An authoritative, somewhat stern, presence, she could cut down an adversary with as little as a raised eyebrow.

"I'm so honored to meet you, Miss Barrymore," Zsa Zsa gushed.

"I understand you were the First Lady of Turkey," Barrymore said. "I've met many a First Lady, but never the First Lady of Turkey. Maybe had it not been for World War I, you and your dictator husband could have revived the Ottoman Empire and presided over it. I hope you fled from Europe with at least half of the Empire's treasure."

Barrymore may have been a great lady, but she was not particularly well-informed about Turkish politics and history, and Zsa Zsa had no intention of correcting her. "I only brought what I could fit into two dozen large suitcases," she said.

The aging actress carefully studied Zsa Zsa: "Your face has the look of the self-enchanted. I suspect that you're the type of a young girl who spends most of her day looking at her image in the mirror, singing, '*I'm so pretty...oh, so pretty,*'"

"It's been such an honor meeting you, Miss Barrymore, but I just saw Lady Mendl enter the room. She's a dear friend of mine, and I must rush over to greet her and welcome her to Hollywood."

Zsa Zsa greeted Lady Mendl like a long-lost friend, with enthusiasm, telling her, "We must get together."

"I'm so sorry, my dear child," Mendl answered curtly. "I'm in Hollywood for such a short time, and my schedule is already overloaded. Perhaps some time in the future."

Behind Lady Mendl, her friend, Cole Porter, was being wheeled in by Cary Grant. He was followed by the Woolworth heiress, Barbara Hutton.

Porter was much gladder to see Zsa Zsa than Lady Mendl had been, and invited her to dinner the following

Ethel Barrymore, the *über*-matriarch of the American Theater, always turned a skeptical eye toward the latest sexpot in Hollywood, which in this case was Zsa Zsa.

"The name will have to go," Barrymore told her.

night. "Perhaps Cary could join us."

Grant took her hand. "I'd be delighted."

"You're my favorite movie star," Zsa Zsa said to Grant.

"But of course, my dear," he said, jokingly. "Who else? I bet W.C. Fields provided me with stiff competition."

Hutton was rather icy and only smiled when Grant introduced her to Zsa Zsa. Ironically, the heiress and the Hungarian would be competing a decade later for the same playboy lover.

Douglas came looking for his date of the evening, as a small band had begun to play dance music in the adjoining room, which opened onto a terrace. When he saw Grant, he kissed him on both cheeks. Apparently, they were old friends. Douglas retrieved Zsa Zsa just as Clifton Webb came into their presence. "Good evening, Clifton," he said.

Webb immediately turned on his heels and headed in the opposite direction.

"You must have done something to offend him," Zsa Zsa said.

"That mama's boy is still mad at me. One early morning, I offered him a ride to the studio. En route, he confessed that he was in love with me and placed his hand on my thigh. At first, I didn't know how to respond. Protest? Show anger? Dismiss him as a pervert? Finally, I decided to laugh the matter off and treat his proposition like a joke. When I did that, he exploded in anger and demanded to be let out of my car. Call it the affair that never was."

In the adjoining room, Zsa Zsa waltzed around the room with Douglas as if she was the star of one of the Vienna Opera Balls. "If only the cameras had captured us," she later lamented. "We would have put Fred Astaire and Ginger Rogers to shame."

Draped in mink, **Lady Mendl (Elsie de Wolfe)** didn't seem to have much time for Zsa Zsa on their second meeting, this time in Hollywood.

"There are so many important people out there demanding to see me," Lady Mendl said.

She wasn't allowed to catch her breath before Eric de Rothschild, of the banking family approached her. In French, he invited her to dance the tango *à la* Rudolf Valentino. With panache, she rose to the challenge.

After the tango, he presented her to Igor Stravinsky, who chatted with her in French.

Her first lover, Willi Schmidt-Kentner, had introduced her to the world of the Russian-born composer, who had been famous since impresario Sergei Diaghilev had commissioned him to compose three ballets for his Ballets Russes. They had included *Firebird* (1910); *Petrushka* (1911), and *The Rite of Spring* (1913).

His father, Fyodor Stravinsky, was of Polish

noble descent, and that gave Zsa Zsa an opening in which to pursue a conversation, as she told of Magda's marriage to Count Jan de Bychowsky.

Stravinsky informed her that since the late 1930s, he'd been living in West Hollywood and that he planned to become a naturalized U.S. citizen. "As you probably gathered, Los Angeles is no longer the backwater it was. Because of refugees, it is becoming a great cultural city. Either living here now or on the way are many European writers, musicians, composers, and conductors—Otto Klemperer, Thomas Mann, Franz Werfel, George Balanchine, and Arthur Rubinstein. In fact, Arthur is here tonight, and I'll introduce you."

"I've also found some good drinking partners who help me pursue my addiction to hard spirits, especially Aldous Huxley and Dylan Thomas. I'm going to write an opera with W.H. Auden. I'll be conducting the Los Angeles Philharmonic at the Hollywood Bowl, and I want you to be my guest at one of the upcoming events."

"I'm flattered," she said. "Never in my wildest imagination did I think I'd have to come to Hollywood to hear the great Igor Stravinsky conduct."

I assume you're a confirmed monarchist like me?" he asked. "I loathe the Bolsheviks. There is Russian royalty here tonight. I'd like to introduce you to her, too."

The talk quickly turned to Nazism. Zsa Zsa confessed that she'd met both Hitler and Goebbels in Berlin as part of her former diplomatic duties in Turkey.

Stravinsky was furious at the Nazis, who had placed his musical compositions on their list of *Entartete* (degenerate) *Musik*.

[Outlawed by the Nazis, music designated by them as "degenerate,"because of its Jewish, socialist, or homosexual origins also included compositions by, among many others, Felix Mendelssohn, Arnold Schoenberg, Walter Braunfels, Erich Wolfgang Korngold, Kurt Weill, Gustav Mahler, Paul Hindemith, along with most forms of modernist music and "Negro jazz."]

"I've lodged a formal complaint (with the Nazis), informing Goebbels that I loathe communism, Marxism, that execrable Soviet monster, and also all forms of liberalism and democratism," said Stravinsky.

"The downside of coming to America is that we often have to tear ourselves away from our lovers," he said. "I'm sure you left

"We European refugees pouring into Los Angeles are giving this cow town some class and adding some culture," said composer **Igor Stravinsky**.

"You're a classic and elegant beauty, not one of these Popcorn Blondes invading Hollywood," he told Zsa Zsa.

strings of lovers in Europe. As for me, I left only one. My own true love, Coco Chanel."

When Stavinsky took her over to meet the Grand Duchess Maria Pavlovna *[born in Russia in 1890],* Zsa Zsa curtsied and bonded with her at once. She

was usually referred to as "Marie," the French version of her name. Her paternal grandparents had been Alexander II of Russia and Maria Alexandrovna.

Until they were interrupted, Zsa Zsa and the Grand Duchess had a spirited chat.

"You're the first person I've met in Hollywood who speaks my language," Marie said. "The world I come from is so different from that of your typical Hollywood movie star."

Stravinsky emerged from the crowd once again and tapped Zsa Zsa on the shoulder. Since Marie wanted to continue talking to Zsa Zsa, she invited her to be her guest at lunch the following day.

In Los Angeles, Zsa Zsa immediately bonded with a lonely and alienated exile, Russia's **Grand Duchess Maria Pavlovna**.

In the *upper photo*, she's seen during her younger days as a member of the Imperial Court. In the *lower photo*, she appears in Hollywood, where she was celebrated as a "royal deity."

When Zsa Zsa turned around, Stravinsky introduced her to Arthur Rubinstein, one of the great pianists of the 20th Century.

"Leave it to Igor to gravitate to the most beautiful woman in the room," Rubinstein said, taking her hand. "Go away now, Igor, and let me have a chance at this divine creature, the Rose of Hungary."

Familiar with Rubinstein's background, she was aware that he was a Polish Jew. In both German and French, they spoke with outrage about "the simultaneous rape of Poland" by Nazi Germany and the Soviet Union.

"I'm giving America a second chance to appreciate my genius," he said. "When I first toured America in 1906, I was not well received. I returned to Berlin destitute and desperate, with creditors pounding on my door. I even considered hanging myself in my room."

"Hopefully, America will open its arms to you faster than it did for me. I'm in Hollywood getting work providing piano soundtracks for films. I assume you're here to become an actress."

"My sister, Eva, perhaps, but I have not made up my mind. I was attached to the most powerful man in Turkey, and I found that exciting. I'd like to find a powerful man in America and get him to marry me. I could be the power behind the throne, the way I was in Turkey. I know this is not a noble ambition, but it's the truth."

"It is so hard to determine what is truth," he said. "My critics say I divide my time among wine, women, and song. That is such a gross lie. I devote ninety percent of my life to women. I am already under your magic spell."

Months later, Zsa Zsa revealed that soon after she'd met him, Rubinstein propositioned her. However, she claimed that she rejected "his indecent proposals. I had arrived with Douglas and I was determined to go home with him, or at least to his home, providing his wife wasn't there. I feared Rubinstein would play Chopin to me all night instead of making our own music together."

[Arthur Rubinstein contined to pursue women almost until his death in 1982. As late as 1977, at the age of ninety, he left his wife, Nela Mlynarska, a Polish ballerina, to go off with young Annabelle Whitestone, though he never got a divorce.

During the heyday of their marriage, "Nela and Arthur" became celebrated for their parties which, in time, became legendary. Zsa Zsa was the guest of honor at several of them. At the last party she attended, the great artist told her, "My offer of bedtime still stands."

She kept turning him down, although pro-  *claiming, "If he made love like he played the piano, it would be a symphony."*

He told her, "When you finally consent to become my mistress, and I know you will, you will find that my love-making, like music, blooms anew each time. The act is always the same, but each time it's different."

"Had I given in to him, he promised me that during the act, he'd play his 1910 recording of Franz Liszt's Hungarian Rhapsody No. 10," *Zsa Zsa said.]*

Rubinstein introduced her to Jascha Heifetz, who was widely regarded as the most influential violinist of the 20th Century. He was at the Rathbone party, with his wife, Florence Vidor, the silent screen actress and ex-wife of director King Vidor.

Zsa Zsa admired Heifetz's talent. Although he

Pianist **Arthur Rubinstein** hailed Zsa Zsa as "The Rose of Hungary" before putting the make on her.

He told her, "I may not be the most beautiful man in Hollywod, but women gravitate to me."

"**Jascha Heifetz** was God's Fiddler," Zsa Zsa claimed. Both of them shared horrors of their arduous journey from bowels of Nazi-occupied Eastern Europe to reach America.

was polite and talkative to her, he treated his wife rather rudely whenever she attempted to say something. Even his friends claimed he was "misanthropic."

Zsa Zsa told him of her arduous journey to reach America. He shared a similar experience, having left Russia in 1917 and traveling by rail to the Far East and thence by ship to the United States.

Heifetz wished her good fortune in her future career, whatever that was. He also whispered to her one of his secrets. "America is teaching me to be more commercial. Not so highbrow. I'd hiding behind a *nom de plume* while writing this song. It's called 'When You Make Love to Me, Don't Make Believe.' I think I'll ask Bing Crosby to record it."

[The song, sung by Crosby, became a big hit during World War II.]

Heifetz asked Zsa Zsa if she were going to petition to become an American citizen, and she said that she was planning to do that. "I became an American in 1925," he said. "The Soviets have attacked me for being a traitor to my home country. Perhaps Hungary will call you a defector, too."

"Perhaps," she said. "Although I love Hungary dearly, it is simply too small a country to contain a woman of my large ambitions. Only America is big enough for me."

Douglas searched for her once again when the band began to play a Viennese waltz. In the middle of the dance, Laurence Olivier cut in. she found it thrilling to be dancing in the arms of Heathcliff of *Wuthering Heights.* He was just as smooth and graceful on the dance floor as Douglas.

At the end of the dance, he invited her over to meet Vivien Leigh. She found them a dazzling couple but rather eccentric.

Olivier told her that he and Vivien were planning to leave Hollywood and return to wartime England. "I don't feel right staying here enjoying the debaucheries of Hollywood while London is being blitzed. If I stayed on, I think I'd be cast as a second lead, dancing around the likes of Betty Grable and Rita Hayworth. I'd probably end up as a footnote in Hollywood history alongside Victor Mature and John Payne."

[In the years to come, Zsa Zsa would frequently encounter Olivier. She once described him as "a dark, romantic hero, but a hero with a tragic flaw. He evoked a neurotic character in a Gothic novel. In many ways, he was the British

version of my Turkish husband, Burhan Belge. Both men were isolated heroes in their own minds, wounded princes looking for a king who did not exist. When I first met the Oliviers, they had only recently been married, but rumor had it that both of them still played the field. I soon learned that Larry was a bisexual going from the bed of a man (Douglas Fairbanks, Jr.) to a woman (Greer Garson.) As for Scarlett O'Hara, she was a great beauty, but certifiably insane."]

At the Rathbone party, Zsa Zsa huddled briefly with Olivier and Vivien. "Before Larry and I leave Hollywood, we'd like to have you to our house for an *adieu.*" Vivien said. "We can even play my favorite parlor game. It's called 'Ways to Kill a Baby.'"

"What a bizarre name for a parlor game!," Zsa Zsa said. "Surely you don't mean that literally."

"I do, indeed," Vivien said. "The players have to concoct unusual and inventive methods of slaughtering infants. The winner is the one who comes up with the most gruesome form of infanticide."

"I fear I would lose such a game," Zsa Zsa said. "I adore babies, though not my own."

At that point, another dashing, debonair Englishman appeared before Zsa Zsa. He was David Niven, a friend of the Oliviers. He had co-starred with Olivier in *Wuthering Heights.*

After kissing both the Oliviers on the lips, he asked Zsa Zsa if he could have the last dance. Searching the room for Douglas, she did not see him and therefore accepted Niven's offer.

As the actor whirled her around the dance floor, he asked her to go to dinner the following night. "I'm not in town for very long, and I desperately need the company of one of the world's most beautiful women."

With many apologies, she turned him down, having already accepted an invitation from Cole Porter and Cary Grant.

"But I have a divine idea," she said. "My sister, Eva, is free, and she's even more beautiful than I am."

"If that be true, then I'd be delighted," he told her.

They were two English beauties unaccustomed to the glare of the California sun when **Vivien Leigh** (*Gone With the Wind*'s Scarlett O'Hara) was photographed with her new husband, **Laurence Olivier**, who'd been a big hit as Heathcliff in *Wuthering Heights.*

When Zsa Zsa met them, they were not just movie stars, but British spies.

157

"Of course, she's still married, but it's all over."

"I'm married too," he said, "but in wartime, all those silly little rules about fidelity are no longer in effect."

"I couldn't agree with you more," she said. "My loss will be Eva's gain."

"Let's make a date to begin a torrid affair when we blow Hitler into bloody bits."

After the dance, Douglas finally located her. She'd accepted his invitation for a "nightcap" at someone's guest cottage nearby. He avoided mentioning the owner of the Bel Air mansion on whose estate they would be temporarily (and anonymously) visiting.

As she was choreographing her exit from the Rathbone party, its host kissed her on the mouth. "You're enchanting."

His wife, Ouida, standing beside him, had a final word for Zsa Zsa: "With your beauty, you could storm a fortress and conquer it. My dear, you must come to all my future parties."

***

Prior to the U.S. involvement in World War II, Zsa Zsa was too busy to fit **David Niven** into her social calender, so she set him up for a blind date with Eva.

Unknown to her (and to most of the film community), he was one of the mysterious players within the underground espionage and propaganda activities of the Brits in Hollywood and elsewhere during World War II.

In the luxuriously furnished cottage, Zsa Zsa began to relax with Douglas. He put her at ease, and she was pleased that he wanted to talk to her before rushing her into bed.

"My greatest thrill tonight was when the dancers moved back and let us take over the floor," she said. "You: Hollywood royalty; me: a poor Hungarian refugee."

"Don't give me that crap. I think in a year—maybe two—you'll own this town or marry someone who does. You're slated for a life of elegance and luxury. You're glamour personified. You have a warm and irrepressible personal style. And I want to be the first."

"The first what?" she asked. "I'm no virgin."

"The first Hollywood actor to seduce you," he said.

"You will definitely have that prize." She hesitated before adding, "But remember one thing, *dahlink:* I have just arrived in Hollywood and I'll be dining with Cary Grant tomorrow night."

"Don't get your hopes up with that limey," he said. "He's been chasing after me ever since he

158

first hit Hollywood."

Zsa Zsa went on to confess that his friend, David Niven, had also invited her to dinner and that she was sending her younger sister, Eva, in her place because she had another commitment.

"I must warn you," he said. "Niv is happily married but still highly susceptible to a beautiful woman," he said. "A few months ago from London, he sent me an eight-page letter, describing in hilarious details an uninhibited amorous adventure he had experienced in the back seat of a car one night. It happened when the city was blacked out during a heavy bombing raid from Göring's *Luftwaffe*. Niv left nothing out. Every detail of every moment of their mutual lechery was carefully detailed."

"That's just what Eva needs after a marriage that has gone stale," Zsa Zsa said.

She went on to tell him that his father, Douglas Fairbanks, Sr., had been her mother's favorite actor. "She never missed one of his movies."

"I've always been plagued by comparisons to my father," he said. "He never wanted me to call him Father or Dad, but demanded that I call him 'Pete.' I don't know where he came up with that name. Later, he told me he regretted naming me Junior, resenting sharing his name with me. He also said he wished he'd named me something like Ralph, John, or Henry. He said there was room for only one swashbuckler in the family—and that was it. For years, I turned down big money by refusing to play swashbuckler roles."

"When I did break into the movies, Elinor Glyn, the gossip journalist who created the term *'It'* for sex appeal, with the understanding that *'It'* was vital for the success of any movie star, told me I didn't have any."

"I'll be leaving Hollywood very soon," he told her. "President Roosevelt has appointed me as a special diplomatic envoy to South America. But when war comes to America, I plan to seek a commission as a reserve officer in the U.S. Navy. My dream is to be assigned to Lord Louis Mountbatten's Commando Staff in England."

"My time in England was too brief," she said. "But I adored it and its people."

"Joan Crawford–I called her Billie—and I went on a delayed honeymoon to England. We were entertained by Noël Coward, Gertrude Lawrence, Bea Lillie, and Prince George, the Duke

In happier days, **Joan Crawford** was married to **Douglas Fairbanks, Jr.**

In bed with Zsa Zsa, he shared one of Crawford's beauty secrets:

"Just before you appear on camera, ice the nipples of your tits. They'll stand up more."

of Kent. It was a glorious time."

"I think there's a danger here, at least for an actress's career in Hollywood," she said. "Myrna Loy told me that she plans to abandon her career. Right now, she's at her peak. But what will she be five or six years from now, if the war drags on that long?"

"What went over big with audiences in 1939 could be *passé* in 1945 or 1946, whenever the war ends. Myrna might appear like a grandmother to the young boys returning home after the war. They'll obviously prefer someone much younger."

"That's a very valid career concern. Niv is also aware of the danger of his running off and signing up. Other foreign-born actors like Cary Grant and Errol Flynn told me they have no intention of joining the service, and plan to stay in Hollywood and make movies."

Finally, as the champagne bottle got emptied, he gave her a long, lingering look. "I was just wondering," he said, "Do I get lucky tonight?"

"I thought you'd never ask. But I have a certain fear. Joan Crawford and Marlene Dietrich are tough acts to follow."

"They were both so different, Joan—or Billie—being more the sexual athlete. Marlene was more self-possessed."

"I fall somewhere in between those categories," she said.

Fairbanks guided her with his usual grace from the sofa to the bedroom.

She didn't arrive back at Eva's apartment until six o'clock the following morning.

"Some party!" Eva said.

Zsa Zsa had almost nothing to say and talked instead about Eva's upcoming date with Niven.

***

Zsa Zsa's luncheon with the Grand Duchess Maria Pavlovna of Russia would mark her life-long fascination with royals-in-exile. Although before coming to America, she had known two kings, Zog of Albania and Farouk of Egypt, the Grand Duchess would mark a milestone in her courting of royal exiles, particularly those who had fled to America.

At their noonday meeting, Marie had advised her "to marry a title," maintaining that a mere movie star had little social standing. It would take Zsa Zsa almost a lifetime before she got around to following the advice of the Grand Duchess.

[Throughout the rest of her life, in the United States, England, and France, she actively pursued men and women with titles, some largely pretend at that point. George Sanders called her a "monarchist who always hoped that Prince

Philip would divorce Queen Elizabeth and marry her."

Zsa Zsa's continuing fascination with royalty was revealed on the opening page of her first memoir, My Story, *co-authored with Gerold Frank and first published in 1960. The opening scene shows her installed at the Plaza Hotel in New York, preparing to fly to Rome for the filming of her seventeenth movie in just eight years. She is writing farewell letters. "One, to the Duke of Marlborough, in Palm Beach to regret that I can't dine with him when he arrives in New York two days from now; another to Prince Parenti, in Capri, to say I will be delighted to attend his party next week; the third to ex-King Farouk, in Monte Carlo, to thank him belatedly for his birthday greeting; and the fourth, to Sir Percy Loraine, in London, who has been my father confessor for twenty years."]*

Her luncheon with the Grand Duchess lasted for more than three hours, as these homesick exiles talked lovingly of their homelands. Marie consumed an extraordinary amount of vodka and told Zsa Zsa an amazing story she'd never forget:

"It was obvious that the love of her life had been her brother, Grand Duke Dmitri Pavolvich of Russia. Their mother, Alexandra Georgievna of Greece, had died giving birth to Dmitri."

"I grew up with Dmitri and spent twenty-four hours a day with him," Marie said. "We did not speak Russian for years, as all governesses spoke English. I loved him dearly. He was the light of my life. Sometimes, we would spend hours in each other's arms, hugging and kissing."

"My greatest disappointment came on December 17, 1916, when I learned that Dmitri had participated in the murder of Grigori Rasputin. I begged Emperor Nicholas to reverse his decision to send Dmitri to the Persian front. But the Czar refused. In a way, it was fortunate. Because of his being stationed far from Moscow and Saint Petersburg, Dmitri escaped murder by the Bolsheviks in 1919."

"I fled from Russia and reunited with dear, dear Dmitri in London. We financed our lives with the jewelry I had smuggled to Sweden before my flight from Moscow. Later, we moved to Paris, where I opened a sewing and textile shop."

After that luncheon, Zsa Zsa claimed she'd made a new friend in the Grand Duchess. She truly liked Marie, and they made plans for a later rendezvous. "There's some big gala being planned in my honor, and I want you to come as my guest. We'll be in touch, my dear."

Before saying goodbye, Zsa Zsa made a rash prediction. Perhaps she'd had too much wine at lunch. "I think Stalin and his men will not be able to control Russians after the war. They may rise up and revolt and demand a return to the monarchy. For all I know, you'll be summoned back as the Czarina of Russia.

A 20th century version of Catherine the Great."

"Just because we're in this dream factory called Hollywood, let's not let our imaginations run wild. But if that happens, I'll make you my first lady-in-waiting."

"Like Queen Catherine's lady-in-waiting, or so I read, that means I'll have to audition all your suitors before they go to bed with you, so you won't end up with a man who's a waste of your time."

"You understand your future duties so very well," the Grand Duchess responded.

***

That evening, Cole Porter and Cary Grant escorted Zsa Zsa to Romanoff's Restaurant. There, Grant introduced Zsa Zsa to "Prince" Michael Romanoff, who ran this Beverly Hills restaurant which was popular with movie stars in the 1940s, most famously so with its nightly patron, Humphrey Bogart.

Treating Zsa Zsa like royalty, Romanoff bowed before her and welcomed her, saying, "I was born Prince Michael Dimitri Alexanderovich Obolensky-Romanoff, nephew of Czar Nicholas II."

After he'd left, Grant, at table, told her, "He just pretends to be a royal prince. Actually, he was a former pants presser in Brooklyn."

"Everybody in town knows Mike isn't a real prince," Porter said. "But it hardly matters. Hollywood is peopled by pretenders."

She thanked Porter for supplying her with tickets to *Panama Hattie* on Broadway "And my escort, that Baron de Rédé! What a man!"

"I saw the show, too," Grant said. "I loved it. In fact, I'm still humming my favorite tune, 'Let's Be Buddies.'" He turned and gave Porter a knowing smile. "I'm sure I inspired the lyrics to that one. Cole and I go way back. Oh, those wild nights at Cerutti's in Manhattan."

[Back in the 1930s, Cerutti's was one of the most popular gay bars in Manhattan, even though such bars were technically illegal at the time. Cerutti's was the favorite watering hole not only of Cole Porter and Cary Grant, but also of "Black Jack" Bouvier, the father of First Lady Jackie Kennedy.]

"This divine creature was known as Archibald Leach back then in the days when I could walk." Porter looked suggestively at Grant. "And do other things."

She suddenly realized that they had once been lovers.

"The show's a big hit, no thanks to John O'Hara," Porter said.

"I don't know him," she said.

"He calls himself an author. But he's a shit-kicker. He mocked the sentimentality of my show and attacked my songs, not only 'Let's Be Buddies,' but 'My Mother Would Love You.' He claims that my decline as a songwriter began with my riding accident."

"*Dahlink,*" she said. "Take comfort in the fact that you're the King of the Box Office. Success, is, after all, its own reward."

"At least two studios are talking about making a movie based on my life," Porter said. "I told them that I'll refuse unless Cary is cast as me."

"Your true story could never be told on the screen," Grant said.

"Neither could yours, you darling man," Porter said. "If you can't print the legend, then hawk the fiction, I always say."

[As improbable as it seems, the so-called life story of Cole Porter finally reached the screen at war's end by 1946. Honoring the composer's request, it starred Cary Grant, and it contained absolutely no references to homosexuality.

The female roles went to Alexis Smith (a lesbian), Jane Wyman (Ronald Reagan's straight wife), Eve Arden (a sometimes lesbian), and Mary Martin (a lesbian).

Director Michael Curtiz later complained, "I made the movie with this homo, Cary Grant, and a cast of dykes."

Within the movie, Curtiz pointedly included Porter's musical number, "You're the Top," knowing that gay audiences would immediately recognize its double meaning.]

Porter informed her that a movie version of *Panama Hattie* with Red Skelton and Ann Sothern would soon be released. "But from what I've seen, I'm not pleased."

"It's being released by MGM," Porter said. "I expect to do better at Columbia with a picture called *You'll Never Get Rich,* starring Fred Astaire and that lovely redhead, Rita Hayworth. Harry Cohn rules the roost at Columbia. He's known for taking advantage of beautiful women who work for him."

"Thanks for the tip," Zsa Zsa said. "Perhaps I should go and surrender my body to him."

"I tried that," Porter said. "I told him I would put up no resistance if he seduced me. He didn't like that. To punish me, he forced me to try out my songs on his staff—you know, telephone operators, secretaries, janitors. All of them loved my numbers, especially 'Since I Kissed My Baby Goodbye.'"

[Porter's optimism about "You'll Never Get Rich" faded after the movie's release. Later, he conceded that it was "A bad score and an even worse picture. But Rita never looked lovelier."]

Grant thanked Zsa Zsa for putting Porter in a better mood. "He's been depressed and irritable. I try to avoid his company, but got trapped into tonight."

"I'm in pain," Porter said. "I think I have to have surgery again on my left leg for the removal of bone growths."

"I'm so very sorry," she said. "I wish you the best."

Still in love with Randolph Scott, **Cary Grant** married Woolworth heiress **Barbara Hutton** on July 10, 1942.

Their fascination with each other soon wore thin.

Grant had an impish look on his face. "Ask Cole about his sex life. That topic always sparks him."

"I wouldn't dare," she said. "He might ask me about mine."

[Years later, author Truman Capote recalled, "Cole liked to describe his sex life in great detail. It excited him to talk about it."]

At Romanoff's, Porter told Zsa Zsa that he resented his critics calling him a practicing homosexual. "That is a vicious lie. I'd say I'm perfect—not practicing."

"These days, I'm more of a *voyeur* than anything," he confided. "Except for Cary here and a few other white boys, I'm fond of black flesh. In New York, I visit this house of male prostitution in Harlem. It's staffed by good-looking, well-endowed Negroes. I sit in an adjoining room and watch the action in the next room through a peephole. Perhaps when you're in New York, you'll join me some night. I'll take you to Harlem."

"It would be my pleasure," she said. "I have never seen a black man nude, much less having sex."

"Unlike me, Cary here is trying to go straight again," Porter said. "He's given up Randolph Scott and plans to marry Barbara Hutton. The press calls them 'The Odd Couple' and 'Cash and Cary'"

"I first met Barbara in 1939 sailing on the *Normandie*," Grant said. "We kept encountering each other in London, Paris, New York, and Palm Beach. One night at the Mark Hopkins Hotel in San Francisco, our relationship became a little more serious. But Hedda and Louella don't give our upcoming marriage a chance."

"*Dahlink,* my dream involves marrying a rich man," she said. "I believe the sexes should be treated equally. There's nothing wrong with the reverse: A poor man marrying a rich woman."

"I'm not exactly a pauper," Grant said. "I'm now making $300,000 a picture. But there's a downside. The bloody reports have made Barbara and me the two most famous people on Earth except for Hitler and Mussolini. The other night, the only way I could escape from the press rats involved taking Barbara by boat to Catalina Island. There, in the Casino, Tommy Dorsey's orchestra was playing, and he had this skinny Italian singer who looks twelve years old, a guy by the name of Frank Sinatra. Barbara thought he was 'a greaseball blessed with a beautiful voice.'"

Before the dinner ended, Zsa Zsa felt outclassed. Grant and Porter were famous men doing important things, and she had little to contribute to the conversation. She had not yet developed the *persona* for which she'd eventually be famous—the one which seemed to transcend any accomplishment she might have made, and which could talk to any person from any walk of life—movie star, king, dictator, playboy, U.S. president—on somewhat equal footing by the sheer force of her effervescent personality.

Before the end of their dinner together, she accepted Grant's invitation to a Sunday night dinner at Buster Keaton's mansion, behind the Beverly Hills Hotel.

"Barbara rented it for the season," Grant said. "Keaton told me he had to take a lot of pratfalls to pay for the dump. I'm choosing Sunday because Barbara's staff is off that night. My guests do their own cooking and washing dishes. I hope you know how to cook."

"I make the most divine goulash," she said.

"I spoke to David Niven today," Grant said. He's bringing your sister, Eva."

"I hope she doesn't upstage me," she said. "She's trying to break into the movies."

"Forget about her for the moment," Grant said. "What can we do to help you break into the movies?"

"I must warn you: I can't dance, I can't sing, and I can't act," she said.

"In that case, you're destined to become a big star in Hollywood," Porter quipped.

"I'm not even sure if I want to become an actress," she said. "It seems so much easier to marry into wealth. I could see myself reigning over Hollywood as a divine hostess. Of course, I'd have to dethrone that adorable Ouida Rathbone."

"In that case, I can help you right away," Grant said. "I'll ask Greg Bautzer to take you to the Sunday night bash. He's the richest attorney in Beverly Hills, and is an aficionado of beautiful women. He's also better looking than any movie star out here. Not only that, but from what I saw in the locker room at this golf course, he hangs all the way down to Honolulu."

"My kind of man," she said. "*Dahlink*, please call this divine creature and summon him from Mount Olympus to my boudoir. Tonight."

***

The sudden appearance of David Niven in Hollywood on the eve of America's entry into World War II remains something of a mystery. He'd been the first of the British actors in Hollywood to volunteer his services to his native England when that country declared war on Nazi Germany.

In 1940, he'd become a British army lieutenant stationed in the south of England. To Laurence Olivier and Douglas Fairbanks, Jr., he had written that during one of his leaves in London, he'd found himself "a tall, Danish blonde model who is an enthusiastic nymphomaniac."

In his autobiography, *The Moon's a Balloon,* he claimed that he took only four weeks off to film a propaganda movie, *The First of the Few.* But his military records reveal that he was "released for civil employment" for a period of five months in 1941.

It was during this leave that he showed up in Hollywood. His presence there became known to several A-list party-goers, including Laurence Olivier, Douglas Fairbanks, Zsa Zsa, and Eva, who dated him.

Niven was always a bit reluctant to discuss what he did during the war. He was rumored to have participated in espionage for producer Alexander Korda, who functioned as Britain's chief spy within the United States. Niven had made a number of propaganda broadcasts for England.

During the months Niven returned to Hollywood, the United States was still officially neutral. "The town was crawling with both German and British agents," he later said. Korda had been instructed by British Intelligence to avoid the scrutiny of both the F.B.I. and the U.S. Senate. Technically, because of America's neutrality, a British agent could have been arrested for spying.

Apparently, Niven provided assistance and performed services for Britain's Special Operations Executive (also known as the S.O.E., or "Churchill's Secret Army,"). His exact duties and accomplishments within its ranks have been lost to history.

Eva knew none of that when Niven escorted her to Cary Grant's party within the rented estate of Buster Keaton. She'd done everything she could to learn about his private life. She knew that he was married at the time to Primrose ("Primmie") Rollo, the aristocratic daughter of a British barrister, but that didn't seem to matter.

Actually, Niven had seduced Barbara Hutton before Grant did, and he'd bedded an even richer woman, too: Tobacco heiress Doris Duke. A Hollywood Lothario, he'd also seduced Norma Shearer, Marlene Dietrich, Carole Lombard, Merle Oberon, Ginger Rogers, Alice Faye, Hedy Lamarr, and Paulette Goddard. He'd even seduced Mae West. In his future loomed Ava Gardner, Rita Hayworth, Deborah Kerr, and Loretta Young.

Eva had heard stories that Niven and priapic Errol Flynn used to stage weekend orgies aboard his notorious yacht, *Sirocco,* during its cruises to and around Catalina Island.

She found Niven the most articulate and sophisticated actor in Hollywood.

He wasn't as handsome as her husband, Erik Drimmer, but Niven had his own style of male flash and charm.

He told her, "Hollywood is hardly a place for intellectuals. It's a hotbed of false values, harboring an unattractive percentage of small-time crooks and con artists."

She knew before the end of the evening that he'd take her somewhere and seduce her. She'd already shared that anticipation with Zsa Zsa. Her older sister had warned her, "Do anything to move out of the orbit of that husband of yours. Him and his damn massages."

At Grant's Sunday night cook-out, Barbara Hutton did not come down from her boudoir to attend the A-list party at which she was the hostess. She stayed in her room all night.

After welcoming Niven and Eva, Grant told them they could locate Zsa Zsa in the estate's (very large) kitchen.

There, Eva found her with an apron covering her gown, making enough goulash to feed a battalion. Eva was introduced to her sister's handsome date, attorney Greg Bautzer, who was showing actress Jean Arthur how to mix martinis.

Eva turned to Niven. "I didn't come to this star-studded party to spend all night slaving in the kitchen. Let's work the room."

Within the enormous living room, Niven seemed to know virtually everyone. Rushing to some emergency in the kitchen, Grant quickly told Eva, "You're better looking than Zsa Zsa. But I'd better be careful: When I told Joan Fontaine that she was better looking than her sister, Olivia de Havilland, that nearly got me blacklisted in Hollywood."

Holding court in a corner, Louis B. Mayer was surrounded by an entourage, mostly actors who wanted to be cast in MGM pictures. Most often called simply "L.B.," he was credited with having created the star system.

MGM's **Louis B. Mayer,** having emerged from a ghetto in the Ukraine, became Hollywood's "merchant of dreams."

Niven whispered to Eva, "Don't be nervous around him. Before heading MGM, he was in the scrap metal business in Brooklyn."

When Eva met him, he was ruthless, brilliant, mercurial, and a keeper of secrets, protecting Greta Garbo while she was a secret agent for the Allies, and getting Clark Gable off on a manslaughter charge.

When they eventually worked their way to Mayer, where Niven introduced her, he said, "You're very pretty. I've heard of you. Are you surprised? I know everything going on in this town, business big and small. Paramount has you under contract, hoping you'll become the next Madeleine Carroll."

"My contract's almost up," she said. "Paramount isn't going to renew."

"Perhaps Metro might consider you," he said.

"I'll call first thing Monday morning," she said, sounding too eager.

"Don't do that," he said. "I have to think about it. If I decide we want you, I'll call you."

Later, Niven introduced her to Constance Moore and her husband, Johnny Maschio, who at the time was arguably the hottest agent in Hollywood. His clients included Fred Astaire, Claudette Colbert, Henry Fonda, William Holden, Lana Turner, and John Wayne.

Eva had never heard of the couple. Iowa-born Moore, who was both a singer and an actress, was a minor star, having appeared in a Buck Roger's serial and also with W.C. Fields in *You Can't Cheat an Honest Man* (1939). She would become better known in wartime musicals.

Maschio seemed fascinated by Eva's look. She didn't know if his interest was sexual or professional. He implied that he might find another niche for her in the aftermath of the loss of her Paramount contract.

"I used to represent Jean Harlow, bless her soul," he said. "I might introduce you to Howard Hughes. He's been searching for years for a replacement for Jean, and your hair is already dyed platinum."

"I saw Hughes' *Hell's Angels* in Budapest," she said. "I thought Harlow was stunning."

"If you're willing, I'll arrange a meeting beween you and Howard," he said.

"That would be thrilling," she answered.

He reached into his coat pocket and removed a small red book. "What's your phone number?"

After that, as she glided across the room with Niven, she told him, "*Dahlink*, you may have already helped my career."

"Okay, but when you meet with Hughes, don't wear panties."

"What on earth do you mean?" she asked.

"You'll just have to take them off," he said.

Suddenly, a man appeared before them and kissed Niven on the lips. "Eva, this is Charles Greville, the 7th Earl of Warwick."

He kissed her hand. "Let's step out on the terrace." He turned to Niven. "I just heard you'd slipped into Hollywood and you haven't even called me yet."

On the moonlit terrace, she was somewhat shocked to learn that the Earl of Warwick wanted to become an actor. Under the stage name of Michael Brooke, he'd appeared in *Dawn Patrol* with Niven and his best friend, Errol Flynn.

She found it hard following their conversation since it was too personal, but the Earl kept glancing at her, seemingly admiring her beauty.

After half an hour, he asked her to accompany him to a gala reception a few days later. "Louis B. Mayer is throwing it for me and I need a date." He turned to Niven. "Of course, I don't want to move in on your turf, ol' boy, David, but Errol Flynn and I believe in sharing."

"She's all yours," Niven said. "Besides, I'll be leaving in two days, taking that long, turbulent trip back to England and dodging—I hope—Nazi U-boats."

After the party, Niven, in someone's borrowed car, did not take Eva home, but drove her to a dimly lit residence in a neighborhood of Los Angeles that was unfamiliar to her.

Without telling her whose house it was, he invited her inside. He had his own key, although the house obviously wasn't his.

In its living room, she spotted a perfectly tanned and "absolutely gorgeous" *[her words]* Errol Flynn. "It was Captain Blood and Robin Hood in one marvelous package," she recalled later to Susan Hayward.

To her, as a devoted movie fan, he was the Knave of Hearts, the Hollywood Swashbuckler, and, according to press reports about his private life, the greatest rogue of them all. She'd heard rumors that he had prematurely aged because of all the booze, drugs, and debaucheries, but he was one of the most handsome men she'd ever met. Not only that, he was charming and suave and spoke with a slight British-Australian accent.

As he stood up and looked down at her shorter frame, she was dazzled by his eyes, just as he seemed mesmerized by her stunning beauty. "His eyes were a beautiful brown flecked with gold," she said. "They twinkled as he spoke." Taking her hand, he smiled at her, revealing his pearly white teeth. He bowed slightly and kissed her hand, and seemed reluctant to return it to her.

"Do my eyes deceive me?" he asked. "Or am I staring at the new Hungarian version of Lana Turner? Niv told me he was bringing you home tonight."

"For the first time in my life, I'm at a loss for words," she said. "How could I, an unknown daughter of a Hussar, find myself in Hollywood with its two most devastatingly charming men? Perhaps this is all a dream."

"Let's have a drink and return to reality," Niven said. "My hours in Hollywood are numbered, and I want to take advantage. "

"As always, Niv, my home is yours to do with as you wish," Flynn said.

"That's what I love about Errol," Niven said. "When we lived together, there were no boundaries, no rules. Love was made to be shared."

"I fear that even in Budapest, we're not that sophisticated," she said.

Over champagne, Niven told Eva, "When I first met Errol, I thought he was rebellious, randy, and a bit too arrogant and aggressive for my taste. But we found we had a mutual interest in booze, mischief, and women, and we became soulmates and fuck buddies."

Niven had first met Flynn at the hotel, Garden of Alla, named for its original owner, actress Alla Nazimova. "He was dating Lili Damita, the actress. Lili and I were sharing Marlene Dietrich at the time."

Niven later described Flynn as "a great athlete of immense charm and evident physical beauty, crowing lustily atop the Hollywood dung-heap."

"When we first met," Flynn said, "Niv and I sniffed each other like two dogs, each thinking the other was a fag,"

"We got to know each other better when we worked together when I was given a part in one of Errol's movies, *The Charge of the Light Brigade* (1936)," Niven said. "It was directed by Michael Curtiz, who hails, of course, from your home town of Budapest. You should have been hired as a translator on the set. Errol and Curtiz fought all the time. After one dispute, Errol told *Herr Director*, that he was 'as thick as a pig-shit bowl of goulash.' Curtiz shot back, 'You lousy faggot bum, you think I know nothing! Well, let me tell you something, I know fuck *all!*'"

Niv and I moved in together at this house on North Linden Drive, just off Sunset Boulevard," Flynn said. "A black-and-white *faux* Tudor place that became the rowdiest address in Hollywood—marijuana, orgies, and hot and cold running babes."

"Errol was generous in sharing the pretty girls, but tight with the purse strings," Niven said. "I had to pay for all the booze and groceries."

"But I was adorable, was I not?" Flynn asked.

"At least you knew where you stood with him," Niven said. "He was always dependable—He let you down every time. Actually he was a bloody shit, but you must overlook the faults of your dearest buddy. Guys like Clark Gable and Spencer Tracy didn't let stardom go to their heads. But Errol always let fame go to his head."

Playacting at war, **David Niven** *(left)* and **Errol Flynn** *(right)* appeared on screen together in *Dawn Patrol* (1938).

Offscreen, they became "fuck buddies," or so they told Eva when she was seduced by both of them before the rooster crowed.

"Yet I'm always great fun. Admit it," Flynn said.

That you are, my dear, prince of a man," Niven said. "Except you have some bizarre habits. Errol is always interested in the size of other men's penises. He believes in taking measurements and comparing them with his own. One night I was in his bed, pounding Carole Lombard. He rushes into the bedroom and pulls me off her when I'm my most impressive. Right away, he measures me."

"As you gathered, life with me is never a bore," said Flynn.

[Marlene Dietrich told biographer David Brett that Carole Lombard was a frequent visitor when Niven and Flynn lived together. "Carole was a very good friend of mine who spent much

of her time with these twilight boys," Dietrich said. "One morning when I went over to Flynn's house, I found him in bed with David Niven. They maintained that they were not gay in the conventional sense, but just fooling around for fun. None of us thought that was such a big deal, though. Lots of actors slept with each other if there were no women around."]

After the three of them (Flynn, Niven, and Eva) had finished off a bottle of champagne, Flynn offered to open another. But Niven stood up and took Eva's hand. "My dear friend, we must retreat to your boudoir," he said to Flynn.

Flynn kissed Eva good night on the lips.

Niven took her hand and led her to the master bedroom, the scene of countless seductions and orgies. "Come, dear girl," he said. "It is time to reveal to you why Merle Oberon fell madly in love with me and wouldn't leave me alone."

Unknown to Eva at the time, Flynn was watching all the action through a one-way mirror.

***

Eva didn't return home until around eleven o'clock the following morning. Zsa Zsa was there, but Drimmer had left for work. Zsa Zsa was eager to know what had happened. "Did you and Niven do the dirty deed?"

For reasons of her own, Eva decided not to tell Zsa Zsa what had transpired that morning after Niven had departed for his flight to New York.

She would later share those lurid details with Susan Hayward.

"Well, tell me," Zsa Zsa demanded. "What was Niven like in bed."

"Have you ever been fucked by a beer can?" Eva asked. "You must try it sometime."

***

Zsa Zsa's experiences at Cary Grant's Sunday night party were completely different from those relayed by Eva. She had been accompanied by "the most dashing lawyer on the planet," as he was called: Greg Bautzer. She had "poached" him from Joan Crawford, who had in turn stolen him from a teenaged Lana Turner.

Zsa Zsa later recalled, "Every big name actress in Hollywood except for Katharine Hepburn wanted Greg, and many of them—including Ingrid Bergman and Ginger Rogers—were also his clients. He also represented men such as Howard Hughes. He was once engaged to that sarong girl, Dorothy Lamour."

Appearing on her doorstep, Greg Bautzer, in Zsa Zsa's words as she later

171

recalled, was "just too dreamy to be true. He was perfect-looking—his handsome face, his courtly manner, those Chiclet white teeth, that physique, that cultured voice. Surely after midnight, he stalked Hollywood as a serial killer. I have learned that any man who looks perfect really isn't."

"When he arrived at our little apartment, I'd already heard that he had been seen at a premiere with Joan Crawford the night before," Zsa Zsa said. "I was worried that that oversexed bitch had worn him out, but he seemed as fresh as the Edelweiss in spring. I practically swooned like a schoolgirl at the sight of him. It wasn't just his looks, but his magnetic personality."

"If I had been on a jury and he was defending a murderess who'd been caught red-handed with the bloody axe, I would have found the defendant not guilty. I would have taken him to the minister right away, although I'd been warned that he was not the marrying kind."

Although a pauper, Zsa Zsa also dazzled Bautzer, wearing a Chanel gown from a Paris fashion house, paid for by Burhan Belge. She wore what diamonds and rubies she'd rescued from Eastern Europe.

At the party, Bautzer introduced Zsa Zsa to Frank Rothman, who *The National Law Journal* once defined as "a legendary litigator" and which included him several times on its list of the 100 most influential attorneys in America. In the early 1950s, he would become one of the key attorneys in Bautzer's law firm before resigning to run Metro-Goldwyn-Mayer Studios.

"When Greg was dating all those Hollywood beauties, he was already on the way to becoming a Hollywood legend known for his sexual prowess," Rothman later said. "He could even satisfy Joan Crawford, and very few Hollywood studs could do that."

"Bautzer was a trial lawyer through and through," Rothman said. "If a movie star happened to murder someone, she contacted Bautzer even before she called the police. Of course, his fast living and heavy drinking got him into trouble now and then. There were a few drunken driving charges."

"Hollywood's most eligible bachelor," **Greg Bautzer,** was a movieland Don Juan, and handler of shady deals among the stars, legal authorities, and in some cases, the Mob.

He was known for his legal talent and for his prodigious talent in the boudoir of stars who included Lana Turner, Ava Gardner, and Ronald Reagan's Jane Wyman.

"Because of his looks, Bautzer was often asked to sign a movie contract, but he turned down all film offers, although Louella Parsons suggested he was a combination of Clark Gable, Cary Grant, and Robert Taylor, with a touch of Errol Flynn and a dash of Tyrone Power for good measure."

An hour later at the Buster Keaton estate, Zsa

Zsa found herself wearing a pink apron with red valentines. She was instructing some of the other guests in the art of preparing a genuine Hungarian goulash.

Having been warned in advance that the guests had to do the cooking, and not knowing what she'd find in Barbara Hutton's larder, she had brought along the ingredients which were essential for the concoction of "Jolie's Hungarian goulash." They included Hungarian paprika she'd hauled all the way from Budapest, chicken fat she'd purchased at a Jewish deli, caraway seeds, and even gingersnaps. Regrettably, her cooking assistants were more skilled in front of a camera than in front of a stove—Mary Astor, Lucille Ball, Joan Bennett, and Claudette Colbert.

After dinner was served, Zsa Zsa was introduced to Louis B. Mayer, who told her he'd met her sister, Eva. "Obviously, beauty runs in your family. Your mother must have been the Bombshell of Budapest."

"That and more," Zsa Zsa said.

Bautzer discussed with Mayer what he considered a legal coup. He'd arranged for Joan Crawford, a single mother, to adopt a baby girl, whom she'd named Christina Crawford.

"Crawford will make a lousy mother," Mayer said.

"But I secured affidavits from Gary Cooper, Barbara Stanwyck, and Margaret Sullavan attesting to Joan's wonderful motherly qualities."

"As if those bed-hoppers would know a god damn thing about motherhood," Mayer said.

After Mayer, more introductions followed, beginning with actress Rosalind Russell. Grant told her to try to watch the screwball comedy— *His Girl Friday* (1940)—he'd previously made with Russell.

Before meeting Russell, Bautzer gave Zsa Zsa the inside scoop. The actress had just married the Danish American producer, Frederick Brisson, son of a famous actor, Carl Brisson. "Freddy and Grant had been lovers. Cary grew bored with Freddy and passed him along to Rosalind. It's a lavender marriage."

"I adore the color, but I've never heard it applied to a marriage," Zsa Zsa said.

"That's when a male homosexual marries a lesbian to cover up their true sexual preferences. Sometimes a homosexual will marry a straight woman who, shall we say, is 'understanding.' Hollywood is filled with such arrangements. That guy Mayer, whom you just met, hates what he calls 'faggots.' Nothing can destroy a Hollywood career out here faster than being identified as a homosexual."

Zsa Zsa enjoyed talking to Russell, who was pleased to have worked with Grant in *My Girl Friday.* "Before that, I was afraid I was being cast as a clothes horse, a sort of hothouse orchid in a stand of wildflowers. An impeccably dressed lady is always viewed with suspicion when she struts out onto the screen with beautiful clothes and charming manners. The audience immediately senses she's in a position to do the hero no good."

"But if I ever become a movie star, I'll insist on being a clothes horse," Zsa Zsa said. "To me, that's what it's all about."

As Bautzer and Zsa Zsa worked the room, he spotted Dolores Del Rio. "Let me introduce you to her."

"She's stunning," a jealous Zsa Zsa said.

Bautzer seemed to know all the sleeping arrangements of Hollywood stars. "In addition to countless men, she's also been the lover of Greta Garbo. In fact, her beauty has been considered in a class with Garbo's but when Dolores opens her mouth, she sounds more like Minnie Mouse."

Del Rio had been hailed as "the female Rudolph Valentino" when she shot to international fame as a star of the Silent Screen. A cousin of former matinée heartthrob Ramón Novarro, she was called "The Princess of Mexico." At the time she met Zsa Zsa, she was engaged in a torrid affair with her "toy boy," Orson Welles, who told people, "She is the great love of my life."

But Bautzer explained to Zsa Zsa that they weren't appearing together in public as a couple.

At Grant's Sunday night cook-out, Del Rio was accompanied by the German novelist Erich Maria Remarque, who had gained fame in America for his 1929 novel, *All Quiet on the Western Front,* which had been made into an anti-war movie starring a young Lew Ayres.

"With Orson unavailable, Marlene arranged for Erich, her lover, to escort Dolores, who is her dear friend," Bautzer said. "I spoke to Marlene today. She was entertaining Edward G. Robinson at four this afternoon and George Raft after ten o'clock. All three of them have made a movie together called *Manpower* (1941)."

"Surely Dietrich doesn't trust her man to a woman as glamorous as Del Rio," Zsa Zsa said.

"That's not the point. Of course, Marlene expects Erich and Dolores to fuck tonight. Welcome to Hollywood."

Face to face with Del Rio, Zsa Zsa thought her skin looked like it had been dipped in porcelain.

"You must tell me the secret of your beauty," Zsa Zsa said.

"I sleep sixteen hours a day and I appear only in moonlight, never in the harsh sun," Del Rio answered. "My most ardent fans tell me I have better legs than Dietrich and better cheekbones than Garbo. You, too, are beautiful, my dear."

"I imagine you're on a special diet as well," Zsa Zsa said. "I eat too much chicken fat myself."

"At lunch, my maid serves me an orchid omelet and at night I consume a plate of perfect gardenias on a silver platter."

"I'd better try that myself."

Bautzer told Del Rio that Zsa Zsa wanted to break into the movies.

"Oh, *señorita*, you've arrived in Hollywood too late," Del Rio said. "I'm sure you've read that I'm box office poison, and I'm in good company—Garbo, Dietrich, Joan Crawford, Mae West, and Katharine Hepburn. The traditional glamour of the 1930s is giving way to the dirty and exhausted look of Vivien Leigh fighting the Civil War. Also, the public is bored with the Latin temperament and all those exotic, two-dimensional parts I played. Real glamour is dead."

"But I was planning to promote myself as a super-glamorous figure, the rival of Dietrich, who is not as young as she ought to be."

"Forget it," Del Rio said. "With the war coming up, Mayer thinks Hollywood will be promoting the girl-next-door type, the guys the servicemen will have to leave at home."

"That cuts me out," Zsa Zsa said. "I would look like the girl next door only if the neighboring address was the Palace of Versailles."

Zsa Zsa envied her beauty, little knowing that in the years to come, Del Rio and Zsa Zsa would be sharing some of the same men— Erich Maria Remarque, Porfirio Rubirosa, and—before the decade ended—Welles himself.

Suddenly, the famous German writer, Erich Maria Remarque, came into Zsa Zsa's field of vision, as he returned with a drink for Del Rio. She introduced him to Zsa Zsa, and the author of *All Quiet on the Western Front* addressed her in German. She found him "devastatingly alluring."

While Del Rio and Bautzer chatted, Remarque discussed Nazi Germany with her. She was aware that Josef Goebbels, the Nazi Propaganda minister, had publicly condemned and burned the novelist's works.

When Zsa Zsa met the reigning diva of Mexico, the exotic **Dolores Del Rio**, she didn't know that the great *Latina* beauty had already seduced her future husband, George Sanders, Del Rio's co-star in *Lancer Spy* (1937).

"Every part of her was beautiful—even her toes," said her escort for the evening, Erich Maria Remarque, the novelist.

"You may have Jewish blood in you," he said. "Actually, I don't. But Goebbels claims that I'm a descendant of French Jews and that my last name is Kramer. Goebbels also lied and said I did not see active service during World

175

War I, and he revoked my German citizenship in 1938. Sometime in this decade, I plan to become an American citizen."

Out of hearing distance of their escorts, he asked her if she would give him her telephone number. "I always need a beautiful woman on my arm when I arrive at a party. Marlene is often occupied, and your escort tonight, Greg, is the most overbooked stud in Hollywood. All the big name actresses want to date him."

"As I'm well aware," she said.

"I'm married," Remarque said. "To an actress, Ilsa Jutta Zambona. We first married in 1925 and that was for love. I remarried her in 1939, not for love, but as a means of protecting her from being deported from Switzerland and repatriated to Germany, where she'd have faced death from the Nazis. Even during our first marriage, we continued to see others."

"All the best marriages allow that," she said, being deliberately provocative. "I'd be honored to be seen on the arm of such a celebrated author." Before coming to the party, she'd written her phone number on two dozen pink cards. She reached into her purse and handed him one.

"I can't wait until our first rendezvous," he said, smelling the card. "A perfumed card. How very alluring. Up to now, I always thought only Marlene did that."

The handsome and stylish novelist, **Erich Maria Remarque**, a German-born intellectual who was seriously involved with Marlene Dietrich, was always a man of mystery to Zsa Zsa. She planned to move in on him.

She'd heard that this platinum-heeled wanderer was attracted to lots of vodka, dangerously fast cars, and spectacularly beautiful women.

"I'll wait for your call," she said. "There's an old Hungarian saying: There's a time to love and a time to die. I've just arrived in Hollywood. This is my time to love."

Ironically, the title (in English) of Remarque's 1954 novel was *A Time to Love and a Time to Die.* Did Zsa Zsa provide the title for that novel more than a decade before he wrote it?

A few hours later, Bautzer was added to Zsa Zsa's lengthening list of lovers.

"Unlike many men, particularly some of those who play great lovers on the screen, Greg lived up to his reputation," Zsa Zsa said. "He not only possessed the equipment, but had a finely honed technique. No surprise. He'd been practicing ever since he turned thirteen. I could easily fall in love with him, but I dared not. To love him would only invite heartache. He was one rooster who had to sample every hen in the barnyard."

176

With Zsa Zsa's help, Eva packed her possessions, especially the chic wardrobe she'd acquired in Budapest, in preparation for her move out of the apartment she shared with Drimmer. Zsa Zsa had found another small apartment within a ten-minute drive. It was barely large enough to contain their wardrobes, but they decided to move in anyway, since it was all they could afford.

Zsa Zsa had told Eva, "It's amazing…We have almost no money, yet invitations are coming in from some of the biggest names on the coast. I'm so grateful we escaped from Europe with enough jewelry and clothing to look like rich sisters. Ethel Barrymore, for one, thinks I made off with the treasury of the Ottoman Empire. In Hollywood, appearances are everything. If people think you're rich, they invite you. Of course, being beautiful also helps."

Eva's final goodbye to her husband "was without passion, violence, or denunciations," as she'd later tell Zsa Zsa and write to Jolie. "We had no money and nothing to divide, so that was the easy part. The initial physical attraction had worn off after a few months. He was still as beautiful as ever, but Hollywood was filled with beautiful men, some of them rich. He agreed that I would file for divorce. He would not contest it. I suspected he'd fallen in love with another woman. Or perhaps he just wanted to play the field. Many women, I realized, desired him…even homosexuals because he was so handsome."

As he was heading out the door for the final time, she asked him, "Would you like to kiss me goodbye?"

He turned and looked at her. Without hesitating, he said, "I'd rather not, if you don't mind."

"And that was that," she said. "In time, my divorces would become routine."

"Knowing that her access to the tiny but emotionally charged apartment would soon be over, she was determined to have a final cup of coffee, and a final contemplative moment or two, in what had been her living room. As she sat in the otherwise stripped-down room, sipping her coffee, she heard a knock on her door. Thinking Drimmer had returned, and as she had surrendered his key to the landlord, she answered. As she did, she encountered a very troubled Greta Garbo.

"Miss Garbo…" She didn't know what to say to the great screen diva.

"Forgive the intrusion," she said. "My name is Garbo. I'm a screen actress."

"I know who you are, Miss Garbo," Eva said. "Won't you come in?"

"I really don't want to intrude, but thank you." She stepped inside, with great hesitation.

"Oh, you're moving out…I had hoped to find Dr. Drimmer here. I have been unable to reach him. This morning I seriously injured my back lifting something, and, of all the doctors in Hollywood, he seems to be the only one to bring me relief."

"He left this morning," Eva said, nervous over being in the presence of such an august personage. "He may have told you: We're getting a divorce. He said his address is uncertain."

Eva invited Garbo to sit down and join her with a cup of coffee. To her surprise, Garbo accepted. "I know you and he are planning to separate. In fact, he has proposed to me that I become his second wife. I'm not in love with him, and I turned him down. He stormed out of my house, and I've been unable to reach him since."

"I don't need to tell you," Eva said. "Swedish men can be very stubborn. And in my country, Hungary, the men can become violent toward women if they don't get their way."

"You're a Hungarian!" Garbo said. "I like Hungarians. They have the soul of the gypsy. I don't want to become Erik's wife, but I want to retain him as a friend and as a doctor."

"He knows where I'm moving today," Eva said. "Perhaps he'll contact me. If so, I will tell him how urgently you need him."

As they sat across from each other, Eva intently studied Garbo's fabled face. The older actress wore no makeup except for some mascara, and she was attired in a dull brown jacket and slacks.

Sipping her coffee, she said, "I have come to view Erik as a friend, and friends are very scarce. I hate to lose even one, although eventually I have had to shut the door to many. I am so tired these days, and in such pain with my back."

"Making movies must be very tiring," Eva said.

"That's true, of course, but it is the movies which have become tired of me," Garbo said, "Particularly with the war, when so many off my fans in Europe can't see my films. There is another point to make. The so-called loose morality of the 20s and 30s is dead and gone. Mayer told me that during the war years to come, MGM will turn out mostly wholesome, patriotic pictures featuring the typical American girl next door. That obviously excludes me."

"Are you really through with films?" Eva asked. "If you change your mind, I'd love to appear in a movie with you, even the smallest part. I'd even play a prostitute."

"Thank you for the offer," Garbo said. "Mayer wants me to make this silly movie, post-*Ninotchka*. This time, I'll be playing a Russian resistance fighter in a film called *The Girl from Leningrad*. I found the script depressing, and I'm rejecting it."

"Your absence from the screen will be such a loss," Eva said. "The screen has never known such a glamorous image. With your face and talent, I thought you'd be performing in films into our 80s. You are a timeless wonder."

"Images, images," she said, sighing. "I was always being shaped and molded by someone else. Masseuses worked me over; designers tried clothes on me like I was a department store mannequin; makeup people shaped my face; different hairdressers came up with curls, bangs, no curls. I bit my nails and sobbed. I shouldn't confess this, but I once considered suicide."

"You may be leaving the movies, but I'm desperately trying to break into them," Eva said. "My contract at Paramount wasn't renewed. I don't know what look to adopt."

"Dear one, war is coming to America," Garbo said. "For as long as it lasts, five or six years, there will be roles for you. I predict you could play a glamorous blonde Nazi spy in picture after picture, which will surely deal with espionage. Trust Mata Hari here."

"That's a wonderful idea, and I am fluent in German," Eva said. "Of course, that means I'll end up getting arrested by the F.B.I. and never in the arms of the leading man."

"My mother always told me that a half-slice of cherry pie is better than no pie at all," Garbo said.

"I was shocked to hear you say the war could drag on for five or six years," Eva said. "That would mean millions of lives being sacrificed."

"I know that, and for that very reason, I know how to end it if only I had the courage," Garbo said.

"How could you end such a thing?" Eva asked. "You're only one person—and a woman."

"I don't know if I should tell you this..." Garbo paused for a long moment. "But I feel you would understand. I have this daydream. I know that Hitler adores my acting, and *Camille* was one of his favorite movies. He wants me to return to Berlin and make German films. He told Goebbels and others that I am an extraordinary specimen of the Nordic race."

"If you make Nazi films, how would that end the war?" Eva asked.

"I would only pretend to agree to make

Eva Gabor poses for a publicity still for Paramount in 1942. Eva's ambitious mother, Jolie, had wanted to be an actress, but the dream eluded her.

In spite of her disappointing beginning, Eva was determined to act. Until she grew disillusioned with the comparison, she fancied herself as "The Next Garbo."

179

films for Goebbels," Garbo said. "It would just be an excuse to meet Hitler. I would carry a revolver in my purse. During our meeting, I would assassinate him. Of course, that would mean ending my own life."

"An incredible scheme," Eva answered. "It's so crazy, it might even work. You'd become a legend, ranking up there with Cleopatra and Catherine the Great."

"Instead of those two ladies, I more or less saw myself as a heroine like Joan of Arc," Garbo said.

"I could never do something like that," Eva said. "I'm such a coward, more like a screaming Madame du Barry being hauled off to the guillotine in Paris."

"You are a very lovely young woman, and as long as your beauty lasts, you will always find a way to support yourself, even in a world being engulfed in war."

"My parents are still in Hungary, and so is my sister Magda," Eva said. "I fear for their safety."

"Personally, I think that both my native Sweden, neutral for now, and Hungary will be overrun by the Nazis," Garbo said.

"I keep urging my parents to escape from Budapest," Eva said.

"Good advice," Garbo said. "But there may be no safe place to run to."

Garbo rose slowly, her face reflecting her back pain. "Please try to find Dr. Drimmer for me."

"I will," Eva promised, although I may have seen him for the last time."

At the door, she reached for Garbo's hand, who seemed a bit reluctant to offer it.

"Forgive me for being so bold," Eva said. "it's not like me—but I'd love to meet with you again. I find you fascinating."

"Most people who meet me claim that I'm boring," answered the Swede.

"Not me, believe me," Eva said.

'Your offer of friendship is most kind and rather rare these days," Garbo said. "I'm not sure what the daughter of a Viking warrior, whose soul is swept by Arctic winds and endless snow, would have in common with a Hussar's daughter fighting off the Turkish invaders."

Sensing that Garbo was about to exit, Eva sought to say something to retain her presence a bit longer. "It seems we do have something in common other than Erik. Both of us are ending one way of life and trying to figure out what the next chapter will be."

"At least for the duration of the war, I'll find a house with a garden behind a walled compound in Beverly Hills where I can work in my garden during the day and walk at twilight along the Pacific shore," Garbo said. "I want a refuge from the world. I want nothing to be expected of me. I will be drifting. I don't want anything to upset my routine—no husband, no other women, no children, nothing but silence and an escape from the world. As you see, my dear creature, I would have nothing to offer you."

To Eva's surprise, Garbo then gave her a long, lingering kiss on the lips. And then she was gone.

When Eva eventually settled into her new apartment with Zsa Zsa, she wrote Garbo a letter with her new address. "I adored your visit, the memory of which I will treasure for as long as I live. We talked of images. I finally figured out who you are. You are Frigga, the wife of Odin, the Norse goddess who appears in the Arctic sky only when the moon is at its most luminous."

Her note was never answered.

***

Over lunch the following day, Eva revealed to Susan Hayward, her new confidant, what happened on the night David Niven took her to Errol Flynn's home. Eva hadn't dared give Zsa Zsa the complete story.

"David had an early plane to catch, and he woke me up to kiss me goodbye with one of those 'we'll meet again' promises. I'm sure he says that to all the girls."

"You mean you were left alone in the house with Errol Flynn?" Hayward asked. "This sounds raunchy."

"And it was," Eva said. "At around ten that morning, I sensed some presence in the bedroom. When I opened my eyes, Errol was standing over the bed with an impressive erection. He didn't demand sex, or even ask for it. He just took it."

"Lucky girl," Hayward said. "I bet you fought him off like a fierce tigress before submitting to his manly charms."

"That really wasn't what happened," she said. "I found him irresistible," Eva said. "What would you have done? One of the world's major heartthrobs, the dream of millions of women around the globe, comes to your bed and wants sex. You're going to resist? Not likely."

"Did he live up to his reputation?" Hayward asked.

"Not only that, but it was one of the most glorious fucks that I may ever experience. I learned his sexual secret. He powders the head of his penis with cocaine before insertion. It drives a girl wild."

"You're getting me hot and bothered and I've got to return to the set," Hayward said. "Are you seeing Flynn again tonight?"

"Perhaps," she said. "I'm going to that Louis B. Mayer reception for the Earl of Warwick. His Lordship has invited me as his date."

"Hot damn!" Hayward said. "You'll meet more stars than there are in the heavens, as Mayer so loudly proclaims."

She was right: As the Earl of Warwick escorted Eva into Mayer's compound, she felt that nearly all the major MGM stars, and lots of minor contract players, had turned out for the bash.

"I don't think any of them could afford to reject an invitation from Louis B. Mayer," the Earl whispered to her.

At least ten acres of flowers must have been felled for the gala. In case of rain, large tents had been placed on the grounds. All the men, mostly actors, wore smartly tailored tuxedos, and the actresses were attired in stunning *haute couture* gowns. The MGM orchestra provided music, and Beluga caviar was washed down with French champagne. Lobster was the meat of choice. "Everybody seemed to kiss everybody else on the lips," as she remembered the event.

As the event's guest of honor, the Earl of Warwick got special attention from Mayer. He also seemed to remember having met Eva, but at this event, no mention was made of any possible contract.

Mayer ushered them over to meet one of his relatively recent "discoveries." Eva and Lord Warwick were introduced to a stunning, sultry brunette, Hedy Lamarr, whom Mayer was loudly acclaiming as "The most beautiful woman on Earth."

When Lamarr spoke to Eva in her lilting Viennese accent, she claimed that she had become "*vonderful* friends" with Zsa Zsa during her stage appearance in Vienna. Lamarr asked Eva for Zsa Zsa's phone number, claiming that she had been trying to get in touch with her.

During the time Lord Warwick, Lamarr, and Mayer stood talking together, Eva seemed completely left out. Zsa Zsa may have liked Lamarr, but Eva was very jealous of her. "It seems that *Gentlemen Prefer Brunettes,*" Eva later said.

Later in the evening, after a bit too much champagne, Lamarr joined Eva in the powder room. She'd switched to speaking in German. "Mayer doesn't know what to do with me," she complained to Eva. "He assigns me the wrong roles. He doesn't know how to handle a blue blood. He's better at making stars out of chorus girls like Joan Crawford."

"At least you're getting to work with Clark Gable and Robert Taylor," Eva said.

"Both of them are here tonight," Lamarr said. "If you're so interested in them, I'll introduce you. Talk about miscasting: Mayer has assigned me to a picture called *White Cargo* (1942). I'm to play a South Seas native girl—with bronze makeup, of course—named Tondelayo. Can you imagine such an outrage?"

[Ironically, the same Hollywood miscasting would be repeated with Eva in 1949 when producer Sol Loesser cast her, a petite blonde with a Hungarian accent, as a raven-haired Polynesian temptress, with bronze makeup, in a forgettable picture called Love Island.*]*

Exiting from the powder room, Lamarr kept her promise and walked Eva over to meet Clark Gable. He was talking with singing star Jeanette MacDonald, with whom he'd co-starred in the 1936 *San Francisco.*

He chatted about working with Lamarr on the set of *Boom Town* (1940), which had also co-starred Spencer Tracy and Claudette Colbert.

"I had this fight scene with Spencer," Gable said. "We rehearsed it with some sparring matches. He's always been jealous of my star billing. He landed a punch in my million-dollar face that broke my upper plate of false teeth and busted my lip."

[Other sources maintain that it was Tracy's stand-in, not the veteran actor himself, who landed the punch.]

"That's not all," Gable said, "With my temporary dentures, I came back onto the set two days later for a kissing scene with Claudette. She kissed me so hard she broke my temporary dentures. Production had to be shut down until I got new teeth. Now Hedy here knows how to kiss without breaking a man's teeth."

Both MacDonald and Lamarr soon drifted off, leaving Eva alone to talk to Gable. False teeth or not, she found him an awesome, magnetic personality, "oozing masculinity."

Even without his star role in the 1939 *Gone With the Wind,* he was hailed as the King of Hollywood, coming from a rough-and-tumble life that had included working the oil fields of Oklahoma during the 1920s.

"With Hedy, I never got into trouble with Carole," Gable told Eva, referring to his wife, the blonde actress Carole Lombard. "She told me that she knows the type of women I like, and Hedy wasn't it."

"But I suspect little blondie here might be the one," came a voice coming up behind Gable. It was Lombard herself. "If you don't mind, cutie, I've come to rescue my husband. I've already had to assign Lana Turner her walking papers tonight. I don't need another dumb blonde moving in my territory. We Indiana cunts like to protect our property. My former husband, William Powell, is here tonight. He goes for blondes. Chase after him. Now, get lost."

Eva was horrified at Lombard's rudeness and potty mouth, and she'd

Carole Lombard and **Clark Gable** posed for a publicity still in the 1930s at MGM, when they were first falling in love, although both actors had other entanglements at the time.

"I knew he was going to plug me," Lombard said. "But when, god damn it?"

183

never heard a woman call herself a cunt.

She was rescued by her date, Lord Warwick, who had encountered some true European bluebloods, whom he wanted her to meet.

Perhaps he wanted to show her off, because all night, she'd been the object of leering glances from many of the males. As she glided across the room—"Like a swan,"—she'd recall—she spotted Robert Taylor surrounded by an entourage of adoring males. She decided she would never be able to break through to him. Besides, he was married to Barbara Stanwyck, not that that mattered in Hollywood to those seeking "big names."

Lord Warwick introduced her to Eric de Rothschild, who had danced the tango with Zsa Zsa at a previous party. Eva also met the Baroness Renée de Becker (*née* Rothschild)

"Renée was a darling," Eva later said. "But her claim to fame was that she once possessed the most expensive piece of furniture in history."

[Eva was referring to the console table once owned by Marie Antoinette. It was made in 1781 by Jean-Henri Riesener, Louis XVI's ébéniste (cabinet-maker) who delivered it to the Palace of Versailles. The elegant console stood on tapered legs encrusted with gilded bronze mounts in the form of lacelike garlands, tassels, and fringe.

After a series of owners, including the Baroness de Becker, it was acquired by the British Rail fund. It was later auctioned off, in 1988, by British Rail. A private collector in London purchased it for nearly $3 million.

"Imagine being famous for owning a piece of furniture," Eva said.]

Hubert von Pantz as he looked in 1986. Eva met him in 1942, when he was younger and much handsomer.

Arriving in America after a torrid romance with Coco Chanel, von Pantz lamented the loss of his 15th-century Palace of the Bishops in Salzburg. Gestapo Chief Heinrich Himmler and his SS officers had turned it into their vacation retreat.

A far more memorable aristocrat Eva met was the Baron Hubert von Pantz, who was known in international society for his torrid romance with French fashion designer Gabrielle (Coco) Chanel.

He was the owner of the 15th-century summer palace of the bishops of Salzburg. In need of cash, he'd converted it into a vacation retreat where celebrities such as Cole Porter mingled with royalty who included Juliana, the future Queen of the Netherlands, who spent her honeymoon there.

The baron told Eva that when the Nazis annexed Austria, his castle was confiscated. "It is now a private hideaway for the Gestapo Chief Heinrich Himmler and SS officers," Von Pantz lamented. "I feel a kinship with you. After all, I as an Austrian and you, as a Hungarian, were once part of the same great empire. If it wouldn't infringe on Lord Warwick's territory, I'd like to invite you to a party so I can talk with you some more."

"Lord Warwick and I hardly know each other," she said. "There is no ownership here, no commitment."

"Good," he said. "I need a lovely lady to accompany me to this gala at the home of Countess Dorothy di Frasso."

"I've heard of her," she said. "She and Gary Cooper toured Europe together. I've met Mr. Cooper."

"She now has a boyfriend even more intriguing than Mr. Cooper," he said.

"I'd be delighted to go with you," she said.

As they were making the arrangements, Eric de Rothschild emerged as the band struck up the music for a tango. She accepted his offer to dance with him.

She'd later tell Zsa Zsa, "Eric, your Rothschild banker friend, can dance the tango better than Valentino in *The Four Horsemen of the Apocalypse*. But it's the Baron von Pantz whom I find intriguing."

[Zsa Zsa had been boasting to her younger sister of her links to royalty, and Eva enjoyed retorting with some blue-blooded name dropping herself.]

"What did you and the Earl of Warwick do after you left Mayer's party?" Zsa Zsa asked.

"Oh, nothing much," Eva said, being very non-commital. "He drove me back to this dump we're living in. Perhaps a kiss on the cheek."

"I don't believe a word you're saying," Zsa Zsa told her. "Unlike me, you were never a very convincing liar."

In just a few days, Eva would have a very different story to tell Susan Hayward over lunch.

***

 A few weeks after her arrival at Eva's apartment in Hollywood, Zsa Zsa assessed their situation. "We have no money and we're living in this rat's nest. Of course, we have our clothing and what jewelry we've managed to acquire. What we don't have is money. Tomorrow, I'm going to try to launch my career in films. If that doesn't work, I suggest we continue our party going and that each of us latch onto an American millionaire sooner rather than later."

And so they did.

CHAPTER FIVE
Hollywood Discovers Magyar Chic

 Zsa Zsa had been so well received by the elite Hollywood colony at parties, she'd quickly earned a reputation as a glamorous Hungarian social butterfly. She hoped to parlay that small acclaim into a movie contract with some film producer. Eva had managed to win a contract with Paramount, and Zsa Zsa felt she was far more flamboyant and ultimately more desirable than "my mousy little sister."

She told Eva, "With your paycheck about to be cut off, someone in this little rathole we inhabit has to bring home the cheese."

One bright, sunny morning, she woke up determined to storm the office of Alexander Korda, the producer and director who had returned to Hollywood in 1940. The year before, he'd married screen beauty Merle Oberon, who had co-starred with Laurence Olivier in *Wuthering Heights.*

Born into a Hungarian Jewish family in 1893, Korda had first worked in Hollywood from 1926 to 1930, when it was making the transition from Silents to Talkies.

Before Zsa Zsa left Budapest for Hollywood, Vilmos, her father, had told her, "Even if Jolie and I can't send you money because of the war, there's always your Uncle Korda to help you. The same Hungarian blood flows through his veins as through yours, and I know he will come to your rescue."

At the age of four, Zsa Zsa had been taken to London by Vilmos, where he'd called on his old friend, Korda, during the period he was working in the British film industry.

In his office, Korda pronounced Zsa Zsa "a real beauty. One day, when she's older, I'll make a big star out of her."

What he really wanted was a loan from Vilmos. Throughout his life, Korda was often in financial trouble, and he borrowed freely from friends and business associates. In a memoir, Zsa Zsa made the outrageous claim that Vilmos had lent Korda a million dollars, which had caused a serious rift between Jolie and her husband. There is no evidence that Vilmos ever possessed a million dollars, much less that that amount had been lent. He may have lent some money to Korda, but hardly that amount, which would have been a vast sum in those days.

Zsa Zsa had been thrilled to hear of Korda's success, beginning with *The Private Life of Henry VIII,* starring Charles Laughton, who had won a Best Actor Oscar for his role in 1933. Korda's most recent success had been *That Hamilton Woman* (1940), starring Vivien Leigh.

For her debut in films, Zsa Zsa even had a role in mind. Jolie had taken her to see Korda's silent picture, *A Modern Dubarry* (1927), starring his first wife, Maria Corda, who spelled her name with one letter different from that of her husband. The story was based loosely on the life of Madame du Barry, mistress of Louis XV. Zsa Zsa was hoping Korda would have the script reworked and tailored for her as a talkie.

At the time Zsa Zsa contacted Korda's office, he was the British equivalent of a ruthless studio boss, and famous on both sides of the Atlantic. In London, he'd been instrumental in launching the careers of both Vivien Leigh and Laurence Olivier. Before their marriage, he'd had an affair with Leigh. A man of immense charm, Korda could also turn violently on people who worked for him.

As a boy raised on the *puszta* of Hungary, he'd made good as a producer and a starmaker, and on a rare occasion, Winston Churchill had even written scripts for him.

When Zsa Zsa had called his office, he'd agreed to see her the following morning at eleven o'clock. She'd awakened early and had worked on her face and wardrobe for hours, selecting a dress that was chic and well styled but not too flamboyant. As she studied her image in a mirror, she'd decided that she had never looked lovelier and had more or less forced Eva to agree with her.

Zsa Zsa wanted **Alexander Korda**, that Hungarian "*wunderkind*" from the puszta" to transform her into a star, as he'd done with his wife, Merle Oberon, and with his former mistress, Vivien Leigh.

"Instead," she said, "he treated me like a stripper—'off with your clothes.'"

Later that morning, she was ushered into Korda's office by his secretary. To Korda, she immediately said, "Vilmos sends his love, and wonders if you'll ever return to Hungary."

"Not bloody likely," he said. "Jews like Vilmos should be getting the hell out of Budapest, not going back there."

Knowing how busy he was, she got right to the point. "Uncle Korda, forgive my boldness, but I want a contract like my sister, Eva, got at Paramount. Perhaps one for seven years. Otherwise, I might be penniless."

He looked her up and down. "You're certainly not that fat little salami Vilmos brought to my office in London! I'll consider a contract. But, remember this—in Hollywood, you can't ask for something without giving something in return."

"My gift in return will be my beauty and talent as reflected in your movie," she said.

"Take off your clothes," he demanded.

In a memoir, Zsa Zsa admitted that she was devastated. She turned and silently left his office, never to mention her encounter with Uncle Korda ever again.

That night she was going to a party in Malibu at the beach house of Darryl F. Zanuck, an even bigger producer than Korda. At some point during the evening, she hoped to corner him and ask for a contract at 20th Century Fox. Surely, Zanuck couldn't be as crude as Uncle Korda.

***

The chance came for Zsa Zsa to meet one of Hollywood's most powerful producers, Darryl F. Zanuck. Greg Bautzer invited her to what she called "a majestic beach bash" at Zanuck's retreat in Malibu. It was established that she would drive herself to the party, as he would be two hours late. The guest of honor was Dolly O'Brien, a gorgeous, blonde, and beautiful millionaire who specialized in marrying and divorcing rich men.

Zsa Zsa would later recall, "If I ever had a role model, it was the rambunctious heiress born in New York at the turn of the century and married when she was only fifteen. Though called Dolly, her final name ended up being Laura Linola Hylan Heminway Fleischman O'Brien Dorelis. She coasted through international society on her beauty—her youthful face was defined as 'timeless,'—and on her charm, wit, and honesty."

"I was later known for being outspoken and for saying outrageous thing," Zsa Zsa said.

"I learned it all from Dolly. The night we met at Zanuck's house, we adored each other, though we came from different backgrounds. In between marrying rich husbands, Dolly told me she was in

Cigar-smoking producer **Darryl F. Zanuck**, or so it was said, seduced half the starlets at 20th Century Fox during midafternoon "fuck breaks."

Zsa Zsa hoped for a Fox contract, but ended up "being treated like a common whore."

Hollywood to sample at least a dozen toy boys before flying back to New York. I had never heard the word 'toy boy.' I think Dolly invented it."

"One of my husbands, Julius Fleischmann, the margarine king, insisted I marry him, even though I told him I didn't love him," Dolly told Zsa Zsa. "We lived on this lavish estate on Long Island. There, I met J. Jay O'Brien. He was dashing polo player and former dancer, and the world's greatest lover, though penniless. I fell madly in love with him and asked Fleischmann for a divorce. He settled $5 million on me. Would you believe my luck? Right after my divorce and after I married O'Brien in 1924, he fell from his polo pony and died. If I had waited a few weeks longer, I would have wound up with $66 million. Let that be a lesson to you, Zsa Zsa."

"In addition to O'Brien's talent as a lover, he turned out to be a great business man," Dolly said. "We made a fortune in real estate in Palm Beach. In fact, we became the king and queen of the social set down there. But my darling died last year of a heart attack. To get over him, I'm getting pounded by the biggest and best studs in Hollywood. After the loss of my husband, these men are making me a woman again."

Zsa Zsa and Dolly went into a bedroom to change into their bathing suits. When they came out, Dolly introduced her to her date, who turned out to be Johnny Weissmuller.

Born to German-speaking parents in an ethnically Hungarian village within

what was part of the Austro-Hungarian Empire in 1904, he was still in marvelous shape, which he exhibited in a bathing suit whose cut resembled something akin to a jock strap.

She knew of his swimming prowess in the 1924 and 1928 Olympics, where he'd won five gold medals and been splashed on

Dolly O'Brien, pictured above in her role as a Palm Beach socialite, became a sort of role model for Zsa Zsa.

Dolly gave her some advice: "Marry for money, even an old geezer, and arrange for toy boys on the side for your sexual pleasure."

Dolly O'Brien agreed with her friend, Tallulah Bankhead, about screen Tarzan **Johnny Weissmuller.**

"Dahling," Tallulah once said to him. "You're the kind of man a woman like me must Shanghai and keep under lock and key until both of us are entirely spent."

the front pages of every newspaper in Budapest.

She thought he was a Greek Adonis, and she had not been surprised when he'd gone to Hollywood to become the screen's most memorable Tarzan.

Rather spare on details, Zsa Zsa in her first memoir wrote of this "soft, cloudless night" in a house in Malibu overlooking the Pacific. However, she refused to give Zanuck's name, referring to him as "Mr. Cord," even though all of *tout* Hollywood knew she was describing Zanuck.

Dolly, Bautzer, and Weissmuller joined Zsa Zsa for a swim in the Pacific under the full August moon, and later sat around a bonfire in their bathing suits. Zanuck's chef had prepared the most delicious barbecued steaks. "I wanted to get the recipe for Jolie," Zsa Zsa later said. So far, she'd seen little of Zanuck, who had remained inside the house.

"Greg sat next to Dolly," Zsa Zsa said. "I don't think it was his intention to seduce her, but he wanted to become her lawyer, taking over her interests in California. Johnny and I spoke in German about the Old World, although I kept staring at that crotch of his. After all, I figured he wanted to display it or else he wouldn't be wearing such a revealing bathing suit. He might as well have been nude."

At one point, Zsa Zsa excused herself to go back into the house. On the far corner of the terrace, she spotted the lit tip of a cigarette. "You found me at last," came a drunken male voice. "Come over here," he ordered.

She remembered laughing nervously, but, as she admitted in her memoir, "It was obvious that he wanted to make love to me."

She didn't explain that very well. What he did as she approached was to lower his bathing suit and display his penis.

As biographer Mart Martin wrote, "Zanuck liked to expose himself and masturbate in front of stars or starlets he was pursuing. He said it was 'to get those broads' juices running.' He also like to open his pants in his office at Fox and pull out his erect penis in front of various female stars."

These had included Wendy Barrie, Dolores Costello, Linda Darnell, Alla Nazimova (a lesbian), Gene Tierney, and Merle Oberon. Later, Bella Darvi, Juliette Greco, Corrine Calvet, and Marilyn Monroe would be "treated" to this exhibition.

"You've had nothing until you've had me," Zanuck told Zsa Zsa. "I am the biggest and the best. I can go all night and all day."

As Ava Gardner later recalled, "The only thing bigger than his cigar was his cock, which he's not too shy to show or put into use."

Zsa Zsa tried to make excuses to leave.

He told her, "Look, baby...how much? I'll pay it—I'm no piker." He reached into the pocket of his pants, which had been placed on the adjoining chaise longue, and pulled out a fistful of bills. He flung them at her.

As she wrote, "Hundreds of dollar bills fell about me."

"There's plenty more where that comes from—take it!"

Traumatized, she remembered fleeing from the terrace and rushing outside the house, where she got into Eva's battered old car. The keys were still in it. "I shot out of the driveway onto Pacific Palisades and drove wildly, weaving in and out of traffic. My tears almost blinded me."

Later, as she lay awake in bed, she was still sobbing because she'd been treated like a tart by an "arrogant, vulgar man." She was aware that Zanuck ruled Hollywood, or at least a good part of it, but she had her pride. "After all, I've known men who ruled countries."

Finally, Bautzer arrived at midnight. In her *negligée*, she let him in. "I know what happened. Darryl pulls these stunts all the time with starlets, or even with big stars. He summons actresses to his office every afternoon for notorious 'fuck breaks,' as he calls them. Everybody at Fox knows that. Tyrone Power, who is bisexual, is the biggest star at Fox. But Zanuck takes him to the sauna on the lot and demands that this big box office attraction go down on him."

"He can't pull stunts like that with me," she protested.

"It will work out," Bautzer said. "I've arranged for Darryl to give you a proper audition next week. He's got this script he wants you to read with Carole Landis. It will all happen in a suite at the Beverly Hills Hotel. He's assured me it's legitimate. I would recommend that you go. He knows I'm backing you. If you'll forgive him, and if your reading with Carole goes well, I'll negotiate a movie contract with you at Fox."

Before too long, Bautzer had her laughing and enjoying the bottle of champagne he'd brought. He'd promised to hold her in his arms for the night.

"I noticed about Zanuck," she said, "that he has oversized buckteeth. When he comes into a room, his teeth precede him by at least three seconds. He'd make a great Bugs Bunny."

***

Over luncheon with Susan Hayward, Eva had a chance to update her on her affair with the Earl of Warwick. "I don't think it's going anywhere, but at least it's amusing. It was not quite a repeat of that night when David Niven took me to Flynn's house, but almost. His Lordship now allows me to call him Charlie. We've become quite familiar."

[Charles Guy Fulke Greville, 7th Earl of Warwick, 7th Earl Brooke (born 1911, died 1984, sometimes known to his friends as "Fulkie"), was a British peer and the last Earl of Warwick to live at the family seat (Warwick Castle) before its sale in 1978. Using the stage name Michael Brooke, he

192

became the first British aristocrat to star in a Hollywood movie, a lead role in The Dawn Patrol *(1938) alongside David Niven and Errol Flynn. This would be his only mainstream movie. Paramount dropped him shortly after it was completed.]*

As Eva relayed to Hayward, the Earl of Warwick also drove her to Flynn's Mulholland House for what he called a nightcap. As before, Flynn was waiting in his trophy-filled living room with champagne and amusing stories to tell.

He told them that his wife, Lili Damita, whom he called "Tiger Lil," had walked out on him, taking "Baby Sean" with her. He was referring to his son, Sean Flynn. "She's divorcing me on grounds of cruelty, as if I could be cruel to anyone."

"I'm amusing myself by giving nude parties," he said. "Last night, Lupe Velez…"

"Who is this woman?" Eva asked.

"A Mexican actress," Flynn said. "She stripped down and danced for my guests. She has an amazing ability to make her breasts dance independently of each other. But I was the star attraction. I came out with a full erection. Tyrone Power had gotten me camera ready with that suction pump mouth of his in my bathroom. I came out and played the piano with my erect cock."

"I have no tales from Hungary to top that," Eva said.

"We British are a bit kinky, but I can't match that story either," the Earl said.

"I want something new and different other than sex," Flynn said. "I was in Jamaica and I became addicted to cockfighting. No, not that kind of cock. I came up with this great idea, sport." (He called the Earl of Warwick "sport.") "On Sunday afternoon, I'm going to start having cock-fights at my bachelor pad here. My guests will get to see roosters bite each other's heads off."

"How gruesome," Eva said. "I'd rather attend the sex parties."

"I'm trying to think of everything I can to amuse myself," Flynn told then. "After all, army doctors tell me I have only a few months to live."

"But you look like the perfect specimen," she said.

"I'm being severely criticized by the press for not becoming active in wartime service," he claimed. "I volunteered, and I've been examined twice. The doctors politely tell me I have an 'athletic heart,' whatever the fuck that is. Not only that, by my lungs are

Charles Greville, the 7th Earl of Warwick, may have called one of England's greatest castles, Warwick Castle, home, but his secret desire was to become a movie star. He billed himself as "Michael Brooke."

193

in bad shape. I was rejected. One doctor told me I have only two years to live, if that."

Eva gasped with surprise and remained silent as the Earl of Warwick gallantly responded, "Looks are deceiving. You look robust enough to live for another century."

"I can't let word of this get out," Flynn said. "It could ruin my career as a screen hero. Fans will think every sword fight on the screen might be my last."

As the hour grew late, the Earl of Warwick took Eva to bed. "He was a master of seduction, like Flynn himself," Eva told Hayward, "His Lordship had had vast experience with the courtesans and ladies of England."

In the middle of their intercourse, a nude Errol Flynn barged into their bedroom, sporting an erection.

"I didn't know how I could accommodate him and Charlie, too," Eva recalled. "But Errol had a different vision. As Charlie was mounting me, Errol mounted Charlie, entering him from the rear. It would be a first for me, but not the last. I was just beginning to experience the ways of the New World."

[Eva's relationship with the Earl of Warwick extended into the late 1970s. They saw each other infrequently, making love in Hollywood, New York, Palm Beach, London, and Paris.

He introduced her to many pillars of British society. At a reception in a Mayfair townhouse, the Earl introduced Eva to Margaret Campbell, newly minted as the Duchess of Argyll, thanks to her marriage in 1951 to Ian Douglas Campbell, the 11th Duke of Argyll.

Before introducing her, the Earl had filled Eva in on details about a Duchess whose notoriety would increase as the years went by. For a brief period, he had been engaged to marry her in 1930. "When it comes to lovers, she had them all," he said, naming both the playboy prince, Aly Khan and Glen Kidston, the record-breaking aviator and racecar driver whose other lovers had included best-selling novelist Barbara Cartland and the bisexual Silent Screen vamp, Pola Negri.

The notoriously adulterous Duchess, **Margaret Campbell**, may have been the first woman in England to use the newly invented Polaroid camera for pornographic purposes.

She liked to be photographed performing fellatio on famous men.

The list of Margaret Campbell's lovers also included the automobile czar, Baron Martin Stillman von Brabus, and the publishing heir, Sir Max Aitkens, the 2nd Baron Beaverbrook. One of her most notorious affairs was with the bisexual Prince George, Duke of Kent (1902-1942), whose other lovers had included both Laurence Olivier and Noël Coward.

At the party, Margaret was most gracious to Eva. "It seems that both of us are celebrated beau-

ties," the Duchess rather immodestly said.

"Apparently, it's going to be a rose garden all the way for me from now on," she told Eva. "I wish the same for you. If only you could find the right man, like I have. My biggest challenge now is vying with that whore, the Duchess of Windsor, for position on the list of the world's Best Dressed Women. I'm now a duchess and the mistress of a historic castle."

"You are my role model," Eva said. "If I could only persuade Lord Warwick to marry me, I, too, would become the mistress of a very historic castle. Warwick Castle. All it needs is Errol Flynn dashing about in green tights."

After Eva spent a few hours at the party, Margaret kissed her goodbye as she was leaving with the Earl. Her final advice to Eva was, "Go to bed early and often."

When not in the same city, Eva and Margaret corresponded with each other. In 1960, Eva was in London and the Earl of Warwick was on the French Riviera. Margaret invited Eva to one of her parties, and even arranged for an escort: Duncan Sandys, a Conservative Member of Parliament who had just divorced Diana Churchill, the daughter of Sir Winston Churchill, to whom he'd been married for fifteen years.

Like the supreme diplomat he was, Sandys was elegantly tailored and a perfect gentleman—"at least while he was dressed," Eva later told her friends. "Instead of raw sex, he was partial to fellatio. He had children, though, so at some point he must have done it the old-fashioned way."

In 1963, Eva was loyal to both the Earl of Warwick and to Margaret when she was caught in one of the most notorious divorce cases in 20th century British history. In suing for divorce, the Duke of Argyll accused his wife of having eighty-eight affairs, including an ongoing relationship with the Earl of Warwick. The case became fodder for the tabloids.

The first Polaroid camera in England had been sent to Duncan Sandys in his role as Britain's Minister of Defence. Apparently, Margaret borrowed the camera for some Polaroid shots of herself fellating her lovers. In these pictures, she wore only her signature three-strand pearl necklace.

The photograph showed her fellating two different men. Their faces were not shown, and British tabloids publicized them as "the headless men."

A guessing game ensued. Who were these men, each shown in a full-body closeup, fully erect, Most of the speculation centered on Douglas Fairbanks, Jr., and on the Earl of Warwick. Finally, it was widely assumed that the men were Fairbanks and Sandys. Zsa Zsa and Eva, perhaps through the duchess, obtained copies of these Polaroid shots of the two naked-and-headless men. Zsa Zsa and Eva—collectively, between the two of them, at least—had seduced each of the three men. Eva immediately eliminated the Earl of Warwick, "That is not Charlie's penis," she proclaimed.

195

Zsa Zsa concluded that one of the headless bodies was that of her former lover, Fairbanks, Jr. "Perhaps the court should also summon Dietrich before a final judgment is passed."

"I didn't have to be a female Sherlock Holmes to figure out that the second man was Duncan Sandys himself," Eva said. "After all, he owned the camera, and we'd only recently had an affair."

The Duke of Argyll won the divorce case, the judge declaring that Margaret was a highly sexed woman "who had ceased to be satisfied with normal sexual relations and had indulged in disgusting sexual activities to gratify a debased sexual appetite."

Zsa Zsa joked to her friends, "Oh, no, dahlinks, the judge was describing me!"

Eva and the Earl of Warwick called on Margaret Campbell one final time in 1978, fifteen years before her death in 1993. "She'd fallen on bad days and had declared bankruptcy," Eva said. "Her beauty had faded along with her money, and she could not pay her hotel bills. Charlie gave her two thousand pounds that day. Margaret had long ceased to be my role model. I feared I'd end up like her if I weren't careful. A sad, sad story of a once fabled beauty. But, as Marilyn sang in that song, 'We all lose our charms in the end.'"]

***

Over lunch with Susan Hayward, Eva said, "When I'm with you, all I do is talk about my love life. Other than your disappointment in the pictures you've been assigned, you'd told me nothing of what's going on under the sheets with you."

"I've been striking out ever since I got to Hollywood," she said. "I was meant to play Scarlettt O'Hara. I've never quite gotten over the loss of that. I've also been on a losing streak with men."

For many years, the fiery redhead, **Susan Hayward**, was a confidante of Eva's. She was one of the first actresses in Hollywood to seduce Ronald Reagan.

She and Zsa Zsa often went for the same man—John F. Kennedy, Porfirio Rubirosa, even businessman Hal Hays.

"Instead of getting Scarlett, I ended up in bit parts in that 1938 Grade B flick, *Girls on Probation*. On that shoot, I fell for another B picture actor, Ronald Reagan. I think he's handsome in a slightly offbeat way—no Clark Gable, but good looking, clean, and wholesome."

"We began a passionate affair," she said. "Instead of some of these two-minute men in town, I'd call Ronnie the forty-minute man."

"After that, both Ronnie and I were assigned to a

movie called *Brother Rat*. There was this mousy looking girl named Jane Wyman in it, too. Would you believe he went for that bitch instead of a glamorous fiery redhead like me? Men…who can figure?"

"Howard Hughes saw my picture in a magazine, and he ordered his pimp, Johnny Meyer, to arrange for us to meet—ostensibly to promote my career, although his real aim involved getting me into bed."

"I made him this chicken dinner, which he found disgusting, and I also told him that redheads make better actresses than blondes because we're more in touch with our emotions."

Suddenly realizing that Eva was a blonde, Hayward quickly added, "Of course, present company is always excepted from my generalization. I bet you're going to become one of the best blonde actresses in Hollywood, your fame ranking right up there with Lana Turner's. She, of course, doesn't know how to act at all."

The best lay I've had in Hollywood was from Gary Cooper when we made *Beau Geste* in '39."

"I agree," Eva said. "He was my best lay, too."

"There's not been one hot guy in the last five movies I've made," Hayward said, "Except maybe Rod Cameron who had a small part in *Among the Living* (1941)."

"He was my substitute for Gary Cooper," Eva said.

"Holy shit, Eva," Hayward said. "Is there any guy I can name in Hollywood you haven't slept with?"

"Clark Gable and Robert Taylor," Eva answered. "But they're at the top of my list. I've already met Gable and spotted Taylor at a party. Both men, though quite different, are my types. I like both pretty boys and the rugged masculine type. How about you?"

"I only like men who have bigger balls than I do," Hayward said.

***

Eva's career was going nowhere, but her social calendar was filling up fast. First, the Earl of Warwick was taking her to the home of Samuel and Frances Goldwyn, who were throwing a giant lawn party for the Earl's friend, the British statesman, Leslie Hore-Belisha.

Scheduled for the following evening, Baron Hubert von Pantz had invited her to a party thrown by the Countess di Frasso, who had acquired a new boyfriend after Gary Cooper had dumped her.

When she'd told Susan Hayward about the Di Frasso party, Hayward said, "At least you and I have something in common with the countess bitch. All three of us have been fucked by Gary Cooper."

At the home of the Goldwyns, some fifty people, including many big name stars, had turned out for the reception in honor of Hore-Belisha, a name unfamiliar to her.

Whereas she had no interest in him at all, she was anxious to meet Goldwyn. Without telling the Earl of Warwick, she had a dream that he would be stunned by her beauty and might put her under exclusive contract.

She had seen many of the movies he'd produced, including *Dodsworth* (1936), *Wuthering Heights* (1939), and *The Little Foxes* (1941).

She had been told that the producer was famous for his "Goldwynisms," including "I don't think anybody should write his autobiography until after he's dead," and "Include me out.'"

She had been warned that Goldwyn was a tyrannical dictator but when she talked with him, she found him exceedingly polite. Learning that he'd been born in Warsaw, she spoke of her sister Magda, letting it be known that she was the Countess of Warsaw, although she no longer held that title.

He'd been born Schmuel Gelbfisz before changing his name in England to Samuel Goldfish. He, of course, later substituted the more sonorous "-wyn" for "fish."

Consistent with so many of her early ambitions, nothing ever evolved between the producer and her. "A spot did open at Goldwyn Studios for a blonde like me, but he gave the contract to Virginia Mayo, a leggy chorus girl bit player with big rosy cheeks and nearly crossed eyes. I could have decorated those glossy comedies that called for a blonde, but Goldwyn just didn't fall for the Gabor charm."

At the party, Eva once again encountered Baron Hubert von Pantz, whom she later described "as the most charming Austrian I've ever met." He made the final arrangements to be her escort at a gala staged by the Countess Dorothy di Frasso.

Von Pantz eventually introduced Eva to the party's guest of honor, Baron Hore-Belisha. She was astonished at his background. After the popular and charismatic Alfred Duff Cooper had resigned as Britain's Secretary of State for War, Prime Minister Neville Chamberlain had replaced him with Hore-Belisha. "An outcry went up across Britain," he told them. "I was called a warmonger and a Bolshevik. In January of 1940, I was sacked and accused of dragging Britain into World War II with the exclusive intention of protecting Jewish people on the Continent."

"All sane people know that isn't true," the Earl of Warwick said.

"Anti-Semitism is alive and thriving in Britain," the baron said. "Also the Royal Family is seriously pissed at me because I supported Edward VIII during the Abdication Crisis."

"I have just two questions to ask you," the Earl said. "First, I read in *Time* magazine that you married French actress Jacqueline Delubac."

"That is absolutely false," the former minister said.

"I also heard that on the eve of World War II, you flew to Paris to recruit Coco Chanel as a spy for Britain."

"Another lie," he said. "If anything, I think Chanel's sentiments lie on the other side."

Eva was later puzzled. Was the former Secretary of War suggesting that the French designer was a Nazi collaborator?

At that point, Frances Goldwyn emerged to rescue Hore-Belisha from a dialogue that was escalating rapidly into an intense debate about wartime politics, and Eva never got to ask that question.

She turned to the Earl. "An afterparty at Flynn's Mulholland House?" she asked.

"It will be my pleasure," he said, "except Errol won't be there tonight. We'll have the place to ourselves."

"What fun!"

***

In Los Angeles, German speaking Baron Hubert von Pantz, known at the time as "a collector and connoisseur of celebrities," and the owner of the legendary Palace of the Archbishops in Salzburg, arrived on Eva's doorstep to escort her to the lavish social event staged by the notorious countess Dorothy di Frasso.

En route, Von Pantz ordered his driver to pick up Ludwig Bemelmans, the Austro-Hungarian-born American writer and illustrator of children's books. Eva had read his first children's book, *Hansi,* published in 1934, and was thrilled to meet him.

The next stopover involved picking up his companion, Lady Mendl, the interior decorator, Elsie de Wolfe, a name Zsa Zsa had mentioned frequently during her sometimes competitive dialogues with Eva.

The next day, when Zsa Zsa learned that Eva drove to the di Frasso party in the same limousine with Lady Mendl, she raged with jealousy. Up until then, she had pretended that Lady Mendl was her bosom-buddy and friend. But now, flushed with envy, she raged: "She has no time for me in Los Angeles, yet makes time to go out with my little sister. *THAT BITCH!*"

At the celebrity-studded party, Von Pantz introduced Eva to the American-born darling of between-the-wars café society, Countess Dorothy di Frasso. Famous for her hobnobbing with royalty, gangsters, movie stars, and politicians, she had numbered Josef Goebbels, Mussolini, and Hermann Göring among "my dear friends" during the 1930s.

The professional hostess, Elsa Maxwell, had defined her as "the great broncobuster of the banal, bathos, pathos, and hypocrisy—that makeup what we call modern society."

Born the daughter of a wealthy leather goods manufacturer in New York State, the imposing countess had raven black hair, sky blue eyes, and a once-celebrated figure that had shifted its proportions rather unattractively in the years that followed the end of her torrid affair with Gary Cooper.

She had been famous since 1912, when she'd married British aviation pioneer Claude Grahame-White, who had organized Britain's first airmail service. While courting her, he'd landed his plane on the White House lawn, inviting President William Howard Taft to "come fly with me." That stunt, and the bravado with which he accomplished it, had made Grahame-White instantly famous throughout the United States.

By 1916, the marriage had flown south. Dorothy filed a legal petition "for the restitution of her conjugal rights." Or, as the wealthy aviator told the press, "Imagine filing a petition to get at my cock." His comment wasn't printed. Although the court had granted Dorothy the right to her husband's sex, he ignored the decree and continued finding other women for his bed.

After their divorce, Dorothy married Count Carlo Dentrice di Frasso, former member of the Italian Parliament. Forever after, she was known as Countess. "I have the money, he has the title," she told the press.

The Countess **Dorothy di Frasso** was known by the company she kept. Her friends included both Mussolini and the Nazi propaganda minister, Josef Goebbels. Her greatest prize was the taciturn but strikingly handsome **Gary Cooper** (*pictured with her above*).

When he left her, she took up with gangster Bugsy Siegel.

The countess replaced Cooper (Eva's former flame), with the notorious murderer, extortionist, and gangster Bugsy Siegel, a handsome, blue-eyed Lothario, professional killer and co-founder of Murder, Inc. Eva had never heard of him. That situation was about to change.

The Countess introduced Eva to Bugsy, who had re-located to Hollywood. He and actor/gangster George Raft had grown up committing crimes on the streets of New York's Hell's Kitchen. When Bugsy first arrived in Hollywood, Raft had managed to get him into the beds of some of its biggest stars, including Jean Harlow, who had died tragically in 1937.

When Eva met Bugsy, he was having a drink with a young singer, who had become his most recent friend. "This skinny guy is Frank Sinatra," Bugsy said.

"Glad to meet you, babe," Sinatra said.

"She was not impressed with him, little knowing at the time that he would become her future lover.

"Incidentally, if you want to live, don't call my friend here by his nickname," Sinatra said. "He hates that. His name is Benjamin Siegel. You can call him Mr. Siegel."

Sinatra later drifted off, but Bugsy seemed enchanted with Eva. "Once he focused on you," she later said, "he was rather charismatic. He was dangerous but exciting. Only in time did I learn how ruthless he was. I was told he was not only mixed up in murder, but in drugs, extortion, prostitution, gambling. We basically talked about our European roots. He, too, had been born into a Jewish family in what is today Ukraine. His criminal record was long, going back to his teenage years when he was indicted for armed robbery, rape, and murder."

He talked about growing up on the tough streets of Hell's Kitchen. "We were poor, I had no way of making money. I started this protection racket. I hustled the pushcart merchants. If they didn't give me a dollar bill, I would incinerate their goods."

He found that amusing. She did not.

"The greatest thing the government ever did for us guys was Prohibition," he told Eva. "Bootleggers got rich."

"I got a lot of my pals here tonight," he said. "I'd like to introduce you to them, show you off, so to speak. You're gorgeous. You've met Sinatra. My other pals are my old Hell's Kitchen buddy, George Raft. Clark Gable is here. So is Cary Grant. Dorothy even invited her old flame, Gary Cooper, who's become a pal of mine. Phil Silvers is here, too. He's a laugh a minute."

"I don't want to name drop, but I've already met Clark Gable, Cooper, and Grant," she said. "I've seen Raft in gangster movies, and I've never heard of Phil Silvers. He's not a big name in Budapest."

Before Bugsy and Eva could begin "working the room," the Countess came to rescue her gangster, and Von Pantz appeared to escort her to a table on the lawn presided over by the Countess. Bugsy sat on her left, Lady Mendl on her right.

Thanks to her vast experience as an international member of *haute* society, the Countess was an entertaining hostess. She told a shocking story about Bugsy

"I thought he was gorgeous," Eva said the first night she met **Bugsy Siegel.** "He was also the most masculine man I'd ever met."

"As I was soon to find out, he also became one of my greatest lovers—and certainly the most dangerous."

201

when he'd lived with her at her lavishly restored Villa Madama outside Rome.

"One night I invited Mussolini and his visitor from Berlin, Josef Goebbels, for dinner. Believe it or not, Benjamin here didn't know that the Nazis wanted to destroy the Jews. Before putting on his dinner jacket, he had this .38 strapped to his chest. When he learned of their anti-Semitism, he threatened to go downstairs and kill them. His exact words were. 'I gonna blow that goddamn WOP'S brains out and then take out the Kraut too.'"

"Then he threatened to go to Berlin and 'shoot the nuts off Hitler.' I had to tell him that Hitler would require only one bullet, as the *Führer* was known for having only one testicle. The other one had never descended at birth."

The dinner table laughed with hilarity at this revelation.

"Benito owes me one for saving his life," the Countess said. "Not to mention Josef. But I'm mad at Benito and may never forgive him. He's seized my beloved Villa Madama and turned it into a vacation retreat for himself."

After dinner, Eva and Von Pantz were invited to a boxing ring which had been built within the Countess's gardens. Every Friday night, she staged what she called "gladiator fights."

She told Eva and Von Pantz, "I adore blood sports. I hire these tough, beefy fighters from Canada, Mexico, South America, and even Europe. My rules are simple—no boxing gloves. I don't want them to kill each other, but drawing blood is acceptable. In case of serious injuries, I have an ambulance standing by. My boxers are nude. I dispense with that stupid rule of not hitting below the belt. They are engaged to attack each other's genitals. Once a boxer from Toronto nearly ripped off the genitals of this fighter from Mexico City."

Eva managed to sit through only ten minutes of that evening's gladiator contest before retreating in horror into the house. There, she found Cary Grant sitting alone on a sofa, drinking a glass of wine.

"Is Barbara Hutton here tonight?" Eva asked. "I haven't seen her."

"Barbara doesn't like to go to Hollywood parties," he said. "People always crowd around her and make a fuss over her, the Poor Little Rich Girl. People have no manners, really. They are always asking her about her money. One constant question put to her is, 'How does it feel to have so much money?'"

"What does she say?" Eva asked.

"She claims it feels very nice," Grant said. "When people meet Barbara, they seem to expect to encounter some raving maniac, shouting orders to a staff of servants. She's not made for the Hollywood scene. Nor am I, for that matter. But enough about me," he said. "Here, have a glass of wine and come sit with me and tell me how you plan to conquer Hollywood."

She felt as provocative as Zsa Zsa usually was. "I want to become a big movie star, and you can help me."

"In what way?" Grant asked.

"You can demand that I be hired as your female co-star in your next movie."

He looked surprised. "That I will, dear girl," he said, rising from the sofa. "But tell me: Are all women from Hungary as blunt as you? Let me think about it. Don't call me, I'll call you."

At that point, Sinatra entered the room. He'd apparently been in the bathroom. Through the corner of her eye she saw another figure emerge from the same bathroom, but did not want to appear to be staring to see who it was.

"Come and watch the fights with me?" Sinatra said to Eva. "They have to mop up the blood in buckets."

"I detest seeing men bloodying each other."

"Don't worry," he said. "I'll get us a seat far enough back so the blood won't get on your pretty white dress."

***

[Although she saw him infrequently in the years ahead, Baron Hubert von Pantz did not disappear from Eva's life completely.

After the War, Von Pantz returned to Austria and, ironically, discovered that Henrich Himmler's SS officers had abandoned his Schloss *in better condition than he'd left it. "They probably used slave labor during its renovation," the Baron said.*

Amid the ashes of Europe in the aftermath of war, he devised a scheme to lure rich Americans into his castle hotel. "They were nouveau riche after the war, and I devised a plan whereby they could mingle with nobles who had titles but no money. A rich American widow might find a bona fide prince as her tennis instructor."

"Rich American women like Gloria Swanson were awed by titles, and many poor nobles were desperately in search of wealth," Von Pantz said.

Although there was no real romance between Von Pantz and Eva, he found her a "lovely friend, always entertaining." After the war, she made four different trips to his hotel, at which time she encountered princes, barons, dukes, and other bluebloods. She met publisher William Randolph Hearst, Sr., and his mistress, Marion Davies. The American brewer August Anheuser Busch showed up on one occasion, and Eva was his guest at a keg party where the beer flowed.

On separate occasions, both Bing Crosby and Bob Hope were guests. On a more elevated status, the Duke and Duchess of Windsor arrived.

"I found it hard to break through to either of them, Eva said. "He still thought he was the King of England, and she definitely acted like she was the empress of some country—perhaps India."

During one visit, Eva met the nineteen-year-old Prince Alfred von

Auersperg, the handsome, penniless scion of an old Hapsburg family, who was then a tennis pro. "He was a blonde Adonis and had a reputation in Europe as a lady-killer," Eva said. "He was German, a walking advertisement for Hitler's Aryan race, but he was far from anti-Semitic. He literally devoured me after only two nights, and I was mad about the boy, as Noël Coward would sing. Regrettably, the Von Auersperg family estates were on the wrong side of the Iron Curtain, and he had lost vast holdings."

During the peak of Eva's affair with Prince Alfred, Martha Sharp Crawford, an American heiress and socialite, showed up at Von Pantz's exclusive retreat.

Eva revealed to her friends that when the beautiful prince learned that "Sunny" Crawford, as she was called, had inherited between $75 and $100 million (estimates varied) "he moved from my suite to her suite, leaving only a pair of dirty underwear. Later, in 1957, I read about their marriage in the society pages. I was not invited to the wedding. The marriage ended in 1965 after the couple produced two children."

In 1966, Sunny married Claus von Bülow, a British socialite of German and Danish ancestry. Subsequently, she became known as Sunny von Bülow.

In 1982, her husband would be convicted of attempting to murder her by an insulin overdose, but the trial verdict was overturned in appeal. A second trial found him not guilty. Sunny's story was dramatized in the book (1986) and subsequent movie, Reversal of Fortune, *by Claus's attorney, Alan Derschowitz.*

Although jealous of the prince and Sunny, Eva did not rejoice in their tragic endings.

Prince Alfred died in 1992 after lingering in an irreversible coma for nine years following a 1983 auto accident in Austria. Sunny lived for almost twenty-years in a persistent vegetative state until her long-delayed death in a New York nursing home in 2008.

Sunny's family always remained convinced of Claus' guilt, as did Eva.

"Even if I hadn't been so jealous, I should have warned this Sunny that her beau had a roving eye," Eva said. "He flirted and then flirted some more. Since he was absolutely gorgeous and a great lover, he got nearly every woman he went after. He cheated on Sunny constantly. On two different occasions—once in New York and again in London, he even came back to my bed. I just couldn't say no to him. I think that in his way, my

Prince **Alfred von Auersperg** was a sexy but impoverished scion of a feudal estate confiscated by the Communisrts.

He turned his body into a "love machine," tempting the American "princess" and multi-millionaire, **Sunny Crawford**.

Prince Charming loved me, but I simply wasn't rich enough for him. Otherwise, I would have become Princess Alfred von Auersperg. With our blonde hair and coloring, we would have had the world's most beautiful children, a boy and a girl."]

***

Before leaving her Los Angeles apartment, Zsa Zsa carefully studied every aspect of her makeup and her designer clothing. "If I must say so myself, I look like I just stepped out of a dream," she told Eva.

At the Beverly Hills Hotel, she took the elevator to the suite of Darryl F. Zanuck for their second encounter. As she pressed the buzzer, she hoped this time their meeting would go smoothly, unlike their initial (exhibitionistic) exchange at his Malibu beach party.

That morning, Greg Bautzer had confirmed that this time, Zanuck would grant her a legitimate audition "with no damn casting couch maneuvers."

Unlike the last time, Zanuck was sober when he greeted her, offering her a champagne cocktail, which she refused. He made no mention of their previous encounter.

As she sat on his sofa, he listened intently to her career ambitions. She spoke glowingly of her success on the Viennese stage with Richard Tauber, and of how the press had described her during recent years, as "The Toast" of London, Vienna, and America, respectively._

"With your looks, you'd be ideal for light musical comedies, "Zanuck said. "How's your singing and dancing?"

"I'm skilled at neither," she said. "I think I'd be better playing a glamorous, spoiled rich girl, perhaps a society figure. The hero could develop a crush on me, but ultimately interpret me as a vapid sophisticate. In the end, he could desert me for his true love, a drab American housewife type, but one who is loving and sincere. I see myself playing a female version of Casanova, a kind of Constance Bennett type stacked up against a young, wholesome newcomer like Anne Baxter."

"You may have hit it right," he said.

At that point, they were interrupted by the appearance of a young blonde actress who emerged from the bedroom into the living room.

Unknown to Zsa Zsa at the time, Carole Landis had already become Zanuck's mistress. The beautiful, vulnerable Polish-American daughter of a railroad mechanic from Wisconsin had dropped out of high school at 15 for a career in show-biz. She had drifted to San Francisco, where she became a nightclub dancer. At the age of eighteen, she'd gone south to Hollywood, where she eventually landed on Zanuck's casting couch. After a series of lackluster films, she'd shot to stardom when she'd made *I Wake Up Screaming* in 1941 with Victor Mature and Betty Grable.

Zanuck presented each of them with scripts to read, a rather silly plot about two sisters arriving in New York to make it big on Broadway. The complication is that both of them fall in love with the same man, their director.

At the end of their respective readings, Zanuck proclaimed both of them perfect, although he surely didn't mean that. The Zsa Zsa part called for an all-American girl, not one with a Hungarian accent.

"I haven't selected the director yet, but I'll have him call you," he said.

Then he ordered champagne from room service. This time, Zsa Zsa joined them in a toast. She felt increasingly uncomfortable with the drift of the conversation, which dealt with how many male stars had tried to seduce Landis since her arrival in Hollywood.

Both Zanuck and Landis laughed at how silly the movie, *One Million B.C.,* with Victor Mature, was, but they appreciated its success at the box office.

Looking over at Zsa Zsa, Zanuck said, "As a lover, Victor Mature is a tough act to follow, but I'm one of the few guys in Hollywood who can measure up to that hunk of beefcake."

After they were finishing off a second bottle of champagne, Zsa Zsa realized that Bautzer had been misinformed. Zanuck was just as lecherous as he'd been that night in Malibu. She'd later tell the attorney, "Without the slightest hesitation or embarrassment, Zanuck suggested that Landis and I should 'get it on' while he watched."

Later, she claimed she'd risen quickly to her feet, grabbed her wrap and purse, and made for the door. "It was clear to me that I was not going to become the new love goddess of Fox."

Her assertion about Zanuck's request was made even more believable when the producer's biographers claimed that Madame Claude *[real name Fernande Grudet]* reported that Zanuck had made similar requests of her girls.

Madame Claude ran an exclusive call girl service in Hollywood, at which Zanuck was one of her best customers. "He'd select two very beautiful women and insist they make love to each other. He would become excited watching them. When they'd finish their love-making, he would select one of them as his sexual partner."

After her second failed meeting with Zanuck, Zsa Zsa became despondent about her career. Divorced from Burhan Belge, she decided that marrying a millionaire might be a more viable option for her than a movie career.

She discussed this with Bautzer, who had no intention of marrying her himself. "It seems to me that every high school beauty queen, every waitress, every five-and-dime salesclerk, every hooker or hoofer on Broadway, arrives by train at Union Station wanting to break into the movies. They probably have twenty-eight dollars in their purse. Little money, big dreams. Maybe one out of a thousand will get somewhere, if only fourth or fifth billing in some B picture. I don't like those odds."

An opportunity for her man-hunting campaign appeared with a call from her new friend, Marie, the Grand Duchess of Russia. King Vidor and his wife, Florence (the former Elizabeth Hill) were throwing a Romanov-inspired costume ball in honor of Marie.

"I want you to go with me as part of my entourage," Marie said. "Of course, you'll need an escort. I have the wardrobe to dress you as a Romanov princess. I also have a great surprise for you, a gift from my beloved brother, Dmitri."

[Marie had already told Zsa Zsa about her deep emotional attachment to her brother, Grand Duke Dmitri Pavlovich, the cousin of Czar Nicholas II and one of Rasputin's assassins. Dmitri had been the murderer who had cut off Rasputin's mammoth penis and preserved it in alcohol for future generations to gaze upon.]

The **Grand Duke Dmitri Pavlovich of Russia** *(photo above)* was the cousin of Czar Nicholas II. His sister, Marie, the Grand Duchess, was in love with him. The young duke's affair with Coco Chanel led to Zsa Zsa acquiring a chic *haute couture* wardrobe.

Arriving at Marie's residence, Zsa Zsa was treated to some Russian delicacies before being ushered into the vast wardrobe closet of the Grand Duchess—a very large room unto itself.

"It took me at least a dozen changes of gowns before I found the one right for me," Zsa Zsa recalled. "I remember it well. With its plunging *décolletage*, it was an emerald green silk with gold accessories. Of course, I had to take it to my seamstress the next day to make for a perfect fit. But in that gown, I looked like the Queen of Russia."

The surprise came later, as Marie ushered her into an alcove where there were sixteen boxes housing designer gowns from Paris. "I never told you this before, but the love of Dmitri's life was not me, but Gabrielle Chanel, whom he called by the silly name

That mad Russian mystic, **Grigori Rasputin**, *(photo immediately above)* was murdered in a conspiracy engineered by a group of nobles who included the Grand Duke Dmitri *(top photo)*.

Dmitri was so impressed with the size of Rasputin's mammoth penis that he cut it off and preserved it in alcohol, as an insult to the psychotic visionary.

of Coco. She had many other lovers, but Dmitri was one of her favorites, and he was madly in love with her. The affair did not last."

"However, she gave him sixteen gowns she'd designed and suggested them for me. They don't really fit me, and they are not my style. But I think they would look terrific on you. They come in a number of colors, all except green. Chanel never works with green."

Like a joyful and excitable child, Zsa Zsa opened each of the packages and found the gowns stunning, especially one in basic black. Most of them fitted her, requiring only minor alterations.

Zsa Zsa immediately hugged the Duchess and thanked her profusely. Her budget at the time would not have allowed her to purchase even the least costly of the lot.

"Of course, these gowns have been worn once or twice, but who's to know?" Marie asked.

After Zsa Zsa tried on the gowns, Marie discussed a possible escort for Zsa Zsa, eventually concluding that the German novelist, Erich Maria Remarque, would be ideal. "I even have a stunning outfit worn by Dmitri. In it, Remarque would truly resemble a dashing Romanov Prince."

At a recent party, Remarque had indicated an interest in Zsa Zsa, so she called him. He agreed that he would escort Zsa Zsa to the Romanov ball, and that he'd come over to Marie's residence for a fitting of the costume the Grand Duchess had devised. "All I'm doing is sitting here drinking and lamenting my writer's block."

"I have only one regret about Erich," Zsa Zsa told Marie, after she'd hung up the phone.

"What on earth?" she asked. "He's the perfect escort."

"It's not that," Zsa Zsa said. "I'm jealous that Garbo and Dietrich got to sample him first."

***

[Within a year of the spectacular Romanov costume ball, a distraught Marie called Zsa Zsa with very sad news: "Dmitri is dead." Her voice sounded as if she were on the verge of suicide.

Immediately, Zsa Zsa rushed to console her friend, whose life had been so tragic. "I held her in my arms and we cried together. In my heart, I knew she would never get over her brother's death. He was truly the love of her life."

Over the years, Zsa Zsa stayed in touch with Marie, even when she left America and settled in Buenos Aires. "Marie never forgave the United States for recognizing the Soviet Union, which she always denounced as an evil empire."

"Marie was a true monarchist, and was devoted to maintaining the old titles of the European aristocracy," Zsa Zsa said. *"She was very distressed when people of noble birth did not maintain their titles."*

When Zsa Zsa learned about Marie's death in 1958, at the age of sixty-eight, she wanted to journey to Lake Constance in West Germany, where she was buried in a family vault at Mainau, beside the grave of her brother Dmitri.

"The Grand Duchess was one of the most tragic figures I ever met," Zsa Zsa said. *"I once tried to interest various producers in filming the story of her life. Of course, I'd play the Grand Duchess. Stewart Granger expressed an interest in playing Dmitri. Had she been alive, I'm sure Marie would have been delighted at my decision to marry Frédéric Prinz von Anhalt, in 1986, when I assumed the title of Princess von Anhalt, Duchess of Saxony."]*

***

Biographers have defined the novelist, Erich Maria Remarque, as "extraordinarily good looking, deeply romantic, and a serial womanizer."

Arriving at the home of King and Elizabeth Vidor, Remarque, with Zsa Zsa on his arm, dazzled the celebrity-studded crowd. Their Romanov costumes were judged the most authentic at the party, except for that worn by the guest of honor herself, Grand Duchess Maria Pavlovna of Russia, who was the only *bona fide* Romanov there. Many stars, such as Clark Gable (who had already met Eva), Barbara Stanwyck, Kay Francis, Alice Faye, James Stewart, Fred Astaire, Henry Fonda, and director George Cukor, were introduced to Zsa Zsa for the first time. They would not forget her.

Many stars had heard of her. Her status had evolved from being the First Lady of Turkey to the last Empress of the Ottoman Empire. Her most vicious critics asserted that she'd had an affair with Josef Goebbels in Berlin.

Her most significant introduction was to Charles Chaplin, whose movie career was all but over. Chaplin seemed enchanted with Zsa Zsa's beauty, and within a week, they'd be engaged in a torrid affair.

As a touch of irony, Chaplin's estranged wife, the New York born actress Paulette Goddard, was also a guest at the ball. Zsa Zsa noted Remarque's eyes taking in the beautiful actress every time she walked past. Eventually, he would marry her.

Zsa Zsa later recalled, "Goddard would chalk up marriages to both of these world famous figures, Remarque and Chaplin, whereas I would get to enjoy their charms as only a passing interlude."

Chaplin already knew Remarque, and Zsa Zsa stood between the comedian and the novelist as they discussed Goddard. "She is a childlike creature of whim," Chaplin said, "entirely different from her screen roles. She is naïve,

209

just like a little child who must be handled gently. She knits my sweaters, and is a tomboy pal to my sons. I had wanted her to be in all my pictures, but, alas, that is not meant to be. In fact, in the future, even my movies are probably not meant to be, with perhaps an exception here and there."

Zsa Zsa's brief but passionate romance with Remarque was launched the night of the Romanov ball. "The most compelling thing about Erich was when he looked at you," she recalled. "He just seemed to pull you, like gravity, into his orbit. When the inevitable request came to join him in his boudoir, I was helpless. I had to give in to his desires. He was a world class lover."

For several weeks, she dated Remarque when he wasn't going out with Ingrid Bergman, or else taking detours to Joan Crawford's boudoir.

Gossip columnist Louella Parsons was a keen observer of Zsa Zsa's affair with Remarque, at least as it played out in public.

"It wasn't really a romance," Parsons proclaimed at parties, but not in print. "It was more of an escort thing. He was always perfectly groomed with those impeccable Continental manners. To me, he was a dour German whose spirits could be momentarily lifted by Zsa Zsa's effervescent personality. For a time, Greta Garbo chased after Remarque, but that was a case of the melancholy Prussian meeting the melancholy Swede."

When Remarque heard Parson's evaluation of him, he did not challenge it. He found Zsa Zsa a good and sympathetic listener to the tragedies of his life. He spoke frankly about his past:

"I am melancholy," he admitted. "It took me a while before I decided to write novels. I started out as a writer sending fashion dispatches from Paris to Berlin for publication in *Die Dame*. That's the German equivalent of *Vogue*. I also covered car races and wrote jingles for tire manufacturers—that is, when I wasn't playing the piano in an insane asylum."

In his dates with Zsa Zsa, she found he'd thought of everything in advance—the transportation, the choice of menu, reservations, even the most romantic setting for a seduction. "There would be two champagne cocktails—never more than that—followed by a sensual undressing," she said. "He'd made love to some of the world's most beautiful women, and he never left the bed of a lady, or so I gathered, until she was completely satisfied."

"When not performing in bed, he had a string of amusing stories to tell, some charming, others filled with horror. He was mildly interested in gossip, but mainly he still relived the horror of Nazi Germany. He predicted that Hitler would end up destroying half of Germany by inviting bombing from the Allies. We were not perfectly mated, though. He was very sedentary, spending hours in his library, whereas I was more gregarious."

"He claimed that it had been 'that little dwarf' *[a reference to Goebbels]* who kicked him out of Germany."

"The bastard made me surrender all my cash and my art collection before he'd grant me an exit visa," Remarque said. "Fortunately, most of my funds from *All Quiet on the Western Front,* which was the best-selling novel of the 20th century, was in non-German currencies in other countries, mainly France, England, and the United States. I had shipped out my Utrillos and Cézannes to Switzerland, so those paintings, at least, were safe."

"I could not convince one of my sisters, Elfriede Scholz, to flee from Germany. She remained behind with her husband and her two children, but I fear the Nazis will kill her just to get back at me."

[Remarque was right. In 1943, Goebbels ordered the arrest of Elfriede. In Hitler's extra-constitutional People's Court, she was found guilty of "undermining morale." She had previously stated that the Nazis would lose the war. Judge Roland Freisler declared, "Your traitor brother is unfortunately beyond our reach—however, you will not escape us. You will be beheaded on December 16, 1943."

As a final insult, the cost of Elfriede's court trial, imprisonment, and execution was billed to her sister, Erna Remarque.]

Today, I am a depressed Prussian in exile in the Land of the Lotus," Remarque lamented. "In my native land, I'm reviled as a 'Jew traitor.'"

"My brief time with Zsa Zsa is filled with happy memories." Remarque told his friends. "The openness of her face is its secret. She said what she believed. If she didn't like somebody or something, she did not conceal it. Her face promised nothing—and therefore, everything."

"My love affair with Erich was like picking a wild flower," Zsa Zsa said. "The blossom began to die almost from the moment it was plucked, even though you put it in water. He was the *grand*

During her romance with novelist Erich Maria Remarque, Zsa Zsa learned of his tragic past. One of his sisters, **Elfriede Scholz** *(photo above),* was sentenced to a "judicial murder, a beheading" on a charge of "undermining morale."

Ironically, Elfriede's husband at the time was a Nazi soldier, fighting in horrifying circumstances on the Eastern Front.

During happier times, a very young **Erich Maria Remarque** posed with his beautiful sisters, **Erna** *(left)* and **Elfriede** *(center).*

Each of the three would be punished and/or murdered as "payback" for Erich's role as a novelist and anti-Nazi dissident.

seigneur of my life, well versed in art and literature. I learned much from my most civilized suitor."

"I delighted in Zsa Zsa's youthful zest," he said. "She saw the world very differently from me and was a strong individualist filled with opinions, even if she didn't really know what she was talking about."

"Our affair inevitably came to an end," Remarque said. "It ended too soon, but it was inevitable. Two vigorous personalities such as ours could only clash. As I watched from afar as she moved into her future, I suspected that she would break not a few hearts and empty many bank accounts on her road to romance."

In the white heat of romance, he sent her a love letter when he was in New York and she was still in California.

"I love you more than yesterday, and yesterday more than before yesterday; that for the first time my life is full since I am with you. I love, adore, worship, and embrace you with every thought in the most pitiful way."

She cherished the letter until years later, when she read in biographies of movie stars that he'd sent the exact same letter to Greta Garbo, Marlene Dietrich, Hedy Lamarr, and Paulette Goddard.

***

One evening at twilight, Eva walked along Hollywood boulevard, looking for a bookstore. She wanted to find an encyclopedia-type volume that documented the famous stars of Hollywood, beginning with the Silent Films of the 1920s.

Every week, she was meeting actors with whom she was unfamiliar. In Budapest and in London, she'd seen only a limited number of American films and knew only the biggest name stars like Gary Cooper, Bette Davis, and Claudette Colbert. She had not seen the films of many of the newly minted stars like Alan Ladd, Veronica Lake, and Victor Mature.

At some point, she became aware of a slow-moving black limousine following her as she moved along the sidewalk. At first, she thought some driver was going that slowly because he was searching for a street address. But her intuition finally told her that she was being spied upon and stalked by whomever was sitting in the back seat of that limousine and issuing instructions to his driver.

At first, she was tempted to run inside a store and perhaps call the police. But she soon decided that she had made no enemies in America, and that no one would have any reason to want her dead. In her fantasy, she imagined that it was

212

some studio head or director who had spotted her walking, and who had decided on the spot that she should be in the movies.

If she ran away, she might be throwing away a career. She was not afraid, as she stopped by the curb and waited for the limousine to come to a stop, which it eventually did. The windows of the vehicle were blacked out, so she couldn't see who was seated in the rear. Then the uniformed chauffeur got out from behind the wheel and approached her.

"Miss Gabor, please forgive the intrusion," he said with a German accent. "But Mr. Benjamin Siegel is in the limousine, and he requests your presence. He is going to a big gala, where some of the top movie stars of Hollywood have been invited. He'd like to be your escort at this event."

"But I can't…" She tried to issue a mild protest, even though she was powerfully intrigued. "I have nothing to wear."

She agreed to talk to Bugsy, and the chauffeur opened the car's rear door for her. With trepidation, she climbed into the limousine to find a formally dressed Siegel inside. He looked strikingly handsome. She'd heard that like Greg Bautzer, Zsa Zsa's escort, Bugsy had actually turned down a Hollywood contract for starring roles as a leading man. To her, he looked as gorgeous as any top star in Hollywood.

Bugsy explained to her that a lavish party was being held in a private home north of the city, and that the Countess Dorothy di Frasso had taken sick at the last minute and could not attend. "I need to show up with a beautiful woman," he said. "If I arrive with just a male bodyguard, people will think I'm a homosexual."

"I doubt that anyone would think that about you, Mr. Siegel," she said. "*Not you.* Thank you for the invitation, but I'm not dressed properly."

"That will all be taken care of," he said, "after we arrive at the party. I telephoned your apartment and spoke to your sister, Zsa Zsa. She told me that I could locate you wandering from bookstore to bookstore on Hollywood Boulevard. I called this fag costume designer, George Orry-Kelly—Cary Grant used to be his kept boy—and ordered him to deliver a dozen gowns, the latest *couture* from Paris, to a bedroom over the club where I'm taking you."

"I have a perfect measuring rod in my head for determining a woman's size. Try on all of them until you find the one which makes you look best. As for the other eleven gowns, take them home as a present from me. Also, that diamond bracelet you'll find on your dressing table is also a gift from yours truly."

She was excited at the prospect, figuring that with her new wardrobe, she could compete with the fortune in *haute couture* that Zsa Zsa had acquired from the Grand Duchess Marie.

Driving north along the coast, she was thrilled, thinking she was heading for an exotic adventure.

He complimented her on her beauty. In response, she told him, "Forgive me for saying so, but you are the most perfectly groomed male I ever met."

"I work out at the Beverly Hills Athletic Club every day, and then spend an hour under the shower, one entire hour. I have my own special barber and hair stylist. I have my hair snipped and shaped very day. I'm also shaved, and the finest lotions are applied to my skin. My fingernails are brushed every day and applied with a fresh coating of neutral polish."

"I imagine that no actor in Hollywood facing the camera devotes that much time," she said. "It's amazing you find time to do anything else."

"The secret is that I almost never sleep," he said. "I believe I'll have plenty of time to sleep in the grave. In my profession, a man doesn't live to a ripe old age."

After driving north along the Pacific Coast Highway, Bugsy's chauffeur turned inland near the southern edge of Malibu. He headed up a steep driveway, stopping at a mammoth iron gate, where two well-armed security guards were posted.

"Good evening, Mr. Siegel," one of the guards said, immediately recognizing the male passenger in the back seat. The gate was opened.

Bugsy's car pulled into a lot filled mostly with Cadillacs and a scattering of Rolls Royces. Taking her arm, Bugsy escorted Eva to the main entrance of a mansion which looked like it belonged on the antebellum set of *Gone With the Wind.*

The mob loved to hear **Frank Sinatra**, "that skinny boy from Hoboken," sing at their gatherings—and they paid him well.

When Eva met him, it did not occur to her that Sinatra would one day become her ardent lover.

This is a very exclusive private club," he told Eva. "I'm a member. Wait till the guys get an eyeful of you."

The mansion's enormous steel-plated main door was opened by a dignified butler dressed in tails. She stood in the hallway under a trio of mammoth Murano crystal chandeliers.

"I'll meet you later at the reception," Bugsy said, conferring her to the care of a maid, who escorted her upstairs. She was dazzled when she stepped into a lavishly furnished suite. Spread out before her were a dozen Orry-Kelly gowns in various colors. She was tempted by the shocking pink and the canary yellow, but settled for a champagne-colored satin gown that showed off her *décolletage.*

214

"It made me look blonde all over," she later said.

Bugsy complimented her when she entered the reception room. He led her from there to a large dining room with a stage at one end. The room was filled with mostly middle-aged men who sat drinking whiskey and champagne at tables filled with a bevy of Hollywood beauties.

She was on her second glass of champagne when a speaker announced the appearance of Frank Sinatra, who had been hired to entertain the Mob that night. "You'll love his singing," Bugsy accurately predicted.

He was right. She'd met Sinatra before, but had never heard him sing until tonight. It would be the beginning of many such nights in her life.

"Frankie come out, sings a few numbers, and pockets $10,000 in cash," Bugsy told her.

At the end of his show, Sinatra joined Eva and Bugsy at table. "You're looking great, doll," he said to her. "Benjamin here sure knows how to pick 'em. I'm taking lessons from him."

Sinatra looked at the entrance. "I'm waiting for my shack-up tonight," he said.

In a few minutes, a rather gaudily dressed red-haired woman, wearing too much makeup, joined their table. She was introduced only as "a showgirl," and she seemed to already know both Sinatra and Bugsy.

"You're late, bitch!" Sinatra said to her. "Don't let it happen again, assuming there's going to be a next time."

After some idle chit-chat, Sinatra and the showgirl departed, and a short while later, Bugsy escorted Eva to the suite upstairs, where a maid had carefully laid out each of the gowns. "I know I promised you a diamond bracelet, but I was afraid one of the maids would steal it. He reached into his pocket and produced a stunning piece of jewelry.

She thanked him profusely.

Then a waiter delivered two bottles of chilled French champagne. Over a glass, he discussed her hopes for a film career and wondered how he might be of assistance.

"I was told I have the face and body to make it on the screen," she said.

"I agree on the face," he said. "As for the body, I need to see more of it so I can make a thorough evaluation."

"You're on," she told him.

He grabbed her and kissed her. As she'd later tell Susan Hayward, "He practically ripped off my gown. I had to have a seamstress repair it before I could wear it again. He was ever so eager."

She had little to say about the actual seduction, only telling Greta Keller that, "I now know why Mae West and Marlene Dietrich keep dialing Bugsy's private number."

That night marked the beginning of a torrid but troubled friendship. Eva would later deny even knowing Bugsy, although they were seen together by dozens of people. She did tell Hayward, "My affair with him was made all the more exciting because you never knew when assassins would break down the door and blow us away with a machine gun."

***

As Eva continued to date Bugsy Siegel in secret, she became aware of where she stood in the pecking order. First came Countess Dorothy di Frasso, whom Eva already knew. Next in line and moving rapidly toward the top of the list was the beautiful Virginia Hill, the ultimate gun moll for the mob.

A distant third was Wendy Barrie, an English actress who'd shot to fame in *The Private Life of Henry VIII.* Since her migration to Hollywood, she'd been starring in "B" pictures, often quickie vehicles. Rumor had it that her film career was stalled because of her close association with Bugsy.

Eva did not want to endure the same fate, so she remained a distant fourth in Bugsy's life and was only linked with him in the press three or four times, most of them obscure references, long forgotten.

Although powerfully drawn to Bugsy sexually, she did not want his notoriety to adversely affect her career.

Ultimately, she came to conclude that Hill was the only woman Bugsy ever loved. At the time when all these women, among others, were dating Bugsy, he also had a wife and two daughters. In 1929, he'd married Esta Krakower, his childhood sweetheart and the sister of contract killer Whitey Krakower. The late Jean Harlow, Bugsy's former flame, had been the godmother of his daughter, Millicent.

As the underworld's greatest beauty, **Virginia Hill** led a lurid life.

Reporter Ed Reid claimed, "She was a flesh-and-blood computer of silk, satin, and a whore's instincts."

Hill herself was the most notorious gun moll in the history of America, having slept with most of the Mob's big name crooks before Bugsy discovered her. A beautiful, auburn-haired green-eyed Southern belle from Alabama, Hill was one of ten children, the daughter of a hard-drinking mule trader and tombstone polisher.

Making her way to Chicago while still a teenager, she had been cast in a girly show called "Elephants & Fleas" at Chicago's Century of Progress Exposition. There, she'd attracted the attention of gangster Joe Epstein, who became her sugar daddy. Her trail of gangster lovers eventually

216

led to Bugsy Siegel.

For his second night of seduction, Bugsy drove Eva to Falcon's Lair, the former home in Los Angeles of Rudolf Valentino. Hill, who had temporarily leased it, was in Chicago at the time.

Eva had seen only one of Valentino's pictures, but she at least knew who he was.

[Valentino's biographer, Emily W. Leider, defined Valentino as "the ultimate Hollywood heartthrob, though often called a tango pirate, gigolo, powder puff, and Adonis. His androgynous sexuality was a lightning rod for fiery and contradictory impulses that ran the gamut from swooning adoration to lashing resentment. The press often reviled him for being too feminine for a man, although millions of women found him the alluring savage lover who embodied women's forbidden sexual fantasies, including rape."

Near the upper terminus of Benedict Canyon, Falcon's Lair, at 2 Bella Drive, was a two-level, sixteen-room Spanish-style villa with a red tile roof, stucco walls, grand fireplaces, and wood-beamed ceilings. In its heyday, it had been the setting for lavish parties attended by neighbors who had included Charlie Chaplin, John Gilbert, Marion Davies, Buster Keaton, Harold Lloyd, Mary Pickford, and Douglas Fairbanks, Sr.

"It was a fun evening," Eva later recalled to Zsa Zsa and Greta Keller. "Bugsy dressed up like *The Sheik* that Rudolf Valentino had played on the screen. We fantasized that Valentino's bed was actually an Arabian tent in which he planned to rape me and make me his woman. It was so, so romantic."

As a result of moving within Bugsy's orbit, it was inevitable that Eva would eventually meet gangster-actor George Raft, one of Bugsy's closest friends and his chief mentor on the Hollywood scene. Along with James Cagney, Humphrey Bogart, and Edward G. Robinson, Raft had epitomized the movie gangster of the 1930s. He'd been the lover of Mae West (his *Night After Night* co-star in '32), nightclub owner Texas Guinan (famous for her phrase, "Hello, suckers!"), Billie Dove (when she wasn't giving Howard Hughes

The stars and hookers **George Raft** bedded—ranging from Lucille Ball to Lana Turner and Mae West—referred to his penis as "Black Snake."

His closest friend, Mack Grey, claimed, "Screwing was his game. He could get it up in the morning and put in a whole day at it."

As he appeared in the 1921 silent classic *The Sheik*, heartthrob **Rudolf Valentino** *(photo above)* and George Raft were gigolo dancers working the "tea rooms," hustling rich female patrons out of their money.

When not dancing with women and prostituting themselves to them, these roommates made love to each other.

syphilis), Marlene Dietrich, and Carole Lombard (his co-star in the 1934 *Bolero)*.

Raft sounded an ominous note when Siegel excused himself to visit the men's room. When Bugsy was out of earshot, Raft told Eva, "Bugsy—and I never call him that to his face—is fearless, more than any man I know. When danger threatens, he's the first man to jump into the fray. He starts shooting while the rest of us pansies are still sitting around trying to figure how to bump off a squealer. No man has more guts than Bugsy Siegel."

Even the cheerfully optimistic Betty Grable, the pin-up Queen of millions of U.S. soldiers during the horrors of World War II, got involved with Raft. When her husband, bandleader Harry James was away, on tour with his "Music Makers," Grable often dated Raft, occasionally joining Bugsy and Eva in their nightclub visits. One night at Ciro's, Eva had watched as Grable and Raft

stepped onto the dance floor together. "It was the sexiest dance I'd ever seen a couple perform. Raft told us that he was the world's first X-rated dancer. 'I was very erotic,' he told me. 'I used to caress myself as I danced.'"

During one of the their double dates, when Raft and Bugsy drifted off to the men's room together, Grable told Eva that Raft had fallen for her when she was fourteen years old and had a small role in the film *Palmy Days* (1931) in which he'd starred. "After a few frustrating dates, he decided to wait a year or two for me to grow up. From the first time I slept with him, I referred to his dick as 'Black Snake,'" she said.

[In the 1930s, Raft and Valentino lived together as sometimes lovers. Both of them spent their evenings working as gigolo dancers in the "tea rooms" of New York City. Female patrons selected one or the other, paying them to dance with them. Later, both Raft and Valentino rented themselves out as

Betty Grable posed with her back to the camera in this picture that became the most famous pinup of World War II. Some soldiers even took it to the trenches with them.

Why is her back to the camera? Because she was pregnant at the time. Unknown to her, she also had a condom that had become entrapped within her vagina for four months, which caused Tyrone Power to break up with her because of the smell.

male hustlers. Sometimes a rich woman took both of them home to bed.

Grable later dropped Raft, preferring Harry James instead. She claimed Raft was a "latent homosexual. During our affair, he spent more time beating me than bedding me."]

On the town with Eva, Bugsy "greased" his way into the town's poshest places—The Cocoanut Grove, the Brown Derby, Romanoff's, and Ciro's—with hundred dollar bills.

Bugsy dated his gun moll, Virginia Hill, more frequently than he did Eva. Once night when she was available, Eva accepted an invitation from Errol Flynn for an evening at Romanoff's.

It was at this celebrity-studded restaurant that Eva once again spotted Hill. "She was sitting at a table with Bugsy, and they were talking with Humphrey Bogart. Bugsy had certainly been good to his mistress. I'd gotten a diamond bracelet from Bugsy, but this Hill dame was dripping in sable and sparkling with so many diamonds and rubies she looked like a Christmas tree."

Siegel included among his friends and associates some of Hollywood's top movie stars, as well as many of the leading gangsters of the 30s and 40s, especially Charles ("Lucky") Luciano, Frank Costello, Albert Anastasia, Vito Genovese, and Joe Adonis.

One weekend, Bugsy invited Eva to Palm Springs, where they stayed in a villa owned by Mickey Cohen, Siegel's chief lieutenant. Eva thought Cohen was charming enough, but asserted that he resembled "an ugly toad."

On several occasions, Bugsy took Eva to the horse races at Santa Anita Park, near Los Angeles, where he bet heavily (and often successfully, thanks to inside information) on the outcomes. To the IRS, Bugsy claimed he earned his living through legal gambling.

In September of 1941, it looked like Bugsy's world was suddenly unraveling. To Eva's shock and horror, he was charged with murder.

***

As two glamour-obsessed sisters living the high life in Hollywood, Eva and Zsa Zsa were dismayed when they discovered that their joint bank account had dwindled to less than one-hundred dollars. Zsa Zsa inaugurated a scheme to sell more of her jewelry, but during the Depression, the gem market had become glutted as bankrupt once-rich people pawned their gold, silver, diamonds, and rubies. Complicating matters, many European Jews, fleeing Nazi death camps, had often escaped with no money, only their smuggled jewelry, flooding an already-depressed market with undervalued ornaments.

Both Eva and Zsa Zsa still had their wardrobes and enough jewelry to wear to parties, but very little cash for food or rent.

Eva was even tempted, in a desperate measure, to sell the diamond bracelet Bugsy Siegel had given her. When she went to the bank to draw out most of their remaining savings for payment of back rent, she was astonished to find that some mysterious donor had deposited $10,000 into their account. She immediately suspected that the largesse had come from Bugsy before he was hauled off to jail.

She'd later tell Zsa Zsa, "It felt like I'd broken the bank at Monte Carlo."

Both sisters were relieved by their reprieve from financial disaster. They continued their pursuit of careers in films, but no prospects opened for them. Their phone calls went unanswered. "Samuel Goldwyn, Louis B. Mayer, and Darryl F. Zanuck would have us as trinkets to show off at parties—we're Hungarian *exotica*—but they don't want to put us on the screen," Eva said.

"Maybe on our backs," Zsa Zsa retorted,

Lady Mendl didn't seem to have any time for Zsa Zsa after meeting her again in Hollywood. But after she was introduced to Eva, the socialite changed her mind and invited both Eva and Zsa Zsa to a catered luncheon in Bel Air.

Each of the sisters dressed carefully, wanting to appear elegant but not too ostentatious in daylight. Jolie had told them, "Don't sparkle too much during the day…If you do, it will diminish your glitter in the evening."

Deciding to splurge on a taxi, both Eva and Zsa Zsa looked stylish in designer dresses and high heels when they were ushered out onto a terrace for their reunion with Lady Mendl. She immediately complained about the heat. "California is better suited to rattlesnakes than to people. Give me Mayfair any day."

Over a pre-luncheon cocktail, Zsa Zsa and Eva were given permission to call Lady Mendl "Elsie." *[Her maiden name had been Elsie de Wolfe]*

"I have several commissions for interior decoration here in Hollywood," she said. "It seems that I'm the first woman interior designer in America. Up to now, that profession seems to have been the exclusive domain of homosexual men such as that actor, William Haines."

Born in 1865, the year America's Civil War came to an end, Lady Mendl seemed fully aware that she had entered "the September of my years. Actually, it's something more akin to December, really."

Several times, she complimented Eva and Zsa Zsa on their beauty. "I bet your parents in Budapest constantly praised your stunning looks," she said. "Not in my case. Both of my parents repeatedly told me what an ugly girl I was when I was growing up. My mother's cousin, the theologian, Dr. Archibald Charteris, was Queen Victoria's chaplain at Balmoral Castle in Scotland."

"When I turned seventeen, he arranged for

Les Grandes Desmoiselles

Long before gay marriage was even an idea, **Elsie de Wolfe** *(right)*, later known as Lady Mendl, lived in a loving relationship with **Elisabeth Marbury** *(left)*, the literary agent of both Oscar Wilde and George Bernard Shaw.

220

me to be presented at the Court of St. James's in London. Overnight, the ugly duckling became a swan. That night, at an elegant gala, I was the belle of the ball. I decided to show such sparkling wit, like you ladies, that I was soon invited to all the big London society parties."

"One night I met Elisabeth Marbury, the playwright's agent. She became the love of my life. Soon, we were being entertained by her favorite clients, Oscar Wilde and George Bernard Shaw. The press described us as 'willowy de Wolfe and the masculine Marbury.' In Manhattan, we purchased Washington Irving's home on Irving Place."

"We spent the summers at Versailles. *[In 1903, Marbury had purchased a villa on the grounds of the palace at Versailles.]* When I was sixty years old, I married Sir Charles Mendl. I did it for three reasons: The publicity, the money, and the title—each a valid motivation in its own right. Please retain that bit of wisdom when you're older."

After their luncheon together, Eva retained fond memories of Lady Mendl. She once told an interviewer, "She was the first woman I ever met who dyed her hair blue. She could do headstands well into her 70s. And how many women do you know who flew on an airplane with Wilbur Wright in 1908?"

Before Zsa Zsa and Eva kissed Lady Mendl goodbye, she confided to them her secrets for "living the fabulous life."

"All of these things, pastiche, *good clothes, vitality, love of adventure, lively interests, must fail unless one waves over them the magic wand of self-control and a cheerful attitude towards life. Nothing ages a woman like worry or a bad temper. I try always to be an optimist. I refrain from discussing my troubles. Never complain, never explain. Complaints create discontent, and they are ruinous to the equanimity which makes the wheels of life turn smoothly. As for explanations, they require too much energy and they are often futile."*

Both of the Gabor sisters later asserted, "Lady Mendl gave us our credo for living."

***

Zsa Zsa

Throughout America, Hedy Lamarr had become an overnight sensation when she appeared with Charles Boyer *["Come with me to the Casbah"]* in *Algiers* (1938). She followed that with one hit after another—*Lady of the Tropics* (1939) with Robert Taylor; *I Take This Woman* (1940) with Spencer Tracy; *Boom Town* (1940) with Spencer Tracy again, but this time with Clark

Gable in the lead; and *Comrade X* (1940), once again with Gable. Except for Boyer, Lamarr slept with all three of these leading men.

She had married screenwriter and producer Gene Markey, but was planning to divorce him.

[Markey had more or less "sandwiched" his affair with Lamarr between marriages to other actresses, as he'd previously wed Joan Bennett and would later marry Myrna Loy, while simultaneously maintaining an affair with Lucille Ball when Desi Arnaz was out of town.]

Lamarr had heard that Zsa Zsa, whom she'd previously befriended in Vienna, was in Hollywood, but had been unable to reach her until she encountered Eva at a party.

Within the week, Lamarr called Zsa Zsa and invited Eva and her to her residence for dinner. *[Shortly before their arrival that day, Lamarr had bid adieu to James Stewart after a session of "love-in-the-afternoon." They'd completed the filming of* Come Live with Me *(1941). As Stewart recalled, "I polluted myself with Hedy." That was his expression at the time for having seduced a woman with whom, presumably, he was not in love.]*

The Gabors were informed that the opera diva, Budapest-born Ilona Massey, would also be attending their dinner. In Hungary, Massey had been a friend of Jolie.

As Lady Mendl archly observed, "There seem to be an awful lot of good-looking blondes from Central Europe running around Hollywood these days, each a candidate for a role in a Viennesse operetta. **Ilona Massey** *(photo above)* is an example of what I mean."

[Billed as "the new Dietrich," Massey had been introduced to American audiences in Rosalie *(1937), a glossy operetta in which she'd co-starred with Nelson Eddy. She did not live up to her billing. Her voice was deemed as too light for the screen, and her acting talent, such as it was, was too slight and too mannered. After her meeting with the Gabors, she would interpret the role of Baroness Frankenstein in* Frankenstein Meets the Wolf Man *(1943), opposite Lon Chaney, Jr.*

Massey had married the former model turned actor, Alan Curtis, but was in the process of divorcing him. They had co-starred together in New Wine *(1941), a movie about Franz Schubert (1797-1828), the Austrian composer.*

The Gabors immediately promised to go see New Wine. *Massey said, "In real life, Schubert was chubby and homely, but my Alan, even though I'm divorcing him, is slim and handsome."*

Maasey ended up playing a femme fatale *spy in the last "official" Marx Brothers comedy,* Love

Happy *(1949), in which she had to compete with another blonde, an upcoming starlet named Marilyn Monroe.*

The last Zsa Zsa ever heard from Massey was in 1959, when she asked her to join her in front of the United Nations, protesting the arrival in New York of Soviet premier Nikita Khrushchev. To the American press, Massey denounced the dictator for the "rape of my native Hungary."

Zsa Zsa did not show up as part of the organized protest, telling friends, "Of course, I'm horrified at what the Soviets are doing to my beloved Hungary. But I'm just not the street fighter type, like Magda during the war. My guerilla activities are best demonstrated in the bedroom loving, not fighting."]

Regrettably, the meeting or reunion of these four women—Eva, Zsa Zsa, Hedy, and Ilona—was not filmed. They were among the four most beautiful women to ever emerge from Central Europe.

The champagne flowed, and there was much babbling in Hungarian and German about what a failure men were. Zsa Zsa and Eva had already divorced their respective first husbands, and divorces for both Hedy and Ilona were being finalized.

Massey told the Gabors that in Budapest, she had never experienced the rich, elegant life they had. "I knew nothing but misery and hunger, and I didn't know the taste of meat until I was seven years old. I was raised on Sauerkraut. Today, I'm well fed, well dressed, and have a home. What else is there for me to want?"

"A rich husband," said Zsa Zsa.

The Gabors learned that Lamarr had lived with Massey when she'd first arrived in Hollywood.

"She buried the English language after I murdered it," Lamarr said, jokingly.

"When we weren't dating, we spent our nights perfecting our English, or at least trying to," Massey said. "We made countless mistakes. When I met Clark Gable, he taught me one of my first phrases in English. I was to come up to a man and say, 'I want you to fuck me.'"

Zsa Zsa envied Lamarr's success in Hollywood, but the MGM star seemed disenchanted with her life and her career. "I changed my name. Louis B. Mayer renamed me Lamarr after Barbara La Marr of the silent screen. I had to change my native-speaking voice and suppress my ethnicity and former background in Austria, especially the Nazi links of my former husband, Fritz Mandl. I slimmed down my body and whittled away at my soul until I had no soul left to inhabit. That's what Hollywood does for you. After a while, you don't know who you are."

"You may be right about that," Zsa Zsa said, her imagination fueled by the champagne and the company. "Instead of a career, I think I'll become a housewife. Of course, I'll insist that my husband provide me with two dozen servants to run a forty-five room household. I'll need an annual wardrobe budget of $250,000, and I'll insist that I have three custom-made automobiles in my private garage. Naturally, I will need a private butler who resembles Robert Montgomery as he was in 1932."

"Not me," Eva said. "I want to become the biggest star in Hollywood since Jean Harlow."

"That's all right with me, providing you don't dye your hair brunette," Lamarr said. "I've got a lock on sultry brunette roles for years to come."

[Discussing her reunion with Lamarr during the years that followed, Zsa Zsa became catty: "Hedy claimed she detested Hitler, but I noticed that she carried around the gold cigarette case the Führer *had given her when she was still married to Fritz Mandl. On it was embedded a diamond-studded swastika."*

Zsa Zsa and Lamarr were friends at the time of their reunion dinner with Ilona and Eva in Los Angeles, but in their future, they would ferociously compete for some of the same men, including Charlie Chaplin, Errol Flynn, Erich Maria Remarque, and at one point, a young John F. Kennedy. Their bitter denunciations over who had "bedding rights" to actor George Sanders, along with their ongoing competition for the same movie roles, eventually ended their friendship.]

As the evening wound down, Eva grew tipsy and fell asleep on the sofa in Hedy's living room. When Massey and Zsa Zsa departed together for Ciro's on a manhunt, Lamarr promised Zsa Zsa that she would see that Eva got home safely in a taxi.

Eva never told Zsa Zsa exactly what happened the night she slept over at Lamarr's house, but she exited hurriedly from the building at three o'clock in the morning. She later admitted to Susan Hayward that Lamarr, in a *négligée,* had entered her bedroom during the early morning hours and had made advances to her. "I told Hedy that even though she was a very beautiful woman, I did not go that route."

Her boss, Louis B. Mayer, defined **Hedy Lamarr** *(photo above)* as "The world's most beautiful woman."

After the MGM mogul saw her running nude through the woods in *Extase* (1932), he put her under contract, warning her that "At MGM we make only decent films. And don't tell anyone that your husband (Fritz Mandl) makes munitions for Hitler."

[Unknown to the Gabors at the time, Lamarr seduced women as well as men, as she admitted in her 1966 autobiography, Ecstasy and Me: My Life as a Woman. *Her lesbian life began at a Swiss boarding school and continued throughout her sojourn at MGM, when she seduced several women*

in the studio's wardrobe department, and several starlets as well. "The men in my life have ranged from a classic history of impotence to a knife-wielding sadist who enjoyed sex only after he'd tied my arms behind me with the sash of his robe."

Long after her older adult fans of the 1940s had departed from this Earth, Lamarr would improve the lives of 21st-century consumers, even if many of them didn't know who she was. She's been credited as "The Mother of the Cellphone." During World War II, she patented an early system of causing radio signals to hop from frequency to frequency—a means at the time of scrambling communications and concealing their content from hostile agents. That technology later evolved into an essential component of cellphone transmissions.

Lamarr patented her invention with George Antheil, the composer and concert pianist who had helped her develop it. In 1959, their patent expired.]

***

A few nights later, Zsa Zsa herself became disenchanted with Lamarr for a very different reason. Zsa Zsa had spent a great deal of her dinner with Lamarr extolling the virtues of Erich Maria Remarque. "I have practically forced him to sign a blood oath that he prefers me to that German trollop, Dietrich."

Dining at Ciro's with Greg Bautzer, Zsa Zsa spotted Lamarr in the distance, entering the restaurant with Remarque, each of them beautifully dressed. Zsa Zsa was horrified. "The bitch didn't even let on that she knew Erich. But now I realize that she has made me look like a fool."

Bautzer seemed to know all the secrets of every star in Hollywood. He told Zsa Zsa that Remarque and Lamarr had had a torrid affair in 1937 at the chic Swiss resort, St. Moritz.

Their affair lasted until she left for London. "That's when Erich met the love of his life—Marlene Dietrich," Bautzer said. "Hedy has all the qualities that Erich demands in a woman: Stunning beauty, talent as an actress, sophistication, a fluency in German, and a *louche* reputation."

As witnessed by Bautzer, Zsa Zsa sighed in despair. "Other than Clark Gable and Robert Taylor, the two most desirable bachelors in Hollywood are Erich Maria Remarque and a certain handsome devil with an endowment larger than it should be: Greg Bautzer. For these prizes, I must compete with some of the most desirable women on the planet—Hedy Lamarr, Marlene Dietrich, the list goes on. In your case, we can add Ingrid Bergman and Dorothy Lamour, in a sarong, no less. Not to mention a very young Lana Turner."

"Now Zsa Zsa, you must admit that you like playing the field like any man with a roving eye," Bautzer said. "You haven't taken up yet with Charlie Chaplin, Errol Flynn, and Howard Hughes, but that's only a matter of time."

In addition to being a savvy lawyer with a prestigious list of movie star clients, Bautzer was also blessed with the gift of prophecy.

***

Eva avidly followed the legal troubles of Bugsy Siegel, who in September of 1941 was charged with murder. Murder, Inc. was accused of killing Harry ("Big Greenie") Greenberg, who was threatening to become an informant for the police. Bugsy was accused of ordering Big Greenie's murder before he could deliver, in court, evidence against Bugsy's criminal activities.

Bugsy was arrested and taken into custody, where Superior Court Judge Arthur Crum ordered that he be held without bail, because it was suspected that he'd take flight before the trial. Bugsy hired the famed Hollywood attorney, Jerry Giesler, to defend him.

A high-profile criminal lawyer, Giesler was on the dawn of defending both Errol Flynn and Charlie Chaplin in two separate cases, both of which involved alleged sexual misconduct.

Bugsy's arrest became notorious because of the preferential treatment provided to the gangster during his incarceration. Over a period of forty-nine days, he was granted eighteen "jail leaves," from 9am to 4pm, ostensibly to allow a dentist to work on his teeth. An examination by a prison dentist, however, revealed that he had perfect teeth.

During one of those leaves, Clark Gable and his wife, Carole Lombard, spotted Bugsy entering Lindy's Restaurant with the actress Wendy Barrie on his arm.

On three of his jail leaves, Bugsy ordered a bullet-proof limousine to pick up Eva and deliver her to his palatial thirty-five room mansion in Beverly Hills. She later told Susan Hayward, "I arrived in time for a late breakfast, and we made love all day until he had to return to the jailhouse at around four that afternoon."

Bugsy told Eva that he'd hired "a pretty young man—very effeminate—to take care of me in jail, serving as my personal valet. He even irons my uniforms."

Before entering prison, Bugsy had ordered his tailor to create couture versions of prison uniforms from soft material, because he'd objected to wearing the same prison garb of the other inmates. He also ordered that his meals be catered by Romanoff's, because "I can't swallow the shitty grub these losers eat." His favorite dish, which he requested two or three times a week, was roasted pheasant.

One headline blared: *BUGSY GETS RED CARPET TREATMENT IN*

HOOSEGOW.

In January of 1942, to the horror of law enforcement agents, the indictment against Bugsy was dropped because of insufficient evidence.

Within days, Bugsy resumed his social life among the elite of Hollywood, and he was seen escorting the Countess Dorothy di Frasso, Wendy Barrie, or Eva to exclusive Hollywood parties.

Carole Lombard had died in a recent airplane crash on January 16, 1942, during a tour selling war bonds. She'd been rushing back to Hollywood in bad weather to rescue Clark Gable from the arms of Lana Turner. Shortly afterward, Bugsy was released from prison. Free at last, he visited Gable on several occasions, finding him "morbidly depressed, almost suicidal."

Bugsy decided that the best way to conquer Gable's "gloom and doom was to get him laid." One night, he proposed to Gable that he spend an evening with Eva, whom he'd met and had been attracted to at a Hollywood party.

"At first, I thought I should turn down the invitation," Eva confided to Susan Hayward. "After all, I'm not a common prostitute. But Clark was the King of Hollywood. Who in Hollywood was turning him down?—not Lana, not Loretta Young, not Marion Davies, not Norma Shearer, and certainly not the late Jean Harlow or Lupe Velez. He had them all. He didn't even say no to director George Cukor, who seduced him back when he was a struggling young actor."

Eva and Gable agreed to meet at his residence for a private dinner. Prior to that, Gable had been spending most of his evenings being consoled by his long-time flame, Joan Crawford.

At nine o'clock one evening, Bugsy's chauffeur delivered Eva, with Bugsy in tow, to Gable's residence. After a drink with them, the gangster disappeared, leaving Eva alone with Gable.

Eva never told Zsa Zsa what happened that night, but she did confide in Hayward.

In the bedroom where Gable had made frequent love to Lombard, he asked Eva to wear a gown designed for his late wife by Irene Sharaff. He also asked her to spray herself with Lombard's favorite perfume.

"It was spooky," Eva told Hayward. "It was as if he wanted me to become the reincarnation of Lombard. I felt very uncomfortable. Not only that, but the sex was no good. I was relieved later when he ordered a taxi for me."

Magda

"I should have warned you," Hayward said. "Even before Carole's death, Clark was known as a lousy lay."

***

It had all begun at the Ritz Hotel in London, weeks before the invasion of Poland. Magda was still married to her tall, well-

227

muscled count, Jan de Bychowsky, but she didn't love him any more, if she ever did. The thrill of being the Countess of Warsaw had quickly faded.

At the hotel's reception for ambassadors to London, Magda had depleted her household budget on the purchase of a stunning white gown created in one of the *haute couture* houses of Paris. She'd visited London's best hair stylist, who had previously styled the hair of actresses Vivien Leigh and Merle Oberon. As Magda told him when he'd created a new look for her, "My flaming red hair looks…well, like it's on fire. *Vonderful!*"

As she walked into the reception with her handsome, broad-shouldered count, once a celebrated member of the Polish Light Cavalry, all eyes turned to gaze upon her. The room was buzzing as to her identity. During one of Zsa Zsa's many trips to London, she had become the toast of the city. Now, it was Magda's turn to dazzle.

She was in the throes of what reporters would later label "the Gabor curse," meaning a roving eye for every man and a tendency for what one writer called "sexual wandering."

Their eyes met simultaneously. He was the distinguished Dr. Carlos Almeida Afonseca de Sampayo Garrido, the Ambassador Plenipotentiary for Portugal in Budapest, who was in the middle of a short ambassadorial visit to London.

As he recorded in his diary, "Her hair was the color of the reddest leaf that falls in the autumn. She had almost dancing eyes that sparkled from their darkest recesses which spoke of mystery and intrigue. Her skin was the color of the whitest porcelain. Including her lips and her nose, her face looked as if chiseled by the most talented of sculptors. I immediately fell under her spell."

Within a few weeks of meeting Dr. Garrido, Magda had followed his trail back to Budapest.

Although Dr. Garrido never told her his age, he was approximately sixty-five years old when his affair with her began. He was a diplomat of the old school, and often appeared in a morning coat with gray spats. Distinguished-looking, he appeared to be no more than fifty years old.

***

In 1941, reunited with Jolie in Budapest, and delighted to be out of war-ravaged Warsaw, Magda told her mother that she'd become Dr. Garrido's "secretary." But from the way she described him, Jolie knew there was so much more to the relationship than that.

During one of her first nights after her return to Budapest, Magda asked Jolie to prepare an authentic Hungarian dinner for her new "boss."

The ambassador arrived for dinner with a bottle of aged French cognac.

Jolie found him enchanting. They spoke of the war and Hitler, which was the talk of everybody at any gathering.

In his capacity as the Portuguese ambassador to Hungary, Dr. Garrido was perceived as a liberal within a Europe that was "swimming in a sea of fascism." Goebbels had sent several cables to the Portuguese dictator, Antonio Salazar, urging that Dr. Garrido be replaced with a diplomat who was more reassuringly pro-Nazi.

Dr. Garrido was keenly aware of the Jewish blood in the Gabor family, and he understood the potential danger the family faced.

Back in Budapest, Magda fell in love with **Dr. Carlos Garrido**. He was Portugal's ambassador to Hungary and an avowed anti-Nazi.

Through him, Magda became a heroine of the Hungarian Underground, secretly battling the forces of Hitler then occupying her homeland.

The morning after her dinner, Jolie telephoned Magda at her apartment. "*Dahlink,* Carlos is divine. But he should be pursuing an affair with me instead of with my oldest daughter. During the coming months, though, he may be very useful to us. I'm sure you will be glad that you took up with such a powerful man. After all, the embassies of the Western democracies have already fled from Budapest."

Within a few weeks of the debut of her working relationship with Dr. Garrido, Magda became aware of his precarious health. "I might look good on the outside, but inside, I'm falling apart. I have a very bad heart. At any minute I could go."

She was horrified to learn this news, and was even more alarmed when he showed her a dozen glass vials which he'd obtained in Zurich. "If you ever see me keel over, or perhaps collapse on the floor, tear the cap off one of these vials and pour the contents into my mouth. Hopefully, I'll be able to swallow. If you don't, I'll have only minutes to live."

One Friday afternoon, in anticipation of a weekend in the country, Dr. Garrido's chauffeur drove them to his summer villa in the Budapest suburb of Galgagyörk, some thirty miles from the city limits.

He strolled with her hand in hand through the ten acres of gardens and parks which surrounded a once-fortified Magyar castle dating from the early 1600s.

Before nightfall, she learned that the site was a centerpiece of anti-Nazi espionage, some of which was conducted from within nearby caves where Hungarian partisans found safe havens stocked with food, wine, blankets, medicine, and clothing.

In the basement of the castle, three experts labored at monitoring devices,

229

having learned how to decipher the codes the Nazis used in their transmissions between Berlin and the German embassy in Budapest. "We want to know what Hitler is telling his SS. It's well known in the diplomatic community that the *Führer* is a raving lunatic."

Within a short time, Magda became an acknowledged member of the Hungarian Underground. Only Jolie would know about this, as she did not feel it was safe to tell Vilmos, who would probably have opposed it based on fears for his daughter's safety.

Jolie told Magda, "You are the bravest of my daughters, but I fear for your life. Eva and Zsa Zsa are living luxurious lives in Hollywood in and out of the beds of every handsome movie star in California. You, Magda, are a true patriot."

Dr. Garrido was aware of the inner secrets of the Hungarian government, and for reasons of his own, he wanted to rescue and protect Hungarian Jews. When he'd first arrived in Budapest during October of 1938, there were about 800,000 Jews living in Hungary.

Dr. Garrido and Magda were systematically invited to dinners and receptions staged by Miklós Horthy, who held the title "His Serene Highness the Regent of the Kingdom of Hungary." He'd achieved the rank of admiral in the Austro-Hungarian Navy.

Under pressure from Nazi Berlin, Horthy had sponsored the first Hungarian anti-Jewish law in 1938, which had limited the numbers of Jews in the government and in professions which included law, medicine, and academia. Although he'd publicly defined himself as an anti-Semite, his actions proved otherwise. As the war deepened, he became more protective of Hungary's Jews than many of his colleagues.

Horthy was aware of Magda's Jewish blood, but always treated her like a grand lady, addressing her as "Countess."

According to Dr. Garrido, Horthy had an uneasy alliance with Hitler and the two men often sparred. Eventually, the *Führer* would arrange for Horthy's overthrow. At the outbreak of war, Horthy had allied himself with Hitler primarily because he feared an invasion from the Soviets. Dr. Garrido claimed, "He's obsessed with the communist threat. His attacks on Stalin are almost psychotic— not that Stalin doesn't deserve them."

In his struggle to define the lesser of two evils, Horthy committed Hungary, with great reluctance, to the Axis agenda, inciting western journalists to label Hungary as "the Jackal of Europe."

In June of 1941, Hungary became part of "Operation Barbarossa," and declared war on the Soviet Union. It sent troops to invade, fighting alongside the Nazis during their siege of Leningrad.

The first massacre of Jewish people on Hungarian territory took place two months later. Near the end of summer of 1941, some 20,000 Hungarian deportees were slaughtered by SS troops. This was the first large-scale massacre of the Holocaust.

Within a relatively short time, Magda became one of the heroines of World War II. In Budapest, she drove a truck for the International Red Cross. Thanks to the influence of Dr. Garrido, she had a high priority driver's permit, and as such, she was allowed to bring aid to wounded Polish soldiers. Many of them had been moved to a Nazi-controlled Prisoner of War camp, and were living in horrible conditions on the outskirts of Budapest

She brought them food and clothing, which she'd rounded up from the attics of partisans in Budapest. In exchange for their Polish army uniforms, they were given civilian clothing as a means of camouflaging their eventual escapes to the West.

Magda was terrified during her morning visits to the camp. SS guards in their ominous black uniforms often stopped a vehicle and shot its driver and occupants merely because they looked suspicious.

As a Red Cross Worker, Magda in time was credited with aiding some 4,500 Hungarian and Polish soldiers. Several hundred managed a hazardous escape to neutral Portugal, and some of them even made it to England. Many of these defeated soldiers would otherwise have been slaughtered, even though many were seriously wounded or crippled for life.

One of the SS soldiers guarding the entrance of the POW camp was a big, beefy German known as Heinz. He was particularly obnoxious to Magda and made lewd propositions to her. At one point he

Miklós ("Nicholas") Horthy (*top photo. on the cover of an English-language version of his memoirs*) ruled uncomfortably as the Regent of Hungary, maintaining an uneasy and much-compromised association with the Nazis.

Referring to how he was forced to take sides— Adolf Hitler vs. Josef Stalin—Horthy lamented "The English have a word for it: 'Caught between a rock and a hard place. Both of them were bloody butchers.'"

In 1938, a commemorative postcard was issued, depicting both **Hitler** and **Horthy**, with Horthy's much-respected wife, **Magdolna**, configured almost as a Holy Intermediary, "trapped" in the middle.

231

pulled out his penis. "Now tell me, 'Flame,' see what I've got that's a big as any salami in Hungary." She endured his lecherous behavior only as a means of entering the camp, where many prisoners came to view her as a sainted version of Florence Nightingale.

Medical supplies were limited, but she brought what she could to dress the wounds of the soldiers. They still referred to her as the Countess of Warsaw, and welcomed her visits. From friendly shops, she brought salami and bread, as much as her organization could afford, but it was never enough to go around.

Dr. Garrido feared that Hungarian soldiers would be slaughtered on the Russian front, and indeed they were. One morning, in front of Magda and Dr. Garrido, a Nazi colonel arrived to remove the four Hungarian security guards assigned to guard the Portuguese embassy. They, too, were being sent to the Russian front. The arrogant colonel told them, "You won't be needing security guards very much longer anyway. Heinrich Himmler and the SS will soon be overseeing all police duties within Hungary."

At one of Jolie's final dinners, Dr. Garrido echoed a warning similar to what Burhan Belge had previously communicated. "Europe is on fire. Soon it will burn Hungary. Your days here are numbered. I will protect you as best as I can, but what power I now have may be taken away soon. Both of you must think of life in another land. America comes to mind."

***

Back in Hollywood, Bugsy had been pleased with Eva's ministrations to Clark Gable, and rewarded her with a flashy ruby ring and a red gown designed by Orry-Kelly to wear with it.

He invited Eva to show off the ring and gown a few nights later at a lavish party that socialite Elsa Maxwell was hosting for Richard Gulley, a British *bon vivant* and cousin of Anthony Eden, the British statesman who had made love to Zsa Zsa so long ago in London.

The party was the venue for what became one of the most whispered about scandals in Hollywood. Fortunately for both Bugsy and Eva, what happened that night never made the newspapers.

Within Maxwell's social orbit, and hosted by her as a house guest, was the American heiress and socialite, Evalyn Walsh McLean. In 1908, she'd married Edward Beale McLean, the heir to the publishing empire associated with *The Washington Post* and *The Cincinnati Enquirer*. McLean's closest friends and confidants, other than Maxwell, included Alice Roosevelt Longworth and Florence Harding, the widow of President Warren G. Harding.

McLean was famous as the owner of the Hope Diamond, which her husband had purchased for her in 1911 from Pierre Cartier for a price that's generally believed to have been $300,000, although some sources define the price as having been closer to $180,000.

At parties, as part of an evening's diversion, McLean had a reputation for hiding the Hope Diamond on the ground floor of whatever house she was staying in and inviting the guests to go on a search for it. She rewarded the winner with a thousand dollars from her vast fortune. The world famous diamond might be hidden in the dirt around a houseplant, or perhaps under a cushion in the far corner of a sofa.

She persisted in this foolish game even though the residence in which she was staying was often uprooted as guests frantically searched for the Hope Diamond. Whenever she brought the diamond out of safekeeping during her party preparations, she always hired a pair of security guards to watch over it.

Before the party, Bugsy told Eva that he wanted to play a trick on McLean. He'd bribed one of the security guards for information about the location of the diamond, and persuaded Eva to cooperate with his plan, commissioning her to retrieve the diamond with the understanding that she'd be instructed as to its whereabouts. After she found it, she was instructed to spirit it out of the house, hiding it within her purse. Bugsy told her that he wanted to play this dirty trick on McLean as a means of ending, forever, her foolish and cavalier game ("Finding the Hope") of hide-and-seek.

He promised Eva that he'd drive over the next morning to return the diamond. "But in the meanwhile, that old bitch will piss her pants thinking someone made off with her precious stone."

Although reluctant, Eva finally agreed to participate in this game which seemed rather silly to her. Before agreeing, she asked a very pertinent question: "Just what in hell is the Hope Diamond? I've never heard of it."

Bugsy could answer that very well, because the previous evening, he'd read an overview of the diamond's history.

[The Hope Diamond is the most famous stone on Earth, but its owners were said to be cursed for life for having possessed it.

The point of origin of the 45.52 carat diamond is unknown, but it is believed to have been discovered in India. It is estimated that it was formed some 1.1 billion

Society hostess **Elsa Maxwell** was dubbed "the Eighth Wonder of the World." Privately, she told friends, "That's not a bad title for a fat old dyke from Keokuk, Iowa."

She boasted, "I've known seven Presidents of the United States, entertained a dozen kings, and I am on a first name basis with half the titleholders in the *Amanach de Gotha*."

years ago. It's pear-shaped, with a size that has been compared to a pigeon's egg or a fat walnut. Its color is a steely blue-violet, a color which caused Elizabeth Taylor to proclaim, "It matches the color of my eyes. Someone should buy it and give it to me."

With ultraviolet lighting, the diamond produces a red phosphorescence, a sort of glow-in-the-dark luminosity, which continues to glow for some time even after the light is switched off.

The first documented owner of the diamond was a French merchant-traveler, Jean-Baptiste Tavernier, who may have stolen it and brought it to Paris during the ancien régime. *He sold it to King Louis XIV in 1668 when the stone weighed in at 115 carats. The king ordered the court jeweler to cut it down to about 68 carats.*

During the French Revolution, the stone disappeared. Smuggled out of France, it eventually reappeared in London. It was there that some jeweler performed a "butcher job," shearing the diamond down to something approaching its present-day size of 45.52 carats.

The stone eventually passed through many hands, eventually becoming the property of the Anglo-Dutch banker, Thomas Hope—whose name has been associated with it ever since. Hope owned the diamond until his death in 1839.

After that, the diamond passed through a series of hands until it was acquired by Edward Beale McLean and Evalyn Walsh McLean.

Upon her death in 1947, McLean willed the diamond to her grandchildren,

who fought over it before finally selling it to America's most famous jeweler, Harry Winston.

Under great urging, he eventually donated it to the Smithsonian National Museum of Natural History in 1958, which still owns and exhibits it today. In an amazing story, Winston insured the diamond for $145.29 and mailed it to the Smithsonian in a simple box wrapped in brown paper.

The Smithsonian is said to have insured the stone for $250 million, but because of the history and legends associated with it, the Smithsonian defines it as priceless.]

Evalyn Walsh McLean owned the most famous gem in the world, "The Hope Diamond." She was the most outstanding hostess in Washington during the 1940s.

At one party, she entertained Vice President Harry S Truman, five cabinet members, three Supreme Court justices, thirty-eight senators, and Lord Halifax (the British Ambassador).

Before his arrival at Maxwell's party, Bugsy had told her that a bribed security guard had tipped him off as to where McLean had buried the diamond. She'd placed it in a jar of cold cream in the medicine cabinet in a ground floor bathroom.

At some point, Eva was instructed to

use the facilities and to retrieve the diamond. "Wrap it in tissue and place it in your purse. As for the cold cream, it will only beautify your already beautiful hands."

At the party, McLean told Eva, "The Hope Diamond is supposed to be associated with a curse. But I don't believe in those silly superstitions."

[Whether a curse or not, McLean suffered a series of tragedies during the course of her ownership of the stone. Her oldest son, Vinson Walsh McLean, was killed in a car accident. Her husband ran off with another woman and eventually died in a sanitarium. The family newspaper, The Washington Post, *went bankrupt. Her daughter, Emily Washington McLean, died of a drug overdose. One of her grandsons was fatally shot during the Vietnam War.]*

The party itself was a glittering success, and once again, Eva dazzled *tout* Hollywood with her beauty She even received a compliment from Louis B. Mayer, although he still hadn't mentioned any potential MGM contract.

But another film producer, the fabled aviator and billionaire, Howard Hughes, paid special attention to her when Bugsy introduced them. His date for the evening was the beautiful but very short blonde actress Veronica Lake, with her trademark peek-a-boo bangs.

As Eva remembered it, "Wherever I was in the vast living room, Hughes' eyes were following me. When I met him, he had little to say to me, but it was obvious that he had earmarked me as his next conquest. He was busy at the time making his most notorious film with Jane Russell, *The Outlaw* (1943) It was a western about someone nicknamed Billy the Kid. But I had a strong suspicion that I just might end up starring in his next movie, if I played the game right."

At some point during the evening, Eva excused herself "to powder my nose," and disappeared inside the bathroom. As instructed, she dug into the cold cream jar and found the precious stone. She cleaned it, wrapped it in tissue, and placed it inside her purse.

THE HOPE DIAMOND

When Eva attended one of Mrs. McLean's parties, she didn't tell her she planned to "steal" **the Hope Diamond** later that evening.

Elsa Maxwell called the Hope Diamond "a singularly ugly stone. It also carried a damn cursed. I warned Evalyn she was heading for trouble unless she got rid of that stone, but she didn't believe me.

I was right!"

As she later remembered, "I looked as innocent as Heidi when I came out of the bathroom." She and Bugsy stayed at the party only fifteen more minutes before departing. But not before Maxwell pronounced Eva "a divine creature," giving her a "wet one with tongue" before letting her escape.

En route to Bugsy's mansion, he explained that kiss. "Elsa is a notorious lesbian, known for being able to agitate a woman's cli-

235

toris better than any man." *[According to writer Philip Bedstone, he actually used the word "agitate."]*

Back at Bugsy's residence, he placed the Hope Diamond in his vault before coming to bed to make love to Eva.

At around 3am, there was a loud buzzing from his doorbell and a commotion in the foyer. Bugsy was aroused by his butler, who was dressed in pajamas and a robe. "Sorry to disturb you, Mr. Siegel, but Mr. Giesler *[Attorney Jerry Giesler]* is in the hallway, demanding to see you."

Putting on a robe, Bugsy kissed Eva and headed down the stairs to confront his lawyer.

Eva slipped out of the bedroom to overhear them in the hallway below.

Lana Turner once told Frank Sinatra, "If you murder someone, don't call the police. Call **Jerry Giesler**."

Unknown to most biographers, the savvy attorney *(photo above)* might have saved Eva from going to jail when Bugsy Siegel implicated her in a plot to make off with the Hope Diamond.

Giesler told Bugsy that one of the security guards had confessed, accusing Bugsy of leaving the party with Eva and the Hope Diamond.

"I was going to return it in the morning," Bugsy protested. "We were just playing a joke."

"The police don't believe that and are on their way here now," Giesler said. "Give me the diamond, and I'll get it back to McLean RIGHT NOW. If we're lucky, no charges will be pressed, and the newspapers won't hop onto this story."

The diamond was returned to its rightful owner, who wanted no scandal. After that, the incident was merely whispered about, becoming part of Hollywood lore.

The Elsa Maxwell party marked the end of McLean playing her wicked party game.

For Eva, there was fallout from the party. She'd picked up a "stalker" by the name of Howard Hughes.

CHAPTER SIX
How to Marry a Millionaire

For three days, Eva suspected that Howard Hughes was stalking her. If she showed up with an escort at a restaurant, he was dining nearby. If she attended a party, he managed to attend the same party, keeping his eyes on her. She was puzzled as to how he knew where she was going to be on any given night. Had his agents tapped her telephone?

Until she was introduced to him by Bugsy Siegel, she'd never heard of Hughes. At first, she'd confused his name with the director, Howard Hawks.

Bugsy filled her in on a thumbnail biography of the Texan billionaire. Orphaned as a millionaire at eighteen, he seized control of the Hughes Tool Company, the linchpin of his future fortune. In the late 1920s, he'd arrived in Hollywood to make movies, including the wildly popular *Hell's Angels.* This film established Jean Harlow as a top star who'd go on not only to have an affair with Hughes, but to become the reigning bombshell of the 1930s.

Eva fitted the profile of what Hughes considered desirable in a woman. He preferred those who were recently divorced, referring to them as "wet decks."

Opinions about him varied, Joan Crawford claiming, "He would fuck a tree." Paulette Goddard said, "He'd have five or six girls a day, and perhaps a boy or two on the side. It was kind of chaste, because he did it only one way." She was referring to Hughes' fondness for oral sex.

At the age of fifteen, Hughes was seduced by his paternal uncle, Rupert Hughes. From that experience, he entered a lifetime of dissipation, the Hollywood columnist James Bacon calling him "the greatest swordsman."

He did not always get rave reviews. The Hollywood publicist Wilson Heller said, "Two of his girlfriends told me he wasn't worth a damn as a lover. He was just no good in the sack. The gals claimed that all he wanted to do was look and fondle."

Marlene Dietrich told her director, Josef von Sternberg that, "We get along well since, as you know, I prefer oral sex."

Across the street from Eva's apartment, she noticed that a battered old car was parked there between 2 and 5am in the morning for three nights in a row. Bugsy told her that the owner and driver of the car was Hughes himself.

"He's harmless," Bugsy assured her. "He's just checking you out to see who might be coming in or leaving from your apartment."

"Why would the richest man in America be driving a car that even I, a pauper, wouldn't be seen in?"

"Howard's an eccentric," Bugsy said. "You've got to understand that about him."

"What does he want with me?" she asked.

"To date you," he answered.

"He has a hell of a way of going about it," she said. "Why doesn't he just call me?"

"I've got a better idea," he said. "I'll send a limousine for you at eight o'clock tomorrow night. It'll deliver you to my home. Howard will be in the living room waiting for you, and we'll just see what happens."

"Won't you be just a little bit jealous?" she asked.

"I believe in sharing my good fortune with Howard," he said.

"I see," she said. "You also believe in sharing yourself—Di Frasso, Wendy Barrie, Virginia Hill…"

"I'm not going to admit that," he said, "because you know my heart belongs just to you..and only to you. Dames come and go, but you'll be the one I marry. We'll have ten kids. Now be ready tomorrow night before my limo arrives. Howard is a tit man, so wear one of those gowns that plunge down to your navel."

Howard Hughes *(photo above)*: America's famous aviator (also a movie producer) lived in a shadowy, dark world which became a nightmare of his own making. For a brief time, this Lothario included Eva in his all-star cast of lovers, both male and female.

"The gender of his desire didn't matter— Only that she or he was beautiful," said Johnny Meyer, his former pimp.

When Eva talked to Susan Hayward the following day, she learned a lot more about Hughes, including the fact he was a fabled aviator who had broken world records. He was also a seducer of beautiful women and men, including both Gary Cooper and Bette Davis. His weekend with Clark Gable in San Francisco turned out to be a sexual dud, but he scored better with Katharine Hepburn, Hedy Lamarr, Carole Lombard, Ginger Rogers, Gene Tierney, Lana Turner, Robert Taylor, Errol Flynn, Cary Grant, Randolph

Scott, Tyrone Power, and Norma Shearer.

On the night of her rendezvous with Hughes, Eva gave her own assessment of herself. "I looked like a dream in baby blue satin."

At Bugsy's residence, she stepped out of a long black limousine and was shown into the living room, where Hughes awaited her. He didn't drink, but offered her a glass of champagne.

During the first ten minutes, he hardly said a word. "The less he talked, the more I blabbered," she said. "Susan had told me to expect long periods of silence from him."

Finally, he addressed her. "I'm considering signing you to an exclusive contract for seven years, with an option to renew for another seven years."

"Mr. Hughes, I'd be delighted. "That would be the answer to my dreams."

"It's no secret that I'm mesmerized by your beauty," he said.

In reference to what happened next, Eva supplied only the roughest sketch to Hayward, with whom she'd lunch a few days later. Eva didn't mention to Zsa Zsa that Hughes had seduced her, because she suspected that Zsa Zsa wanted to set up her own rendezvous with the aviator/producer.

"You don't have to tell me what he wanted to do," Hayward said. "He's the world's leading expert at cunnilingus."

"When he sought his own relief, he certainly didn't prefer it in what you Americans call the missionary position," Eva said.

"In technical English, it's called intermammary intercourse," Hayward told her. "That means sticking his big thing between a woman's breasts. I will say one thing for Howard: They do grow them big deep in the heart of Texas."

Eva told Hayward "That night I thought Howard and I had the house to ourselves. Bugsy was gone for the week. In the middle of the night, my throat felt parched. I put on my robe and sneaked out of the room, heading for the kitchen for a glass of orange juice. There, I found Robert Taylor in his underwear raiding the icebox. Here was my dream man—practically naked."

From the look on Eva's face, Taylor must have sensed that she was aware of what was going on between Hughes and him. It was the talk of inside Hollywood. "To my surprise, he was bluntly honest with me—there was no at-

When Eva first met matinee idol **Robert Taylor**, he was involved in affairs with both Howard Hughes and Lana Turner, his co-star in *Johnny Eager*.

Taylor was married at the time to Barbara Stanwyck, then the highest-paid woman in America.

But he also found time for Eva.

tempt to cover up what he knew I knew. After all, he could have claimed the status of a male house guest who was just hanging out…but he didn't. I liked that about him."

"You and Howard?" Eva asked. "I didn't know."

"We're the best of friends," Taylor said. "I owe him a lot. Long ago, I signed this contract at MGM. Mayer got me on starvation wages. Whenever I need a new car, help with my mortgage, a tailor-made wardrobe, a Rolex, or someone to pay the bills. Howard is always there with a checkbook."

"I would say it's a convenient arrangement," she said.

"Thanks," he said. "I knew you wouldn't judge me. Howard and I both get what we want."

He kissed her lips and bid her good night.

After climbing back upstairs, she slipped into Hughes' bed, where he was gently snoring.

She fell into a deep sleep and didn't awaken until 10am the following morning. She felt a man's presence n the bed. When she turned over to look into her bedmate's face she discovered that it wasn't Hughes in bed with her, but Taylor himself. As he slept soundly, she took in the beauty of his face.

During her luncheon with Hayward, the actress pressed her for additional details.

"I slipped into the bathroom to take nature's call and to make myself glamorous," Eva said. "After all, a girl wants to look her best when America's heartthrob wakes up beside her. Let me put it this way. Bob woke up and took care of that part of my anatomy that Howard hadn't satisfied. Bob may not have the world's largest penis, but he sure makes do with what he has."

"So where do you go from here?" Hayward asked.

"I'm taking my cue from Bugsy," Eva answered. "He's dating three other women. As for me, I'll date three men—Bugsy, of course, Howard, and Bob."

"For some penniless refugee from Hungary, you are now dating the three most sought-after men in Hollywood. If these guys have a wife somewhere, it doesn't really matter. Watch out for Barbara Stanwyck, though. She's jealous of Bob, even though they sleep in separate bedrooms. On the nights he's out of the house, she's bedding down with Marlene Dietrich or Joan Crawford…perhaps her new flame, William Holden, who extends mercy fucks to aging actresses."

***

In her memoirs, Zsa Zsa admitted to have both known and dated Charlie Chaplin. But she concealed the extent of their affair, defining it as just three dates, which she said were spent innocently riding roller coasters and eating hot dogs.

Although he was fifty-three years old when he began courting Zsa Zsa, Chaplin did not go out on dates with the innocence of a high school boy escorting a teenage girl to the senior prom.

In the throes of a third divorce, he still had his roving eye, which had fallen on Zsa Zsa at a party. He told friends that the Hungarian beauty reminded him of his former wife, Paulette Goddard. Chaplin was the only person who saw any similarities between Zsa Zsa and Goddard. About the only thing they had in common was that each of them was sleeping with Erich Maria Remarque.

Zsa Zsa claimed in a memoir that "Charlie was as much of a god as Kemal Atatürk, but was a simple man."

Chaplin was about as simple as Albert Einstein's Theory of Relativity.

Wherever she'd gone in Hollywood, Zsa Zsa had heard stories about the sexual prowess of Chaplin, who referred to his genitalia as "my twelve-inch penis—it's the eighth wonder of the world." Mae West agreed, claiming, "Chaplin is short and his nose average, but his pecker is really big-time."

His second wife, Lita Grey, said that, "There were nights when Charlie was good for as many as six 'bouts' as he called them, and in succession, with scarcely five minutes' rest in between. When I married him, he said, 'I'm a stallion, Lita, and you'd better resign yourself to it.'"

His Hollywood conquests were legendary, ranging from Aimee Semple McPherson, the most famous evangelist in America, to Marion Davies, mistress of William Randolph Hearst. Zsa Zsa also learned that Hedy Lamarr had sampled Chaplin's "weapon" before he fired it at Zsa Zsa herself.

Chaplin also had a dark side, as future star Marlon Brando noted in 1967. "He was sadistic, a mean man. Like me, he was bisexual. He once told me, 'the most beautiful form of life is the innocent rosebud of a very young boy just starting to bloom. The same could be said of the genitals of a teenage virgin girl, too."

By the early 1940s, Chaplin had seduced more than a thousand women, often prostitutes in brothels which he constantly frequented since his arrival in Hollywood, sometimes summoning as many as five different girls in one night, according to the madams of that era.

Chaplin told his friends, "This Zsa Zsa Gabor evokes my libidinous curiosity." Those quaint words were his exact speech.

During the brief time they were engaged in their affair, Chaplin rarely seemed available in the evening. He always had some other engagement. On several occasions, she attended luncheons at his residence in Beverly Hills. In most cases, after the other lunch guests had departed, he followed the meal with a "love in the afternoon" session in his bedroom, where The Little Tramp lived up to his billing.

At one luncheon, she met actor Sir Cedric Hardwicke and the American novelist, Sinclair Lewis, two names with which she was unfamiliar. Most of their conversation was about a play, *Shadow and Substance,* in which Hardwicke had recently starred. Both men were suggesting to Chaplin that he should acquire the film rights.

At another luncheon, Zsa Zsa was introduced to Orson Welles, who would play a role in both her private and professional future. He wanted Chaplin to write a play about Bluebeard Landru, the celebrated French murderer.

Chaplin promised Zsa Zsa that if he opted to sponsor the project, he'd assign her the role of one of Bluebeard's ill-fated wives.

"I could get any name actress in Hollywood I want," he boasted. "But I don't want someone famous. I am searching for an unknown, a beautiful woman who can inspire my flagging ambition to make another movie. You have a champagne complexion, a striking figure, a promising bosom, and lovely hair. Of course, I'd have to do a screen test. My fear is that the camera will not capture that effervescent personality of yours. The camera is a tricky monster. It can make beautiful girls unattractive and ugly girls stunning."

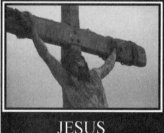

JESUS

Based on his success portraying Hitler in *The Great Dictator,* **Charlie Chapin** *(upper photo)* wanted to "move upstairs" and portray Jesus Christ in his next film, in collaboration with Igor Stravinsky.

He suggested that Zsa Zsa would be ideal as Mary Magdalene.

"Just by looking at you, though, I can tell you have a great deal of talent. You are so fresh, so very much alive."

Unknown to Zsa Zsa at the time, he was delivering that same pitch to another starlet, Joan Berry (a name sometimes spelled as Barry). She had an unfortunate trait, though—a fondness for shoplifting, which sometimes led to her arrest. On a number of occasions, Chaplin had to bail her out of jail.

For decades, Chaplin had been "fretting and fussing" over a movie script. "If I ever finish it, I will offer you the role of Mary Magdalene,"

"A fallen women," Zsa Zsa joked. "Type casting."

"For years, I have dreamed of using the Virgin Mary and the Crucifixon as a dramatic subject," he said. "I've even involved Igor Stravinsky in the project I've named *The Passion of Christ*—I would star as Christ, of course. The setting would be the stage in a tawdry nightclub. The patrons would be drunk and boisterous and not aware of the drama unfolding before them."

"That would be some drama indeed," she

said. "But religious people, like the Catholic Church, would find it offensive."

"To hell with them," he said.

The movie would be one of many that Chaplin flirted with, but never realized.

"I couldn't depend on him to put me in a movie, but I could always count on him being reliable in bed," she told her friends. "He assured me he was sterile and that I need not worry. He found a diaphragm unaesthetic."

According to Zsa Zsa, Chaplin ended their brief affair with a phone call. He told her, "You're too smart for me. It's over between us. I do not prefer to make love to women who are intelligent."

For his farewell present, he sent her a Cocker Spaniel, having learned that she adored that breed of dogs. She maintained that she and Eva were practically penniless at the time and could not afford to feed the dog.

"We fed it with the orchids our dates had presented to us," she claimed.

That story is more romantic than accurate. She did not mention that Bugsy Siegel had deposited thousands of dollars into the bank account she jointly maintained with Eva, enough to supply good meals to the Cocker Spaniel and to both sisters as well.

Even though Chaplin ended their affair, he would remain in Zsa Zsa's life throughout the course of her upcoming marriage.

***

Eva

On Eva's first formally designated date with Robert Taylor, it wasn't a question of whether or not he'd seduce her. He'd already done that. All he could do was assure her that "Love is better the second time around."

He spent most of their dinner together complaining about how low his weekly salary from MGM was; how bossy his movie star wife, Barbara Stanwyck was; and how newspapers were mocking him as a "pretty boy." When he'd appeared in *The Gorgeous Hussy* (1936), with Joan Crawford, reporters asked, "To whom does the title apply?"

That movie had also starred Franchot Tone, who was married to Crawford at the time. "On separate occasions," Taylor told Eva, "both of them pursued me, and I didn't put up much resistance."

As a bisexual, Taylor had been a Romeo in the 1930s, seducing actress Virginia Bruce, his co-star in *Times Square Lady*. And before he suddenly dropped her, he'd taken the virginity of Thelma (Pat) Ryan when she worked as an extra on *Small Town Girl* (1936). She ended up marrying Richard Nixon on the rebound.

His other flings had been with Howard Hughes, Errol Flynn, John Gilbert,

Tyrone Power, Lana Turner, and Greta Garbo, with whom he'd co-starred in *Camille* in 1936. Garbo had said of him, "So beautiful—and so dumb."

To prove to the homophobic Louis B. Mayer that he was "completely heterosexual," Taylor also made several visits every month to a brothel maintained by MGM, who hired young women who did not get signed by the studio boss as starlets.

"Everyone calls me Bob Taylor," he told her. "But I think my real name would have had greater marquee value—Spangler Arlington Brugh."

Some actors she'd met, such as Gary Cooper, had told her very little about themselves. In contrast, Taylor seemed to delight in talking about himself. On their first time out, she couldn't recall one question he'd asked her about her own life. Nevertheless, she found him amusing and very sensitive about certain subjects.

"Every day I read something in the papers about how pretty I am. I'm a red-blooded male and, for your information, I've got hair on my chest. That wasn't fake fur rubbing against your breasts."

Ever the courtesan, and as an encouragement to conversation, she said, "You must get a lot of fan mail?"

"You wouldn't believe most of it," he answered. "Tons of girls and homosexuals write in, and they are constantly insisting that they want to see my legs—one even wanted to see my tits. Mayer said MGM male stars had never seen fan letters like that before. One letter said, 'I held my breath hoping Bob Taylor would show his legs at some time or other, but he did not. I would like to know just why we are deprived of those two very important features. It was signed by a guy named Richard Barths."

As if to explain why he was dating other women, despite his status as a married man, he said, "I recently told Barbara Stanwyck, whom I called 'The Queen,' that I wanted a divorce. She cut her wrists in a feeble suicide attempt. I'm still with her, but I'm often away for months at a time. If we lived under the same roof night after night, I'm sure we would have separated years ago."

"I haven't made love to her in a year. I told her I had a prostate problem. She told me, 'There's always oral sex, Junior.' She calls me Junior. With Lana Turner, I didn't have a problem getting an erection, and that wasn't a problem I had with you."

"Forgive me for asking, but everybody I talk to insists that Stanwyck is a lesbian," Eva said.

"She is. And not just with her favorites, Joan Crawford and Marlene Dietrich. Would you believe that in the 1920s, in New York, she had an affair with Marjorie Main. Obviously, Main didn't look like the dishrag she does today. Like Barbara, she was a lesbian hoofer in the 1920s."

"It's hard to imagine her with Main," Eva said.

"I can imagine that more easily than I can Tallulah Bankhead with Hattie McDaniel."

"You mean Mammy from *Gone With the Wind?*"

"One and the same."

"I've never understood lesbianism. I have nothing against it. With a man, you've at least got something to work with, but with a woman, one only faces another hole."

"I'll explain it to you some day," he said, smiling.

Taylor continued with his endless self-assessment: "I'm always being taken advantage of," he said. "Like on a recent trip when I was flying to Kansas City on this promotional tour. I fell asleep on the plane. Apparently, I was snoring with my mouth open. This damned reporter, Ruth Robinson, stuck her tongue in my mouth and started kissing me. I woke up fast."

"Eva Gabor is no exception. I'd like to take advantage of you, too, you beautiful doll."

"What are we waiting for?" he asked. "My car is outside."

En route to a guest cottage on the Howard Hughes estate, she told him, "It's thrilling to be riding off into the night for a rendezvous with the man in America every woman wants."

"You are a lucky girl," he said. "In the men's room I checked out my appearance in the mirror. Even I would fall in love with Robert Taylor and beg him to give me a tumble."

***

The Gabor sisters' unofficial godmother, Greta Keller, had emigrated from Vienna to Berlin to New York, landing in Hollywood with her new husband.

The then-fabled Austrian chanteuse was eager for news of all three sisters, especially Zsa Zsa, with whom she had the closest relationship, first developed during their time together in Vienna in the 30s. Since then, she'd visited Jolie several times in Budapest, and the two of them had formed an affection and surprisingly durable bond.

In Hollywood, Greta was singing in night clubs, making some recordings (including her version of "Lili Marlene"), and also doing some film work in roles that demanded a sophisticated Continental dame.

When she phoned Zsa Zsa, she invited her to have lunch with her in the MGM commissary, where she was appearing in an uncredited role as the Baroness von Steinkamp in a movie entitled *Reunion in France* (1942).

The picture otherwise starred Joan Crawford and John Wayne, and the plot dealt with French underground forces of liberation in Paris in the wake of the country's Nazi takeover.

Chatting away in German, Greta and Zsa Zsa caught up with what had happened since they'd left Europe. Both women had divorced their first husbands, and Greta had married an aspirant actor, David Bacon, who was under exclusive contract to Howard Hughes. The aviator/producer was billing Bacon as "the handsomest man in Hollywood," although that title was arguable.

He was the son of one of the most prominent and socially connected families of Massachusetts. "David's family makes Kate Hepburn's clan look like white trash," Greta claimed.

Zsa Zsa was fully aware that Greta was a bisexual and that she had had a fling with Marlene Dietrich when both of them had appeared on stage together in Vienna in the play entitled *Broadway*.

During Greta's extended singing gig at the Algonquin Hotel in Manhattan, Greta Garbo had become her number one fan, attending her performances two or three nights a week. In lesbian circles, Garbo and Keller were collectively identified as "the two Gretas," and were rumored to have engaged in a sexual fling that lasted for five months.

On the coast, Greta had not only married Bacon, but had launched herself into an affair with another bisexual, Pola Negri, the silent screen vamp and former rival of Gloria Swanson.

As Greta confessed to Zsa Zsa, "That night, I met this lost and lonely boy [*meaning David Bacon*] at Pola's house and practically adopted him. He aroused a latent motherly instinct in me."

Zsa Zsa told her that she and Eva had already banished their respective first husbands, and that Magda had left her Polish count and was living once again in Budapest.

"That's not the safest place in the world to be," Greta said.

"Eva and I are—the Americans have an expression for it—playing the field," Zsa Zsa said. "Both of us are looking for that elusive millionaire who will present us with diamonds and encase us in mink, before we divorce the devils and sue them for al-

From Germany came *(left figure)* **Marlene Dietrich**; from Sweden, **Greta Garbo** *(center)*, and from Austria, **Greta Keller** *(right)*.

These bisexual expatriates were part of the lesbian underground in Hollywood that came to be known as "The Sewing Circle."

imony."

"That's always a noble profession," Greta said.

At some point, they were joined at their luncheon by a beautiful young starlet, Ava Gardner, who was appearing in an uncredited role in *Reunion in France,* playing a shopgirl named Marie. Before Gardner's arrival, Greta had revealed, "She's sleeping with the producer." The reference involved Joseph L. Mankiewicz.

As a faithful reader of the gossip columns, Zsa Zsa had heard of Gardner, who was married at the time to pint-sized Mickey Rooney, who since the late 1930s had been a box office bonanza.

"Some people say Elizabeth Taylor and I are whores," **Ava Gardner** *(photo above)* told Zsa Zsa.

When Gardner spoke, Zsa Zsa was startled by her Tarheel accent from the tobacco fields of North Carolina.

Ava and Zsa Zsa would, on occasion, "double up with the same men— Richard Burton, Porfirio Rubirosa, and even gangster Johnny Stompanato, among many others.

"Yes, I'm just a l'il hillbilly gal, but that's what turns them on, honey chile," she claimed.

As they chatted, Gardner said, "I came to Hollywood to marry a tall, dark, and handsome man, and I married a midget. I prefer the quiet type in a man. In contrast, Mickey is 'on' day and night."

"But I've got to give him credit," Gardner continued. "If I ever become a star, or ever make something of myself, I owe a debt to Mickey. He's taught me a lot about the business. But I must confess to you gals that after the first six weeks, the magic was gone. Besides, he's out whoring six nights a week. He's even fucking Norma Shearer."

Robert Taylor suddenly walked by, heading toward a booth where Clark Gable sat waiting for him.

Zsa Zsa looked over at their table. To Gardner, she said, "I'll take Gable and give you Taylor."

"That's fair," Gardner said. "But I intend to have both of them."

At that time, Zsa Zsa didn't know that her baby sister had already seduced both Taylor and Gable. Zsa Zsa, and especially Greta, complained about life as it existed in Hollywood. Greta attacked the "droopy palm trees, the horrible architecture and billboards, the dime stores with gum-chewing clerks, and the garish movie houses."

Then, in hushed tones, Gardner confided that "Crawford has already invited me to her dressing room, where she made a pass at me. She's asked me over Saturday night. She told me her 'brats" wouldn't be there, and we'd have the joint to ourselves."

"Are you going?" Greta asked.

"Hell, yes!" Gardner answered. "I may be a country girl, but I've learned from Mickey that who you fuck in this town determines how bright your star will shine. Everybody does it, so I'm told, except Greer Garson."

Crawford herself was having lunch that day in the commissary with one of her co-stars, Philip Dorn. On her way out, she stopped by the table where Gable and Taylor were seated, sat down with them, and ordered a final cup of coffee.

Heading out, she spotted Gardner with her two dining companions and smiled at her. Crawford had already met Greta. "Joan," Gardner said, "I'd like to introduce you to Zsa Zsa Gabor. She's from Hungary."

Crawford appraised Zsa Zsa with a very skeptical eye. "Never heard of the place." Suddenly she picked up Zsa Zsa's luncheon plate, tossed its contents into her face, and stalked out of the restaurant.

"Thank god I wasn't eating spaghetti," Zsa Zsa said ruefully, wiping her face with a napkin.

Gardner assisted Zsa Zsa in her transit to the women's room, where she helped her wipe her face and clean her dress.

"Why would that Crawford bitch do that to me?" Zsa Zsa asked.

"On the way to this crapper, I figured it out," Gardner said. "Crawford obviously thinks Greg Bautzer belongs just to her and her honeypot alone."

"That must be it," Zsa Zsa said.

During the years ahead, Zsa Zsa would wreak revenge on Crawford by conducting an affair with her second husband, actor Franchot Tone.

"Let's put it this way, *dahlink*," Zsa Zsa said. "Miss **Joan Crawford** *(photo above)* and I were not destined to be friends."

"Marilyn Monroe and Jack Kennedy may have been lovers, but Crawford seduced both of them."

"I'm glad Crawford hasn't found out about me," Gardner said. "Greg and I have gone out on three dates, but he takes me to obscure places. And we certainly don't want to run into Mickey."

Back at table, Greta told Gardner and Zsa Zsa, "Hollywood is a small town within a tangled web. Everybody seems to be dating everybody else. Howard Hughes is dating my husband, for now, at least, and I assume that he hasn't discovered either of you yet. I'm sure that in time, however, he will."

There was an irony in what she predicted. Once again, Eva had beaten out the competition, including her sister, having already crawled between the sheets with Hughes.

Both Gardner and Zsa Zsa, however, would position themselves as conspicuous fixtures within Hughes' future.

***

248

One late afternoon, in anticipation of a dinner party, Zsa Zsa and Eva arrived at a mansion in Santa Monica with twelve bedrooms, nine bathrooms, and a swimming pool. It had been leased by their godmother, Greta Keller, and her new husband, David Bacon, who officially lived there together. At the same time, David's boss, Howard Hughes, maintained a bungalow in the Hollywood Hills as a love nest where Bacon spent many a night with him.

The Gabor sisters were told that Bacon, who was one of the anticipated guests at the dinner, was at Hughes' bungalow gathering up his possessions, and that he'd be joining them later with a male friend, Peter Lawford. David and Hughes had had a major argument. Originally, Bacon had been promised the role of Billy the Kid in Hughes' controversial upcoming film, *The Outlaw* (1943).

"Apparently, Hughes fell for another young actor, Jack Buetel," Keller said. "Hughes fired David from the picture and replaced him with Jack."

Greta told them what a proud man her husband was, and how distinguished his pedigree. His stepfather, Gaspar G. Bacon, a socially prominent Boston Brahmin, was a close associate of banker J.P. Morgan and later served as U.S. Secretary of State under Theodore Roosevelt, and as Ambassador to France under William Howard Taft.

"David is involved in a very dangerous scheme," Greta said, "and I fear for his safety. He's writing a memoir describing his love affair with Hughes, and has made him aware of that. He doesn't plan to actually submit the manuscript to a publisher, but he thinks Hughes will settle at least forty thousand dollars on him as a means of assuring that it will never be published."

"I should think it would be worth three million," Zsa Zsa said.

Greta Keller, the unofficial godmother of the Gabor sisters, entered into an unconventional marriage with Boston Brahmin, David Bacon.

Bacon had signed a contract with Howard Hughes to star in a picture, *The Outlaw*, co-starring Jane Russell.

But then came along Jack Buetel, and Bacon was off the picture.

David Bacon *(photos above)* was murdered while writing an *exposé* of his former boss, Howard Hughes. Greta warned him how dangerous it was to attempt blackmail, especially on a man as powerful as Hughes.

In a prophetic warning, she told him, "He can hire someone to murder you."

"Blackmail is a very dangerous game, especially when you're dealing with one of the most wealthy and powerful men in America," Eva said.

At the time she said that, Eva had not admitted to her own sexual involvement with Hughes either to Greta or to Zsa Zsa.

"David is stubborn and very determined," Greta said. "When he makes up his mind to do something, nothing seems to stand in his way."

Bacon arrived about an hour later with his new lover, Peter Lawford, an exceedingly handsome British actor, who had signed with MGM in 1942. He'd been assigned a small role in MGM's wartime hit, *Mrs. Miniver,* starring Greer Garson.

Both Eva and Zsa Zsa found the two young men handsome and charming. Zsa Zsa thought "Peter and David make a perfect couple."

The elephant in the room was Greta herself. The Gabor sisters were intrigued with this permissive and highly promiscuous union, a gay American WASP aristocrat married to an aging daughter from the dying twilight of the Austro-Hungarian Empire.

"*Dahlink,*" Zsa Zsa later said. "The marriage was so unconventional and sexually ambiguous as to be positively amoral. I adore people who don't follow boring middle-class morality. Greta and David revived the decadence that sophisticated Europeans had immersed themselves in for centuries."

During the course of the evening, Eva found no common ground with either Lawford or Bacon. Zsa Zsa would later proclaim, "Lawford was exceedingly superficial—like I am, *dahlink.*"

Zsa Zsa later said, "He was a party circuit boy that I was always encountering at parties in the 40s, 50s,

David Bacon's last known lover was a bisexual young British actor, **Peter Lawford,** who was trying to make a name for himself in Hollywood films.

Even though he was never noted as a great lover, everybody seemed after him, including Elizabeth Taylor and Noël Coward.

and even the 60s. Sometimes he would escort Marilyn Monroe, who was making a play for my then-husband, George Sanders. On other occasions, it would be Elizabeth Taylor. She and I were both sharing the love-making of Nicky Hilton."

"On one occasion in Santa Monica, Lawford was hanging out for the weekend with a handsome young politician, John F.

The silent screen vamp, **Pola Negri,** pictured here in tight close-up, had been involved with everyone from Charlie Chaplin to Rudolf Valentino.

When Greta Keller first arrived in Hollywood, Negri became her lover.

Kennedy."

"Did I like Peter Lawford?" Zsa Zsa asked. "No, I didn't. We had too many conflicts of interest in our respective games of love. Everyone I ever met, from George Cukor to Noël Coward, asserted that Lawford was a lousy lay. He was mostly the oral type. But no one ever made such libelous statements about Zsa Zsa Gabor."

***

A few months before Greta's dinner party in Santa Monica, Zsa Zsa had met a tall Texan who would change her life. Their meeting occurred at Ciro's restaurant in December of 1941. It wasn't just her orbit that was changing: The entire world was undergoing rapid change. The Gabor sisters were in a state of neurotic panic for Magda, Jolie, and Vilmos as tensions increased between the Nazis and the Soviets.

The debate over whether America should enter World War II ended on Sunday, December 7, 1941, when the Empire of Japan attacked Pearl Harbor. Nazi Germany, in the immediate aftermath of that bombing, declared war on the United States.

America accelerated its mobilization for a long, drawn-out war. Young men nationwide lined up at draft boards to enlist.

But thoughts of war were forgotten, or at least postponed when Greg Bautzer invited Zsa Zsa for dinner and dancing at Ciro's, where the stars hung out. She accepted his invitation, opting to ignore Joan Crawford's implied threat to "keep your hands off my man."

"Crawford was telling people that she would ruin me in Hollywood if I continued to go out with Greg," Zsa Zsa said. "She said I would never find work here. I thought it was an idle threat because Crawford herself was getting kicked out of MGM and couldn't find a good movie role for herself."

Eva wanted to go to Ciro's too, thinking some producer might spot her. Zsa Zsa called Bautzer asking if there was anything he could do, and he arranged for his partner, Bentley Ryan, to be Eva's escort for the evening.

In compliance with Eva's search for a unique "blonde" identity, Zsa Zsa had dyed her naturally blonde hair to a tint she defined as "American red," *[That was an unusual description since "red" in America was no different from "red" as defined in Europe.]*

In her assessment, Zsa Zsa claimed that their quartet made the most spectacular entrance of the evening at Ciro's. "I was dazzling in my shimmering dark blue satin with turquoise embroidery. Ryan was striking enough to decorate a magazine cover, and Eva and Greg, as usual, looked regal." The two couples attracted the attention of the entire room.

Most of the patrons knew who Greg Bautzer was, and even a few, especially those employed by Paramount, were already aware of Eva's identity, being defined by some as "Howard Hughes' latest conquest." But Zsa Zsa was a mystery. Some identified her as the latest mistress of Charlie Chaplin—"Paulette Goddard's replacement."

Across a crowded room, hotelier Conrad Hilton asked the *maître d'hotel*, "Did Helen of Troy just walk into Ciro's?"

Only that morning, columnist Louella Parsons had written, "Mrs. Burhan Belge is even prettier than her sister, Eva Gabor."

Then Zsa Zsa spotted him. As she'd later relate in a memoir, "He was six foot two, exuded power, looked like Atatürk and Vilmos, and resembled an American cowboy from the Wild West—all rolled into one. For a moment, I felt dizzy."

She asked Bautzer. "Who is that man staring at me?"

The attorney knew virtually everyone in Hollywood—and all their secrets. "That's Conrad Hilton, the hotelier. A Texas millionaire. Before he finishes, he'll own every deluxe hotel in America, from the New York islands to California."

"My kind of man," she said.

"I'll let you in on a dirty secret," Bautzer said. "Conrad Sr.; his son Nicky; and his brother Carl have three feet of cock among them, but I'm not going to tell you how it's distributed."

The founder of Hilton Hotels and Zsa Zsa's second husband, **Conrad Hilton, Sr**. *(photos above)* was a powerful man, hailing from Texas. He started out with nothing. A bellboy in Dallas once lent him money to buy a hamburger and Coke. Hotel by hotel, he built an empire.

During his marriage to Zsa Zsa, he had to share his wife with his oldest son, Nicky Hilton, although at the time, he was not aware of that, of course.

The trio Bautzer was referring to included Conrad Hilton, Jr., born in 1926, and whom Papa Hilton had nicknamed "Nicky." The other reference was to Conrad, Sr.'s brother, Commander Carl Hilton, a coast Guard officer stationed in Key West.

At that point, Hilton, Sr., was crossing the room. "He's coming over here," she said.

"Don't get carried away, *señorita,*" Bautzer said. "He's old enough to be your grandfather."

[In a memoir, Zsa

Zsa did some fuzzy math, claiming that she was seventeen years old at the time and that Hilton, Sr., was sixty-one. The hotelier had been born on Christmas Day in 1887, in San Antonio, New Mexico, which would make him fifty-four years old at the time of his meeting with Zsa Zsa.

Zsa Zsa had been born in 1917, which would have made her twenty-four at the time, hardly the age of a high school senior.]

The age of a man did not seem to matter to Zsa Zsa. "After all, love is blind, *dahlink.*" Jolie had always taught her daughters that the right age for a groom should be twice the age of the bride, minus seven.

After being introduced, Hilton asked Zsa Zsa to dance. She remembered that he held her so close, she could hardly breathe. Before the end of the dance, he'd offered her $20,000 to fly with him to Key West for a visit with his brother. Claiming that she was "grossly insulted," she turned him down, but did not reject him completely.

At table, Hilton continued to be outrageous. "Both of you sisters are beautiful," he told the Gabors. "But I think it's Zsa Zsa that I'm going to marry. Maybe Eva on the side as first mistress."

"The man was tasteless," Eva said. "He may have had millions, but that didn't allow him to ignore social protocol."

Observing him up close, Zsa Zsa liked what she saw except for his baggy suit. "But I knew the best tailor in Hollywood, so that wasn't a problem."

During the dance, he'd told her that he didn't speak Hungarian and that he had a difficult time wrapping his tongue around the correct pronunciation of her name. "I'm going to call you Georgia." At first she thought he was referring to the Soviet state of Georgia, but he explained that he meant the Georgia depicted in *Gone With the Wind.*

"He had on this tacky necktie, with three of his hotels embroidered on it," she said. "In some ways, he reminded me of Vilmos, especially those striking blue eyes that evoked a Viking warrior arriving in Scotland to rape its women. After being made love to by Atatürk, what was left for me but to be captured by this Gary Cooper-like man—a real rough and rugged, ride 'em cowboy from Texas? He even wore a ten-gallon hat with boots and spurs."

"He told the assembled personalities at the dining table that his favorite sport involved shooting rattlesnakes and then having his chef sauté the reptile for dinner and serve it with Lone Star Hot Sauce."

Zsa Zsa quickly determined that he was free to marry. He told her he'd divorced his first wife, Mary Adelaide Barron, in 1934, and had not married since. They'd had three sons, including Nicky, William Barron Hilton, and Eric Michael Hilton.

Once again, Hilton escorted Zsa Zsa to the dance floor. "Georgia, you're a card," he said.

She knew what a card was, but didn't see how that applied to her. "*Dahlink,* cards are flat. As you can see, I'm anything but flat."

"How right you are," he said.

"His eyes looked all the way down to my navel," she later recalled. "Fortunately, I was wearing plunging *décolletage.*"

Back at table, she evaluated him once again. "I *theenk* I am going to marry you."

"You *sink* you're going to marry me?" he said, mimicking her Hungarian accent.

As related in his memoir, *Be My Guest,* Hilton said. "I, a confirmed bachelor, to whom marriage from a religious standpoint *[he was a staunch Catholic]* was forbidden fruit, thought that was a fine joke."

He turned to Zsa Zsa. "Then why don't you marry me?"

In his memoir, in reference to their dialogue, he wrote, "But four months later, the joke was on me."

In Zsa Zsa's words, "the 'courtshipping' began that night."

The Hollywood columnist, Sheilah Graham, wrote "*Tout* Hollywood viewed the pairing skeptically. It was love at first sight, Zsa Zsa's first sight of Hilton's wallet."

***

 After being dumped by Paramount, Eva floundered in Hollywood for six months with not one single job offer. She'd also lost a husband *[through her divorce from Erik Drimmer],* but, unlike what had happened at Paramount, her divorce had been an event of her own choosing.

"Divorce, divorce, *tsk, tsk,*" she said. "In America, divorces are almost as common as marriages today."

Since Hollywood didn't want her, Eva decided to knock on the doors of Broadway theaters in Manhattan. She sold her battered Mercury for thirty dollars "to some sucker," packed her mink coat, gowns, and jewelry, and took the train on the long cross-country transit from Los Angeles to New York. In Manhattan, she hoped to find a new man (or several new men), a new life, and a new career.

She checked into a seedy hotel in the Times Square area, and for the first few weeks, life looked bleak. Through the lobby of her hotel walked drug pushers, prostitutes, and con men, along with many addicts and alcoholics.

Then, to her surprise, her talent agent in Hollywood began to badger her with telegrams, urging her to return to the West Coast. "David O. Selznick wants you," one telegram promised. She even received an actual film offer in which she'd play the small role of a beautiful Nazi spy, a Mata Hari type. She turned it down, informing her agency, "It's more suited to Signe Hasso, the mistress of my former husband."

When Eva was finally convinced that "Hollywood would stop making motion pictures unless I returned to star in them," she boarded the train once again, this time traveling in the opposite direction, eventually disembarking at Union Station in Los Angeles.

Once back, she lived temporarily with Zsa Zsa. Eventually, she was offered a contract at 20th Century Fox, paying $125 a week. She decided to sign, since she could not get an appointment with Selznick. "He had time for Madame Chiang Kai-shek's wartime visit, but not for Eva," she said, bitterly.

"The closest I could get to Selznick was to become a car hop on roller skates, serving him a mustard-coated hot dog with Sauerkraut on the side," she said.

At Fox, Darryl F. Zanuck had no roles for her, but ordered her enrolled in acting classes as a means of sharpening both her talent and her fractured English. She referred to her first months at Fox as "a platonic relationship—it had not been consummated."

In the meantime, she was allowed to perform in a play, *The Affairs of Anatol,* being staged at the Hollywood Theater. It was already familiar to her, as it had been written in 1923 by Arthur Schnitzler, a Viennese dramatist who had died in 1931. His father had been the prominent Hungarian laryngologist (throat specialist), Johann Schnitzler (1835-1893). Both of his parents had been Jewish.

Jolie had branded Schnitzler a pornographer because of his frank descriptions of sexuality, which had been cited in the writings of Sigmund Freud. Amazingly, the playwright had kept an 8,000-page diary of his sexual conquests—often with three or four women at the same time. He'd also kept a record of every orgasm he'd ever had.

Josef Goebbels didn't like the sexually explicit plays of **Arthur Schnitzler** *(photo above)*, the Viennese playwright, and neither did Adolf Hitler, ordering them banned. Even the Gabor matriarch (Jolie) found them offensive.

But in Hollywood, Eva agreed to appear in one of Schnitzler's plays, even though she interpreted his personal diary as "pornographic."

"Back in Budapest, Jolie was very disappointed with Eva for appearing in what she referred to as "one of Schnitzer's garbage plays."

Both Adolf Hitler and Josef Goebbels had denounced Schnitzler's work, defining it as "Jewish filth." In Berlin, copies of all of Schnitzler's plays went up in flames, along with the works of other Jews who had included Albert Einstein, Karl Marx, Franz

Kafka, and Sigmund Freud.

In the United States, Cecil B. DeMille, in 1921, had directed and produced Schnitzler's *The Affairs of Anatol* as a silent film starring Gloria Swanson and the doomed Wallace Reid. Another famous actress of that era, Bebe Daniels, had played the role of "Satan Synn." The original play, which had starred John Barrymore, had opened on Broadway in 1912.

The play's reprise in Los Angeles reunited Eva with Philip Merivale, with whom she'd previously co-starred in the lackluster *Pacific Blackout* (1941).

One night, Bette Davis, then at the peak of her career, attended the play and went backstage to congratulate Merivale and Eva. Then Davis asked them to stage a morale-building charity performance of the play at the USO for American Servicemen, many of them soon to be shipped off to fight for their country in the Pacific Theatre.

The actors agreed, and the performance received loud applause from the servicemen. Then, in her dressing room, Eva changed into a low-cut dress and put on "Joan Crawford fuck-me high heels," before going out to meet dozens of men from all branches of the military.

Davis herself was a witness to a major event in Eva's life. She remembered a tall, dark, and handsome man walking through a line of women volunteers, heading straight for Eva. "He was a knock-out," Davis recalled, "with that golden tan, that starched white uniform, those broad shoulders, and that gorgeous face. His hair evoked Jean Harlow's. Prematurely gray at the temples, it was sun-bleached on top. He seemed to want Eva, but I would have surrendered my virginity to him had I not already lost it long ago."

"My name is Charles Isaacs," he said.

"He looked resplendent in his Coast Guardsman uniform," according to Eva. "He reminded me of my former Hussar lover in Budapest. Perhaps he was not as beautiful as Erik Drimmer, my ex, but he could give Clark Gable and Errol Flynn some competition. He had a youthful face, a wholesome smile, a boy-next-door quality. He was very down to earth, extremely sensitive, and con-

At the Hollywood Canteen, at a party *(left photo)* during World War II, Eva met her dreamboat, Charles Isaacs, who became husband #2. "Before the night was over, I learned that he was not only handsome, but very rich, too."

In this 1942 publicity still *(right photo)*, **Eva Gabor** was instructed by the photographer to "look like a sex kitten."

siderate of women. That uniform, so I suspected, concealed a body that would make women swoon."

He asked her to dance, and she remembered that his seductive breathing in her ear made her "want to follow him to the end of the Earth. I knew how the night would end, and I'd only known Charles for five minutes.. Both Zsa Zsa and I, meeting our second husbands—hers being Conrad Hilton—knew we were going to marry and soon."

"Performers at the USO weren't supposed to leave with servicemen, but Charles and I broke the rules that night," she said. "In the parking lot, I expected to get into some battered jalopy and be driven to some horrible little bedroom. I didn't know one car from the other. But Charles owned a deluxe vehicle more suited to a bigtime star. It had been custom made."

"I had stars in my eyes like a lovesick schoolgirl when he drove me to his home," she said. "I was shocked when his butler opened the door and invited me into a large and luxuriously furnished living room for a late supper of French champagne, chunks of lobster, and Beluga caviar, my favorite food and drink."

Before three o'clock that morning, Isaacs asked Eva "to become my woman," and she was eager to fulfill his request. "He was so manly, so overpowering in his sex appeal. I also felt it was my duty to provide love to him in exchange for his duty guarding the California coastline. I was told that if the Japanese ever conquered California, their soldiers would take beautiful girls like me and install us in whorehouses where we'd be raped as often as twenty times a day."

As Eva remembered it, "It was dawn before I extinguished Charles' insatiable desires. He put out all my fires. I didn't think I'd be able to make love for at least a month. The very next day I learned that Charles liked to make love in the morning, in the afternoon, and also at *après* dinner sessions. What a man! He attacked with a powerful weapon attached to a great body."

"The best news came the very next day. Charles was worth millions in real estate. He was also well connected in Hollywood, entertaining stars, directors, and producers at his home. I had known him less than twenty-four hours before he proposed marriage, and I accepted. I wanted to nail him before some low-grade prostitute like Veronica Lake nabbed him. He was a gentleman who preferred blondes."

"Talk about a reversal of fortune for me," she said. "Before I met Charles, I was counting my pen-

Before Eva entered the life of Charles Isaacs, he was emotionally involved with the mentally disturbed movie star, **Frances Farmer** *(photo above)*.

"Living with her was a journey into hell," he confiided to Eva.

nies. I gave quarter tips. Charles tipped with ten-dollar bills. His mansion came with servants. In just one day and night, I went from an out-of-work actress who didn't always have car fare to a kept woman who was assigned her own chauffeur."

During her first afternoon in Isaac's residence, she wandered into his library, where she found a picture on his desk of the emotionally disturbed movie star, Frances Farmer. It made her aware that she was not the first blonde in his life.

When he came in and saw her looking at Farmer's portrait, he said, "Frances and her mother lived with me for a time. Her mother, Lillian Farmer, was quite a character. She had worked tirelessly to breed a chicken in the patriotic colors of red and blue. She used interbred strains of Rhode Island Red, a White Leghorn, and an Andalusian Blue Chicken."

Lillian took her hen to Washington, and even got Eleanor Roosevelt to look at it. The First Lady turned it down, because she didn't want America represented by a chicken, the symbol of a coward. Then Lillian tried to get Congress to make her '*Bird Americana*' the national emblem of America instead of the eagle. But her idea was rejected."

"Frances and I didn't work out," he said. "She's mentally ill."

[During the course of Eva's marriage to Isaacs, he visited Farmer several times at the sanitarium where Lillian had had her committed. During her confinement there, she was sexually assaulted by both male and female orderlies. Some of the hospital staff sold her sexual favors to drunken soldiers from the nearby Fort Lewis Army Base. These young men were allowed to gang-rape Farmer for ten dollars a session.]

"With Charlie, before and during my marriage to him, I could do no wrong. I was right, even when I was wrong. He never seemed to be in a foul mood and went along with whatever request I made. He made me wonder if all American men were that easy to manipulate."

***

Ironically, before she left for America, Jolie had advised Zsa Zsa, "Please don't rush into another ill-fated marriage. If you must marry, though, make it a hotel director."

Months later, from Hollywood, Jolie received a letter from Zsa Zsa in which her daughter informed her, "I'm going to marry the most famous hotelier in the world."

Years after their marriage, it was revealed that Conrad Hilton came very close to calling off his wedding to Zsa Zsa. He flew to an austere

Catholic retreat in the desert of New Mexico, where he lived with priests in their monastery. For a week, he mulled over his decision. A devout Catholic, he didn't want to be cut off from his church, which did not recognize divorce. Flying out of New Mexico, he had made up his mind. "I will not marry the Hungarian glamour queen."

In Los Angeles, he invited her to the Beverly Hills Hotel for lunch. She was making a rejection of her very difficult for him. As Eva later revealed, Zsa Zsa spent four hours getting ready to see Conrad—"and Zsa Zsa looked stunning." Over lunch, she poured out her love and devotion to her prospective husband.

Even so, he was still determined to call off the marriage. After lunch, he invited her for a stroll through the hotel's gardens Finally, he found enough courage to tell her, "My Catholic church just means too much to me. I'm very faithful. I've been unable to get a dispensation from the Vatican. Because of my divorce from my first wife, I can't marry you."

Sobbing, she fled, soon after colliding with two friends, Walt Disney and Spencer Tracy, who were emerging from the hotel's dining room. Seeing what a bad condition she was in, Tracy volunteered to drive her back to her apartment, although he was much too drunk to take the wheel. Somehow, they made it to Eva's apartment, but not before he put his hand on her knee and "made a lewd proposition to me."

Eva recalled that Zsa Zsa shut herself up for four days and nights, crying constantly. Shortly before midnight on the fourth day, she came to the phone to hear a Texas drawl:

"Little darling, I can't live without you. Let's get married!"

***

Before their wedding, Conrad wanted to introduce Zsa Zsa to his 82-year-old mother, Mary Laufersweiler Hilton. He flew with her to El Paso, Texas, and on the flight there, Zsa Zsa became panicky, fearing that the elderly woman would view her as no more than a gold-digger.

When Conrad had been in the U.S. Army during World War I, his father, Augustus Halvorsen ("Gus") Hilton, had died in a car accident in Texas.

After the piercing blue eyes of Mrs. Hilton had carefully evaluated Zsa Zsa, she pronounced that she liked the Hungarian beauty. "Your Georgia, as you call her, has a lot of spunk and is one gorgeous little hussy. Better than you deserve, you *roué.*"

When Conrad left the living room, she whispered to Zsa Zsa, "Before Connie started buying up every deluxe hotel in America, he sold coffins. Texas and New Mexico were pretty much frontier when he was a boy. I always feared the

Indians would abduct me and turn me into a squaw. I still sleep with a gun under my pillow. If an Indian breaks in on me, I'll send that redskin to his happy hunting grounds in the sky."

Fearing he would not marry her, Zsa Zsa had kept Conrad at bay during their four-month courtship. She admitted that he was obsessed by her and her body, claiming, "He was burning to have me. I was determined he wasn't going to get any until I had that wedding ring on my finger."

From Tiffany's he'd presented her with two rings, advising her to choose which of the two (one with a small diamond, another with a larger stone) she preferred.

Zsa Zsa, a European who was universally recognized as one of the most glamorous. women in the world, met her mother-in-law from the wild western frontier.

Ironically, **Mary L. Hilton** *(photo above)* approved of her.

"I was no fool," she later said. "I had to choose the smaller diamond, even though I hated it. We Gabors know our diamonds. Had I selected the larger diamond, I would have been exposed as a gold-digger. *Dahlink,* that was the last time in my life I ever chose the smaller diamond when offered a choice by a man."

With Eva designated as her matron of honor, Zsa Zsa Gabor married Conrad Hilton on April 10, 1942 at the Hotel La Fonda in Santa Fe, New Mexico, at the foot of the Sangre de Cristo Mountains. "It was twilight," Zsa Zsa said, and over the mountains was a stunning sky of pink and purple. The place was garlanded with flowers, mostly white lilies and white gardenias. It was a dramatic setting."

Before the wedding, she'd met her three stepsons-to-be: Conrad Nicholson, nicknamed Nicky, born in 1926; William Barron, born in 1927; and Eric Michael, born in 1933.

A lot of Conrad's fraternity brothers from Tau Kappa Epsilon showed up for the wedding, as well as Republican cronies from the New Mexico State Legislature, in whose body Conrad had served when he was in his early twenties. Many of his male friends from his World War I Army days also attended.

At the reception, Zsa Zsa was overcome with grave doubts about the world into which she had married. After all, she'd been the mistress of Atatürk, the father of his country, the former political center of the great Ottoman Empire.

She'd come from a background of intelligence and international sophistication. She found herself socializing with "primitive cowpokes with their vulgar jokes and their hearty back-slapping guffaws."

An old man, who introduced himself as "Red" and who claimed that he managed a hotel in El Paso, came up to her. "I'm known as the biggest lady killer in the State of Texas, where the competition is terrific. Everything's bigger in Texas, including me, if you get my drift. I saw Connie in the locker room. You're in for a treat, gal, and so is he. I told him he was going to get some red-hot Hungarian paprika tonight."

Conrad didn't come to the bridal suite until five o'clock that morning. He was drunk and staggering. He fell down on the bed and told her they had to catch an early morning flight, leaving at seven o'clock for Chicago.

***

The following night at the landmark Blackstone Hotel in Chicago, Zsa Zsa experienced her honeymoon night. As she admitted in a memoir, her husband was "a wonderful lover, virile, well endowed, and masterful." She also claimed to Eva and friends that Greg Bautzer had not exaggerated. "It was more than ten inches long and very thick."

The next day, she learned that Conrad was closing the deal on buying the Blackstone. She heard him on the phone negotiating and felt she came to know him better. "He was as ruthless as Atatürk," she said. "One time I heard him yell into the phone, 'If that shithead double-crosses me, I will have the bastard killed.'"

"In bed, he was loving to me," she said. "But nearly every waking hour during the day, he was no cuddly Teddy Bear. He was all business. When he came to bed, he demanded and took his pleasure."

Before he left Chicago, he proclaimed, "I've pulled off a great package deal, a ribbon tied around my Georgia and the Blackstone in the same day."

During their first forty-eight hours of marriage, Conrad realized he had very different spending habits from Zsa Zsa. Whereas thrift had been his lifetime motto, she believed that money was meant to be spent.

With only $5,000 in cash and $20,000 in credit, he'd built a hotel chain beginning with one hotel in Cisco, Texas. By the time of his marriage to Zsa Zsa, he had acquired nearly two dozen hotel properties.

On looking back at his wedding,

"A man's best friend is his mother." Or so said young **Nicky Hilton** *(left)*, when he met his new stepmother, **Zsa Zsa** *(center)*.

Conrad Hilton's other son, **Barron**, is on the right in this photo from 1944, snapped two years after the Gabor/Hilton wedding in New Mexico.

Against her better judgment, Zsa Zsa soon found herself in a torrid affair with Nicky. As she told Eva, "Little boys grow up in the most delightful ways."

Conrad said, "Our marriage was doomed from the start. I could afford it, but glamour, I found, was expensive, and Zsa Zsa had raised glamour to the last degree. She also knew more days in which gifts would be given than appear on any holiday calendar."

After breakfast, Conrad excused himself to meet with lawyers associated with the sale of the Blackstone. Left alone in their bridal suite, Zsa Zsa was astonished when a bellhop let Nicky into the living room. He didn't even knock.

Only seventeen years old at the time, he moved toward her and took her in his arms. He pressed his body tightly against hers, and he kissed her passionately, inserting a darting tongue.

She was shocked by his aggression, although, as she admitted later, "He was strangely appealing."

He looked through the double door into the bedroom of the suite, spotting the unmade bed. "I should have been here last night making love to you instead of Dad. But don't you tell him that. He'd beat me half to death."

"Nicky, *dahlink*, you're adorable and ever so handsome," she told him, "But you really should not take advantage of your new stepmother like that."

"To hell with that," he said. "When you married Dad, you didn't gain just one new man in your life. You gained two new men in your life. I'm much more virile than my poor old Dad, as you shall soon see. New get dressed for lunch. I want to show off my new red hot mama in the restaurant downstairs. When you walk through that door, you'll no doubt produce fifty erections." He stepped back. "Look what you've already done to King Kong here."

***

In her memoir, *Orchids and Salami,* Eva had virtually nothing to say about her marriage to Charles Isaacs, a union which officially extended from 1943 to 1949. The actual marriage lasted for only a few months. Her explanation for not writing about her married life was this: "I can't say more about it because I do not believe it is right for me to say more."

Officially, she was married during one of the most momentous periods of her life, from the final years of World War II to the 1950s. Eva began dating other men after only six months of marriage to Isaacs. Why he allowed it is an unanswered question. He seemed to tolerate the most outrageous behavior from his wife.

Jolie had given her some advice long ago back in Budapest: "If one isn't happy with a husband, she should get a good lover on the side, perhaps more than one good lover. A woman can never have enough good lovers, especially on Christmas, birthdays, and on Valentine's Day, when she should make it clear that she's partial to diamonds—no small stones, please."

During the beginning months of her marriage, Eva evolved—thanks partly to her husband's connections—into one of the top hostesses of Hollywood. She didn't quite rival Ouida Rathbone, but A-list producers, directors, and movie stars came and went from the home she shared with Isaacs.

At her first big dinner party, her guest of honor was David O. Selznick, the fabled producer of 1939's *Gone With the Wind*. Despite her hopes that he'd sign her to a contract, Eva had not even succeeded in persuading him to schedule an appointment.

Ironically, she found herself hosting a dinner party in his honor. Meeting her, he was most gracious and pretended he'd never heard her name before. During the time she knew him, he never mentioned that contract she sought, and she felt it would be ill mannered to bring it up while she was entertaining him as a guest in her home.

Selznick's date at the Isaacs manse was the brunette actress Jennifer Jones, who, officially at least, was married to the handsome bisexual actor, Robert Walker. As Eva recalled, "Jennifer was the hottest ticket in town at the time, having won a Best Actress Oscar for her 1943 role in that sappy religious drama, *The Song of Bernadette.*" Jennifer and Eva were the same age, although Eva never admitted that.

For her first appearance as a Hollywood hostess, Eva wore a stunning black satin gown. Jennifer admired it and told her that by coincidence, she had com-

missioned her dressmaker to create one that was almost exactly the same. "We'll have to make it a point not to show up at the same parties," Jones cautioned.

Eva never completely adopted Jennifer as a role model. Yet within the context of her marriage to Isaacs—in ways similar to Jones during her marriage to Walker—Eva would date men on the side, keeping her outside affairs camouflaged as much as possible.

"A woman needs a husband who is understanding about a woman's need for outside diversions," Eva said.

She became known for continuing to date Bugsy Siegel, Robert Taylor, and, as a sometime thing, Howard Hughes. There were even some occasions when she was seen leaving Errol Flynn's house shortly

Actress **Jennifer Jones**, in mink, attends a Hollywood premiere with her husband, **David O. Selznick**, who had produced *Gone With the Wind*. Jones had dumped her husband, actor Robert Walker, to marry Selznick.

Eva stuck around to help Walker mend a broken heart.

The bisexual French star, **Claudette Colbert**, had some advice for Eva about living arrangements within the context of a heterosexual marriage:

"Always maintain separate residences, and live apart to keep love alive."

before dawn. Sometimes after a raucous party at Flynn's house, she would remain behind for a sleep-over. As she joked, "With Flynn, you never got much sleep." Often, when she staggered back to the Isaacs' manse, he had already left for that day's duties with his Coast Guard unit.

On at least three separate occasions, the recently wid-owed Clark Gable summoned her back to his residence for yet another sleepover. Once again, she donned one of the *négligées* worn by Carole Lombard and sprayed herself with the dead star's perfume.

During one of Eva's parties, she was enchanted by the Paris-born movie star, Claudette Colbert. "I want to push myself into Selznick's orbit tonight," she confided to Eva. "I want him to cast me in a picture with Jen-nifer Jones."

[As it came to pass, Colbert and Jones, Selznick's mis-tress, eventually starred together in the memorable Since You Went Away (1944).*]*

Colbert had arrived at the party with a young actress, whose name Eva never remembered. She'd been told that Colbert was mostly a lesbian, having survived a torrid affair with Marlene Dietrich. A bisexual, she'd also seduced many male stars, including Gary Cooper and Maurice Chevalier.

During her chat with Colbert, Eva was told, "To keep love alive, a man and a woman should always have separate residences." Colbert eventually followed her own advice during her marriages to actor Norman Foster and Dr. Joel Press-man, a physician.

"I would be so much happier if Charles let me have my own private apart-ment at another address at least twenty miles away," Eva said. "He could make an appointment to see me whenever he wanted. I think it's called 'conjugal rights.'"

"I agree with you," Colbert said. "A wife should live elsewhere, and her husband should call for an appointment. That would give a woman time to clear anybody out of her bedroom and make herself look super glamorous before re-ceiving her spouse."

The second great star of the 1930s Eva met at her party was the very beau-tiful Loretta Young, who had been in films so long she'd even appeared on screen with Rudolf Valentino in his landmark movie, *The Sheik (1921)*. Known for her lady-like gentility onscreen, she was the complete opposite in person. Young obviously knew that Eva occasionally dated Bugsy Siegel.

She revealed that Bugsy's thirty-five room Hollywood mansion had gone on the market, and she'd deposited $8,500 down on the asking price of $185,000. Young told Eva that she and her husband, advertising executive Thomas A Lewis, had taken out a sizable mortgage.

However, when they hired an exterminator, he diagnosed that the house had serious structural damage from termites. According to the terms of the sales contract, Bugsy was responsible for the cost of any termite damage.

"When I took him to court, the judge ruled in my favor, and granted me the return of my escrow money," Young said. "But instead of paying up, your gangster is threatening me."

Three nights later, on a date with Bugsy, Eva learned that her mob friend was doing far more than threatening Young. He'd ordered one of the mobsters in Murder, Inc., to assassinate her.

Years later, Eva claimed, "I was responsible for saving Young's life. I begged so hard for Bugsy to spare Loretta, that he called off one of his boys— and just in time before she got a bullet in her head. That, of course, would ultimately be Bugsy's fate."

In the aftermath of her first big party, Eva summed up her new status within A-list Hollywood. "They raved about me as a hostess, but as a struggling actress, the bastards slammed the door in my face. I was definitely traveling in the fast lane now that I had a handsome, wealthy husband."

"Charles, as far as I know, was straight, and he'd had his share of women," Eva said. "But at Hollywood parties, he was always surrounded by homosexual men. A lot of men who are straight object to that, but Charlie seems to love to be the belle of the ball. What is the male equivalent of belle, *dahlink?*"

On the night of her first party, Isaacs had to retire before midnight because he was scheduled to get up at 5AM to report for duty with the Coast Guard.

Eva saw her last guest out at around two in the morning. As she was switching off the lights on the terrace, the shadow of a man emerged from the garden. She didn't know how long he'd been standing outside the house looking in at the party-goers.

At first, she was going to scream until he said, "It's okay. I'm Jennifer's husband, Robert Walker."

She knew who he was. "He looked so desolate, I invited him in for a drink. Even though he was married to Jennifer and had two sons with her, all of Hollywood knows that Selznick is stealing her from

Loretta Young *(photo above)* found herself in a contract dispute and later in a bitter feud with Bugsy Siegel involving the transfer of a building she discovered had termite damage. *"LORETTA ATTACKS BUGSY'S BUGS"* screamed a headline.

Eva intervened and possibly saved Young's life when the gangster ordered Murder, Inc., to have her killed.

Robert." She knew he'd specialized in boy-next-door roles, and she found him softspoken with a friendly, yet sad, face.

He interpreted Eva as a sympathetic soul. "I can't compete with Selznick," he said. "He can offer her the world. Make her a bigtime star. What do I have?"

She had heard that he'd become an alcoholic, and there were reports of a mental disorder. He more or less confirmed that when he confessed that he was contemplating suicide "because of the loss of my beloved Jennifer."

She felt awkward talking to this strange man while Isaacs was asleep upstairs, so she agreed to telephone him the following day and talk some more.

"Thank you, thank you," he said. "Everybody takes Selznick's side. I'm a nothing. In Hollywood, you go where the money is."

After her first audition as a Hollywood hostess, Eva pronounced herself a success, based on the initial reports in the press.

"But it wasn't enough," she claimed. "Giving great parties and hiring handsome waiters was not my idea of a career goal," she said. "I still wanted to be a big star, and I could not give up that dream and settle down, even if my husband was a millionaire."

***

In Budapest, Jolie received a telegram from Zsa Zsa. "Connie marrying me has made me almost the happiest woman in the world, but I cannot be the happiest without you."

The telegram was more reassuring and loving than it was accurate.

At least for the moment, Zsa Zsa had decided that her career would be as Mrs. Conrad Hilton, glamorous woman of Hollywood, wife of a fabled hotelier, and fabulous hostess of Bel Air. At one point, she told a reporter, "I am the uncrowned Queen of Bel Air, and for the first time I've become a mother."

She was referring to her newly acquired stepsons, Nicky and Barron Hilton, who had moved in with their father and her. The youngest son, Eric, age 12, preferred to live with his mother.

From the beginning, there was tension between Nicky and Conrad, Sr. One evening, just after Conrad had returned home from a business trip, he and Zsa Zsa kissed passionately.

From a sofa nearby, Nicky watched with fascination. "Dad, what does a fellow have to do to get a kiss like that from Zsa Zsa?"

Impulsively, Conrad bashed Nicky in the face, leaving his nose bleeding profusely. She rushed to the aid of the stricken teenager, fearing he'd been given a concussion.

Conrad stormed upstairs to his bedroom, his retreat from the world. Furnished in a Spartan Spanish style, it evoked a monastery. Before Zsa Zsa moved in, he'd told her that, "I would never share a bedroom with a woman."

Even before her marriage, she'd been allowed to decorate what they defined as her own bedroom. The first piece of furniture she ordered was an elaborate four-poster. "I wanted to wake up like Scarlett O'Hara in *Gone With the Wind.*" She selected white lace curtains and covered the walls in a violet-tinted chintz. When her bedroom was decorated to her liking, she said, "Now I feel like Miss Scarlett. When is Clark Gable coming to rape me?"

Migrating from room to room, she began to redecorate the entire house on Bellagio Road, which was built in the Andalusian style with a red tile roof and large panoramic terraces overlooking the golf course of the Bel Air country club. Next door lived Basil and Ouida Rathbone, where Zsa Zsa had first been introduced to *tout* Hollywood in 1941.

She was not satisfied by redecorating just the house: She wanted to remake the man as well. "I tossed out his baggy suits and burned his ties with his hotels painted on them. I drove him to the best tailor in Beverly Hills and ordered two dozen custom-made suits. I even ordered a dozen pair of elegant leather shoes and told him to wear his boots only in the Southwest. Alas, I could change the outer man, but not the inner man. Although elegantly dressed, he remained a Texas cowboy."

"I also had to change Connie's sleeping arrangement," she said. "I fired his twenty-eight-year old secretary, a beautiful girl with a big bust who competed with Lana Turner for the title of 'The Sweater Girl.'"

She was replaced with the rather drab Mrs. Olie Wakeman, who turned out to be an amazing business woman and a brilliant organizer of Conrad's rather sloppily run office. She began to manage his affairs with more skills than he'd ever known.

In a memoir, Zsa Zsa claimed that "my marriage to Conrad meant the end of my freedom." That was not true. For a wife, she had almost unlimited freedom. Her husband was usually gone four nights a week.

Sometimes, he'd disappear for almost a month, including several visits to Mexico. Even when he was in Bel Air, he'd turn down offers to go out with her, allowing her the freedom to disappear into the night with an "escort."

He'd tell her, "I'm too tired to go out. I want to go to bed early so I can get up at 6AM to play golf."

Even though he'd lost his Lana Turner wannabe secretary, Conrad was like the legendary sailor who had a girl in every port, except his ports were cities such as El Paso, San Francisco, Houston, Chicago, and New York.

"Connie never believed that I loved him, even though I did," Zsa Zsa claimed. "But I loved him in my fashion, *dahlink.* To him, I was forever the little Hungarian gold digger. But I didn't always get the gold."

She cited her desire for a Cadillac to match the color of her hair. She ended up getting a secondhand blue Chrysler that had been owned by Greg Bautzer when he was dating Lana Turner.

"That car reminded me of the color of our old kitchen stove in Budapest. Every time I got behind the wheel, I smelled Sauerkraut and potatoes cooking."

Although she was often turned down, she kept making requests for gifts. "The next time you buy me a present," she told him, "I would appreciate sapphires to match the color of my eyes."

During the first weeks of marriage, she had felt empowered to buy anything she wanted. But after tallying up her expenses for the first three months, Conrad became enraged. He called her into his study and tossed her bills into the air.

"From now on, "I'm putting you on a strict budget of two-hundred and fifty dollars a month— that's that! Your clothes, the beauty parlor, your lunches with the ladies, all of it has to come out of your allowance. I, of course, will take care of all household expenses."

"*Dahlink,* in Europe when I was a girl, Vilmos gave me $300 a month to spend while I attended boarding school. That was in Switzerland. This is Beverly Hills, 1943, the most expensive city in America."

On her limited budget, Zsa Zsa rose to become recognized as the best dressed woman in Hollywood. How did she do it?

She approached the designers and made a deal with them. She would wear one of their best gowns for just one night and would loudly proclaim their talent to *tout* Hollywood. She'd return the gown the next day, "after giving you a million dollars worth of publicity," she'd tell a designer. "As you know, on me, the gown will dazzle."

Many designers presented her with the gown in gratitude. She complained to Eva, "Connie makes five million dollars a year, and expects me to get by on peanuts."

"Connie may have objected to the money I spend on myself, but he respected my business sense," Zsa Zsa claimed. One night, he came to her and asked, "Which shall it be? The Plaza in New York or the National in Cuba? For the moment, at least, I can buy only one of them."

"The Plaza, *dahlink,*" she answered, remembering where she had spend her first night in America. "After all, I don't want to be homeless the next time I visit Manhattan."

Zsa Zsa also claimed that Conrad used her elegance

Multi-millionaire **E.F. Hutton**, in a photo snapped in the 1920s.

Hutton told Zsa Zsa that had he seen her first, he would have proposed marriage.

and beauty to gain financial backers. Her most memorable encounter transpired one night at the Plaza Hotel when she met E.F. Hutton.

[Born in 1875, Edward Francis Hutton was one of the most fabled American financiers and the co-founder of the prestigious investment firm, E.F. Hutton & Co. From 1920 to 1935, he was married to Marjorie Merriweather Post, the General Foods heiress. They had one child, actress Dina Merrill, who married actor Cliff Robertson.]

After dinner at the Plaza, Hutton told Zsa Zsa, "We're going to put up the money for Connie mainly because of the good taste he showed in marrying such a young, beautiful, and smart girl who is the epitome of elegance and charm. My only regret is that I didn't get to you first."

After many negotiations, Conrad did buy The Plaza, although he got bored with all the rich elderly ladies who hung out in the lobby. One night, after too much to drink, he threatened that he was going "to put on my Stetson and my boots and shoot 'em all."

"*Dahlink,* she protested, "that would not be discreet. We would get bad publicity."

During the spring of 1943, Conrad telephoned Zsa Zsa in Bel Air. "I've just bought another hotel, the Roosevelt in New York. It's next to Grand Central Station. It's got 1,079 rooms, and I've seen all of them."

"I don't care about the number of rooms," she said. "How many floors?"

"Twenty-three," he said. "My buying the Roosevelt is just a prelude for my next big move, the Waldorf-Astoria."

"I'm already Queen of The Plaza, *dahlink,*" she said "At the Waldorf, I will have to be the Empress."

Conrad summed up his own marriage. "Being wed to Zsa Zsa brought me, in many ways, more laughter and gaiety than I had ever known in my personal life. But it brought me headaches and heartaches as well. It was a little like holding on to a Roman candle—beautiful, exciting, but you never were quite sure when it would go off. And it is surprisingly hard to live the Fourth of July every day."

At a party at the Hilton's home in Bel Air, Elsa Maxwell remarked, "Zsa Zsa and Connie are like two splendid ships that pass in the night over the North Atlantic. They quickly move on, but leave a magnificent afterglow in the moonlight. Zsa Zsa is like the thunderstorm of glamour. For some, it is too, too much."

Conrad told Maxwell, "My wife has many addictions, including thousand dollar flacons of perfume. After feasting on a cup of black coffee and a piece of Melba toast at breakfast, she begins to prepare her face for lunch."

"It might take an hour for her to select what designer scarf to wear," he said. "Selecting a brooch is like an Axis power deciding whether to declare war on the United States."

"After lunch and a beauty sleep, the dressing ritual for dinner begins, including a luxurious bath in perfumed waters. Making up her face takes two hours. Selecting the right outfit is crucial. I've seen her burst into tears of indecision in trying to find the right hat to wear."

Whenever Conrad was in town on a Sunday morning, he attended Catholic services at a church in Beverly Hills. He insisted Zsa Zsa attend the services with him.

On her first visit, in the church's courtyard, he introduced her to some of his friends there. They included Mary Pickford, Loretta Young, Kathryn Grayson, and Mrs. Spencer Tracy, whose husband was comfortably installed in a bungalow with Katharine Hepburn on the estate of George Cukor.

At the end of the sermon, the congregation made its way toward the rail to receive communion. As a divorced man, Conrad could not participate in this ritual. He remained behind with Zsa Zsa, kneeling in his pew.

"To be deprived of the Sacrament was the price I had to pay for marrying Zsa Zsa," he later said. "I went on praying as fervently as before, but now I felt adrift, cut off, spiritually isolated."

***

That Monday morning, Zsa Zsa left the house at around ten o'clock, driving to Rodeo Drive on a shopping expedition. She needed a scarf, "but not any scarf...the right scarf."

A terrible driver, she struggled to park her car (the blue Chrysler formerly owned by Bautzer). The space was tight, and she collided with both the bumper in front of her and the bumper behind her.

Seeing her distress, a tall, shabbily dressed man appeared, emerging from a battered old car. "Pretty lady," he said, "let me park that car for you. I'm an expert driver. I also fly airplanes, if you want a bird's-eye view over Los Angeles."

She looked him up and down. Behind his unshaven mask, she sensed that he was quite handsome, but his suit was ill-fitting, his tieless white shirt dirty. He wore a pair of old tennis shoes with his big toe sticking through the fabric of one of them.

"No, thank you," she said. "I'm perfectly capable of parking my own car."

"Are you sure this is your car?" he asked. "It looks like Greg Bautzer's car."

"How impertinent." She got out of the car and locked the door, even though it was angled precariously into the street.

Arrogantly, she walked across the street, "not looking back at that bum."

Photographer Paul Hesse, with whom she had an appointment, had been waiting for her and witnessed her confrontation.

"Zsa Zsa," he said. "I'm impressed. I didn't know you knew the great Howard Hughes."

"You mean that tramp was Howard Hughes, the richest man in America?" she said. She looked back across the street, but Hughes had disappeared.

In a memoir, Zsa Zsa would write, "Nothing happened between me and Howard Hughes."

When Susan Hayward read that, she said, "Does anyone believe that? If such a person exists, tell them I have this beautiful, uninhabited island in Hawaii that I'll sell to them for a hundred dollars."

***

Robert Walker called Eva the next morning and asked if he could pick her up and drive her to Malibu where he had a cottage. Charles Isaacs had announced that he'd be away for the weekend on military duties in San Diego, so she accepted Walker's offer.

Walker intrigued her, and she was sympathetic to his plight. Producer David Selznick, no great beauty, was stealing his wife, Jennifer Jones.

Behind the wheel, driving north, Walker told her, "They say money is sexy but power is sexier. When you've got both money and power, like Selznick, that's a winning combination. The girls tell me I'm good looking. But women often want a lot more than a handsome face."

Eva later confessed to Susan Hayward, "Bob brought out the mother instinct in me. I felt he was coming unglued emotionally. I knew he was drinking too much. His career was getting off the ground, but he feared that Selznick would use his power in Hollywood to destroy his chances. He was a sad case, but I liked him and felt sorry for him."

In his rented cottage, Eva and Robert changed into bathing suits. He often took his two sons, Robert Walker, Jr., and Michael Walker, to the cottage on weekends, but they were involved with their mother (his wife) that Saturday and Sunday.

Eva and Walker ambled along the beachfront for an hour before spreading out their beach blankets.

Walker's estranged wife was on his mind. He told her that he'd met the aspiring actress, then known as Phyllis Isley, when they were attending the American Academy of the Dramatic Arts in New York City in 1937. "We were married in Tulsa—that's in Oklahoma—in January of 1939, and we moved to Hollywood to find work in films. Two years later, Selznick discovered her and began grooming her for stardom," he said. "Fortunately, she had already given birth to our two sons. Perhaps to keep me busy, Selznick got me work at Metro, where I've just finished a movie called *Bataan* (1943). During its filming, I've made two friends, the best I've ever had, Robert Taylor and Phillip Terry."

"I know Mr. Taylor," Eva said, giving no indication that they'd been lovers. "I don't know Terry."

"He's married to Joan Crawford, poor guy," Walker said. "She's a man-eater, just like Judy Garland."

"Dorothy from *The Wizard of Oz?*" Eva said. "Andy Hardy's girl friend? I find that hard to believe."

"When you've been around Hollywood long enough, you soon learn that actors aren't as they appear on the screen," he said. "I idolized Judy. "When I was shooting *See Here, Private Hargrove* (1944), the director told me that Judy was working on a picture on the next sound stage. He knew her, and I begged to be introduced to my idol. He took me over to meet this dear sweet girl."

"When I encountered Judy in her dressing room, I turned my idolatrous eyes upon her. Her face brightened, and she gave me not a sweet smile, but a sexy one. I couldn't believe the way she talked. She's just a young gal, but she sounds off like a supreme sophisticate."

"We chatted for several minutes, most of the time with her hand on my knee," he said. "I learned later that Judy likes to come up to men and grab their crotches. On the dance floor, she's been known to unzip a guy when he's got her in a tight embrace."

Robert Walker and **Judy Garland** were cast together in *The Clock* (1949), her first dramatic role, and a movie in which she did not sing.

"I idolized her screen image," Walker told Eva. "But Judy Garland off the screen was an aggressive man-eater. She didn't even ask you...She just unzipped you."

"I find that shocking," Eva said, "though I've been in Hollywood long enough to believe anything."

"When I got ready to go, Judy stood real close to me and talked like Mae West."

"I've heard a lot about you, honey," she told me. "That whorish wife of yours doesn't deserve a cute little hunk like you. Drop around some night and see me, and we'll have a few belts and get to know each other like Adam did the night Eve got him to bite into that fucking apple."

"I got her drift all right, but I didn't come around," he said. "Three days later, there was a knock on my dressing room door. When I opened it, Judy was standing there. I just couldn't believe how aggressive she is. I had on just a pair of underwear. The first thing I know, she's pulled down my underwear and is going down on me——right in my dressing room. Fortunately, she'd locked the door when she came in. I've been secretly dating her ever since…that is, when she has a free moment. She says that she'll get her husband, Vincente Minnelli, to cast me with her in picture called *The Clock* (1944)."

"Well, I guess the casting couch in Hollywood works both ways," she said. "Women, too, can put men on the casting couch."

As the sun was setting over the Pacific, Walker suggested they go back to the cottage to "wash the sand off."

It contained two bathrooms. As she was showering in one of them, a nude Walker pulled back the curtain and entered the shower stall with her.

As she'd later relay to Susan Hayward at lunch the following week, "I didn't resist. We both knew it was going to happen. I like to think I helped him get over Jennifer…at least for a night. But that evening in Malibu had a second act after the end of our performance in the shower."

Fully dressed, Eva joined Walker in the kitchen, where he was ordering take-out. "We've got guests for dinner. Bob Taylor and Phillip Terry. They like to escape from their respective wives, Barbara Stanwyck and Joan Crawford. Those wives of theirs like to snip off their balls whenever they're home. They have to get away from time to time to restore their manhood."

"It'll be great seeing Bob again," she said. "And I'd like to meet the man brave enough to marry Crawford."

"Oh Eva, thank God you're a sophisticated European. If you were a typical American girl from the sticks, I might have to warn you. When they were making *Bataan* with me, Bob and Phillip fell madly in love. They're still in the throes of passion and can't keep their hands off each other. So be duly warned."

"Bring 'em on."

***

Four days after Zsa Zsa's abortive car parking encounter with Howard Hughes, he called her. "Miss Gabor," he said. "I've bought the rights to this unpublished novel set in old San Francisco. There are roles in it for two glamorous German sisters."

"Both Eva and I speak fluent German, and it is said that we are glamorous," Zsa Zsa said.

"Actually, I am very well acquainted with your sister Eva," Hughes said. "A wonderful girl. So beautiful, so charming. I've seen two of her movies. Bad script, bad directing, but she projected a magnetic personality. The two of you on the screen together would be a dynamic, bubbly combination. You might end up becoming Hollywood's next great sister act."

"What do you mean?" she asked.

"Like Constance Bennett with Joan Bennett, or Joan Fontaine with Olivia de Havilland."

That's very flattering, Mr. Hughes, and you must forgive me for my rudeness during my attempt to park that car," she said. "You were most kind to volunteer your services."

"It's natural you might have thought I was a car thief," Hughes said. "But I promise you I'll be better groomed if you can meet me for lunch today at one o'clock at the Beverly Hills Hotel. I've rented a bungalow in the gardens of the hotel."

"I'd love to talk over movie roles for Eva and me," she said. "It sounds exciting, *dahlink*. Of course, I'll have to chastise Eva for not telling me how well she knows you already."

"I'd rather you didn't," he said. "I don't want to get embroiled in any sibling competition. I also know your husband. He's getting on in years. He really shouldn't let a lady who looks like you wander around alone in Los Angeles."

"If you know my husband, then you know he's wed first to his hotels, with me as a distant second."

"Let's forget about him at lunch," Hughes said. "I've got one of the hottest film properties in Hollywood to discuss with you."

Over lunch in the dining room of the Beverly Hills Hotel, Zsa Zsa wore "Chanel black with diamonds." *[her words]*.

Hughes was not particularly well groomed, but at least he'd shaved. He wore a clean suit with a white shirt and no tie. The *maître d'hotel* always suspended the restaurant's dress code for Hughes.

Over lunch, Hughes was gracious to Zsa Zsa. He outlined the plot of a movie that seemed intriguing:

"Two beautiful sisters share a mansion in San Francisco during the city's heyday before the earthquake," Hughes said. "One of them, against her father's wishes, runs off with a handsome dock worker. During her absence, her father disinherits her and soon after, dies of a stroke. The dock worker eventually deserts the sister who married him, and she's forced to move back in with her (now rich) sister, who has inherited the family house and fortune. The rich sister agrees to support her errant sibling, but assigns her to the maid's room."

"Along comes San Francisco's most dashing and eligible bachelor. "I'm considering either Errol Flynn or Robert Taylor for the role. The remainder of the drama concerns the poor but beautiful sister's attempt to lure her rich sister's husband into an adulterous affair as an act of revenge, with the intention of ruining their marriage."

"I think Eva and I could play that," Zsa Zsa said. "Of course, I would be cast as the rich sister."

"That goes without saying."

By the end of the luncheon, Hughes had informed her that he was going to fly the director, Howard Hawks, on a sightseeing tour above Greater Los Angeles. "Would you like to come with us? Hawks is interested in directing you and Eva in my movie."

She told him she'd be delighted, but when Hughes drove her to the airport, he learned that Hawks had had an emergency and could not join them.

"Let me show you Los Angeles, alone with me, from the point of view of an eagle," he said.

She was most willing, and was awed by the coastline, having grown up in landlocked Hungary. But it went on and on until San Francisco came into view. Luring beautiful women, or handsome young men, into his plane and flying them north from L.A. was a frequent seductive technique used by the Aviator. Both Norma Shearer and Rita Hayworth had already been seduced this way.

Zsa Zsa expressed her dismay, but was also excited to be seeing San Francisco for the first time.

As a married woman, she opted to be very discreet about her "lost weekend" in San Francisco.

Hughes had booked two adjoining suites at the Fairmont Hotel. It was obvious that he had carefully planned this trip in advance.

In her suite, Zsa Zsa encountered the finest hairdresser in the city. After she'd had her hair styled, the female manager of the best *haute couture* house in the city arrived with a choice of five gowns. Zsa Zsa selected the most expensive one.

Then, as yet another "get acquainted" gift from Hughes, she was presented with a stunning string of pearls.

Years later, Zsa Zsa admitted to her "godmother," Greta Keller, that at some point, she left the connecting doors between her suite and that occupied by Hughes unlocked. "He took advantage. After all, I wasn't going to let Eva get ahead of me."

[That episode in San Francisco launched one of the most bizarre romantic entanglements in the history of Hollywood.

As only a man of great wealth and power could pull off successfully, Hughes began simultaneously but secretly dating not only the two Gabor sisters, but the two most famous sisters in Hollywood, Joan Fontaine and Olivia de Havilland. Before the conclusion of the dramas that evolved from all this, each of the four women would deserve an Oscar for her respective performance.]

***

275

Eva

Gossip maven Louella Parsons may have launched Hughes' affair with De Havilland when she wrote, in error, that the actress, who had played Melanie in *Gone with the Wind,* had accepted an engagement ring from Hughes after "a whirlwind courtship."

Parsons got it wrong: Hughes had never met De Havilland.

Ironically, it was at that point that Hughes—inspired by Parson's column—actually began his pursuit of her.

During De Havilland's first date with Hughes, he told her that because of his intervention with David O. Selznick and then-director George Cukor, he'd won for her the role of Melanie in *Gone With the Wind.*

De Havilland may have fallen in love with him. There was talk of marriage, more from her standpoint than his.

He had announced to Johnny Meyer, his publicist (actually, his pimp), that he didn't plan to marry until he was fifty. "But he probably changed his mind," Meyer said. "He was always a bit crazy. In addition to Jack Buetel and Faith Domergue, he was still dating Ginger Rogers. Then, during a brief period of less than a month, he proposed marriage to five separate women: Ginger Rogers, Olivia De Havilland and her sister, Joan Fontaine, and both of the Gabor sisters."

Eva and Zsa Zsa each dated Hughes secretly, but not discussing their respective liaisons with him, even to one another. Hughes emotional "entanglements" were gossiped about at the time, but descriptions of the extent of his madness didn't appear in print until years later.

"Joan was the first to spill the beans," Meyer said. "When she realized that Olivia was falling in love with him, she broke down and told her that Howard had simultaneously proposed marriage to her too. And later, when Eva and Zsa Zsa realized that there would be no movie about two rich sisters in San Francisco, they drifted away too."

The only confidante Eva had during the course of all this was Susan Hayward, who was sympathetic since she, too, had been wooed, disastrously, by Hughes. Eva fed her stories of events that transpired during her dates with Hughes: "He has strange eating habits, ordering a butterfly steak with only twelve peas," Eva said. When the waiter arrived with more peas that that on the plate, Howard sent it back to the kitchen. On our first night out, when the bill arrived, he told me he never carried any money. I had to pick up the dining tab for the world's richest man."

Eva told Hayward that Hughes kept insisting on giving her flying lessons, "but I'm no bird. Being up in a small plane caused me to panic. What would I do if I encountered a Japanese bomber trying to bomb Los Angeles like they did Pearl Harbor? I much preferred to go dancing."

One night at Hugo's Garden Room, Hughes demonstrated his skill at the fox-trot. "He was also a pretty good rhumba dancer," Eva said, "but, of course, no Cesar Romero."

"One night at Hugo's, we double dated with Ronald Reagan and his young wife, Jane Wyman. She didn't relate to me, but Ronnie liked me a lot. Under the table, he put his hand on my knee, and I secretly patted it, hoping to encourage him for one night when he was free. Jane seemed rather possessive, and obviously knew that her husband had a roving eye."

"I would dress in fabulous *couture,* and Howard would show up in some old jalopy," Eva said. "One night it was raining heavily—'cats and dogs,' as the Americans say—and I got into this death-trap. The damn roof was leaking, ruining my gown."

"The next day a messenger from Hughes arrives with a $5,000 gift certificate from one of the finest dressmakers in Hollywood. It was from the same place where Stanwyck and Crawford go shopping, probably on the same days I'm hanging out with their husbands, Robert Taylor and Phillip Terry. Hollywood is such a grand place. It makes you feel wonderfully decadent."

Hughes eventually stopped proposing marriage to various women at random. Johnny Meyer said, "He got tired. It was too incestuous. Howard not only balled Ginger, but had for a long time conducted an affair with her husband, Lew Ayres. He had both Joan and Olivia to deal with, with the gold-digging Gabors hot on his trail, too. Eventually, he chose the coward's way out. He just disappeared."

Hughes had met and been captivated by a sexy wannabe starlet, Norma Jean Baker, who later changed her name to Marilyn Monroe. He was also making romantic overtures to Ava Gardner, Mickey Rooney's ex-wife.

Shortly before the breakup of her relationship with Hughes, Zsa Zsa at a Hollywood party renewed her contact with Elsa Maxwell. "I had a dream last night," she told Maxwell. "I was married at the same time to both Conrad Hilton and Howard Hughes. Both of them died and I became their sole heir, making me the richest woman on earth. With this new power, I proposed marriage to a bachelor prince about to inherit a kingdom from his dying father."

"Keep working at it, you dear girl," Maxwell assured her, "and I think your dream will come true. The best I can do at the moment is to introduce you to Prince Rainier of Monaco. It's not much of a kingdom, but at least you can become its Princess.

***

The telephone at the Hilton manse had an urgent ring. It was three o'clock in the morning when Zsa Zsa, in bed alone, was aroused by her maid. At first, she thought something might have happened to Conrad, who was in Texas at the time.

"It's Greta Keller," the maid said. "She seems desperate to speak to you."

Arousing herself from sleep, Zsa Zsa removed her eye patch and went to the phone.

"Oh, dear one, please come at once," came a desperate, sobbing voice. "Something dreadful has happened. My poor David has been murdered."

At Greta's house, Zsa Zsa was introduced to the silent screen star, Pola Negri, a close friend of Greta's She asked a nurse to take Zsa Zsa to Greta's bedroom.

Only a small bedside lamp was lit when Zsa Zsa entered the room of her recently widowed friend. Wearing no makeup, Greta's face was streaked with tears.

"I warned David," she said, "He was foolish to have threatened Hughes. He didn't have to kill David himself. He hired somebody to do it for him."

Slowly, through Greta's tears and choking throat, her account of the tragedy unfolded.

Bacon had left their house late one morning with his new boy friend, Peter Lawford. "Both of them looked so beautiful in their white bathing suits. They were going to spend the day on the beach at Santa Monica."

Four hours later, a maroon-colored British-made sports car—a gift from Hughes to Bacon—was seen lurching along Washington Boulevard in Venice, an area of Los Angeles about four coastal miles southeast from Santa Monica.

The driver was manning the wheel like he'd drunk a huge amount of liquor. There were no other cars on the road—if there had been, he'd surely have crashed the car.

The driver of that car was Bacon himself. He suddenly slammed on the brakes and rolled to a stop, his front wheel jumping up onto the curb. Sheila Belkstein was walking her German shepherd that afternoon, and later reported what she'd seen to the police.

"I was walking my dog near a field of cabbage. At the sound of brakes, I spun around. My dog barked hysterically. From the car emerged a man wearing only a white bathing suit which showed blood stains. Across the street was a gas station. The attendant there saw Bacon and called the police."

Belkstein got to Bacon a few moments before he died. "Help me!" he called out to her. "Oh God, please help me. He fell to the ground. He was dead. A stiletto was lodged in his back.

A coroner later revealed that the stiletto had pierced his lung, and that he had bled to death internally. A thorough examination of his body revealed no bruises, no signs of struggle. Police surmised that Bacon had known his assailant.

For weeks, his death was the talk of Hollywood. Several years later, the youngest-ever editor of *The Saturday Evening Post,* Cleveland Amory, listed the Bacon murder as one of the "Top Ten Unsolved Murders of the 20th Century."

"I can't prove it, but I know that Howard Hughes either killed David or hired someone to do it," Greta claimed to Zsa Zsa.

"What about Peter Lawford?" Zsa Zsa asked.

"Peter left my house about an hour ago," Greta said. "He told me that before the murder, he was summoned to a hot dog stand and little bar across the street where he was wanted on the phone."

"The bar was behind a fence. Peter said he picked up the phone and someone, a male voice, threatened to expose his affair with David. He was warned that his career was about to be ruined. Apparently, he was on the phone for some time. When he returned to the beach, David was gone. He'd obviously gotten into the car and driven somewhere for help. He apparently didn't know where Peter was."

"Peter has pleaded with me not to involve him in anything I told the police," Greta said. "He burst into tears in front of me. His career means everything to him. I promised him I wouldn't, because I do not believe for a moment that he had anything to do with David's murder."

Zsa Zsa arrived back at the Hilton estate at 7AM the following morning. She hadn't told Greta that she, too, was intimately involved with Hughes.

Apparently, Zsa Zsa never confided to anyone, not even Eva, (or especially to Eva) the details of the David Bacon murder.

Her decision was probably selfishly motivated. At that point, she believed that Hughes could launch her as a movie star.

Robbery had been ruled out. Bacon's blood-soaked leather wallet had been tucked into the elastic band of his swimming trunks. When, in the aftermath of his murder, it was found by the police, the wallet contained one hundred dollars in twenty dollar bills, along with a nude picture of himself. It had been snapped on the beach perhaps two or three weeks previously. No one knew who had taken the picture. It might have been snapped by Lawford.

Although Zsa Zsa may have been deeply troubled by Greta's accusation, she chose not get more deeply involved. Jolie had always taught her daughters, "Regardless of the disaster suffered, it is over, and you must be off into another day. Nothing is ever gained by lying around lamenting the past. It's only today and tomorrow that should occupy your every waking moment, even your dreams."

Three nights later, Zsa Zsa met for a discreet reunion with Hughes at his mansion. No mention was ever made of the murder of David Bacon.

***

Eva

It was convenient for Eva that Charles Isaacs was gone for most of that week, because she entered what future friend, Merv Griffin, called "the most promiscuous period of Eva's life." As Griffin once confessed to Rock Hudson, "Eva has something in common with the two of us. She thrives on handsome hunks."

In her relationships with "the two Roberts," Taylor and Walker, and Joan Crawford's husband, Phillip Terry, Eva discovered that many actors in Hollywood were bisexuals. Nothing in particular in her background had prepared her for this, except perhaps her exposure to the world of the Hussars. During the heyday of the Austro-Hungarian Empire, bisexuality among Hussars was rumored to have been accepted and indulged.

Like Zsa Zsa, Eva evolved into a woman who was accepting and indulgent with bisexuals. She soon learned that although each of them was married to women at the time, Taylor, Walker, and Terry were sleeping with each other. As she told Susan Hayward, "I felt like a mother confessor, den mother, mistress, and cook for them, even if my kitchen skills, unlike Jolie's, were limited to opening a can."

The concept of Walker and Taylor as lovers and bedmates soon became commonplace to her. She called Walker "Robert" and Taylor "Bob."

"Jennifer Jones was spending her nights with David Selznick, so I was catching Robert on the rebound," Eva said. "Bob was married to Stanwyck, who preferred girls and who seemed to want her husband only as arm candy. And Phillip was free most nights because Joan Crawford had started dating other men."

Terry was actually a German, having been born to immigrants, Frederick Andrew Kormann and Ida Ruth Voll, in San Francisco in 1909. Twenty years older than Eva, he was rugged and very handsome in a masculine kind of way.

He'd had a colorful "only in America" background. He'd worked as a roustabout and a rig builder in oil fields. He had been a football player at Stanford University before enrolling in London's Royal Academy of Dramatic Art (RADA) in 1933. As he confessed to Eva, "I became a plaything for the vast homosexual underground in the British theater. They were all after me—Noël Coward, Laurence Olivier, John Gielgud."

In his pursuit of an acting career, he'd landed in

Phillip Terry *(above)* and Robert Taylor were maried to two of the most glamourous women in Hollywood, Joan Crawford and Barbara Stanwyck, respectively, but these bisexual husbands often spent their nights together.

Hollywood, where he was spotted by an MGM talent scout in 1937. He was assigned a bit part in *Mannequin* (1938), a film that otherwise starred Joan Crawford.

Crawford took one look at Terry and "auditioned him," eventually marrying him on July 21, 1942, at the Hidden Valley Ranch in Ventura County, California. Just before the ceremony, the happy couple gave their names as "Lucille Tone" and "Frederick Kormann." A reporter, alerted that a celebrity couple might be married that weekend, saw those names. "But I didn't realize that Lucille Tone was THE Joan Crawford. But who in hell had ever heard of this Phillip Terry Kraut?" *[In 1942, anti-German sentiment was at its peak in America.]*

It was during the course of their marriage (1942-1946) that Joan adopted her first child, a daughter, whom she named Christina Crawford. After Crawford's death, Christina wrote her controversial memoir, *Mommie Dearest.*

An Unhappy Family at Play

Phillip Terry *(left)* races along with **Phillip Terry, Jr.** Joan Crawford changed his name after she divorced Terry.

In a dirndl, Crawford playacts at being a mother. On the far right is her adopted young daughter and nemesis, **Christina Crawford** *("Mommie dearest, I hate you").*

In 1978, after Joan's death, Christina published her notorious autobiography to forever tarnish her mother's reputation. It was adapted into a campy movie starring Faye Dunaway.

The film version of that book, starring Faye Dunaway impersonating Crawford, became even more notorious than the book. Dunaway stepped into the role after Anne Bancroft bolted. "I just couldn't do that to Joan," Bancroft later claimed.

Eva was a frequent visitor to the apartment for which Walker, Taylor, and Terry jointly paid the rent as a hideaway during their escapes from their respective wives. Of the trio, Terry was clearly her favorite.

Biographer David Brett defined Terry as an "anglicized, muscle-bond six-foot-one, 180-pound slab of beefcake," and that's exactly what attracted Eva to him—that and his charm and consideration of women. "He was almost as handsome as Franchot Tone *[Crawford's second husband]* and equally bisexual, but more discreet. His current *amour* was none other than Robert Taylor."

Eva also told Hayward, "In seducing Terry, I was getting back at Crawford for tossing that plate of food at Zsa Zsa in the MGM commissary."

"I was more of a mother than a lover to Walker," Eva said. "He was such a kind and gentle soul until he drank a quart of liquor. Then he often turned violent and started lashing out at the world. He was still in love with Jennifer. On a few occasions, he threatened to purchase a gun and shoot Selznick."

"As for Bob Taylor, he was the most beautiful male animal in Hollywood," she said. "But he was somewhat under-endowed and not that great between the sheets. He was also visiting a psychiatrist twice a week, dealing with his own homosexuality."

During the time that Eva was secretly dating Taylor, he was also conducting a torrid affair with Tyrone Power whenever they happened to be able to arrange it. Ironically, Power would eventually become the great love of Eva's life.

In later life, she observed, "When I got to Hollywood in the 1940s, it was so incestuous. Everybody, male or female, was sleeping with everybody else in all sorts of combinations. I've lost touch, but perhaps it's the same today."

As for Phillip Terry, throughout the course of World War II, he worked in a factory, claiming that his wife was at home busily rejecting film offers, searching for a script that would put her back on top again. "I would have taken any role, and she was rejecting every script sent to her. She only wanted a role worthy of an Oscar."

Away from their respective spouses, Eva and Terry spent many nights listening to music and reading poetry together. "He had a quiet masculinity, a gentle passivity," she said. "But in bed, he became a tiger." He did confide to Eva that in his sexual relationships with both Taylor and Walker, "I was the man." But she had already suspected that.

"He might have been bovine in the living room, but he was all bull in the bedroom," Eva claimed.

Terry had seemed destined for stardom after Hedda Hopper referred to him as "a combination Clark Gable and Cary Grant." Terry was subsequently offered roles in two major films: *The Lost Weekend* (1945), playing the alcoholic brother of Ray Milland; and *To Each His Own* (1946), co-starring with Olivia de Havilland. Both those roles won Oscars for its lead actors. After that, however, Terry's career went into decline.

During much of his time with Eva, Terry complained about life in the Craw-

Partly for dramatic effect, **Joan Crawford** feigned illness during the Oscar ceremony of 1945. Her role of a ferociously loyal, long-suffering mother in *Mildred Pierce*; 1945 was a candidate for the Best Actress Award.

When it was announced that she had won, there was a virtual stampede of friends, colleagues, reporters, and photographers who raced to her home in Brentwood.

As cameras rolled and photographers clicked, the film's director, Michael Curtiz handed Crawford her statuette in bed, where she was discovered "camera ready."

ford household. "She wants me to be her butler during the day, then a stallion in bed at night," he said.

After she won her long-awaited Oscar for her role in *Mildred Pierce* (1945), Crawford, according to Terry, became "more ballsy" than ever.

He ran to Eva's arms one night after Crawford viciously attacked him in the aftermath of her big win.

"I have the Oscar now, and I don't need you anymore. Besides, you're too much like the weak character of Monty in *Mildred Pierce*. You enjoy me being the breadwinner. You even like to be called 'Mr. Joan Crawford.' You lack Gable's charisma and also Fairbank's gregarious, showoff nature. Franchot Tone beat the hell out of me, but at least he never bored me."

In the wake of that denunciation from Crawford, Terry pleaded with Eva, "Honey, Joan just snipped off my balls. Would you go to bed with me and restore my manhood?"

Crawford was later quoted as saying, "Marrying Phillip Terry was the biggest mistake of my life."

In contrast, Eva once claimed, "Not marrying Phillip Terry was the greatest mistake of my life."

***

Before, during, and after her marriage to Conrad Hilton, William S. Paley (1901-1990) maintained an ongoing affair with Zsa Zsa, despite her denials.

His father, Samuel Paley, was a Ukrainian Jewish immigrant who came to America and became a millionaire through the manufacture of cigars.

Young Paley did not want to follow in his father's footsteps and instead became the chief executive of the Columbia Broadcasting System (CBS). He created that conglomerate from a small radio network into one of the foremost radio and television operations in the United States.

Zsa Zsa met Paley before he went to London during the war to serve in a branch of the Office of War Information under the direction of General Dwight D. Eisenhower.

During her initial involvement with Paley, he was married to Dorothy Hart Hearst, who had previously wed John Randolph Hearst, the third son of press baron, William Randolph Hearst, Sr.

As Paley came of age, he had become notorious for his constant womanizing. His conquests even included the iconic actress, Louise Brooks. When he broke off from her, he gave her a monthly stipend for life.

Zsa Zsa remembered her first date with Paley, which took place at an obscure beach club in Malibu. "He wore a very revealing bikini, unusual for American men in the early 40s. His shirt was wide open; he was barefoot, and he looked a bit like Aristotle Onassis."

In spite of what she wrote in a memoir, her affair with Paley lasted for several years. She remembered him as a perfectionist. He told her that when he built the new headquarters of CBS on Sixth Avenue in Manhattan, he supervised everything. He even devised the recipe for the hot dogs served at the CBS concession on the ground floor. "What a man!" Zsa Zsa raved. "What talent…What a genius!"

Zsa Zsa confided to Greta Keller and others that, "In my own way, I was in love with Bill for years. We frequently talked of marriage, but I never really got to know him. He was a hard man to get close to, except when having sex, of course, *dahlink.*"

"Once or twice, I crossed Bill," she admitted. "He had a reputation for being Mr. Cool and never losing his temper. That was not the case. He had a terrible temper. When he got mad, I was afraid of him. He was a very disturbed man, always troubled by life. Frankly, I think he was hiding an inferiority complex—not as a lover. He was great at that. His setbacks or disappointments in the business world caused him great anguish. Instead of celebrating his successes, he wallowed in his defeats."

"Even though I was not his wife, Bill was terribly jealous," Zsa Zsa said.

"Once, I mentioned another lover, and he slapped my face. When he was with me, he treated me like I was married to him. He pretended to be nice to Conrad, but secretly, he loathed him because he was my husband. He constantly told me, 'You should belong just to me.'"

His second wife, Barbara Cushing Mortimer, whom he'd married in 1947, was called "Babe" by her friends. "She was constantly voted one of the best dressed women in America."

"Bill himself had great taste in both décor and design," Zsa Zsa said. "Because of Babe, he learned a lot about women's *couture*. On my first dates with him, I appeared elegant and grand until I painfully learned that that was the exact opposite of what he wanted. He had had enough of that being married to his 'Babe.' What he wanted from me was for me to dress and act like Marilyn Monroe. To be frank, *dahlink,* he preferred me as a blonde bombshell. In his words, 'I want to date a sexy broad.'"

Earl Wilson, one of New York's most popular gossip columnists, read Zsa Zsa's second memoir, including her denial of an affair with Paley. He later said, "Zsa Zsa is unbelievable.—you can't believe a damn thing she says."

For years, Paley arranged rendezvous with Zsa Zsa almost every two weeks, during his scheduled trips from New York to Hollywood. He even asked her to cut the ribbon when he opened the new CBS building on Fairfax in Los Angeles.

In her memoir, she claimed they drifted apart as the years went by, and that she accidentally encountered him when they ran into each other on Park Avenue in Manhattan.

She quoted Paley as saying: "What about making love today? I'll give you a wonderful TV show if you sleep with me."

She alleged that she rejected him, although she was tempted by the man himself and not by the TV show. "It was the mention of the TV show that stopped me from succumbing to Bill Paley. Without the mention of the TV show, we might have been lovers."

"That was such bullshit," Wilson claimed. "I knew Bill Paley for years. He told me he'd been fucking Zsa Zsa since World War II. She would have done anything to headline a TV show for CBS. That had been a very private dream of hers, as she wanted to become a female Jack Paar or Johnny Carson. If Bill had offered her a show like that, she, on bended nylon, would have gone down on the fucker right in front of Tiffany's. I understand tht Zsa Zsa didn't want to look like a whore when she dictated her first memoir back in 1959. It was still the Eisenhower era, and women weren't supposed to sleep around when they were married."

***

As a would-be starlet at 20th Century Fox, Eva knew it was inevitable that she'd be summoned one afternoon to the office of studio boss Darryl F. Zanuck.

As biographer Mart Martin wrote: "Every afternoon at 4PM, was Zanuck's sex break. At that time, a girl, selected by Zanuck himself, from the 20th Century Fox lot, would come to his office. Once she entered, the door was locked from the inside. Thereafter, no calls or interruptions were permitted, and all work in the offices adjacent to Zanuck's ceased. When he was finished, the girl left by a side door, and Zanuck unlocked his office for work to resume. Rarely did the same girl come twice, but there were exceptions."

When Eva was taking lessons from a voice coach, a messenger handed her a note. She was to report to Zanuck's office at 4PM. It was already 3:30PM, so she had little time to "paint a new face on myself and wear something provocative." Someone from the wardrobe department brought her a gown that had been worn by Betty Grable in *Moon Over Miami* (1941).

Eva claimed that she felt Zanuck would advance her career. "I was also bored and unhappy in my marriage to Charles, in spite of his millions."

"A few months later, she expressed regrets about her infidelities. "I could not go on living with Charles, knowing that he was madly in love with me, thinking that I am his life and on the side I am playing around with someone else."

That "someone else" should have been expressed in the plural.

Infidelity was not exactly on her mind when she entered Zanuck's office, and he locked the door behind her.

Facing him for the first time, she encountered a self-styled Superman. As his biographer, Marlys J. Harris, noted, he had "self-confidence and gall. He styled himself as a writer, producer, a man of action, a soldier, a groundbreaker, a leader, a creative genius. Everything he touched was charged with an electricity of his own that defied nature and made it special."

Eva later mockingly referred to Zanuck as "the producer who discovered Rin Tin Tin, the dog who saved Hollywood."

When producer Alexander Korda had instructed Zsa Zsa to remove her clothes in his office, she had refused and walked out. But when Zanuck made the same request of Eva, she agreed to disrobe. "After all, *dahlink*," she later said, "I was proud of my figure. I'd certainly dieted enough to keep it in shape."

She found herself lying on the producer's well-worn casting couch, where so many other big-time stars or starlets (Carole Landis, Dolores Costello, Linda Darnell, and Gene Tierney, among others) had been before.

As Eva later confided to Susan Hayward, "Zanuck was rather verbal. Most of the talk consisted of him extolling the size of his penis. During the act, he asked such questions as 'Have you ever been plugged by a whopper like mine?'"

Zanuck broke his rule about preferring once-only sexual encounters. He liked having sex with Eva so much that he began to date her, even though both of them were married at the time.

In a gossipy town like Hollywood, Virginia Fox Zanuck, his wife, soon learned about the affair between Eva and her husband.

"These liaisons mean nothing to Darryl," she said. "Sometimes they last no more than an afternoon or evening. He always comes home to me."

Virginia was a former actress, and he respected her opinion, often reshooting a filmed scene or even tossing out a script if "Mrs. Zanuck doesn't like it."

She had discovered talent, including Tyrone Power, who eventually became Fox's more reliable box office attractions. It would be years before Eva would personally uncover the charms of Power.

During her dates with Zanuck, she discovered that if he needed to urinate, even if it were in front of Ciro's, with both women and men watching, he would whip out his penis "and piss like a horse," Eva claimed.

"'Bullshit' was his favorite word," she said. "The only big thing about him was his penis. His body was short and skinny. He was arrogant. One night at Ciro's, the waiter served an overcooked dish of pasta. Darryl tossed it back in his face. That was a trick also practiced by a future lover of mine, Frank Sinatra."

During the war, Eva saw Zanuck very infrequently, as he'd been commissioned as a colonel in the reserves. He was assigned the job of coordinating Hollywood's efforts to make training films and propaganda features. He was later transferred to London, where he was installed in a suite at Claridges, the best hotel in that city.

He would later tell Eva of his adventures, as when he participated in a perilous night time air raid above German-occupied France with Lord Louis Mountbatten.

He never really came through on his promise to make Eva a star at Fox, but he did get her a role, however, in *A Royal Scandal,* starring Tallulah Bankhead improbably cast as Catherine the Great of Russia. Before signing Eva, he warned her, "Watch your step, gal. Tallulah might end up loving your pussy as much as I do."

***

As a "hotel widow," Zsa Zsa began to host her own A-list Hollywood parties at Hilton's Bel Air mansion. Nearly all the stars accepted her invitation, unless they had already accepted an invitation to a party at the home of Ouida and Basil Rathbone next door. Ouida had become seriously angry at Zsa Zsa's attempt to upstage her as the most important hostess in Hollywood.

One night, a drunken Errol Flynn showed up on Zsa Zsa's doorstep. He had not been invited, but was well-received by the hostess because despite his notoriety, he was one of the leading box office attractions in America.

Earlier, he'd told his pal, Bruce Cabot, "I've already fucked one Gabor sister…Why not the other? I hear there's a third one in Hungary, but I'm not going to risk my life to fly to Budapest to plug her. I'll wait until she, too, arrives in Hollywood, as you know she will."

Zsa Zsa later recalled, "Errol was a flirtatious devil. He was about the handsomest man I'd ever seen. It should be against the law for men to look that great."

In a memoir, she had written, "I did not fall prey to Errol Flynn's much vaunted charms. Conrad was out of town, and Errol and I danced together. He whispered to me, 'Darling, come to my house and sleep with me tonight,' his voice pulsating with passion. 'When you wake up in the morning, you will look out my window and see stallions outside—and then you will see what a stallion I am.'"

As it happened, she didn't return to his home with him that night. She waited until the following evening when he invited her to a dinner party at his home on Mulholland Drive."

He liked to pull stunts on female stars, including putting a snake in the dressing room of Olivia de Havilland. For Zsa Zsa, he planned something sexier. As he told actor Bruce Cabot, "I'm hiring Freddie as one of the waiters tonight.'

Cabot knew what that meant.

[In Hollywood legend and lore, there were three different Freddies—one in the 1930s, another in the 1940s, and one—whom Joan Collins encountered— in the 1950s. Each of these Freddies had a thick penis that extended for more than a foot. These young men, whose real names have been lost to history, hired themselves out for sex with the stars (they serviced both men and women) or sometimes as party gags.]

"The Perfect Specimen," as he was known, swashbuckling actor **Errol Flynn** liked to show off his chest and everything else he had.

He told his friend, Bruce Cabot, "I've already had one Gabor. Why not another?"

Flynn on several occasions had had sex with the 1940s version of Freddie. He'd also devised a gag to use on unsuspecting female guests. He acquired a large salad bowl and arranged for an opening to be drilled into its side.

At the dinner party, at which Zsa Zsa was his guest of honor, he ordered Freddie to produce an erection as a means of "plugging the hole" in the side of the salad bowl. The chef then placed greens in the bowl, and Freddie, outfitted as a waiter, "served the salad" to whomever Flynn had designated.

Zsa Zsa, as she lifted the greens from the bowl onto her plate, screamed when she encountered "a huge, pulsating salami hiding there."

David Niven's biographer, Graham Lord, wrote that "penises were a constant Flynn-Niven preoccupation" when those two actors lived together. Freddie was often a major attraction at their parties. The guests of Flynn and Niven were astonished at Freddie's ability to perform autofellatio."

Freddie didn't always serve his penis with salad. One night when Hedy Lamarr was the guest of honor, Freddie's mammoth organ appeared atop a silver tray otherwise spilling over with hors d'oeuvres—quail eggs, caviar, smoked salmon, thin slices of raw beef, and tiny prawns.

A hungry Hedy Lamarr was rather aggressive that night, stabbing at the hors d'oeuvres with a fork. Howling in pain, Freddie dropped the tray and retreated to the bathroom for emergency First Aid.

A few hours later, after that raucous X-rated dinner, Zsa Zsa assumed that the house was emptied of guests, except for Flynn and herself. As he'd done with so many other women before her, the swashbuckling star invited Zsa Zsa out onto his terrace to take in the panorama over the sparkling lights of Los Angeles.

"Everything looks so beautiful by moonlight," she said. "All the ugliness is gone."

"You don't need the glow of the moon to enhance your beauty," he assured her, repeating a line he'd used so many times before.

At another party at her Bel Air home, Zsa Zsa told Mickey Rooney about her experience at Flynn 's dinner party. After listening to her, he relayed his own story about another Flynn dinner party he attended with Clark Gable, Spencer Tracy, Robert Taylor, and Wallace Beery. "We knocked on the door, and it was opened by a pair of exquisitely beautiful female twins—they were absolutely nude!"

Zsa Zsa would later tell Greta Keller, "Errol from time to time had been charged with rape. But he didn't have to rape me. I was a willing victim. He was just as romantic in life as he was on the screen. Imagine, both Captain Blood and Robin Hood wrapped into six feet, two inches of thrilling manhood."

Her memory of their romantic nights together were ruined three weeks later when at a party, Hedda Hopper informed her that there was a two-way mirror in Errol Flynn's bedroom.

"You must have put on quite a show," the gossip maven said. "For Bruce Cabot and perhaps his other two drunken buddies, Alan Hale and Guinn (Big Boy) Williams."

"I didn't feel that before, but after that, I felt I had been raped," Zsa Zsa said.

She vowed never to speak to Flynn again.

***

Eva

In the wake of David Bacon's murder, the bisexual actor, Peter Lawford, wasted little time in finding a new male lover. At MGM, he met Robert Walker—Eva's sometimes *amour*—through their mutual friend, Van Johnson.

The promiscuous Lawford was also seducing A-list female stars, as many as he could, including June Allyson, Lucille Ball, Ava Gardner, Judy Garland, Rita Hayworth, Janet Leigh, Elizabeth Taylor, Lana Turner, and even Jane Wyman, wife of Ronald Reagan.

Lawford made additional amorous detours to the beds of the visiting Londoner, Noël Coward, and to that of the unsexy director, George Cukor, who later denounced him as "a lousy lay."

Lawford's ill-fated affair with Tom Drake (Judy Garland's "Boy Next Door" in the 1944 film *Meet Me in St. Louis*) was said to have temporarily broken that actor's heart.

Lawford even ended up in the bed of "Miss Priss," Clifton Webb, who later turned his attention to chasing another pretty boy, Robert Wagner.

Eva kept Susan Hayward abreast of her ongoing relationships with Walker and Lawford. Hayward told Eva, "I'd trade both of them, anytime, for two good studs like Gary Cooper and Johnny Weissmuller."

"Opposites are said to attract," Eva told Hayward. "That would explain Peter's attraction to Walker, or vice versa. Robert constantly attacks Peter for his values, including seducing big name actresses for the sole purpose of furthering his career."

He avoided the social aspects of Lawford's life, preferring to see him in private. "I hate big parties," Walker said, "and I loathe Peter's socialite friends. I don't even own a tux. I can't play the Hollywood game the way Peter does."

Walker's criticism of Lawford could also have been directed at Eva. She, too, played the Hollywood game, tossing lavish parties for the A-list. However, she never invited Walker to any of her galas, fearing he would detest them, or perhaps get drunk and make a scene. She also was worried that he might come to regard her as being as superficial as Lawford .

"Sometimes, Peter would make Robert mad, and he'd go into one of his moods and not speak to him for days," Eva said. "During those times, he attacked Peter viciously and told me really sad stories about his life."

"That limey bastard is Hollywood's biggest cocksucker," Walker told Eva. "One day we went to the beach, and he spent most of the day in the men's toilet. Both the latrine and the stools were exposed, with no partitions for privacy. He must have sucked off a dozen guys. When beach boys went in to take a leak, they got relived in two ways. Toilet sex is fairly common in the Los Angeles area."

"Not in Budapest," said Eva. "We prefer the boudoir."

Biographer Mart Martin claimed, "Intercourse didn't interest Peter Lawford that much, due to his predilection for oral sex. Prostitutes knew Lawford as an excellent $50 oral sex trick, and he also seduced 'call boys,' male hustlers, young male extras, and studio messengers."

According to Eva, "Peter Lawford was the most promiscuous actor I ever met in Hollywood—that is, until I was introduced to Frank Sinatra."

Eva never knew what mood Lawford would be in. As he told her, "I have frightening depressions. I have great days, then one like death. Why? I don't know—I have everything."

What he didn't have was a supportive mother. He complained to Eva about Lady May Lawford, who once announced to his boss, Louis B. Mayer, that her son as a homosexual. Lady May even asked Mayer to try to "find some treatment to rid Peter of this scourge."

One night at Santa Monica Beach, Eva, Walker, and Lawford camped out for the night. Peter Lawford hoped to fit in some early morning surfing before reporting to the studio.

"The boys taught me much about Hollywood's sex life, but I flopped as a surfer," Eva said. "I also refused to go motorcycle riding with them. I felt the wind would ruin my hairdo."

At the time of Lawford's involvement with Walker, he was also intimately linked to Van Johnson as well as to actor Keenan Wynn and his wife, Evie. Rumors were rampant in Hollywood that the foursome was involved in a sexual *ménage à quatre*. In 1947, when Evie divorced Wynn and married Johnson a few hours later, Hollywood wags speculated, "Which of them will gain custody of Peter?"

Although she knew Lawford over a period of many years, Eva claimed that she did not have sex with him. "I never knew where his mouth had been the night before. I found Robert sexy, but Peter did not appeal to me, even though I thought he was good looking. Most of his fans did-n't know this, but one of his arms was withered, and he constantly tried to conceal that flaw."

At one point, even Walker and Eva ceased to have sex. "He just wanted to lay his beautiful head on my breasts and sob."

"Sometimes when Robert called me, I couldn't see him, because Charlie had come home," Eva said. "That made him angry and he became abusive, even denouncing me. But he'd call the next day and sound very sweet on the phone. He didn't seem to remember how abusive he'd been."

"He liked to do wild, reckless things with me," Eva said. "One night when he slept over at my house, he wanted to put every liquid he could find into a blender—orange juice, tomato juice, juice from a

Robert Walker was photographed in 1946 under arrest in Kansas for disorderly drunkennes

pickle jar, Scotch, vodka, gin, rum brandy. We each drank three of these concoctions which he called 'Walker's zombie drink.' The next morning we woke up nude on the living room floor with the worst headaches in recorded history."

At one point, Eva tried to define to Hayward her attraction to Walker and Lawford. "Charles is such a decent, kind, and respectable husband to me, but I have this wild streak in me," Eva said. "I long for adventure, excitement. Peter and Robert provide that for me, as both of them are bad, bad boys. They are like time-bombs, ready to go off at any minute. Charles never explodes, never loses his temper. Peter and Robert go completely crazy two or three times a night…at least."

"What's my ultimate conclusion about Peter and Robert?" Eva asked herself. "I think both men love women but prefer sex with men. As regards that, I always say, 'to each his own.'"

***

Zsa Zsa set out to become, in her words, "one-hundred percent American," taking golf lessons from the Bel Air pro, William Novak; voice lessons from the best coach at MGM, Helen Vogeler; and tennis lessons from the world-famous champion, Bill Tilden.

During the course of her brief affair with Charlie Chaplin, Tilden, with Zsa Zsa, would challenge Chaplin and his partner, Gussie Moran, to spirited games of tennis.

Both Chaplin and Zsa Zsa had become extremely fond of William Tatem Tilden II, nicknamed "Big Bill," considered at the time one of the greatest tennis players of all time. For a period of seven years, he was the premier tennis champion in the world.

Scion of a wealthy Philadelphia family, Tilden was gracious to Zsa Zsa. He'd suffered a great loss with the early death of his three older siblings and his semi-invalid mother. His father had sent him to live with a maiden aunt where he resided until 1941, when he was 48 years old.

Without any concrete evidence, Zsa Zsa, during her discussions with Chaplin, had assumed that Tilden was a homosexual.

The athlete's biographer, Frank Deford, claimed his early family losses caused Tilden to spend all of his adult life attempting to forge father-son relationships with a long succession of youthful tennis protégées, of whom Vinnie Richards was the most noted.

Kenneth Anger, in *Hollywood Babylon,* claimed that Tilden preferred "a bevy of fresh-faced ball boys, pre-pubescent Ganymedes in clinging white seersucker shorts. "In Vladimir Nabokov's novel, *Lolita,* Tilden the tennis player turned up as Ned Litam—"Ma Tilden" spelled backward—Lolita's tennis teacher in that novel about heterosexual child molestation.

During his heyday, Tilden had played tennis with Rudolf Valentino, Louise Brooks, Ramon Novarro, Clara Bow, and many other stars, including Errol Flynn, Spencer Tracy, Tallulah Bankhead, Katharine Hepburn, and Greta Garbo.

Chaplin and Zsa Zsa often lunched with Tilden, finding his diet amazing. "No vegetables, no fruits," Zsa Zsa said. "Just steak and potatoes for breakfast, lunch, and dinner."

In front of Zsa Zsa, Chaplin warned Tilden that he was tossing away the huge sums of money he earned. He maintained a suite at the deluxe Algonquin Hotel in New York, and often financed unsuccessful Broadway shows that he'd written, produced, and starred in.

When he was twenty-nine, an infected fingernail forced him to undergo an operation in which the tip of the middle finger of his serving hand was amputated. Amazingly, he re-emerged on the tennis court as skilled as ever.

Nicky Hilton soon joined in playing tennis with Zsa Zsa, Chaplin, and Tilden on tennis courts owned by the Little Tramp.

One late morning, Zsa Zsa arrived there and went into Chaplin's changing room, where she came upon Tilden performing fellatio on teenaged Nicky. She quietly excused herself and stood outside.

Nicky, apparently, was "too far gone and must have held Tilden's head in place until he climaxed," to judge from the sounds.

Although usually indiscreet, Zsa Zsa knew how to keep a secret when she wanted to. She never mentioned the scene she'd witnessed to Chaplin, who was often accused of child molestation himself. She also never confronted Nicky or Tilden with what she'd caught them doing, and she certainly never told her husband, Conrad Hilton.

Tilden was arrested in November of 1946 on Sunset Boulevard by the Beverly Hills police. He was charged with a misdemeanor for soliciting a 14-year-old boy for sex. He served seven and a

A convicted child molester, **Bill Tilden**, was hailed as the world's greatest tennis player. Here, Tilden *(right figure, above)* is seen giving lessons to a young man to whom he was attracted.

When he was arrested, Hollywood turned against him, with the high-profile exception of Zsa Zsa and Charlie Chaplin, who remained his loyal friends.

half months in prison. He was arrested again in January of 1949 after picking up a 16-year-old hitchhiker and "performing a sex act on him." This time he served ten months.

After that, Tilden was shunned by the Hollywood elite, except for two loyal friends, Zsa Zsa and Chaplin. They continued to be loyal to him and to play tennis with him on Chaplin's private courts. Chaplin also aided Tilden financially when he struggled to pay his legal fees.

When a reporter asked Zsa Zsa why she remained loyal to Tilden, "a known child molester," she answered: "Oh, *dahlink,* who among us hasn't committed an indiscretion from time to time? The crime is in getting caught."

***

Dressed in red satin and encased in sable, Zsa Zsa drove to the Town House Hotel to pick up Conrad and take him to a dinner party at the home of an insurance executive.

He rushed out of his office and tossed a recent newspaper into her lap. He hadn't even unfolded it. Suddenly, he had to go back inside to take an emergency call. Waiting for him in the car, she casually opened the paper for a view of a glaring headline that horrified her: NAZIS SEIZE BUDAPEST.

BUDAPEST, March 19, 1944—Hitler's storm troopers began marching into this Hungarian capital at dawn today and by noon the entire city was occupied. The SS has begun rounding up Jews and "dissidents."

When Conrad returned to the car, she screamed at him: "Jolie, Vilmos, Magda…the Nazis are going to execute them…I just know it!"

CHAPTER SEVEN
Hungarian Rhapsodies in
Amerika! Amerika!

Two months before the Nazi takeover of Budapest, American bombers launched an early morning attack on the Hungarian capital, bombing strategic targets. One bomb fell right behind the Embassy of Portugal where Dr. Carlos Almeida Afonseca de Sampayo Garrido and Magda occupied the master bedroom. Other bombs leveled areas near Jolie's apartment, destroying centuries-old villas, coffee shops, and theaters, along with a secret depot storing weapons.

In April of 1944, without a single bullet being fired, the Hungarians had capitulated to the powerful Nazi advance. "Within twenty-four hours, it was as if Goebbels himself was running every newspaper and broadcasting bulletins over every radio," Magda said.

For a brief time in April, even after the Nazi takeover, Jolie tried to maintain her luxurious lifestyle, seemingly ignoring the threat. "I was like Nero playing my fiddle as Rome burned," she later recalled. "Magda understood the danger. I did not."

On a Friday night, Jolie had driven her Mercedes to the Arizona Club in the center of Budapest. It was a chic rendezvous mostly patronized by wealthy Jews from the business and professional communities. Jolie was friends with the owners, a popular Jewish singer and her husband, who accompanied her on the piano.

Jolie had ignored the warnings and hosted a large dinner party for the Gabor family. The champagne flowed. "It would be the last such gathering we ever had," she lamented, years later. "The matriarch of the family, Francesca Tilleman, attended, wearing her mink coat and a stylish hat.

Jolie remembered getting drunk on champagne. Her mother, Francesca, had warned her that this might be the last champagne the family would have. "I'm sure that the SS will raid our cellars."

The matriarch, who had taken a young lover in the wake of the death of her husband, had only days to live before being executed by the SS for the "crime" of being a Jew.

Based on his status as a wealthy representative of the (neutral) nation of Portugal, Ambassador Garrido had already paid out the equivalent of $100,000 U.S. dollars to an informant within the inner sanctums of the Gestapo. That informant had kept him abreast of the intentions and actions of a military organization which the Ambassador defined as "a terrifying group of thugs."

Early one morning, Dr. Garrido learned that the Gabor family's name had been added to a list of undesirables earmarked for extermination.

Magda had not spent the night with him, but was asleep in her own apartment. Garrido advised her that he was sending his chauffeur-driven Embassy car, with its Portuguese flag conspicuously flying, to transport her to the relative safety of his Embassy.

He was alerted that the Gestapo had learned that Magda had long been a member of Hungary's underground resistance; that she had edited an illegal anti-Nazi newspaper; and that she had helped Polish soldiers, now fighting with British forces in Egypt, during their escapes from Nazi POW camps.

Magda did not have time to pack any of her most prized possessions. She managed to throw her jewelry into a suitcase and was on the street within fifteen minutes of the warning from Garrido, with a mink coat thrown on over her *négligée.*

When the driver from the Portuguese Embassy arrived, Magda persuaded him to take her to Jolie's apartment. In desperation, Magda used her key to get in, finding her mother still in bed in her lace nightgown, sipping a rich Turkish coffee. Magda ordered her mother to put on some clothes, collect her jewelry and valuables, and leave with her at once.

"The Nazis won't bother me," Jolie foolishly said. "I can't go because I've invited friends of mine to a luncheon at The Hungaria today at one o'clock."

"If you don't get out of that god damn bed, the only date you'll have to keep is on a cattle car to Auschwitz."

Magda was finally able to force her mother to leave. Jolie later lamented, "I had to leave everything behind. I escaped only with my jewelry and a few furs."

Magda then ordered her driver to take Jolie and herself to the apartment of Vilmos. Unlike Jolie, he immediately ascertained the imminent dangers, and without any fuss, went willingly with them in the Embassy's limousine.

When the driver deposited the Gabors at the Portuguese Embassy, Jolie expressed horror at the living conditions she found there. More than seventy refugees from the Nazis were already living there in appalling squalor.

Dr. Garrido had reserved a private room upstairs for Jolie and Vilmos. At first, Jolie protested to Magda, "I divorced your father years ago, and now Mr.

Ambassador expects me to sleep in the same bed with him?"

"*Nuci,* in case you haven't heard, there's a war on," Magda told her. "You can either occupy this room, or join the refugees downstairs in the courtyard."

Magda herself would share Dr. Garrido's bedchamber.

The next morning over breakfast, Jolie told Magda, "We had sex last night. If it was good once, it can be again."

Sex was the last thing on Magda's mind. She could not depend on the local Hungarian-language radio broadcasts for accurate news. Dr. Garrido's informants kept them posted on the Gestapo's actions within Budapest. The news reaching the Embassy horrified both the Ambassador and the Gabors.

One thousand Jewish lawyers had been rounded up and taken to the banks of the Danube, where a firing squad was waiting to assassinate them. Jolie also learned what had happened to the patrons of the Arizona Club. The SS had demanded that every patron there turn over his or her money and jewelry. A plane waited for them at the Budapest airport "to fly them to Switzerland."

The Jews duly obeyed. En route, in air space over Austria, SS members opened the plane's exit hatch and threw each of the screaming passengers to their deaths 20,000 feet below.

Jolie had maintained a friendship with a young Jewish man who was skilled as a decorator. He was very pretty and a bit effeminate. The Gestapo arrested him, cut off all his fingers, and then tied him down where he was sodomized by nearly two dozen Nazi soldiers before they tortured him to death.

In the courtyard of the Embassy, Magda and Jolie encountered a young mother who had a small girl with her. She told them that to sustain life for her starving child, she had traded a ten-carat diamond for a stale piece of moldy bread. At one desperate point, she cut her wrists and drew blood to give a child a drink in lieu of other nourishment.

Magda later revealed to Zsa Zsa and Eva in Hollywood that many of their friends and extended family had been rounded up by the Gestapo and taken to Tattersall. That was a well-known riding academy where Magda and Zsa Zsa had learned to ride horses when they were young.

At Tattersall, these victims, including the Gabor family's lawyer and their family physician, both of whom were Jews, were machine-gunned to death along with hundreds of others. Later, their bodies were thrown into a mass grave dug by slave labor on the outskirts of Budapest.

Dr. Garrido decided to transfer the Gabors to this country villa at Galgagyörk, a Budapest suburb. Surrounded by gardens, the villa was officially designated as an annex of the Portuguese Embassy, and as such, enjoyed diplomatic immunity. Life in the center of Budapest was becoming too dangerous.

Meanwhile, it was being loudly noted by the Nazis that the Ambassador from Portugal was anything but neutral, and that he was siding with the Allies on many important diplomatic issues. Consequently, Goebbels pressured the Portuguese dictator in Lisbon, Antonio Salazar, to recall Dr. Garrido and to replace him with an official more sympathetic to the Nazis.

As Magda remembered, for nearly a month, the Gabors lived "like it was the halcyon days of Hungary between the Wars." Afternoon tea was served in the garden, and at dinner, the women wore gowns. Dr. Garrido came and went from the main office of the Embassy, but no longer took his *protégée* with him, fearing that his car might be stopped and Magda arrested en route.

Suddenly, and without warning, a group of about a dozen terrorists stormed the villa, Heavily armed, they were clad in black clothing, their faces concealed by masks. Their unidentified leader wore a long pair of black boots extending up to his thighs. As he barked orders, Magda noticed that those boots looked scruffy.

Pointing machine guns at the Gabors and at the villa's other guests, most of them aristocratic Jews, he ordered them to go to their rooms and return with all their money and jewelry. SS men were assigned to accompany them in case one of them tried to hide their valuables. "Anyone not turning over every valuable item will be executed on the spot," the terrorist leader warned.

The bandits occupied the Portuguese-owned villa for about an hour before driving off in three separate vehicles. The occupants of the villa, including Magda, gathered in the building's living room to await instructions from Dr. Garrido.

Garrido talked to them for about two hours, informing them that his position in Hungary was growing more dangerous by the minute, and that he feared that Salazar would succumb to the pressure from Berlin and have him replaced.

As he was talking, a dozen Nazi storm troopers raided the villa. Their leader told Dr. Garrido that they were responding to a report that terrorists had robbed the occupants of the villa.

In a bizarre twist, sharp-eyed Magda noticed that their commander wore the same boots as the terrorist's leader. It was one and the same man. The identities of the terrorists had been revealed.

With their permission, Dr. Garrido went immediately to his ground-floor office to lodge a formal protest with the Hungarian government.

During his absence, the Nazi leader grabbed Magda's arm. "You have been identified as Magda Bychowsky, and you're wanted for questioning by the Gestapo. You must come with us."

Jolie, with Vilmos at her side, stepped up to protest. "We're her parents, and we insist on going with our daughter."

"The more Jews, the merrier," the sadistic leader said. "It just means we'll have to dig a deeper grave."

From her lover, Magda had learned that the first stop for captives was an interrogation by the Gestapo, followed by a trip to one of the "killing fields" outside Budapest, where they'd probably be shot.

As she was being dragged along the corridor that opened into Dr. Garrido's office, she learned why he had not come to her rescue. His heart had failed him, and he was lying on the floor of his office, dying.

She broke from her two SS captors and darted into his office where she reached into his desk and removed a vial of medicine. Following his instructions, she got him to swallow its contents, knowing that if she failed to make him swallow it, he'd have only moments to live. As he gulped, gagged, and choked, the medicine had the instant effect of reviving him.

When he became aware of his surroundings, she helped him to his feet. "I am the Ambassador from Portugal," he told the SS men. "If you take Magda or any of the Gabors, I insist that you arrest me, too."

The stormtrooper's leader did not immediately acquiesce to Dr. Garrido's request, even though he probably realized how inappropriate it would be to arrest, without specific instructions, an ambassador from a neutral country.

Outside, a large black car was waiting for the captives. An SS officer forced Jolie and Vilmos into its back seat. Magda was ordered in next. But when Dr. Garrido attempted to join them, the SS officer blocked him.

Impulsively, Magda placed her foot outside the car door, planting it firmly on the ground. The SS officer slammed the door on her leg, but she kept it firmly in position anyway, despite the agonizing pain. She kept doing that even when she feared that her leg would be broken, or perhaps even severed. She later recalled the almost unbearable pain.

The door did not close, and Dr. Garrido quickly joined the Gabors in the vehicle's back seat.

In an amazing turn of events, after their car had traveled about two miles along the road leading to Gestapo headquarters in central Budapest, two squad cars of the Hungarian police gave chase. In a surprise move, the SS officers stopped their car and got out, running into the fields, leaving Dr. Garrido alone in the car with Vilmos, Jolie, and Magda with her injured leg.

When the Hungarian police arrived at their car, their chief officer, who had obviously been briefed, apologized for the arrest of the ambassador. One of the policemen

Because of her heroic effort as an underground warrior against the Nazis, **Magda** was praised by Jolie.

"You are my bravest daughter," she told her." You saved us from the firing squads that killed many other Jews along the banks of the Danube. I will be forever grateful to you."

was ordered to drive the Gabors and the ambassador back to the villa at Galgagyörk.

Vilmos was let out first, followed by Dr. Garrido and Jolie. Magda required assistance. However, instead of helping her out of the vehicle, the policeman slammed the door of the car with Magda still inside. Then the driver accelerated, aiming his vehicle quickly out of the driveway.

Vilmos, Jolie and Dr. Garrido were informed that Magda would be escorted to police headquarters, where a report had to be filed before she'd be returned, unharmed, to the villa.

Dr. Garrido assured the officer that he would immediately file a protest. From his office, Dr. Garrido telephoned the German Ambassador to Hungary, who agreed to contact Germany's Chief of Diplomatic Protocol.

Later, however, when Garrido telephoned the local police headquarters, he was told that Magda was not on the premises—nor had she been brought there at all. Garrido, still weak from his near-fatal heart attack and his traumatic experiences of the previous hour or two, demanded her return.

As revealed in latter-day dialogues with Magda, she had not been taken to police headquarters, but to a recently configured nerve center and torture chamber maintained by the Gestapo.

She was ushered into a large office where she confronted an SS colonel wearing enormous Nazi military head gear.

"Your Excellency," he said to Magda. "Despite the unusual circumstances, it is an honor to meet the Countess of the former city of Warsaw. I am Adolf Eichmann. Yes, enjoying the same first name as that of our beloved *Führer.*"

***

Otto Adolf Eichmann was born in 1906 to a soldier who served in the Austro-Hungarian Army during World War I. In time, he, too, joined the military on the side of the Nazis, where he rose quickly to become an *SS-Obersturmbannführer* (lieutenant colonel). He was charged with the monumental task of managing the logistics of the mass deportation of the Jews to ghettos and extermination camps throughout Nazi-occupied Eastern Europe, including Hungary.

Eichmann arrived in Budapest in the immediate wake of the Nazi takeover of Hungary in 1944. Soonafter, he sent a message, through underground channels, to the Western powers, proposing the establishment of a "Blood for Goods" program wherein Hungarian Jews would be traded for Allied trucks and vital supplies. When the Allies rejected his proposal, he ordered that 430,000 Hungarian Jews, more than half of the country's total Jewish population of 800,000, be sent by rail to the gas chambers at Auschwitz.

Shortly after their arrivals at the death camp, the Jews were gassed. This was part of Eichmann's orders to carry out "The Final Solution" to the existence of Jews in Hungary. Eichmann's program was carried out between May 15 and July 9, 1944.

[Exactly what happened to Magda during her custody under Eichmann may never be known. She never shared the details of her experience with either Dr. Garrido or with her parents. But when Eichmann was arrested in 1960, she revealed a few insights. He had been living quietly in a suburb of Buenos Aires when he was kidnapped by agents of Mossad and flown to Israel to stand trial.

In 1944, fearing she would be tortured, Magda was taken to a room where two SS officers stripped her of all her clothing and tied her nude body to a cot. Within a half-hour, Eichmann entered the room. Without removing his uniform, he unbuckled his trousers and proceeded to rape her. When he was finished, he called her a "Jew bitch" and slapped her face several times.]

Intently, almost obsessively, she followed Eichmann's trial in Israel, where he was indicted on fifteen criminal charges, including crimes against humanity and war crimes. When he was executed by hanging on June 1, 1962, she said, "I am dancing on the monster's grave. There is a special torture chamber waiting for him in Hell."

During her incarceration at Gestapo head-quarters, Magda had assumed she'd be tortured and forced to reveal the names of key members of the Hungarian underground. But, surprisingly, she was not.

After her rape, she was delivered back to the villa at Galgagyörk where Dr. Garrido, Vilmos, and Jolie had been waiting for her. The ambassador had summoned a doctor to examine her leg and treat it.

She was experiencing some degree of traumatic shock. Even though she was, at least for the moment, in safe surroundings, she seemed to fear that the Nazis were coming to take her away at any minute. At random moments during the days ahead, she would suddenly burst into tears, reliving some past horror.

Adolf Eichmann, a mass murderer, was sent to Budapest by Hitler to carry out "The Final Solution" against the Hungarian Jews. Magda became one of his more prominent victims.

When he was executed in 1962 in Israel, with a sense of overpowering sadness, she "danced on the monster's grave."

One of the most evocative photographs from Hungary in 1944 was of a poor Jewish refugee and her shabbily dressed children on their way to the death camps at Auschwitz.

"None of us is safe, even within this Embassy," Dr. Garrido warned. "All of us must begin making plans tonight to escape from Hungary."

That night, Magda kissed Dr. Garrido. "You have given my parents and myself the gift of life. I'll be eternally grateful. But time is running out."

***

 Cut off from her husband, Conrad, Zsa Zsa led a lonely life in her wing of the Hilton manse in Bel Air. Barron and Nicky Hilton were away at military school in New Mexico.

Conrad came and went from the house without telling her. Her only companion was a shy and neurotic, but loving German shepherd named "Ranger." He accompanied her through the gardens and around the house, but ran and hid if somebody approached.

In looking back, Zsa Zsa claimed that she knew her marriage to Conrad was over one Saturday night when he returned to their beautiful home on Bellagio Road from a business trip.

After dinner, she put on her most stunning Parisian *négligée* and "painted on my most glamorous and seductive face."

Walking down the corridor, where her bedroom lay three doors away from his own boudoir, she knocked lightly on his door. There was no answer. She tried the knob, only to find he'd locked the door from the inside.

"He no longer wanted me," she lamented.

The following Monday morning, Conrad left the house at 6am. Zsa Zsa didn't rise until eleven.

Her maid informed her that Father Jack Kelly had phoned, asking to come by that afternoon for tea at 4pm, and she agreed to see him.

She knew at once that Conrad had asked Kelly to talk to her.

Five hours later over tea, the priest came to the point, telling her that the first Mrs. Conrad Hilton was still alive, and that in the eyes of the Catholic church, Zsa Zsa wasn't officially married.

"Poor Mr. Hilton, who is one of my most faithful church members, lives day and night with the torment of having divorced his first wife," Kelly said. "You can end his suffering by divorcing him. That way, he can be accepted once again into his faith where he belongs—and no longer living in sin with you."

Zsa Zsa rose to her high-heeled grandeur. "GET OUT!" she shouted at the priest. It was the remark about living in sin that she could not tolerate.

Her nights became an agony of horror. Tormented with visions of Vilmos and Jolie being shot, and of Magda being raped by the SS, she couldn't sleep.

She began a reliance on pills, both uppers and downers. As the weeks passed, she grew increasingly dependent on them. She also suffered great guilt, feeling she'd deserted her parents for a life of luxury in Hollywood. "Life here involved gossiping about who was having an affair with whom, what movie deals were being made, and what Louella or Hedda had said in their latest column," Zsa Zsa said. "As far as Hollywood people were concerned, Hungary existed on the other side of the moon."

Afternoons were often spent on the terrace of Eva's apartment. Zsa Zsa found that only European men understood her dilemma, pain, and guilt. Eva seemed less obsessed with the war, and was still dreaming of a career in films. "She was denouncing everyone and everybody for not giving her the break she felt she so richly deserved," Zsa Zsa said.

The great German director, Ernst Lubitsch, often joined Zsa Zsa on Eva's terrace to discuss the war and its politics. She remembered him "as a little man with infinite tenderness."

His urbane comedies of manners had earned him a reputation as Hollywood's most elegant and sophisticated director. His films were promoted as artworks "with the Lubitsch touch."

Born in Berlin in 1892, he came from a Jewish family and had appeared in some thirty German-language films as an actor between 1912 and 1920. His last appearance as an actor had been with Pola Negri in *Sumurun (1920)*.

Emigrating to Hollywood, he evolved into a well-respected director, helming stars who included Mary Pickford, Negri herself, even Jeanette MacDonald. Zsa Zsa had been thrilled when Lubitsch directed Greta Garbo in *Ninotchka* in 1939.

Ironically, in 1945, he would offer Eva a film role in *A Royal Scandal* in which Tallulah Bankhead portrayed Russia's 18th-century monarch, Catherine the Great.

Lubitsch and Zsa Zsa didn't talk about movies, but about what was happening to their fellow Jews amid the flames of Europe at war. Bitterly, she blamed herself for leaving Magda, Vilmos, and Jolie behind.

"But you did what you could," he told her. "You urged them to leave. They were stubborn. They didn't listen to you. Don't blame yourself. You've been a good daughter. They must take some responsibility for not heeding your warning."

A cigar chomper like Darryl F. Zanuck, the great Berlin-born German director, **Ernst Lubitsch** provided comfort for Zsa Zsa during his long talks with her about the war raging in Europe and the plight of his fellow Jews.

Both Zsa Zsa and Lubitsch felt that Hollywood was too self-involved to care that millions were being slaughtered by the Nazis.

303

The comfort he offered was only temporary. Alone, she confronted "nights without end" and cried herself to sleep. She often grew irritated with Eva, accusing her of being selfish and not showing concern for the plight of the Gabors they had left behind.

With increasing frequency, Zsa Zsa depended on pills. Without admitting it, she had become an addict.

Occasionally, she pulled herself together in her capacity as a hostess. She wore perhaps too much jewelry and seemed to float through a party without really seeming to know anyone there.

Louella Parsons recalled one of her encounters with Zsa Zsa. "I asked her if she planned to pursue a screen career," Parsons said. "But she didn't seem to know who I was, and everybody in Hollywood knew who I was. She actually welcomed me to the film colony and wished me luck in getting work in character roles. I thought she'd lost her mind."

At times, Zsa Zsa became irrational, one night blaming her jewelry as the cause of her family's suffering. She'd often spend nights with her jewelry, trying on one gem after another, usually beginning with the pearls her grandmother, Francesa, had given her, and invariably including the ruby necklace which Vilmos had presented to her in commemoration of her wedding to Burhan Belge.

One rainy, windy night in Bel Air at around midnight, she became overcome with guilt for owning so much jewelry when her family was probably starving. She was staying that night in a suite within the Hilton Town House Hotel.

Impulsively, she gathered up her jewelry, walked out onto her terrace, and tossed it six floors down to the grounds below. Fortunately, the doorman concluded that the gems had come from her suite. He gathered up her collection, except for a "misplaced" diamond necklace, and returned them to her. Zsa Zsa's necklace eventually turned up around the neck of the doorman's girl friend.

As he later told Conrad, "Mrs. Hilton didn't seem to realize what she had done. She seemed to have no memory of throwing her jewelry off the terrace."

When Conrad returned from his frequent trips, he no longer accompanied her out on the town, and he didn't even have dinner with her, retreating instead behind the locked door of his private bedchamber.

A woman as heavily sexed and as young as Zsa Zsa could not continue for long "living the life of a nun," as she put it.

In spite of her addiction to pills, she continued to stage elaborate dinner parties, inviting mostly expatriate Europeans who talked seriously about the homelands they'd abandoned.

One of her favorite guests was the Austrian actor Paul Henreid, who arrived with his wife, Elizabeth ("Lisl") Gluck, whom he'd married in 1936.

Zsa Zsa confessed to Lubitsch her growing attraction to Henreid.

"It began with a flirtation over the dinner table when his wife wasn't looking," she said. "It was those sleepy eyes of his that attracted me. He was also suave and sophisticated. I had thrilled to him in two movies I'd seen months earlier."

She was referring to *Now, Voyager* and *Casablanca,* both released in 1942.

In *Now, Voyager,* co-starring with Bette Davis, Henreid had delivered one of the most iconic scenes in movie history by lighting two cigarettes at the same time and handing one of them to Davis.

He'd also immortalize himself as the freedom fighter, Victor Laszlo, in *Casablanca.* Although second in line to the more famous Humphrey Bogart, he ended up with Ingrid Bergman in the final reel during the most famous good-bye-at-the-airport scene in film history.

"We also spoke the same language," Zsa Zsa said. Henreid had been born in Trieste (now part of Italy) when it belonged to the Austro-Hungarian Empire.

She claimed that there came a point when she could no longer be alone in her wing of the Hilton manse. She confessed, "Even when Conrad is home, I am still alone. I can't reach through to him. He frightens me, too."

"Paul was the kind of man I was accustomed to knowing in Europe," she said. "He was the very opposite of Conrad. He reminded me of the land I'd left behind."

She was aware of his reputation—in fact, he later entitled his autobiography as *Ladies' Man.* And so he was. He was reputed to have seduced many of his leading ladies, including French actress Michèle Morgan, as well as Bette Davis, Hedy Lamarr, Olivia de Havilland, Eleanor Parker, and perhaps even Ingrid Bergman, who was also pursued by Bogart in spite of her frequent denials. "Joan Bennett said yes, but Katharine Hepburn told him to knock on some other door," Zsa Zsa later recalled.

"Sometimes my entire day revolved around the hour when I could drive over and meet with him," she said. "He understood me. And, yes, after intercourse, he lit two cigarettes for me like he'd done for that bitch, Davis."

"There was never any question of

Bette Davis enjoyed the romantic attention of Austrian actor **Paul Henreid** both on and off the screen when they co-starred together in the classic 1942 film, *Now Voyager.*

When Conrad Hilton began locking his bedroom door to Zsa Zsa, she, too, was driven into the arms of this "Ladies' Man" (as Henreid accurately entitled his autobiography).

his leaving his wife," Zsa Zsa said. "I didn't want him to. We knew our affair had the chance of a plucked flower. But when it was in full bloom, it was pure ecstasy for me. I felt comfort, protection, with his arms around me. I felt like nothing could harm me. He was not the most beautiful man in Hollywood, but he knew his way around the ladies. No wonder he was so popular in the boudoir."

In his 1984 memoir, Henreid claimed that his wife, Elizabeth, received an anonymous letter. It read:

"You are probably unaware that your husband is having an affair with Zsa Zsa Gabor. When he isn't shooting, she picks him up at the studio parking lot and they drive away, leaving his car there. They return several hours later. He gets into his car and drives away, and she drives away in her car. I have documentary proof of this in photos. If you'll meet me at Sunset and La Cienega at nine tomorrow night, I'll turn this proof over to you—for a hundred dollars."

At that point, and based on the implications of that letter, Zsa Zsa and Henrieid decided not to continue their affair.

After breaking off with Henreid, Zsa Zsa's mental condition continued to deteriorate at an even more rapid pace. She told Eva and others, "Without love, I have no reason to go on living. There are those in Hollywood, mostly women, who are jealous of me. Married to a multi-millionaire and living in luxury in Bel Air. They don't seem to realize that a life without love isn't worth living. It is existing."

On some nights when her personal crises bubbled over, she would drive to Eva's apartment and spend the night with her.

On one such very early morning when she couldn't sleep, she rose at around 3am and headed for the bathroom. She didn't turn on the lights, because she didn't want to disturb Eva, who was sleeping in the bed nearby. In the darkness, she dropped a glass. The sound of it breaking awakened Eva, who grabbed a flashlight. When Eva opened the bathroom door and shined the light into her sister's face, Zsa Zsa became hysterical and started screaming.

Somehow, in her mind, Zsa Zsa perceived that the Nazis had broken into the apartment and were about to haul her away. She continued screaming and weeping.

Eva called a doctor who rushed to the apartment. He gave Zsa Zsa a shot to sedate her. An ambulance was summoned.

She was unconscious when she was taken to a hospital in Santa Monica. When she woke up, she had no memory of what had happened the night before.

The doctors diagnosed her as having had a breakdown. "They kept me on a diet of sleeping pills," Zsa Zsa later recalled. "Eva came to visit. Conrad did not show up. I was in a fog during my stay—which lasted about a week—in that hospital."

My worst experience there was when two men, dressed in white uniforms, arrived to deliver me to the funeral parlor," Zsa Zsa said. "I panicked, thinking I had died. The men had the wrong room. A woman patient had died in the room next to mine. It was horrible. I started screaming once again, and this time a doctor shot me with something that knocked me out for two days."

After about a week, Eva arrived to drive Zsa Zsa back to her apartment.

Zsa Zsa told her, "I'm leaving Conrad. I don't plan to return to Bel Air. I'm flying to Washington to see if I can get some intervention in helping Magda, Vilmos, and Jolie out of Hungary—if they're not already dead."

"After that, I'm going to fly to New York and stay in a suite at the Plaza. After all, Conrad owns that hotel, and I'm still his wife. I want to be in New York to welcome our family if they can manage to escape to Lisbon. From there, we can arrange onward passage for them to New York and that Statue of Liberty."

***

As a means of reciprocating their hospitality, the Paul Henreids often invited both Eva and Zsa Zsa to their rather intimate dinner parties. The guests were mostly European expatriates.

An exception was a handsome young man, Philadelphia-born Hugh Marlowe, a stage and screen actor whose career was wallowing in mediocrity. Critics claimed that on film, he was "the embodiment of stoic uptightness."

When Eva met him, he was yet to immortalize himself playing Celeste Holm's playwright husband in *All About Eve* (1950), starring Bette Davis and Anne Baxter.

When he was introduced to Eva at the Henreids', he was a house guest of the couple and one of Henreid's best friends. Just like Eva with Charles Isaacs, Marlowe was in the throes of a divorce from his wife, E.T. Stevens.

Elizabeth Henreid recalled Marlowe sitting on their sofa, with Eva huddled on the carpet at his feet. "She was such a lovely blonde, and she'd positioned herself so that she was exposing maximum cleavage. Hugh was all eyes."

During the course of the dinner party, Elizabeth wrote, "Hugh and Eva had eyes only for each other. Occasionally, she would glance nervously at me. I wasn't Hugh's wife. I had no claim on him. Perhaps she'd heard rumors."

At the time, gossips claimed that Paul and Elizabeth were locked into a *ménage à trois* with Marlowe.

Before settling in for the evening, Eva spoke to Elizabeth on her terrace. She was blunt. "Does Hugh belong to you?"

Elizabeth laughed at the suggestion. "Oh, please, this is not another Van and Evie Johnson/Kennan Wynn kind of household. You can have him, sweetheart. I'll stick to Paul. He may be dull, but he's mine. Didn't you come with someone?"

Indeed, she had, although Eva later could not remember the name of whoever had brought her, only that he was a rich stockbroker from New York who invested in movies.

"He's not really for me," Eva confessed. "I accepted his invitation because he has millions of dollars, a Rolls-Royce, and a chauffeur."

Elizabeth looked at the discarded beau, finding him a dapper man, somewhere on the shady side of eighty.

A sophisticated hostess, Elizabeth even suggested that Eva was welcome to share their guest room with Hugh if she so desired. "It was obvious to me she so desired," Elizabeth said. "She was hot to trot."

That night, Eva launched an affair with Marlowe that lasted for nearly eighteen months. Of course, she wasn't always available. "My dance card was always overbooked," she later jokingly recalled.

As it happened, the Henreids were sitting in their living room having a drink with Marlowe, their houseguest, when Eva called one night to cancel a date with him at the last minute.

One of the most famous car conversations in movie history took place when **Hugh Marlowe** *(right figure in photo above)* departed to find a gas station after running his car out of gas. That left **Celeste Holm** *(left)* alone in the car with Margo Channing (center), a role interpreted by **Bette Davis** in her greatest role.

Eva and Marlowe conducted a months-long affair. "He was a bit dull, *dahlink*," Eva told Zsa Zsa. "But he hit the spot."

With drink in hand, Marlowe rose to answer the phone. "It's me, *dahlink*," Eva said. "I won't be able to keep our date. Something's come up, if you'll forgive the expression. Last night, I fell in love with another man."

After about fifteen minutes, Marlowe reported to his friends and hosts: "I don't understand it. Yesterday…well, she swore devotion and her love for me. We even discussed marriage. This sudden change of mind…It doesn't make any sense."

"Actually, you look a bit relieved to get this Hungarian bombshell off your plate," Henreid said. "Come on, have another drink and forget her."

Years later, during the recitation of the story to party guests at Merv Griffin's house, Eva said, "I lied to Hugh. I said. I'd fallen for another man. But I was never good at math. At the time, I was also in love with four other men…or was it five? As I told you, *dahlinks*, I never could count."

***

At long last, Darryl F. Zanuck, at Fox, secured Eva a minor role in *A Royal Scandal (1945),* with the understanding that it would be directed by Zsa Zsa's friend, Ernst Lubitsch, and that it would star the indomitable Tallulah Bankhead as the Russian Czarina, Catherine the Great. A young and beautiful Anne Baxter was cast as her chief Lady-in-Waiting, Anna Jaschikoff.

Charles Coburn was assigned the role of Chancellor Nicolai Iiyitch, with William Eythe interpreting the role of the romantic male lead, Lieutenant Alexei Chernoff.

This film would represent Lubitsch's second attempt to bring the life story of Russia's Catherine the Great to the screen. He'd already filmed *Forbidden Paradise* in 1924, a silent movie starring Pola Negri as Catherine.

Lubitsch had trepidations about working with Bankhead, who was known for her tendency to fly into sudden rages. Before Bankhead signed her $125,000 contract, Lubitsch had arranged for it to be sent to at least ten other actresses. Consequently, he eagerly accepted an unexpected, last-minute call from Greta Garbo, who had retired from the screen after the failure of her previous film, *Two-Faced Woman* (1941). Previously, both Lubitsch and Garbo had enjoyed great success through their collaboration with *Ninotchka* in 1939. Millions of Americans were lured into the movie houses by that film's slogan: GARBO LAUGHS.

When Lubitsch was reunited with the elusive Garbo, she approved of the script he'd sent her. "I played a long shot sending it to Garbo, never thinking she'd agree to do it," Lubitsch recalled.

Impulsively, without checking with Zanuck at Fox, the director more or less went ahead and promised the role to Garbo, even though Fox would have to pay off Bankhead.

To Lubitsch's shock, Zanuck and Fox Studios' New York-based sales department were dismissive of Garbo. "We don't want the bitch back on the screen, at least not at Fox," Zanuck claimed. "Her last picture bombed, and she did better in the European market than in America. Because of the war, we've lost the European market, so we'd better stick with the dyke we have instead of the dyke who wants to make a comeback at Fox's expense."

[The word dyke had come into usage in 1942.]

Thanks to Zsa Zsa's friendship with Lubitsch, Eva discovered this pre-production hassle before she reported to work on the picture. There, she had been cast as Countess Demidow, a Lady-in-Waiting within Catherine's court.

When she first met Eva, Bankhead seemed charmed by her, and invited her into her dressing room for a drink.

The next day, Eva joined Bankhead for costume fittings. "Remember, *dahling*," Bankhead said to her. "My gown has to dazzle. You are only a Lady-in-Waiting."

Within fifteen minutes, Eva was privy to one of the most startling arguments ever to take place on the Fox lot: **GRETA GARBO VS. TALLULAH BANKHEAD.**

Without having checked with anyone at Fox, Garbo had assumed that the picture was hers, and arrived at the studio for wardrobe fittings. The staff was startled to see Garbo making an entrance onto the site, and immediately assumed that she had arrived to wish Bankhead good luck. Rumor had it that these superstars had engaged in a brief sexual fling with each other during the early 1930s.

Eva was a witness to their encounter, although her presence was completely ignored by Garbo. Nonetheless, Eva would spend the next few years "dining out" on what she witnessed that day between the formidable *über*-divas.

As Garbo walked in on Bankhead, it was immediately obvious that there was no love lost between them. The romantic encounter they had shared together *[in 1931 at the home of the screenwriter, Salka Viertel, when Garbo had scandalously arrived at a formal dinner party wearing jodhpurs]* was a distant memory.

Garbo was her usual blunt self, wasting no time in silly talk, getting immediately to the point. She stood back and skeptically observed Bankhead being fitted into a lavish ball gown that was probably more spectacular than anything the real Catherine the Great ever actually wore. Imperiously, Garbo gave Eva not the slightest indication that she even knew Bankhead.

Practicing her best Southern manners, Bankhead at first attempted to introduce Garbo to Eva.

"I'm not here to talk to some blonde thing," Garbo droned, but to acquaint you with a change in casting. It's regrettable that I have to work as a messenger boy for Fox. I just assumed that Lubitsch had told you. From this moment on, I'll be playing Catherine the Great. The role of that Czarina is part of my destiny."

"Miss Garbo, I would be the first to welcome your return to the screen," Bankhead said. "But I've already been signed. Not only that, I've accepted my first paycheck and spent a huge chunk of it."

"Lubitsch told me that you will be paid and bid a sweet *adieu, "* Garbo said.

"I know your pictures haven't done well, especially that last turkey, *Two-*

Faced Woman," Bankhead drawled. "I tried to sit through it, but got diarrhea and had to run out. It's true that America has grown tired of your emoting. But you're still big in occupied Paris. Edward R. Murrow told me that Nazi soldiers crowd into speakeasies every night to watch you in *Anna Karenina* and *Ninotchka*. *Mata Hari* is the favorite of the SS boys. They adore you as a German spy."

"At least I made some great pictures, unlike some other 'actresses' who came to Hollywood," Garbo said.

"Need I remind you that my last picture for that divine Mr. Hitchcock was called *Lifeboat?*" Bankhead said. "They lined up around the block to see Mama Tallu."

"Dear me, you were just playing yourself in that trifle," Garbo said. "The role of Catherine the Great calls for a European woman. I have proved my greatness in playing Queen Christina."

"You mean that Swedish dyke?" Tallulah said.

"I mean, *that* Queen Catherine did not speak like an Alabama pickaninny."

"*Dahling,* I don't know who taught you Southern dialect. But if you ever go below the Mason-Dixon Line, I suggest you not call a white Southern belle a pickaninny."

"Lubitsch explained to me that it would be wrong for you to attempt to

Director **Ernst Lubitsch** *(center)* fell directly into a war between two *über-divas,* **Tallulah Bankhead** *(left)* vs. **Greta Garbo** *(right).* Garbo is shown as she appeared playing the bisexual Swedish queen in *Queen Christina.*

Garbo had been misled into thinking she was also going to portray another queen on screen, Catherine the Great. To Lubitsch's astonishment, he learned that "the money people in New York" preferred Bankhead over the great Garbo. The message to the director was blunt: "We prefer the dyke we have, instead of the dyke who wants the job."

Cast in a small part in *A Royal Scandal*, Eva was an eyewitness to "two tarantulas contemplating regicide during pre-production wardrobe fittings

Catherine," Garbo said. "You were brought to Hollywood to become the second Garbo. You failed miserably at that. Unfortunately, I've sat through your pictures. You are not a screen actress, but a stage actress who in front of the camera seems to be projecting to the last row in a balcony on Broadway. You should have studied my close-ups more carefully if you were trying to imitate me."

"I think I'm just as strong-willed and just as horny as Catherine ever was," Bankhead said.

"You must select your film roles more carefully," Garbo said. "That is, if there are to be any more film roles. I heard you came to Hollywood to play Scarlett O'Hara. She is supposed to be sixteen years old when the film opens. The role in *Gone With the Wind* that was suited to you would be Belle Watling."

"Are you aware she's the mistress of the local whorehouse, and that I'm a lady?" Bankhead said.

"You've played whores before," said Garbo. "I saw you onstage in Maugham's *Rain*. You were like the cheapest slut on Place Clichy in that one. I didn't come backstage to congratulate you because I was too embarrassed."

"Miss Garbo, you have played far more whores than I have," Bankhead claimed.

"As for your makeup, it is too garish for Catherine. You must have raided the makeup department. You're not an Indian putting on warpaint to massacre the white settlers. Fortunately, I don't need to paint a face on myself—a little lipstick, a dash of powder, perhaps the quick brush of an eyebrow pencil. On me, false eyelashes are not needed."

"I found that out," Bankhead said. "Remember when I first met you, I pulled them to see if they were real. Let's not get too carried away with all that natural beauty. You forget that I first met you when you passed through New York. You were an un-retouched Swedish dumpling, with frizzy hair, buck teeth, and, lest I forget, the shadow of a double chin, puppy fat accumulated by eating too many Swedish pancakes with sugar-coated lingonberries. Makeup, of course, could never do anything for those clodhopper feet of yours. And then you took up with that dreadful Mercedes de Acosta. To me, she always looked like some mouse in a topcoat."

"Mercedes was a celebrated Spanish beauty," Garbo said. "Not like your former lover, Hattie McDaniel, all 350 pounds of pure black Mammy."

Word spread quickly to the executive offices of Fox that Garbo was on the lot, feuding loudly with Bankhead. An emergency call was placed to Lubitsch in the hopes that he would diffuse what was escalating into an explosive confrontation. Lubitsch made a call to the wardrobe department and got Garbo on the phone. "I had the horrible duty of telling her that Fox didn't want her. It was one of the most painful things I've ever done as a director."

After Garbo put down the receiver, she took what Bankhead defined as "French Leave," departing from the Fox lot never to return. She was seen later that day aboard a flight to New York.

Three years later, in October of 1948, Garbo and Bankhead would compete for another imperial role, this time that of Elizabeth of Austria in Jean Cocteau's new play, *The Eagle Has Two Heads*. Before Garbo could make up her mind, Bankhead signed for the role. "With the play, *dahling*," she recalled, "came a young actor, Marlon Brando, who was called upon by me to perform boudoir duty."

Years later, columnist James Bacon asked Bankhead to confirm the rumor about Garbo showing up to challenge her for the role of Catherine the Great during a pre-production wardrobe fitting for *A Royal Scandal*.

"Yes, *dahling*, it is true and so embarrassing for her," Bankhead said. "When I saw her, I said, 'Greta, *dahling*, and here we are, still surviving after all these years. You with your face lifted and your vagina dropped, and me with my vagina lifted and my face dropped."

***

The following day, secure in her status as a viable star after her confrontation with Garbo, Bankhead met the film's co-star, a very beautiful and very young Anne Baxter. The young actress immediately antagonized Bankhead, who later told Eva, "The cuntie is an arrogant little snob just because she's the granddaughter of Frank Lloyd Wright. The no-talent bitch has nothing to be snobbish about."

That afternoon, Lubitsch also introduced Bankhead to her six feet tall co-star, William Eythe. Bankhead defined the dark-haired, twenty-four year old actor as "handsome like a man should be—not some powder puff like Robert Taylor."

She told Eva, "The only thing I heard that was wrong with him involved a punctured eardrum that kept him out of the war. I understand that all other parts of him are in working order. *Photoplay* called him 'a wonderful catch.' Well, I'm planning on being on the receiving end of his ball...make that *balls, dahling*."

Homage to Aunt Tallu
(Tallulah Bankhead)

The author remembers Miss Bankhead fondly because of quotes such as this one: "I've tried several varieties of sex. The conventional position makes me claustrophobic and the others give me a stiff neck or lockjaw."

Appearing in *A Royal Scandal*, based very, very loosely on the story of Catherine the Great. were **Anne Baxter** *(left)*, **William Eythe** *(center)*, and **Tallulah Bankhead** *(right)*, clad in the wardrobe department's idea of what the imperial empress might have worn.

Director Ernst Lubitsch later claimed, "There was more scandal going on off screen than on. Off screen, both Baxter and Bankhead were forcing Eythe to perform "double duty"—at least until Eythe's jealous lover, actor Lon McAllister, showed up to reclaim his stud.

Within a few days, Bankhead was raving to Eva about having scored a home run with Eythe. "He gave me my biggest thrill since I came to Hollywood with the intention of fucking that divine Gary Cooper."

"Eythe was an equal opportunity fucker," Lubitsch said. "Within the week, he was also secretly plowing Anne Baxter. It's a wonder he had any energy left to perform on camera."

Bankhead befriended Eva and was very supportive of her. She confronted Lubitsch, telling him, "You watch that girl. She's going to be a big star. I should think you could find more for her to do in the picture."

Lubitsch suspected that the bisexual Bankhead was more intrigued by the prospect of promoting an amorous relationship with Eva than boosting her standing as a film star—and he was right.

On Monday morning, when cast members reported to work at the studio, they were informed that Lubitsch had suffered a heart attack over the weekend and that he was recuperating in a hospital in Santa Monica. Because he'd be in no condition to continue his involvement in the movie, Zanuck had turned its direction over to Lubitsch's young assistant, Otto Preminger.

That choice of director suited Bankhead better than Lubitsch. She and Preminger had been friends for years, ever since she'd used her influence with her friend, Harry S Truman, to get the Preminger family out of Nazi-controlled Austria. Bankhead had also learned that Preminger had been her biggest champion during the hassle over which star should play Catherine the Great—Garbo or herself.

She learned that Preminger had told both Zanuck and Lubitsch, "I will not double-cross Tallulah. If you sign Garbo and fire Tallulah, I will walk off the picture."

314

Bankhead appreciated that kind of loyalty.

Unlike Baxter and Bankhead, who were still overworking Eythe as he performed double duty, Eva, as she later claimed, didn't get intimate with anyone on the film set.

The sexual popularity of Eythe on set came to an abrupt end after two short weeks, when Lon McCallister, a Los Angeles-born former child actor, showed up on the set to retrieve his boyfriend.

Eva was the first to meet him. He was only four years younger than she was, but his height of 5'6" made him look forever boyish. Bluntly, he told Eva, "I've come to rescue Billy—he's my boyfriend—from those two tarantula divas who have been panting over all that man-flesh, or so I'm told."

Since he didn't have a job at the

The former child actor, **Lon McAllister,** came of age but never got beyond his height of 5 feet 6. After hearing of the off-screen escapades of his lover, William Eythe, on the set of *A Royal Scandal,* he showed up to reclaim him.

After losing Eythe's services, the bisexual Bankhead turned to a pursuit of Eva.

Called in to finish the picture after Lubitsch fell ill, the tyranical director, **Otto Preminger** may have been a horror to the rest of the cast, but he was forever loyal to Bankhead.

She'd used her influence with President Truman to get his family rescued from Nazi-occupied Austria.

time, McCallister decided to remain on the set for the duration of the shoot. "When you find a cock as big as Billy's, you got to hang on to it for dear life."

[Eva bonded with McCallister and Eythe and remained friends with them for years. As the decades passed, and as their movie careers slipped into oblivion, she persuaded Zsa Zsa to lobby their cause with Conrad Hilton. Her older sister agreed, and subsequently, arranged work for both actors in appearances in Hilton Hotel commercials.

With sadness, in January of 1957, Eva attended Eythe's funeral. He had died at the age of thirty-eight, after suffering from hepatitis and acute liver disease.

McCallister fell into Eva's arms, sobbing. "Without Billy, he told her, "I can't go on living."

Actually, he did, dying on June 11, 2005, from congestive heart failure at the age of eighty-two.]

The first day on the set, lunching with Eva, Bankhead gracefully responded to the loss of Eythe as a lover. "Obviously, he prefers the midget *[a reference to McCallister]* to my overworked vagina. Let's press on, *dahling,* to my next conquest."

315

Another visitor to the set was Frank Lloyd Wright, wanting to watch his granddaughter perform in front of a camera. In reaction to this request, Bankhead stormed off the set, refusing to emote in front of the fabled architect. "I'm not his fucking granddaughter."

Preminger finally persuaded her to appear, but Bankhead deliberately flubbed her line—thirty times—until Wright grew impatient and left the set.

When Preminger asked why she'd done that, she answered, "Darling, he's a known anti-Semite and a Republican Nazi."

A third visitor to the set was actor John Hodiak, coming to visit his bride-to-be, Anne Baxter, with whom he'd appeared in the 1944 film *Sunday Dinner for a Soldier.* They had fallen in love, and planned to be married. Despite road-blocks imposed by Baxter's family, the couple would eventually marry in 1946.

Eva said that Bankhead "was in triumph when she learned that Baxter had fallen for Hodiak."

"I had that beer can of his first," she claimed, referring to their joint appearance together in *Lifeboat* (1944).

News of actor **John Hodiak's** "beer can" that he stuffed into his pants was already known when he showed up on the set to meet with his bride-to-be, **Anne Baxter**.

The couple *(depicted above)* had fallen in love during World War II when they'd made a morale-builder, *Sunday Dinner for a Soldier,* together.

Eva, too was attracted to this hot Ukranian, but she had to wait until he both married and divorced Baxter.

Baxter trusted Eva to entertain Hodiak when she was in front of the camera. Eva had read in *Photoplay* that Hodiak was "the next Clark Gable," although that same appellation had also been applied to other actors, including James Craig.

Eva learned that Hodiak was the son of immigrants from the Ukraine. And although she was involved in a torrid affair with Hugh Marlowe at the time, she admitted to Bankhead that she found Hodiak "powerfully masculine. He's soft-spoken and radiates sex appeal, but in a quiet way, not flashy like Errol Flynn. All John has to do is stand in one spot, light a cigarette, blow out the smoke, and the dames will come flocking to him."

[The Hodiak/Eva Gabor affair would be postponed until 1952, in the wake of his divorce from Baxter after six unhappy years of marriage

Eva would be the first woman Hodiak called for a date after dumping Baxter. "I followed in Tallulah's footsteps and got my man, although that sneaky bitch, Janis Paige, was also moving in on him. A catfight was brewing."

Eva, perhaps influenced by Bankhead, also became something of a diva on the set, challenging Preminger about his camera angles and repeatedly accusing him of trying to make her look unattractive. He was outraged—"all that from a little stinking Hungarian twat."

As a means of wreaking revenge on "that two-bit Budapest whore," Preminger cut every reference to her and each of her scenes out of the movie.

She burst into tears when she went to a theater in the Los Angeles area to see it with friends. "I'd told everybody about my being in it. Preminger, that ass, cut what little part I had. I simply didn't exist."]

***

Back at the annex of the Portuguese embassy in Galgagyörk, Magda was still trying to recover from her rape by Adolf Eichmann and her leg injury. In the adjacent bedroom, Jolie frequently heard her oldest daughter cry herself to sleep.

In the violent twilight of the Third Reich, Dr. Garrido warned her that diplomatic niceties "are no longer being respected by those monsters. The Nazis are arresting, raping, pillaging, and murdering thousands, even millions, at random. You are no longer safe here."

The Soviet Army was advancing from the East, and even with the enemy at their gates, the Nazis continued their systematic execution of Jews. Those same Nazis would soon die with Soviet bullets in their hearts and heads.

Dr. Garrido had learned through his paid informant at Gestapo headquarters that Magda's name had been added to the list of the top ten most-wanted "enemies of the Nazi regime in Budapest," and slated for execution.

"When the SS arrives to arrest you, they will have orders that will supercede any diplomatic privilege," he told her. "You will be taken away, perhaps along with Vilmos and Jolie, too."

The following morning, after telling her that, Dr. Garrido was ordered by the Portuguese dictator, Antonio Salazar, to surrender his ambassadorial post to a replacement arriving soon from Lisbon. Garrido had been reposted as the Portuguese ambassador to Bern, and was ordered to relocate to Switzerland within forty-eight hours.

Garrido told her that once he was established in Bern, that he could arrange air transport to fly her from Switzerland across Nazi-occupied France and neutral Spain into Lisbon. But first, she had to get there. He made her emphatically aware that even a vehicle flying the flag of neutral Portugal would not be a safe way to transport her across Nazi-controlled borders into neutral Switzerland.

Whereas Garrido had been ordered to fly from Hungary to Switzerland, it was understood that his personal property and his private papers would be transported by truck. The vehicle carrying his household goods would undoubtedly

317

be stopped and searched, but as long as it didn't contain anyone wanted by the Gestapo or by the Hungarian or Austrian police, it would probably be allowed to pass.

Dangerous political prisoners had already been smuggled out of Hungary within a secret and very cramped compartment concealed beneath the floor of a truck associated with the Portuguese Embassy. Although the ride would be long and difficult, it was decided that the only way Magda could avoid detection involved being concealed this way.

"It's a ghastly trip," he warned her. "Fumes, noise, bumping, dirt, and grime. In safe, secluded spots, you'll be let out to eat and relieve yourself. But it will be the most uncomfortable and frightening trip you'll ever take."

It was agreed that once she arrived in Lisbon, he would arrange for lodgings within a luxurious villa of a friend of his while awaiting transport by ship to New York. "All ships going to America are overbooked these days, but I will use whatever influence I have left to get you on board."

Then he informed her that although the "replacement" Portuguese ambassador to Hungary, Teizeira Baranquino, would be sympathetic to the plight of Vilmos and Jolie, "he'll have no real power to protect them during the final days of the Nazi Occupation of Hungary. Those bastards are more intent on exterminating Jews than in defending Budapest from a Soviet attack from the East."

She was aware that her parents might not survive the hundreds of miles of an arduous trip beneath the floor of a bouncing truck. Dr. Garrido believed that since there was no warrant for their arrest, they might follow later within a conventional vehicle flying the flag of Portugal.

"I will feel so alone with my daughters out of Budapest," Jolie had told Magda. "Vilmos is begging me to stay until he is granted a Portuguese visa, which hasn't come through yet. I already have mine. He does not. And of course, I can't leave Paul Savosdy. I'm still madly in love with him."

"This is no time to think about your love affairs," Magda chastised her. "You can always find another lover. Zsa Zsa, Eva, and I can't find another mother."

The night before Magda's escape, a young aide delivered a message to them. Jolie's apartment, overlooking Elizabeth Bridge in Budapest, had been completely destroyed by an Allied bomb.

Jolie broke into uncontrollable sobbing. Magda recalled that during happier times, if a maid broke a single cup, Jolie would often become hysterical. Now, all her possessions, clothing, furniture, and paintings, were gone after just one blast. Fortunately, she had escaped with all her jewelry.

"It's amazing that America, our hope for freedom, was also the force that destroyed my home. If anything was telling me to leave Budapest, it was that single bomb."

As Jolie told Magda, as part of a tearful farewell, "If I must die, I will die in peace, knowing that my daughters have made it to safety."

[It was later learned that a few hours after Magda's escape beneath the floorboards of the Embassy's truck, an order was issued by the Gestapo: ARREST MAGDA BYCHOWSKY.]

***

In an attempt to rescue her family, Zsa Zsa flew to Washington, D.C. During her time in the hospital, she had read that Conrad Hilton was one of the twenty most powerful men in the United States. She believed, therefore, that by announcing herself as Mrs. Conrad Hilton, she could get some of the power brokers in Washington to cooperate with her hopes of allowing Magda, Jolie, and Vilmos to enter the United States through the Port of New York.

When she checked into a hotel in Washington, she turned on the radio. At the noon hour, she heard the terrible news. One wing of Conrad's Bel Air manse had been razed by fire. It was the wing in which she lived with all her family memorabilia, clothing, and personal possessions. She'd left behind many choice pieces of her jewelry. The announcer claimed that there had been only one living creature who perished in the flames. It was her dog, Ranger. She burst into uncontrollable weeping.

Ouida Rathbone, her next-door neighbor, was the first to have spotted the fire. In a desperate search for more information, Zsa Zsa placed a call to her in Bel Air.

"Oh, Zsa Zsa, it was so terrible," Ouida said, between sobs. "I stood in your front yard and I could hear Ranger's howls. I begged the fireman to save her, but by then the fire was too advanced. Your poor dog died a horrible death, over my screams of SAVE THE DOG! It was too late."

Zsa Zsa went into mourning as if she'd lost a beloved member of her family—which actually, she had.

Three days later, she had pulled herself together and set about the task she had embarked upon: Her mission in Washington.

She called first on Dr. Vasco Garin, First Secretary of the Portuguese Embassy in Washington, D.C. She carefully explained her family's connection to Dr. Garrido and the Portuguese Embassy in Hungary. Garin told her that Portugal accepted war refugees only if the United States guaranteed their admission into America. However, since the Gabors were Hungarians, and since Hungary had declared war on the United States, the Gabors would have to be classified as "enemy aliens" and therefore not allowed to enter America.

Zsa Zsa remained in Washington for two frustrating months. "I knocked on every door."

Dr. Munir Ertegün was the Turkish Ambassador to the United States. He and Mrs. Ertegün were emphatically aware that Zsa Zsa was the former mistress of Atatürk, and both of them paid great attention to her, but could provide no help.

Mrs. Ertegün did procure an invitation for Zsa Zsa to one of the parties hosted by Gwendolyn (Gwen) Cafritz, who was one of the most prominent hostesses in Washington. Cafritz competed with socialite Perle Mesta as the U.S. capital's "Hostess with the Mostest." During a period stretching from the end of World War II until the early 1970s, their lavish, widely publicized parties were famous for influencing the course of legislative policies and for mingling Hollywood celebrities with politicians.

Cafritz extended her invitation to Zsa Zsa after learning that "Connie Hilton's wife is Hungarian." Both women had been born in Budapest.

At the Cafritz party, Zsa Zsa once again was introduced to the Duke and Duchess of Windsor, along with the power elite of the U.S. capital.

Zsa Zsa wore her finest diamond-and-ruby necklace, but was outdazzled by Cafritz, who wore a diamond-and-emerald necklace featuring 13 oblong emeralds and 145 marquise diamonds, each within a setting of platinum and gold.

Zsa Zsa told her that before leaving Bel Air, "I was awakened by this man brandishing a gun. He looted my jewelry, even a Hand of Fátima that Atatürk had presented to me in Ankara."

[In 1965 and again in 1969, Cafritz would experience two famous robberies herself. During the latter, four masked gunmen punched, kicked, and forced her to open a safe, while other members of her household slept undisturbed in a distant wing of her house.]

At her party, Cafritz was warm and hospitable to Zsa Zsa, discussing the problems she had finding a good servant and also the hardship her household was undergoing because of wartime scarcities. Zsa Zsa begged her to introduce her to an influential politician who might help her.

"Here comes Lyndon," Cafritz advised. "He's going to ask you to dance. Press your case, dear, as you press up against him. Don't be surprised if you're greeted by Jumbo."

Not as hip as she later became, Zsa Zsa didn't know what "Jumbo" meant. But she soon learned, as the Texas politician held her close.

Lyndon B. Johnson told her he was a close friend of her husband. After the dance, during which he held her far too close as she experienced "Jumbo" first hand, he invited her for a drink.

When she poured out the details of her plight to him, he suggested that they retire to a room he kept at the Mayflower Hotel for further discussions. "You'll soon learn how things work in Washington: One good favor deserves another. We call it 'reciprocation.'"

She later regretted rejecting his offer. "Had I known that one day he'd be President of the United States, I would have gone back with him to the Mayflower. But I never believed that a crude country boy like Johnson would ever become president. Had I been seduced by him I could add to my *resumé* that I slept with three Presidents of the United States."

In her memoir, Zsa Zsa did not "out" Johnson, but wrote about "a courtly Senator who held my hand. All evening he nuzzled me," while assuring her that he might be of aid. She also falsely wrote that he was from a state she could not recall. But whereas the episode was not published in her memoirs, she "dined out" on news of her encounter with LBJ throughout the 1960s, during his Presidency and beyond.

In spite of her turning down his sexual advances, Johnson may have helped Zsa Zsa after all. Soonafter, she received a call informing her that the U.S. Secretary of State, Cordell Hull, would receive her the following morning in his offices at ten o'clock. She dressed in a black dress with a black overcoat.

She remembered a slender, gray-haired man who treated her with great courtesy. When she became speechless in his presence, he brought her a glass of water. "A war was going on, and he didn't have much time, but he listened to my dilemma," she said.

He explained that the Soviets would soon be controlling Budapest, and that he didn't have any influence with them. "Because they are Hungarians, and because Hungary is at war with the United States, the Gabors are enemy aliens. I can classify them as American allies only if they reach Lisbon. If they can do that on their own, I will speed up their clearance into the United States."

At a party in Washington, Zsa Zsa later regretted that she turned down a proposition from rising Texas politician, **Lyndon B. Johnson**, to return with him to his suite at the Mayflower Hotel.

"I didn't get to experience the full treatment of what he called his 'Jumbo,' but I sure felt it pressing up against my vagina as we danced."

In Washington, Zsa Zsa met with Secretary of State **Cordell Hull**. He told her the bad news:

"Because Hungary has declared war on the United States, your parents are classified as enemy aliens."

She was so grateful that she kissed his hand. "I should be the one kissing your hand, beautiful lady," Hull said.

She flew out of Washington that afternoon, heading for the Plaza Hotel in

New York. For an indefinite time, that would become her new address. Her husband's address would be the Hilton Town House Hotel in Los Angeles.

On her first day in New York, she called Eva and told her where she was, and how things had gone in Washington. She never left her suite during the entire second day and retired early. The ordeal in Washington, the anxiety, and her fears had weakened her.

At around midnight, she sensed the presence of someone in her bedroom. She bolted awake and switched on her bedside lamp. In the doorway was framed the figure of a nude young man.

***

Before abandoning Hollywood ("it abandoned me, *dahlink*"), Eva secured a small part in one final movie, *The Wife of Monte Cristo,* released in 1946.

Dorcas Cochran's screenplay had little to do with the novel by Alexandre Dumas *père.*

The director was the super-masculine Edgar G.Ulmer, who had been born in what is now the Czech Republic. In Vienna, he had been an art director for Max Reinhardt's widely respected *Theater in der Josefstadt.* When he came to the United States, he directed the low-budget *Damaged Lives* (1933), an exploitation film exposing the horrors of venereal disease. One reviewer wrote: "After watching this horror, no one will ever have sex again."

The Black Cat (1934), which he directed, starring Bela Lugosi and Boris Karloff, became the biggest hit of the season for Universal Pictures.

The male star of *Monte Cristo* was John Loder, who had married Hedy Lamarr in 1943. The sultry brunette star and Ulmer had long been lovers, their affair beginning in Europe. Loder seemingly knew of Ulmer's affair with his wife, but it caused no tension between them.

Although Loder had two children with Lamarr, his marriage to her was coming unglued, and each of them was seeing other people. During Loder's fling with Dinah Shore, Lamarr was also slipping around for sexual trysts with the handsome actor and furniture maker, George Montgomery, Shore's husband.

When she met Loder, Eva knew him only as Lamarr's husband. The British-American actor, over a period of several decades, would eventually make at least one hundred movies beginning with *Dancing Mad* in 1925.

In *Now, Voyager,* (1942*),* he'd played a wealthy widower engaged to Bette Davis. Off screen, Loder had a brief affair with Davis. He later said, "I think Bette seduced me out of curiosity. She wanted to learn first hand what turned

322

on the most beautiful woman on earth, meaning Hedy, of course."

Until Loder came along, Eva had no conflicts with Lamarr about men. "Leave those jealous feuds to Zsa Zsa and Hedy," Eva said. But upon meeting Lamarr's husband, she was powerfully attracted to him, especially when she learned that his marriage to Lamarr was all but over.

Eva made friends with Lenore Aubert, who had been cast as the film's female lead, the Countess of Monte Cristo. A year older than Eva, Aubert had been born in Slovenia when it was still part of the Austro-Hungarian Empire. Later, she married a Jew, Julius Altman, and immigrated to the United States after the Austrian *Anschluss* of 1938.

After that, Aubert began to find work in American films, including *Bluebeard's Eighth Wife* (1938). On the set, Eva met Aubert's husband, Altman, who worked in the garment business in New York. When Eva moved there, he beefed up her wardrobe by helping her procure her designer clothing at cut-rate prices.

Eva later dismissed her own small part in the low-budget *Monte Cristo* swashbuckler. "I took the role of the Countess, Mme Lucille Maillard, because it was the only thing offered to a young *ingénue* like me. The pay was virtually nothing. Fortunately, I still had a rich husband to pay the bills. Lenore's wardrobe was more beautiful than mine, as was her jewelry. She was also beautiful, but not in my category, *dahlink*. Some vicious queenie hairdresser gave me a hideous coiffure, with my hair piled in ringlets on top of my head. Far more devastating were friends who saw the movie. They claimed that my voice sounded more like Zsa Zsa's."

Women were attracted to Loder because of his looks. Lamarr had openly praised "his physique and his strength. As a bedtime partner, I had only one complaint about him. He wore his shorts under his pajamas."

Loder was the subject of an underground rumor in Hollywood. It was said that he could make love to a woman nineteen times over the course of a two-day weekend.

One day, Eva kidded him about this assertion in his dressing room. "I can prove it to you if you'll go away for the weekend

John Loder, seen here with **Eva Gabor** in a scene from the B-movie, *The Wife of Monte Cristo* (1946), was once married to Hedy Lamarr.

Loder lives in Hollywood sexual lore for his studly ability to function for more rounds in bed with a woman than any other actor on the screen.

Women, including Eva, often put him to this marathon test.

with me to Palm Springs. The trick is to get lots of exercise and plenty of sleep before the marathon. Then, after things get started, I rest about two hours between each roll in the hay, and get by on about six hours sleep."

In a spontaneous moment of recklessness, Eva agreed to test his claim, and consequently disappeared with him for three nights in the desert.

She later reported to Aubert, "John lived up to his boasting. Nineteen times! It was remarkable, unbelievable. For me, it was a once-in-a-lifetime experience. Never again. No more sexual marathons for me, no setting of records. As a lady, I prefer quality more than quantity. Those last six times with John weren't as good as they should have been."

Loder admitted to Ulmer, "As you, of all men, know, I'm married to the world's most ravishing brunette, but every now and then, a man becomes famished for blondes."

Lamarr later learned about her husband's adultery with Eva, and other female stars, and ultimately divorced him. Loder told Eva and Ulmer, "Hedy is accusing me of adultery, but isn't that like the pot calling the kettle black?"

***

Jolie

In war-ravaged Budapest, both Jolie and Vilmos realized that time was running out for them. Every day, they were in danger of being hauled off to a death camp. Magda had escaped, but they had remained behind.

The death toll within the city was appalling. At least five thousand Hungarians had already been murdered, and an equal number hauled off to Nazi-run slave labor camps. Nearly 15,000 residents had been deported to uncertain fates.

In a desperate move to obtain a Swiss entry visa, Jolie had gone to the unofficial Swiss consul in Budapest and offered a bribe. She would surrender her five-story apartment house in exchange for an entrance visa. She later said that the consul must have been the last official in Budapest who would not accept a bribe. He rejected her offer.

At the time, neutral Switzerland was besieged with thousands of Nazis fleeing from Germany, knowing—even if Hitler didn't—that the Nazis had lost. These Germans were hoping to use Switzerland as a launch pad for their eventual escape to such South American countries as Paraguay or Argentina.

Fortunately, one of Jolie's old beaux, André Zalábondy, contacted her after a silence of almost fifteen years. Rather chubby, he had pursued her for years without much success. In Budapest, he'd sold villas to wealthy aristocrats. But for reasons not entirely clear, he'd fled from Hungary and established a base in Spain. It was rumored that Zalábondy was a black market courier allowed to operate even in countries controlled by the Nazis. He also had powerful connections among the government officials of neutral Switzerland.

He had never liked Magda, finding her too aggressive, but from Lisbon, she had contacted him and asked for his help. Zalábondy was never known to do a favor for anyone without compensation, so some deal was struck to arrange safe passage for Vilmos and Jolie, plus their entourage, for travel across Nazi-occupied Austria and through parts of Southern Germany into Switzerland, even though no one in their party had the proper transit visas.

Throughout the endeavor, Jolie seemed more intent on rescuing her lover, Paul Savosdy, than she was in saving her ex-husband, Vilmos. So far, despite his Jewish birth, Savosdy had managed to avoid the Gestapo. Jolie believed that he had not been immediately executed because of his involvement in food distribution through his firm, Mendel's, which had been a major food exporter before the war. Savosdy had been assigned the task of feeding some 5,000 prisoners in a deportation camp. He later lamented, "I was given not enough food for 2,000." The prisoners included many members of the Jewish elite, plus an array of countesses, turncoats, princesses, collaborators, and government ministers, all of them awaiting execution.

During her one visit to Esterházy Schloss, the elegant seat of the Savosdy family, Jolie had noted crosses affixed the walls of virtually every room. Her lover's Dresden-born parents had been born Jews but had conspicuously converted to Catholicism during one of the pogroms that afflicted that city.

Even so, Savosdy's parents, including his mother, whom everyone called "The Princess," had been arrested, tortured, and dragged out of their luxurious castle and deported to a concentration camp.

Jolie sensed that Savosdy himself would be next. The Nazis no longer needed him, having commandeered most of the country's stocks of food for themselves, and no longer concerned with sending them to the starving inmates of concentration camps.

"I've got to save Paul," Jolie said. "My passion for him is so great, I'd make any sacrifice. My love for him is so intense, it's a sickness."

A reign of terror fell over Budapest during January of 1945, when the Soviets began their occupation of the eastern part of the capital. In Jolie's words, "They robbed and raped and stole."

Allied bombs, most of them American, rained down almost daily. In the Nazi-held territories of Hungary, Jews were still being slaughtered. Then, when the Soviet troops moved in, they slaughtered Nazis. Random fires broke out across the city, and there was massive looting.

Jolie had arranged for her mother, the family's reigning matriarch, Francesca Tilleman, to be provided with sanctuary within the Portuguese villa at Galgagyörk, But shortly after she got there, Francesca bolted, preferring to remain within the center of Budapest with her son, Sebika, and her three other daughters. Sebika was married to a woman known as Manci with whom he had produced a twelve-year-old girl, Anette.

Jolie worried nightly about her family, as American and British bombs rained down upon Budapest. Whenever that happened, she huddled in the cellar of the villa until the airplanes departed back toward the west.

During the interim between the departure of Garridos and the arrival of the new Portuguese Ambassador, a young Portuguese *chargé d'affaires* and his wife had taken over the administration of the Embassy, running things from headquarters within Budapest's Ritz Hotel and the embassy's "annex" in Galgagyörk. Unlike the Swiss consul, they were not opposed to accepting expensive gifts, including jewelry from Jolie.

The young Portuguese couple agreed to transport Savosdy to Galgagyörk in exchange for shelter and refuge. Savosdy relinquished his remaining food supplies, including the last of his canned hams, to the *chargé d'affaires*. "Both Paul and I ended up singing for our supper...really for our lives," Jolie recalled.

[Until her sister-in-law moved with the other refugees into the Portuguese villa, Jolie had never defined Manci as a rival, referring to her as "the little brown mouse." For months, she had denied Sebika conjugal rights, blaming it on "female trouble." Ostensibly, at least, she kept a daily appointment with her doctor.

It was later discovered that nothing was wrong with her equipment. Instead of consulting the doctor, it was revealed that she was visiting his brother, an engineer, and engaging in torrid sex with him instead of with her husband.]

When she was at last reunited with Savosdy, Jolie invited him to her bedroom, where they made love. There was talk of marriage, although he reminded her, "You are four years older than me...and I'm being kind."

She shot back, "That's the most romantic proposal I've ever heard."

The morning after Savosdy's arrival at the villa, Jolie—who had not been able to sleep—arose early, and pulled back the curtains for a look out at the garden.

Right below her, she spotted Savosdy walking with Manci, holding her hand. "I was a queen in feathers and marabou and beautiful hats and perfumed," she later wrote. "At the villa, they called me Madame du Barry. Yet Paul had left me to eat my guts out while he fastened those precious blue eyes on Manci, the mouse. Make it rat. I'd saved him so he could make love to my brother's wife."

Her brother, whom Jolie had affectionately called "Seby," was relatively safe—at least for the moment—because he'd obtained a job as a chauffeur for the Nazis. Jolie warned him that when the Soviets took over, he would probably be executed, but he refused to listen. "No harm will come to me, but I want

Manci and my daughter to stay with you in the Portuguese villa," he had said.

The following morning, clearance had been arranged for a four-vehicle caravan, each of its units waving the flag of Portugal, to depart from Budapest and head west, with the understanding that it would contain Jolie, Vilmos, Manci, Anette, and other refugees with enough clout to have been able to arrange the necessary payments.

Sebika remained behind with his mother, Francesca, and the other Gabors. Tearfully, Jolie packed their meager possessions and, with her ex-husband, got into one of the vehicles.

Jolie recalled her final goodby to "Seby" and her mother. She would never see them again.

There would be many stops along the way. The first was at the Austrian border, where the caravan stopped for a toilet break. Savosdy emerged from the men's room, buttoning his trousers. He stood beside Jolie, looking at Manci, who was seated in one of the vehicles. He then turned and kissed Jolie on the mouth, giving her a bear hug. "I am not in love with you," he said.

With a bitter sense of irony, she later wrote, "And this is how I left Hungary."

***

For the remainder of their passage through Nazi-occupied Austria and Southern Germany, Savosdy sat in the rear of the vehicle, holding Manci's hand, with Anette sitting on his opposite side. In a middle seat, Jolie sat with two Hungarian generals, along with two men she remembered only as "Count Mylot" and "Baron Gudman."

With many stops and searches *en route* the four vehicles managed to avoid Allied bombs still raining down from above. Strewn beside the Autobahn were many vehicles still burning from recent attacks.

Word reached them that the Soviets were moving rapidly toward Berlin, which had already been bombed virtually beyond recognition. Hitler was said to have retreated to his bunker, along with Eva Braun and, among others, the Goebbels family.

Ahead of the caravan, she noticed several vehicles racing toward the Swiss border. Soldiers were tossing their Nazi uniforms out the windows and slipping into civilian clothing they'd stolen along the way.

Because their van was overloaded, Jolie was ordered to abandon her luggage. "Everything I possessed except the mink coat on my back was left along the Autobahn for some lucky woman."

Since they didn't have Swiss entry visas, they were detained in the border town of Sankt Margrethen. The prices the locals charged the desperate refugees for food was unbelievable, a chicken costing as much as $3,000 in American dollars.

Fortunately, Savosdy had packed a large garlicky Hungarian salami in his suitcase. "I knew Paul had fallen for Manci when he cut her a very large slice of the salami, giving me a thin cut," Jolie said.

The entourage spent the night in a little hotel. Amazingly, Zalábondy knew of their whereabouts, and telephoned Jolie at the hotel. He told her that he'd arranged for her to cross the border, and that when she and Vilmos got to Bern, $5,000 would be waiting for her at the Portuguese legation.

Defining themselves as citizens of Portugal, the Portuguese delegation crossed the Swiss border that next morning, driving to Zurich for the night. It was here that Savosdy told her that he and Manci were going to remain in Zurich to start a new life together, even though she was still married to Jolie's brother.

She later claimed that Savosdy knocked on her hotel door later that night. "It will be my last farewell present to you," he said, standing before her and removing his clothes. He crawled into bed with her.

"This memory of me will have to last a lifetime. I will never see you again."

Back in the van the next morning, she was trying to hold back her tears. Vilmos told her, "You are better off to be rid of that butcher." *[He referred to Savosdy that way because of his involvement in the meat-packing business.]*

Traveling across rural areas of France, where the Nazis had retreated after the Liberation of Paris in August of 1944, Jolie was shocked to find fresh roses and a large box of chocolates waiting for her at the Spanish border, compliments of Zalábondy. "I was treated like royalty, even given a luxurious hotel suite in Barcelona."

Zalábondy came to call on them and invited Vilmos and Jolie to an elegant dinner at his villa outside Barcelona. "He was pretty much as I remembered him," she recalled, "but a lot fatter." He also informed her that he was the best friend of General Francisco Franco, the notorious dictator of Fascist Spain.

During the ride back to Barcelona, Vilmos asked Jolie, "What does he expect from us? At some point the piper will have to be paid. His generosity is not *gratis.*"

Years would pass before Jolie learned why Zalábondy had been so generous. He had heard that Zsa Zsa was divorcing Conrad Hilton, who was said to be settling ten million dollars on her, a rumor that later turned out to be untrue.

At some point prior to all this, Zalábondy had met with Conrad in Los Angeles. It is not known who arranged the meeting, perhaps Zsa Zsa herself.

A deal had been conceived and hatched. With the blessing of Franco's government, Conrad was invited to build a luxurious Hilton Hotel in Madrid on land owned by Zalábondy.

***

With Dr. Garrido—reposted to Bern—out of her life, Magda, in Lisbon, wasted no time in replacing him. Almost overnight, she became the mistress of a *grandée* of Spain at his luxurious villa in Estoril, 15 miles west of Lisbon.

He was José Luís de Vilallonga, the Spanish Marquis de Castellbell, who was six years her junior.

Of all her lovers, this tall and handsome *roué* was the most colorful, and led a life worthy of a movie plot. He is best remembered today for interpreting the film role of José da Silva Pereira, the dashing Brazilian multi-millionaire whom Holly Golightly (played by Audrey Hepburn) planned to marry in Blake Edwards' 1961 *Breakfast at Tiffany's,* whose plot was based on Truman Capote's novella.

Years before, his father, the nobleman Salvador de Vilallonga de Cárcer, wanted to toughen up his sixteen-year-old son. To that effect, he forced Vilallonga to join the National execution platoon, fatally shooting captured Revolutionary soldiers opposed to the Fascist dictator, Francisco Franco. "I shot at least one young man every day. On arguably my finest day, I murdered eight young men who weren't allowed to finish their lives. All this killing made me very confused."

At the time he met Magda, Vilallonga had become disenchanted with Franco's Fascist regime. After the publication of his first novel, the fervently anti-Franco *Ramblas End in the Sea* in 1954, he was banned from ever re-entering Spain. and sentenced in absentia to imprisonment for sedition. Every three months thereafter, he was retried (in absentia). In every case, the severity of his punishment and the length of his imprisonment was increased. After several of these "retrials," the combined totals of his various sentences called for jail time of more than 300 years.

He became a foreign correspondent and would later write four autobiographical books about his numerous love affairs, including the one he shared with Magda in Lisbon.

Later in life, he claimed, "I didn't write about all my affairs. It would have taken ten volumes, not four. For example, when I lived in Argentina after the war, I didn't claim I was regularly plowing Evita Perón, for fear of what might happen to me."

"Magda Gabor was my greatest seduction. I called her 'The Princess.' Somehow, she remained a grand lady while performing the vilest acts on a man. It was amazing. My time with Magda was sheer bliss. She wanted me to get a divorce and marry her, but I had no intention to do that—not until I'd spent the last pound of my heiress wife."

During his adulterous affair with Magda, Vilallonga often talked about his wife, the Hon. Essylt-Priscilla Scott-Ellis, whom he'd recently married. "When she fell asleep on our wedding night, I slipped away and spent the rest of the evening in a brothel filled with French prostitutes."

Vilallonga called himself "a seducer of beautiful women and a cad. I'm a hardened alcoholic who, without taking precautions of any kind, slept with more whores than a porcupine has quills."

His wife was the daughter of Thomas Scott-Ellis, 8th Baron Howard de Walden, one of the wealthiest peers in England. A former debutante who'd been nicknamed "Pip," Priscilla had joined Franco's forces during the Spanish Civil War.

Vilallonga's father, Salvador, had opposed his son's marriage, publicly accusing his rebellious daughter-in-law of "sleeping with half of the Spanish Army, if not the entire Nationalist Force.

Magda's lover in Lisbon was the dashing Spanish *grandée*, **José Luís de Vilallonga.**

As a 16-year-old, during the Spanish Civil War, he launched his career by executing eight anti-Franco soldiers a day. He later turned against the Spanish dictator and was forced into exile.

Vilallonga is remembered today for playing a stylish cad, a Brazilian multi-millionaire, who seeks to run off with Holly Golightly in *Breakfast at Tiffany's*. Here he is seen with **Audrey Hepburn**, who played Holly in that classic movie.

This unchivalrous assertion prompted Lord Howard de Walden to challenge him (without success) to a duel.

Magda defined Villalonga as "the most skilled of all my lovers. Two weeks into our affair, I told him I'd fallen in love with him and wanted to marry him. He told me that 'any woman who falls in love with me is making a dreadful error and heading for horrible humiliation.'"

After Villalonga spent his wife's inheritance and sold off her valuable collection of modern art to finance his spending sprees, he divorced her in 1972.

Renowned for his indolent air and lanky elegance, he sailed the finest yachts, rubbing shoulders with Aristotle Onassis, the Rothschilds, and the Kennedys. (He aggressively pursued Jackie.)

He edited Spain's version of *Playboy* and personally selected and "auditioned" the centerfolds. He also wrote a racy column, called "Letters from Paris," for the soft-porn scandal weekly *Interviú*.

When Franco died and the Spanish monarchy was restored, Vilallonga returned to his native Spain, where he wrote a best-selling biography

330

of King Juan Carlos.

In a drunken interview during the late 1970s, Vilallonga claimed that during the filming of *Breakfast at Tiffany's* "Audrey wouldn't get enough of my Don Juan swordsmanship. Truman Capote told me I had the most magnificent penis he'd ever seen."

When Vilallonga died at the age of 87 in 2007, his obituary in *The London Telegraph* called him "a playboy, wastrel, fortune hunter, and bit-part actor."

He wrote his own epitaph:

HERE LIES THE DON JUAN OF THE 20TH CENTURY:
AT LAST HIS LOVERS KNOW WHERE HE'S SPENDING THE NIGHT.

***

 In her memoirs, Zsa Zsa, the lady, would deny affairs with such men as Howard Hughes or Errol Flynn. Yet in those same memoirs, she willingly made an even more damaging admission, asserting that she fell in love and had a voluntary affair with her stepson, Nicky Hilton.

He was that young man standing nude in the doorway of the bedroom of her suite at the Plaza Hotel in New York City.

As she frankly admitted, "I had always loved Nicky Hilton, my stepson; now I began to love Nicky, the man. He was sexy and exciting, but not quite as dazzling as Conrad."

"It was a night of grand passion," she later told Greta Keller. At the time, her unofficial godmother was singing at the Stanhope Hotel in New York, and Nicky and Zsa Zsa attended three of her evening concerts. No one, not even Walter Winchell in his syndicated column, noted their joint appearance in the audience. Since Conrad was out of town, people assumed that Nicky was merely functioning as a diligent and attentive stepson and escorting his mother to dinners and night clubs. No one seemed to notice that they were holding hands under the table.

"A love affair like ours wasn't so unusual," Zsa Zsa told Greta. *[Ironically, Greta herself, when she was in her eighties, would end up with a lover, Wolfgang Nebmaier, in his twenties.]*

"Actually, Nicky was closer to my age than I was to Conrad's age." Her stepson was born in 1926, which made Zsa Zsa only nine years older than he was.

"In many ways, I was instrumental in restoring Nicky's manhood," Zsa Zsa claimed. "All of his life, he'd lived in his father's shadow. Nicky liked to drink and to carouse and didn't really apply himself to running the hotels. He wanted to party. Conrad constantly attacked him and belittled him. Instead of building him up and supporting his son, he tore Nicky down."

"During the long years of our affair," she said, "I constantly praised his manhood. He was a stallion. Ever since he was fourteen, both homosexuals and hot-to-trot females had sought him out. He was handsome, rich, and possessed a magnificent weapon that he'd inherited through Conrad's genes. Both of them were Texas bulls."

Nicky photographed badly, but in person, he was extremely handsome, speaking in a soft Texas drawl. He was tall and broad-shouldered and wore tailor-made suits from Savile Row in London. Even as a teenager, he had a reputation as a playboy, his dark brown eyes suggesting mischief and desire.

Even though he looked like he'd just graduated from college, he was a man of the world, having launched affairs with members of both sexes. He was at ease moving within high society, as he'd spent his early teenage years meeting movie stars, industrial tycoons, presidents, senators, and fading members of the European aristocracy.

"Yes, Nicky was bisexual," Zsa Zsa said, "which did not come as a shock to me ever since I'd seen Bill Tilden going down on him on Chaplin's tennis courts. Homosexuals restored his sense of manhood by the constant praise heaped onto that weapon of his. Even Tyrone Power, Eva's future all-time lover, 'bottomed' for him. I had never heard that expression before I came to America, but I thought it apt."

"Nicky might have indulged in sex with homosexuals, but I can assure you he was always the man in such situations."

"He had such a commanding presence with women," she said. "It was amazing for one so young. Over the years, there were many reports of his violence toward women, especially from his first wife, Elizabeth Taylor, but during our affair, which lasted for years, he always treated me with great respect, love, and tenderness."

"Perhaps I exaggerate. He could get a bit rough in the bedchamber, but in a way that most women would adore. From reading American romance novels, which sell in the millions, I think women like to be devoured by a strong man who is a skilled swordsman. I can assure you that no woman ever left Nicky Hilton unsatisfied."

As a teenage boy, he'd also been pursued by movie stars with voracious sexual appetites. He jokingly called them "child molesters, but in my case, the child wanted to be molested."

An example of a star who Nicky had seduced (or vice versa) was Joan Crawford, who had once bedded Jackie Cooper when he was sweet sixteen. One night when Nicky checked into the Plaza Hotel, Crawford telephoned his suite and invited him over for cocktails.

He confessed that he accepted Crawford's invitation. "She was ready to go," he told Zsa Zsa. "We did it on the living room floor of her suite. She couldn't wait until we got to her bedroom. It would have been a memorable experience for me, but she had the most awful breath."

Lana Turner had been another of his conquests. "She even made a movie (*Weekend at the Waldorf;* 1945) at Dad's hotel."

The hotel heir didn't really work, although in time, he held two major posts—one as the vice president of the Hilton Corporation, and the other as the manager of the swanky Bel Air Hotel, which he referred to as "my fuck pad."

It was at this hotel that Zsa Zsa would prepare her famous "Dracula Goulash" for Nicky before bedtime in the privacy of his hotel suite.

Debates about fidelity never came up between Nicky and Zsa Zsa. Over the years, when he wasn't with her, he was seen with actresses such as Denise Darcel, Terry Moore (rumored to have married Howard Hughes), or else with socialites like Kay Spreckels and Hope Hampton. Ironically, Conrad, Sr., had previously dated both Spreckels and Hampton.

[In 1955, Spreckels, aged 39, became the fifth and final wife of Clark Gable.]

Zsa Zsa was well aware that Nicky occasionally pursued women who had previously visited his father's boudoir. He was always after that final approval whenever he heard one of them say, "You're a better lover than your father."

"Nicky was a wonderful lover," Zsa Zsa told Greta, "but he was more than that. He was a supportive friend. We could even complain about our other lovers with each other. There was another compelling reason that made my affair with Nicky so exciting. When I married Conrad, he was almost the grandfather type, though still reasonably virile."

"With Nicky, I was getting a younger version of Conrad, which his first wife had gotten, but which I never got to experience because of the difference in our ages."

"As much as they disliked each other, Nicky was definitely his father's son. They were men used to getting their way. Women were theirs to command. Both had forceful personalities, and both were strong and terribly sexy."

"The subject of marriage did come up on occasion," she claimed, "but only when we'd had too much champagne. We decided almost from the beginning that

"**Nicky Hilton** *(photo above)* was a Texas bull, just like his father, my husband Conrad," Zsa Zsa said. "Perhaps I'm indiscreet, but I fell in love with him, even though he lacked the excitement of his father. He had everything else. Also, *dahlink*, he was much closer to my age than my husband.

"I wouldn't be the only woman on the planet who fell in love with her stepson. It's far better than a young man having sex with his mother."

333

it would be too scandalous for me to divorce Conrad only to marry his son. After all, I didn't want to be dropped from the social register."

Zsa Zsa also told Greta, "When I became Nicky's lover, I honestly felt that I had gone to bed with Conrad for the final time. As soon as I got back to California, I was going to file for a divorce. But my plan didn't work out. There was an unexpected rape looming in my future."

***

 Eva was the first to admit that she had not been a good wife to her millionaire husband, Charles Isaacs, who doted on her. "He was in love with me; I was not in love with him, although he was rich and handsome, two very compelling reasons to marry a man."

She'd grown bored with her role as a Hollywood hostess, and she didn't want to feel any more guilt "when I had a string of beaux on the side." Her list of outside romances still included, among others, Phillip Terry, Robert Taylor, Hugh Marlowe, Bugsy Siegel, and Robert Walker. ("He needed more comforting than love-making.")

Her film career was going nowhere, especially after every trace of her small involvement in *A Royal Scandal* ended up on the cutting-room floor. Tallulah Bankhead had telephoned her twice, urging her to come to New York, where the actress promised to invite her to parties where she'd meet *Who's Who* in "The Theater."

One Sunday, when Isaacs returned home from his Coast Guard duties, Eva had already booked her train ticket and packed her luggage.

Phillip Terry, freed from the clutches of Joan Crawford, had driven by in a station wagon earlier in the day and had hauled her excess luggage into storage at a Los Angeles depot. He also gave her a "farewell fuck," as he put it, knowing their sexual intimacy was all but over. Both Terry and Eva had already agreed that it was time for each of them to move on.

During the course of Eva's last attendance at a Hollywood party, columnist Hedda Hopper asked her, "Why do you want to work as an actress? As the wife of Charles Isaacs, you can buy the studio."

Eva complained to Susan Hayward that, "No one understands my commitment to acting. It's something I've dreamed about as a little girl growing up in Budapest. I've got to pursue my dream; otherwise, my life will turn into a nightmare."

Isaac's best friend, a stockbroker named Ralph Fabor, said, "Eva was the love of Charles' life. He catered to her demands shamelessly. She wanted something: He got it for her. He told me that she was his lifetime partner. Sad to say, because of his premature death, that one commitment he would honor."

"Charles just did not understand how much I wanted to be an actress," Eva said. "I wanted that more than anything, and I was willing to lie on casting couches, whatever it took. I didn't want to be *just* the wife of a rich man. I wanted to be known as Eva Gabor, not as Mrs. Charles Isaacs. Unfortunately, my husband did not realize that. He thought that by providing me with a lavish lifestyle, turning me into a Hollywood housewife, he would please me and that I would stay with him. How he misjudged me."

Ironically, the month Eva deserted him, his doctors told him that he was riddled with cancer. The malignant cells had spread throughout his body, and he had only a short time to live.

"But it wasn't the cancer that killed him," Fabor said. "It was the loss of Eva. He never recovered from his broken heart. Usually, he was a guy who could roll with the punches. But her abandonment of him and the cancer thing—it was all too much. He lost his will to live."

Eva later regretted her impulsive decision, referring to it as "the mistake of my life. He was literally dying the day I told him I was leaving," she admitted in a candid newspaper interview, using a direct approach which in itself was unusual for her. "I've paid for that mistake dearly. I'm still haunted by it. I let ambition, not compassion, rule me."

"I knew Charles would continue with the marriage, even if I confessed I was unfaithful to him. But I could not go on the way I was. I felt guilty sleeping in his bed, cheating on him, and living off his rich purse."

As Eva wrote in her memoir, "And so, as the sun set behind the corner of Hollywood and Vine, I headed East, leaving behind the great film city, which didn't even know that I had gone."

Jolie later chastised her for leaving Charles. "*Dahlink*, you should have stuck around and inherited his millions. You would have been fixed for life. After you buried him, you could have gone and done anything you liked, even the theater. But you would show up at auditions in diamonds and mink instead of living in a seedy hotel near Times Square."

According to some reports, Eva was given a million dollars by Isaacs. She informed her longtime companion, Camyl Sosa Belanger, however, that "I didn't take a penny from him."

Later, when Jolie got to Hollywood, she called on Isaacs, since his divorce from her daughter hadn't yet been finalized. "I had heard how virile and handsome he was. Not the man I encountered that day. He was emaciated. A manservant had to carry him out onto a chaise longue for tea with me in the garden. His face had a yellowish color to it, and he looked like he weighed no more than eighty-five pounds. The cancer was eating his body alive."

He spoke to Jolie about his great love for Eva "Look at me," he said. "What kind of husband could I make? My life is over. I can only be grateful that she came into it and provided me love and comfort for the short time she did."

"What is it with my daughters?" Jolie later asked. "They married million-aires and then they walked away from them. That's not how I trained them as courtesans. Maybe in the future, they would learn their lessons better. But that didn't happen all at once. Like a sister act, both Zsa Zsa and Eva would enter into disastrous third marriages. What's a mother to do?"

***

 As World War II wound down in 1945, Magda, followed by Jolie and Vilmos, found a temporary home in Lisbon, the capi-tal of Portugal, which had supposedly remained neutral through-out the war.

"*Nucika,*" came Magda's voice over the long-distance phone, calling from Lisbon to her mother in Barcelona. "Oh *Nucika,* you made it to Spain. Lisbon is only a flight away. The Nazis are behind us."

Both women were crying over the phone at the sound of the other's voice, but because of the high expense involved, they agreed to relay the bulk of their respective news until Jolie's arrival in Lisbon.

In Spain, the sponsor who had navigated the way for Jolie and Vilmos, André Zalábondy, informed them that he was *persona non grata* in Portugal, and as such, he would not be able to accompany them.

At the end of their train ride across Iberia to Lisbon, Jolie and Magda fell into each other's arms, crying and hugging, before Jolie released her daughter for the embrace of Vilmos, who seemed bewildered by his new surroundings.

Jolie was shocked at Magda's appearance. She looked emaciated, and some of her hair had fallen out. Magda blamed it on her shattered nerves. "I didn't know which members of my family were going to be executed."

Unlike Spain, where they'd been treated like royalty, Jolie complained about their rude reception at the Portuguese frontier. "We were stopped, searched, and treated like all the other penniless *émigrés.*"

On their way to the best hotel in Portugal, the Palacio Hotel in Estoril, Magda described her new circumstances as the mistress of José Luís de Vilal-longa, a *grandée* of Spain.

"If you don't put some meat on those bones of yours, he'll drop you!" Jolie (undiplomatically) warned her.

Before they arrived at the hotel, Magda informed them that all three of them would have to remain in Portugal until the end of the war.

When she saw the elegant and impressive Palacio Hotel, Jolie had to warn her daughter, "*Magduska,* Papa and I have escaped, but we have no money left.

336

Everything was left behind, including $200,000 in jewelry which I had deposited in a bank vault, fearing it would be seized at the border by the Nazis. They take everything."

"But Portugal is very cheap, "Magda assured them, "and José will take care of everything within reason. But we must be frugal."

Eva and Zsa Zsa had also agreed to help. Each of them would contribute $500 a month to their parents' welfare.

"With that, and with what José gives us, you can live in luxury here," Magda assured them.

After the bellhop escorted them to their room, Jolie protested. "But only one room! I am a divorced woman!"

"The hotel is overcrowded," Magda said. "Everyone from Nazi officers to Allied commanders, along with half the spies in Europe, have booked all the rooms."

Finally, the next morning, Magda arrived with good news. "José has used his influence. You now have two rooms, although each is rather small." Then she noticed that of the twin beds, only one had been slept in.

Jolie explained, "I went to lie on Vilmos' shoulder, hoping he would console me. We remembered the good times, and one thing led to another."

"Oh, *Nuci,* you're impossible," Magda said, "and after all the trouble I went to."

Magda remembered looking at her father, who had once been a dashing Hussar. "His hair was gray, and he'd gotten fat. He was without his property, family, and friends, except for us. He longed for Hungary. I feared he would not adapt to America."

Worried about the future, Jolie remembered being very despondent one night. She allowed herself to be picked up in the bar of the Estoril Palace by a blonde, handsome, blue-eyed Nazi.

Later, as she explained to Magda, "I felt dirty and used, although at first, I'd been flattered that such a good-looking devil found me attractive as a woman. I sat in the bathtub for an hour trying to wash off the Nazi slime."

Jolie was eager for news of Zsa Zsa and Eva. Jolie was horrified when she learned that Zsa Zsa was divorcing Conrad Hilton, but predicted that the hotelier would settle millions on her.

Jolie went on with presuppositions about Eva: "I've told everybody that Eva is a big star in Hollywood. She sent me all these pictures of herself posing in gowns at lavish parties, or else in bathing suits in front of deluxe swimming pools. I figure that if Garbo makes $10,000 a week, Eva must be making at least $5,000 a week."

"She's penniless," Magda said, "and she's about to divorce her millionaire husband. She never made it as a star, or even as a starlet, in Hollywood. She moved to New York to look for work on Broadway."

"I thought the $2,000 I sent her for her new teeth would have made her a great beauty and a star!" said Jolie, dismayed.

Throughout the remainder of World War II, Jolie and Vilmos remained installed at the Hotel Palacio in Estoril, amid members of faded monarchies deposed by the seismic changes that had recently swept over Europe.

Magda visited her parents daily, often for lunch. The Gabors were already ensconced there when the Soviets took Berlin and when news spread that Hitler had committed suicide. Before the end of that summer of 1945, the U.S. President, Harry S Truman, launched the Atomic Age by bombing the Empire of Japan into unconditional surrender.

It was on December 1, 1945, that a fur-clad Jolie stood at the port of Lisbon, bidding Magda and Vilmos good-bye. She was sailing alone to New York aboard a dismal freighter. Vilmos and Magda would follow as soon as transport became available.

Jolie looked worried: "I haven't seen Eva since 1940, or Zsa Zsa since 1941. I know they've changed. But what has America done to them?"

She kissed Vilmos and Magda as she sobbed, "I must start a new life. I'm beginning over again with nothing."

Left on the shore holding her father's hand, Magda also realized that she, too, would have to create a new life and identity in America. Only the night before, José had told her that he was leaving Estoril to accept a job in liberated Paris now that the war was over.

Without saying so, he made it clear that a former girlfriend was waiting for him in France.

After waving goodbye to Jolie, Magda turned to Vilmos: "Within six months in America, maybe less, I will find a new husband."

***

Zsa Zsa—never an example of marital fidelity—blamed Conrad's adultery on the guilt he suffered for having divorced his first wife against the teaching of the Catholic church.

Just prior to her divorce from him, Zsa Zsa received an elegantly engraved invitation to a lavish party on Long Island. Conrad wanted her to attend the gala with him. Thinking it might be fun, she agreed to go, although she'd never heard the name of the hostess before. Conrad had insisted that the hostess "is a dear friend of mine."

In a chauffeur-driven limousine, Conrad and Zsa Zsa arrived at a gated mansion in Southampton, at an estate once frequented by vacationing members of the Rockefeller family.

Taking Zsa Zsa's arm, Conrad led her through the garden until a butler escorted them to the building's largest living room. Instead of furniture, the latest owner had installed a mammoth indoor swimming pool in the floor. In it, lotus blossoms floated. "It was all very Dorothy Lamour and South Seas," Zsa Zsa recalled.

She was amazed by the number of beautiful girls in shapely, skimpy bathing suits and by the array of handsome young men who lounged around the pool, drinking tropical drinks as if the estate were a Caribbean manifestation of paradise.

In the mansion's main hall, the hostess stepped out to greet them, kissing Conrad full-frontal on the lips. Zsa Zsa was startled by the fact that she was completely nude. She was a beautiful, fairly young blonde, evoking Lana Turner, and she wore her hair long and flowing. Zsa Zsa later wrote in a memoir, "I was startled, but attributed the unconventionality of the situation to America, to my unfamiliarity with strange American customs, and even stranger American parties."

After enjoying some food from a buffet table loaded with champagne, lobster, and caviar, Conrad disappeared behind a door that was padded and upholstered with red velvet. Then the hostess reappeared with a good-looking young man who appeared to be no more than nineteen.

The madam directed Zsa Zsa into her study, with the young man—who wore a see-through bikini— trailing behind.

Once inside, she shut the door. "This is Ramon Garcia," she said.

"Hello, beautiful lady," he addressed her with accented English.

"He's from Cuba, and he used to perform in stage shows in Havana," the hostess said. "He was billed as 'El Toro.'"

With one quick move she snapped off his bikini, a garment which had been specifically designed for fast, theatrical unfastenings. "Here's why."

Later in her life, Zsa Zsa would tell her friends, "Not until I met *[the Dominican playboy]* Porfirio Rubirosa, had I ever seen such an appendage. He resembled something you'd see on one of those XXX-rated mosaics the Romans installed in their villas in ancient Pompeii."

"I thanked the hostess and complimented Ramon on his obvious physical attributes, but then fled I from the study," she said. "I went on a search for Conrad."

"At first I hesitated, but then I opened the red velvet door and entered a room thick with the smell of incense. A beautiful young girl lay nude on the bed, and I came face to face with Conrad, who was just zipping up his pants."

Before the night ended, she was made aware that those handsome young men, as well as the many beautiful young girls lying around the pool, were for hire.

She wrote, "My husband, the love of my life, had taken me to a whore-house."

She later claimed, "That was his way of signaling the end of our marriage. If I still had a residue of love left for him, it disappeared that night. It was an outrageous thing to do to me to end our marriage."

But Zsa Zsa was wrong. The marriage didn't end that night. It had a final round to go.

***

A few weeks later, Zsa Zsa—thanks to her association with Conrad—was staying *gratis* in a suite at the Waldorf-Astoria in Manhattan. It was there that she learned that Conrad had been involved in a ski accident and that he was re-cuperating within the suite she had previously occupied at The Plaza, also in New York.

A call came in from her about-to-be-ex-husband, who told her that he was in bed with his leg in a cast. "I agreed to make a mercy call on him," she said.

She admitted that the first hour of her visit to Conrad's bedroom passed pleasantly enough. He'd obviously not learned of her affair with his son, Nicky.

"We talked about the ski accident, but made no mention of our upcoming divorce."

She later wrote in a memoir, "Then (incredible as it sounds, but quite be-lievable if you had known Conrad, his forceful nature, and his intense virility), he raped me."

Nine months later, a daughter, and Zsa Zsa's only child from all of her mar-riages, was born. "I named her Francesca Hilton."

Zsa Zsa became the only Gabor sister to ever give birth to a child. All other potential Gabor babies were aborted.

CHAPTER EIGHT
What's Love Got to Do With It?

Her turbulent life was changing too rapidly for Zsa Zsa. She was not only plotting to divorce Conrad Hilton, but had fallen madly in love with her stepson, Nicky.

She could not come up with any game plan for her future, and felt adrift. The only thing she had to hold onto was Nicky, but he was considered unreliable. "One day, he'd be beside you in bed. When you woke up the next morning, he might be calling from Texas or Los Angeles. He was a creature of impulse. But so adorable."

She'd long ago ruled out marriage to Nicky, but she wondered if she should find another millionaire husband like Conrad Hilton. If so, who would it be? Obviously, not any of her previous lovers. Her intuition and experience told her than such previous conquests as Howard Hughes and Greg Bautzer probably wouldn't be suitable as marriage material.

Instead of another marriage, she wondered if she should pursue a career as an actress. In frank moments with herself, she admitted that she wasn't as talented as Eva, and that even her sister's career seemed to be going nowhere.

Zsa Zsa was also nervous in her interchanges with Jolie, Magda, and Vilmos, fearing that they might become a burden on her after fleeing, penniless, from their saga of wartime horror in Europe. She feared that unless Conrad settled enough money on her, she wouldn't be able to take care of them.

When Nicky wasn't in her suite with her in New York at the Plaza, she feared she was sleeping her life away. Her doctor had advised her to take sleeping pills "whenever you need them."

"Well, I needed them most of the time," she said.

When she did go out with friends in New York, they sometimes evaluated her as something akin to a zombie. One night at a club, "I was the dullest woman in the world."

July Garland sat next to her. "You need a happiness pill," Garland recommended.

"Never heard of such a thing," Zsa Zsa said.

"It's Benzedrine," Garland said. "I thrive on it. Keeps me perky all day."

The next day, Zsa Zsa sought out a "Feelgood" doctor in Manhattan, who agreed to prescribe "all the Benzedrine you want—it's perfectly harmless and not habit-forming."

Over the course of the following week, she discovered the perfect solution: Benzedrine to keep her alert throughout the day, and sleeping pills at night to sink her into a coma. At some point, the sleeping pills didn't work—but the Benzedrine did: "I was alive and perky all day and all night."

"I came home at dawn, usually having been out all night with Nicky," she said. "While he snored in a deep sleep, I'd take a perfumed bath, go shopping, and return to the Plaza at four o'clock when he got out of bed. I was on a twenty-four-hour-a-day schedule, which was awful for my shattered nerves."

After her living quarters in Bel Air burned to the ground, she defined the Plaza Hotel in New York as her temporary home. One morning, high on Benzedrine, she decided to redecorate. Dressed in her finery, she went on a shopping binge. First, came a bed with a price tag of $5,000. *[It had previously belonged to Joséphine Bonaparte, and had presumably—occasionally, at least—been visited by Napoléon.]*

That same day, as a supplement to her other dog, a boxer named Josephine, she adopted a French poodle—"an idiotic, jealous little Frenchman." She named him Harvey.

Forgetting (or deliberately ignoring) the $250 monthly budget imposed on her by Conrad, she ordered a dozen copper-colored gowns from the fabled dressmaker Hattie Carnegie to match her flaming hair. "It seemed that I was the only woman in New York, or at least the first, to wear a platinum gray mink. I still had enough jewelry to adorn myself in rubies and diamonds. Sometimes I dressed simply. If I wore a silk shirtwaist, I made sure the buttons were ten-carat diamonds created by Van Cleef & Arpels."

"No one else would do but Nicky. He was my love machine. He wanted sex all the time. I'd just look over at him, and he'd attack me. What a voracious appetite he had for sex. His stamina was truly amazing."

Then, without warning, her world came tumbling in on her one day after Nicky flew to Los Angeles. She awakened in a sanitarium, and at first didn't remember how she'd gotten there. She couldn't move her arms, and soon discovered that she was encased in a straitjacket.

Slowly, her memory came back. At her suite within the Plaza, she'd been introduced to a man who identified himself as "Rudolph Stein," claiming he was a producer from Vienna who wanted to cast her as the lead in a Broadway play he was financing.

She'd been lured out of the Plaza and into a car, which had taken her up-state to a castle-like hotel on the Hudson. In the foyer, she'd encountered two men in white, one with a goatee and a hypodermic needle.

At first, she thought they were robbers, trying to steal her diamonds. She fought them with all her remaining strength, but she was overpowered. The needle plunged into her arm. Blackness.

As she slowly regained consciousness the next day, she saw those two same men in white approaching her bed. Another long needle. More blackness.

So it went for weeks. She later recalled them as "days and nights of horror, invented by Dante."

The two men in white were her almost constant companions, sometime re-lieved by a nurse. She remembered being constantly injected with those nee-dles.

Once, she tried to escape, battling a burly night nurse she later likened to the Bitch of Buchenwald. "I fought her, but she struck me across the face. Then the dyke grabbed a pillow and smothered me until I passed out."

She later deciphered that one of Conrad's last maneuvers as her husband in-volved having her confined to a sanitarium. Perhaps he'd found out about her affair with his son. She sobbed frequently, lamenting that Nicky never came to visit, until she learned that Conrad had refused to tell him where she was. "No one came, not Nicky, not Conrad, not Eva. I was alone."

Finally, another night nurse, a kindly, rather fat Irish woman, looked after her. "She was so sweet and kind," Zsa Zsa said. "She told me that I didn't be-long in here. She was my ally and agreed to slip a note out of the sanitarium to my lawyer in New York."

Two days later, her lawyer, Barnet L. Arlan, and a friend of hers, Hamlin Turner, visited her at the hospital. Turner later filed a sworn affidavit about her condition:

"She was in a shocking physical condition. She'd been brutally assaulted about the face, nose, and body: She'd been given insulin shock treatments tri-weekly, and, as a result of hypodermic injections, she displayed to me two large, infected areas on both thighs which resisted healing and were open and festering."

Arlan swung into action, filing a writ of *habeas corpus* with the courts, charging that Zsa Zsa had been wrongfully detained. He accompanied her in a chauffeur-driven limousine to a branch of the New York Supreme Court in the Bronx for a hearing.

The judge asked her a lot of questions, even though her responses were often incoherent. She even mumbled about Atatürk, a name unfamiliar to the judge.

She also told him that she was married to Conrad Hilton.

He seemed to take pity on her. In his final ruling, he said. "I don't think you should be committed just because you daydream that you're married to a famous man like Conrad Hilton. Just the other day, I dealt with the case of a woman who claimed she was Mrs. Clark Gable. Women all over the country have harmless daydreams about being married to famous men. Even I, a judge, once dreamed about Betty Grable. You don't appear to be a menace to anyone. The writ is sustained. You're to be discharged."

***

Jolie

On December 31, 1945, in the aftermath of World War II and recently released from a mental institution, Zsa Zsa joined Eva on the pier to welcome their mother to New York. Impatient to get to America, Jolie had booked passage aboard the *Mirandello,* a cork-carrying freighter that was one of the oldest Portuguese vessels afloat.

Eva was the first to enjoy Jolie's embrace, as her mother rushed into her arms sobbing and babbling in Hungarian. She was a bit heavier than before.

Still pale, and looking emaciated from her recent ordeal, Zsa Zsa was next to hug her mother. Eva had agreed to keep from Jolie the secret that Zsa Zsa had just been released from a mental asylum.

Jolie was wrapped in a mink and wearing her best jewelry and a couture dress to greet her daughters, who were equivalently attired in mink and diamonds. Jolie later said, "Eva and Zsa Zsa had so much jewelry, they sparkled like a Christmas tree, but I suspected they'd put on everything they owned to impress me."

During their transit to the Plaza Hotel, where Conrad Hilton had generously provided them with a free suite, Jolie told them she'd been booked into "a closet" aboard the freighter, and that she'd had a brief fling with the vessel's rugged captain. "The ship was a junky cork-carrier," she said, "but I was treated like Marie Antoinette. I always dressed for dinner at night. The menu was always the same: cod stew."

Eva held her mother's hand as she told her daughters that Paul Savosdy had deserted her for Manci, her brother's (their uncle's) wife.

"Manci and Paul," Eva said. "I can't believe it, but anything's possible in wartime, isn't it?"

"I always knew Manci was a slut," Zsa Zsa chimed in. "Poor Uncle Sebika."

344

Jolie said that Magda and Vilmos would be arriving later. The Soviets had conquered and occupied nearly all of Budapest right before they left. Jolie told her daughters, "The fate of the Gabors, including my mother and her sisters, is uncertain. Sebiki also remained behind."

Once they were settled into the Plaza, Jolie confessed she'd given her last hundred dollars as a tip to the freighter's staff, and that they'd been kind to her. She took Eva's hand first, then reached for Zsa Zsa's.

It was Eva who said: "Both Zsa Zsa and I are going through a rough time in our own lives now, but we'll give you what money we can to keep you afloat."

"I don't want to depend on my daughters," Jolie said. "Just give me a little money to open a small shop, and I'll soon be taking care of myself."

In her memoir, Jolie stated (wrongly) that Conrad Hilton and Charles Isaacs had also showed up to greet her at the pier, but Hilton was in Houston, and Isaacs was in Los Angeles at the time.

Emotionally scarred from the ravages of Europe, Jolie had arrived at the Port of New York on the last day of 1945. The following morning, New Year's Day, 1946, represented not only a new day for her, but a new year and a new life.

***

That afternoon, a limousine owned by the Plaza Hotel drove Zsa Zsa, Eva, and Jolie to Zsa Zsa's newly rented home in Bay Shore, Long Island.

When they arrived at the house, its door was flung open and from it emerged Nicky Hilton, who had been searching for Zsa Zsa for weeks. Apparently, someone had tipped him off as to where Zsa Zsa had moved.

Eva stood in astonishment, as Nicky rushed to Zsa Zsa, picked her up in his strong, virile arms, and kissed her long and passionately.

"Who is that young boy with Zsa Zsa?" Jolie asked. "Don't tell me he's the gardener!"

"That's Conrad Hilton," Eva answered.

"But I thought he'd be a man in his sixties."

"No, it's Conrad Hilton, Jr.," Eva said. "He's still a teenager and in love with his stepmother—your daughter."

"Oh, dear," Jolie told Eva, "I can't make moral judgments. I, too, have been in love with a young man—the one who is now making love to your uncle's wife. Let it not be me to cast stones."

Eva introduced Nicky to Jolie, and he kissed her hand. She seemed enchanted by him. Later, when he and Zsa Zsa disappeared into an upstairs bedroom together, Eva told Jolie, "Nicky is very, very rich. I'm urging Zsa Zsa to marry him."

"Vilmos will not approve," Jolie said. "He's so traditional, but I see nothing wrong in my daughter marrying her husband's son...after the divorce, of course."

"Of course, Eva said."

***

Zsa Zsa would later recall her time with Nicky in their Long Island home as "The most idyllic in my life. We were lovers, riding horses on the beach under the moonlight, spending hours in front of a blazing fireplace, making love."

As she'd later tell Greta Keller, who came to visit, "At twilight, we'd walk along the beach with feathery clouds on the horizon. With the sun setting, they turned pink. It was so romantic, like some novel of young love. We'd see tiny hermit crabs scurrying through the sand. The sound of seagulls was in the air. The ocean was rough and we'd fall asleep listening to crashing waves, but only after making love to each other. Every night was filled with beauty, fulfillment, and promise."

In her memoirs, Zsa Zsa wrote that she had been at La Guardia Airport in New York to greet Magda when she arrived alone on an airplane from Lisbon. Zsa Zsa also stated that she'd gone to Philadelphia to meet a freighter carrying Vilmos from Lisbon. Actually, he'd arrived at New York Harbor.

Eva and Jolie had shown up to greet both Magda and Vilmos during their respective arrivals in the New World, but Zsa Zsa, who was not feeling well, had stayed in her rented house at Bay Shore for both events.

After Vilmos and Magda had settled into their temporary lodgings in Manhattan, they were driven, along with Eva and Jolie, to Bay Shore for a visit with Zsa Zsa. All of the Gabors crowded into the small rented house, where Nicky functioned as host, bonding to some small degree with Vilmos, who spoke not a word of English.

"Nicky ingratiated himself with my family," Zsa Zsa said, "especially when he brought them fresh lobsters and plenty of champagne."

With resentment and deep regret, Vilmos told them that he'd lost everything. "The Communists took it all...everything. I have nothing now. I was such a rich man."

Other tragedies were on their way. On the Monday following their arrival in Bay Shore, a messenger arrived in a car sent by the Plaza Hotel with a telegram for Zsa Zsa. She read it and screamed before collapsing.

Jolie rushed to her side and picked up the cable. The Nazis, before abandoning Budapest, had executed the remaining occupants of the Portuguese

Embassy's annex, including Francesca and Sebika Tilleman. They had been hauled into the building's courtyard and shot, their bodies left to rot. They were eventually discovered by the invading Soviets.

Zsa Zsa remembered the next few days at Bay Shore as among the gloomiest of their lives. "I could be thankful that my immediate family escaped intact, but my heart was sad. Nicky did what he could to cheer us up, and I'll always be grateful to him for that."

Kissing Nicky goodbye a week later, Zsa Zsa flew back to Los Angeles, and found herself a lawyer to press for her divorce. She'd met Claudette Colbert at several parties, and asked her for a recommendation, although she'd been tempted to turn to Greg Bautzer. She would have hired him, except for the fact that he was a close friend of Conrad's.

Later, she'd regret having used the lawyer Colbert recommended.

For her appearance in court, Zsa Zsa attired herself in a battleship gray suit and hid her hair under a cloche hat. Her face was mostly obscured with a funereal veil. "I wanted to look like a bereaved widow."

In front of a superior court judge in Santa Monica, she sobbed, "Mr. Hilton preferred his butler to me. He wouldn't fire the man, even though he refused to speak to me. I was told that if I didn't like the butler, I could pack my clothes and leave."

One newspaper headlined its story about their divorce: *THE BUTLER DID IT.*

Leaving the courthouse, she told reporters, "I couldn't compete with his greatest love, his hotels."

Zsa Zsa always regretted the divorce settlement of $35,000 in cash and $250,000 in alimony, to be paid over the next decade unless she remarried. Zsa Zsa would later claim, "I settled for peanuts, and I could have taken him for millions."

When Jolie learned the details of the settlement, she said, "Her lawyer was so nice, so polite, and so stupid...a jerk. It was a stupid, stupid divorce, not even a permanent suite at The Plaza. Wherever Zsa Zsa goes in the future and stays at a Hilton, she must pay herself. Ridiculous!"

***

More than anyone, Eva helped Jolie recover from the death of her brother, her mother, and her other relatives. There was even a rumor that they hadn't been shot by the Nazis, but killed by an American bomb that had fallen directly on the Portuguese Embassy Annex in Galgagyörk.

"We'll never know exactly what happened," Eva said. "Let's

go forth and meet whatever challenge we've got to face here in America."

Jolie was a survivor, although she did admit that on two different occasions, she contemplated suicide—once by jumping out a window at the Plaza Hotel and another by jumping from the Empire State Building.

"Stop thinking about suicide and open a shop," Eva advised her. "You did very well in Budapest. You can do the same in New York. The war is over, and Americans have a lot of money to spend."

Eva met with Zsa Zsa and they sold some of their jewelry, enough to accumulate $7,200, which they agreed to give to Jolie to invest in a shop on Manhattan's Madison Avenue. With it, Jolie managed to rent a "hole in the wall" between 62nd and 63rd Streets, from a couple returning to Paris during the aftermath of the war. The rent was $126 a month, a price Eva thought was very cheap for Madison Avenue.

"But *Nuci!*, what are you going to sell?" Eva asked.

For $3,600, from a wholesaler's showroom on Fifth Avenue, Jolie acquired a small inventory of upscale costume jewelry.

Within a month, she realized that her "tiny little shop of horrors," as she defined it, had failed miserably. She sold her inventory to a cosmetician and her lover, a showroom salesman, whom Eva had met casually.

When Eva invited her to come and live with her in California, Jolie closed up her shop and flew to Los Angeles. A few days after her arrival, Eva asked her mother to accompany her to the home of her estranged husband, Charles Isaacs, to remove the remainder of the wardrobe she'd left in his closet.

A butler escorted Jolie inside and directed her into the garden, where Isaacs was sitting in a chair. She had been prepared to dislike him—after all, Eva was divorcing him—but this sick, dying man won her sympathy.

"For a brief time, I became a mother to him," Jolie later confessed. "He had nothing but praise for Eva and told me how much he'd always loved her. My heart went out to him. Oh, if only Paul Savosdy had been that loving and considerate of me."

Jolie had planned to breeze into the Isaacs mansion, pick up Eva's clothing, and depart. But she spent four hours with him and accepted his invitation for lunch the following afternoon. "I'm so lonely," he told her. "Your coming over is the brightest thing that has happened to me in weeks."

Back in Eva's apartment, Jolie praised Isaacs so much that she infuriated her daughter.

"*Nuci,* you might as well face facts. Right now, I'm balancing five men in my life—all of them handsome, some of them rich, some very, very rich, and each of them famous in a certain way. I want you to know that I love each of these boyfriends more than I ever loved Charles. He's sweet. But a man has to be more than sweet for me to love him. A woman wants a forceful man, not some weakling who will give in to her every demand."

"You must meet one of my beaux," Eva said. "His name is Bugsy. He's very handsome, very virile, and extremely charming. He's picking us up tonight and taking us to Ciro's. Look your most glamorous."

That evening, after spending an hour getting dressed and prepped, Jolie faced Bugsy Siegel, who arrived at nine o'clock. Eva warned her mother that Bugsy was just a nickname and that Jolie should call him Benjamin.

"He was handsome, like Eva said, but I felt there was something danger-ous about him," Jolie recalled. "He had a chauffeur, and I learned that his lim-ousine was bullet proof. Also, there were two men who looked like gangsters sitting up front, in addition to the chauffeur. This Bugsy was charming and beautifully dressed, in spite of that stupid nickname."

"When I had lunch with Charles the next day, he told me that Bugsy Siegel was one of the most dangerous men in America, the founder of Murder, Inc. I think Eva was getting money from this Al Capone type creature."

The following afternoon, Eva and Jolie had a fight when her mother de-manded that she drop "this Bugsy creature as your escort. I heard assassins one day might shoot him. He has people murdered. Is that the kind of man you want?"

"He's developing this fabulous palace, the Flamingo Hotel, in a town called Las Vegas," Eva protested. "It's out in the desert about 285 miles to the east of here. It will be a very plush hotel with a casino, suites, palm trees, gardens. All the movie stars from Hollywood will frequent it, and Bugsy is going to give me my own show room. I'll be a headliner doing a continental review, a sort of Hungarian version of Marlene Dietrich."

"It sounds like a fantasy," Jolie said.

"Like hell! It'll become an American Monte Carlo! I will never leave Bugsy. In fact, I want him to marry me. He's promised to make me the Queen of Las Vegas. I'll become famous all over the country."

"You might become a candidate for the graveyard," Jolie warned. "Fortu-nately, I have this divine black dress and a gorgeous black hat with a flowing veil to wear to your funeral."

"Oh, *Nuci, Nuci,* you will never understand me. You'll never understand America. You're strictly Old World. The Austro-Hungarian Empire is dead and gone. We're living on a new continent where people are different."

Much to Eva's disapproval, Jolie began to visit Isaacs every day. She no-ticed that in his condition, he was growing more and more dependent on her with each passing day. One night at dinner, Jolie horrified Eva by surmising: "I think Charles is falling in love with me. If he weren't dying of cancer, I think he might ask me to marry him when his divorce from you comes through. Too bad he's ill. I adore him, and he adores me."

The gangster Bugsy Siegel was a visionary, dreaming of becoming "The King of Las Vegas," with the fabulous **Flamingo Hotel** as his palace. He even promised to make Eva the "Queen of Las Vegas," with her own showroom and stage.

Ironically, it would be Zsa Zsa, not Eva, who opened in her own one-woman show at the Flamingo, a hotel that Conrad Hilton ended up owning.

"You accused me of daydreaming about Bugsy, marriage, stardom, and Las Vegas," Eva said. "Now I think you're off on some wild fantasy about Charles. Be realistic. It'll never happen. He'll be dead."

"I even met his mother," Jolie said. "She, too, adores you. She's a real estate princess in ermine and diamonds. She was brought up in Switzerland."

"That $20,000 diamond bracelet I wore the other night didn't come from Bugsy," Eva said. "It was a Christmas gift from my mother-in-law."

"How very generous," Jolie said. "I think you'll regret the day you walked out on the Isaacs family."

Eva became infuriated.

The tension between Eva and her mother grew more intense. Every day, there was an argument. One night, Jolie said, "You really misled me in Budapest, sending those pictures of you in Hollywood. You're not a star. Maybe you get a little walk-on at some community theater in Los Angeles. You waste all your time at tryouts and auditions, or else spend the day hounding agents to get you a job," Jolie said. "You're going nowhere with this so-called career of yours."

Perhaps in retaliation, but to an increasing degree, Eva started ordering Jolie around, demanding that she run errands for her, that she maintain her wardrobe, and insisting she cook and clean house. "She must have thought I was a housemaid, cook, and bottle washer. Me, a lady."

"She goes out every night," Jolie complained to Greta Keller. "One night I opened the door to the apartment and Robert Taylor was there. *The* Robert Taylor, Garbo's lover in *Camille*. I couldn't believe it!"

When Eva caught Jolie stealing canned goods, everything from pea soup to hams, from Isaac's pantry, she scolded her. "You must understand!" Jolie protested. "He has so much! I need to ship food to friends of mine in Budapest who are starving to death."

Relenting from her hard position toward Jolie, Eva mused, "I've taken diamond bracelets from the Isaacs family," Eva said. "I even made off with three Cadillacs—imagine that. When I first arrived in Hollywood, I rode around in a piece of junk. When I decided I wanted a raspberry-colored bathtub, I ordered one and charged it to Charles."

"Forgive me," Jolie said, "but I also stole a pair of his leather shoes to mail to Vilmos. I counted twenty-eight pair of them in his closet. He won't miss them. Now he wears only bedroom slippers every day."

One late afternoon, Eva came home sobbing because she'd lost out on yet another movie role.

In an attempt to comfort her, Jolie said, "Stardom has eluded you. You've got to admit that and try something else."

"I WANT TO BE A GOD DAMN ACTRESS!" Eva shouted at her. "CAN'T YOU GET THAT THROUGH YOUR THICK SKULL?"

"Oh, Eva, Eva….," Jolie said. "You've never talked to your mother like that before. Cursing and shouting at me. Me, your *Nuci,* who wants only what's best for her daughter. America has changed you, made you tough and hard."

For the first time in her life, Eva slapped Jolie's face and stormed out of the living room.

The next day, Jolie packed and moved out. With a ticket paid for by Isaacs, she was flying back to New York. "Eva is self-enchanted," she told Isaacs when she visited him for a final goodbye. "When her Filipino houseboy started patting my *derrière* and making lewd propositions, I knew it was time for me to leave."

When she kissed him goodbye, Isaacs was in tears. Both of them knew they'd never see each other again.

Eva had been gone all day. Later, Jolie learned that she'd been with Robert Walker, who had tried to commit suicide over his desertion by Jennifer Jones.

"When I was in New York, Zsa Zsa had taken me to see this Miss Jones in a movie called *Love Letters.* I couldn't understand why any man would want to commit suicide over *that* woman...so unappealing."

When Jolie was in Manhattan again and installed in the suite which Conrad had provided for her at the Plaza, she phoned Eva.

She had been hoping that Eva would have apologized to her for slapping her, but she hadn't.

In Hollywood, Eva picked up the phone. When she heard it was Jolie, she slammed down the receiver.

Jolie did not become overly upset, knowing that Eva's hostility toward her would eventually fade. In the past, they'd had many disagreements, and Jolie had long ago concluded that Eva was her most difficult daughter. She told her friends, "Eva is becoming the most American of all my daughters, not always respectful of their mothers the way they are in Hungary."

Francesca Hilton entered the world in March of 1947. Before Zsa Zsa became impregnated in the aftermath of her rape by her husband, Conrad Hilton, as a farewell to their marriage, she'd never thought about motherhood, or even desired it. "Babies were never my concern. But once my little girl was born, I looked into her little face and felt complete."

"Of course, *dahlink,* I wasn't going to sit around the house all night nursing a baby," she later said. "Haven't you ever heard of a babysitter or a nanny? As soon as I recovered my figure, I was back to dating since I was now a free woman."

"During my incapacitation, my darling Nicky was photographed with a number of showgirls. But as soon as I was in working order again, he was a frequent visitor to my boudoir."

"What I didn't foresee in the months ahead as competition was from, of all people, this child co-star at MGM, little Miss Elizabeth Taylor. She was embarking on her decades-long career as an international slut, and my Nicky was one of the victims of this devouring creature. Miss Taylor and I would have many conflicts in the future over the same man—take Richard Burton as one example."

Vilmos was still in New York at the time of Francesca's birth, and he visited Zsa Zsa at Doctors Hospital. He expressed disappointment when he heard that the newborn was a girl. "Three daughters I have, and not one of them will give me a grandson."

Jolie pretended to be overjoyed at the news of the baby, but privately she admitted, "The idea of me being a grandmother is ridiculous. Just look at me. I'm far too young to be anybody's grandmother." She was fifty-one years old.

The night she had to rush to the hospital to see Zsa Zsa, Jolie stood up a young man with whom she'd made a date. Even though she'd dismissed his social standing—"that of a lowly worker in a hamburger place,"—she was intrigued by his good looks and obvious virility. She learned that his full name was Peter Howard Christman.

She went every day to Hamburger Heaven, where he talked to her, but never asked her out. Finally, he wrote to her, explaining how shy he was. She called him and set up a rendezvous with him for March 10, 1947.

But when she was suddenly summoned to the hospital, she decided not to alert Christman, fearing that if he ascertained that she was a grandmother, he'd have nothing further to do with her.

Days later, her potential beau confronted her about her non-presence at their previously scheduled rendezvous. Jolie explained that she had become a grandmother and that because of the sudden birth of the child, she had been unavoidably detained.

"That makes no difference to me," Christman responded. "I'm actually forty-eight years old—and not the boy you imagine me to be."

Christman not only escorted Jolie out on the town that night, but accompanied her during one of her visits to Zsa Zsa and Francesca in the hospital. An attendant thought he was "Mr. Gabor," the father of Zsa Zsa's child.

That night at her apartment, Jolie admitted, "I helped Peter get over his shyness. By dawn, he was shy no more."

Conrad Hilton, the newborn's father, was somewhere in Texas and sent a telegram, but made no follow-up plans to see his new daughter. "Friends sent flowers," Zsa Zsa said, "but not one rose from Conrad."

After their stay in the hospital, Zsa Zsa and Francesca Hilton arrived at her luxurious penthouse apartment on the East Side of Manhattan. "With a nurse for my new daughter, I was free to start dating again, now that I had shed Conrad, who I decided was too old for me."

"I, too, was not the type to sit at home, listening for the baby to cry. Once the bachelors and adulterous married men heard I was single again, my phone began to ring."

"By some coincidence, my first two dates were with men who would one day become very powerful—a future U.S. president and a future king of an oil-rich country in the Middle East. Both were rich—one handsome, the other not."

***

One of the first invitations Zsa Zsa accepted was to the garden party of her newly minted friend, Bunny Mellon. "As a horticulturist, this very rich and powerful lady had one of the most beautiful gardens I'd even seen. Against a backdrop of gorgeous roses stood a handsome young man who seemed to exude charm and charisma. Bunny, that dear lady, introduced me to this dashing man, who had a gleam in his eye when he looked at me."

He was John F. Kennedy.

In her first memoir, Zsa Zsa coyly remembered that she "looked through my old date book" and came across Kennedy's name. But she didn't need a date book to remember that she had dated the future president of the United States. The details and implications were imbedded in her brain, as was her on-again, off-again affair with the young politician. In fact, in the 1960s, she dined out on references to her former romantic link to him.

But in her memoir, she merely mentioned him as one of the men she had dated, providing no further explanation or detail. Of course, the memoir was published in the year (1960) that Kennedy ran for president, so perhaps she was merely being discreet as a means of protecting him from adverse publicity, and thereby currying favor with the new regime.

Zsa Zsa is always listed on the databases that gossips and historians assemble on who slept with JFK over the years. Based on what Zsa Zsa said and revealed over the decades, a mosaic of her intimacies with JFK can be pieced together.

"At the time I first met him, I think he was a congressman or something, speaking with a delightful Boston accent," she said. "I had met his father, Joseph P. Kennedy, when he was the Ambassador to the Court of St. James's in London before the War. Papa Kennedy came on to me, as he did to every other beautiful woman, so I was told. I just assumed that Jack was the acorn who fell from the same tree."

"I was with my first husband, Burhan Belge, when I met Kennedy *père,* and he was with his wife, Rose. We never had a chance to connect—that would come later in Palm Beach. But first, the son: I had heard that the Kennedys were very rich, and wealthy men were not to be ignored. If they were also handsome and charming, that made such men all the more appealing."

"After our first three minutes of talking and flirting with each other, he allowed me to call him Jack," she said. "I had been calling him 'Your Honor,' although I learned that was not the proper way to address a congressman. He was with some other woman that night. I learned later that it was this lovely Palm Beach socialite, Durie Malcolm. They were said to be secretly married, but Papa Kennedy did not approve and later had the marital records in Palm Beach destroyed."

"Before I left Bunny *[Mellon's]* party, I was able to slip Jack my perfumed social card, which was printed in conch-shell pink. That night I dreamed about him. In my dream, he became my husband number three. The next morning, I tried to get used to my new name—Sari Gabor Belge Hilton Kennedy. It was awkward-sounding, but I could live with it."

"Being the aggressive, hot-to-trot young man that JFK was in those days, he telephoned the next morning as I was eating my lavish breakfast of one poached egg, black coffee, and a piece of unbuttered Melba toast."

"On our first date, at the Stork Club, I discovered that Jack had been active in sports —football at Harvard, a member of the intercollegiate sailing team— before a back injury. He graduated *cum laude* as a class officer. He also had a brilliant mind. When he was very young, he wrote a best seller called *Why England Slept.*"

"Since he came from such a powerful family, I thought I'd spend the evening listening to him talk about himself. Not so. His accomplishments seemed the last thing on Jack's mind. He was the greatest listener I've ever known. He was the rare American who even knew who Atatürk was. He wanted to know all about him, and he was interested in the trip that I, along with Burhan, took to Nazi Germany where I met Hitler himself and, of course, that little weasel, Goebbels."

"When a woman talked to him, the rest of the world didn't seem to exist for him," she claimed. "He focused completely on the woman he was with at the time. He absorbed my every pronouncement as if I were delivering the Ten Commandments. He seemed to understand me. What a seductive technique!"

"Even though he didn't talk much about himself, his character came through to me at that early stage in his life. Apparently, heroic service in the Navy during the war had matured him. He seemed to be heading somewhere fast, and he knew what he wanted."

"Before our first intimacy, I had ruled out my dream of marrying him" she said. "It was that gleam in his eye. As we passed through the Stork Club, he encountered at least five ladies who, to judge from the look on their faces and their greetings, seemed to have intimate knowledge of his anatomy."

"One of the women I was introduced to was Gene Tierney, the movie actress," Zsa Zsa said. "In spite of her buck teeth, she was hailed as one of the screen's great beauties. I'd seen her in *Laura* (1944)."

Most Hollywood historians claim that JFK and Tierney met in August of 1948 when he was introduced to her on the set when she was filming *Dragonwyck*. But Zsa Zsa always insisted that Kennedy already knew Tierney that night in 1947 at the Stork Club.

"Women have a way of sizing each other up on first meeting, and I just knew I would be competing with Tierney over men in our future. Obviously, Jack was one of those men. I didn't know at the time that others, including Prince Aly Khan and George Sanders, my future husband, would be added to the list."

"Back at my penthouse apartment in New York, the night was lovely. So was I. Gorgeous, in fact. So was my date. It would be the beginning of many such nights in the future. After an hour of talking and drinking in the living room, I encountered what he called 'my implement' in my boudoir."

"I am not the first of many of his lovers who can-

"He was handsome and rich, a fresh-faced Irishman with a gleam in his eyes," Zsa Zsa said of young **John F. Kennedy.**

"I knew from the first moment we met that he was going to end up in my bed."

"He was one of those aggressive young men whom women can't resist. When he saw what he wanted, he went after it, using charm as a weapon."

355

didly admit that the future President of the United States was not among the world's greatest lovers. He was probably better than Hitler, but that's about it."

"Even so, being in bed with him was thrilling because of his charm and kisses. He was so boyish, so endearing. Because of his bad back, he preferred the woman to be on top."

"Over the years, I have both agreed and disagreed with some of the assessments of Jack the lover. He once made a controversial statement that once he'd had a woman, he moved on. 'The conquest is more important than the final act itself.' I'm sure that was true in some cases, but not in mine. He came back for more time and time again—in Los Angeles, Washington, New York, Palm Beach, wherever."

"His former roommate at Harvard, Charles Houghton, claimed that JFK felt women 'were a useful thing to have when you want them, but when you didn't want them, he put them back.' That was true in the sense that he didn't waste a lot of time in the afterglow, including cuddling around the fireplace. When it was over, it was over. He swung into action again, making urgent phone calls, arranging his next moves. He was definitely a man who was going places. And that was the Oval Office, where he became one of our most popular presidents."

"Let me say this in his defense: When he was in bed with a woman, fleeting though the time might be, he was all there for her. She felt like he Queen of Sheba. Of course, after he got what he wanted, he jerked back into a new reality. You either accepted him on his terms, or you were out of the game. I wanted to stay in the game, so I played by his rules. In fact, we were birds of a feather, flocking together. I treated certain men in much the same way he treated women."

"The morning after, he gave me a quick kiss and was on his way," she said. "At the door, he promised, 'I'll call you.' He always said that whenever he was leaving. He meant it, too. The only problem was that you didn't know whether he would ever call you again. Certainly not the next day. Maybe weeks would go by, even a year or so. Don't get the wrong impression, *dahlink*. I wasn't exactly sitting near my phone waiting for Jack to call. I was out pursuing my own agenda. My datebook was always full, and invitations came daily from very important men, both in America and from abroad, whenever they were in New York."

"Of course, some of these dates were more meaningful than others. You might wonder how some of these men arriving in New York ever managed to contact me. I was in the same position as Nancy Davis (later Reagan) in Hollywood. Our private phone numbers were passed around a lot."

***

"Joan Crawford had her own reasons for throwing that plate of food in my face in the MGM commissary," Zsa Zsa claimed. "I'm sure Greg Bautzer preferred me to her. I was so much younger, of course. Historians—that is, scholars of ancient history—claimed that Crawford was born in 1904, but *dahlink*, don't you believe it. I have it on good authority that she was a waitress at the Last Supper."

In addition to Bautzer, Crawford had other reasons to be jealous of Zsa Zsa. Douglas Fairbanks, Jr., Crawford's first husband, had already seduced Zsa Zsa, who was now dating Franchot Tone, her second ex-husband, whom she'd divorced in 1939. And eventually, another Gabor (Eva) seduced Crawford's third husband, Phillip Terry too.

"These were all fine men, and very good looking," Zsa Zsa said. "Crawford should have held onto at least one of them. But I'd heard that this bitch, a star of blue movies in the 1920s, was very difficult to get along with. I never starred in a stag movie—well, maybe one, but that was a setup, *dahlink*."

At the time that Zsa Zsa began to date Tone, he was married to what Zsa Zsa defined as "that B-actress blonde, Jean Wallace, a former chorus girl not unfamiliar with casting couches."

[Some of Zsa Zsa's critics blamed her for breaking up the Wallace/Tone marriage in 1948, but Tone had cheated on Wallace with women other than Zsa Zsa. Wallace later married another famous actor, Cornel Wilde, a bisexual who'd had an affair with Laurence Olivier when they'd toured together in Romeo and Juliet.

A swashbuckler, a sort of dime store Errol Flynn, Wilde became known as "The King of Beefcake Bondage," because he, on occasion, stripped to the waist and was whipped by a villain.

"All I knew about Wilde was that his parents were Hungarian Jews," Zsa Zsa once said. "Frankly, I think Franchot should have stayed married to Wallace. After her, he married that tramp, actress Barbara Payton, who ended up a drug addict and a ten-dollar-a-night hooker. Poor Franchot, he was such a kind and decent man."]

Both from Hollywood gossip and from extended dating with Tone over a period of years, Zsa Zsa learned much about a man whom Crawford defined as "sedate, until he beat you up."

Zsa Zsa found Tone handsome in an unconventional way, and "rather sexy, especially his warm, lyrical, and romantic voice, although I didn't understand what he was talking about sometimes. After all, he'd gone to Cornell, and I hadn't. He was an accomplished actor and had come from a rich, cultivated background. He was also a man of impeccable manners."

Tone confided to Zsa Zsa, "Playing second fiddle to Joan in all those 1930s movies, where I was second banana to Clark Gable, damaged my male ego. My servitude to Joan at home also rankled my manhood. Every night, even if we were alone, she dressed lavishly for dinner. When she came down the stairs, I was supposed to compliment her for at least an hour. Hell, even if Venus de Milo descended those stairs every night, I couldn't go on raving like a madman about how beautiful she was."

On one of his dates with Zsa Zsa, Tone confessed that he might have been the catalyst for the decades-long feud between Bette Davis and his wife. "When Bette and I were filming *Dangerous* back in 1935, Joan arrived unannounced on the set. She found me in Bette's dressing room. How can I put this? I was undressed and could not cover up a raging erection that didn't seem to want to go down."

"After that, every time I came home," Tone said, "Joan would insist that I stand under the shower for at least an hour with a special soap she'd discovered," telling me, "'Who knows what germs you picked up from that poisonous trap, Bette Davis' overripe vagina."

"Nights with Franchot Tone weren't always about sex," Zsa Zsa said. "After all, when I met him, he was in his early forties and past his prime. Sometimes, he shared his dreams with me. He said that ever since he'd filmed *Mutiny on the Bounty* (1935) with Clark Gable, he'd wanted to buy a schooner and sail to some remote island in the South Seas."

In the 1930s, **Franchot Tone** was making love to his wife (**Joan Crawford**, pictured above) both on and off the screen.

"Perhaps I should have married Zsa Zsa," he later said. "Our on-again, off again affair lasted for decades. We turned to each other between lovers and between marriages."

"I want to spend the rest of my life there with my lady love," he told her. "An idyllic setting without photographers, no scandal mongers, no studio bosses."

"He once invited me to the Canadian woods north of Toronto, where he'd vacationed as a boy, fishing, hunting, camping, water skiing. I had to turn him down. Those activities weren't my thing, although I did like horseback riding."

When pressed by Greta Keller, Zsa Zsa revealed that Tone was a great lover. "I may have been among the first to label him "Jaw-Breaker. A penis doesn't come any thicker than his, at least not from my experience."

Over the years, Zsa Zsa learned that many Hollywood insiders defined Tone as a bisexual. A famous story circulated about Tone and Errol Flynn. It was said that after they attended the funeral of their mutual lover, actor Alexander

358

Ross, they went home together and made love to each other. Ross had committed suicide in 1937, his slated roles at Warner's going to newcomer Ronald Reagan.

"Harry Warner told me that every man in Crawford's inner circle, such as William Haines, was either homosexual or bisexual," Zsa Zsa claimed. "Even Tone's chief rival, Clark Gable, had slept with a lot of men in the 1920s when he first arrived in Hollywood. Of course, *dahlink*, that could have been for career advancement instead of for sexual desire."

Crawford's first three husbands were bisexual," Zsa Zsa said. "Perhaps he learned all that from his mother, Gertrude Tone, a political activist who was in love with the famous writer, Dorothy Thompson, for many years."

In her highly unreliable memoirs, *A Portrait of Joan,* published in 1962, Crawford devoted very little space to Zsa Zsa's romancing of her former husband. The only insight she provided in that book was this simple sentence: "At a party at Earl Blackwell's, Franchot arrived with Zsa Zsa Gabor wearing the diamond studs I'd given him."

[Zsa Zsa elaborated later on the incident:

At their table, Zsa Zsa asked Tone where he'd gotten the diamonds he was wearing. "I never saw you wear those before."

Zsa Zsa claimed that before he answered her, Tone glanced lovingly in the direction of Crawford's table, and told Zsa Zsa, "From my darling," indicating his former wife.

Zsa Zsa became furious that he'd referred to Crawford as his darling and that, "you're wearing diamonds that she gave you when you're out on a date with me. How could you be so insensitive?"

Later, Zsa Zsa claimed, "I got my revenge on Franchot. Back at my home, I held him off for three hours before I'd agree to have sex with him. Call it payback time. No man calls another woman darling when he's out on a date with me."]

***

From her newly established base in Manhattan, Jolie became very frank with Zsa Zsa, bluntly advising her to "quit wasting your time chasing after such losers as Franchot Tone. You should never marry an actor. Why not a king? Since most of them have been without thrones since the end of the war, try at least for a Prince with money."

Zsa Zsa decided to follow her mother's advice.

In Ankara, as the wife of Burhan Belge, she had met and entertained the Crown Prince of Saudi Arabia as part of his state visit. At a banquet, he did not conceal his fascination with her. "I'm awed by your beauty," the Prince told her. "You would make a fine addition to my harem."

"How flattering," Zsa Zsa said, "but I do only a solo."

"Saud wasn't the prettiest thing walking," Zsa Zsa recalled. "But he was very, very rich."

[Saud bin Abdulaziz Al Saud (aka "Saud of Saudi Arabia"; born 1902, died 1969)—who eventually ruled the troubled kingdom from 1953 until he was ousted for financial mismanagement in 1964—was the second son of the legendary Ibn Saud, the first Saudi King, who reigned from 1932 until his death in 1953. In 1945, he'd made an alliance with the United States, and had sent his son Saud to cement that union.]

In New York, Saud phoned Zsa Zsa for a date, and she suggested he take her to the Stork Club, telling him that it was the most fashionable place to be seen in the city. "How I regretted suggesting it," she recalled. "It was one of the most humiliating experiences of my life."

When they got there, Sherman Billingsley, a former bootlegger and the

Saud bin Abdulaziz Al Saud, the Crown Prince of Saudi Arabia, posed for this picture in 1952, a year before his ascension to the throne.

Zsa Zsa: "I would have accepted his proposal of marriage, but there was no way in hell I would have tolerated all of his other wives. Upon arrival at his palace, I would immediately have kicked them into the desert."

owner of the club, blocked Zsa Zsa's entrance at the door. "Mrs. Hilton," he said to her in front of the Crown Prince. "You and Conrad are welcome here on any night—in fact, I'd view the presence of one or both of you as an honor. But surely you already know that our door policy is not to admit a Negro."

"But Sherman," she protested. "He's not a Negro. He's the Crown Prince of Saudi Arabia, the heir to the throne. He's one of the richest men in the world."

"Don't insult my intelligence," Billingsley told her. "I know a Negro when I see one."

The Crown Prince with Zsa Zsa ended up going to Schrafft's and feasting "on the best ice cream sundaes in the world." When they left, Saud gave each of the three motherly Irish waitresses a $1,000 bill.

[For a period of at least fifty years, the elite of New York ate and drank nightly at the Stork Club. Peter Hamill once wrote: "At 3 East 53rd Street, it was the headquarters of café society: the social merging of the children of the rich with movie stars, gossip columnists, prewar Eurotrash, politicians, judges, some favored cops, a few good writers, and a sprinkling of former bootleggers"

At the time Billingsley turned Zsa Zsa away, he was "shacked up" with Broadway star Ethel Merman.

The notorious Director of the F.B.I., J. Edgar Hoover

and his lover, Clyde Tolson, made the Stork Club their regular hangout whenever they were in New York. Walter Winchell practically wrote his column from a well-positioned table within the club, and Ernest Hemingway once paid for his liquor bill by cashing a $100,000 royalty check his publisher had issued for For Whom the Bell Tolls.

Hamill claimed that Billingsley was privately anti-Semitic, preferring famous, rich, well-born, and good-looking WASPs. He did allow entrance to certain Jews such as Winchell, or one who was internationally famous, such as Al Jolson.

The last "Negro" he barred from the Stork Club was the celebrated black singer/dancer Josephine Baker on October 16, 1951. It created a nationwide flood of bad publicity, and may have contributed to the night club's ultimate demise.

Zsa Zsa later lamented, "My getting turned away with the Crown Prince of Saudi Arabia should have made headlines around the world. But, NO, Baker had to go and hog all the publicity for herself."]

***

Zsa Zsa admitted to her friends that she did indeed go to bed with the Crown Prince. "He even proposed marriage to me, *dahlink*. But that would not have made me the queen when he ascended the throne. In time, the devil became the father of 115 children, and he had so many wives, he was never sure of the count."

[Saud's fiscally conservative replacement, Crown Prince Faisal bin Abdulaziz, overthrew his free-spending father in 1964, seizing the throne for himself. On hearing of Saud's death in 1969, Zsa Zsa said, "I would have married him, dahlink, if he'd agreed to get rid of all those other wives. With me, he would not have needed them. It would have been fun

Sherman Billingsly *(upper photo)* was the king of New York City night life, ruling from his perch at the celebrity-studded **Stork Club**. Below is its main dining room as it looked in 1944 at the peak of its wartime glory. Frank Sinatra, Orson Welles, even General Dwight Eisenhower, when he returned from the war in Europe, patronized the club.

But he barred entrance to Zsa Zsa and Prince Saud of Saudi Arabia, accusing him of being a Negro.

Zsa Zsa called Billingsley "a racist asshole."

helping him spend that $450 million he lost during his reign."]

***

After the departure of Zsa Zsa's Prince from New York, she took up with another royal. This one would have been allowed into the Stork Club or any other exclusive club in the world. He was Ernst Augustus IV, the Prince of Hanover.

Born in Germany in 1914, he functioned as the official head of the House of Hanover from 1953 until his death in 1987. His christening in the summer of 1914 represented the last great gathering of European monarchs before the start of World War I. At birth, as an emphasis on the family links between the royal families of England and Germany, he was awarded, among many other titles, a designation as "Prince of Great Britain and Ireland" by King George V of the United Kingdom.

Decades later, Zsa Zsa once met his son, Prince Ernst Augustus V of Hanover, who had been born in 1954. She was attending a gala in Monaco when he'd become the third husband of Caroline of Monaco, the daughter of Prince Rainier and Grace Kelly.

"Caroline made off with the real catch," Zsa Zsa claimed one night at the Casino of Monte Carlo. "This darling man is worth five billion pounds—that's *pounds, not dollars, dahlink."*

"I always regretted not marrying the father," Zsa Zsa said. "If I had, I would have held, among other titles, that of the Duchess of Brunswick. Instead, much later in life, I became the Duchess of Saxony."

Zsa Zsa's romantic interests shifted after she and Jolie attended a screening in Manhattan of the movie, *The Moon and Sixpence. [Editor's note: this film was re-released in 1948 after a limited initial release in 1942].*

Zsa Zsa always regretted not accepting the proposal of marriage from **Ernst Augustus IV,** the Prince of Hanover, *[born 1914, died 1987, and depicted in the photo above].* "If I'd married him, I would have become the Duchess of Brunswick," she claimed.

"We might also have given birth to the most eligible bachelor on the planet." *[i.e., Ernst Augustus V, born in 1954 to Ernst Augustus IV and Princess Ortrud of Schleswig-Holstein-Sonderburg-Glücksburg].*

"He's one of the richest men in the world, but Princess Caroline of Monaco walked off with him."

An adaptation of the W. Somerset Maugham novel of the same name, it starred George Sanders interpreting the role of the narcissistic but artistically driven Charles Strickland, a bland London stockbroker who abandons his wife and children and flees first to Paris and then to an island in the South Seas to pursue a career as a painter. For viewers, it evoked the legend of Paul Gauguin.

Zsa Zsa linked her arm with Jolie's as they were walking out of the movie house, and announced, "I have fallen in love with George Sanders. He is going to be my next husband."

***

Zsa Zsa's scheme to meet and ultimately marry George Sanders was delayed when, in 1949, she was invited to Palm Beach by the gold-digging heiress Dolly O'Brien. They'd previously bonded at a Hollywood party and had stayed in touch. Zsa Zsa had lived through Dolly's latest marriage and divorce and her roller coaster romance with Clark Gable. She was a blonde who reminded Gable of his third wife, Carole Lombard, who had died in an airplane crash in 1942

Dolly wanted Zsa Zsa to accompany her aboard the train hauling her and her entourage from New York to Florida. "All my friends are converging there, in Palm Beach, including the Kennedy family. They're very entertaining."

"I've already been entertained by one of the Kennedy men," Zsa Zsa shot back.

"Oh *him,*" Dolly said, dismissively. "Who hasn't?"

"Dolly practically had to rent a separate railway car for her massive quantities of luggage," Zsa Zsa said. "She even carried her own bottled water and monogrammed silk sheets."

Aboard the train, Dolly introduced Zsa Zsa to five extremely handsome and well-built young men who would be traveling with them. As biographers have noted, "She liked being surrounded by young men, and it was fortunate she had the money to support her tastes."

"Before we disembark at Palm Beach, you're welcome to sample all of these guys," Dolly told Zsa Zsa, who never revealed if she accepted the offer.

During the long trip South, Dolly consumed an enormous amount of food but never gained weight. "I never had to diet," she told Zsa Zsa. "My daily regimen of eighteen holes of golf keeps me at 112 pounds." Her hair had not one trace of gray, and her face was free of wrinkles, although she said she never indulged in facials. "I'm what's known as a natural beauty."

To pass the long hours aboard the train, Dolly spoke of her romance with Gable, which had begun at the Stork Club in Manhattan in 1944. "Gable is a bit older than I like in a man," she said. Zsa Zsa knew that Dolly was six years older than Gable. "It's better to get men when they're at their sexual peak, at around nineteen or twenty."

One night, Gable had proposed marriage to Dolly, telling her that, "You're the only woman I met who can help me get over Carole."

363

At the last minute, Dolly had changed her mind and married her fourth husband, José Dorelis, the Bulgarian perfume maker, instead. On May 11, 1946 *The American Weekly* had printed an announcement of the event with the headline: *CLARK GABLE DIDN'T GET THE GIRL!*

"Three Years after her latest marriage, and no longer particularly concerned about issues associated with fidelity, Dolly told Zsa Zsa, "Clark and I have decided to give it one last try," Dolly said. "I'm crazy about the guy, but he's slightly flawed. I can't get him to haul ass out of Hollywood, a town I can't stand. Even though we're back together, I don't know how long it can last. He's an inveterate womanizer, and he's even taken up with Joan Crawford again."

"As for marriage," Dolly continued, "try not to let the damn thing last longer than *Gone With the Wind* before you rush to your lawyer to discuss alimony."

Zsa Zsa was caught up in the glamour of Palm Beach. She fitted into this glittering world of the megawealthy as if born to it, even though she later defined it as, "A place of shady characters under blue skies and palm trees. They think they have class but they merely have money. Class, *dahlink,* is something else."

In Palm Beach, Dolly, in Zsa Zsa's words, "was living like a queen. Marie Antoinette would have been jealous. We didn't have to walk even one block. A limousine was always waiting to take us the short distance."

As Dolly's guest, Zsa Zsa moved through a world populated with Kennedys, Vanderbilts, Whitneys, Cushings, and Livingstons.

"The natives change their clothes five times a day and take tea in outdoor gardens under palm trees before going to balls, often costume balls, concerts, or the theater." Zsa Zsa said. "Everybody is sleeping around with everybody else. No husband is safe. Nor any wife, for that matter."

"To all this was added the star attraction, the arrival of Clark Gable," Zsa Zsa said.

Gable was still being called the King of Hollywood, even though other stars were stronger at the box office than he was at the time. In the bright Florida sunshine, he looked far older than Zsa Zsa's screen image of him. "I guess I was expecting Rhett Butler and I got a middle aged man dangerously closing in on fifty. His long years of drinking had caught up with him. He was graying and his face reflected years of rough living."

There were problems involved with dating a star. One day, Dolly asked him to accompany her during one of her shopping jaunts along Worth Avenue. "He was mobbed by autograph fans," Dolly told Zsa Zsa. "I'm Dolly O'Brien, a lady accustomed to being the center of attention, but I was pushed aside by these broads."

"Then the inevitable happened," Zsa Zsa later admitted to friends when she returned to New York. "Dolly had gone with three of her girlfriends to a big luncheon on Miami Beach. Clark didn't want to go, and I feigned a headache. I was left alone in the house with him. When he knocked on my door, as I knew he would, I was in a sexy black *négligée*. I won't exactly say that he forced himself onto me, but I didn't put up much resistance."

She was very frank in her revelations about Gable. "I was only in love with the screen image of Gable. I liked the attention he lavished on me, but I never related to the man himself. He became more of a friend than lover. Jolie later met him, and they became friends. He was very likable."

"Clark, or so I heard, has admitted to friends that he's a lousy lay, and, *dahlink*, I have to agree with him. To put it bluntly, he has a severe case of phimosis. That was a term I learned from a doctor. I don't know if there is a word for it in Hungarian. It's a condition where the foreskin refuses to retreat properly along the shaft of his penis. He was noted for a really bad smegna odor, yet he managed to seduce every big star at MGM, including Norma Shearer and Jean Harlow. Of course, Lana Turner and Crawford go without saying. In time to come, he would even bed Marilyn Monroe before the hearse arrived."

[Zsa Zsa kept her remarks about Gable's sexual attributes relatively contained, unlike Bette Davis, whom she visited in 1949 on the set of All About Eve. *Zsa Zsa had arrived to take George Sanders, one of the co-stars, to lunch.*

During some point in her conversation with Davis, Gable's name came up. "It's just as well I didn't get the role of Scarlett O'Hara," Davis said. "Starring opposite Clark Gable? That would have been a pip. I can't stand a man who has fake, store-bought teeth and doesn't keep his uncircumcised cock clean under all that foreskin. I hear he shoots too soon and messes himself all the time."

"I'd never give a man a bad review the way Davis did," Zsa Zsa said.]

After two weeks together in Palm Beach, Gable and Dolly decided that marriage would be a bad idea, and they parted as friends.

Gable returned to Hollywood, where it was announced, on December 20, 1949, that he had married Lady Sylvia Ashley, who had previously been married to Douglas Fairbanks, Sr.

The day of Gable's exit from Palm Beach, Dolly's maid delivered Zsa Zsa a handwritten invitation to dinner.

It was from Joseph P. Kennedy.

***

"There are two things I remember about Ambassador Kennedy," Zsa Zsa later recalled. "He seemed to have a perpetual twinkle in his blue eyes, and he had a habit of slapping his thigh with the palm of his hand and laughing at his own jokes."

"I arrived in my finery at the Kennedy compound, thinking it was going to be a dinner party for his friends," Zsa Zsa said. "Except for some discreet servants, we were alone. I was told that Rose Kennedy was still in New England. I later learned that he and his son Jack often 'swapped' women. Perhaps Jack had told Papa of my charms."

After two glasses of champagne, Zsa Zsa was in a frivolous mood, and she delivered a hilarious imitation of his Boston accent as filtered by her Hungarian accent. "He laughed so hard he had to wipe his teary eyes with his handkerchief," she said.

Kennedy consumed three hearty courses—"a meat and potatoes man"—while she dined lightly, preferring a small piece of grilled fish and some unbuttered broccoli.

After dinner, he began his well-worn seduction technique for aspiring actresses: "You know, I could turn you into another Constance Bennett."

Not quite sure who that actress was, she asked, "Don't you mean another Garbo, or another Dietrich? I see myself in light, sophisticated comedies."

"I knew Connie in the 1930s very, very well. At the pinnacle of her career, in the midst of the Depression, she was the highest paid actress in Hollywood, pulling in $30,000 a week. A lot of paychecks were $7.50 a week back then."

"I'm impressed with the money," she said.

"I think that if I promoted you right, you could earn that much, but only if I'm managing everything about your career. Total management—nothing less. "You and I as a team might make millions off the right kind of movie. When talkies came, Gloria Swanson made disastrous script choices."

"Do you have a picture in mind?" she asked. "Surely, you must have a lot of writers sending you scripts."

"Now, don't be startled," Kennedy said, "but I'm considering a script about the private life of Adolf Hitler," he said. "I see you cast as Eva Braun, his mistress."

"I've actually met the woman," she said. "I could play her. But the idea of making love to the *Führer* is a bit repulsive."

"I assume that you speak German," he said.

"Yes, fluently," she said. "If I'm Eva Braun, who will you cast as Hitler?"

"That's a real problem," he answered.

"Charlie Chaplin's out," she said. "He's already played Hitler."

He frowned at her. "We're not talking comedy here. It would be a serious picture."

The talk soon turned from movies to moonlight, as he invited her upstairs to his terrace, where he wanted to show her his garden.

She later claimed, "Before I realized what was happening, he'd grabbed me and kissed me, holding the nape of my neck. His other hand was on my formidable breast, a temptation to any man, particularly for one as lecherous as the ambassador. Still, I was a working girl breaking in, and a promise from such a powerful mogul as the ambassador could not be lightly dismissed, even if it led to the boudoir."

As she described it to Greta Keller one night at the Stanhope Hotel in Manhattan, "Like his son, the ambassador was not a prizewinner in bed. But at least he had more staying power than Jack."

Over breakfast the next day with Dolly, Zsa Zsa learned that Constance Bennett had been one of a series of movie stars, some of them in silent pictures, that Kennedy had seduced during the peak of his Hollywood days of the 1920s and 30s. The list most prominently included Swanson, Evelyn Brent, Nancy Carroll, Betty Compson, Viola Dana, Marion Davies (when William Randolph Hearst wasn't nearby), Marlene Dietrich, Phyllis Haver, and perhaps Greta Garbo, although that seduction has never been conclusively documented.

Not all of his conquests were stars. Many of these young women were call girls, starlets, or dancers.

The ambassador had invited Dolly for a game of golf that day. Zsa Zsa had been invited to "tag along" with Dolly if she wanted to watch them play.

"There he stood in the Florida sun wearing white flannels, argyle socks, and two-toned shoes, an outfit that would have been fashionable in 1928," Zsa Zsa said. "He was most gracious to me, calling me 'the world's most glamorous woman,' although that title had been bestowed on me before."

"But throughout the course of the day, there was no talk of a movie contract. No Eva Braun role. He never made a movie about Hitler. I was fast learning that most motion picture scenarios in Hollywood never go beyond a man's dream."

As Dolly and Zsa Zsa were leaving the golf course, the ambassador called to them. "I heard you gals have entertained Clark Gable. But I've got one up on him." He smiled, flashing his teeth. "Unlike Gable's false teeth, these are my own genuine pearly whites."

In 1929, Ambassador **Joseph P. Kennedy** *(left)* was photographed on the beach at Cannes with **James Henri Le Bailly de La Falaise, Marquis de la Coudraye,** who was married at the time to Gloria Swanson. In 1931, he married another famous Hollywood actress, Constance Bennett. Both women were mistresses of Kennedy.

"I had the ambassador, or rather, he had me, but I never got around to De La Falaise," Zsa Zsa said. "The ambassador promised to star me as Eva Braun in a movie about Hitler, but he never did."

Later, Zsa Zsa concluded, "There will be no romance with Kennedy, no prolonged affair. It was what you Americans call a one-night stand. Unlike Swanson, I'm not going to be his next trophy mistress. If he's going to make a star out of anyone, it will be Jack Kennedy. I think he wants the young man to become president one day He's more interested in creating a star politician than he is in developing another hot movie star."

Back in New York, Zsa Zsa resumed her pursuit of George Sanders. The first challenge involved how to be introduced to him.

***

At long last Eva had been assigned a movie role, cast as the glamorous Countess Marina in the 1949 romantic costume drama, *Song of Surrender*, directed by Michel Leisen and starring Claude Rains and Wanda Hendrix.

Gay-friendly Eva bonded with Leisen, and she frequently had lunch with him and his lover, Billy Daniel, the dancer/actor/choreographer. "Every now and then, they had a lovers' spat, and I was the peacemaker," she recalled.

Leisen had previously worked with and/or directed such A-list stars as Jean Arthur, Billy Wilder, Preston Sturges, and Miriam Hopkins. His most famous picture had been *Hold Back the Dawn* (1941), with Charles Boyer, Olivia de Havilland, and Paulette Goddard.

The actor who immediately attracted Eva's attention was Macdonald Carey, a native of Sioux City, Iowa, who was known in Hollywood circles as "The King of the Bs," while Lucille Ball was simultaneously reigning as "The Queen of the Bs."

Carey's best work had been in Alfred Hitchcock's *Shadow of a Doubt*, released in 1943. Carey played a detective on the trail of a killer, played by Joseph Cotten. When Eva met Carey, he was emerging from active duty as a member of the U.S. Marine Corps.

[From 1966 until around 1994, in Days of Our Lives, *as part of the longest running gig in show business, Macdonald Carey played the kindly Dr. Horton. It's his voiceover that recited, at the beginning of each episode: "Like the sands through the hourglass, so are the days of our lives."]*

According to Eva, "I was drawn to many handsome actors, including Macdonald, during what I call my 'white heat' period in the 40s and 50s. Macdonald and I never shared any particular romance. He'd married Elizabeth Heckscher during the war, and was relatively faithful to her. I think he was a good Roman Catholic. But we had our moments."

"Late one afternoon, he drove me home in what became a monsoon," she said. "We parked in a secluded lane and did some what you Americans call 'heavy petting,' I'm not giving a blow-by-blow description, but I learned he was all man and he already knew I was all woman. A lot of things happen during torrential rainstorms in parked cars."

"I visited Macdonald in his dressing room a few times, and learned he had a drinking problem, but he handled his liquor well," Eva said. "He was always smoking a pipe, which eventually led to lung cancer."

Eva also discussed her interchanges on the set of *Song of Surrender* with the film's London-born co-star, Claude Rains. "He was such a distinguished actor and gentleman, it was hard to believe that he was ever in such a low rent potboiler," Eva said. "I'm sure he was doing it just for the money. I told him that when *The Invisible Man* opened in Budapest in 1933, lines formed around the block"

"I was overdressed and looked ridiculous," **Eva** lamented when she saw her publicity stills for *Song of Surrender*.

"I wanted to be Garbo, and here I was cast as the glamourous Countess Marina, which did nothing for me."

[The Invisible Man, starring Claude Rains in his first American screen appearance, and co-starring Gloria Stuart, is usually cited as one of the great horror films of the 1930s.)

"Claude told me an amazing story. He'd been born with a serious Cockney accent and a speech impediment, but in time, he taught elocution to such actors as John Gielgud and Laurence Olivier. He's remembered today by Bette Davis fans for costarring with her in *Now, Voyager* (1942)."

Eva became like an older sister to the female star of the picture, Wanda Hendrix, a beautiful brunette from Florida, who had come to Hollywood at the end of World War II. She'd just recently completed *Prince of Foxes* (1949) with heartthrob Tyrone Power. Ironically, he was the actor who was to become the love of Eva's life.

Hendrix was disappointed with both the direction of her career and with her marriage. "The pictures I've made are putting me on the road to oblivion," she complained to Eva. "That road is already scattered with thousands of bodies. I want juicy parts, but they always go to other actresses. My constant failures on the screen are driving me crazy, that and my marriage to Audie Murphy."

Ironically, Hendrix had become more famous for her marriage than for her movies. She'd wed a Texas sharecropper's son who became the most decorated soldier of World War II, having killed some 240 Nazi soldiers in combat. The baby-faced foot soldier had appeared on the cover of *Life* magazine for his receipt of the Congressional Medal of Honor. Hollywood had honored the war

hero by giving him a movie contract.

Audie's biographer, Don Graham, summed up the soldier's tragic life: "Just beneath the surface of his life lay a numbness, a delayed stress relieved only by bouts of womanizing, nocturnal adventures, reckless gambling, and dangerous practical jokes. Murphy would survive into the Vietnam era as an anachronism of sorts, whose baroque schemes for financial salvation plunged him into the American political and criminal netherworld— a hero badly out of his time."

One of his practical jokes, as he defined them, involved "driving around late at night shooting at niggers," a pastime he'd first practiced growing up in Texas.

Hendrix found Eva a sympathetic soul. She told Eva, "Everything I do, even the clothes I wear, invites Audie to criticize me. Almost every night he has me sobbing. He even attacks the wattage in the living room bulbs. Once he threw pancakes in my face when he claimed there weren't enough blueberries in them. If I stay married to him, I think I'll end up in an asylum."

"Every night, in his nightmares, he fights World War II," she said. "He always carries a .45 around with him, and he's a great shot. One night, he jumped up screaming, grabbed his pistol, and started firing in all directions. He has guns all over the house. He never feels secure unless he's near a gun."

One day, Hendrix showed up for work and couldn't face the camera," Eva said. "She and Audie had had a brutal fight the night before, and she was almost suicidal."

"I beg him to see a psychiatrist, but he refuses," Hendrix said. "Sometimes he points a gun at my head and threatens to blow my brains out. Or else he'll put a gun in his own mouth and threaten to commit suicide."

The World War II hero was suffering from one of the war's worst cases of post-combat stress syndrome, and often experiencing "blackouts," where he couldn't remember what he'd said or done.

Once, Eva joined the unhappily married couple for lunch in the commissary. "I lost my appetite," Eva later recalled. "Audie told us this awful story of being trapped behind enemy lines during the war. He almost came face to face with a Nazi security guard."

"When I was less than a foot away, I caught him by surprise and shot him in the head," Murphy claimed. "My mouth was open. Some of his brain matter blew right inside, and I'm no cannibal."

Instead of lunch that afternoon, Eva settled for black coffee.

Somehow Murphy became convinced that his wife was having an affair with Carey. One afternoon he showed up on the set with his .45. When he spotted Eva, he called her "a Nazi bitch," and fired in her direction. "The bullet just missed my head."

On his way to Hendrix's dressing room, Carey spotted him and tackled him from the rear, wrestling the pistol from him. Security guards arrived, and Murphy was restrained and hauled away in an ambulance.

"He was taken to an asylum," Eva said. "The studio didn't want to call the police and have them come and arrest America's most decorated war hero. It would have caused an awful scandal."

"After the filming of *Song of Surrender,* I decided once again that the movies were not for me, Eva said. "I still nurtured my dream of having that showroom in Las Vegas that Bugsy had promised me."

***

Eva could not really sing or dance, but Bugsy Siegel hired both a vocal coach and a dance instructor to help her prepare for her night club act at the newly opened Flamingo Hotel in Las Vegas. He also signed two different comedy writers to work up an act for her, and commissioned Orry-Kelly to design a spectacular wardrobe for her.

The construction of the Flamingo had been mired in troubles from the beginning. Its original developer, William Wilkerson, had run out of funds, and Bugsy had taken over. At a disastrous Christmas opening in December of 1946, nothing had worked properly, including its air conditioning system, which had utterly failed in the scalding desert heat. In the embarrassing aftermath, the hotel was closed, eventually reopening three frantic months later, in March of 1947.

At one point, Bugsy revealed to Eva, "I've worked this desert outpost before. I provided illicit services to the crews constructing the Hoover Dam." She didn't ask him what kind of illicit services, but assumed that prostitution had been part of the agenda.

"I plan to reinvent myself as a respectable businessman with the Flamingo," Bugsy told Eva. "All the big stars will turn out for your opening night. I plan to have Frank Sinatra get up on stage with you and do two numbers. Lucille

Ball, Lana Turner, Betty Grable, June Haver, and most definitely George Raft will be there to welcome you. I can blackmail Milton Berle and Bob Hope to show up too."

"Getting the Flamingo up and running has been a nightmare," Bugsy said. "Because of wartime shortages, I had to skim building materials from the black market, paying exorbitant prices. But this hotel will have the best gambling, the best liquor, the best food, and the best entertainment in the business. All the high rollers will flock to the Flamingo. Once the word gets out, they'll also be coming to see you."

Eva was thrilled at such an opportunity, and she was especially impressed after her tour of the 93-room hotel. Its cost would eventually soar to $6 million, which would convert into about $65 million in today's currency.

"I'm going to build this place into the richest gold town in history," Bugsy vowed. "American high rollers are going to lose more gold at gaming tables here than what was dug up during the Gold Rush of 1849."

"In your showroom here, you'll be on the entertainment map of America," Bugsy said to Eva. "That is, honey doll, if you keep loving this man of yours."

"You are the man of my dreams," Eva said.

Even though her marriage and divorce from **Conrad Hilton** had transpired years before, he and **Zsa Zsa** always remained on friendly terms. They could even share a laugh on occasion about some of the good times they'd had together.

"I learned from you never to marry a rich man," Zsa Zsa told Conrad. "They're too stingy with their money."

During her affair with Bugsy, Eva made it a point not to pry into his business operations. She didn't want any insights into how he earned money from operations which included dope smuggling, bookmaking, and white slave rackets.

Only because it was widely discussed at Hollywood parties did she learn how he extorted money from Hollywood studios. He would approach a studio chief such as Jack Warner and more or less demand a "loan," an outlay of hard cash that would never be repaid. Privately with Eva, he defined these movie moguls, including Louis B. Mayer, as "klutzes."

What Eva couldn't understand was why these producers and CEOs, including Samuel Goldwyn, kept inviting Bugsy to their homes for cocktails and private dinners, even though during daylight hours, he was extorting money from them. Eva and Bugsy were regularly entertained at such restaurants as Romanoff's with men like Warner and Goldwyn picking up the lavish tabs.

[Ironically, it would be Zsa Zsa, not Eva, who eventually opened with a one-woman show at the

Flamingo. Her act was a sensation. Even her ex-husband, Conrad Hilton, showed up on opening night, as part of his first visit to Las Vegas. Conrad not only saw the act, but bought the hotel.

In the middle of her act, Zsa Zsa, on stage, quipped, "My former husband, Conrad Hilton, is in the audience tonight. As part of my divorce settlement, he gave me five million Gideon Bibles."

Conrad stood up and shouted at her, "Then why don't you read one?"

After he purchased the Flamingo, Conrad never invited Zsa Zsa to appear there again.

Even so, she would maintain friendly relations with him until his death. She showed up with a small Christmas tree in December of 1978.

She found a priest by his side at St. John's Hospital in Santa Monica. In a glamorous outfit, perfumed and coiffed, she had come to say her farewell. "He still had his toupée on, but his false teeth were out, and he looked like a dying old man, not the virile Texan I had known."

She later wrote, "Seeing him this way—Conrad who had been so big, so strong, and so powerful—was one of the saddest moments of my life. He couldn't talk anymore."

He died on January 3, 1979, at the age of ninety-one, leaving $365 million to his beloved Catholic Church. "I think he was trying to buy his way into heaven," Zsa Zsa claimed.]

***

Eva

One night at Ciro's, Eva showed up with actor Hugh Marlowe. Virginia Hill—Bugsy's number one gun moll—decided to visit too. Gangster Joe Adonis, her other longtime "flame," was her escort that night.

As Hill's biographer, Ed Reid, maintained, "There have been many women in criminal history, but never before anything quite like Virginia Hill. Sharp, and smart, completely different. A liberated woman, long before the term was invented. She was relatively free to do her own thing and run as she pleased—but only on a leash of gold held by the Mob. She was a flesh-and-blood computer of silk, satin, and whore instincts."

Eva was in the women's room at Ciro's checking her makeup when Hill entered. "It's about time me and you had a little chat," Hill said to Eva.

"I have nothing to say to you," the astonished Eva said.

"Listen, bitch, I'm Virginia Hill, your worst enemy. You have a very pretty face, and I'd hate to see you lose it. Some boys I know carry around acid in a bottle. The liquid in one of those bottles can change your complexion more than any face cream."

"You wouldn't dare!" Eva said, her alarm mounting.

"Try me!" Hill said, moving so close to Eva's face that she peppered her with saliva. "If I ever catch you with Bugsy again, the boys will make you regret it to your dying day. I assure you, after they're through with you, no man will ever look at you again, except in horror." Then she stormed out of the women's room.

Eva stood there petrified before she began to sob. Encountering Hill had been terrifying. After that, Eva continued to see Bugsy, but only rarely and then under very secret conditions.

In June of 1947, he invited her to spend four or five days with him in a house that Hill had rented in her name. Bugsy was occupying the building with Allen Smiley, his associate and a self-styled movie director. The gun moll had relinquished her lease on Rudolf Valentino's Falcon Lair and in its place had rented this Moorish-style castle at 810 North Linden Drive in Beverly Hills. Hill, who had departed on a shopping expedition to Paris, wouldn't be anywhere near the premises.

Eva accepted Bugsy's invitation, but with the understanding that instead of arriving on June 21, in accordance with the original terms of the invitation, she wouldn't be available until June 24 because of a scheduling conflict.

"When Eva picked up the morning paper on June 21, she screamed at the picture that appeared on the frontpage. That previous night, Bugsy had been assassinated within Hill's rented castle.

Targeted for assassination by Lucky Luciano, gangster **Bugsy Siegel** died a violent death in Virginia Hill's rented castle in Beverly Hills.

The police snapped this death photo and released it to newspapers in all its bloody horror.

With his death, Eva's dream of a Las Vegas showroom of her own came to an abrupt end.

He had been sitting with Smiley reading a copy of *The Los Angeles Times.* French doors in the living room opened onto a terrace. Cigarette butts indicated that the assassin had waited there for hours to get a clear shot at Bugsy with his .30 caliber military M1 carbine. Many shots were fired into Bugsy, including three directly into his head.

At a meeting of the mob's "board of directors" in Havana over the Christmas holiday of 1946, Bugsy had been targeted for murder. Exiled by U.S. authorities from ever entering the U.S. again, and visiting Havana from had become his new home in Sicily, Lucky Luciano had charged Bugsy with stealing millions from the mob. It was understood by Luciano's henchmen that Bugsy's execution would be scheduled for some time during the upcoming spring.

After his assassination, a photo of Bugsy's

lifeless body appeared on the front pages of newspapers across the country. He was depicted lying on a slab in the morgue, his bare right foot sporting a toe tag.

In the aftermath of his death, Eva said, "That Virginia Hill monster sure picked a convenient time to go shopping in Paris. I'm sure she knew that Bugsy was going to be brutally murdered...and in her own home."

In Rome, an American reporter, Mike Stern, approached Luciano in the lobby of the Albergo Savoia. When he was asked about the assassination, Luciano replied, "Sure I murdered Bugsy. Why not? I'm the King of Vice, the King of Dope, and Public Enemy Number One. Now is there anything else you want me to confess to—any baby snatches, ax murders?"

In the years to come, Eva was asked only once about her widely conjectured association with Bugsy Siegel. She responded in anger. "I never met him. I went on two or three dates with George Raft, and I think he may have known Mr. Siegel. I know nothing about America's gangland, other than what I've seen in the movies. Ask Virginia Hill. I couldn't even play a gun moll on screen. A director could hire Gloria Grahame. She'd be great in such a role."

[Time magazine described Virginia Hill as "The Queen of Gangster Molls." In 1951, she was subpoenaed to testify before the Estes Kefauver hearings in Washington. As the magazine later reported, "Hill spent her time on the witness stand boggling Senators with her full grown curves and explanations of just why men would lavish money on a hospitable girl from Bessemer, Alabama."

Indicted for income tax evasion, she fled to exile in Switzerland in 1954. Over the years, confronting fast-dwindling resources, she attempted to blackmail the Italian-American Mafia with incriminating evidence.

On March 24, 1966, at the age of 49, her body was discovered near Koppl, an Austrian town close to Salzburg. Her death was ruled an apparent suicide from an overdose of sleeping pills.

In Hollywood, when she heard the news, Eva said, "Suicide, my foot. She was murdered. Bugsy himself once told me that anyone who attempted to blackmail the mob ended up as a feast for the sharks."]

***

Eva continued to see the troubled actor, Robert Walker. From her discussions with him, she surmised that both Robert and Peter Lawford were dating the same woman, MGM starlet Nancy Davis. Davis would soon be dating Ronald Reagan, even though he had a roster of other women also vying for his attention, including the singer/actress Doris Day.

Walker, who was still mourning the loss of his wife, Jennifer Jones, to David O. Selznick, would sometimes talk about Davis:

"Nancy goes for that vulnerable little-boy-lost quality in me," Robert told Eva. "When I'm around her, I emphasize that particular trait in my character. But I'll soon be losing her, too. She told me that in the long run, Ronald Reagan would be a better provider than I'll ever be."

As the months wore on, Eva noted that Walker's consumption of alcohol had increased. Once, she arrived at his home to find him "plastered" before noon, morosely sunk into the sofa in his living room wearing somewhat soiled underwear.

"I asked to help him, prepare him some lunch, or whatever," Eva said, "but he was mean and surly, ordering me out of his house. I left and never returned, although I wasn't really angry at him. If anything, I felt sorry for him. I feared that he was headed for self-destruction."

"One night, I encountered both Ava Gardner and Robert drunk together at a bar in Malibu," Eva said. "I was with Phillip Terry. I spoke to them, but they virtually ignored me. They were making a picture together called *One Touch of Venus* (1948). I later learned that for Ava, it was just a casual affair. She was devoting more serious attention to Howard Duff. But Robert gave his heart away to Ava, who tossed it back at him."

"He called me once or twice to go out," said Eva, "but at the time, I had my own problems. I couldn't cope with his alcoholism. I was startled when he married Barbara Ford in 1948. She was the daughter of John Ford. I also would have marriages that lasted for only a few weeks."

"In spite of my troubled relationship with him, I was heartbroken to learn of his death," she said.

On the night of August 21, 1951, his housekeeper discovered him hysterical and threatening suicide. She telephoned his psychiatrist, who rushed over and administered amobarbital to sedate him.

Unknown to the doctor, Walker, at the age of 32, had consumed an inordinate amount of liquor that morning. When the sedative combined with the alcohol in his system, it catalyzed a fatal physical reaction. He stopped breathing. All efforts to resuscitate him failed.

Radio stations across America interrupted their regular programming to announce the tragic news.

When she learned of his death, Eva remembered the last time they'd gone out together. He had told her, "As a kid I knew I was never meant to be born into this world. I've spent my life trying to escape this place, wanting to go back to the peace I knew before I entered it."

"Robert's death was the beginning of many Hollywood tragedies in the 1950s and 60s," Eva said. "My challenge was not to become one of the casualties. I had to leave California, perhaps for good, and seek a new life in New York. Once again, my dream was to be a star on Broadway. This time, God damn it all, I made it!"

***

 Disappointed with her reception in Hollywood, Jolie flew back to New York.

Magda met her at the airport and welcomed her back. On the following night, she dined with Vilmos.

He told Jolie, "I'm an old Hussar. I will never fit into the American way of life. I'm going back to my homeland to live out my days in Budapest, even though it's now ruled by the Soviets."

Magda telephoned Eva and convinced her to patch up her relationship with Jolie. "Their little feud was too silly," Magda said. "We Hungarians have such tempers."

In need of money, Jolie reopened her hole-in-the-wall jewelry shop. For an emergency window display, she used whatever jewelry, mostly costume, that she still had left.

From Budapest, she'd received a cryptic unsigned postcard curtly informing her: "The jewelry you had deposited in that Hungarian bank was confiscated by the Russians." She never knew if that were true or not. Perhaps the friend she'd left the jewelry with during the moments prior to her hasty exit from Budapest had stolen it instead.

Gradually, customers started coming into her shop, which for a while became known—thanks in part to word-of-mouth advertising by Magda—as a purveyor of high-quality copies of antique Austro-Hungarian crown jewels. Magda also convinced Jolie to post a *GOING OUT OF BUSINESS* sign. "People will think they're getting steals, and will patronize the shop," Magda assured her mother.

She was right.

Adhering to the old Hungarian proverb, *WHO WAKES EARLY FINDS GOLD*, Jolie arrived for work every morning at 7am, cleaning, dusting, and polishing her inventories of costume jewelry. Magda usually slept until 10:30am, since she had quickly moved into New York's society party circuit in the same way that Zsa Zsa had when she first arrived in New York.

New Yorkers were impressed with Magda's title, and she was addressed as "Your Excellency, the Countess Bychowsky." With her striking red hair, green eyes, and porcelain white skin, Magda quickly became the darling of the megawealthy. She was a desirable guest at dinners, especially whenever a male VIP guest arrived from Europe without a wife or mistress and needed a female partner at lavish dinner parties.

Based partly on Magda's urging, Jolie stopped selling "junk" and began

377

offering quality cultured pearls, some of them from Rosenthal, a high-end purveyor of luxury goods which imported the pearls from the Far East.

It was never clear exactly where Magda was living at any given time, and Jolie was too polite to ask. Her temporary residence at the Plaza had ended in the wake of Zsa Zsa's divorce from Conrad Hilton. She met a Hungarian couple who were flying to Vienna to live. They relinquished to Jolie their $59-a-month lease on a one-room apartment with a sink and a gas range.

The building that contained her new apartment seemed like a good investment when it was put on the market. Now that she was speaking to her youngest daughter again, Jolie urged Eva to purchase it. "It's a steal and you'll probably be able to support yourself from its income."

From California, without seeing the building Eva used her limited funds to buy it. "The first thing she did," Jolie complained to Magda, "was to raise my rent. In protest, I'm stopping all future rent payments."

During her nightly social rounds, Magda touted the glories of Jolie's little shop. Soon, female members of Manhattan's super-rich set were showing up to buy such items as a handmade clasp, a copy of something worn by the 18th-century Empress, Maria Theresa.

The patriarch of the Gabor family, **Vilmos Gabor,** soon realized he was not destined to become an American.

"English is a ghastly language, and America is not a fit place to live in. Even though the commies have taken over Budapest and seized all my property, I'm going back home. There's a little girl waiting for me."

Jolie began to make money. When a shop next door became available after its owner had a stroke, Magda urged her to purchase the lease and expand her premises. Jolie followed Magda's advice. "She was always the most sensible of my daughters, except when it came to picking husbands."

Jolie acquired the lease for $8,000 and asked Zsa Zsa and Eva to give her the final $2,000. Both daughters refused, fearing that Jolie would never be able to pay back the loan.

Consequently, Magda persuaded one of her new friends, socialite Elizabeth Whitney, to purchase $2,000 of cultured pearls, and subsequently, Jolie acquired the new premises.

Whitney and Magda had become "fast friends," and subsequently, the heiress introduced Magda to her upper-crust contacts. Her glittering list of friends included Prince Aly Khan, the world's most desirable bachelor.

Whitney had an estate in the hunt country of Virginia, and invited Magda down for a week. On her first day there, she called Jolie in New York. "You should see the place. It even has a drawbridge and a moat surrounding the castle. When Elizabeth lets down the drawbridge, horses come onto the terrace and through the open doors into the living room. There's horseshit everywhere."

As her male escort during the week she spent at the Whitney's country estate, Magda was assigned a Hollywood writer, William Rankin.

In her next phone conversation with Jolie, Magda asked, "Have you ever heard of the screen writer, William Rankin?"

"No," Jolie said. "Should I?"

"Well, *Nuci,* you will hear of him now, because I married him last night."

***

From the beginning, Jolie was suspicious of Magda's newly acquired husband. In her memoirs she wrote, "Magda got married for a few minutes to something named William Rankin. He is a Hollywood writer who I think was only writing home for money. She got rid of him as quickly as she married him."

In Hollywood, Magda introduced Rankin to Eva and Zsa Zsa. During a conversation with Greg Bautzer, Zsa Zsa learned that "Rankin's only claim to fame was a blow-job he got from Judy Garland" when she was filming *The Harvey Girls* (1946), which had been based in part on a script he had written.

Rankin was a not very successful American playwright and screenwriter who had contributed, often uncredited, to a number of film scripts in the 1930s, including *Pennies From Heaven* (1936) and *Only Angels Have Wings* (1939).

Magda telephoned Jolie almost daily, rhapsodizing about her new husband. "Oh, *Nuci,* he's bought me a mink coat and a red car."

"Can he afford all these luxuries?" Jolie asked.

"He can afford anything, even me," Magda answered.

Two months later, she had changed her opinion. "I threw the bum out. He tried to borrow money from me. He's also an alcoholic."

Almost at the same time as that announcement, bills arrived at Jolie's shop for Magda's mink coat and red car.

Magda's divorce from Rankin wasn't finalized until August of 1947. During that time, she dated other men. At one party, she was introduced to another friend of Whitney's.

The next morning, Magda called Jolie: "I met the most divine man last night. He's asleep in the next room, so I must speak softly. He's worshipped as a deity by millions."

"Who is this divine creature," Jolie asked. "Not another Rankin bum?"

"No, no, *Nuci,"* Magda said. "He's worth tons of millions and known all over the world. He's Prince Aly Khan."

***

At long last, Zsa Zsa's wet dream became real when she met the object of her romantic fantasy, George Sanders.

In April of 1947, the flowering trees in Manhattan's Central Park were in blossom, and she was at last free of her marriage to Conrad Hilton.

"I was the gay *divorcée*," she claimed, "and at the top of the list of any lavish party being thrown in New York. Every wolf in Manhattan was drooling at the mouth for me."

Her historic meeting of Sanders, born in 1906 to British parents in Imperial St. Petersburg, Russia, occurred inside the deluxe apartment maintained by Wall Street banker Serge Semenenko. That apartment was stylishly situated within the St. Regis Hotel, on Fifth Avenue at 55th Street in Manhattan.

When Zsa Zsa appeared in the doorway in a clinging black silk jersey dress, the creation of the then-famous designer "Alexis," all male eyes except one set turned and gazed appreciatively upon her glittering entrance. Her diamonds sparkled. The only man who didn't look at her was Sanders himself, surrounded at the time with adoring women.

Because the host was too preoccupied to introduce Zsa Zsa to her idol, she walked over to him and said, "Mr. Sanders, I'm Zsa Zsa Gabor, and I'm madly in love with you."

He eyed her skeptically. "How very understandable. Very understandable indeed."

"In person, you're just as irresistible as you were on the screen when you played Charles Strickland in *The Moon and Sixpence.*"

"Oh, that dreary thing," he said.

Zsa Zsa later told her friends, "My god, he was even taller than Conrad Hilton. He devoured me with those striking blue eyes of his. I felt he was undressing me. He was ever so good looking, a man of elegance and taste with what appeared to be the body of an Olympic athlete."

"In spite of dreadful manners and arrogance, he was a perfectly preserved male specimen at the age of forty-one," she recalled. "His face was bronzed from the California sun, and he wore Old World dinner clothes with pearl studs on his tailored black silk suit."

Without being invited, she sat down, and he joined her on the sofa. "I don't like attending parties and being surrounded by beautiful women. Actually, I don't particularly like women—they bore me."

"You're speaking about other women," she said. "I've never been boring in my life."

Before the party ended, Erich Maria Remarque had joined Zsa Zsa and Sanders. The novelist and the actor, who were friends, had arrived together at the party. When he saw her, Remarque kissed Zsa Zsa on the lips.

"I had no idea you scandalous international figures even knew each other," Sanders said, "although I don't know why anything surprises me anymore."

When the three of them grew bored with the party at the St. Regis, Zsa Zsa suggested that they return to her penthouse apartment on Manhattan's East Side for a nightcap of vodka "with caviar, of course, *dahlink.*"

As Zsa Zsa prepared drinks and served Beluga, the two men chatted about Remarque's latest novel, *Arch of Triumph.* He reported that it was being adapted into a motion picture, starring Ingrid Bergman, Charles Boyer, and Charles Laughton. *[It was eventually re-leased in 1948.]*

"I found this pre-war novel a bit sluggish," Sanders said. As Zsa Zsa soon learned, he delivered a lot of blunt and often abrasive opinions.

By two o'clock, Sanders announced to Remarque, "Since three is a crowd, do I have to fight a duel over Zsa Zsa tonight? When I was a young man in Chile, a man challenged me to a duel. He caught me with my landlady, who just happened to be his *fiancée.* I wounded my opponent, but didn't kill him. I was kicked out of the country."

"That won't be necessary tonight," Remarque said. "I'm meeting Marlene *[Dietrich]* at the Plaza for early morning cocktails."

"That means I'm staying," Sanders said.

Zsa Zsa later claimed that she was infuriated at Sander's casual announcement that he'd be sleeping over. "Who did he think he was? Did he take me for some tramp? Did he just assume that I would give in to his sexual demands?"

In spite of her private protestation, she did submit to him. After Remarque left, Sanders grabbed her by the waist with both hands and pulled her down onto the sofa. Passionate kissing led to a trip upstairs to her boudoir.

When he woke up beside her late the next morning, he said. "'Zsa Zsa' doesn't suit you. From now on, I'll call you *Cokiline.* In Russian, that means 'sweet little sugar cookie.'"

Two views of the arrogant, cynical (and ultimately, suicidal) **George Sanders**. He was to become Zsa Zsa's third husband, and her most troubled relationship.

When she saw his performance as a self-destructive alcoholic painter *(lower photo)* in *The Moon and Sixpence,* she announced to Jolie that Sanders was "the man I'm going to marry."

And she did.

Zsa Zsa confessed in a memoir that she, indeed, shared intimacies with Sanders that long ago night in Manhattan. She never went into clinical detail, but later claimed, "If I could live my entire life over again, I would spend every minute of it with George. If I live until the end of time, I'll never find another George Sanders."

Zsa Zsa and Sanders would not pledge fidelity to each other except on the day they got married, two years later. During the weeks ahead, Zsa Zsa faced a formidable arsenal of women who were also vying for the actor's affection.

They included Gene Tierney, with whom Sanders had engaged in an affair since 1941 when they appeared together in the film, *Sundown*. Hedy Lamarr had loomed on the horizon ever since they filmed *The Strange Woman* together in 1946. There was also Lucille Ball, with whom he had become attached when they co-starred in *Lured* (1947).

Also on the scene was the Mexican beauty, Dolores Del Rio. Tobacco heiress Doris Duke was also a contender. Not only that, but Sanders was still married to actress Susan Larson, whom he had wed in 1940.

Sanders dated Zsa Zsa frequently, but often they were separated. During those times, he scheduled "reunions" with all of these other fabled women.

Zsa Zsa, however, was not sitting home alone. Although she would have preferred to date Sanders exclusively, she filled up not only her social calendar but her boudoir with an impressive array of men. Multi-millionaire Bob Topping became one of her conquests. "I broke him in for Lana Turner," Zsa Zsa later facetiously claimed. "She made the mistake of marrying Bob. I was far too savvy for that."

***

In Manhattan, Jolie gave the first of many interviews to the press. Some of her comments never saw the light of publication. She told a reporter, "The 1950s are around the corner, a new decade and a new life for me and my fabulous daughters, Magda, Zsa Zsa, and Eva."

"I don't want to exaggerate—the way certain men do about the size of their penises. But the Gabors, especially Eva and Zsa Zsa, are about to become household words in America."

CHAPTER NINE
Public Images, Private Pain

In her efforts to persuade George Sanders to marry her, Zsa Zsa had to eliminate some formidable competition. The first and most unlikely candidate was Lucille Ball, the reigning Queen of the Bs. Her bandleader husband, Desi Arnaz, was frequently gone for long periods of time, performing on the road. At night in almost any city he visited, he found his own harem of willing, nubile girls.

Lucille was not an actress who liked to sleep alone. In the absence of her husband, she launched a series of affairs, including one with Peter Lawford.

In 1947, she became enamored of her leading men from two different pictures, *Lured,* co-starring George Sanders, and *Her Husband's Affairs,* co-starring Franchot Tone. Tone and Lucille were sexually involved even during his marriage to Joan Crawford in the 1930s.

Complicating matters during his involvement with Lucille Ball, Zsa Zsa continued her "sometimes fling" with Tone, who, on occasion, was rumored to still to sleep over from time to time at Crawford's home.

"This Ball creature is moving in on my territory," Zsa Zsa claimed to friends—first with Franchot, then with George."

"I don't know what men see in her," Zsa Zsa said. "She has no breasts at all. Perhaps she fulfills some homosexual leaning in these men, who sometimes prefer a flat-chested boy. Two high-class men like Franchot and George should be ashamed of themselves for running around with this low-class hussy from hell."

Once, when Sanders was with her at her New York apartment, Zsa Zsa picked up an extension of her phone and overheard Lucille talking to him.

"Why in the fuck are you hooked up with the Hilton woman?" Lucille asked Sanders. "What a bitch! What a gold digger! You know I love you. She's completely wrong for you."

During her eavesdropping, Zsa Zsa heard Sanders confirm a date for the following night with Lucille. She chose not to confront him about it. She was

In the late 1940s, **Lucille Ball** *(above)* and Zsa Zsa were locked into a cat-fight as to which of them would get George Sanders. "Love," Lucille said, "I was always falling in love."

The list of her lovers was long, and included Robert Mitchum, George Raft, Peter Lawford, Broderick Crawford, Milton Berle, Brian Donlevy, Henry Fonda, and Orson Welles.

not married to him and wouldn't be for many months to come. And because he was still married to actress Susan Larson, her negotiating position was weak

To Zsa Zsa's annoyance, Lucille and Sanders did little to conceal their involvement. In Hollywood, they were sometimes spotted dining together at a restaurant or drinking together at a nightclub.

In years to come, Lucille once discussed Sanders with Vivian Vance, her co-star in the TV series, *I Love Lucy.* And she made comments to other friends, too. "Desi was the only one who meant anything to me. Most men came and went in my life so fast, I hardly remembered them, except for George Sanders. What a man!"

"He had the best legs of any man in Hollywood. George told me he got his start as a chorus boy dancing on the London stage because a director 'went bat shit over my gorgeous legs.'"

Both Lucille and Zsa Zsa remembered Sanders when, tanked up on vodka, he sometimes struck them, often hard enough to knock them down on the floor. He told his best friend, actor Brian Aherne, "A woman, a dog, and a walnut tree—the more you beat them, the better they be."

Lucille admitted to Vance and others that she had once seriously considered divorcing Arnaz to marry Sanders. "But the arrogant snob never proposed to me, unlike Sammy Davis, Jr., who wanted to marry me. He told me I wouldn't know what sexual pleasure was until I'd tried a black man. In the end, Gorgeous George preferred to wrap those dynamite legs of his around that international tramp and gushing plate of goulash, Zsa Zsa Gabor. Men…who can figure them out?"

***

"Bob Topping, among other specimens, is one of the men I dated while waiting for George Sanders to make up his mind about what to do with me," Zsa Zsa said. "When George was romantically entangled elsewhere, so was I. We have an old proverb in Hungary, 'What is good for the gander is even better for the goose.'"

One afternoon, she received a call from Bob Topping, whom she'd met a few nights previously at a penthouse party in Manhattan. "He wasn't the most gorgeous man I ever dated, but he was a multi-millionaire. Unlike George

Sanders, I knew I wouldn't have to pick up the check, so I agreed to go out with him."

At the Stork Club that evening, he presented her with a pair of diamond earrings. He had a special way of offering the gift, dropping them into a martini glass for her to fish out.

"I hadn't done anything to earn them at that point, but I knew I'd have to pay the piper before the evening was over. Even before he showed up for our date, he'd filled my living room with roses and orchids, so I knew he wasn't stingy like George."

Although she referred to him as Bob, his full name was Henry J. Topping, Jr., heir to a family fortune derived from steel, railroads, and tinplate. "I've heard about steel and railroads, but *dahlink,* what in hell is tinplate?"

At the time Bob started dating her, he was in the process of separating from the B picture actress Arline Judge, a Hollywood-born beauty who in time became more famous for her eight husbands than for her movie roles.

Millionaire sportsman and socialite, **Dan Topping** *(above, left)* became the first husband of **Sonja Henie** *(right),* the ice-skating movie queen.

Zsa Zsa always succumbed to the charms and money of Dan as well as his brother, Bob. "If a girl goes for one brother, she might equally go for the next," Zsa Zsa said. "That's not incest, is it?"

Zsa Zsa later recalled, "Arline and I competed for the number of spouses we'd wed."

Don's brother, **Bob Topping,** is seen here during his marriage to **Lana Turner.** "I turned him down, but Lana went for him, in spite of his Jekyll and Hyde personality," Zsa Zsa said. "I bet she ended up with a lot of black eyes that makeup couldn't cover."

She became very catty in her remarks about Judge: "She married Bob in 1947, and I think during the wedding ceremony, she began plotting her divorce. The honeymoon was hardly over before she announced that she was going to divorce him 'and take everything the bastard has.'"

[Judge was already notorious within the Topping family. In 1937, she had married Bob's brother, Daniel ("Dan") Topping, divorcing him in 1940.]

"There's something indecent about a woman marrying two brothers," Zsa Zsa said. "It sounds incestuous."

[In an ironic role reversal, both Zsa Zsa and Magda would each eventually marry George Sanders.]

"I felt at the time that either of the Topping boys would be great catches in case George fell through," Zsa Zsa said. "Dan was far handsomer than Bob. When I met him, Dan was married to that Sonja Henie thing, the so-called film star—she skated but couldn't act. She'd been an Olympic champion and Hitler's favorite as the ideal Nordic girl."

Bob invited Zsa Zsa for the weekend at the 600-acre Topping estate at Round Hill, Connecticut—an Elizabethan-inspired manor with thirty rooms, a farm, a lake, a greenhouse, and tennis courts. Since she was a horseback rider of renown, Zsa Zsa went riding on horses from the Topping stables.

One weekend, Bob sailed with Zsa Zsa to Bermuda aboard his yacht, *Snuffy,* named after his favorite comic strip character. At the Princess Hotel in Hamilton, he dropped a fifteen-carat marquise diamond into her martini glass, and proposed marriage.

"I no longer believed in returning diamonds to men, but if I had accepted the ring, I'd have been obliged to marry him—and I wasn't ready for that. I had to fish it out and give it back to him. A few months later, he pulled the same diamond-in-the-martini-glass trick with Lana Turner. That dumb blonde accepted."

"The only reason I think Bob married Lana was because she became pregnant, which could destroy the career of a film actress, as shown by the adulterous Ingrid Bergman at the time," Zsa Zsa said. "Regrettably, Lana's baby was stillborn, as was a second baby with Bob."

"My romance with Bob went sour, because he wanted to have babies, and I told him I was no breeder," Zsa Zsa said. "One child was enough for me. If I ever got pregnant again, I was determined to deal with it."

During her brief courtship with Bob, she was brutally exposed to his dark side. By daylight, he could be sweet and generous. But tanked up on a quart of liquor, he demonstrated a Dr. Jekyll and Mr. Hyde personality. He would throw money around recklessly. Once, in Bermuda, he blew $10,000 on a bet associated with the results of a golf putt.

In divorce court, Judge testified that Bob had frequently beaten her and that on two different occasions, he'd shot at her, one bullet narrowly missing her head.

One night, when Bob and Zsa Zsa were dining at the Brown Derby in Hollywood, Judge herself was seated with a beau only five tables away. That morning, in print, Hedda Hopper had referred to Zsa Zsa as an actress. In a loud voice, Judge said derisively, "ZSA ZSA GABOR—AN ACTRESS? The only acting that Hungarian hussy has ever done is on her back!"

Back on the East Coast, through Bob Topping, Zsa Zsa was re-introduced to café society, which Sanders contemptuously dismissed as "all *ennui* and *la dolce far niente.*"

Morning began with the butler delivering Bloody Marys to each of the twelve bedrooms at Round Hill. The drinking continued until the final bottle of champagne was opened after midnight.

"The parties were endless, and the lifestyle of the idle rich completely dissipated," Zsa Zsa said. "All the bedrooms were filled every night with couples...whether married or not, it didn't matter. The Toppings were liberal for their time. Sometimes a couple consisted of two handsome males, or else a rich older man with his young stud *du jour*. On occasion, couples switched partners on Saturday night, and new liaisons were formed on Sunday."

When Bob decided that his heart belonged to Lana Turner, Zsa Zsa switched allegiances and began dating Bob's brother, Dan Topping, who functioned, between 1945 and 1964, as part owner and president of the New York Yankees. In the 1930s, he had also owned, outright, the Brooklyn Dodgers.

"Dan had married the actress Kay Sutton in 1946, but that didn't interfere with his dating," Zsa Zsa said. "If Bob occasionally lost control, darling Dan at times became a maniac, although enchanting. Once, he took me to this out-of-the-way restaurant in rural Connecticut. It had a fireplace. Just for the fun of it, he removed ten-thousand in one-hundred dollar bills from his wallet. He tossed them into the fire. The headwaiter seriously burned his hands trying to retrieve them."

"The Topping brothers pioneered a new lifestyle in America that came to be known as 'come-and-go-husbands,'" Zsa Zsa said. "In a way, they prepared me for my next husband, George Sanders. Talk about come and go."

"Arline Judge and Sonja Henie despised me, but they hated each other even more," Zsa Zsa said. "Dan's kid, the one he had with Arline, told me that his mother said that when he visited his father on the weekends, he should let Sonja have it in the face with her ice skates. Family fun, we call it."

"Bob wasn't the only Topping with a temper," Zsa Zsa said. "One night at Round Hill, Dan got angry at one of the women guests. She had revealed to her husband that Dan had propositioned her. While twelve of us were seated at the table, he ran into the kitchen, assembled an arsenal of heavy iron pots, and re-emerged into the dining room throwing them at his guests."

"The Topping brothers became too much for me," Zsa Zsa said. "I decided to go back to George."

***

Magda

In Manhattan, still in the throes of her divorce from William Rankin, Magda was soon added to Prince Aly Khan's stable of lovers. The list was long, and included Pamela Churchill, and later, Gene Tierney.

Aly Khan was a media headliner, the darling of the paparazzi and the tabloids, who tried in vain to keep abreast of his many romances.

Magda was more overwhelmed by his credentials than impressed—hunter, jockey, pilot, horse breeder, sportsman, daredevil, soldier, multi-millionaire, and religious leader. His family was said to have descended directly from the Prophet Mohammed.

His father, Aga Khan III, was the head of the Ismaili Muslims, which numbered in the millions, mostly in their homelands of Pakistan, India, East Africa, and Indonesia.

In international society, he was hailed as "The Great Lover," and was said to have learned his sexual technique, particularly his stamina, from secrets handed down from the ancient Egyptians.

Sometimes judged as a cosmopolitan maverick among the Ismaelis, he listed his address as "The World." One never knew where he would pop up, living high with *haute* Paris after the war, basking in the glow of the French Riviera or Hollywood and New York, a frequent visitor to Cannes, Beirut, Palm Beach, New Delhi, and Karachi.

At first, Magda compared him to a slimmer version of Orson Welles, and remembered his reputation as an Oriental super stud.

But when she sat with him on a sofa and listened to him talk, she found he was a gentleman of refinement, culture, and exquisite manners. He spoke six languages.

At the party where Magda met the prince, Elsa Maxwell had warned her, "Don't fall for this handsome devil. He's a sybaritic Oriental prince. Enjoy him for tonight because tomorrow, he will be off again to some foreign land and another beautiful conquest. *Prenez garde, mon enfant.*"

"Aly was incredible," Magda claimed. "When he was with Americans, he became a Yankee from New England. When he was with Islamites, he was a Muslim. With a French hostess, he was Jean Gabin; with an English hostess, Laurence Olivier—actually, more Ronald Colman."

"He told me he didn't want to succeed his father as a spiritual leader of millions."

"I want to live in a world of racetracks, night clubs, and gambling casinos, surrounded by only the prettiest women, including you, Magda. I like old wine, new women, and fast cars."

"He also liked to go swimming and dancing. Sometimes we danced until three or four in the morning, cheek to cheek. The waiters would arrive with ham and eggs and chilled champagne. Dare I say, his favorite pastime was making love, which he did with the stamina of a bull."

"When he took me shopping, he was familiar with the houses of Givenchy and Balenciaga. He gave me a diamond-and-sapphire watch from Van Cleef & Arpels."

"I remember waking up one morning in his suite at the Waldorf-Astoria in Manhattan," Magda said. "It was a dull, rainy day. Aly telephoned someone in Palm Beach and learned that it was sunny and bright in Florida. Within two hours, we were on a private plane heading south to the beaches."

"Any woman would have succumbed to Aly's persuasive charm," Magda said. "He was a modern day Casanova. I think he simply could not resist the challenge of a beautiful woman. He was constantly searching for some new feature in his life, some new experience, some excitement."

"I like to go where something wonderful is happening," he told Magda. "Otherwise, I will die."

At a party, Elsa Maxwell asked him, "In a nutshell, what is your philosophy of life, Aly?"

He responded immediately, "Take what you want from life, but be aware you must pay for it."

Eventually, Magda lost Prince Aly to the screen love goddess, Rita Hayworth. Magda called Jolie one morning and said, "It's over."

[In the aftermath of her four-year marriage (1949-1953) to the Aly Khan, Hayworth ruefully observed, "He married Gilda but woke up with me."]

Prince **Aly Khan** and **Rita Hayworth** were photographed during one of the few happy moments in their disastrous marriage.

"I only think of the woman's pleasure when I am in love," the Prince said. "I must have women around me. Life means nothing without them. It didn't necessarily have to be my wife."

Singer-actress Juliette Greco said, "I don't know who didn't have an affair with him."

"As we knew it would be," Jolie said. "But I suspect he hasn't finished with the Gabors, however. After all, I have two other beautiful daughters for Aly to pursue. I'm sure he won't overlook them, especially Zsa Zsa, who might even go for that butterball, the Aga Khan himself."

***

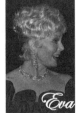

In New York, Eva's agent took her to meet a television producer who was casting a TV drama, *L'Amour the Merrier,* starring Burgess Meredith, whom Eva had met.

The literal English-language translation of its title (*Love the Merrier)* didn't make a lot of sense to her, but she wanted the female lead anyway. When she met with the director, he immediately informed her, "You're far too sophisticated for this role."

The next day, however, he changed his mind and assigned her the minor role of a French girl.

Meredith was impressed with her beauty, and she was awed by his acting ability. He was in the final weeks of his marriage to Paulette Goddard, who had wed him in 1944 after her divorce from Charlie Chaplin.

Hailed as "one of the most accomplished actors of the 20th Century," Meredith was a virtuoso star and a life member of the Actors Studio. Eva had seen him in the 1944 movie, *The Story of G.I. Joe,* in which he had starred as the popular war correspondent, Ernie Pyle.

The critic, Wolcott Gibbs, once said, "Meredith's extraordinary success on stage has practically nothing to do with what he looks like."

The actor himself admitted, "God knows I was not a dashing swain, but in a kind of mongrel way, I chased the foxes," including a pre-Bogart Lauren Bacall.

His list of conquests was impressive—Peggy Ashcroft, Ingrid Bergman, Olivia de Havilland, Ginger Rogers, Norma Shearer, Hedy Lamarr, and Marlene Dietrich.

On his first date with Eva, he invited her to a party that Tallulah Bankhead was hosting within her hotel suite at The Algonquin.

Eva told Meredith of her experience working with Tallulah in *A Royal Scandal,* and he described meeting her when they'd appeared together in *Winter* on Broadway in 1935.

"Tallulah sent word that I aroused her interest, and she swooped down from the sky to pick me off," Meredith claimed. "I realized it was fruitless to resist the siren's summons, so I went to see her."

Meredith went on to claim that during sex with the eminently quotable actress, she had shrieked, "For god's sake, Meredith, don't come inside me! I'm engaged to Jock Whitney!"

When Eva arrived with Meredith at Tallulah's suite at the Algonquin, Tallulah—stark naked—threw open its door. According to Eva, "she grabbed Burgess, tongue down the throat, before giving me that same sloppy experience. At least she was an equal opportunity kisser."

About twenty people were already in the suite, and no one seemed to pay attention to Tallulah's nudity. As hostess, she passed around a silver platter of cocaine for everyone to sample. "It was my first time," Eva said.

A late arrival at the party was actor John Emery, who critics sometimes defined as "the Poor Man's John Barrymore." He had married Tallulah in 1937 in Jasper, Alabama, and they were divorced in Reno in 1941. They had remained friends.

At one point, fueled by cocaine, Tallulah unbuttoned Emery's trousers and shouted to her guests, "Look at this!" She pulled out his flaccid penis. "It's a two-hander and it's not even hard yet!"

Eva wondered how a sensitive-appearing actor like Emery had managed to survive a marriage to Tallulah. When Meredith and Tallulah disappeared together inside her bedroom, Eva chatted with Emery and found him very charming and appealing.

"He was intelligent, exceptionally good looking, and amusing," Eva said. "Unlike Tallulah herself, he had good manners."

He asked Eva if he could call her sometime, and she agreed, giving him her phone number.

After a seduction by Meredith—"for old time's sake, darling," Tallulah had put on a red silk Japanese kimono.

Emery left the party early, and Tallulah pawed him at the door during her goodbye. She must have sensed Emery's fascination with Eva because she called her aside. "Listen, *dahling*, don't be too impressed with John's equipment. Yes, it's very, very long,

When Eva attended her first party in New York, her nude hostess, **Tallulah Bankhead**, threw open the door. She later passed around a platter of cocaine for her guests.

She had been proud of the equipment of her husband, Actor **John Emery**, and often unzipped his trousers to display it for onlookers.

and gets very, very hard. But although the weapon has admirable proportions, the shot is indescribably weak. Try me if you want to be given better head."

At the door, Eva once again felt Tallulah's snake-like tongue seeming to reach the pit of her throat.

Going down in the elevator, Meredith turned to Eva and said, "I talked to Tallulah's best friend, Estelle Winwood, earlier in the evening. She told me that Tallulah has a wonderful heart, but that sometimes it doesn't beat in all the right places."

***

From Hollywood, George Sanders telephoned Zsa Zsa in New York and asked her to come and live with him. Her daughter, Francesca, was reluctantly included in the invitation.

Back in Hollywood, she discovered Sanders living in the house of Gene Tierney, who was out of the country at the time. Sanders and Tierney had begun their on-again, off-again affair when they'd appeared together in *Sundown (1941)*.

Tierney's romance with Sanders had been rekindled when director Joseph L. Mankiewicz had cast them together in *The Ghost and Mrs. Muir (1947)*, with Rex Harrison.

Tierney had already separated from her husband, fashion designer Oleg Cassini. Her beaux had included Howard Hughes, John F. Kennedy, Darryl F.

Zanuck, Tyrone Power, and Mickey Rooney. Somehow, she managed to slip Sanders into her heavily booked datebook.

Zsa Zsa recalled. "Back in Gene Tierney's bed, George proposed marriage to me. Actually, that wasn't quite right. I proposed marriage to him and, after mulling it over, he finally accepted when I threatened to withhold sex from him."

***

During her temporary sojourn within Tierney's house, Sanders announced to Zsa Zsa that he was flying alone to Mexico for a series of meetings, including a reunion with "the most beautiful woman in Mexico," Dolores Del Rio.

"I knew Del Rio and George had been lovers, and I accused him of wanting to resume their affair," Zsa Zsa said.

"The trip is strictly business," Sanders protested. "Everything that went on between us is now ancient history. You know how I hate to pay income taxes. I'm considering setting up a production company in Mexico to avoid them. Dolores, who knows everybody important in Mexico, is arranging a series of business meeting for me."

"If only I could believe you," she said. "You're such a great actor that you're more believable when you lie than when you tell the truth."

While Sanders was south of the U.S. border, Tierney returned unannounced from her trip abroad. She was obviously expecting to encounter Sanders in her home, but instead was greeted by his (new) mistress, Zsa Zsa. It was a difficult encounter.

[In her second memoir, Zsa Zsa placed their meeting at a party. But it was in Tierney's home where the confrontation took place.]

"Blood drained from her face," Zsa Zsa wrote. "I realized that George hadn't told her about us."

Tierney obviously had plans of her own for Sanders and may have been considering him at the time as her future husband.

Shocked to find him living (in her house) with Zsa Zsa, Tierney ordered her out of the home, even though the building had technically been rented to Sanders.

Zsa Zsa climbed the stairs to her bedroom and telephoned Greg Bautzer, who arranged to send movers over to gather up her wardrobe and personal effects. She reached Sanders in Mexico and told him what had happened. He invited her to move into an apartment he owned on Shoreham Drive in Los Angeles.

When she arrived there with the movers, she was terribly disappointed. "It was so small that three fleas would find it overcrowded. Fortunately, George owned an empty apartment next door, and I used it for my extensive wardrobe and a sort of dressing room."

She soon discovered that Sanders had been using the apartment as a hideaway for sexual liaisons. She found a lot of blonde hair in the unmade bed, and more blonde hair stopping up the bathroom sink. To her disgust, she picked up a used "rubber" among the dirty, rumpled sheets on the bed.

"When he returned to Los Angeles, I was going to confront him with this evidence and also to ask him why he had installed an alarm to go off if the bathtub overflowed with water."

On his first night back, Sanders went to Tierney's house and stayed there for five hours. He later told Zsa Zsa that he needed all that time to gather up his possessions.

The next morning, she asked him about the alarm on the bathtub. He told her that in the apartment, he'd had affairs with three Hollywood stars—Ingrid Bergman, Linda Darnell, and Margaret Sullavan. "All three of them had an annoying habit of turning on the water to fill up the bathtub and then forgetting about it. They ruined too many ceilings downstairs, and I had to put a stop to it."

"I also learned the identity of the blonde bimbo," Zsa Zsa said. "The little tramp leaving all those dyed hairs behind was this starlet, Marilyn Monroe. Regrettably, George was about to make a picture with the untalented little hooker."

[Zsa Zsa, of course, was referring to the upcoming 20th Century Fox picture, the 1950 All About Eve, *starring Bette Davis and Anne Baxter, with Sanders and Monroe in supporting roles.]*

Zsa Zsa later wrote that during their time together in the apartment, Sanders insisted on "torturing me with tales of Monroe, calling her a starlet that no one at the Fox commissary wanted to sit next to."

"I find that hard to believe," Zsa Zsa said, challenging his claim. "George was like most men, hopelessly lured to a big bosom and a flea-size brain."

Actually, the reason Fox actors avoided Monroe in those days was because of her involvement with studio moguls Darryl F. Zanuck and Joseph Schenck, each of whom had arranged plastic surgery for her.

"George told me that poetry-writing Monroe was so insecure that if a man asked her out on a date and didn't fuck her, she felt she was no longer sexy."

He also revealed details about his first sexual encounter with the starlet, claiming that one morning, he answered his doorbell wearing nothing but his bathrobe. It was Monroe, clad in a very expensive sable.

"Hello, Mr. Sanders," she said. "I've come to see you." Then she threw open the coat to reveal that she was completely nude underneath.

"I had to make love to her," Sanders confessed to Zsa Zsa. "Otherwise, my reputation was at stake. Had I not done the dirty deed, she would spread the word across Hollywood that I was a homo. In bed, during my workout, Marilyn was too much the professional hooker during ouyr tryst." I prefer to teach young girls sexual tricks. I resent being taught sexual tricks by one so young. She certainly knows the ways of love. She would say things like, 'Howard Hughes loves this,' or 'Peter Lawford just adores this.' Then she would proceed to demonstrate various techniques. Marvelous."

Initially, Zsa Zsa was dismissive of Monroe. "These little dyed blondes come and go in Hollywood. I don't think the public will see much more of Miss Monroe in the future. She'll probably end up disfigured by some hideous venereal disease."

Leaving Monroe in Los Angeles to fend for herself among dozens of other men, Sanders trailed Zsa Zsa back to New York. After some business in Manhattan, he invited her to go on a honeymoon. The only thing lacking during their trip was a marriage license.

***

As a destination for their pre-marriage honeymoon, Sanders wanted to take his bride-to-be on a cross-country trip to show her many of the sights of America. "You'll be a U.S. citizen one day, so you might as well learn that America is not just Hollywood and Manhattan."

Gene Tierney and **George Sanders,** lovers on screen and off, appeared together in this publicity still from their film, *The Ghost and Mrs. Muir.*

Co-star Rex Harrison called Sanders "a perfumed parlor snake both on and off the screen."

Tierney said he was "conceited, erratic, and childish, but so adorable."

Sanders defined himself as "suave, ingratiatingly self-indulgent, with a fatuous honesty--not only irresponsible but unreasonable."

Renting a car, they set out from New York to California with no fixed itinerary. "It was our voyage of discovery," Sanders said.

Zsa Zsa later remembered "picnics along the Mississippi River, ham and eggs for breakfast at Mom & Pop roadside diners on back country roads. I saw motor courts like those where Clark Gable and Claudette Colbert stayed in *It Happened One Night.*"

My husband-to-be was a monster, a self-admitted dreadful man, a professional cad," she said. "But he was my own true love. Although it was heavily masked, he did have his sensitive side. He taught me to enjoy a sunset over the wheatfields of Kansas, or an early morning fog over the Mohave Desert."

On many a night at a truck's stop, over a Blue Plate special, Sanders shared stories of his amazing life. After the Russian Revolution of 1917, the Sanders family fled penniless to Vienna. One of his uncles went with them, salvaging from the wreckage of his fortune only his sable-lined winter coat.

In the old town of Vienna, a drunken Russian *émigré* accosted him with a gun, demanding his coat and his wallet. The uncle had almost no money and his only valuable possession was that coat. The Cossack pulled off his own ragged coat and threw it on the sidewalk, slipping into the valuable overcoat.

When Sanders' uncle got back to the shabby lodgings he had procured for his family, his wife helped him out of the ragged coat, with the intention of cleaning it. To her shock, she discovered that the coat's lining was filled with gold jewelry and diamonds. Obviously the tramp who had made the forced trade never knew that after (supposedly) stealing it from its previous owner.

With that unexpected loot, the Sanders clan made their way to America and a new life.

"As for my own gold and diamonds, I no longer had to worry about those," Zsa Zsa said. "A masked thief had broken into my penthouse apartment in Manhattan as I slept in the nude. He forced me out of bed and made me turn over my jewelry to him. I always slept in diamond earrings, but he didn't seem to notice those. Instead, he demanded the ring on my finger. It was studded with diamonds, rubies, and sapphires. I pleaded with him, and he let me keep it. Good thing that he did. At my wedding to George in Las Vegas, he had not bought me a ring. So I had to lend him the one I still owned, thanks to the generosity of the masked bandit."

Back in Hollywood, Sanders reluctantly attended an A-list party at the Bel Air home of Basil and Ouida Rathbone. On the way there, they drove by the nearby ruins of her former home. Conrad Hilton had not yet rebuilt it.

At the party, Hedda Hopper came up to Zsa Zsa, wearing a wide-brimmed hat that looked like an unkempt garden. "Mrs. Hilton," she said, "Where are you and George Sanders going on your honeymoon?"

In her impudent style, Zsa Zsa shot back, "We've just come from our honeymoon, and will soon be leaving to get mar-

When **George Sanders** played his Oscar-winning role of critic Addison DeWitt with **Marilyn Monroe**, it caused tension with Zsa Zsa. She had wanted him to campaign for her to be cast into the role of the curvy Miss Caswell.

When the part went to Monroe, Zsa Zsa tried to be cast instead as Phoebe, the ambitious newcomer to the theater who, like Eve, pursues success at any cost. "That role went to Barbara Bates," Zsa Zsa later said. "What did it get her? A ticket to oblivion and suicide."

Sanders told Zsa Zsa, "Don't be silly. Acting isn't for you."

ried in Las Vegas."

"Surely, you jest!" Hopper said.

"Not at all," Zsa Zsa answered. "To all prospective brides, I recommend—first, the honeymoon, then the marriage. If the honeymoon is no good, then don't go through with the marriage. A man is like a car. He should be test driven before an actual purchase."

"Now that you are no longer wallowing in the Hilton millions," Hopper asked, "I assume you'll be experiencing a dreadful change in the way you live."

"How right you are. By getting married, I'll lose my alimony payments from Conrad. Not only that, but George is a skinflint. I gave him a 24-carat gold cigarette case, and he demanded that I buy cigarettes with my own money to fill it up."

Zsa Zsa and Sanders were married on April Fool's Day, 1949, at a wedding chapel off the Las Vegas Strip. He rented a minister by waving a ten-dollar bill. "I'd never known him to be so extravagant." Zsa Zsa said.

To stand in as best man, his older brother, actor Tom Conway flew in to Las Vegas. Like his brother, Conway, too, had been born in St. Petersburg.

In the 1940s, Conway had taken over the role of the popular amateur detective, "The Falcon" in nearly a dozen films within that series.

Sanders had originated the role, and Conway was furious at the unfavorable comparisons critics made, with "me coming out on the losing side. I've always lived in George's shadow," he confided to Zsa Zsa. "I love my brother, but at times, I also hate him. I'm very jealous of him. For example, he captured your love, when it should have gone to me. He's always taking roles that I could have done better."

Zsa Zsa later claimed that she was outraged by the behavior of her brother-in-law at a reception following her wedding. "When George left the room, Tom propositioned me. I'm sure that is not the first time a brother-in-law had come on to the bride at a wedding, but it was unforgivable to be so tasteless. Then he said that since I was not available, that he would go after Eva. 'but few men, certainly not me, want to settle for second best.'"

On her wedding night, Sanders told Zsa Zsa, "Now that you are no longer my mistress, and no longer Mrs. Conrad Hilton, but merely Mrs. George Sanders, I don't know if I can get an erection any more."

He also confessed to her, "My moral sense scarcely exists. I'm also a woman hater. Women are so very stupid."

After she returned to Hollywood, the outspoken Zsa Zsa summed up her third husband's character. "I think George wants to be a decadent aristocrat living in 18th Century France before the revolution, or perhaps an Elizabethan rake sodomizing Shakespeare when he wasn't busy writing masterpieces."

As columnist James Bacon said, "You could always count on Zsa Zsa for a great quote. Only trouble was, your editor wouldn't print it."

***

Bored in their small apartment, Zsa Zsa dressed up in her finery and paid an unannounced visit to the set of Sanders' latest picture, *Samson and Delilah,* starring Victor Mature and Hedy Lamarr and directed by veteran Cecil B. De-Mille.

For reasons known only to her, Zsa Zsa claimed in a memoir that she met Lamarr there for the first time, although she'd known her in Vienna and had previously visited her home in Hollywood.

At the studio, wearing full costume and makeup, Sanders appeared before Zsa Zsa as "The Saran of Gaza." She thought he looked dazzling in his tunic. "*Dahlink,* the gold armor shows off your blonde beard and blue eyes. At last you're revealing your studly legs in a movie. That Edith Head obviously knows your best asset."

He snapped at her. "My legs, as you well know, are not my greatest physical asset."

In contrast, Zsa Zsa was not at all impressed when she spotted Hedy Lamarr in her Delilah costume. A few days later, Zsa Zsa told Hedda Hopper, "George looks absolutely fabulous in his costume. But Edith Head didn't do justice to poor Hedy. She looks like a ten-dollar-a-night stripper in some sleazy dive catering to drunken sailors."

Hopper considered the comment, but opted not to print it.

Zsa Zsa's once friendly relationship with Lamarr had moved north into the icefields. She knew that Lamarr and Sanders had had an affair when they'd made *The Strange Woman* together in 1946. Both Lamarr and Zsa Zsa had also had affairs with some of the same men, including Charlie Chaplin, Errol Flynn, Clark Gable, Howard Hughes, and John F. Kennedy. "At least both of us showed our good taste, *dahlink,"* Zsa Zsa later said.

Eva, too, had shared some of Lamarr's lovers. Including her latest fling in New York with Burgess Meredith.

"I've always adored indifferent, unapproachable men," claimed **Zsa Zsa** on her wedding day to **George Sanders** in Las Vegas.

She later recalled their honeymoon in a bleak hotel room. "At first, neither of us spoke. George was thinking of his lost freedom, and I was thinking of my lost alimony from Conrad Hilton."

Lamarr feared that she and Zsa Zsa might one day compete for the same roles should Zsa Zsa decide to become a film actress. "I'm sure that in the future, directors will consider both Zsa Zsa and me for a part." Lamarr told DeMille.

Lamarr was dismissive of Zsa Zsa's marriage. "George Sanders is not a man to wed. Perhaps a brief fling, but hardly marriage. Besides, what is the fun of marrying a man with so little money? What reason could you possibly have?"

"Love, perhaps," Zsa Zsa said.

"Who in Hollywood has ever married for love?" the more cynical Lamarr said.

"That night, George told me why he'd dropped Hedy as his lover," Zsa Zsa said.

"I had cut off the affair because she screams so loudly at curtain call in bed that she wakes up the neighbors," Sanders told her. "Hedy is merely a *poseur,* claiming to be the most beautiful woman in the world when the title clearly belongs to you, my dear."

Before she left the studio that day, Zsa Zsa was introduced to the heavily muscled Victor Mature playing Samson. "Hedda Hopper is going to hate the picture, since she wanted her homosexual son, William Hopper, to be cast as Samson."

He also told her that Cary Grant and James Mason had each been considered before being quickly rejected. More serious consideration had been given to Douglas Fairbanks, Jr., Stewart Granger, Burt Lancaster, Orson Welles, Bruce Bennett, Errol Flynn, Robert Stack, Robert Ryan, and Robert Taylor.

Brothers **Tom Conway** (born "Sanders"; *left)* and **George Sanders** *(right)* were rivals both on and off the screen. They could virtually play the same roles on screen, and often had the same taste in women.

On her wedding day, Zsa Zsa was propositioned by Conway, his brother's best man.

DeMille wanted to honor the newlyweds and invited Sanders and Zsa Zsa to join him in the commissary for lunch. He delivered more casting lore, claiming that for the role of Delilah, Jeanne Crain had been considered, as had Ava Gardner, Rhonda Fleming, Gail Russell, Lana Turner, Jennifer Jones, Vivien Leigh, Susan Hayward, Alida Valli, Greer Garson, Rita Hayworth, and Jean Simmons." DeMille paused. "And are you sitting down? Lucille Ball."

"Well, if Selznick actually considered Ball for the role of Scarlett O'Hara, why not Ball as Delilah?" Sanders asked. Both Zsa Zsa and DeMille knew that Ball had

398

been one of Sanders' mistresses.

"For my own role as the Saran, Cecil here considered Boris Karloff, Michael Redgrave, Ray Milland, John Lund, Macdonald Carey, Charles Boyer, Rex Harrison, and even that nance, Cesar Romero," Sanders said. "I'm sure I was chosen because of my golden legs."

Recalling her meeting with DeMille, Zsa Zsa later told Sanders, "He kept looking down at my feet. He seemed for more interested in my feet than my beautiful face."

"As everyone knows, Cecil has a foot fetish," Sanders said. "That was evident in his close-ups of women's feet in his silent films. Julie Faye, his long-time mistress, often showed her petite feet in close-ups."

"He could never cast Greta Garbo with her clodhoppers in a movie," Zsa Zsa cattily snapped.

Before she left the studio, Zsa Zsa told DeMille, "I wish I were playing Delilah instead of Hedy. Regrettably, I can't act."

"Don't sell yourself short," DeMille told her. "I've known the biggest stars in Hollywood—Valentino, Swanson, Negri, John Gilbert, Garbo. Believe me, my dear, NONE of these legends could act. They had personalities, or as Norma Desmond says in *Sunset Blvd.,* 'they had faces then.'"

Back in her small apartment, feeling trapped in her role as a *hausfrau*, Zsa Zsa grew despondent and complained to her new friend, Pamela Mason, wife of actor James Mason. "I was the Queen of Bel Air. I lived in a mansion with servants. Now I'm doing George's laundry and making him goulash at night. I live in an apartment where fellow tenants are extras, plumbers, mechanics, and waiters. My social status in Hollywood has collapsed.

"This, too, will pass," Pamela said. "Sooner than you think. You'll grow bored and break out."

"But break out where?" Zsa Zsa asked.

"Just wait and see,"

(Left photo) **Pamela Mason** poses with her husband, James Mason, in this family photograph.

In the right-hand photo, Pamela as she appeared on television talk shows, sometimes with her best friend, Zsa Zsa. "To amuse the housewives of America, we often tore into our husbands, snipping off their testicles if the audiences laughed enough at our put-downs."

"Judy Garland, who fucked my husband when they co-starred in *A Star is Born,* told me that I obviously didn't marry him for the sex."

Pamela said. "Welcome the surprises of the future."

***

Fortunately, Richard Rodgers was at home the night *L'Amour the Merrier*—starring Burgess Meredith and Eva Gabor—made its TV debut. The next day, Rodgers called Eva's agent, telling him that he wanted his client to audition for the role of Mignonette in the upcoming Rodgers and Hammerstein Broadway production of *The Happy Time* by Samuel Taylor. It was slated to open on January 24, 1950, at Manhattan's Plymouth Theater.

During the audition, where Eva was so nervous she was shaking, she managed to impress Rodgers in spite of what she considered a very poor reading. He flew her to Boston to audition for the director, Robert Lewis. "I was even more nervous, but he must have seen some quality in me."

That afternoon, Lewis cabled Rodgers in Manhattan. "We've found our *Mignonette.*

In deference to Eva's accent, Lewis changed her character from what had originally been conceived as that of a French Canadian to that of a Hungarian bearing the inappropriate name of Mignonette. "I should have been called 'Ilona,' but it didn't matter. To get this role, they could have called me Brunhild."

Eva had never worked with such a harmonious cast. "It was truly *The Happy Time,*" she said.

Her favorite among the cast members was Kurt Kasznar. "We jabbered away in German." She would remember him as "big, chubby, glib, and dapper...and also as gay as a spring corsage. He was actually mad about the boy, Hollywood's Rock Hudson."

Richard Rodgers *(left)* and **Oscar Hammerstein** were so impressed with Eva that they cast her in their Broadway play, *The Happy Time*, in 1950. The role called for a French Canadian girl, but after they met Eva, they switched the character's origins to Hungary.

"At long last," she said. "My dream had come true. I was a star on Broadway. I thought that star would glitter forever."

In spite of his being a homosexual, he married his second wife, veteran actress Leora Dana, who was also co-starring in *The Happy Time.* Eva also bonded with his bride-to-be.

Dana praised Eva to the press. "No one in the theater ever worked so hard to become a Broadway star," Dana claimed. "Eva could have coasted by on her stunning beauty, but she was dedicated. If the director had wanted it, she would have shaved off that beautiful blonde hair of hers. If the role called for a fatty, she would have packed on fifty pounds. That girl desperately wanted stardom on the stage."

Eva attended the wedding ceremony of Kasznar and Dana, knowing that the marriage probably would not last. "Darling Kurt loved the gay saunas more than Leora's boudoir," Eva told Lewis.

[Leora Dana is still seen on cable TV in the 1958 Some Came Running. *Whereas Shirley MacLaine played the hooker in that film, Leora was cast as the social-climbing wife of small town jeweler Arthur Kennedy.]*

In Eva's play, Mignonette is an out-of-work acrobat who takes a job as a maid with a French family. Her love interest in the play was Richard Hart, a New Englander who had previously appeared in *Green Dolphin Street (1947) with Lana Turner and Donna Reed; and in* Desire

Eva's co-star in *The Happy Time* was the French actor, **Claude Dauphin**. "He fought with De Gaulle's forces against the Nazis in World War II, and was a real hero," Eva said.

"Romantically, Claude and I got nowhere, but Tallulah's ex-, John Emery, became my Stage Door Johnny."

Me *(also in 1947), where he competes with Robert Mitchum for Greer Garson.*

During a month of rehearsals, Eva got to know the other cast members, who included the French actor Claude Dauphin, who was well known within his native France. He told her about his life during World War II when he fought with the free French forces under the direction of Charles de Gaulle.

Eva was amused by the young actor, Johnny Stewart, cast as a twelve-year-old boy, Bibi, who was going through a rough time with puberty. "At first, he resented having to perform our scenes together, all that mushiness, kissing, and what he called sissy stuff," Eva said. "I was supposed to hug and kiss him in a maternal fashion. But during the long run of the play, Johnny grew up. He seemed to have grown an inch every time he came out onto the stage. I soon nicknamed him Hot Lips, and I felt something growing other than his height. Before the play ended, I feared I'd be arrested for contributing to the delinquency of a minor."

During the run of the play, her moment of glory came when *Life* magazine featured her photo on its cover, calling her "a glorious success": and predicting a rosy future for her as a star on Broadway. Zsa Zsa and Magda congratulated Eva but "I knew how jealous they were," she said.

Eva began to appear on television in various roles, which made her even better known. Soon, autograph hunters began to congregate nightly at the stage door. "I had to change from my stage costume and make myself glamorous in mink and diamonds before I faced my adoring public on the street. I felt I had truly arrived. Stardom at last!"

Whenever he was free, actor John Emery showed up backstage to retrieve Eva for a late supper and a night spent in her apartment. "The cast was impressed that I was dating Tallulah Bankhead's former husband, even though they were long divorced."

The son of stage actors—his mother had played little Eva in *Uncle Tom's Cabin*—John Emery had been practically adopted by John Barrymore and his wife, Katherine Harris, which gave rise to rumors that John Emery was the illegitimate son of The Great Profile.

"Personally, I think John tried hard not just to look like John Barrymore, but to actually *be* him as well." Eva said. "That was a tragic mistake to live in someone's shadow like that."

When **Eva** made the cover of *Life* magazine's February 6, 1950, edition, she proclaimed, "I'm the toast of Broadway. But where do I go from here?"

During the course of their love affair, Emery amused her by relating theater lore. He claimed that whenever Barrymore appeared in green tights onstage, he inserted a sock into his crotch. "Just the opposite with me," Emery said. "Directors make me tape my penis up against my belly so that it won't bulge."

He discussed his marriage to Tallulah. "It was like the rise, decline, and fall of the Roman Empire," he said.

One night, Emery proposed marriage to Eva, which would have represented his third trip down the aisle. He'd previously married the Russian ballerina, Tamara Geva, who had been the first wife of the dancer/choreographer George Balanchine. *[Geva had married him when she was only fourteen.]*

Partly because of Emery's legendary endowment, which was highly touted by Tallulah, he was sought out by stars with large sexual appetites, including Rosalind Russell. By the end of his life in 1964, he was living with Joan Bennett, who cared for him throughout the course of his final illness.

"The competition for John's services became too stiff, if you'll forgive the *double entendre,* and I lost him to other stellar lights on Broadway," Eva said. "He also had a devoted gay following."

"In the next few years, I reached my romantic heyday. A parade of gorgeous men, some of the most dazzling on the planet, passed through my life. Some were famous, others merely wanted to be famous, but each one thrilled this little blonde from Budapest."

"I should have kept a detailed diary of my escapades. My 1953 memoir *Orchids and Salami,* was so vanilla, I could have called my second memoir, *The Tumultuous Love Affairs of a Hussar's Daughter.*"

The Rodgers and Hammerstein musical, *The Happy Time,* closed after 614 performances. Eva did not stick around for the final curtain, however, becoming a star on the emerging medium of television instead.

"In just no time at all, I became a household word, *dahlink,*" she said.

***

In New York, Magda was becoming the darling of café society, even more so than Eva and Zsa Zsa who were enjoying social success among the Hollywood elite.

Magda was a frequent guest at the estates of the mega-wealthy in Southhampton, especially in summer. She flirted briefly with an acting career, appearing in minor summer stock productions, mainly in New Jersey and New England.

To support herself, Magda went to work in Jolie's rapidly growing jewelry business. Jolie agreed to pay her $900 a month in wages.

Magda had been matron of honor at her mother's wedding ceremony to Peter Christman. Despite her smiles, Magda frequently warned Jolie that the waiter was marrying her for her money.

Jolie brushed aside such criticism. "At least I have some money coming in from my shop. Remember when I got off the boat, I was penniless?"

Shortly before Vilmos left New York for a postwar life in Hungary under the Soviets, Jolie had asked Christman and Vilmos to dinner. She'd slipped her new husband fifty dollars to pay the bill. Magda tagged along for "the fireworks," but found the dinner peaceful. "Maybe it was because my father spoke no English," Magda said. "Vilmos was a sad, pathetic figure at the dinner. His glory days as a Hussar were long behind him."

"As I predicted, Jolie's marriage to Peter lasted as long as a sickly butterfly," Magda said. "His idea of a fun night involved staying home and having Jolie make him goulash while he listened to Guy Lombardo on the radio. *Nuci* was not destined to lead that kind of life."

Christman came down with such a bad case of pneumonia that it damaged his lungs. His doctor recommended that he move to a dry climate. Fortunately, he'd recently inherited a small little house with an adjoining diner in Arizona. He pleaded with Jolie to go West with him.

"Oh, Magda," Jolie said. "I can't see myself becoming some fat waitress in a roadside diner catering to what Americans call cowpokes."

On the day Christman left, Jolie kissed him goodbye, giving him the Hungarian farewell greeting of "*Isten veled.*" [*(def.)* "*god is with you.*"]

Magda accompanied her stepfather to the airport because Jolie had to visit a wholesaler to purchase more artificial pearls.

"Some very important people were patronizing our shop," Magda said. "Mother had wealthy customers who wanted to look richer than they were, and poor women who wanted to look rich. I was an aristocrat because of my marriage to a Polish count. For her other sales girls, *Nuci* hired French countesses, a German baroness, even a Hungarian princess—the most aristocratic staff in New York. The old European titles meant nothing if you lost everything in the war."

Both Magda and Jolie were in the shop when Nicky Hilton walked in one day to purchase some *faux* emeralds for Elizabeth Taylor, who he planned to marry.

"Two weeks late, Elizabeth herself came in," Magda said. "She purchased a fake diamond-and-emerald necklace. When she did so, she unbuttoned her blouse, revealing her ample breasts before trying on the necklace. She complained to *Nuci* that she regretted that the stones were not real. Mother assured her that with a face like she had and a bust like the one she possessed, she would soon be accumulating real diamonds in her life."

Jolie's shop was attracting the carriage trade, and soon, the press hailed her as "The Queen of Madison Avenue." In some ways, Magda resented all the attention Jolie was receiving. "I wasn't quite like Ann Blyth, Joan Crawford's daughter in *Mildred Pierce,* but there was some jealousy there."

Jolie felt prosperous enough to take Magda along with her the day she signed a contract to purchase a one-family, four-story brownstone on 63rd Street between Madison and Fifth Avenues. The total price was only $42,000, with a $600-a-month mortgage, a remarkable price even in the early 1950s for platinum real estate in Manhattan.

Jolie decided to renovate it and transform it into apartment units. Magda was her first tenant, but for one year, she refused to pay rent until Jolie threatened to evict her.

At a party at the Plaza Hotel, Magda met Sidney Warren, who was described as a "dynamic, intense attorney." At first, Jolie seemed delighted, claiming, "It would be nice to have a family lawyer for the Gabors. We get into so much trouble."

But after she had dinner with Magda and Warren, she changed her mind. That night, she told Magda, "I can tell you don't love him. Don't marry this man. It will be a disaster."

"It's true, I don't love him tonight," Magda said, "but tomorrow I will love him a little more….and the next day, even more, and so on and so on."

"Forget my other two husbands," Magda continued. "This one is for keeps.

He spurns café society and prefers the simple life. We might even buy a farm in New England or Upper New York State and settle down."

"I know you only too well," Jolie said. "That is not going to happen. You are not a farm girl."

For a month, the marriage worked, as Warren moved into Magda's apartment within Jolie's brownstone. He helped her straighten out her tangled financial affairs in the wake of her divorce from William Rankin.

"But on the second month the marital battles began," Jolie said. "From the sound of it, it reminded me of the retreat of Hitler's armies from Budapest as the Soviet troops moved in from the East."

One day, as she returned home from a shopping expedition at a jewelry wholesaler, Jolie encountered her butler Harry. In her memoirs, she wrote that "Harry was black. He was also a fairy."

When Jolie got angry at her black butler, she'd shout at him, "Lincoln should never have freed people like you." But they always made up. It was a relationship that evoked *Driving Miss Daisy* (1989).

She found him depositing Warren's clothing and possessions on the sidewalk in front of her townhouse. Jolie rushed inside the building to confront Magda. "Her face," remembered Jolie, "was the color of her hair."

"You can't just put his stuff out on the street," Jolie protested to her daughter. "It'll be stolen by bums."

"I can throw out his shit and I will!" Magda said. "He and I are through."

Jolie retreated to her own quarters but kept glancing out of her draperies, watching for Warren's return. Finally, two hours later, he showed up. Jolie spotted him. "He looked stunned and paced up and down the street, seemingly not knowing what to do. Finally, he called me from a pay phone."

"You poor man," Jolie said to him. "I can't reason with Magda. She won't listen. I don't know what's happened between you two. Did she catch you with another woman…or, perhaps, with another man?"

"Nothing like that," he said. "I've always been a faithful husband to her."

"Please call a taxi and take your possessions to a hotel before they're stolen," Jolie recommended. "Some tramp would love to acquire your expensive tailor-made suits."

Warren finally gave in and took Jolie's advice. His mother-in-law was never to see him again.

The next day, Jolie had breakfast with Magda. "Sidney had to go," she told Jolie.

The mystery still remains about what Magda discovered about Warren. In her memoirs, Jolie, perhaps for legal reasons, never revealed what she'd learned that morning. She merely wrote that her son-in-law was involved in "things that weren't one-hundred percent kosher."

Jolie's brownstone became one of the most famous addresses in New York, a gathering place of the *glitterati* before the term was invented. Her first tenant, Magda, was already a celebrity in spite of her lack of achievements. Jolie rented her other three apartments to men who were not only celebrities themselves, but magnets attracting "beautiful people" to the premises.

The society impresario, Earl Blackwell, was the first tenant to move in. He was the founder, in 1939, of Celebrity Service and later became famous across the country for creating the best- and worst-dressed lists. Although he had ended his affairs with Cary Grant and Randolph Scott in the 1930s, as he'd confessed in his memoirs, he still remained friends with them when they occasionally showed up at the townhouse, as did an impressive array of celebrities listed in "Who's Who."

Another of the building's tenants was Robert C. Schuler, an advertising and public relations executive. *[Schuler became famous for marrying one of America's premier opera divas, coloratura soprano Patrice Munsel ("Princess Pat") and later, in 1956, for creating, writing, and producing the primetime*

ABC-TV variety series The Patrice Munsel Show, *which ran to huge acclaim for two years. Munsel first sang at New York's Metropolitan Opera in March 1943, when she was 17. Best known for her interpretation of Adèle in* Die Fledermaus, *her other acclaimed opera roles included Rosina in* The Barber of Seville *and Despina in* Cosi fan Tutte.*]*

The final tenant was the most flamboyant of the three, the very effeminate fashion designer, Jacques Fath, one of the three most important figures in postwar *haute couture. [The other members of that trio included Christian Dior and Pierre Balmain.]*

One of the most famous of all post-war fashion designers, **Jacques Fath**, is seen arranging the flow and folds of one of his designs, as modeled by his wife, **Geneviève Boucher de la Bruyère**.

Jolie and Magda often entertained Fath and his male lover, French director Léonide Moguy.

During his residency in Jolie's brownstone, many of Fath's faithful clients came and went, including Ava Gardner, Greta Garbo, and Rita Hayworth. (In fact, Princess Rita had worn a Fath dress during her 1949 wedding in Cannes, France, to Prince Aly Khan.)

Magda and Jolie sometimes dined with Fath and his lover, Léonide Moguy the French film director. In 1945, he'd directed Gardner and George Raft in *Whistle Stop* and had cast George Sanders' brother, Tom Conway, in one of its leading roles.

When society parties were thrown, all the apartment doors were opened, and guests wandered from floor to floor. "You might encounter Elsa Maxwell wobbling down the steps to greet the arriving Duchess of Windsor," wrote "The Voice of Broadway," columnist Dorothy Kilgallen.

"Judy Garland might pop in with John F. Kennedy, or Claudette Colbert might arrive with her latest girlfriend," Magda said. "One night, Doris Duke showed up with a seven-foot-tall Mandingo escort. You never knew who might show up, even Zsa Zsa on the arm of the president of General Motors. I never remember her arriving with her husband."

"A potpourri of Vanderbilts mingled with Bobo Rockefeller, who had made off with six million dollars after divorcing Nelson Rockefeller. One of Jolie's newest customers, Lady Sylvia Ashley, arrived with Clark Gable," Magda said.

A drunken Errol Flynn once appeared, informing Kilgallen, "I've fucked both Eva and Zsa Zsa. Why not Magda? Maybe the old girl herself?"

He was referring, of course, to Jolie.

Kilgallen noted, but couldn't print in her column, that the aging swashbuckler didn't get either Jolie or Magda. Three hours later, he was seen disappearing into a taxi with actor Laurence Harvey. He'd escorted Margaret Leighton to the party but deserted her for Flynn. "I want to know what 'In Like Flynn' feels like," Harvey had told Kilgallen.

To everyone's surprise, Joan Fontaine showed up one night with actor Brian Aherne, whom she had divorced in 1945. There was speculation that the couple might get together again, although he'd married Eleanor de Liagre Labrot a year after his divorce. However, within the hour, Aherne said something that infuriated her former wife and brought out her bitchy side.

In discussing the incident with Magda and Kilgallen, Fontaine became catty, claiming that on her wedding night, Aherne had spent the evening talking about his affair with Marlene Dietrich. "Next, he jumped out of bed and demonstrated ballet steps he'd taught Dietrich's daughter, Maria Riva. It took five nights before the marriage was actually consummated." She turned in panic toward Kilgallen. "Oh, dear heart, don't print a word I said. How unusual for me. I'm the most discreet person in the world."

"Are you and your sister, Olivia de Havilland, on speaking terms?" Kilgallen asked.

Fontaine glared at Kilgallen and headed across the room to enchant Tom Conway, George Sanders' actor brother.

Magda remembered one night that Frank Sinatra showed up without an invitation. "He was by himself and wandered from floor to floor looking very unhappy. I think he was looking for Ava Gardner, who had visited only two nights before."

At one party, Magda found herself surrounded by Elaine Stritch, Betty von Furstenburg, Victor Borge, and Billy Rose.

Igor Cassini, brother of Oleg Cassini, wrote a society column under the name of Cholly Knickerbocker. He had been permanently barred from Jolie's townhouse after writing that she lived off a percentage of the money earned by her daughters, taking a cut like an agent.

"It was I who contributed to my daughters, not the other way around," Jolie protested. "They are the most ungrateful daughters. Just the other night, Eva was on television and the host admired her jewelry. She smiled and said it came from an admirer, suggesting a man who was crazy enough to give her diamonds. The necklace came from me. Here was her chance to plug my shop on Madison Avenue. She knew I supported myself by selling jewelry, and she didn't advertise my store when she could have for free."

"Cecil Beaton showed up one night with Greta Garbo," Magda said. "Hermione Gingold, the ugliest woman who ever lived, visited one night on the arm of Prince Aly Khan. I was shocked to see him again. Without alluding to our affair, he kissed me and invited me to El Morocco later that night 'after I put Hermione to bed, the poor dear.' Later, he sat down on the floor and sampled some food while surrounded by Kim Stanley, Geraldine Page, Anita Loos, and Lily Pons."

"Oh, did I tell you that the distinguished actor, Paul Lukas, tongue kissed me after being introduced?" Magda said. "He told me that since both of us had been born in Budapest, he felt he had that privilege."

With Peter Christman gone from her life, Jolie needed an escort when she went out. Being young and beautiful, Magda never had a problem finding a beau. But, as a middle age woman with expanding girth, Jolie faced more of a challenge.

She'd been invited to the April in Paris Ball at the Waldorf-Astoria, and she needed an escort. She called Princess Marta and asked if her husband, Franz Joseph, the Austrian Archduke and the Prince of Hungary, was available.

[Jolie inaccurately identified the dignitary in question as Franz Joseph. She was probably referring to Archduke Otto von Hapsburg (born 1912, died 2011), who had functioned, from 1916 till the dissolution of the Austro-Hungarian Empire (in 1918), as its last and final Crown Prince, and who spent time, in the aftermath of World War II, living in the United States.]

The Princess said they had another engagement.

Jolie wasn't satisfied with that response. She said, "You and the Archduke design apartments, do you not? Well, I will go on TV and denounce you as bad designers unless you free the Archduke for the night."

At eight o'clock, "Franz Josef" showed up in his tuxedo and escorted Jolie to the gala. Two weeks later, Jolie went on TV, raving about their apartment designs.

Sometimes, when a Hollywood VIP was arriving in New York without his girlfriend, boyfriend, or mistress, Zsa Zsa called Magda and invited her as "arm candy" for the evening.

One night, veteran actor Fredric March arrived to take Magda to a big party at the Stork Club.

"The old letch looked really disappointed when he saw me," Magda recalled. "He treated me like a doormat all evening. He hardly spoke to me. I finally asked him if he wanted me to leave the club."

"No," he said. "Stay with me."

"Then, what is the matter?" she asked.

"It's not you, Magda," March said. "In Hollywood, Zsa Zsa promised me that my date for tonight would be Marilyn Monroe."

One night at a party, Kilgallen asked Magda if she had planned to remarry in the wake of her 1950 divorce from Sidney Warren.

"No, I'm playing the field," she said. "America has the most beautiful men in the world, and I want to know as many of them as I can."

Six years would go by before she met "the love of my life."

***

Jolie flew to Hollywood to visit her recently wed daughter, Zsa Zsa, and to get to know her newest son-in-law, George Sanders, better. Before the end of her three-day visit, she had nicknamed Sanders "The Deep Freeze."

"On my first night at dinner, King George made it clear he had little regard for me and found my granddaughter, Francesca, annoying," Jolie said."Not even a Hungarian Gabor, with all our charm, could melt that Siberian icicle."

"By the time I arrived as their guest at ten o'clock my first night in California, I thought they'd take me out for a late supper," Jolie recalled. "I found both of them in bed. A servant let me in."

"By nine they were in bed the following night," Jolie said. "Poor Zsa Zsa. George wanted to watch wrestling matches. I knew people, so I went out with friends I had made in New York. Clark Gable and Lady Sylvia Ashley took me to the Mocambo. With Lady Sylvia along, it wasn't a romantic date. Clark was just an escort, but ever so charming."

"At the end of my visit, I told Zsa Zsa, "you have become the man's slave, rubbing his back, flattering his bloated ego. I'm sorry you married this cold fish. The Kennedy boy, Bob Topping, and most definitely, the Prince of

Hanover, even Franchot Tone, would have made a better husband. You tossed aside all that alimony from Hilton. I didn't raise you to become some *haus-frau.*"

Zsa Zsa settled uncomfortably into married life. Sanders demanded twelve hours of sleep every night, and he wanted Zsa Zsa in bed with him during that entire time in case "I wake up and have sexual needs."

Back in Hollywood, Sanders demanded that Zsa Zsa sell her New York brownstone, which she did at a loss. Had she held onto it, it would be worth a vast fortune today. He also forced her to sell her classic New York Bentley, also at a loss. With the money from her sales, and with the insurance settlement she collected from the theft of her jewelry in Manhattan, she purchased a splendid fourteen-room mansion on Bellagio Place in Bel Air.

Of course, she had to hire a gardener, as the house included three land-scaped acres. It was completely furnished in Chinese modern, which Sanders detested. "Who are you trying to imitate, Shanghai Lily? You must think you're Marlene Dietrich."

He made a compromise: He would visit the Bel Air mansion on occasion, but preferred to retreat for long periods to his small apartment, which he didn't want to give up.

"I ended up with a sometimes husband, who I'm certain conducted other affairs," Zsa Zsa lamented.

Perhaps in retaliation, but also for her lusty side, she continued to see Nicky Hilton as he planned his ill-fated marriage to Elizabeth Taylor.

Night after night, Sanders berated her for trapping him into a marriage. "I should have married a rich woman. Doris Duke comes to mind. She's crazy about me. Only problem is, she wants a man to spend at least two hours every day making love to her feet and sucking her toes."

In his memoirs, *Confessions of a Professional Cad,* Sanders claimed: "I lived in Zsa Zsa's sumptuous Bel Air mansion as a sort of paying guest. I was allotted a small room in which I was permitted to keep my personal effects."

He never really moved in," Zsa Zsa said. "He brought two suits, one horrible painting, and an ashtray—that was it. Everything else was back in his apartment."

George invited only his friends to the house, and it was a lost and lonely time for me," Zsa Zsa said. "I had no films to talk about. One night we entertained Vivien Leigh and Laurence Olivier. She was a bit crazy, and attacked him throughout most of the evening. When she wasn't belittling him, they talked about how superior the British were to Americans, and how much each of them loathed Hollywood."

"I called *Nuci* in New York, and all she could talk about was Eva's triumph on Broadway in *The Happy Time.*"

***

Once again, as in her marriage to Burhan Belge, Zsa Zsa had wed a man who didn't like her dog. Often, while she was getting dressed, she pleaded with Sanders to walk her gray poodle. She'd placed a rhinestone collar around the dog's neck. He very reluctantly, with resentment, agreed to take the dog for an occasional stroll, although he complained bitterly. "What will people think of me walking this fag dog?"

Zsa Zsa's boring, early-to-bed nights with Sanders were relieved when he signed for a role in *Blackjack* (1950), to be shot on the Balearic island of Majorca, off the Mediterranean coast of Spain. Sanders was the star of the picture, but he had a strong backup cast, including Agnes Moorehead, who was rumored to be a lesbian, and one-legged Herbert Marshall, who had once had a prolonged affair with Gloria Swanson.

Blackjack, alternately titled *Captain Blackjack,* was a Franco-American co-production, with Sanders in the lead playing a sophisticated scoundrel living by his wits on the French Riviera. He was a notorious drug smuggler, and Marshall played a detective on his trail. The film was held up for three years before its release in the United States.

Sanders and Zsa Zsa flew to Madrid. From there, they transferred by train to Barcelona, where boat transportation had been arranged to carry them the rest of the way to Majorca.

In Barcelona, many photographers turned out for their arrival. "George tried to force me out of the pictures."

"Why take a picture of her?" he asked the photographers. "I'm the star. She's a nobody, merely my wife."

The paparazzi did not agree, believing (accurately) that beautiful Zsa Zsa would sell more newspapers than staid, stolid Sanders.

On Majorca, Zsa Zsa thought all the men and women looked as if they'd been painted by Velázquez.

When she first saw the two Englishmen, Sanders and Marshall, together, she said, "Dry was the word for both of them. They had sleepy eyes and a world-weary elegance. Both were at their best playing unscrupulous men and cads. You couldn't really tell that Marshall had had his right leg amputated during World War I."

The production staff had booked Zsa Zsa and Sanders into a luxurious suite at the Hotel Mediterráneo.

The film's director, Julien Duvivier, had scheduled an eight-week shoot, but it stretched out for seven months. Both Zsa Zsa and Sanders grew bored with Majorca, although he'd later change his mind and purchase a home there.

411

"George ate too much, drank too much Spanish wine, gained too much weight, and spent most of his days fantasizing about all the alleged affairs I was having," Zsa Zsa said.

"While George was filming one day, I woke up with an impacted wisdom tooth," she said. "The hotel arranged for a young man named José to take me to a dentist in Palma. I'd seen him in the restaurant at night playing the guitar."

"After dental surgery, José was driving the hotel's Mercedes back when it broke down along the way," she said. "He called a service station. As the garage attendant was repairing the car, George and Herbert Marshall rode by, coming back to the hotel in a station wagon. They didn't stop."

"I arrived back in the hotel suite with my jaw swollen and my gum aching," she said. "George flew into a jealous rage. I could not believe it. He had the strength of a bull, and he grabbed me and dangled me off the iron railing around our terrace. He was threatening to kill me and calling me an adulterous whore. I begged for my life. Finally, he pulled me up. Thank heavens I was wearing a Balenciaga. A cheaper dress might have ripped."

That night, Sanders encountered José in the dining room playing his guitar. "He gave him a twenty-dollar bill, the most expensive tip I'd ever seen him present to anyone," Zsa Zsa said. "There was no scene, nothing. Only two hours earlier, he was going to kill me over José. He was a very attractive boy, and under different circumstances, I might have succumbed to his charm, but not after a wisdom tooth extraction."

"When I could take the boredom of Palma no more, and with my own money, I purchased a plane ticket to Paris, telling George I had to do some shopping."

In Paris, she installed herself in a suite at the Plaza Athénée, "which I paid for myself, *dahlink.* George didn't want me to go to Paris."

Joan Bennett and Walter Wanger read in the papers that I was in town, and they called me, inviting me to dinner at Maxim's," Zsa Zsa said. "I was told that they'd arranged an escort for me."

Outfitted in another Balenciaga, Zsa Zsa later claimed she looked like "I'd stepped out of a dream, I was so lovely. Apparently, my escort at Maxim's thought so too. I was introduced to one of the richest men in the world, the gorgeous, well-

Before her blonde period, **Zsa Zsa** and **George Sanders** were seen at a film premiere in 1951.

She later said, "He was not faithful to me during the marriage. Once, when he didn't come home, I asked him, 'What happened to you?' He said, 'I saw a Spanish woman on the street, so I wanted to know what a Spanish woman was like in bed.' I forgave him. He could do no wrong. He was torturing me, but I just—you know, when you love somebody—I forgave him because I really adored him."

412

mannered and incredibly charming Elie de Rothschild."

As Zsa Zsa later confessed in a memoir, "Elie was very seductive to me."

He was also enchanted by her reddish-blonde hair, peach complexion, and her wit and charm. When Bennett and Zsa Zsa retired to the women's room, Elie confided to Wanger, "I want to go to bed with your friend. We're both married, but so what?"

For years, Jolie had told Zsa Zsa fascinating stories about the Rothschilds, considering them successors to the Bourbons. Their world was one of vineyards, yachts, elegant *châteaux*, stud farms, riding stables, resorts, and theaters.

Zsa Zsa later confessed that she found Elie's looks mesmerizing, with his falcon beak nose, his mischievous smile, his piercing eyes, his chiseled features, and high hairline. "He had a boyish charm and after midnight could be vulgar in a most delicious way. Other than raising grapes, he had another hobby, collecting the world's most desirable women. He also had a famous mistress, Pamela Churchill, who had been married to Sir Winston's son, Randolph Churchill."

The scion of one of Europe's most distinguished and richest families, Elie was a banker but also owned Château Lafite, the most celebrated vineyard in France. A lover of horses and races, he was often seen with his globe-trotting friend, Prince Aly Khan, particularly at Deauville. He was married to Liliane Fould-Springer de Rothschild, but Zsa Zsa had heard from Joan Bennett that "it is a loveless marriage." Actually, Elie had married her by proxy during the four years he spent in a Nazi prison camp. "I was considered an officer *[des Anciens Cuirassiers]* in the French army. Otherwise, as a Jew, I would have been sent to an extermination camp."

After their meal at Maxim's, Bennett, Wanger, Zsa Zsa, and Elie went to Freddie's, which was the most fashionable late night rendezvous in Paris. "Freddie was quintessentially French and, other than Garbo, one of the most beautiful women I'd ever met," Zsa Zsa said. "She modeled her clothes on the outfit that Marlene wore in *Morocco,* that 1930 film she'd made with Gary Cooper."

"All the people in the club, both the straight men and the women, certainly the lesbians, even the gays, were attracted to Freddie," Zsa Zsa said. She even confessed in a memoir that she'd never been attracted to a woman before, until Freddie asked her to dance.

"She held me close and pressed her body into mine, and I began to have fantasies about taking both Freddie and Elie to bed, having the best of both worlds," Zsa Zsa claimed to Bennett. "As Freddie danced with me, she'd cupped one of my breasts," Zsa Zsa said. "It was very erotic. When Elie returned to table, he revealed how Freddie handled a man on the dance floor. She unbuttoned or unzipped his trousers and fondled him as she danced up close."

In her highly unreliable memoirs, Zsa Zsa wrote that Elie drove her back to the Plaza Athénée after some passionate embraces in his chauffeur-driven Rolls-Royce. "Since I was still in love with George, I told him I was staying in room #305. He agreed to come in half an hour after I'd made my entrance into the lobby. Later, at the door of room #305, he encountered a woman in curlers and an angry husband who nearly beat him up, or so he told me.

[There were obvious flaws in that story. First, Elie was well known at the Plaza Athénée, and a friend of the general manager. When he arrived in the lobby of the hotel, he was greeted by the manager, who sent a hundred red roses to Zsa Zsa's suite, along with three bottles of the hotel's best champagne.

Elie did not go wandering off to some double room, but was personally escorted, to Zsa Zsa's suite by the manager. Zsa Zsa later reported to friends that, before receiving him, she had dressed in diamonds and a very revealing black négligée.

The next morning, she telephoned Joan Bennett and thanked her for the introduction, asserting that Elie was one of the world's most skilled lovers. "With his hundreds of conquests, he has learned what a woman wants in bed. I'm madly in love with him. I'd even divorce George Sanders if he asked me to marry him, which he never will, of course."]

***

[After that torrid night at the Plaza Athénée, Zsa Zsa and Elie would begin an affair that lasted throughout most of the 1950s.

"At his stables, I rode horses with him like I did in Turkey," she recalled. "He was one of the world's great art collectors, and I went to galleries with him. But our relationship was fairly clandestine. Once, we visited the Duke and Duchess of Windsor at their small château outside Paris. We knew that that gay couple would keep our secrets."

Elie told Elsa Maxwell, who in turn confided to Zsa Zsa, that he liked her because she was a strong and independent woman. "I do not like a submissive woman, the type who brings a man his bedroom slippers. I could have a million tarts, but I prefer a woman of substance. I will go with a woman like Pamela Churchill, even if she's no raving beauty. She stimulates me. Zsa Zsa is both stimulating and a world class beauty. But it's an aristocratic beauty, not like a Marilyn Monroe, who looks like a gorgeous milk maiden from Norway."

As a standard venue during her outings with Elie, Zsa Zsa always dressed fabulously, because he was one of the world's best dressed men himself. Even the fashionistas of Paris approved of Zsa Zsa's chic wardrobe. The eccentric aristocrat and Parisian society doyenne, Marie Laure de Noailles, told her companion, composer Ned Rorem, that *"Zsa Zsa, as she calls herself, looks so dazzling at night, she could convert the fairies to a more sexual orthodoxy."*

"Elie's art collection was stunning," Zsa Zsa said. *"He had the world's greatest collection of Dubuffets along with Klimts and the inevitable Picassos. He owned such masterpieces as Rembrandt's* The Standard Bearer *and Gainsborough's* The Marsham Children.*"*

"Once, I toured the vineyards with this Jewish playboy and polo fanatic," Zsa Zsa said. *"We dined at his château, where he hired the finest chefs in Europe. Meals were an event. Each exquisite course was served on the finest Sèvres porcelain. He told me because of his long imprisonment by the Nazis, he was having to make up for lost time by extravagantly living the good life. I might add that the good life included his harem of some of the most beautiful women in Europe. I was proud to be part of his collection."*

"I even met Liliane, Elie's wife, who looked as ugly as a toad and may—or may not—have known of our affair. She didn't even wear lipstick. A friend said, 'She looks like a cook, talks like a queen, lives like an empress, and thinks like a philosopher.'"

"Of course, dahlink, things were not always sunshine," Zsa Zsa said. *"Elie was a man of mercurial moods, like George. He was given to childish outbursts. If someone annoyed or offended, he would burst into tears, and I would have to comfort him on my naked breasts until he revived. He said what he thought, no matter how shocking. He, too, would send others into hysterical outbursts after devastating them with his critiques."*

Elie de Rothschild, shortly before his death in 1970, holding up a choice bottle from his vast cellar.

He was one of the most sought-after men on the planet. Zsa Zsa managed to seduce him, although neither ever made a commitment to the other.

"He was a handsome, charming, fun-loving companion, and each new day with him brought something new to do," she said. "He filled his life with adventure—and I was one of those adventures."

Finally, Liliane found out about Zsa Zsa's sexual involvement with her husband. Once, she trailed them in her Austin Mini as they headed to an upscale inn in Barbizon, a chic and verdant refuge within an easy driving distance from Paris. *"Elie knew the back roads, and he knew speed, so we managed to elude this Miss Sherlock Holmes,"* Zsa Zsa said. *"We spent a glorious weekend touring the art galleries there and looking at the merchandise in the antiquaires. We slept in the same bed where Prince Philip had fucked Princess Elizabeth on their honeymoon, with that big penis he is rumored to possess, and which I have yet to find out for myself."*

"In time, I suffered the fate of nearly every mis-

415

tress who ever lived," Zsa Zsa said. *"Elie moved on to younger, brighter faces. He told me that we'd always be friends, whatever that meant."]*

***

"When George Sanders signed to co-star in *All About Eve (1950)* with Bette Davis, Anne Baxter, and this blonde thing *[a reference to Marilyn Monroe],* reporters and photographers swarmed all over my Bel Air home for a feature story: *GEORGE SANDERS AT HOME,"* Zsa Zsa said. "I had to protest to be included in the layout. There was a bitter quarrel. He told me that the photographers wanted to see him, a star, at home. But I protested that many stars at home are photographed with their wives. Otherwise, it looks like a bachelor pad."

During the shooting of *All About Eve,* she visited him at Fox and had lunch with Bette Davis and Sanders. "Davis was enraptured with this super macho actor, Gary Merrill, so I knew she didn't have her lecherous eyes set on George," Zsa Zsa said. "In the commissary, Monroe went past. She was adept at wiggling her ass and batting her eyelashes."

"Merrill had a meeting in the head office with Fox that day," Zsa Zsa said. "Otherwise, Bette would not have been free for lunch." In a memoir, Zsa Zsa claimed, "There was a bed on the set, and every time the crew came back from lunch, it was obvious that Gary and Bette had been using it during the break."

That night, Sanders made violent love to Zsa Zsa in their Bel Air manse. "This was not his style," she said. "I accused him of fantasizing about Monroe while making love to me. That infuriated him. He picked up my nude body and carried me out into the garden, where he tossed me into the swimming pool."

For the final shooting of *All About Eve,* the cast was flown to San Francisco. "We had the room next to Monroe's," Zsa Zsa said. "I told George that she was nothing but a tramp. He kept our door slightly cracked and stayed up half the night spying into the traffic patterns in the hallway outside. Before dawn, at least four members of the crew—not Gary Merrill—came and went from her bedroom. She didn't make it with Hugh Marlowe either, or so I heard. I learned in San Francisco that Hugh had been sleeping with my baby sister, Eva. Again, and I've said it before, Hollywood is nothing, if not incestuous, with everybody sleeping with everybody else."

After the final scenes of *All About Eve* were completed in San Francisco, Marilyn Monroe flew back to Los Angeles with Sanders and Zsa Zsa. Zsa Zsa occupied a window seat, and Monroe sat across the aisle from Sanders. "She wore a very tight sweater," Zsa Zsa said. "Each time I glanced in her direction, she was making eyes at George."

On the set, one of the co-stars, Celeste Holm, had told Zsa Zsa that during the filming on the Fox lot, Sanders had brought a packed lunch to Monroe's dressing room every day.

Sanders invited Zsa Zsa to accompany him to the Academy Award presentation, where he'd been nominated as Best Supporting Actor of the year for his interpretation of Addison DeWitt. To Zsa Zsa's thrill, he won the Oscar that night.

Sanders defined that ceremony as "an occasion filled with delight, with such painful suspense that I never rose above a state of frozen stupification. My bride was delighted that I invited her to this top-flight Beano."

After a brief thank you, he disappeared backstage.

After the conclusion of the event, as the audience filed out, Zsa Zsa sat in her seat, thinking he would come back for her. He didn't. She waited until the auditorium was empty before going backstage, where she found him in front of reporters receiving hugs and kisses from Monroe.

When Zsa Zsa freed him from Monroe and assisted him on his walk to a limousine, he was sobbing. "I can't help myself. Winning this Oscar has completely unnerved me."

"And this from a man who was contemptuous of acting," she said. "He spent half the night crying like a baby. He even went to sleep cuddling his Oscar instead of me. Before he shut his eyes, he held the Oscar up to my face."

"Here is one prize you'll never win," he accurately told her.

Back in Bel Air, with his Oscar prominently displayed on the piano,

George Sanders *(left)* told one of his best friends, actor Brian Aherne, "When **Zsa Zsa** dyed her hair blonde and I dimmed the lights, I could at least imagine that I was fucking Marilyn Monroe."

When Aherne wrote *A Dreadful Man*, a book about Sanders, Zsa Zsa never spoke to him again. "Brian was so very, very mean," she said.

In one of the pivotal scenes in *All About Eve*, **George Sanders** *(left)*, playing the theater critic Addison DeWitt, confronts Eve Harrington (**Anne Baxter**), exposing her lies.

"During the making of that movie, Zsa Zsa was hysterically jealous of me," Sanders said. "She had a reason for grief over Monroe, but not Anne Baxter. I never touched Baxter, on or off the screen. Like the role she was playing, Baxter was a cold fish to me."

"She told me, 'I can't possibly see what Zsa Zsa sees in you. If you were my husband, 'I'd drain you out with the dishwater.'"

Sanders played music all day and sang "Some Enchanted Evening." He decided he wanted to replace Enzio Pinza, the Italian opera singer who had enjoyed wild acclaim during his appearances in the hit Broadway musical, *South Pacific.* When Sanders felt he was good enough, he sent a recording to Oscar Hammerstein and Richard Rodgers in New York.

Sanders was known to Hollywood insiders for his good baritone singing voice. He'd often play the piano at parties and "sing songs of a scurrilous nature for friends." Ella Raines, Cornel Wilde, and even Anthony Quinn praised his voice to Zsa Zsa, but Joan Fontaine found that "he sang ribald ditties in a constipated voice."

Within a week, Rodgers, who had hired Eva for *The Happy Time,* wired Sanders that he'd been accepted as a replacement for Pinza.

But after working so hard for so long on his vocal technique, Sanders bowed out and wired Rodgers that he didn't want the role in *South Pacific.*

"I'm a serious dramatic actor," Sanders told Zsa Zsa. "I do not do musicals."

Ironically, Sanders ended up playing one of the lead roles in the film version of the musical *Call Me Madam* (1953). The film was based on Perle Mesta's life as a hostess in Washington, D.C. "I wasn't worried about Merman moving in on my husband," Zsa Zsa said. "I knew she'd rather be sleeping with Judy Garland than with George."

Finally, party-loving Zsa Zsa could no longer tolerate going to bed at nine or ten every night. She took an inventory of the many gowns in her closet that she'd never worn, stunning designs by Balenciaga or Lanvin.

When she complained to Sanders, he gave her permission to go out on the town with an escort of her choice. At the Cocoanut Grove in the Ambassador Hotel, she was photographed dancing with Wilson Linnett, a handsome, wealthy businessman known as a "lady killer."

Columnists James Bacon and Hedda Hopper speculated, "Where does Zsa Zsa Gabor, the former Mrs. Conrad Hilton, stash her latest husband, George Sanders? She is seen dancing every night with a different escort."

Sanders did accept a dinner invitation from his friend, fellow British actor James Mason, and his witty, outspoken, and charming wife, Pamela.

Pamela Mason and Zsa Zsa found they had much in common, in addition to being married to two famous British actors. Both Zsa Zsa and Pamela would have their own talk shows in the 50s and 60s. Privately, Zsa Zsa gave Pamela "tips" for her book, *Marriage Is the First Step Toward Divorce.*

Before coming to Hollywood, James Mason had been the top box office attraction in England at the end of World War II. Today, the "Yorkshire-born laddie" is considered one of the greatest actors of the 20th Century, and his "languid but impassioned" vocal talent is still obvious in such films as *The Desert Fox*

(1951); A Star is Born (1954), where he co-starred with Judy Garland; and as a pedophile in *Lolita (1962).*

In time, Pamela would become Zsa Zsa's best friend, but the first dinner party Zsa Zsa attended at her home had been a disaster.

"The smell of civet greeted us at the door," Zsa Zsa said.

[A civet refers to any of various carnivorous catlike mammals having anal scent glands that secrete a fluid with a musky odor.]

"The Masons owned twenty-eight cats, none of them housebroken. I don't think Pamela had ever heard of an air freshener. James wore a pink dinner jacket and Pamela appeared in a black *négligée.* She was an awful cook, but we had a lot of witty, outrageous banter at table, James, Pamela, and I enjoyed ourselves, in spite of George's disdain."

Toward the end of the evening, James suggested that Zsa Zsa, faced with all her spare time, should go on TV talk shows.

Rising sleepy-eyed from an armchair, Sanders motioned to Zsa Zsa that it was time to go home. "I could just see Zsa Zsa on a talk show. She'd never make it. She's far too stupid."

How wrong he was.

Literally thousands of talk shows loomed in Zsa Zsa's future, as she became one of the most sought-after guests in the history of television.

***

After divorcing "The Man with 100,000 beds" (Conrad Hilton, Sr.), Zsa Zsa in subsequent years preferred not to remain silent about details associated with their marriage. "In other words, I was the very opposite of Jane Wyman when she divorced my friend, Ronald Reagan," she claimed.

She noted the parade of women who followed her to at least one of Conrad's 100,000 beds. "He pretended to be a devout Catholic, but was self-righteous, pushy, dictatorial, and a woman chaser—pursuing socialites like Hope Hampton and Kay Spreckles, but also actresses like Jeanne Crain and especially tap-dancing Ann Miller—even that French thing, Denise Darcel. I had to look up who Gladys Zender was. From Peru, she became Miss Universe."

"Nicky was closer to Conrad than his other sons, but Nicky always was involved in some scandal or another, including some homosexual ones," Zsa Zsa said later in life. "Conrad wanted to make a hotel man out of Nicky, but the darling boy wanted to be a playboy. He spoiled Nicky and gave him anything he wanted. If Nicky smashed up his new Cadillac, it was quickly replaced."

"On many a night, Nicky came to me, most often for sex, but on some nights, he was so drunk, he cried on my breasts. I was both his mistress and his mother. He lived in his father's shadow and knew he could never measure up to his old man—except in one department, and we won't go into that, *dahlink.*"

"When Nicky wanted a private plane, Conrad bought it for him, but I feared he'd die in a fiery crash because he was so reckless."

Eventually, Francesca Hilton became aware of her mother's involvement with her former stepson, but didn't seem to object. She reportedly claimed that "Nicky and mother embarked on a loving and long-standing relationship."

An MGM starlet, Carole Wells, a friend of Nicky's, told biographer C. David Heymann, "I always considered Nicky a prototypical Cain-and-Abel figure, an idiosyncratic combination of good and evil. He and Elizabeth Taylor were never especially well-suited. He was spoiled silly, while she exuded the air of a pampered *prima donna*. He resented her fame, and she envied his wealth. His money made her so nervous, she bit her nails to the quick and began to wear fake fingernails."

"Nicky often arrived in my boudoir drunk and aggressive," Zsa Zsa said. "Elizabeth back then was put off by that, but I found his feisty, aggressive lovemaking thrilling. Actually, I've found that men who have a touch of violence in them are greater sexual partners than the men who fuck like gentlemen and graciously thank you at the finale."

"I remember the first time Nicky brought Elizabeth to my house when they first started dating," Zsa Zsa said. "Except for her overgrown bosom, she was much smaller than I thought she'd be after having seen her on the screen. Her eyes were beautiful, although she appeared to have double lashes. I thought they were false, but they turned out to be real. What shocked me was that she was a hairy ape. She even had peach fuzz on her face. Her arms were covered in black hair. I could just imagine what her legs looked like. I'm sure I met her the day before she went into electrolysis. Her eyes were marvelous, though. They were blue instead of violet."

"It was one of the saddest days of my life when my precious darling **Nicky Hilton** *(right)* married that **Elizabeth Taylor**," Zsa Zsa lamented.

"I predicted the marriage would not last through the honeymoon, and it almost didn't. Instead of Elizabeth, Nicky slept with prostitutes on his honeymoon night."

"I feared that when he got mad at her, Nicky might kill her. Because he always kept that .38 revolver beside his bed. One drunken night at my Bel Air home, he started shooting out the lights. The neighbors heard gunfire and called the police. I hid Nicky in my clothes closet when the police came and claimed that vandals had broken in, but had fled when they heard sirens. That story even made the newspapers."

"The night before his wedding, Nicky practically made love to me all night. The next morning, I told him quite frankly, "Nicky, please don't marry Elizabeth Taylor. She's wrong for you.'"

"Mama, you're just jealous," he told her. "You're afraid that I'll cut off access to Tiger (an obvious reference to his enormous endowment). That I'll never do. When you're sixty-five, I'll still be banging you two or three times a week."

Both Conrad and Zsa Zsa showed up on May 5, 1950, at the Church of the Good Shepherd in Beverly Hills for Nicky's wedding to Taylor.

Zsa Zsa joined such stars as Greer Garson and Ginger Rogers for the ceremony. Before it began, William Powell told her, "I don't particularly like Elizabeth Taylor, but Louis B. Mayer told me and other MGM stars to get our asses over here today. Greta Garbo was the only one with the balls not to show up, but then, she's out of pictures."

On the steps of the church, Ann Miller appeared on the arm of Conrad Hilton. She deliberately stood next to Zsa Zsa, as if showing off her catch, Conrad himself. "Your loss, my gain, honey," Miller whispered to Zsa Zsa.

On her other side, pint-sized Mickey Rooney whispered to Zsa Zsa, "I got Liz's snatch before Nicky did."

Within two months, Nicky was back in Zsa Zsa's boudoir, holding her in his arms. "Mama, I made a terrible mistake. You were right. I should never have married this MGM creation. She doesn't yet know who she is. She's just an image on the screen. There is no reality to her."

***

Zsa Zsa plotted her revenge on Sanders for his affair with Marilyn Monroe. Continuing her affair with Nicky Hilton was not enough: She wanted someone new and fresh, a sexy Adonis, perhaps not quite the male equivalent of Monroe, but a handsome hunk, preferably British. Sanders had warned her that he'd be more intimidated if she had an affair with a fellow British actor such as James Mason, Laurence Olivier, or the young Richard Burton, than if she bedded Gary Cooper, or Clark Gable.

Her chance came when Sanders invited her to the MGM commissary for lunch with him and his handsome co-star, London-born Stewart Granger, who was

When Zsa Zsa saw this publicity still of **Ann Miller** she said, "Who does this hussy think she is? Esther Williams?"

"That tap-dancing low life has been chasing after Conrad Hilton for centuries, even after I was married to him."

"She even went after Charles Isaacs, Eva's ex-husband, and she seduced Hal Hays, a businessman I was going to marry."

421

making *The Light Touch (1951)* with Pier Angeli, who had not yet mastered English.

At table, Zsa Zsa asked Sanders for a cigarette. "I can't afford one," he shot back at his wife."

This startled Granger, who at first thought that Sanders was joking. When he realized that he was not, he went over to the counter and purchased a package of cigarettes.

Back at table, he removed two cigarettes from the package and lit both of them at the same time, imitating Paul Henreid in the movie *Now Voyager,* with Bette Davis.

When Granger handed the lit cigarette to Zsa Zsa, his fingers caressed her delicate hand.

Sanders observed all this skeptically. "I noticed, Granger, that you nigger-lipped that fag before passing it on to my wife."

"Somebody's got to do it," Granger answered.

Over lunch, Granger expressed his disapproval of the movie script and its director, Richard Brooks. "The bloody sod told me my first day on the set that he would have preferred Cary Grant in my role."

"All of us, old chap, have to sometimes do things we detest," Sanders said. "Like my marrying Zsa Zsa here."

"That did it," Zsa Zsa later said to Pamela Mason. "Before that luncheon ended, I knew that Stewart and I were to become lovers. He was a living doll, devastatingly charming and so handsome, with a voice that could cause a woman to orgasm. No wonder Vivien Leigh and Deborah Kerr were mad about the boy. Of course, Jean Simmons had already molested the hunk with her greedy little paws."

Sanders was seeing a psychiatrist at least three times a week when he was in Hollywood. During his sessions, he constantly talked about Zsa Zsa. The psychiatrist wanted to meet her. But instead of summoning her to his office for a joint session, he decided to throw a party in her honor.

Some thirty guests showed up, but not Pier Angeli, who would later propel herself into a torrid affair with the doomed James Dean before marrying singer Vic Damone.

At the party within the home of his psychiatrist, Sanders rhapsodized about "that stunning Italian beauty, Pier Angeli. She is so lovely, so endearing, so charming. I think she's going to be one of the biggest stars in Hollywood. She's so unlike Marilyn Monroe. Her beauty is ethereal, a gift from the Gods. A director could cast her as the Virgin Mary."

When Zsa Zsa got Sanders alone by the pool, she attacked him viciously. "How dare you rave about another woman's beauty when you're out with Zsa Zsa Gabor, the acknowledged most beautiful woman in the world?"

When he could take it no more, Sanders seized her by the neck with both hands. "I'm going to kill you, choke you to death." Just in time, he came back to his senses.

She ran inside the house, searching for the psychiatrist. "He wants to kill me," she shouted at him. He nearly choked me to death. Call a mental clinic. Tell them to bring a straitjacket."

At that point, Sanders entered the room in tears, kneeling before Zsa Zsa and begging her to forgive him "Just this one final time. Never again will I harm you."

***

The plot of *The Light Touch*, revolved around the theft of a Renaissance-era painting from a church in Sicily and a corrupt art dealer's desperate desire to possess it.

In his memoir, *Sparks Fly Upward*, first published in the U.S. in 1981, Granger didn't think *The Light Touch* was even worth writing about. The film lost an estimated $400,000 and wasn't something he wanted to remember. He did find the space to at least mention Zsa Zsa, concealing his affair with her.

He claimed that he encountered her at the home of James and Pamela Mason, and remembered her as a "non-stop chattering voluptuous lady."

That sounded like a putdown to Zsa Zsa, although she admitted to the voluptuous charge. "Actually, Stewart later told me that 'conversation can be as important in a relationship as sex.'"

[Granger later expressed regret that he had not been more candid and revelatory in his memoirs. "If I had, I would have had a bestseller. Imagine leaving out such tantalizing tidbits as Zsa Zsa Gabor, Grace Kelly, and Ava Gardner, or the night Princess Margaret came on to me. Dare I mention my fling with Elizabeth Taylor when I was living with Jean Simmons, in the house we shared with Elizabeth and my old buddy, Michael Wilding. What about the time I was in love with both Vivien Leigh and Larry Olivier?"]

The dinner party at the Masons became rather raucous, especially when David Niven arrived. The men discussed their first sexual experiences, although Pamela and Zsa Zsa refused to join in the revelations.

Granger claimed that he lost his virginity to "Josette," a young Parisian prostitute when he was in France for a rugby match. He avoided mentioning his wartime, long-enduring affair with Michael Wilding, who became Elizabeth Taylor's second husband, but he did admit to going to bed with Hedy Lamarr.

"Who hasn't?" Zsa Zsa quipped. "Hitler, Goebbels, Mussolini, you name the dictator."

"Hedy told me as I mounted her, 'Now don't come too fast, will you?'"

Granger said.

Niven claimed that he lost his virginity when he was fourteen to "Nessie," a prostitute who "trolled the Dilly," a reference to London's Piccadilly Circus. "I kept company thereafter with her for a year. I didn't have to pay her. She said she'd do me for free. I've had Hedy too. Mae West didn't charge me either. But I felt I should have charged Doris Duke and Barbara Hutton. After all, they're the richest women on the planet."

Mason shocked the dinner table when he claimed that he had still been a virgin at twenty-six years of age when "I met this darling former child actress sitting across from me. She called herself Pamela Ostrer Kellino."

Pamela, who appeared drunk, challenged that statement. "You mean, I was your first woman. I guess you're not counting all the stately homos in Britain like Noël Coward and Laurence Olivier who you bottomed for."

When Sanders went out of town, Granger called Zsa Zsa, because he'd obviously picked up on her flirtatious signals across the dinner table.

Zsa Zsa later told Pamela that "Stewart is a wild and reckless lover…and totally adorable."

Years later, she would meet Grace Kelly at a gala in Monaco. The Princess had made *Green Fire* in 1954 with Granger. She told Zsa Zsa , "Stewart is the most conceited man I've ever met."

Zsa Zsa quipped, "Well, *dahlink*, he's got a lot to be conceited about."

She found Deborah Kerr's assessment more accurate. "Women sense that there's a bit of the brute in Stewart."

Columnist Dorothy Kilgallen observed, "I have never seen anything like the way ladies with high boiling points and high intelligence are falling to

The Light Touch, a failed film, starred **George Sanders** *(left)*, newcomer **Pier Angeli** *(center)*, and **Stewart Granger** *(right)*.

Whereas Sanders became fascinated by Angeli, Zsa Zsa gravitated to the handsome British actor, Granger himself.

"Even though I didn't have to, I was naked under the blanket," **Stewart Granger** later said.

"It make me more authentic in the role, and it gave the gay men on the crew a thrill when I stripped down. So why not?"

pieces over Mr. Granger—and that includes Zsa Zsa Gabor."

Zsa Zsa retained fond memories of Granger. "He was handsome, suave, and debonair. His real name was James Stewart, which he had to change for obvious reasons. He would have been ideal cast as James Bond in the 007 series."

"On the first night I saw him in the nude, aside from his obvious attraction, he showed me battle scars from World War II. He also told me that when he first arrived in Hollywood, Cary Grant put the moves on him. He also shocked me when he claimed that he'd plotted to kill Howard Hughes when he wouldn't stop pursuing his wife, Miss Simmons. He also said that Hughes was 'a dirty, double-crossing, Machiavellian son of a bitch.'"

"If not for Errol Flynn's swashbuckler roles, Stewart might have been a bigger star," Zsa Zsa claimed. "I later met him in London in the 1980s. His hair had turned gray, whereas I was still a dazzling blonde. He still had that stone-cracking grin that causes women to drop their knickers. He made bedroom eyes at me and told me that even at this advanced stage in life, I could still put my high heels under his bed any night."

***

 Knowing that *The Happy Time* would not run forever on Broadway, Eva signed with a television agent and told her, "I'm ready to make bags of money on the Tube, even though many stars hold it in disrepute. But if it's good enough for Helen Hayes and Maurice Evans, it's good enough for me."

The agent booked Eva on a number of test spots and sent out pictures of her for cheesecake, as part of campaigns that evoked Paramount's studio publicity when she was a starlet during the war.

She had already appeared on such shows as *Leave It to the Girls,* "where the *vimmen* always won the battle, if not the *var*," Eva claimed.

She also accepted roles in live dramatic series, including *GE Theater, Philco Playhouse,* and *Climax.* "I learned the hard way. In those days of live television, anything and everything that could go wrong went wrong. In one production, the wall of a set fell in on me, but, like the Phoenix, I rose from the ashes as if nothing had happened."

Her biggest break came when she was offered the role of Helena in a TV production of Chekhov's *Uncle Vanya.* She was intimidated at first, knowing how many talented actresses had previously interpreted the role. She fretted about it for a full sleepless night before accepting it the following morning.

Before filming began, she was reunited with Leora Dana, with whom she'd starred in *The Happy Time.* She also met the production's star, Boris Karloff. As she later wrote, "I'd never seen him before without the nuts and bolts. He didn't look like a man who had eaten a smidgen of human flesh."

Beginning in 1953, while still appearing on Broadway, she was offered *The Eva Gabor Show,* a TV talk show usually featuring theatrical personalities. It ran from 8 to 8:15pm, which meant that she had to break speed records rushing to the theater in time to slip into her maid's costume in time for her appearance in *The Happy Time.*

In Hollywood, Zsa Zsa told George Sanders that she was jealous about Eva being the star of her own TV show.

Eva's first guest was actor Richard Hart, the star of *The Happy Time.* "That interview went so easy, but others were a disaster, *dahlink.* " She cited a socialite who came on drunk after downing eight martinis backstage. "One actor come out and leered at me during the show. He kept inching closer and closer. I had to rebuff his advances right on camera. It became the first sponsored rebuff in TV history. Somehow, I managed to wiggle away from this octopus."

The press played up her glamour image, sometimes referring to her as "The Baby," at other times as "Miss Rich Dish." One headline got it wrong—*THIS GIRL WANTS A HUSBAND WHO'LL BE THE BOSS.* "In my next marriage, I want to be the boss," she had said.

Her greatest exposure came not from TV but from advertising billboards. She was selected as "Miss Valen-*Tie* " in 1951 by the Men's Tie Foundation. A poster with her likeness appeared in 28,000 retail stores from New York to California.

"I ask myself more questions than *Hamlet* as I ponder which shoes to wear," said **Eva Gabo**r, appearing above in two publicity shots from 1951.

"All any girl needs at any time in history is simple velvet and basic diamonds."

"I'm always being asked what divides the European male from the American male, and I have the answer: The Atlantic Ocean!"

Between posing for ads and TV appearances, Eva toured in a road show version of *Her Cardboard Lover.*

Eva found this play a good vehicle for her talents. It had already been brought to the screen three times, the last movie in 1942 starring Norma Shearer, Robert Taylor, and George Sanders. When Eva saw the movie, she said, "I got Robert Taylor and Zsa Zsa wound up with George."

In the plot, a rich woman hopes to discourage a former boyfriend from pursuing her. She hires a young songwriter in need of money to pay off gambling debts, to pretend to be her boyfriend. The "phony" boyfriend is actually in love with her.

"During the tour, I slept in fleabags,

including an especially seedy hotel in Memphis," Eva claimed. "I was told that *The Cardboard Lover* would be a dismal failure, but we played to packed houses."

Sometimes, Eva was invited as a guest on other TV talk shows. An invitation came in from Faye Emerson, who was in the throes of a divorce from Elliott Roosevelt, the former president's son. The appearance was on CBS's 1950 *The Faye Emerson Show.* Its hostess telephoned Eva, suggesting that she dress conservatively because of "my uptight audience."

"I came out looking like I was taking up collections for the Salvation Army only to find Emerson in plunging *décolletage.* I'd been had. Her breasts captured all the attention. The show should have been called *Cleopatra Meets Rebecca of Sunnybrook Farm.*"

"I later forgave Faye for pulling that trick on me," Eva said. "She introduced me to the man she was soon to marry."

[Eva was referring to Lyle ("Skitch") Henderson, who became a household word when he was the musical conductor of Johnny Carson's Tonight Show. *Emerson's marriage to Henderson hit the skids in 1957 when he was involved in a scandal with some teenage girls. Subsequently, Carson dropped him from* The Tonight Show.

Years later, after Emerson retired, Eva visited George Sanders on the island of Majorca, where he had a home. Hearing of her visit, Emerson, who also had a home on the island, invited Sanders and Eva for dinner. They found her living

Eva Gabor *(above, right)* emoting as a serious actress in *Her Cardboard Lover*

"Norma Shearer made her farewell to the screen in 1942 in this vehicle, but I wanted to revive it," Eva said. "Regrettably, I didn't have Robert Taylor to appear with me in it, the way Shearer did."

Faye Emerson *(both photos above)* became famous for showing *décollétage* on television. She didn't want Eva to compete with her, so she tricked her into dressing conservatively.

When Eva came out and greeted her host, she claimed, "Faye showed her tits, except for the nipples, and I looked like an old maid schoolteacher in my high-necked dress. After the show, I threatened to take Elliott Roosevelt away from her. She startled me by telling me, 'You can have him!'"

the life of a recluse with Anne Roosevelt, the divorced wife of John Roosevelt, Elliott's brother.

On the way back to his home that night, Sanders at the wheel told Eva, "Someone should write a book just on FDR's children and their former spouses—what a tangled web."]

Back in the early 1950s, Eva's TV appearances attracted a lot of media attention.

One TV critic wrote that "Fluffy best delineates the difference between Eva and Zsa Zsa. Despite Eva getting a jump as the first Gabor sister on TV, Eva's public image was based on sophistication, continental understanding, and sweetness; she lacked the tartness and bite of Zsa Zsa. In the 1950s, Zsa Zsa was destined to be the public favorite, just as she had been Mama Jolie's favorite at home. But Eva paved the way for Zsa Zsa's appearances on TV."

Looking back on Eva's TV career, a *Vanity Fair* writer in 2006 defined Eva as "a game performer with a wholesome, even cheerful, sensuality that came under the continental sophistication that was supposedly her calling card—she came across like Sally Field doing a party impression of Marlene Dietrich."

"Oh, *dahlink,* if you think all this work on TV and in road shows left no time for romance, you would be dead wrong," Eva said. "In the 1950s, one divine man after another came and went from my life, often too quickly. I was, however, too busy to check to see if they were married. I always thought it was too personal to ask a beau if he were married. After all, it was an invasion of privacy."

***

"If all Ukrainians are like John Hodiak, then book me a seat on the next plane to Kiev," Eva said during her brief fling with him in the wake of his 1952 divorce from Anne Baxter. *[Along with Tallulah Bankhead, Eva had appeared with Baxter in* A Royal Scandal.*]*

Alfred Hitchcock had cast Hodiak in his *Lifeboat* (1944), a film starring Tallulah Bankhead. During the shoot, Tallulah invited Hodiak to her dressing room. "I absolutely demand that you fuck me, *dahling,*" she ordered. "I've always had this thing for Poles, if you get my drift."

[Hodiak was Ukrainian.]

"I met John when he was going through a crisis and was uncertain of his future career," Eva said. "He often talked about his life and his indecisions. He seemed deeply troubled. In 1949, movie exhibitors had labeled him 'box office poison.'"

Louis B. Mayer had wanted him to change his name from Hodiak when he'd signed a seven year contract with MGM, but he'd refused.

"John may not have been the best looking man in Hollywood, but once a woman saw him in the nude, she'd go for him bigtime," Eva said. "I think he managed to seduce many of his leading ladies, including Judy Garland, Lucille Ball, Lana Turner, Ava Gardner, and Hedy Lamarr, the usual suspects. Word of John's physical assets had spread quickly through the Hollywood grapevine to the reigning screen beauties of the 1940s."

Regrettably for Hodiak, many matinee idols of the 1930s, including Clark Gable and Robert Taylor, had returned from the war, and leading roles eluded Hodiak. He often appeared with these better-established idols, whose availability forced him to accept second or even third leads. He made *Command Decision* with Gable in 1948. "But in that picture, instead of getting the girl, I had Van Johnson chasing after me," he ruefully told Eva.

"I'm getting tired of second fiddle roles," he told her as he lay with her in bed smoking a cigarette after intercourse. "Always the star's brother, or whatever. I just wasn't cut out for that. I know I'll never be another Gary Cooper, so I'm going to Broadway to try my luck there."

He did appear on stage in New York in *The Caine Mutiny,* but returned to Hollywood to film *The Trial (1955)* alongside Eva's future lover, Glenn Ford.

Before he left for New York, Eva had proposed marriage to Hodiak, but he turned her down. "I was hurt once by Anne. I don't want to be hurt again."

"John was terrified of life," Eva said. "He even got butterflies in his stomach when he had to make an entrance into a party. He was afraid of meeting people. He was so sensitive that even the slightest criticism would cut him to the quick. He was not made for Hollywood, where the attack knives were always being sharpened. I think the bastards finally got to him."

"Every time he went out with me, he always brought me a present," Eva said. "He was the exact opposite of Zsa Zsa's stingy George Sanders. John once bought this six-room house and moved the entire Hodiak clan into it, including his three siblings and their families. He supported them. No wonder Baxter divorced him."

The last time I encountered him, it was in New York, and it was quite by accident," she said. "I always had fond memories of him, but he didn't look well. He'd suffered from hypertension for years. He told me that he had frequent dizzy spells. Two

Eva had to wait until Anne Baxter no longer wanted **John Hodiak** as a husband before taking up with him. He is pictured above as he appeared in *Lifeboat*, Tallulah Bankhead's best picture.

"John was a lost and lonely soul, and I even proposed marriage to him. He gracefully turned me down," Eva said.

months later, at the age of forty-one, he collapsed and died of coronary thrombosis."

"He was a sad, dear man, and I wept when I heard that he'd gone."

***

Eva always claimed that she had "discovered" the handsome Basque actor, Jacques Bergerac. That was before he fell in love with two other blonde actresses, Ginger Rogers and Dorothy Malone, and married both of them.

"Zsa Zsa and I shared some of the same men with Ginger," Eva said. "They included…Let's see: Howard Hughes, Greg Bautzer, Burgess Meredith, David Niven. Unlike Ginger, we never got around to Desi Arnaz, Jean Gabin, Cary Grant, George Montgomery, Dick Powell, or Jimmy Stewart. Ginger, however, danced her way to all of them."

Eva appeared with Bergerac in a 1950s NBC television show called *NBC.* "Within fifteen minutes, I'd developed a crush on him."

Growing up in Biarritz, the chic Atlantic resort in southwestern France, Bergerac became a lawyer, but changed career directions and became an actor. He is best remembered today for his appearance in *Gigi (1958),* directed by Vincente Minnelli, who reportedly was thrilled by the male beauty of two of its stars: Bergerac's and that of Louis Jourdan, who was once voted "the handsomest man in the world."

"There was something magical about **Jacques Bergerac**," Eva said. "When he walked into a room, women swooned. He was always beautifully bronzed and had such a masculine body—and a lot of other attractions."

"He got away from me. But lucky Ginger Rogers. Lucky Dorothy Malone."

The assessment of both Eva and Rogers is the same: Bergerac was extraordinarily handsome and totally charming. "He was the kind of man women flirted with, or did something else with, *dahlink*," Eva claimed.

"I've always considered Basque men the most beautiful in the world," Eva said. "Of course, they are also known for being temperamental."

Having grown up on the beaches of France, Bergerac liked to swim, play tennis, and end the evening dancing. "I think I fell in love with him when we took our first swim together," she said. "He toweled me dry and rubbed my back with this fragrant lotion that evoked the smell of almonds."

"My memory of him is still vivid," she said. "If he had any flaw at all, it was a tendency to develop a boil on his *derrière.* Otherwise, he was perfect. He also seemed to have a fixation on the legend of Eva Perón, who was dying of cancer in Argentina. He told me, 'Any woman named Eva is a woman to love and cherish.'"

Bergerac was a fan of the bullfights. "Personally, I think bullfighting is barbaric," Eva said. "But had we been in Spain, I'm sure he could have talked me into going. I agreed with Rogers, who said that "Jacques could talk a pig out of the curl in its tail.'"

Eva noticed that not just beautiful women, but homosexuals were attracted to Jacques, who was straight, fending off their advances.

Rogers faced that problem with him when they went to visit the Georgian-style home of Noël Coward in the south of France.

"After lunch, Jacques and Noël left me alone while they disappeared for a tour of the house," Rogers wrote in her autobiography. "When half an hour had passed, I summoned the butler and told him I was ready to go and would be in the car. Jacques appeared sheepishly in ten minutes, but nothing would soothe my ruffled feathers. Because of this incident, Noël Coward, the man, was lessened in my eyes."

When Eva heard that Bergerac and Rogers were divorcing in 1957, she attempted to call him, but never got through. Rogers told friends that she had discovered that Bergerac was being unfaithful, although she maintained, "He was still my knight in shining armor."

"*Dahlink,* a woman must realize that when she marries a man as gorgeous as Jacques Bergerac, of course he will be unfaithful," Eva said. "Half the world wanted to crawl into bed with this Basque Adonis—and many of them did."

***

Because of her increasing recognition in television, Eva was lured back to Hollywood to star in an occasional movie, beginning with the 1952 release of *Love Island.* Her leading man, Paul Valentine, was cast as U.S. Navy pilot Lt. Richard Tabor, who crash lands on a remote island in the South Pacific.

There, he encounters a beautiful Balinese beauty, Sarna, as played by Eva. "Yes, *dahlink,* the producer, Sol Lesser, cast me, with thick Hungarian accent and all, as this native girl. I wore a flowery hat, a raven-black wig, and a sarong *à la* Dorothy Lamour."

Eva found Valentine handsome and compelling, and within the week added him to her list of conquests. "After all, I had to make love to him on camera. Why not off?"

The native New Yorker had adopted the name of "Paul Valentine" after his appearance with Robert Mitchum in the 1947 *Out of the Past,* one of the greatest of all *film noirs.* Prior to that, he had billed himself as Valin Valentinoff, or as Val Valentine.

Before meeting Eva, he'd been a ballet dancer and had starred in Broadway musicals such as *Follow the Girls* and *Gypsy Lady.* During his brief film career, he worked not only with Mitchum, but with Jane Greer, Joan Fontaine, Richard Widmark, Robert De Niro, Ray Milland, Susan Hayward, and the Marx brothers.

At the time of Eva's fling with Valentine, he had just emerged from a divorce from the striptease artist, Lili St. Cyr, whom he'd married in 1946. She was one of the top three strippers in America, her competitors being Gypsy Rose Lee and Ann Corio.

St. Cyr was tabloid fodder, not only because of her husbands (she was married six times), but because of the brawls over her and her suicide attempts. Her trademark act was "The Flying G." At the end of each performance, a stagehand would pull on a fishing rod attached to a quick-release on her G-string, and the flimsy garment, as the lights dimmed, would fly into the balcony.

Her performances were constantly denounced as "immoral, obscene, and indecent."

Before meeting St. Cyr, Eva had learned from Valentine that his former wife had been involved in an affair with the emerging starlet, Marilyn Monroe. At the time, Eva's knowledge of Monroe was very limited, although she'd seen *All About Eve,* wherein Monroe briefly emoted with Eva's (then) brother-in-law, George Sanders.

Zsa Zsa had constantly complained to Eva that Monroe was having an affair with her husband. After learning this about Monroe, Eva could hardly wait to inform Zsa Zsa that Monroe was a bisexual.

[Anna Freud, who analyzed Monroe during a week in London in 1956, also determined that she was a bisexual

Lili St. Cyr's fifth husband, actor Ted Jordan, would write a book in 1989 entitled Norma Jean: My Secret Life with Marilyn Monroe. *In it, he backed up Valentine's claim that St. Cyr had engaged in lesbian sex with Monroe.]*

When Eva met St. Cyr, the stripper expressed resentment of her former lover, and seemed terribly jealous of Monroe's increasing acclaim. "When I met Monroe, she was a mousy, brown-haired gal with a high, squeaky voice," St. Cyr charged to Eva. "She stole my whole *persona*—my way of dressing, of talking, my movements. She learned to become a sex goddess because of me. Now she's the rage of the nation. I feel I've been raped."

One evening, Valentine took Eva to Ciro's in Hollywood to see St. Cyr perform as "The Anatomic Bomb." Her act was later denounced as "lewd and lascivious," and she was hauled into court. Once there, she charmed the mostly male jury, insisting that her act was both "refined and elegant." She won the hearts of the jury, who acquitted her of any so-called crime.

Eva's confidant, Susan Hayward, who had once worked with Valentine, was eager for details about Eva's affair with her former flame. "Dear heart, now you're reduced to taking my sloppy seconds," Hayward said, teasing Eva.

"Oh, Susan," Eva said, "Watch that acid tongue of yours or else you're likely to get my quiche in that beautiful face of yours. You don't want to end up with egg on your face, now, do you?"

"From what I've seen of this turkey you're in, you're the one who's going to end up with egg on her face when this movie is released."

Hayward was right.

"The film was dumped on the market with no promotion," Eva claimed. "The producer, Sol Lesser, obviously realized what a disaster it was. Lesser did better promotion for one of his male stars, Bela Lugosi, than he did

Eva Gabor in *Love Island*

with me. He also did well with promotions for the hunks in those Tarzan movies—Johnny Weissmuller, Lex Barker, and that beefy Gordon Scott. Apparently, Lesser was better at promoting beefcake than my cheesecake in a sarong."

One critic called *Love Island* "the dullest, stupidest, and most worthless film ever made."

It was later suggested that the public had to wait until Zsa Zsa starred in *The Queen from Outer Space* before a worse performance could be viewed. Lesser thought so little of *Love Island* that he did not renew the copyright and today it is in the public domain.

[In 1958, Eva encountered Lesser at a Hollywood party, and they laughed at "what a joke" Love Island had been. He told her that he was retiring from films. "I have reached the age that one either finishes on top or far below. I've decided to end on top, so I'm leaving." He spent his remaining years restoring many of his early films, dying in 1980.

He'd told Eva that his greatest regret was not having a copy of his "lost film," The Last of the Barbary Coast, shot in 1915, when he had lived in San Francisco.

He'd heard from the authorities that they were going to shut down the Barbary Coast, a raucous district of brothels, gambling, "peg houses,"

"My performance in *Love Island* with **Paul Valentine** *(lower photo)* was interpreted as High Camp even before the term was invented," **Eva** claimed. "It was producer Sol Lesser who cast me as a raven-haired South Seas island temptress."

"The scriptwriter should have explained why a girl with a Hungarian accent was found on this remote island," Eva said. "At least I got Paul Valentine off screen. He'd been married to that stripper, Lili St. Cyr. Marilyn Monroe not only stole Lili's *persona*, but had a lesbian romp with her, too."

*(where sailors sodomized young boys), dope dives, and saloons. Shot on loca-
tion in these dives, it was the first truly lurid "exploitation" film and made so
much money for Lesser, he was able to purchase a chain of movie houses.*

*After spending time that night with Lesser, Eva said, "I feel that all the
films I've made will suffer the fate of Sol's movie about the Barbary Coast. No
one will want to preserve one of my films, especially* Love Island.*"]*

***

Months later when a writer for *The Hollywood Reporter* asked Eva about
her romance with Paul Valentine, her face flushed with anger. "Why don't you
ask Ronald Reagan?" she said. "He invented the term '*LeadingLady-itis.*' During the making of most films, the leading man often succumbs to the charms
of his leading lady. When the film is wrapped, so is the romance. Both the male
and female stars pick up the pieces of the lives they left behind. That's how the
game is played in Hollywood. I hardly invented the game, *dahlink.*"

Eva told Susan Hayward, "If Ronald Reagan can develop *LeadingLady-
itis*, I can come down with a case of *LeadingMan-itis*. On every film I make, I
view myself as a total failure if I don't find some gorgeous man to seduce. Of
course, I was stuck with Boris Karloff, but most often I hit the jackpot. In my
new picture, *Paris Model (1953),* I've trained my sights on Robert Hutton and
Tom Conway."

"I've heard nothing but fabulous things about Hutton," Hayward said. "But
isn't Tom Conway your brother-in-law?"

"Just because Zsa Zsa is married to his brother, George Sanders, doesn't
mean I can't sleep with Tom," Eva protested. "Is there a law in America that a
woman can't sleep with her brother-in-law? In Hungary, *dahlink,* it's a time-
honored custom."

In *Paris Model,* quickie producer Albert Zugsmith linked four stories by
using the same Paris original gown, a garment the script defined as "Nude at
Midnight." It was first worn most glamorously by Eva herself, who portrayed
the character of a "good bad girl," Gogo Montaine, in the first of the film's four
sub-plots. Her date for the evening is Tom Conway, who was cast as the Maharajah of Kim Kepore.

In the next sequence, the gown is illegally copied by Betty Barnes (Paulette
Goddard), who makes a social gaffe when the wife of her boss shows up in the
same design.

In the film's third mini-plot, Marion Marmelee (Marilyn Maxwell) wears
the gown to coerce her husband's boss into giving him a "promotion.

Finally, Marta Jensen (Barbara Lawrence) dons the gown in hopes that her
erstwhile beau, Charlie Johnson (Robert Hutton) will pop the question. Conway

434

returns for an appearance in the final sequence.

Eva carried through on her threat, and within two days, she was seen at Ciro's dancing with Hutton. "He's God's gift to women," she later proclaimed. The son of a hardware merchant, he was also the cousin of Woolworth heiress Barbara Hutton, who, years later, would tangle with Zsa Zsa for boudoir rights to the playboy, Porfirio Rubirosa.

"I'm following in Lana Turner's footsteps," Eva announced to her friends.

She was referring to Turner's dating of Hutton when she filmed her greatest movie, *The Postman Always Rings Twice.* A Hollywood writer headlined the story of her real-life romance with Hutton as *LANA'S BIGGEST THRILL.* Other actresses who'd had the privilege of going to bed with Hutton were amused at the double meaning of that headline.

When Eva first met Hutton, he'd begun a downward cycle of playing in Westerns and mostly B movies. But for a while during the war, he'd been a leading man. He was not drafted into the Army and consequently, got many lucky breaks in Hollywood through what was known as "victory casting." Many big stars, such as Robert Taylor, Tyrone Power, and James Stewart, even Clark Gable, had voluntarily joined the military. With these actors unavailable because of their military service, many B-list actors, previously assigned to fourth or fifth billing, rose quickly and became romantic leads.

"Everyone told me I looked like Jimmy Stewart," Hutton told Eva. "Some roles that Jimmy might have played went to me."

His most famous role was in the 1944 film, *Hollywood Canteen,* in which he played a young soldier who falls in love with a beautiful actress, Joan Leslie.

Hutton confessed to Eva that when he'd made *Destination Tokyo (1954),* with Cary Grant and John Garfield, "Cary fell for me big time. I'm ashamed to admit it, but I gave in to him because he's such a big star."

"*Dahlink,*" she said. "That's nothing to be ashamed of. I, too, would have given in to Cary Grant if he'd asked me."

[Years later, Eva got in touch with Hutton and sent her condolences when she'd read that he'd broken his back in an accident near his home in Kingston, New York, where he'd been born.

"That poor, dear boy, who was such a dahlink,

Robert Hutton, who was one of Barbara Hutton's cousins, never made it big in Hollywood, but he was a big thrill to such blondes as Lana Turner and Eva. "I dated him—perhaps more than just dated—when we appeared together in *Paris Model,*" Eva said.

"Poor Bob only became a star when the really big stars such as Gable and that divine Tyrone Power joined the war effort. When the male stars came home from the battlefront, Bob's moment of glory faded."

spent the last years of his life in a dreary medical care facility," Eva said, *"a hopeless basket case. Sometimes hearing about what happens to Hollywood stars makes me want to cry. I fear my own final days."*

Robert Hutton died at the age of 74 in 1994.]

During the shooting of *Paris Model,* Eva bounced back and forth between Hutton and a sexual tryst with Conway. "Instead of romantic endearments whispered in my ear by Tom, we spent most of our time discussing how he felt about living in the shadow of his famous brother, George Sanders," Eva said.

"My career was always been overshadowed by George," Conway claimed. "To make it even worse, we are the same type—tall, suave, and, dare I say it myself, handsome. My critics, however, say I don't have George's personal style. Nor, according to these birds of prey, do I possess his wit and charm."

Sanders had scored a hit with his detective film series, in which he played "the Falcon," a amateur detective. When Sanders bowed out of the series, Conway took over, starring in nine Falcon detective movies by 1946. "George was seriously pissed off when my Falcon films grossed more than his."

"I hate playing detective, and it seems I'm stuck with them for life," Conway told Eva. "After the Falcon, along came another detective role, Bulldog Drummond. I'm even playing Sherlock Holmes on radio, but fans of Basil Rathbone are writing in that they miss him in the part. And as you know, I replaced Vincent Price in the radio mystery series, *The Saint.* George had already played that character in a movie a decade before. Now I'm also playing the debonair police detective, Mark Saber."

Conway had nothing but praise for Zsa Zsa, claiming that he had attended her wedding to his brother, George. "When it came time to kiss the bride, I gave her some tongue, and I think it turned her on. I don't think her marriage to my brother is working out. She's strong and independent, and he wants a woman willing to light his cigarettes, pour his drinks, bring him his slippers, and go to bed with him whenever he's horny. Zsa Zsa is not that kind of dame. He always wants to keep her in the background, but she's an upfront kind of gal."

George had reasons to keep his first wife, Susan Larson, hidden," Conway said. "She was a waitress at The Brown Derby when George met her. He always told people who asked that he didn't take her to parties because she'd bore people to death."

"He can't say that about my sister," Eva quipped.

"Indeed," Conway said. "But he had a better reason to hide Susan. She was always bordering on the psychotic. She ended up in a mental institution."

"I hope that George doesn't drive Zsa Zsa to that point," Eva said. "Hilton put her away in an asylum for a few weeks."

At one point, Conway confessed that his own marriage to actress Lillian

Eggers was coming unglued, and that he was shopping around for another woman to marry. "How about it, Eva?"

She told him she was flattered, but turned him down.

"Look at the publicity we'd get," he said. "Two famous sisters marrying two famous brothers. We'll give the scoop to Louella."

"That is not the most romantic proposal I've ever heard," she said. "I don't want to settle down. I tried that with Charles Isaacs, and I was faithful to him for only three weeks, if that. I simply can't resist temptation. Whenever a leading matinee idol comes up to me and says, 'How about it?' I always give in. Call me Madame Sin."

"I'll confess I have a reason for wanting to marry you," Conway said. "George is the darling of the social set, especially the British expats. He's often entertained by the Ronald Colmans, although Ronnie doesn't like him. Benita adores him, however. He hangs with the Boyers, the Ronald Reagans, Brian Aherne, Douglas Fairbanks, Jr., and the Joseph Cottens. I'd like to move into that circle. With you as my arm candy, I think I can break into it. You might be the best thing that ever happened to me. I bet you could even get me to cut down on my booze."

"That's not a reason for me to marry you," she said. "Let's be friends. Sleep together—or not—depending on our moods. I desire freedom. I found marriage too restrictive."

"My dear, you're the most liberated woman I've talked to," he said.

"I don't have the reputation, but it is I, not Zsa Zsa, not Magda, who is the most promiscuous of the Gabors. For some reason, when I meet a man, I invariably glance in the direction of his crotch. But I do it ever so discreetly."

***

To break the boredom of her *hausfrau* life with George Sanders, Zsa Zsa had been expanding her *haute couture* wardrobe in anticipation of accompanying him to London. He'd signed with MGM to co-star in an adaptation of *Ivanhoe*, based on the novel about medieval England by Sir Walter Scott. His fellow stars included such big names as Elizabeth Taylor, Robert Taylor, and Joan Fontaine.

Zsa Zsa had prepared for weeks for the trip, but on the morning of departure, Sanders announced to her, "You're not going. You would find London boring, and, besides, having a wife along would cramp my style."

She burst into tears and sobbed throughout the day, calling Eva, Jolie, and Magda to complain. "Being the wife of George Sanders is not big enough for me. I want more than that in my life."

That summer of 1951 loomed dismally in front of her. Unlike the other Gabors, she had nothing to do. Eva was touring the summer "straw hat" circuit in regional theaters, and Magda was being wooed by a series of both eligible and not-so-eligible suitors. Jolie was playing around with boy toys while selling a lot of jewelry at her boutique.

Jolie informed Zsa Zsa that Eva and Magda were competing to see which one could have the most suitors.

Zsa Zsa's prediction about the Nicky Hilton/Elizabeth Taylor marriage evolving into a disaster had come true. Nicky no longer visited Zsa Zsa as regularly as he used to, perhaps appearing once a month. Among other girlfriends, he was rumored to be dating Marilyn Monroe, who Zsa Zsa insisted on calling "that tramp starlet."

Eva had previously confessed to Zsa Zsa that Tom Conway had seduced her during the making of their film, *Paris Model.*

Zsa Zsa was surprised when Conway himself called her late one night, a sense of panic in his voice. He'd been appearing on a TV series called *Bachelor's Haven,* a televised "advice to the lovelorn" program where letters from women were read on the air.

The panelists were supposed to come up with a glib solution to whatever problem was cited. Conway explained that every program featured the wife of a celebrity. For some reason, Janet Leigh had to cancel, and consequently, he urgently needed a replacement for the following morning's show.

The thought of an appearance before live cameras sent Zsa Zsa into a panic. "I wouldn't know what to say."

"I've never known you to be at a loss for words," Conway said.

"Besides, I'm not an actress."

"You don't have to be," he said. "The show calls for the wife of a celebrity."

"I have nothing to wear," she protested.

"Only fifty designer gowns," he answered.

Finally, Conway convinced her to arrive the following morning at CBS Studios in Hollywood. She spent most of the night deciding on what to wear, finally selecting a simple, very tasteful Balenciaga black dress which would set off her diamonds.

That morning at the studio, Conway greeted her with his familiar "snake tongue kiss," before complimenting her on how fabulous she looked.

Another of Eva's colleagues in *Paris Model* was her brother-in-law, **Tom Conway** *(photo above).* She was willing to make love to him, but turned down his proposal of marriage.

"I feared he wanted the publicity and desired me as arm candy more than he wanted a wife," Eva said.

"George told me I was too stupid to go on television," she said.

"You're one of the wittiest women I know," he said, "a female Oscar Wilde."

Johnny Jacobs was the moderator of the show, whose panelists included Kay Aldridge, wife of the oil tycoon, and Paul Coates, a columnist for the *Los Angeles Mirror-News.*

As the cameras rolled, Jacobs whistled at the number of sparkling diamonds Zsa Zsa was wearing.

"These are nothing, *dahlink,* she said. "Only my daytime diamonds."

The audience burst into laughter and then applause. Zsa Zsa was off and running.

Question after question was put to her by viewers, and she always had a ready comeback.

One woman asked, "Do you believe in large families?"

"Oh yes, *dahlink,* Every woman should have at least three husbands."

One housewife asked, "My husband is a traveling salesman, but I know he strays even when he's at home. What should I do?"

"Shoot him in the legs," Zsa Zsa answered.

Another woman asked, "I'm breaking my engagement to a very wealthy man. He gave me a beautiful home, a mink coat, diamonds, an expensive car, and a stove. What shall I do?"

Caressing her diamond bracelet, Zsa Zsa looked directly into the camera and said, "You have to be fair, *dahlink.* Give him back the stove."

Each of Zsa Zsa's answers brought a wild response from the studio audience, and the CBS switchboard was flooded with calls of approval from future Zsa Zsa fans, many of whom wanted to see more of "this Hungarian dame with the diamonds."

The producer of the show, William Brennan, asked her to sign to become a regular on *Bachelor's Haven,* for which she would be paid thirty-six dollars for every appearance. "Sounds like fun," Zsa Zsa said, agreeing to the low paycheck.

The next morning in Bel Air, Zsa Zsa was still immersed in her beauty sleep. Her maid, who looked a bit like Hattie McDaniel in *Gone With the Wind,* arrived with her breakfast tray. "Good morning, ma'am," she said. "Your phone's been ringing off the wall. It seems the whole world is trying to get in touch with you. Forgive me for saying so, but you're the biggest thing since a man discovered he could get an erection."

The first call Zsa Zsa returned was to Pamela Mason, who told her, "I've just read *The Hollywood Reporter.* They've called you the most beautiful girl ever to have appeared on television."

Then she returned Tom Conway's call. He assured her, "You were sensational, doll." Then he invited her on a date to Ciro's that night.

"But wouldn't George get jealous?" she asked.

"He's too busy to notice, "Conway assured her. "And anyway, in London, he's spending every night with Pamela Churchill."

The memory of how she had sustained an affair with Pamela's boyfriend (Elie de Rothschild) must have crossed Zsa Zsa's mind

"You're launched!" Tom continued. "If George doesn't watch out, you may become a bigger star than he ever was."

In a very provocative sign-off, she said, "Please come over, *dahlink*, at eight o'clock. You don't need to bring your pajamas. You'd fit perfectly into a pair of red silk pajamas I recently bought for George, a pair he's never worn."

The calls that morning seemed endless, not only from columnist James Bacon, but from Louella Parsons and Hedda Hopper. Sidney Skolsky took time off from panting after Marilyn Monroe for an interview with Zsa Zsa, as did a reporter from *Daily Variety*. Skolsky would be the first to label Zsa Zsa's quips as "Gaborisms."

The Associated Press had filed a story that morning—*A STAR IS BORN OVERNIGHT.*

Three days later, without an appointment, agent/mogul Russell Birdwell pulled up in his new Cadillac in front of Zsa Zsa's Bel Air manse. He wanted to take her on as a client, to supplement a roster that already included Howard Hughes, Joan Blondell, and Marlene Dietrich.

Birdwell was known as the P.T. Barnum of Hollywood publicists. During his tenure with David O. Selznick, he had launched a nationwide search for an unknown to portray Scarlett O'Hara in *Gone With the Wind*. Birdwell was also the agent who'd made Carole Lombard a household name.

As part of his effort to impress her with his press and publicity muscle, Birdwell had already devised "a Zsa Zsa campaign that would rival the 1944 launch of the D-Day landing on the beaches of Normandy."

In her living room, he dazzled her with what was in the offing. It included front page coverage in 225 Sunday newspapers owned by William Randolph Hearst, Sr. *Collier's* wanted her for a magazine cover, as did *Look, Paris-Match*, and the *London Picture Post*. "And *Cosmopolitan* wants to put you on its cover," Birdwell said.

"There's something even bigger about to happen," Birdwell told her. "Philippe Halsman, the best photographer in America, wants to fly to Hollywood to photograph you for the cover of *Life* magazine."

The first afternoon that Zsa Zsa went shopping in Beverly Hills, she was mobbed by fans seeking her autograph. "Everybody wanted to touch me, talk to me, or get my signature. When I got home, tons of letters came in, often from men who wanted to marry me. Many of them enclosed photographs of themselves with full erections. Those were my favorites, *dahlink.*"

Every night, Zsa Zsa went out with either Birdwell or with Conway. Hollywood viewed her "dates" with Birdwell strictly as publicity stunts. And whenever she was seen out and about with Conway, her loyal brother-in-law, he was interpreted as an appropriately restrained escort during her husband's absence in England.

In a memoir, Zsa Zsa did not fully admit to an affair with Conway. However, she did write that they dated when she was grappling with all of Sanders' adulterous affairs. "I was prey to the manipulations of George's younger brother, Tom Conway." That statement was probably true, except that Conway was Sanders' older brother, not his younger one.

"With George out of the way, Tom formulated the perfect scenario by which to undermine him," Zsa Zsa enigmatically wrote.

Birdwell later said, "I knew that Tom Conway and Zsa Zsa had an affair during the months Sanders was in London filming *Ivanhoe.* He told me so himself, and Zsa Zsa admitted it too."

"I may have been responsible for Zsa Zsa keeping the affair going," Birdwell continued. "I had learned from Sanders' best friend, Brian Aherne, that months before Sanders met Zsa Zsa, he'd been banging Magda. Neither Sanders nor Magda had ever told Zsa Zsa about this affair."

"When Zsa Zsa learned about it, she was furious, even threatening to get a divorce. As unreasonable as it was, since she didn't even know Sanders at the time, she felt both her husband and her sister had betrayed her. Zsa Zsa was also grateful to Conway. After all, he'd helped launch her into stardom."

"She admitted to me that when she'd first experienced a climax with Conway, she'd shouted, 'George, oh George,'" Birdwell said. "According to her, Conway snapped at her, 'Forget about my rotten brother, and concentrate on the man who's plugging you now.'"

During the course of her secret affair with Conway, Birdwell, as her new publicist, escorted Zsa Zsa to premiers and to A-list Hollywood parties, showing her off in front of producers and directors. "He treated me like he'd done with Lana Turner, giving me the full star treatment, even though I didn't deserve it…not yet," Zsa Zsa said. "A chauffeured limousine, photographers waiting as I stepped out of the car in sable and diamonds. A whole new life almost overnight had opened up for me."

One night, while Birdwell was dancing with Zsa Zsa at Mocambo's, she attracted the attention of director Mervyn LeRoy, who had done so much to launch Lana Turner.

He approached Birdwell's table, where the publicist introduced him to Zsa Zsa. Not ten minutes of talk had passed before LeRoy offered her a starring role in MGM's newest and most expensive musical, *Lovely to Look At,* co-starring Kathryn Grayson, Howard Keel, and comedian Red Skelton.

"No test is needed," LeRoy said. "I've seen you on television. You photograph beautifully. You're a natural."

Birdwell chimed in: "Mervyn, we've got a new Marilyn Monroe here without benefit of the nude calendar. A woman of class and beauty who doesn't have to shake her tits and wiggle her ass to attract attention. The public will adore her."

***

Blissfully unaware of what was happening back in Hollywood, and perhaps not really caring, the self-centered Sanders wrapped *Ivanhoe,* kissed Elizabeth Taylor and Pamela Churchill goodbye, and left London aboard a plane headed back to California.

He'd wired Zsa Zsa to meet him at the airport. "My little *Cokiline*, your loving son is returning to the nest," he'd wired her, giving details. But when he landed, he found no one waiting for him, including Zsa Zsa, who had other commitments that day at MGM.

He stopped at a newsstand to catch up on the local trade papers. Once there, he was stunned to spot his wife on the cover of *Life* magazine. "What in hell has she done to merit a *Life* magazine cover?" he asked the befuddled vendor.

He read the article before leaving the newsstand, only to discover that Zsa Zsa was the most talked about personality in Hollywood.

In October of 1951, **Zsa Zsa** graced the cover of *Life* magazine. Almost overnight, with virtually no credentials, she'd become a star.

"My God," he said. "She's become a star overnight. Who needs acting talent in this god forsaken place called Hollywood? I said she was too stupid to go on television, but I overlooked something. Hollywood has a long tradition of making stars out of stupid people. How could I have missed that?"

"I don't want to be bitchy, *dahlink*," she told Pamela Mason, "and Eva is my baby sister, but I looked so much more glamorous on the cover of *Life* than she did."

442

CHAPTER TEN
Don't Ask For Forever

Based in part on her growing fame, Zsa Zsa came into intimate contact with three legendary women—Marlene Dietrich, Greta Garbo, and Tallulah Bankhead.

***

DIETRICH

Back in her Bel Air manse, George Sanders, fresh from shooting *Ivanhoe* in England, invited Marlene Dietrich for dinner. Zsa Zsa had wanted Greta Keller to come as well, knowing that she and Dietrich had had an affair in Vienna during their stage appearance in a play called *Broadway,* but Greta was in New York appearing in concert.

Leaving the dinner arrangements to the cook, Zsa Zsa spend all afternoon preparing her makeup and her wardrobe to meet the legendary star. She feared Dietrich might have heard of her offer to appear in films at MGM and would be envious.

In Paris, Zsa Zsa had acquired a stunning gown by Christian Dior. Through an arrangement with Jolie, she wore a diamond-and-ruby necklace that belonged to Harry Winston, but was said to have been owned by Maria Theresa, the Empress of Austria.

Dietrich arrived alone at Zsa Zsa house. Sanders had refused to tell Zsa Zsa how he had met and knew the Berlin-born star, and she didn't really want to know.

In contrast to Zsa Zsa's glittering outfit, Dietrich wore slacks, a white silk blouse, and a pearl necklace. Her makeup had been skillfully, even artfully, applied to give her a peachy complexion and to conceal any tell-tale lines. She also had applied the "reddest of red" lipstick. She greeted Zsa Zsa with a passionate kiss on the mouth before planting the same on Sanders. When introduced to Zsa Zsa after the kiss, Dietrich stood back and appraised her figure, a bit too skeptically for Zsa Zsa's comfort.

Then she did something that shocked Zsa Zsa and even caused minor distress to Sanders, who did not shock as easily. She went to a phone and dialed the number of her husband, Rudolf ("Rudi)") Sieber, whom she'd married on May 17, 1923 at the registry office in a Berlin suburb. Although still married, they had long since turned their marriage into a friendship.

"Forgive me," Dietrich said to Zsa Zsa. "But I must get my husband, Rudi, on the phone. I need to tell him that I have found the perfect woman for him, a woman he can love and devote his life to so he will not spend eternity searching for a replacement for me."

Sanders had already told Zsa Zsa that Sieber and Dietrich were living apart and pursuing other loves. Dietrich's action came unexpectedly to Zsa Zsa, and seemed like a social gaff, since Zsa Zsa was at least pretending to be faithful to her husband, although he was more blatant about his affairs.

Within minutes, Dietrich had Sieber on the phone. "I've found her," she said. "The right woman for you. She is Mrs. George Sanders, and she is beautiful."

After some brief discussion in German, which Zsa Zsa understood, Dietrich handed her the phone. In her memoirs, Zsa Zsa admitted that both she and Sieber were "extremely embarrassed" to be introduced over the phone in this way.

Zsa Zsa later said, "Seiber and I had no interest in each other, and to this day, I can't understand why Marlene put us on the phone together. It also seriously pissed off George, but since it was Marlene, he quickly forgave her."

Over drinks, Dietrich recalled her long ago wedding day. "Weddings are supposed to be happy occasions, but mine wasn't. Rudi had a fiancée named Eva May. She was madly in love with him. Right after our wedding, we received news that she had been rushed to the hospital. She had slashed her wrists. She survived that, but the following year, she took a revolver and shot herself in the heart because Rudi had left her."

Nearly everyone's happiness is gained at the expense of someone else's," Sanders said.

"That's true," Dietrich said. "Many men have killed themselves over me, but I cannot be held responsible if these silly fools fall in love with me. What about you, Zsa Zsa? Have men died for you in Europe? Kings, princes, counts, whomever?

"Unlike you, Miss Dietrich, I'm not a *femme fatale,*" Zsa Zsa said. "More of a *hausfrau.*"

"My dear, I find that hard to believe," Dietrich said. "Housewives rarely land on the cover of *Life* magazine. Wherever I go, there is talk of Zsa Zsa Gabor. We ladies of a certain age are fearing the new arrivals from Europe. You're not going to replace me, are you?"

Don't worry, Marlene," Sanders said. "You and Zsa Zsa have completely different styles."

"You are called 'The Last Goddess,'" Zsa Zsa said. "That means exactly that. Of course, there will be those who come after you, but they won't be goddesses. You and Garbo, and a few others, were women of mystery, allure, and enchantment. Those qualities won't be found on the screen. Instead, the 1950s gets a nude Marilyn Monroe and those who feel all they have to do is show their breasts."

"You are so very kind," Dietrich said. "I find comparisons so odious. When *The Blue Angel* was released in America, critics said I have Garbo's eyes but Gloria Swanson's nose. To hell with that. I have my own eyes, my own nose. No one compared anybody else's legs to mine. My legs are my trademark. When I arrived in Hollywood, it was said that I had come to dethrone certain hollow temptresses—and I did. Swanson never made it in talking pictures until *Sunset Blvd.,* a picture that deliberately called for a bad actress."

"I beat out Pola Negri, and Tallulah failed to make it in Hollywood. Only Garbo endured for a while. Katharine Hepburn and I survived, but she is hardly a goddess. It was written only last week that I am too old to be a woman of mystery, too obvious."

"You are a timeless wonder," Sanders assured her. "

"That I doubt," she said. "Time, that relentless enemy of all women, marches on. The other week, I had drinks with Tallulah. She said that all of us legends, in time, become caricatures of ourselves."

"Oh, *dahlink*," Zsa Zsa said. "Not me. I've hardly ventured out the door, and reporters are already claiming that I'm a caricature of myself."

"You are a very interesting study," Dietrich said. "I've heard you on TV. You seem to link sex to every remark. It's amazing how you work sex in. You do not speak of love. I wonder if you've ever been in love."

"Very much so!" Zsa Zsa said. "I was—and *am*—madly in love with George, even though he doesn't put his slippers under my bed every night."

"If you marry a man for love, you are running a great risk," Dietrich said. "The risk of being painfully hurt. Marry for whatever reason—companionship, money, security, fondness—but never, never, my dear, marry for love. It's a poison pill."

Dietrich, Sanders, and Zsa Zsa talked until way past midnight. The two women did not become friends, and they would compete at least on one occasion for the same starring role.

Sanders carefully observed both of them. He later said that "Zsa Zsa was exactly what she appeared to be, blurting out the first thing that came into her mind, regardless of how indiscreet."

"In contrast, innocence was never the mode of Marlene," he said. "She was always conscious of her effect and the impression she was creating. I never knew anyone with such self-awareness. That's why she was so provocative on screen. When Zsa Zsa goes on the screen, what the viewer sees is what she is."

"Zsa Zsa dazzles by her wardrobe, her diamonds, and her beauty," he said. "She shocks by what comes out of her mouth, which apparently television audiences find devastatingly funny. All Marlene has to do is stand absolutely still, perhaps smoking a cigarette, and audiences find her fascinating even if she doesn't say a word. Few actors can do what Marlene can. Above all, Marlene is a star. Zsa Zsa a mere personality. To me, a star is a woman who can be fabulous without doing anything at all. Garbo, for instance."

After Dietrich departed for the night, Sanders learned exactly what Zsa Zsa thought. "She started throwing things at me," he later told Brian Aherne. "She accused me of preferring Dietrich over her."

"The only reason you're not involved with Dietrich right now is that she's old enough to be your grandmother," Zsa Zsa said. "Imagine coming into my house and trying to palm me off on some cast-off husband of hers—the nerve of that woman. I will plan no more dinners for your concubine."

"I want to leave you with one image," she said. "Have you ever concentrated on what Dietrich looks like when she emerges from her shower in the morning, dripping wet and with no makeup, and with a body that appealed to Goebbels and Hitler in the 1920s? One that could play a witch or a crone today?

***

GARBO

In a memoir, Zsa Zsa started to write quite candidly about her relationship with Greta Garbo, but she drew the curtain before supplying the rich details.

Their first encounter came when Sanders accepted an invitation to dinner at Brian Aherne's house in Santa Monica. Other guests included Lady Sylvia Ashley Gable (but no Clark), David Niven, and a rather effete Clifton Webb.

Garbo was the last guest to arrive. She wore brown corduroy trousers, a drab pullover sweater, and an anorak the color of tree bark.

Zsa Zsa was enthralled by Garbo's biscuit-colored hair and a face that was almost unlined, with its delicate nose made for sniffing only the most subtle of perfumes. "Her teeth were like pearls, and her eyelashes lush, though not in the freakist category of heavy-lidded Elizabeth Taylor," Zsa Zsa said.

In behavior equivalent of what he'd displayed with Dietrich, Sanders never told Zsa Zsa how he'd met Garbo. When he introduced her to Garbo, he said, "My wife has a wild crush on you."

As Zsa Zsa remembered it, "That was one of the first times in my life I actually blushed."

Garbo took it in stride, replying, "So many women do, so many men." She looked carefully at the beautifully made up and elegantly dressed Zsa Zsa. Speaking as if she were not there, Garbo said, "Your wife...she is so very beautiful."

Garbo spoke mostly with Aherne at the party and never talked to Zsa Zsa, but she did bid her good night. Sanders escorted her to her car. When he returned, he told Zsa Zsa, "You don't need to be so in love with her any more. When I kissed her, she smelled of cheap soap, whereas it must take a ton of flowers from the Côte d'Azur to make the perfumed soap you use."

Sanders was not with her when Zsa Zsa met Garbo the second time, the occasion being a party honoring Rex Harrison, who at the time was a hit on Broadway as the star of *My Fair Lady*. Aherne was the host once again at his townhouse on 62nd Street in New York.

This time, Zsa Zsa was more candid in her memoirs, claiming that "Garbo spent most of the evening standing behind the bar flirting with me. Rex was all over Garbo, and Garbo was all over me. I nearly melted."

Later that night, Zsa Zsa accepted Garbo's offer to drive her home, which was a suite at the Savoy Plaza Hotel.

In front of the hotel, Garbo asked her, "Darling, would you like to come to my apartment?"

"I was paralyzed," Zsa Zsa said as Garbo leaned over and kissed her on the lips. "I couldn't help kissing her back, because she was so overwhelmingly strong, and so beautiful. I've never had lesbian tendencies, but if I had ever had them, the woman of my life would definitely have been Greta Garbo."

And so, as far as Zsa Zsa's official memoirs go, the story abruptly ended.

But Sanders, Aherne, Greta Keller, Pamela Mason, and even Jolie herself, claimed at various periods that the Garbo/Zsa Zsa infatuation continued at infrequent intervals over a number of years.

From what her friends have said about what she'd told them, some rough outline of their relationship can be ascertained:

Once at a party at Aherne's house, Sanders told the dinner table, "From what I have gathered about Greta and Zsa Zsa, there has been some massaging of the vertebrae, fondling of breasts, deep kissing, and then goodbye without any guerilla activity. Trespass into Greta's most private world is *verboten.*"

Zsa Zsa was fond of quoting to friends whatever Garbo told her. She said the great star was "a forlorn and vulnerable woman concealing herself behind a series of masks she put up to keep the world out."

"I am a misfit in life, a sad person," Garbo told Zsa Zsa. She also gave strange advice, suggesting that whenever Zsa Zsa took a bath, she should always tie her hair with a yellow ribbon—"no other color." More advice included the use of only unpasteurized milk in tea.

One night in Manhattan, Garbo invited Zsa Zsa for a dinner which she prepared herself in a small kitchenette. It consisted of unsalted butter on bread, slices of ham, a strong-smelling cheese, and Swedish beer.

She had one grammatically awkward pet phrase that she used several times a night. "I must always be on guard that my goose will not be cooked."

Sometimes, Garbo spoke of love. "I view relationships as a drab necessity. In love-making, I do not prefer the staccato."

Zsa Zsa didn't know what that meant, but was too intimidated to ask.

"My trouble in life is not love," Garbo said. "I cannot talk of love because I have never experienced it, and therefore know nothing of it. My main trouble in life is finding a pair of shoes that comfortably fit me."

Zsa Zsa remembered another dinner at Garbo's apartment in New York, which began with what she called *kahr-vee-yeyarr.*

"When she served the caviar, I noticed that her hands, unlike her face, were weatherbeaten. She wore a man's white shirt that perhaps dated from the 1930s and was yellowed by time."

"We drank vodka, and she prepared some grilled lamb chops and steamed vegetables. Her favorite brand of cigarettes was Old Gold."

Later that winter night, the winds grew colder, but Zsa Zsa in a mink coat agreed to accompany Garbo for a walk through the frozen canyons of New York. "I like the ice and rain and wind," she said. "After all, I'm a Swede."

When Zsa Zsa departed from Garbo, the star warned her, "Remember, you are forbidden to phone me. It is I who will call you."

Zsa Zsa claimed, "I learned some of Garbo's little secrets. She keeps sardines and crackers under her bed for nourishment at night." Zsa Zsa chose not to tell her dinner companions how she acquired that boudoir revelation.

"Sometimes, when I dined with her, she let the conversation lag," Zsa Zsa said. "I soon learned not to fill in the gap with my chatter. When Garbo came out of her reverie, she sang in a low soft voice, 'Nobody knows the troubles I've seen but Jesus.'"

Once in Santa Monica, Zsa Zsa was invited to walk along the beach with Garbo at twilight. "She wanted to run for a time, although she had far more stamina than I did. She told me, 'We must keep our bodies in Olympic trim.'"

"One night at twilight, we spotted a bird with a wounded wing being pecked to death by greedy sea gulls," Zsa Zsa said.

"This is a sight that Tennessee Williams might have written about," Garbo said.

She said that her former lover, Mercedes de Acosta, once wrote a script for her called *Desperate,* in which she would dress as a man.

"Irving Thalberg at MGM rejected it and fired Mercedes," Garbo said. "He didn't think my dressing as a man would be good box office. I'd love to play Dorian Gray." She turned to Zsa Zsa. "You'd be perfect cast as a woman I destroy. I've also considered playing Georges Sand wearing velvet trousers and smoking a cigar. I've also had a fantasy about becoming St. Francis of Assisi on screen."

"Garbo lives in a state of self-enchantment," said Zsa Zsa. "She is egotistic and does not want to go out of her way to help anybody else. She is filled with tragic regrets and bad memories about what happened to such men as John Gilbert and Mauritz Stiller. She once told me that she only became a free woman 'when I withdrew from adulation.'"

Zsa Zsa remembered the last time she saw Garbo and what she said: "I wanted to be a writer or a painter, but I stumbled into what is called acting, and what I labeled as being a mannequin for Louis B. Mayer, a dreadful creature. But I do have a reason for living."

"Oh, please tell me," Zsa Zsa pleaded.

"I wait for the spring, when I can buy glazed apricots."

***

BANKHEAD

Whereas Eva had worked on *A Royal Scandal* with the formidable Tallulah Bankhead, Zsa Zsa had yet to meet the star Marlene Dietrich had defined as "the most immoral woman who ever lived."

Confessing to more than 500 love affairs with both women and men, Bankhead had married only one of them, Eva's former beau, actor John Emery.

No day passed that she did not consume two bottles of bourbon and smoked a hundred cigarettes.

In an attempt to save radio from being consumed by television, she had been cast as the hostess of *The Big Show.* In this serialized radio venue, she invited an array of celebrities, among them Dietrich, Ethel Merman ("You don't look a day over sixty, Ethel"), Douglas Fairbanks, Jr., Gary Cooper (her former lover), Ethel Barrymore, Gloria Swanson, and Judy Garland.

George Sanders had already been a guest on her show twice. *"Dahling,"* she told him. "I'm trying to grow old gracefully."

He retorted, "And so you have, my dear."

She attracted an audience of 30 million viewers, and Sanders decided it would be a good break for Zsa Zsa to go on the show with him as part of a husband-and-wife skit. He telephoned Bankhead's scriptwriters, assuring them, "Zsa Zsa will be great. She's the hottest thing in Hollywood."

Zsa Zsa had never heard of Bankhead's show, and did not know that the guests most often traded insults back and forth with its hostess.

Bankhead, of course, had an acid tongue. On her show, she accused Bette Davis of impersonating her in her creation of the character of Margo Channing in *All About Eve*. On the air, Bankhead called Davis a hag and said. "Wait until I get hold of her. I'll tear every hair out of her mustache."

She often had confrontations with guests backstage. When Jerry Lewis arrived an hour late for a rehearsal, Bankhead burst into his dressing room, denouncing him as a "son-of-a-bitch."

When Edith Piaf (whose English was not first-rate, thereby making her unequal to the task of defending herself with counter-quips) came on, Bankhead said, "The Little Sparrow looks like something I'd reject on my breakfast plate."

In later years, Zsa Zsa could have handled and perhaps triumphed over Bankhead's quips. But at the time of her booking on *The Big Show,* she was relatively inexperienced in live media.

Sanders escorted Zsa Zsa into the studio, where she was instructed to look over the script. Half an hour later, Bankhead barged in, giving Sanders a tongue kiss. Then she turned and appraised Zsa Zsa skeptically. "So this is Mrs. George Sanders."

"Actually, I want to be introduced as Zsa Zsa Gabor. I will always be known by that name. Mrs. George Sanders is merely my present designation."

"I see," Bankhead said. "Cocky little thing, isn't she, George?"

"You don't know the half of it, my dear," Sanders answered.

The script dialogue horrified Zsa Zsa, especially when she realized that her husband would be expected to say lines which included, "That's no lady, that's my wife. I don't really see much of her, but I keep her around to wash my socks."

"I refuse to allow George to say that," Zsa Zsa protested. "It makes me sound like some washerwoman."

"The line stays as it is, *dahling*," Bankhead said. "It's a funny skit. I'm the host, and I call the shots."

"I think the skit is insulting to me, and I won't participate," Zsa Zsa said. "I'm walking out."

"Nobody, you little bitch, walks out on Tallulah Bankhead."

Zsa Zsa stormed out of the studio anyway, and Sanders caught up with her in the parking lot. "I went to a lot of trouble to get you on this spot. Now, get your Hungarian fat ass back into the studio."

"I'm going home, and you can't stop me," Zsa Zsa said.

"You do that, and I'm walking out on the marriage," Sanders threatened.

She fled that day and found comfort that evening drinking with Greer Garson and Rosalind Russell, who dropped by her Bel Air house to see her.

By the following morning, news of Zsa Zsa's walkout on Bankhead had appeared in Walter Winchell's column, as well as within Dorothy Kilgallen's "Voice of Broadway." The *New York Journal-American* offered a contest with prize money for the best answer to the question: "Was Zsa Zsa right when she resented the slur on her marriage?"

All the Gabors lined up behind Zsa Zsa, Magda asserting that the script "was untrue and undignified."

Zsa Zsa was at MGM when her maid called to tell her that Sanders had arrived at her home with a moving van. Although he had very few of his possessions within the Bel Air house, he wanted his piano, which had been paid for by Zsa Zsa.

Ironically, Zsa Zsa was giving an interview to *McCalls* when she heard the news. When she came back to the interview, the reporter's first question to her was, "Now, Zsa Zsa, tell us how you keep a man?"

After five nights, she grew heartsick from missing Sanders. She made him a ham sandwich and put it in a bag with a bottle of milk, his favorite nighttime treat, and drove over to his apartment. When she came in, he was in bed watching a Western on TV.

She fell into his arms, and he seduced her, telling her that he hadn't had time to pick up another woman during his absence from Bel Air. The next morning, she persuaded him to come back to her house.

Years later, she recalled, "I didn't know it at the time, but the marriage was doomed even though he returned. I had no idea a playboy looming on my horizon would have my private life splashed on every frontpage in the nation."

*   *   *

Zsa Zsa had read in a newspaper that the handsome, rich, and charismatic John F. Kennedy was in Los Angeles. As regards his appeal to women, the line formed on both his left and his right, so she didn't expect he'd call her in remembrance of their previous encounter. But call he did at four o'clock that afternoon at her home in Bel Air.

He'd obtained her unlisted phone number from someone. "It's been too long," he said. "I've missed you. "My god, you're famous. You're so publicized, I can't pass a newsstand without seeing your face on the cover of some magazine."

"When it comes to magazine covers, Elizabeth Taylor and Marilyn Monroe have me beat," she said. "You must have encountered both of them on your visits out here in the 40s."

Elizabeth, I know, of course," he said. "Robert Stack introduced us. If I've met Marilyn before, I don't remember. If I did, she sure didn't look like she does today. But I didn't call you to talk about other women. I want to know how you've been."

"I'm not the innocent virgin you deflowered so long ago," she said, teasing him.

"Zsa Zsa, come on," he said. "You weren't innocent when you popped out of the womb."

"I won't debate that," she said. "At least, I'm more experienced than when we last met."

"So am I," he said. "A schoolboy no more. Oh, I meant to ask you. How is married life?"

"Frankly, I can recommend to you that you stay a bachelor," she said. "Marriage is such a roller-coaster ride that one can easily fall off. Trust me, I've already tried it three times."

"A little bee buzzed by and told me that George Sanders is not in town."

"If that's a come-on I can inform you that champagne, caviar, and me, a vision in pink chiffon, will be waiting for you tonight at eight o'clock."

"Don't wear any outfit that will make it hard for you to shed," he said. Before he hung up, he delivered a "love ya."

Indeed, he showed up exactly on time. Pamela Mason had to wait until the next day for a report. "How was it?" she asked Zsa Zsa. "Are you madly in love with him? Are you divorcing George?"

"I adore Jack Kennedy," she said, "but there are serious problems. He puts up a good front, but he's really a basket case. He has to do it on his back."

"What exactly do you mean?"

"There are medical problems—very, very serious ones," she said. "He looks gorgeous on the outside, like Errol Flynn. But inside, also like Errol, he's falling apart. In his condition, I don't understand how he can have all the sex he's reported to enjoy with so many women. He seems to have lost weight, and he didn't have that much to lose. He has horrible pains in his abdomen, and even has so much back trouble I had to kneel down and put on his socks."

"At least he took off his socks during love-making," Pamela said. "Some men don't even go that far."

"He takes cortisone, Nembutal, and I don't know what else," Zsa Zsa said.

"He sounds like a walking pharmacy," Pamela said.

"Don't get me wrong," Zsa Zsa said. "I am very fond of him. He amuses me. I'd even marry him if he asked me. But Joseph Kennedy would never allow it, especially if he wants Jack to become president some day, like around 1964."

"Are you going to see him again?" Pamela asked.

"Only if he calls me," Zsa Zsa said. "I'm not going to pursue him."

"I'm not getting enough details about last night to satisfy my voyeuristic curiosity," Pamela said. "Can't you tell me more?"

"All right, I'll let you in on his darkest secret," Zsa Zsa said. "After intercourse, he likes to pluck out three of a woman's longest pubic hairs to keep as a souvenir."

"Maybe he keeps all that hair in a scrapbook with labels. It sure beats stamp collecting."

Gossip about JFK quickly disappeared when Zsa Zsa told her that she was taking an emergency trip to Paris to visit the houses of fashion. Sanders had alerted her that for many dress movies of that era, actresses were sometimes asked to wear their own wardrobes, if suitable.

That doesn't make sense to me," Pamela said. "On modern pictures with a contemporary setting, the credits read 'Gowns by Edith Head,' or whomever. Are you sure George is right about this?"

"Whether he is or not, it gives me an excuse to fly to Paris," Zsa Zsa said. "Come with me."

"I'd love to, but I can't," Pamela said.

Since Sanders hadn't phoned her in two days, Zsa Zsa traveled all the way to Paris without telling him. However, she did leave him a note.

In her favorite city, she quickly renewed her love affair with Elie de Rothschild, whom she visited at night, frequenting fashion houses during the day. When a reporter from *Paris Match* got too curious about her relationship with the baron, she dismissed him. "We're just dear friends, *dahlink*."

On June 14, 1952, Zsa Zsa found herself sitting in the first-class compartment of an Air France plane departing from Paris' Orly Airport, heading for Boston.

"A young girl, sort of prim and proper, had the seat opposite me," Zsa Zsa said. "She rudely kept staring at me throughout most of the flight. She wasn't very attractive and had this kinky hair and bad skin. As the hours dragged on, she finally got up the courage to speak to me. She complimented me on the beauty of my porcelain skin, and had the nerve to ask me how I took care of it. There was no way in hell I was going to give her my beauty secrets. Because I was Zsa Zsa, the customs men in Boston cleared me at once—not this ugly little duckling with the pimpled skin. To my surprise, I found Jack in the waiting room. He rushed to me, hugged me, and lifted me off the ground. Obviously, he wasn't in back pain that day."

"Oh, *dahlink*," Zsa Zsa said to him. "You seem in the mood for a repeat performance." She was referring to his seduction of her during his previous visit

453

to Hollywood.

"Can't now," Jack told her, "But I'd love to. You'll always be my sweetheart. You know I've always been in love with you."

"At that moment, the Little Wren from the airplane appeared," Zsa Zsa said.

"Zsa Zsa, I want you to meet my *fiancée*, Jacqueline Bouvier. Jackie, this is Zsa Zsa Gabor, the best thing to come out of Hungary since goulash."

"I'm honored, I'm sure," Jackie said in a tiny, almost meek voice.

"Miss Bouvier shot daggers at me," Zsa Zsa claimed. "For the first time, I think she realized that I had been having an affair with her future husband. I told Jack what a beautiful girl he had. I also warned him, 'Don't you corrupt her morals.'"

Jackie looked straight into Zsa Zsa's eyes. With a little smirk, she replied, "He's already been there, done that."

[As Zsa Zsa entered the valley of the shadow of death in 2011, her last husband, Frédéric Prinz von Anhalt, showed prospective buyers around her 28-room Bel Air mansion.

He stopped in the living room and pointed out an oil painting of an olive-colored satin canopied bed. "That was the site of most of her great love affairs." the prince said, "Her first seduction in that bed was of a young man named John F. Kennedy."]

George Sanders used to announce that, "I wouldn't marry a wife more famous than myself." But as Zsa Zsa's name became a media event, he faced that dilemma.

When Sanders went out in public with her, it was she who was surrounded by autograph hunters. After obtaining Zsa Zsa's autograph, one young woman asked him, "Are you important, too?"

"No, I'm just Mr. Gabor, a tag along," he said sarcastically.

***

With an MGM film contract clutched in her hand, Zsa Zsa arrived at the fabled studio. "I've come here, I see it, and I plan to conquer it."

The arrangement from MGM involved a Technicolor musical with three far more talented stars than Zsa Zsa—MGM's "songbird," Kathryn Grayson; the handsome and macho baritone, Howard

Keel; and tap-dancing Ann Miller, who had been her major competition for the love-making of Conrad Hilton. *Lovely to Look At* was a garish remake of the 1935 *Roberta,* which had starred Irene Dunne, Fred Astaire, and Ginger Rogers.

Unlike the paltry salary that Eva had received as a starlet at Paramount, MGM offered Zsa Zsa $10,000 a week. As a gimmick for her portrayal of a French model, Mignon, Zsa Zsa spoke in French, and English subtitles were inserted into the context of the final cut.

Zsa Zsa recalled her first day at MGM when she arrived early in the morning and was sent directly to makeup. Seated before a long mirror, and wearing no makeup, were Lana Turner and Grace Kelly on one side of her, and Elizabeth Taylor (her rival for the affections of Nicky Hilton) and Ava Gardner on the other side. "Talk about intimidation," Zsa Zsa said.

Bursting into the room came the flamboyant Sydney Guilaroff, Hollywood's most famous hairdresser. "Okay, girls, put on your lipstick," he told this bevy of beauties. "I don't fix up dogs."

Grace Kelly was the first to leave makeup, and Zsa Zsa was the first to subsequently denounce her. In Zsa Zsa's memoirs, she wrote, "Even then, I was aware that Grace has more boyfriends in one month than I had in a lifetime."

No friend of Zsa Zsa's, Ann Miller reported the nasty crack to Kelly, the future princess. "Me, the nymphomanic? Zsa Zsa Gabor is fucking her way through the phone book. I heard that when she lived in Ankara, she slept with the entire Turkish army!"

Grayson bonded with Zsa Zsa, and they became friends for years to come. Afraid of the camera, Zsa Zsa froze. "Somehow, my lines just would not come out." Grayson called for a break and invited Zsa Zsa to her dressing room, where she supplied her with three shots of vodka. When she appeared again on camera, Zsa Zsa was relaxed enough for the take.

Watching the rushes, director Mervyn LeRoy told the press, "The camera loves Zsa Zsa. It does more than that, it caresses her and make her luminous. She is blessed with a kind of screen glow that few stars have. Carole Lombard had it, but not many others."

Back at her Bel Air residence, Zsa Zsa discovered Sanders in the kitchen having a homemade dinner with Clark Gable.

She revealed her first day stage fright to Gable. Instead of a sexy heartthrob, the aging matinee idol was more of a kindly Dutch uncle. "Don't worry about it. Do what I do. Regardless of the role, I am always Clark Gable, and I've done all right. Just be yourself. As Zsa Zsa, fans will love you."

She didn't take Gable's advice, and the following day employed an acting coach. Elsa Stanoff was acclaimed as the finest acting teacher in Hollywood, and she went to work to teach Zsa Zsa acting—"Something you obviously know nothing about." In spite of her stern lectures, Zsa Zsa came to regard her know nothing about." In spite of her stern lectures, Zsa Zsa came to regard her affectionately, nicknaming her *"Apfel Strudel."*

Pamela Mason was correct in assuming that MGM did not need Zsa Zsa's recently acquired Paris couture. The gay designer Adrian, one of the best known in the business, worked with her, designing the bell-skirted, bare-shouldered look that she had already adopted as her trademark. She appeared wearing black, in sharp contrast to the Easter egg-colored outfits worn by Grayson and the film's other female star, Ann Miller.

As Zsa Zsa confessed to Pamela Mason, she found the film's male star, Howard Keel, "Hollywood's sexiest macho baritone. He was strikingly handsome, a man made to fulfill the dreams of loving women. But, alas, he walked around the set like a lovesick puppy, drooling over Kathryn," who had previously co-starred with him in *Showboat* (1951) with Ava Gardner.

One day, Keel invited Zsa Zsa for lunch when Grayson was otherwise occupied with the director, LeRoy.

Much of the time was spent "mooning over his unrequited love for Kathryn" and complaining about his current role. "My charcter of Tony is a likable horse's ass but conceited," Keel claimed.

He told Zsa Zsa that he and Grayson could not turn off their love for each other. "I go home and down eight martinis, telling my erection to go down. I'm married, you know. It's amazing that Kathryn and I have such restraint that we haven't run off somewhere together, but we didn't want to hurt the people who love us."

Zsa Zsa told him that she'd heard from LeRoy that Marilyn Monroe had lobbied for three months for the role of Mignon. "When she learned that the role went to me, she broke down and sobbed," Zsa Zsa claimed.

Zsa Zsa was surprised when Keel confided that he'd met Monroe when he was twenty-one and she was only thirteen. "She was called Norma Jean Baker then, and stood about five feet, five inches. She looked much older. I asked her to go dancing with me one night, even though she was real San Quentin jailbait. I was known as somewhat of a ladies' man, and she made me feel like an old *roué.*"

MGM's songbird, **Kathryn Grayson**, became a friend of Zsa Zsa's, not a rival. She even helped Zsa Zsa to get over her stage fright by tanking her up on vodka.

When Keel's posthumous memoir was published in 2005, he described his early date with Monroe. But he left out one tantalizing detail, which he confided to Zsa Zsa:

"Norma Jean and I ended up getting familiar with each other's anatomy in my new Chevrolet coup," he said. "I'm so tall it was god damn awkward, but Norma Jean and I got the job done. For a thirteen-year-old, she was no virgin."

456

Then Zsa Zsa launched into an attack on Monroe, primarily because of her affair with Sanders. "The girl must work Santa Monica Boulevard every night. I don't think I've met a man in Hollywood who hasn't slept with her."

Kurt Kasznar, Eva's friend from Broadway, stopped by and chatted briefly with Keel and Zsa Zsa. When he'd gone, Keel called him, "a real hoot. He always manages to come into my dressing room as I'm stepping out of the shower. He likes to see me dry off and put on my underwear."

As a relatively unknown part of Hollywood lore, MGM's handsome baritone, **Howard Keel**, molested a thirteen-year-old Norma Jean Baker

"Take it as a compliment, *dahlink*," she said.

In his memoirs, Keel claimed that Zsa Zsa was "a hell of a nice gal, and I loved her. Had I not been hung up on Kathryn when we made *Lovely to Look At,* I would have thrown Zsa Zsa in my car and headed for a wild weekend in Palm Springs."

Away from the studio, Zsa Zsa in her home life with Sanders became almost intolerable. Two stormy egos clashed repeatedly. "Things got really bad when I told him that my star is ascending as yours declines."

Sanders called her a bitch and told her he'd already seen *A Star Is Born.* He began to spend days, even weeks, at his hideaway apartment.

"I knew he was seeing other people, which freed me to date other men as well," Zsa Zsa said. "I went on with my life without George."

As their marriage crumbled, Zsa Zsa and Sanders became involved, respectively, with both halves of a formerly married couple, Porfirio Rubirosa and Doris Duke.

"Rubi" was the most famous playboy gigolo of Europe and the Americas, and Duke, the tobacco heiress, was the richest woman in the world.

***

A second film role for Zsa Zsa emerged immediately. *We're Not Married (1952)* was directed by Edmund Goulding and brought Zsa Zsa onto the set of the same picture that also featured Marilyn Monroe, her arch rival. Fortunately for the sake of harmony, they did not share any scenes together. The film also starred Ginger Rogers, Fred Allen, Victor Moore, David Wayne, Eve Arden, Paul Douglas, Eddie Bracken, and Mitzi Gaynor. The plot concerns how various couples react when they lean they are not legally married.

In the film, Zsa Zsa was cast as Eve Malrose, a gold-digging young bride who marries an aging millionaire (Louis Calhern), with the intention of divorcing him and making off with his millions. In the end, each of the couples except Zsa Zsa and Calhern remarry.

Monroe had had a brief fling with Calhern, an actor from Brooklyn who was born in 1895, during the making of that classic film noir about a jewelry heist, *The Asphalt Jungle.* Calhern, an erudite character actor with an imposing beak-like nose, possessed a lot of charm.

Monroe dropped by to pay her respects to Calhern, and he introduced her to Zsa Zsa.

When Zsa Zsa had first learned of Monroe's affair with her husband, she had publicly raked her over the coals in the press by attacking her "outrageous behavior."

Zsa Zsa told James Bacon, "Of course, Hollywood has always needed so-called actresses who can play sluts. In lieu of talent, Monroe uses her body to attract reporters. I understand she makes herself available to them."

When confronted with Zsa Zsa's remarks, Monroe shot back, "I never noticed Miss Gabor in church taking up a collection for the poor."

"Dahlink," Zsa Zsa said to Monroe at the time of their inaugural face-to-face. "How nice of you to drop by, perhaps to give Louis acting lessons. I must admire your dress. It was obviously sewn on you. What do you do when you have to take a shit?"

Monroe gave Zsa Zsa an icy stare. "Is it true you told Sidney Skolsky that I make money only with my tits and ass? That my talent is above my waist and below my navel?"

"I chatter so much to so many people, I don't remember saying that," Zsa Zsa said. "But it is so clever and so accurate that I probably did."

On screen, **Zsa Zsa** played the gold-digging wife of veteran actor **Louis Calhern** in *We're Not Married.*

Off screen, he introduced her to her rival, Marilyn Monroe, who had dropped by to service the aging actor in his dressing room.

"You may denounce me as a slut, but at least I don't carry the burden of having gone to bed with Adolf Hitler."

"Dahlink, you are confusing rumors about Hedy Lamarr with me."

"Perhaps I am, but perhaps not," Monroe responded.

"I understand you know my husband, George Sanders," Zsa Zsa said. "Is it true you have a problem with hygiene?"

Before Monroe could answer, Calhern took her arm. "Would you excuse us, Zsa Zsa? Marilyn and I have some unfinished business. Unlike the gold-digger bride you're playing in this movie, Marilyn likes me for my aging body."

The couple disappeared.

458

Then, Zsa Zsa was approached by a former Marine, Lee Marvin, who had been cast as "Pinky" in *We're Not Married.*

"How about it, babe?" he asked her. "While Marilyn is getting plowed by an antique dick, how about you going for some fresh meat?"

At first, Zsa Zsa looked startled at such a direct, vulgar approach, but she decided to handle it with humor and style. She kissed Marvin on the mouth. "The meat is probably still too fresh for me. It needs to age a bit."

She turned and walked away as Marvin whistled at her shapely buttocks.

***

Two days later, Zsa Zsa learned that Monroe was just a small trout. Sanders, during her absence, had netted a far bigger catch, a major-league barracuda.

At a party at Ciro's, Doris Duke came up to him and kissed him passionately. "Darling, didn't we have fun this afternoon? You're terrific."

Sanders didn't even look embarrassed. He said, "Doris, may I present my wife, Zsa Zsa Gabor."

"Oh, the Romanian refugee," Duke said, before taking Sanders' hand. "Come dance with me."

Furious, Zsa Zsa stood looking on with a plate of food from the buffet in her hand. Her husband was dancing with the richest woman on the planet, a siren who had just trivialized and humiliated her.

"I was consumed with jealousy," Zsa Zsa said. "I could compete with any woman on equal terms. I could match myself beauty for beauty, sex appeal for sex appeal, against any woman. But I could not compete with a tycoon who filled banks in Zurich with gold bars."

Ginger Rogers, who had recently completed her involvement in *We're Not Married,* approached and stood next to Zsa Zsa. She introduced her to her handsome Basque lover, Jacques Bergerac, who had recently had an affair with Eva.

Zsa Zsa later reported she was awed by the male beauty of Rogers' latest lover. "He bowed and kissed my hand, and I fell in love…sort of."

"Look at my errant husband dancing with the tobacco queen," Zsa Zsa said to Rogers.

Rogers stared at Sanders and Duke, who seemed enraptured with each other. "Whatever Doris wants, Doris gets, regardless of the price tag, or so I've heard," said Rogers.

"Do you think I've lost him?" Zsa Zsa asked.

"If a poor boy has a chance to marry a rich, plain woman, or a beautiful one with no money, the choice is easy for most men," Rogers said.

Bergerac confronted her, flashing anger. "You don't mean me?" he asked. "Do you, Ginger?"

She kissed him on the lips. "Present company is always excepted, my darling boy. You're the type of man who marries only for love." She didn't bother to conceal the slight touch of sarcasm in her voice.

When Sanders and Duke finished dancing, he joined the heiress at her table, not even looking over at Zsa Zsa.

Brian Aherne later said that Duke and his best friend, Sanders, "were well suited for each other. Each of them was jaded, sophisticated, and obviously bored with the world, and each of them was a notorious cheapskate."

Sanders confided to Aherne that after he divorced Zsa Zsa, he planned to marry Duke. "There's no greater aphrodisiac than money."

Rogers invited Zsa Zsa to join Bergerac and her at her table. As they sat down, the handsome young actor John Bromfield appeared. He had arrived at Ciro's with his wife, the French actress, Corinne Calvet, whom he'd married in 1948. Their relationship was crumbling at the time. Bromfield had just had a fight with Calvet, who had stormed out of the club. Rogers knew Bromfield and invited him to join their table. She introduced him to Bergerac and Zsa Zsa.

"Let Duke have Sanders," Rogers advised "You and I are sitting with the two most beautiful men in Hollywood, John Bromfield and my beloved Jacques. Where are the god damn photographers now that we need them?"

Indiana-born Bromfield had a macho record—football player, boozing champion in college, service in the Navy, and he'd also harpooned two whales. In the 1948 film, *Sorry, Wrong Number,* both of its bisexual co-stars, Barbara Stanwyck and Burt Lancaster, had propositioned him off-screen.

Unknown to the general public, Zsa Zsa had always been jealous of the much younger Calvet, who was born in Paris and had studied criminal law at the Sorbonne.

She'd done radio, stage, and film work in France in the 1940s before Hal B. Wallis brought her to Hollywood where she'd starred in *Rope of Sand (1949),* opposite Burt Lancaster and Paul Henried.

There weren't that many movie roles for women with foreign accents, and Zsa Zsa felt that Calvet had snared many of the parts that would otherwise have been ideally suited for her. The roles that Calvet appeared in had not called for a strong actress, so Zsa Zsa thought she could easily have played in them with her limited range.

Bromfield was most charming to Zsa Zsa, and she could have easily been captivated by his striking looks and courtly manners. But she knew his studio had forced him into a marriage of convenience with Calvet as a means of masking his private homosexual tastes. She believed that although he was paying attention to her, he would much prefer to have gone off into the night with the equally good-looking Bergerac.

Bromfield did take her home but, as she later reported, "All I got was a peck on the cheek, although I practically begged him to come inside for a nightcap...or whatever."

It was on that particular night at Ciro's that Zsa Zsa swore revenge. She knew that Porfirio Rubirosa had been Duke's former husband, and that she was still in love with him and was constantly pursuing him, trying to get him to remarry her. In a memoir, Zsa Zsa wrote, "I was determined to have an affair with Rubirosa. I knew that if I carried out my threat, I would hurt Duke and get revenge on George for going off with her."

As she looked up, she spotted Duke and Sanders disappearing through the main door. She was certain that the heiress's chauffeur was waiting on the sidewalk outside with a limousine.

***

[Years later, Zsa Zsa's jealousy and fury against Calvet would be revealed on a radio "chatfest." Seemingly unprovoked, and with Calvet nowhere near the recording studio, Zsa Zsa launched into an attack on Calvet. "She's about as French as a Cockney born within the sound of the Bow Bells. My former husband, George Sanders, knew her years ago in England. She spoke not a word of French but had a thick Cockney accent. She's a total fraud, masquerading as a Parisian femme fatale."

When Calvet heard about this, she was furious. She told a reporter, "I am amazed that such a silly, false, and peculiar accusation was made by Miss Gabor. A lady I do not even know. I'm surprised it's getting so much publicity. I will sue, of course, because such a charge can ruin a career."

Trained as a lawyer, Calvet met her attorney

Holding a glass of champagne and a cigarette holder, French star **Corinne Calvet** was told to "look sexy and cheap like a hooker" when this publicity still was taken.

Jealous of her, Zsa Zsa accused her of being a fraud: "She's actually a Cockney from London."

Calvet sued for libel.

and within forty-eight hours had filed a libel suit against Zsa Zsa. The suit, demanding a million dollars, was filed in the Santa Monica Municipal Court.

Calvet's attorney, Stanley Foy, faced journalists, claiming that "Corrine is a Parisian, the daughter of her petite mama and père, Pierre and Juliette Munier Dibos. She was born Corinne Dibos on April 30, 1925, and we have records from Paris to prove that."

When she filed charges, Calvet appeared in Santa Monica beautifully dressed. She told a reporter that "Zsa Zsa's mouth should be washed out to the tune of $55,000 for damage to my career, and $500,000 to punish her."

The catfight never went to trial, and was settled privately in Calvet's favor. It was rumored the Zsa Zsa shelled out $50,000 to get her to drop the case.]

***

Before she was to begin a twelve-week nationwide tour with *Her Cardboard Lover,* Eva flew to Los Angeles for some rest and recreation. The first invitation she accepted was from Kurt Kasznar, with whom she'd become friends during the Broadway run of *The Happy Time.*

At a party within Kasznar's home, she was introduced to Mel Ferrer, a gaunt actor with dark eyes and continental charm, even though he'd been born in New Jersey. He'd launched himself into show business by dancing as a chorus boy on Broadway.

When Eva met him, he was both an actor and a director and a founding member of La Jolla Playhouse, south of Los Angeles, near San Diego.

[Critics at the time claimed that La Jolla Playhouse was noted for "a series of astonishingly dull plays." Disbanded in the 1960s, it re-opened in 1983 under the supervision of Des McAnuff. In 1997 the La Jolla Playhouse celebrated its 50th anniversary. Mel Ferrer was in the audience.]

As Eva remembered it, she and Ferrer spent the first half of their talk in "civilities that did little to conceal our fierce sexual attraction to each other."

Slender and gallant, Ferrer at six foot three towered over her. He was urbane, stylish, and articulate, her kind of fantasy man, with an unusual mixture of Cuban and Irish blood.

She was curious about his marital status, learning that in 1937, he'd married the aspiring actress and later, sculptor, Frances Pilchard. He divorced her in 1939 but remarried her in 1944, the relationship lasting a decade. In 1954, he divorced Pilchard again to marry Audrey Hepburn.

"I caught Mel between wives," Eva later claimed.

Ferrer had dropped out of college after time spent at Princeton. Among his many jobs was as a disk jockey in the wilds of Texas and Arkansas. He'd even had a bout with polio.

She also knew that he had credits as a director. She asked him if he were related to José Ferrer, an even more famous actor whom he'd directed on Broadway in *Strange Fruit* and the highly popular *Cyrano de Bergerac.* "The only two things we have in common is our name," he said. "José chases after every woman he sees, and I go after only a few Helen of Troys who come along, including the one I'm sitting here chatting with tonight."

After two hours of talk, Ferrer announced "Have I got a play for you. You'd be ideal as the female lead in this play, the only woman in a cast of ten Gaelic men."

In 1952, Ferrer was planning to produce, direct, and tour, nationwide, with a play, *Strike a Match,* hoping to eventually bring it to Broadway. He was putting up some of his own money, raising the rest from backers Randolph Hale and Charles R. Meeker. The play had been written by Roger Smith.

*[*Strike a Match *was set in a New York City bar ("any" bar) during the cold winter of the present, with flashbacks to a warm summer when love was still young. Pat O'Brien played Ernie—the cantankerous bartender —while Eva and Richard Egan played estranged lovers in search of a resolution over his inability to deal with failure and his squandered talent. If she accepted, Eva would be cast as Kay, once "the happiest woman in the world," but no more.]*

After the party, Ferrer drove Eva back to her hotel, where she invited him to spend the night with her. Before dawn broke, she'd agreed to drop out of the road tour of *Her Cardboard Lover*—"The director can find a hundred actresses who'll jump at the chance to take over my role" and to begin rehearsals in La Jolla for *Strike a Match.*

Before she met the rest of the cast, she and Ferrer became almost inseparable. As she'd tell Susan Hayward, her friends, and Jolie, "Ferrer was skilled as a lover. He approached sex like he was playing a role on Broadway and delivers a fine performance. It was very hygienic, no dirty stuff. He is a real gentleman."

On the first day of rehearsals, Eva met O'Brien, the star of the show. She remembered him as a character actor from those gangster movies of the 1930s with Humphrey Bogart and James Cagney. By 1952, O'Brien's film career was in decline.

This publicity photo of **Mel Ferrer** was taken during his production and direction, in 1952, of *Light a Match.*

"Long before Audrey Hepburn sank her claws into Mel, he was mine," Eva proclaimed.

"Pat had a great deal of Gaelic charm and he always seemed high on Irish whiskey," she said. "On stage, he could deliver the wisecracks and snappy *repartée*, and offstage, he told wonderfully embarrassing stories about his days in Hollywood, including revelations about his best pal, Spencer Tracy, and his curious bonding with the unlikely Katharine Hepburn."

Eva admitted that had she not been romantically engrossed in Ferrer, she would have actively pursued Richard Egan, her romantic co-star. He had a talent as an actor, a rugged physique, and good looks.

"One night when I was angry at Mel, I made a play for Richard," Eva confessed, "but got nowhere. He was a devout Roman Catholic and told me that one day when he got married, it would be for keeps."

[Egan was a man of his word. In 1958, he married Patricia Hardy and was still with her on the day of his death in 1987.]

Eva developed a complaint about the Catholic Church after being introduced to her ruggedly handsome co-star, **Richard Egan** *(photo above)*, who appeared on stage with her during the road show of *Strike a Match*.

"As a director, Mel cracked the whip," Eva recalled. "We had some bitter fights about my interpretation, but we usually made up at night. He would infuriate me at times, mocking my Hungarian accent. He often accused me of not giving a scene my all. But ultimately, I think he brought out the best in me."

One afternoon, he told her, "You are much too concerned with looking beautiful than you are in playing Kay. You aren't taking the role seriously."

"I burst into tears," she said. "I was trying to give it everything I had."

She enjoyed working with the all-male cast, calling it "the happiest bunch of actors I ever appeared with."

"They brought out my maternal instinct. On the road, I had to see that they got their underwear laundered before it was time to catch the next train. I was their social secre-

"A woman like myself is presented with this sexy, beefed-up man, but he's been indoctrinated by the Catholic Church, who has put it in his head that he should be faithful to his wife. Have you ever heard of anything more absurd, *dahlink?*"

"The Gang's All Here." The stars and writer of *Strike a Match* are *(left to right)*, **Mel Ferrer, Pat O'Brien**, playwright **Roger Miller, Richard Egan**, and a perky **Eva Gabor.**

"As the only woman, I tried to be a wife to the all-male cast," Eva provocatively told reporters.

tary, their maid, their valet. I got them out of the trouble when they picked up the wrong women on the road. Two of the more handsome actors fell in love with each other, and I was often a referee as they went through their lovers' quarrels."

Strike a Match had its premiere in at the La Jolla Playhouse on August 20, 1952. Eva in general got good reviews. "She is a great beauty and has a certain talent, though limited," wrote Critic Ralph Vent. "On stage, she has a certain mischief, grace, and enchantment, more vanilla *soufflé* than *chili con carne*."

The play moved to Los Angeles and San Francisco, before opening in Houston and San Antonio. "Texans like big musical comedies," she said. "The people of the Lone Star State want to keep Shakespeare locked in the closet."

Eva was seeing America for the first time as the play continued a tour up and down the East Coast with the rowdy team of actors. She slept in B&Bs, small inns, hotels, and sometimes above gambling casinos. Her accommodations ranged from tiny closets to luxurious suites.

During the run of the play, she met many of Ferrer's friends, including handsome Gregory Peck on whom she developed a crush, and Joseph Cotten. She also met some of Ferrer's women friends, including Dorothy McGuire and Jennifer Jones.

Jones by now was Mrs. David O. Selznick, having divorced the late Robert Walker, Eva's former boyfriend. "I'm sorry he's dead," Jones said, but his alcoholism and his homosexuality became too much for me."

Strike a Match closed in Memphis, after playing to an audience of 3,500. At curtain call, the staff picked Eva up and tossed her into the air.

"It was *Auld Lang Syne,*" she said. "*Strike a Match* never lit up Broadway. The flame flickered out that night in Tennessee."

When asked what happened to her love affair with Mel Ferrer, Eva told Pat O'Brien, "He's met Audrey Hepburn, and I never expect to see him again. If he has that enchanting little doll, what does he need with me?"

"Don't worry, honey," O'Brien assured her. "A gal who looks like you needs only to stand for five minutes on a street corner before another beau comes along."

***

As an actress, throughout the duration of her career, Eva was confined mostly to involvements with road shows, but she never abandoned her hope of becoming a film star. Zsa Zsa's involvement in roles within four films (any of which might have gone to her) rekindled Eva's ambition.

Finally, her agent succeeded in signing her for a movie role, even though it was silly. It was for the female lead in *Captain Kidd and the Slave Girl,* re-

Eva appears with her co-star, **Anthony Dexter** in *Captain Kidd and the Slave Girl.*

"I was the most gorgeously gowned slave girl in the history of the world," she claimed. "I found Tony incredibly sexy, the living incarnation of Rudolf Valentino."

"The silent screen heartthrob died before I was 'officially' born, but Tony re-created the thrill for me in his full Sheik drag."

leased in 1954.

The film starred Anthony Dexter as Captain Kidd, an actor who bore a striking resemblance to the "the Sheik" himself, silent screen heartthrob Rudolph Valentino. Dexter had portrayed Valentino in the 1951 film, *Valentino,* with Eleanor Parker.

On the morning Eva met Dexter, he was walking around bare-chested, getting into character in preparation for some publicity shots.

Both Dexter and Eva laughed about their respective roles in the film. She made fun of the scripted demand that she run around a desolate Caribbean island wearing stunning ballroom gowns and being perfectly groomed and coiffed. "Call it a director's fantasy," she said.

Over lunch, Dexter told her that there had been a nationwide search for an actor to portray Valentino in advance of his previous film. Of 75,000 applicants, 400 were selected for screen tests. "I appeared shirtless, with wild eyes emoting, and with my nostrils smouldering. I got the part!"

"I specialize in playing real life characters," he said. "Things like *Captain John Smith and Pocahontas (1953),"* he said. "But I'll never escape the curse of too close an association with the Valentino image."

He told her he'd made a big mistake in his career. He broke from Edward Small, the producer of the original *Valentino* film "because he wanted me to go on playing characters equivalent to Valentino's."

"Guess what?" he asked Eva. "I found that other producers also wanted me to play characters inspired by Valentino, but for far less money. Oh, the hazards of show business."

Eva's affair with Dexter began one afternoon when neither of them was needed on camera. He knocked discreetly on the door of her dressing room. To receive him, she covered her nudity with a silk robe.

As she later told her intimates "We didn't waste a lot of time with preliminaries. Even though he'd been born in Nebraska, he was an exotic. He had silky smooth skin and was great at making love to a woman."

"Thus began our affair," she said. "There was no talk of love, no long-term commitment. Pure and simple, it was about sex. Tony certainly had the equipment for it."

"As was well known at the time, I always try to seduce my leading man. That's part of my trademark. Most of my leading men are easy marks, a term I learned from American gangster movies. Occasionally, I strike out. But sometimes, I've even won over a gay male."

One evening, while dining with Dexter at Ciro's, he made a confession that surprised her. "I was more inspired by the private life of Valentino that by his movie roles," Dexter said. "He started as a gigolo in New York, dancing, and fucking rich old ladies for their money."

"Ever since I appeared on screen as Valentino," Dexter continued, "I get offers coming through the mail from obsessive Valentino fans—mostly wealthy women, but occasionally from men."

"At times, I have long dry spells between jobs," Dexter continued, "and when times get really tough, I hire myself out as a male prostitute, dressing up as an Arab Sheik, which, as you know, is the role Valentino was most identified with."

"I'm not sure my sessions with these people are about sex, although sex is part of it. It's about my fulfilling some long ago fantasy they had in their youth when they were enthralled by this tango dancer. They're not having sex with me, but with some long-dead figure who thrilled them repeatedly on screen."

"That's a bit ghoulish," Eva said, "but anything to keep the bills paid."

By the end of the 50s, or the 60s, at the latest, most of the world will have forgotten Valentino, and I will have to find another way to moonlight between acting jobs," he lamented.

"Of course, after that dinner conversation at Ciro's, I couldn't resist," Eva said. "Tony dressed up one night for me in his sheik drag, and I found it most exciting. Those customers who booked him for sexual gigs sure got their money's worth from that guy."

We dated two or three more times," she said, "when I was in town."

One night, he called her and in-

Eleanor Parker appeared with **Anthony Dexter** in a film (*Valentino*, released in *1951; photo above*), which had almost nothing to do with the actual life story of Rudolf Valentino, the silent screen legend who had died amid great outpourings of public grief almost 30 years before.

"After that role, I was forever asked to play Valentino-tyle characters," Dexter said. "Not only that, but obsessive fans—both male and female—paid me ridiculous amounts of money to dress up like the Sheik and descend like a rapist into their boudoirs."

vited her to Pasadena, where a theater was showing his latest film, *Fire Maidens of Outer Space* (1956).

"I want to show you how low I've sunk," he said, before she sat through this "horrible piece of crap. I didn't tell him that, *dahlink*, but praised his performance even thought the whole movie was ridiculous."

"The next day, I called Zsa Zsa and told her all about it. "I fear my older sister mocked Tony, but I guess he had the last laugh on her. Two years later, Zsa Zsa herself appeared in a disaster called *The Queen of Outer Space.*"

***

Even though it meant a six-month separation from her husband, Zsa Zsa was finally persuaded to sign as the star in *Moulin Rouge (1953)*, a drama which would become her greatest film role. She would be cast as Jane Avril, the legendary Parisian *chanteuse* and can-can dancer who had entranced the great artist, Henri de Toulouse-Lautrec.

José Ferrer had already signed to play the difficult lead role. Because the historical figure of Toulouse-Lautrec was a dwarf with a deformed body, Ferrer would have to use a set of knee-pads to walk on his knees with his lower legs strapped to his upper body.

Until the film's British producer, James Woolf, and his lover, actor Laurence Harvey, had showed up on her doorstep in Bel Air, Zsa Zsa had been reluctant to sign for the role.

"These two charming devils" could be very persuasive, and before the night was over, Zsa Zsa had agreed to star in the picture.

Woolf told Zsa Zsa, "You are more like Jane Avril than any other woman I could imagine. A hedonist who lives only for love and the admiration of men, and a beautiful vision at that." He told her that Avril had once proclaimed, "I will be twenty-five forever."

Even before signing, Woolf had told Zsa Zsa that the film's director, John Huston, was opposed to casting her in the picture. "He prefers Marilyn Monroe."

"Doesn't everyone?" Zsa Zsa snapped.

James Woolf, partnered with his brother, John, had founded two independent production companies, Romulus Films and Remus Films, and as such, were active as film producers in the 1950s and 60s. They had launched their film careers with the tedious and long-winded *Pandora and the Flying Dutchman* (1951), starring Ava Gardner and James Mason. Their greatest triumph had come that same year when they backed *The African Queen,* co-starring Humphrey Bogart and Katharine Hepburn.

Woolf told Zsa Zsa that their mentor, Alexander Korda, had warned them that "we'd lose our shirts. Two old people going up and down an African River? Who's going to want to see that?" Korda had said.

Huston had also directed that picture and Woolf had a good relationship with him, but Zsa Zsa feared that he'd be difficult with her since he'd originally objected to casting her.

Huston had told Woolf, "Gabor's talent wouldn't even fill a thimble."

"I adored Larry *[i.e., Laurence Harvey]*," Zsa Zsa later said, "and we became great friends, although he was quite snobbish. He was outrageously gay, and Woolf was madly in love with him and was doing much to make him an international star."

"Larry speaks disparagingly of women," she said. He had told her, "Dealing with a woman is like dealing with a known crook. It is not possible to fall into their beds without finding yourself caught in one of their cunning little webs, like a Black Widow spider."

"Even though he was disparagingly called "Florence of Lithuania," a reference to both his status as a homosexual and to his native country, he told Zsa Zsa, "I'm not bothered by that."

Before the end of her meeting with Woolf and Harvey, Sanders arrived. He urged his wife to sign for the picture. She later told Woolf and Harvey, "With me on location for this film in England and Paris, George will be free to pursue his affair with Doris Duke."

"Larry detested George, but George found him amusing," Zsa Zsa said. "He later told me that Larry was 'a cross between Shakespeare and Madame du Barry.'"

Zsa Zsa's return to Paris was greeted by *Paris Soir* with an article that stated, "Zsa Zsa, *la femme la plus chic du monde.*"

The shooting of *Moulin Rouge* began in Paris

The real **Jane Avril** (1868-1943), was the daughter of a courtesan and an absent father. Abused as a child, and suicidal, she ran away from home and was treated at a sanatorium for what was identified as "female hysterics" until her exposure to dancing reportedly cured her "movement disorders." When she was released, she was taken in by the madam of a Parisian brothel.

After reigning as the most sought-after entertainer in the history of Paris, she remains in the public eye because of the illustrations painted of her by Toulouse-Lautrec. The photo above was snapped in 1893 during the peak of her popularity as the featured dancer at the *Moulin Rouge* and the *Jardin de Paris.*

She died, impoverished, lonely, abandoned, and miserable, in a retirement home during the Nazi occupation of Paris and the darkest days of World War II.

Zsa Zsa's portrayal of the famous dancer in her film, *Moulin Rouge,* did not reflect the recurrent tragedies of the dancer's unhappy life.

Zsa Zsa appears as the dancer and stage entertainer, Jane Avril, in her most memorable film, *Moulin Rouge,* centered around the life of the artist, Henri de Toulouse-Lautrec.

"I had something in common with Jane Avril," Zsa Zsa claimed. "Both Jane and I planned to be twenty-five forever."

in the summer of 1952. On her first night, Huston invited her for dinner at Maxim's. Over dinner, he announced, "I'm going to sleep with you. I must have you."

"That macho nose of his was only an inch from my mouth," she said. "In our booth at Maxim's, he practically wrapped himself around me. I refused his sexual demands, but feared that did not bode well for me. He didn't handle rejection easily, so I was told."

Her fears were well grounded. Throughout the rest of the shoot, he humiliated her in front of cast and crew, especially when visitors came onto the set. One night, in front of some fifty people, he ordered his cinematographer, Ossie Morris, "To move in for some extreme close-ups. That way, we'll see just her beautiful face, which will camouflage the fact that she can't act."

Sanders phoned her, telling her that he was flying to Rome to make a film, *Viaggio in Italia* or (in the U.S.) *Journey to Italy,* for Roberto Rossellini starring his wife, Ingrid Bergman. Bergman had deserted her husband, Petter Lindström and child (Pia) in Hollywood to marry the Italian director, which had caused an international scandal and practically destroyed her Hollywood career.

Since it was well known that Rossellini was a regular patron of Rome's best bordellos, Zsa Zsa suspected the Bergman would be free on many a night, perhaps for a dalliance with Sanders. After all, Alfred Hitchcock had spread the word in Hollywood that "Ingrid Bergman would do it with a doorknob."

Over the course of her career, Bergman had become known for seducing her leading men, including Humphrey Bogart during the filming of *Casablanca,* despite denials from both sides. On her list of seductions would eventually appear the names of Leslie Howard, (her first seduction of a leading man), Burgess Meredith, Gregory Peck, Gary Cooper, Joseph Cotten, Bing Crosby, Omar Sharif, Spencer Tracy, and Anthony Quinn.

Far away in Paris, the cast and crew of *Moulin Rouge* were given the day off to celebrate Bastille Day (July 14, 1952) the French equivalent of America's Fourth of July. Select members of the cast and crew were invited to dine at the most exclusive restaurant in Paris, La Tour d'Argent, its windows overlooking the Seine and Notre Dame Cathedral.

Unknown to Zsa Zsa, a well-connected VIP, in Paris at the time, telephoned Huston and asked if he could be seated next to Zsa Zsa at the restaurant. Huston responed to the VIP, "I failed to get her out of her panties, but you might succeed."

At table at Tour d'Argent, Zsa Zsa was startled when her escort turned out to be Prince Aly Khan, an international seducer of women, one of whom had been Magda Gabor. Zsa Zsa had read in the press that the prince's marriage to screen goddess Rita Hayworth was on the verge of collapse.

"Your Highness," Zsa Zsa said to him. "I'm honored to be at table with you."

He flashed his award-winning smile at her. "You're one of the few women in America I've longed to meet."

"I'm flattered, but also wondering who those other American women are," she said. "No doubt Mamie Eisenhower. I hear that Ike neglects her something awful."

Aly Khan laughed. "Of course, it's Mamie, you dear woman. How did you guess?"

She later recalled that at the time, she was a vision in pink. "Madame Schiaparelli, who was promoting her shocking pink in the fashion world, would have been proud of me. I wore this pink gown of pleated taffeta like an accordion, along with pink gloves, pink shoes, and everything set off with sparkling diamonds."

Hawkeyed by Huston, Zsa Zsa flirted with Khan throughout the dinner. After the final champagne was served, he invited her to walk with him through the streets of Paris, which were lit with lanterns for the Bastille Day celebrations.

"He held my hand as we strolled through the city, which had never seen or looked so romantic," she said. "We visited three little *boîtes* on the Left Bank before dawn. We sat in darkened corners in these dives, and he got cozier and cozier with me. I desperately wanted him to make love to me."

Back at her hotel, she discovered that the prince, like Elie de Rothschild before him, had already filled her living room with roses, along with silver buckets of champagne chilling.

Weeks later, she praised his stamina to such friends as Pamela Mason and Greta Keller, even to Jolie herself. "I made him forget all about Gene Tierney and Rita," she said.

"He was a true stallion," she said. "He could go on for hours. He told me that when he was a sixteen-year-old boy, he had been trained in *Imsák,* an Arabic sexual technique. He placed two silver buckets of ice, in which the champagne had chilled, on each side of the bed. When he was about to climax, he'd

471

thrust his arms—no, not that other appendage—into the ice to delay his ejaculation."

"Dahlink, forgive me for being so vulgar, but he was celebrated for his skill at cunnilingus. He couldn't get enough of my honeypot. I bet I thrilled him more than that overripe, overused Venus's Flytrap of Pamela Churchill."

Her prince charming spent every night with her until her departure for additional filming in London, where he promised to join her as soon as possible.

"I understood why he couldn't go with me," Zsa Zsa said. "Rita Hayworth had flown into Paris to reclaim this prized stallion."

***

Upon her arrival in London, Laurence Harvey and James Woolf invited Zsa Zsa to drive with them to Stratford-upon-Avon for the weekend. They saw a production of Shakespeare's *Julius Caesar* and took in historic sites associated with the Bard.

On Monday, when she showed up at the studio, Huston asked her if she'd gone to Anne Hathaway's Cottage.

"I believe we had tea with her," Zsa Zsa said.

Huston burst into derisive laughter based on how Zsa Zsa didn't know that Hathaway had turned into dust centuries ago.

"It was the first of the humiliations suffered from this dreadful man," she said. "At school, we studied Goethe and Schiller. I never got around to Shakespeare."

Throughout the rest of the shooting of *Moulin Rouge*, Huston introduced Zsa Zsa to every visitor to the set as, "Here's the little gal who had tea with Anne Hathaway."

After watching Zsa Zsa perform, the cinematographer, Ossie Morris, claimed that "Gabor moved like a tank, so Huston hired Colette Marchand to show her how to move." Marchand had been cast in the movie as a prostitute, Marie Charlet.

In addition, Huston hired veteran actress and acting coach Constance Collier, a frequent companion of Katharine Hepburn, to teach her how to act.

Zsa Zsa liked Collier, later calling her "one of the most stately old dykes of England. I'm sure in her long career, she at one point became familiar with Katharine Hepburn's nether regions."

Whenever Zsa Zsa had to perform in a scene at the Shepperton Studios outside London, Huston would pointedly ignore her, concentrating instead on playing poker with a member of the crew. He never looked over at her. "At the end of the scene, he'd proclaim, "You did right, little girl."

He would constantly shout at her, "If you go dead again at the end of a line,

I'll shoot you, so help me!"

On of her big numbers involved descending a pair of stairs singing "The Song of Moulin Rouge."

Huston approached her. "My dear," he said, "you know nothing about acting, singing, or dancing. I'm going to put the picture of a heart on the camera—and you're to walk down the staircase, if you can manage that much. Wiggle your Hungarian ass and just keep your eye trained on that heart."

In a stunning crêpe dress, she came down the stairs "with a pink angel face and a picture hat so wide-brimmed even Hedda Hopper wouldn't wear it," Morris said.

In spite of Huston's contempt, the crew applauded Zsa Zsa's scene. Of course, her singing voice had to be dubbed.

Zsa Zsa and **Laurence Harvey** having a gay old time together during a party at her Bel Air manse.

George Sanders defined Harvey as "a cross between Shakespeare and Madame du Barry."

After her spirit was deflated by Huston, her mood was lifted when Prince Aly Khan flew into London. Before arriving at her hotel suite, he'd ordered champagne in silver buckets and dozens of red roses.

Showing up at her door in black tie, he found her "bathed in champagne colors to match our drink of choice for the evening."

In a memoir, she called him "the most charming, the most debonair, the most thoughtful companion any woman could ever wish for. We danced cheek to cheek—that is, *dahlink,* when we weren't back at my hotel suite for constant love-making."

He invite her to the races at Ascot, and when photographers took their picture, one London tabloid hailed them as the most glamorous couple in England.

"Aly had to return to Paris, but he invited me for a vacation at his villa in Cannes," she said. "It was a sad day for me when I had to turn down his invitation. Frankly, since he was divorcing Rita, I had a fantasy that he would ask me to become his next wife. Alas, that was one invitation that was not to be."

Somewhat despondent, she showed up on the set of *Moulin Rouge* for her final scene. Huston approached her and startled her by saying, "I don't know how in hell to direct Jane Avril in this scene where she says goodbye to Toulouse-Lautrec. We'll just turn the camera on you for you to do your stuff."

In panic, Zsa Zsa decided to say whatever came into her head. She leaned over toward the deformed dwarf and artistic genius, Toulouse-Lautrec (José Ferrer) as she improvised. "Henri, *dahlink,* I hear you are dying. I just came to say goodbye. I'll see you soon. Now I have to run. I have the most beautiful man in the world waiting for me at Maxim's."

Huston yelled out, "CUT! Print it! Let's call her one-take Gabor."

As he leaned over to kiss her goodbye, he said, "In Paris, you missed the fuck of your life when you turned me down. Any pussy I attack, I leave a limp dishrag."

With her prince back in Paris, Zsa Zsa was entertained by Count John Gérard de Bendern during her final night in London. At the chic Les Ambassadeurs nightclub, she spotted a dark-skinned man seated with Ayisa, the Maharani of Jaipur, and Princess Hohenlöhe (*née* Patricia Wilder, and nicknamed "Honeychile.")

Count Bendern identified him as the Dominican playboy, Porfirio Rubirosa.

"He's not my type at all," Zsa Zsa said. "He's no Atatürk, no Hilton, no Sanders. Actually, he looks like my first husband, Burhan Belge. I have no wish to be reminded of that Turk. No way is this Rubirosa going to add me to his list of seductions."

***

Almost daily, Jolie reminded Magda that she was too dependent on her financially. One morning, Magda overheard her mother talking on the phone. "I have a third daughter, and she's actually the biggest talent in the family. On the stage or in film, she would be a much better actress than either Zsa Zsa, who can't act at all, or Eva."

Magda never learned what kind of acting job her mother was pursuing for her, but Jolie's recommendation was rejected by whomever was on the other end of the line.

"My oldest daughter was very unhappy," Jolie later said. "She would not admit it, but she was jealous of Eva and Zsa Zsa. She also had stage fright. When she was offered the role of Peggy in *The Women* for a road tour, at the pay of $1,500 a week, she went into a kind of panic. Her nerves, you know."

During this period of her life, which Magda defined as an "intermission," she fell in love with Tony Gallucci, a handsome, sexy, and charismatic building contractor who also owned and ran a plumbing factory.

Night after night, Magda pondered marriage to Gallucci, but feared his alcoholism was growing worse.

One night, he came over and had a dinner cooked by Jolie. Magda told Jolie that she and Gallucci planned to get married. "Tomorrow is the big day," Magda said, "and you must come to our wedding."

Later that evening, she asked Gallucci to walk and exercise her chocolate brown French poodle, who she had named "Coco" in honor of Coco Chanel.

After four hours, he had not returned, prompting Magda to walk the streets trying to find Coco. Finally, the dog appeared, racing toward her on the sidewalk with her leash missing.

Two days later, she learned that Gallucci had gotten drunk, crashed overnight at the apartment of a former girlfriend, and had married her two days later.

That afternoon, Magda took an overdose of sleeping pills and, unconscious, was discovered by Jolie, who immediately called a doctor. After rushing to her apartment, he forced her to vomit up the pills.

That night, Jolie discovered a will that Magda had drawn up, leaving everything she owned to her gay butler, Harry. "Not a cent, nothing for me, her mother who had done so much for her." Jolie was adamant and went for three weeks without speaking to Magda.

In the meantime, Magda hired an agent, Jeffrey Jones, who arranged a few acting roles for her. By accident, Jones and Magda ran into Gallucci on the street. After their awkward hellos, she asked her former beau to return with her to her apartment.

Once inside her home, she offered Gallucci a drink of her best Scotch whisky. As he started to drink it, she cracked a whip, knocking the glass from his hand. He tried to protect himself from the cracks of the whip, but she beat him severely.

When Jolie heard his screams, she rushed to Magda's apartment and wrestled the whip from Magda. What Magda was doing with a horse whip in her apartment was never explained.

Jolie called an ambulance for Gallucci. At the hospital, a doctor treated him for flesh wounds, finding that he had no internal injuries. After he was bandaged up, Jolie stayed with him until 8pm. He was released the next day, and Jolie was there to take him to his apartment in a taxi.

Once inside his apartment, she prepared a home-cooked meal for him. It was agreed that he would tell his wife that he had been mugged on the street.

Some connoisseurs of Hungarian flesh considered **Magda Gabor** the sexiest of the Gabor sisters.

For a brief period, she tried for a theatrical career, as when she posed for this publicity shot.

Prince Aly Khan and even George Sanders discovered Magda's allure before they got around to sampling Zsa Zsa and/or Eva.

Magda refused to see him. Nor did she apologize, although the horse whip had come very close to putting out Gallucci's left eye. Of course, Jolie was anxious to avoid a lawsuit.

As she invariably did, Jolie forgave Magda her transgressions. In two weeks, Magda entered El Morocco on the arm of a "Count Yailotzie." Jolie's escort for the evening was a twenty-eight year old Hungarian jewelry wholesaler who had fled from Hungary before the Nazi takeover. Although he had a wife and three children on Long Island, he was spending most of his nights in Jolie's apartment. She was paying his bills.

In the middle of their drinks, a waiter approached the table and told Magda that she was wanted on the phone.

She excused herself and went to take the call at a booth. It was Gallucci on the other end.

"Oh Magda, your beating me with that whip made me realize that I love you, and only you," he said. "I don't love my wife. I want you back. My wife's not here. Can you come to my apartment tonight…right now! I'll die if I can't hold you in my arms and transport you to heaven, as I usually do."

Without telling Jolie or the count goodbye, Magda disappeared from El Morocco and wasn't heard from for a week.

Long before she became Gallucci's wife, she lived with him on and off as his mistress until he eventually got a divorce.

***

"My luck ran out on seducing my leading man when director Richard Brooks cast me in *The Last Time I Saw Paris,"* Eva said. The film starred a stunningly beautiful Elizabeth Taylor, and the leading men included Van Johnson, Walter Pidgeon, and Eva's friend from Broadway, Kurt Kasznar. All three actors were gay.

"Roger Moore, later of James Bond fame, made his Hollywood debut in this film," Eva said. "Van, Walter, Kurt, and I wanted him, but as far as I know, all of us struck out, including Donna Reed, who was also cast in the movie."

The move was loosely based on F. Scott Fitzgerald's short story, *Babylon Revisited.* It was filmed on location in Paris and also on the MGM backlot. The title of the movie was based on the song by composer Jerome Kern and lyricist Oscar Hammerstein II, which had won an Oscar when it made its film debut in *Lady Be Good* in 1941.

[Because of a copyright oversight, MGM failed to renew the copyright on the film, and it entered the public domain in 1972.]

Eva's role was of Lorraine Quarl, described as a professional *divorcée,* and her screen appearance was one of her most glamorous, although the youthful beauty of Elizabeth Taylor was the true dazzler of the film.

Elizabeth's role was based loosely, very loosely, on Zelda Fitzgerald.

Eva later recalled, "I'll never forget my first scene with Elizabeth. She wore the most glamorous red chiffon gown. Her hair had been cut shorter than usual, which inflamed Louis B. Mayer, who didn't like it. I thought she looked so young, so beautiful. Yes, I was jealous."

"Van and I were driven to the MGM backlot that day in the same car. I had on this yellow coat I was supposed to wear. But I got drenched in a downpour when I stepped out of the car. The idiots didn't even have an umbrella. My hair and my coat were ruined. This could only happen to me. Here I was appearing in a scene with the most ravishing girl in the world, and I looked like a little wet rabbit."

"I had great fun hanging out with 'the boys,'" Eva said. "Van, Walter, and Kurt were amusing and Roger Moore was unavailable. I thought Elizabeth might be rude toward me, because of Zsa Zsa's involvement with Nicky Hilton, her former husband. But she was polite and rather charming. I already knew her from the makeup department of MGM. One day, she invited me to lunch."

In the commissary, she whispered a secret," Eva said. "She told me that she was pregnant, presumably from Michael Wilding, that English actor who had become her second husband after Nicky."

When *The Last Time I Saw Paris* was released, Eva, outclassed by the name stars, was virtually not mentioned in the reviews. Bosley Crowther of *The New York Times* defined it as "a bistro balderdash of lush, romantic scenes." *Time Out* claimed that Pidgeon stole the show and that the film "borrowed *clichés* from *Casablanca* and countless 'American in Paris' yarns." *Variety* found "Miss Taylor delectable, but occasionally quite dull."

"Next time around, I'll come out better," Eva vowed.

The cast of *The Last Time I Saw Paris* included *(left to right)* **Eva Gabor, Walter Pidgeon, Donna Reed, Van Johnson,** and **Elizabeth Taylor,** whose character was very vaguely based on Zelda Fitzgerald.

"I was outclassed," Eva said. "Most of the male stars were gay, except for Roger Moore, who was otherwise occupied. Alas, what's a girl looking for love to do?"

***

[In the years to come, Eva maintained a casual relationship with Elizabeth Taylor, mainly because she lied and claimed that she never had an affair with Elizabeth's then-husband, Richard Burton. Taylor learned that Zsa Zsa had had an affair with Burton, which the actress did not keep a secret, but loudly proclaimed on occasion.

Taylor once said, "I think Zsa Zsa wants to sample all my husbands, and that includes not only Nicky, but Eddie Fisher. She's probably had Mike Todd and Michael Wilding, too."

In October of 1991, Eva was invited—along with her escort, Merv Griffin—to Taylor's wedding to truck driver Larry Fortensky. She joined 160 other guests (who included Gerald and Betty Ford and Ronald and Nancy Reagan) at Michael Jackson's Neverland ranch.

"After the wedding, everybody was kissy-kissy," Eva said. "The Gloved One (Michael Jackson) didn't want to kiss me, but two former U.S. presidents did. When both Reagan and Ford started to plant a kiss on my cheek, in each case, I moved my head a little and got their kisses on my succulent lips."

"I kissed only two U.S. presidents. Zsa Zsa got to know two presidents more intimately, one a Republican, the other a Democrat, so I would call her bipartisan."

Over a final champagne toast with Taylor, the new bride said to Eva, "If I believed half of what I read about myself, I would truly hate me."

"Oh, dahlink," Eva said, "you've got the best revenge on all your critics by living well and so glamorously...and now by taking on a young husband."]

***

In Hollywood, Zsa Zsa signed with producer Sidney Franklin to star in *The Story of Three Loves,* to be directed by Vincente Minnelli. It was a 1953 romantic anthology film for MGM, with an all-star cast which included Pier Angeli, over whom she'd once gone into a jealous rage with George Sanders when they'd co-starred in *The Light Touch.* The stellar cast also included Ethel Barrymore, Leslie Caron, Kirk Douglas, Farley Granger, her friend James Mason, Agnes Moorehead, and Moira Shearer.

Zsa Zsa's segment with Granger appeared as a sub-section of that film entitled "Mademoiselle," During its filming, she met child actor Ricky Nelson. "He would grow up in the most delightful ways," she later said. The other stars of that sub-section included Caron, Granger, and Barrymore. Zsa Zsa's role was exceedingly small. Cast as a nameless "Flirt" at a bar, she tried to entice Granger.

"That was quite an acting job we put on," Zsa Zsa later said, "since that gorgeous-looking man was gay as a Hungarian goose."

"Besides, our gay director, Mr. Minnelli, was chasing after Farley, but seemingly getting nowhere," Zsa Zsa said. "I don't know how Judy Garland put up with that one."

Granger remembered Zsa Zsa's role as that of "a ravishing blonde in a scarlet dress that emphasized her milky white cleavage. She had a captivating smile and a killer Hungarian accent."

"Her part was small, but when she arrived with the entire hair, makeup, and wardrobe departments in tow, fussing over her as if she was royalty, she made a very big entrance," Granger said.

That same year (1953), another gay director, Charles ("Chuck") Walters, also cast her in *Lili,* reuniting her with Leslie Caron, the *ingénue* "coming of age" star of this romantic melodrama, set in France, from MGM.

Caron played a touchingly naïve French girl, a role that earned her a Best Actress Oscar nod.

Zsa Zsa bonded with the film's director, who was noted for having previously directed Esther Williams' musicals, each of which involved underwater "ballet swimming."

Zsa Zsa remembered spending a weekend with Walters and his lover, John Darrow, who had been a juvenile movie star in the late 1920s.

"They'd built this charming little house in Malibu," she said. "It was all plum-colored carpets and chocolate walls. John and Chuck danced the night away."

"When we weren't dancing, Chuck attacked Minnelli. They were competitors. No love was lost between those two."

"Although they were lovers, John and Chuck were also competitive with each other." Zsa Zsa said. "Each wanted to be the center of attention,

"Farley Granger was a beautiful man," **Zsa Zsa** claimed when she appeared with him in a segment for the MGM film, *The Story of Three Loves.*

"In my scene with him, I flirted with him at the bar. Off screen, we talked about his boyfriend."

John with a few drinks got a little rough at times, and called Chuck a faggot."

"The year I made *Lili* for him, Chuck agreed to dance on screen with Joan Crawford, who hadn't made a musical in some twenty years. The film was called *Torch Song* (1953). I went to see it, *dahlink*. Could you believe at one point, Crawford appeared in black face. She called it 'Caribbean makeup.'"

Zsa Zsa found the two male stars of that film, Mel Ferrer and Jean-Pierre Aumont, captivating. "My sister Eva had staked out Mel, so I went for Jean-Pierre, that French hunk of a man, very sexy, very romantic. This dashing Frenchman, a woman slayer, was also a war hero," she said.

French actor **Jean-Pierre Aumont** claimed that this photograph of him was the handsomest ever taken of him.

For years, Zsa Zsa hung an autographed copy of it in her bathroom.

[During World War II, Aumont won the Legion d'Honneur *and the* Croix de Guerre *for his military service.*

As a Jew, he had to flee from France after the Nazi takeover, but he later joined the Free French forces fighting in North Africa.

When Zsa Zsa met him, his 1940s marriage to "Cobra Woman," the exotic Maria Montez, had ended with her death in 1951.]

"I was fortunate that I got to meet this adorable hunk before Grace Kelly dug her feline claws into him," Zsa Zsa said. "I adore Grace, *dahlink*, but you don't trust her around a man."

In *Lili*, **Zsa Zsa** confronts **Leslie Caron**, the French actress.

"We were such different types that Leslie and I were never competitive," Zsa Zsa said. "My direction was to play this role as beautiful, witty, and self-important."

"Aumont was a wonderful lover," Zsa Zsa claimed. "He'd picked up some skills in the bordellos of Algeria during the War, or so I believed. He was courteous, handling a woman like a lovely piece of porcelain. His finely sculpted body became a tool of pleasure for a woman."

"I thought our romance would end as soon as *Lili* was wrapped, but we saw each other a few more times, both in Paris and at my home in Bel Air. He was always welcome."

"If anything was wrong with him, it was too great a concern about his image," she said. "He was overly sensitive to the slightest criticism in the press. He liked to be written up as a great actor and war hero, but when he started dating Grace, reporters often attacked him. He was called an ambition-crazed gigolo using Grace for publicity. He was also labeled a dubious adventure and a minor league Casanova."

"I remember once he called me around April of 1955," she said.

"Guess what?" he challenged Zsa Zsa. "Albert Einstein died on April 18, and the press devoted more space to Grace buying me an ice cream cone."

One dark night in Paris, Zsa Zsa invited Aumont to her favorite nightclub, Freddie's. "Again, he was very upset by the press. Louella Parsons had written that he had attempted suicide over losing Grace to Prince Rainier."

"The road was slippery, and my car ran off into an embankment," Aumont told Zsa Zsa. "I fractured a rib. It was not a suicide attempt."

The legendary, much-adored French singer, Edith Piaf, was in the club that night, and consequently, Freddie had little time for Zsa Zsa. But she did drop by their table. Freddie was loving and friendly to Zsa Zsa, but seemed to hold Aumont in contempt.

With a bite of sarcasm, Freddie told Aumont, "Miss Kelly apparently would rather be called Princess of Monaco, Duchess of Valentinois, Marquise de Baux, Countess of Grimaldi, and be referred to as 'Most Serene Highness' instead of being known merely as Madame Aumont."

"*Merde*," he said. "If Rainier would bestow titles like that on me, I'd fuck the bastard's fat ass every night."

"I will never marry just for a title," Zsa Zsa vowed.

How wrong she was.

***

In 1952, quite by coincidence, Porfirio Rubirosa met Zsa Zsa in an elevator going up to their respective suites at the Plaza Hotel in Manhattan. He later recalled his vision of her. "Her blonde hair was swept up, and she was clad in a fabulous mink coat. She had two poodles on the leash. I have known many a woman in my day, but hardly one as glamorous and stunning looking as Zsa Zsa Gabor."

"Madam, I'm Porfirio Rubirosa. May I ask what you are doing in New York?"

"I'm here to attend the premiere of my picture, *Moulin Rouge*," she said.

"Is your husband, George Sanders, in town, too?" he asked.

"He's in Naples shooting a picture with Ingrid Bergman and Roberto Rossellini," she answered.

He then invited her for a drink with Generalíssimo Rafael Leonidas Trujillo, the dictator of the Domincan Republic, who was visiting the United States on a goodwill mission.

She thanked him, but declined his offer, claiming she had an appointment with her hairdresser.

"Perhaps later," he said.

"Perhaps," she said, getting off the elevator with her poodles.

At the time, she recalled that Rubirosa was just a name to her, one she read frequently in the gossip columns, mostly because of his ill-fated marriage to Doris Duke, the mistress of Zsa Zsa's husband.

"Even without meeting him, I'd once vowed to seduce Rubirosa as a revenge against George for sleeping with Doris," Zsa Zsa said. "But even though I'd been rude to Rubirosa in the elevator, I suspected he wouldn't take my first refusal as final."

Alone in the elevator, Rubirosa pressed the down button, which carried him to the reception desk. There, he arranged to have his suite moved to the suite adjoining Zsa Zsa's. He had one question: "Is there a connecting door between the two suites?"

The receptionist assured him there was, "but it must be unlocked from the lady's side."

Once inside her suite, Zsa Zsa decided to take a beauty nap before meeting her hairdresser. One reporter described the rest of Zsa Zsa's day as a scene torn from the pages of a romantic "bodice ripper."

When she awakened two hours later, she found the living room of her suite filled with the most beautiful red roses she'd ever seen, each flower seemingly handpicked and selected for its exceptional beauty. The heady aroma of the roses perfumed the entire suite. She found a note which read: "For a most beautiful lady, Rubi." He had enclosed his card, identifying him as "Don Porfirio Rubirosa, Minister Plenipotentiary, The Dominican Republic."

Long before the tabloids discovered the adulterous romance of Elizabeth Taylor and Richard Burton, 1950s headlines blazed with news about the notorious affair of **Zsa Zsa** with Dominican playboy, **Porfirio Rubirosa.**

Although he seduced redheads and brunettes, he had a particularly affinity for blondes—Veronica Lake, Jayne Mansfield, Kim Novak, Evita Perón, and inevitably, Marilyn Monroe.

The phone rang. It was Rubi. She remembered that "his voice was the most seductive I've ever heard. It was like a caressing whisper in a mauve-colored fog that evoked romance and intrigue."

He wanted to come by her suite, but she told him that her hairdresser was on the way up. There was no way she wanted to entertain Rubirosa in curlers. She declined his second invitation for a drink, but left open the possibility that she might be available after the premiere of *Moulin Rouge.*

He informed her that by coincidence, he was occupying the suite immediately adjacent to hers, with a connecting door.

"What a coincidence," she said before ringing off.

After an hour with the hairdresser, she was left alone in her suite, since she'd given her maid the day off. In preparation for the evening's gala, she tried on a $50,000 gown, the most exquisite she'd ever worn. It was made of baby lamb skin that fitted her like a second skin. She took in her figure in the full-length mirror and liked what she saw.

However, she couldn't get the gown zipped up in back. Impulsively, she telephoned the suite of Rubirosa next door, apologizing for the intrusion and inviting him over to zip her up. "Would you be so kind?" she asked. "I'll unlock the connecting door."

He readily agreed, and within minutes was in her suite, where she had a chance to observe him more closely. Previously, when she'd spotted him from a distance at a London nightclub, she had not been impressed. Up close, and with a keener observation, she changed her mind, a woman's privilege.

At the age of forty-five, with graying temples, he appeared in excellent physical condition. She would later describe him as having the body of Adonis. From the elevator, she'd remembered his sun-burned cheeks and his cerise tie. From constantly playing polo, he was slightly bow-legged. His jet black, nappy hair had been straightened, and he wore it slicked back like a shiny ebony helmet. Even though plastic surgeons had worked on it, his nose was still wide. Critics claimed he looked like a monkey. She found him sexy and charismatic.

At long last, she found herself alone in a room with "the Romeo of the Caribbean," the "Don Juan of the 20th Century," as he was described in the tabloids.

Like Zsa Zsa, Rubi had been married three times before, first to the nymphomaniac, Flor de Oro, the daughter of the Dominican dictator *[Generalissimo Rafael Trujillo]*, and later to the actress, Danielle Darrieux, the highest paid film star in France. He'd already wed and divorced Doris Duke, but only after she'd given him a private plane, a 17th-century townhouse in a chic neighborhood of Paris, and an income for life.

As he zipped up Zsa Zsa's gown, his fingers caressed her bare skin, sending shivers through her body. "It made me dizzy with desire," she later said. "He arouses passion in me, and his voice was so close to my ear, it felt like kisses of endearment."

He'd later claim, "Her beauty was dazzling. So many women have passed through my portal, but none quite as lovely as Zsa Zsa. She had peach perfect

In Paris, tobacco heiress **Doris Duke** married the world's most famous gigolo, **Porfirio Rubirosa**.

Rubi was constantly pursued by rich women who wanted to check out the rumor about his famous "equipage."

His equipment was defined by various witnesses (who were many) as "priapic, indefatigable, and grotesquely proportioned." Duke claimed that he could "excite a woman beyond the threshold."

skin, an ample bosom, a Venus de Milo figure, and blonde hair piled up on her perfectly shaped head with these luscious red lips. Everything was set off with sparkling diamonds. I was overwhelmed. I, a man who had been intimate with some of the most glamorous women of the 20th century, including Evita Perón of Argentina."

After he'd zipped her up, she agreed to meet him in the Persian Room at the Plaza Hotel after the movie premiere. As he'd done with a thousand women before her, he helped her on with her sable coat. "He was so close to me, I could feel his breathing on my neck," she later said. "He gave off an intoxicating aroma. Not since Atatürk had I met such a masculine creature."

At the premiere, she made a dazzling appearance, much to the delight of photographers and her fans. At one point, John Huston stood beside her, proclaiming, "Technicolor and Zsa Zsa Gabor made this picture."

Outside, a two-story giant cutout of her cast the glow of her incandescent beauty over Times Square. Fans mobbed her for autographs.

She later claimed, "From that moment, I was drunk on my own power. For the first time, I was infused with pride at my own achievement, little knowing that this would be the highlight of my film career, that producers and directors in the years to come would shun me because of my notoriety, giving me roles where I was no more than a caricature of myself."

After the premiere, she returned to the Plaza and headed for the Persian Room, where she found Rubi sitting with Prince Bernadotte of Sweden. "Before drinks were over, I knew I had a choice of men, both of whom seemed eager to seduce me. What was it to be? The prince or Rubi? I chose Rubi."

The trio conversed in French and English. "Rubi devoured me with his piercing black eyes. Whenever he could, his hand brushed against mine, sending electric shock through my body. He was almost primitive in his desires."

As she relayed to Pamela Mason back in Hollywood, "I noticed he had his diplomatic trousers tailored much tighter than the norm. My eyes focused on his crotch, which seemed on exhibit. It looked as if he'd stuffed three very thick socks into his trousers."

The intrigue did not end in the Persian Room. The next day, Zsa Zsa woke up, finding herself sleeping next to a nude Rubi. His passion for her had only been relieved at eight o'clock that morning. It was now two in the afternoon.

She'd later recall, "I woke up before him. Before I lived through the past few hours, I thought Atatürk and Prince Aly Khan were the world's greatest lovers. Rubi dethroned them. He knew how to manipulate a woman's body to give her the greatest pleasure a man is capable of giving. He could transport you to heaven and then let you descend on pink, fluffy clouds. He attacked all parts of a woman's body, leading her to discover erotic zones she never knew existed before."

"I was so miserable, yet so happy," she recalled. "George was indifferent to me, supercilious, even hurting me far more than anyone knew. Then there was Rubi. Because I was overexcited and overmiserable, and because I was lonely for a man, I had said yes to Rubi."

A cable was resting on the coffee table in her suite. It was from Sanders, who was in Italy filming *Voyage to Italy*, and suffering from food poisoning from the polluted fish caught in the Bay of Naples. He'd changed his mind. Initially, he had refused her request to travel abroad with him. Now he wanted her to fly at once to join him during the final weeks of shooting the Rossellini film.

Faced with indecision, she cursed the world. Why did society make a woman choose between a husband she still loved and a lover she could no longer live without?

***

Zsa Zsa flew to Rome and then took another flight south to Naples, where Sanders in a rented Fiat met her at the airport. He told her that they'd be staying in Ravello, a scenic hill town on the southern end of the Amalfi coast, a town that for the moment, at least, was awash with American film crews and Hollywood movie stars.

Even in Hungary, she'd heard of this enchanting town forty-one miles south of Naples. It had attracted artists and celebrities for years, including André Gide, Richard Wagner, Greta Garbo, and D.H. Lawrence, who wrote *Lady Chatterley's Lover* here. Incidentally, Zsa Zsa had always wanted to play Lady Chatterley in a film. Boccaccio had dedicated part of his *Decameron* to Ravello, but currently, her nemesis, John Huston, was using it as the location of his latest film, *Beat the Devil*, starring Humphrey Bogart, and Jennifer Jones.

Sanders and Zsa Zsa checked into the Villa Cimbrone, which had entertained everyone from Henrik Ibsen to Virginia Woolf and Tennessee Williams.

Before she'd unpacked, Sanders practically attacked her for a session of love-making. "Rubirosa he was not," Zsa Zsa said when she got angry at her husband.

The next day was a Saturday, and Sanders didn't have to work. In a memoir, she articulated an abbreviated version of what took place on her first full day in Ravello.

Over breakfast, Sanders confided to her that his alltime sexual fantasy involved watching her make love to a Catholic priest who had never before been sexually intimate with a woman.

She was shocked by this, interpreting the proposal as outrageous. However, she agreed to meet with a young Catholic priest who was eager to be introduced to her. "I admit I was curious. I expected some gray-haired old robed man to arrive and was shocked when I met Guido."

[That was the name she used in a memoir. Actually, his name was Mario Sorrento.]

The priest who showed up for lunch on a terrace overlooking the sea was not what she expected. To her friends, and to her ghost writer, she recalled, "He looked like Alain Delon when he made that picture *Purple Noon* years later, in

1960. Guido wore a form-fitting T-shirt and tight blue jeans that didn't make you tax your imagination very much. Not only was he handsome, but he was charming and spoke English with such a beautiful accent. He was also hot to trot, wanting to take me over to a friend's house for an afternoon of lovemaking, his first time, although I think some of the male priests had molested him. Apparently, all of this had been arranged with George, who would voyeuristically observe the action."

On the Amalfi Coast, Zsa Zsa encountered the cast of John Huston's *Beat the Devil*. Seated from left to right are **Jennifer Jones, Humphrey Bogart,** and **Gina Lollobrigida**, the stars of the picture.

Zsa Zsa knew Bogie from Hollywood. He told her, "When Jennifer Jones isn't getting marching orders from her husband, David Selznick, by cable, she's being chased around the Amalfi Coast trying to escape from the clutches of a tall, aggressive lesbian."

Huston told Zsa Zsa that Lollobrigida made Marilyn Monroe look like Shirley Temple.

"I turned him down, but I did accept an invitation to go horseback riding with him in the hills the following day, when George was busy shooting his film," she said. She did admit in a memoir that "Guido took me in his arms and devoured me with kisses. George was miles away and missing the experience of his life…as a voyeur, that is."

Guido *[i.e., Father Sorrento]* took her to a remote little inn in the mountains known mainly to off-the-record Italians.

Zsa Zsa wrote that she found Guido "intensely attractive," and that she "had to control herself."

[As it happened, she controlled herself the same way she'd controlled herself in New York with Rubi. Consequently, she introduced Guido to his first sex with a woman. It would not be their last session.]

She confessed that every time she visited Italy during the years to come, she made it a point to call on the irresistible "Guido" (Father Sorrento).

Visiting Sanders on the set the following day, she met Rossellini, who held her hand too long. She found Rossellini "fat and balding. I could not believe that Bergman had risked everything to run off with this adulterous toad."

As he chatted with her, he told her, "I can see now that I married the wrong film star. Ingrid won't even give me a blow-job. She likes it only in the missionary position, as the Americans say."

Finally, she heard the voice of Ingrid Bergman coming toward her. "I've always wanted to meet Mrs. George Sanders," Bergman announced.

Shaking her hand, Zsa Zsa snapped back, "A delight to meet you, too, Mrs. Rossellini."

They did not become friends.

After Bergman departed, Zsa Zsa complained to Rossellini. "Calling me Mrs. Sanders is so bourgeois and unglamorous."

"I agree, my dear," Rossellini said. "Why don't you get even with Ingrid and come back to my suite with me?"

"I would love to," Zsa Zsa said, "but I've got a date this afternoon with a priest. To make a confession, *dahlink.*"

Ingrid Bergman, depicted above, had virtually destroyed her Hollywood career when she ran off and married Italian director Roberto Rossellini. When introduced to them, Zsa Zsa was not impressed with either of them.

Rossellini propositioned her, but she thought he was a "fat toad." Bergman insulted her.

"Bergman was equally obnoxious when she met Jennifer Jones working nearby on *Beat the Devil*," Zsa Zsa said. "She reminded Jennifer that she'd had her husband, David O. Selznick, before Jennifer had married him."

Sanders had the following day off, and so did Humphrey Bogart, who was shooting *Beat the Devil* nearby. He invited them to walk down to and through the little town of Amalfi on the coast, which he told them had a wonderful waterfront tavern.

En route, Zsa Zsa complained that she wasn't wearing the right shoes.

They'd just passed a local shop. Bogie told Sanders to buy a pair of sandals for his wife.

"I can't afford them," Sanders said."

At first, Bogie thought he was joking before concluding that he meant it. "You cheap bastard," Bogie said, walking up the street to the store and returning with a pair of comfortable *espadrilles* for Zsa Zsa.

She had another reason for liking Bogie:

He had recently given an interview in which he claimed, "The two women I most admire in America are Zsa Zsa Gabor and Ingrid Bergman." She was surprised that he had left out Lauren Bacall, and could forgive him his bad taste in including Bergman on that list.

That night, Zsa Zsa found Sanders deep in depression, even threatening suicide. He was furious at Rossellini, although he had only kind words for Bergman. Apparently, whenever Rossellini shut down production to visit the bordellos of Rome, Bergman had been spending cozy evenings with Sanders.

"There's no god damn script," Sanders said. "Either I get new lines every day from this WOP, or I have to improvise as I go along."

That night, Sanders was interviewed by a reporter from Rome. He indiscreetly said, "Like all women, my wife resembles the Queen Bee who ultimately extinguishes her mate. Her pattern is clear. She's caught me. She's breaking me in. When she utterly owns me, she'll trample on me. Zsa Zsa Gabor is my married mistress. Or perhaps a lady pirate stealing hearts."

The next day, after another session of love in the afternoon with Guido, Zsa Zsa returned to her suite at the villa. Once there, she found that Sanders had opened a cable that had arrived from Rubi. He read it aloud to her:

NO WORD FROM YOU. MISS YOU. LOVE YOU SO MUCH. WIRE ME. RUBI.

Then Sanders dropped the cable on the floor. "Cokiline, you've conquered the great Rubirosa. He's in love with you. What a conquest. I'll answer his cable for you."

In spite of her protests, he picked up the phone and called reception, asking them to send a cable to Rubi in Paris. He dictated it: *MON CHERI. I LOVE YOU TOO AND CANNOT WAIT TO SEE YOU AGAIN. ZSA ZSA.*

That night when Sanders went to dinner, she stayed in her bedroom, calling Rubi in Paris. They talked for an hour.

She told him that the following day, she was obligated to fly all the way to Las Vegas, with transfers through Rome and New York. She had an engagement at El Rancho.

He told her he had only one night free, but that he'd fly all the way from Paris to Las Vegas to catch her performance. "And other things," he added.

***

In Las Vegas, Rubi arrived in time to attend Zsa Zsa's one-woman show at El Rancho. He applauded wildly and sent five mammoth bouquets of roses onto the stage at the end of her act.

Within an hour after that, he was in her bed within her luxurious suite at the hotel. She later told her intimates that, "We made love until the dawn, when he had to fly out again to return to France, with a promise to meet again soon."

She later attempted to characterize their shared feelings for each other. "We were like two children: pleasure-seeking, hedonistic, perhaps spoiled and self-ish, but full of an unquenchable lust for life and an insatiably strong appetite for excitement. Rubi and I both suffered from the same curse. Life held too many possibilities for us. It was as if there was too much potential surrounding me, too much love, too much excitement. We were too greedy for life and too greedy for each other."

She repeated what Rubi had told her the night before, "I am, and will always be, a man of pleasure. In my native land, I was called a *tíguere,* a tiger. Born of low origins with big aspirations, Tigers rise up in the world. They are hunters. When a man is a tiger, he will tell lies, practice treachery, and commit violence if it's warranted. He will do anything to achieve his ends. What was I supposed to do? Go to work in a factory for six dollars a day?"

From her jewelry shop in Manhattan, Jolie called Zsa Zsa the afternoon Rubi flew out of Las Vegas. "He is not husband material," she warned her daughter. "He is an international gigolo preying on the world's richest women. For a husband, he is not good."

Zsa Zsa refused to heed her warning. "*Nuci,*" you must understand. Rubi is a disease of my blood. I cannot live without him."

By a coincidence of luck, Zsa Zsa was offered a starring role in a film to be shot in Paris. There, she would hook up with Rubi once again. Her first foreign film would be called *L'ennemi public n° 1* (aka *El Enemigo Público No. 1*; aka *Public Enemy no. 1).* It starred Fernandel, France's top comic actor, famous for his horse-like teeth. She would play a gun moll named Lola.

For the sake of appearances, she booked into a suite at the very posh Plaza Athénée, but spent most of her nights at Rubi's townhouse on rue de Belle-chasse, a gift from Doris Duke at the time of their divorce.

When Sanders heard of this, he told a reporter, "So many princesses, countesses, and even a queen *[a reference to Queen Alexandra of Yugoslavia]* have slept at Rubi's townhouse that he had become a baron by process of bedroom osmosis."

When she wasn't working with Fernandel, Zsa Zsa and Rubi became almost inseparable. "He had such power over me, I had no will of my own," she

489

later said. She adored the interior of his townhouse, which carried the aroma of tobacco and leather. He'd decorated the downstairs living room with polo gear and trophies he'd won.

Dinners were lavish events. His woman chef had once cooked for Trujillo, and she introduced a series of Caribbean delicacies to their VIP guests. With Zsa Zsa as his hostess, Rubi received the cream of European society. One night even Prince Philip arrived by himself, although she suspected he had arranged a rendezvous for later in the evening. "Rubi and His Highness talked polo for most of the night, when not drinking champagne and eating Beluga caviar," she said.

Later that night, Rubi slapped me around, accusing me of flirting with Philip," she claimed. "He was ferociously jealous and had a real Latin temper. Once, while driving through Paris, he accused me of looking at a handsome young man on the sidewalk. Without warning, he braked the car and slapped me, his eyes blazing like hot coals."

"On another night, we went to the popular nightclub, Freddie's, where its namesake kissed me on the lips," Zsa Zsa claimed. "Freddie and I were just friends, but when I came back to the table, Rubi grabbed my arm and twisted until he practically broke it. 'So, now you like women, too, you lesbian slut,' he said."

Observing them at a party in Paris, Elsa Maxwell said, "They reminded me of two flames shooting toward each other, yet having no control over their flight."

During her time in Paris, Rubi announced to her that he was going to Deauville for four nights. She made use of his time away, entertaining on separate occasions both Elie de Rothschild and Prince Aly Khan at her hotel suite. "When Rubi suspected that I was having an affair with his friend, Aly, he seduced his estranged wife, Rita Hayworth, as an act of revenge, I understood that, as I'd had a few revenge fucks in my day."

Fashionistas hailed Zsa Zsa and Rubi as the best dressed couple in Paris. Rubi's tailor, Pierre Cagna, remembered coming by to fit him for three suits. "Miss Gabor's dressmaker was there, measuring her for a

"La Gabor Becomes a Gun Moll."

In the film they made together, both **Zsa Zsa** and the French comic, **Fernandel**, wore heavy spectacles as part of their wardrobes.

Fernandel played Public Enemy No. 1, and Zsa Zsa was cast as a female gangster.

"In a way, it was type casting," she told the French press. "But I steal hearts, not money from banks."

gown," he later told reporters. "I will always remember the vision of her beauty. She wore only a flimsy brassiere and panties embroidered with sequins, the latter coming as a surprise. At the time, I thought only burlesque dancers wore panties like that."

Although Rubi lived on the largesse of money given to him by rich women, especially Duke, he spent some of that loot on Zsa Zsa. In Paris, he presented her with a turquoise-and-diamond necklace from Van Cleef & Arpels. From Bulgari he purchased a diamond brooch with rubies fashioned into roses. From Cartier came a dazzling bracelet of blue diamonds and an Art Deco cluster of rubies.

He took her to the House of Dior to purchase both daytime dresses and evening gowns. "He knew more about women's clothing than Coco Chanel, or so it seemed," she claimed. "Surely, he must have a gay streak in him. He also told me what gowns made me look ravishing, and those I should never wear. I trusted his fashion sense completely."

When she wasn't needed at the film studio outside Paris, she and Rubi rose in the late morning and went to Fouquet's on the Champs-Elysées for breakfast. There, he always reserved a table where patrons of yesterday had included Sir Winston Churchill, Franklin D. Roosevelt, Charlie Chaplin, Maurice Chevalier, Marlene Dietrich, and Mistinguett. "He always downed a dozen raw oysters from Brittany, telling me that he had to eat those to live up to his sexual reputation."

She attended games of polo at the Bagatelle. "All the players wore white helmets," she said. "But Rubi stood out in a ruby-colored helmet in honor of 'Rubi.'"

Once, she stood next to a José Luís de Vilallonga, the Spanish writer, who, coincidentally, had been Magda's lover in Lisbon during the closing months of World War II. He'd left Magda and had settled in Paris. He described Rubi on the polo field: "He became a savage, covered with blood and displaying a macho competitiveness in the extreme. You could tell that he would gladly give up his life rather than face defeat."

Photographers followed them nightly as they made the rounds, often dining at Maxim's and ending the night in such fashionable *boîtes* as *l'Elephant Bleu.*

Soon, reporters were hailing their affair as "The Romance of the Decade." In the 1950s, they became what Elizabeth Taylor and Richard Burton were in the jet-setting 1960s.

At the end of Zsa Zsa's film commitment in Paris, they were often separated. But they frequently came together to attend the race car season, spring on the Riviera, August in Deauville, and time spent in Bel Air, where he lived at her home.

When not with her, he swamped her with cables and flowers, urging her to divorce George Sanders. "If you do not, *ma chérie,*" he warned in one cable, "I will kill myself."

When he cabled her or called her, he used the code name of "Mr. Perkins." She eagerly awaited these communications. "Rubi is a sickness for me," she proclaimed.

She later said that the notoriety caused by her involvement with Rubi practically wrecked what might have been a much more successful film career. "I was almost destined to carve out the same kind of career Marilyn Monroe did. But producers wouldn't hire me for the big pictures, giving them instead to that former hooker."

When Rubi wasn't around, she dated other men. "But these were rather harmless encounters. John F. Kennedy, in spite of his marriage, continued his attachment to me, popping in every now and then when he got the urge. When I refused to make some charity appearance for him in Boston, he threatened to turn me over to his younger brother, Bobby. He never did, although I would have been tempted."

As the months went by, Rubi's urgings to divorce Sanders grew more passionate. Finally, he sent an ultimatum cable.

"I love you, darling," it read. "But after reading your last cable, I see that you are not willing to separate and come here. So be frank and decide once and for all. Love, Rubi."

In spite of that ultimatum, she still wavered, still maintaining she was in love with Sanders.

One day, she picked up a newspaper and was shocked to see a tabloid spread featuring Rubi holding hands with Barbara Hutton.

She mockingly said, "Well, he has bills to pay. But Hutton is a comedown for him. He was once married to the richest woman in the world. Hutton is only the second richest woman in the world. Duke has earned more in tobacco than Hutton has by selling her junk trinkets at those Five-and Dime Woolworth stores."

Finally, Zsa Zsa concluded, "After he's ripped off Hutton, Rubi will come running back to me. He loves me, not this ugly, dried-up prune of a woman. I also hear she's frigid."

A few days later, the question of divorcing Sanders was not decided by Zsa Zsa but by Sanders himself. Her lawyer notified her that Sanders had filed for a divorce in California.

She immediately telephoned Rubi with the news.

At long last she would be free to marry him, because, as she said, "I could not spend one day or one night of my life without constantly thinking of Rubi and my desire for him."

***

Zsa Zsa publicly proclaimed, "Rubi is all male whether he talks to you, dances with you, walks with you, you know he is a man, thinking only of you and always of you as a woman to be taken and possessed and kept away from other men because, being so feminine and desirable, you are their natural prey."

She was absolutely astonished that wherever she went, she faced the same question from both men and women: What is the exact size of Rubi's penis? At first, the indelicacy of such a question shocked her. Surely no female celebrity in the history of the world had ever faced such a question before.

Throughout the United States and Western Europe, especially in London and Paris, a customer in a restaurant asked a waiter for a "Rubirosa" whenever he wanted a peppermill. Café society nicknamed Rubi "Rubber Hosa."

Even his third spouse, Doris Duke being rather indiscreet, claimed, "It was the most magnificent penis that I had ever seen."

Jerome Zerbe, society photographer, claimed, "It looks like Yul Brynner in a black turtleneck sweater."

His intimate friend, restaurant owner Manouche, said, "It was long and pointed and it hurt. It was never hard and never soft. It was nothing for Rubi to take on two or three women in a night. By late at night, when he was good and drunk, he didn't give a damn what kind of legs were opening."

It was rumored that in certain European bordellos, he often ordered a beautiful young boy, his lips painted red, to come to his room for sodomy. "What a tight fit," he told his gay friend Jimmy Donahue, a cousin of Barbara Hutton. "They scream, which excites me, but I hope it is a scream of pleasure." Donahue claimed that Rubirosa was a true hedonist. "He would fuck anything that wiggled."

Whenever Rubi got up to go to the toilet, he could always count on a string of voyeuristically inclined men trailing him to the urinal. One night at Maxim's, a rich industrialist from Milan asked him how large his organ was when erect. "I really don't know," Rubi told him. "It takes so much blood to get it up, I always pass out."

Late at night at intimate drunken parties, Rubi sometimes balanced a chair with a telephone book on it on his erection. He claimed that for "virility, I eat a dozen oysters a day and drink a Japanese black mushroom tea."

Those who had seen him erect, and they numbered in the hundreds, claimed that his penis was six inches in circumference. Most seemed to agree that his sex organ was "eleven inches long and thick as a beer can." Truman Capote, who had seen Rubi's penis erect, wrote that it was an "eleven-inch octoroon dick."

The peekaboo blonde-haired movie goddess of the 1940s, Veronica Lake, disputed these sightings, and claimed that when fully erect, the penis of Rubi could extend a full thirteen inches. "I should know, because I measured it one night at one of my famous orgies. I guess some of his other girlfriends, and that includes Jayne Mansfield, Marilyn Monroe, Ava Gardner, and Susan Hayward, didn't excite him as much as I do. I don't want to sound immodest, but I'm always frank even if the truth hurts."

Even Elsa Maxwell weighed in on the size of Rubi's penis: "He was the best hung man in international society. It was his calling card into society. Women heard about it, talked about it, dreamed about it, had to see it, hold it, and have it. He was not the kind of man to deny them that pleasure."

A hit Cuban song, "Que Es lo Tuyo, Rubirosa?" (What Have You Got, Rubirosa?) was, of course, a reference to his penis.

The French referred to the state of his penis as *toujours prêt* ("ever-ready").

Rubi's temper flared when he was drunk. He resented talk about his penis, and when the subject came up, he was often belligerent.

One night at Maxim's, a tipsy Zsa Zsa called him, "My Ding Dong Daddy from Santo Domingo."

She was "rewarded" with a hard slap in the face that bloodied her nose and sent her sobbing to the women's room. That would not be the only time he struck her.

His penis appeared to be in a permanent state of semi-erection, and he sometimes wore a heavy duty jockstrap. He had athletic supporters designed specifically for him with the image of a tiger emblazoned on them.

When pressed by someone about Rubi's sexual prowess, Zsa Zsa tried to evade the question. "Let's put it this way, *dahlink*. I always call him 'Big Boy,' and will say no more."

***

Sander's filing for divorce shocked Zsa Zsa. She said that in spite of outside love affairs, which included both Rubi and Doris Duke, she "somehow imagined that George and I would stay married until the day we died. I was devastated by the news."

It was later revealed that Sanders had been goaded into action by all the publicity Zsa Zsa and Rubi had received when they were in Manhattan on a joint visit in the autumn of 1953. She was in town to film a television show, and at night, she and Rubi were photographed wherever they went, be it dining at "21" or dancing at the Stork Club. In her "Voice of Broadway" column, Dorothy Kilgallen widely reported on this very public affair, as did Walter Winchell.

494

Sanders told his friend, Brian Aherne, "That woman is determined to humiliate me in front of the world."

Those exact words were used in his petition to the court seeking a divorce from her. He also charged that she had "subjected me to inhuman treatment and all this has allowed my health to deteriorate."

The attorney, Jerry Giesler, advised her to countersue, which she did. "All this still seemed unreal to me," she lamented.

As divorce proceedings dragged on, Sanders and Rubi would have only one encounter, and that was during Christmas in 1953, when Zsa Zsa gathered her sisters and her mother together at her home in Bel Air.

Rubi flew in for this family gathering. "It was my way of introducing Jolie to her new son-in-law-to-be," Zsa Zsa said.

During the celebration, Zsa Zsa, in front of Rubi, said, "I just wish George could be here." She would later regret saying that.

His hot temper flared up, and he stormed upstairs to her bedroom to pout.

After putting Jolie to bed downstairs, and waving her sisters off in their separate cars, Zsa Zsa walked up the steps to confront Rubi.

He had seemed despondent throughout the Christmas dinner. She apologized for making that remark about missing Sanders, but he had a more pressing problem.

"I just got back from the casino in Deauville," he told her. "Barbara [Hutton] was there. She's begging me to marry her, but I'm in love only with you. If you don't agree to marry me, I will marry Barbara."

"I'm not prepared to make a decision like marriage," she protested. "As you know, Magda, Eva, and I have to open tomorrow night in Las Vegas at the Last Frontier."

Unknown to Zsa Zsa, Sanders had waited outside during their Christmas dinner, along with two hired detectives he later characterized as "Laurel and Hardy."

He planned to invade the house and confront Zsa Zsa and Rubi, but he held back until Jolie had gone to bed and Eva and Magda had driven away. "If I had barged in on all the Gabors, it would have been like a rowboat confronting the Spanish Armada," he told the detectives.

At what he viewed as the right moment, he and the detective appeared within Zsa Zsa's garden carrying an expandable steel ladder, which was leaned up against the exterior wall of her second-floor bedroom.

Sanders himself mounted the rickety ladder, going all the way to the top rung. The lights were out as he leaned forward to peer inside. Regrettably, part of the ladder had been resting directly against the glass. Suddenly, as he was peering inside, the glass shattered.

He heard Zsa Zsa scream inside the bedroom. Rubi was perhaps rushing for his revolver, the one he secretly carried around with him because of assassination threats from his enemies.

The all-glass window continued to shatter as Sanders fell into the bedroom. A nude Zsa Zsa reached for her robe and switched on the lamp beside her bed.

"Oh, my god!" she shouted. "It's George!"

As she later claimed, "There George stood in a blue turtleneck sweater and faded blue jeans. He looked so handsome, so big, bronzed, and bearded, a blue-eyed giant of a man, much more beautiful than Rubi could ever be."

Sanders got his first full-on view of a nude Rubi. As she later said, "George gazed upon Rubi and his appendage, right before Rubi disappeared into the bathroom, locking the door behind him. George would dine out for years to come describing the fabled glory of Rubi's sex organ."

Zsa Zsa rushed over to see if he'd been injured by the shattered glass. He was unharmed. He told her, "I'm an old man, too old to be climbing ladders to catch my wife in bed with some Caribbean Negro stud."

While Rubi remained in the bathroom, she invited Sanders downstairs, where she presented him with a brandy and her Christmas present. No mention was made of Rubi, and after twenty minutes, Sanders left peacefully. He never really explained the purpose of this Christmas night raid, perhaps not even understanding it himself.

Within half an hour, Rubi came downstairs fully dressed and ready to go. He confronted her.

"You won't admit it, but you're crying like a silly little fool. You're still in love with this scoundrel."

Then he stormed out the door, slamming it behind him and not telling her if he planned to fly to Las Vegas or not.

"Other than that, *dahlink,*" Zsa Zsa reported to Pamela Mason in a phone call the following day, "it was an old-fashioned Yuletime celebration, complete with an apricot-stuffed Hungarian goose."

***

[On April 2, 1954, on what would have been their fifth wedding anniversary, Zsa Zsa and Sanders were granted a divorce in a crowded courtroom in Santa Monica.

He was in Spain making a picture, and he didn't contest her countersuit. In Madrid, he told the press, "Zsa Zsa needs some kind of passion play to restore her life."

A municipal judge granted the divorce. Zsa Zsa later said. "George Sanders was part of my life. Like a child, my father, my family. He was the love of my life."

"After I divorced her, or she divorced me, whatever, Zsa Zsa and I became harmonious friends," Sanders said. "In the future, there would be rare conjugal visits on certain occasions. We'd even star in a movie together."]

***

Magda wanted to break out of her career rut, where the only acting jobs available seemed to be appearing in rather mediocre plays on the straw-hat circuit. She dreamed of a show business gig that would propel her into national publicity, the kind both dreaded and enjoyed by Zsa Zsa and Eva.

Magda wanted to appear in a sister act, featuring all three Gabors in a hotel showroom in Las Vegas.

In the late spring of 1953, she'd read that Tallulah Bankhead was opening at the Sands in Las Vegas. Like herself, Magda knew that Tallulah was no musical comedy star like Ethel Merman. Partly motivated by what she'd be able to apply to her own nightlife ambitions, she booked a plane ticket to Las Vegas to catch Tallulah's show at the Sands.

Many of the most stellar members of *tout* Hollywood had flown to Las Vegas to watch Tallulah—who could neither sing nor dance—bomb in front of a Las Vegas audience.

Despite those predictions, Tallulah was a success, although she privately admitted, "I was "lousy." In the show's aftermath, *Variety* defined her as a "socko entertainer." She opened with pure stand-up comedy, pretending she was "a virgin" at the gambling casinos. She then spun into a dramatic monologue, "Telephone Call," written by her friend, Dorothy Parker.

She might have sounded like a frog croaking at mating season, but Tallulah even managed to sing renditions of "I'll Be Seeing You" and "Bye Bye Blackbird."

Magda went backstage to greet Tallulah, even though the star and Zsa Zsa were feuding. But when she spotted Magda, Tallulah was graceful and cordial, kissing her on the lips. "Welcome, *dahling*!" she said. "With this stint of mine, I'm officially launching myself, once a great stage actress, into popular vulgarity." In a makeup-smeared white robe, Tallulah did not mention Zsa Zsa. She opened her robe to expose her newly lifted breasts. "Just gaze upon these knockers, *dahling*. Marilyn Monroe, eat your fucking heart out."

Magda discussed her plan to open a three-way act featuring herself and her sisters. As regards questions about how to handle whatever showroom would host their act, Tallulah advised, "Take them for all you can get. I'm getting $20,000 a week, far less than Liberace and Marlene, but the wolf is always at my door, *dahling.*"

"Magda was surprised when Tallulah invited her back to her suite for "champagne and cognac, perhaps a little cocaine if Rock Hudson hasn't exhausted my supply."

Later, in Tallulah's suite, Magda was startled to see Hudson emerging from her bedroom with a suitcase. He had a plane to catch back to Los Angeles. He kissed Magda "hello and goodbye and gave Tallulah a wet one with tongue," according to what Magda witnessed.

After he'd gone, she said to Tallulah, "Friends of mine told me that Rock is gay."

[That word had come into general usage by 1953 to mean homosexual.]

"He is, *dahling*, a far better cocksucker than I am," Tallulah said. "But the dear boy likes to occasionally give mercy fucks to antique pussies like Joan Crawford and myself. He also on occasion has fucked Liberace. He's already plowed those aging heartthrobs, Tyrone Power and Errol Flynn, but mostly he likes handsome, well-built young guys like himself."

[In her confessions, Zsa Zsa had hinted at her own streak of lesbianism. But until Magda began rehearsing for her Las Vegas debut, no one had ever mentioned lesbianism in regard to her. In Las Vegas, however, rumors began to circulate about Magda being intimately linked with Bankhead and later with Marlene Dietrich.]

Weeks later, Zsa Zsa was said to have been indiscreet and told Pamela Mason and others that Magda had a lesbian affair with Tallulah that night.

Of course, along the way, there could have been a sexual detour, as there so often is with people in show business.

[In the 1960s, Ted Hook, Tallulah's secretary and companion, revealed to this author that his boss admitted that she'd had a brief three-day affair with Magda in Las Vegas when she was performing at the Sands.

The very gay Hook, a former chorus boy, expanded on Tallulah's involvement with women. "My God, she even fucked Winston Churchill one night in London, where she also managed to bed Dame Sybil Thorndike and Beatrice Lillie. Add to that list the singer Gladys Bentley, Katharine Cornell, Marlene Dietrich, Joan Crawford, Patsy Kelly, Billie Holiday, Lilyan Tashman, Laurette Taylor, and Mammy—Hattie McDaniel—from Gone With the Wind.*"]*

Before leaving Las Vegas, Magda was given some final words of advice from Tallulah.

"Good luck with your show. Show the world you're a far better performer than Mrs. Sanders and Eva. But deliver some self-deprecation on stage, along with bravado."

"And, *dahling*, don't spread the word I'm a sex maniac."

***

Back in New York, Magda went immediately to her theatrical booking agent and presented him with a big challenge. Get some Las Vegas casino to put up the money to produce a show featuring the three Gabor sisters.

He told her he thought it was hopeless, mainly because none of them knew how to convincingly sing or dance. She told him to try anyway.

It came as a shock when agents for the Sahara, the Sands, and the Last Frontier were receptive to the proposal. Because of the success they'd had with Marlene Dietrich and Tallulah Bankhead, it was presumed that the Gabors, "with all their glamor and goulash" would be a big hit, because all of them were known as beautiful, sexy women.

As one booking agent in Vegas said, "Each of the Gabors has the morals of a rattlesnake, and audiences will go for that big time."

On stage in Las Vegas for the first time together, the three Gabor sisters *(left to right;* **Magda, Eva, and Zsa Zsa**) sold glamour and mocked their own images as gold-digging sexual predators.

Both Zsa Zsa and Eva criticized Magda for "trying to capitalize off our fame." Even though Magda was the least experienced of the famous trio, she virtually stole the show, which greatly upset her jealous siblings.

Magda soon grew tired of "the showbiz grind," not wanting to make the sacrifices necessary for a career in entertainment. "Besides, through inheritance, I became the richest Gabor and no longer had to work," Magda claimed.

Each hotel, without even seeing the Gabor act, bid for their services, The Last Frontier offered the highest bid with an amazing $500,000 package for a show that technically didn't exist. The hotel was willing to put out that kind of money because, as the general manager said, "the Gabors will be a three-ring circus, and will get press around the country."

When Magda called Eva to announce the deal, Eva immediately rejected it, in spite of the money. "There's no way I want to be billed as a sister act with you and Zsa Zsa. Do you want us to become the MacQuire sisters? How about the Andrews Sisters? We could sing 'Don't Sit Under the Apple Tree With Anyone Else But Me.'"

It took a lot of convincing, but Eva finally agreed to go along, providing certain demands were met, and, most important of all, if Zsa Zsa signed on as well. Without Zsa Zsa, there would be no act.

Magda found Zsa Zsa even more resistant than Eva. A distracted Zsa Zsa was also in process of divorcing a man she claimed she still loved, and having a romantic tryst with another man she maintained she couldn't live without.

"We'll satirize ourselves, mocking men and love," Magda claimed. "The Frontier people have agreed to hire two of the best scriptwriters in Hollywood."

It sounds to me that big sister Magda is trying to cash in on the growing fame of her little sisters," Zsa Zsa charged. "Eva can already draw an audience on her own name. As for me, *dahlink,* I've already played the Flamingo with a one-woman show, and every night was a sell-out. You've never appeared in a night club before. Audiences might not go for your red hair and peculiar charm."

Finally, it was the money that convinced Zsa Zsa to go along, that and the massive publicity she knew such an act would generate.

Magda on her own flew to Las Vegas to meet with the people at the Frontier. The writers had been hired, and the show had a name, *THE GABORS— THIS IS OUR LIFE.* The script would be peppered with light banter about sex, in imitation of a venue previously established by Tallulah.

Another major potential roadblock for Magda involved presenting the collective demands of her sisters to the general manager of The Last Frontier. The Gabors wanted personal maids, separate suites, the best hairdressers and makeup people, and each demanded her own personal press agent. Zsa Zsa already had a press agent in the form of Russell Birdwell, and she wanted the hotel to pick up the tab for his services as well.

Magda agreed that the sisters would wear designer gowns, which would be paid for by the hotel. In a development that genuinely surprised Magda, The Last Frontier approved and granted the demands of each of the three divas.

Magda knew that both Eva and Zsa Zsa had had a lot more onstage experience than she'd had—especially Zsa Zsa who had been a sensation with her one-woman show.

Magda decided to check out the competition as a means of gauging how that formidable diva, Dietrich, was faring in her own one-woman show. Magda understood the obvious: she could learn a lot just by watching how an actress whose real talents lay on the screen pulled off a live act onstage.

She didn't want to go to the show alone, so she called Zsa Zsa in Bel Air, hoping she might know someone willing to escort her.

On the phone, Zsa Zsa came up with what she called "the perfect solution"

"As you know, *dahlink* , Cary Grant and I are friends," Zsa Zsa said. "Strictly platonic. I heard he's in Vegas to see the shows. He goes there quite a lot, even though he's not a gambler. As you know, he's handsome, elegant, charming, and suave. Perfect for you. You don't have to worry about putting out later, although your room service waiter, assuming he's good looking and well built, might be a target for Cary."

"Not only that, but Cary knows Rubi and was once married to Barbara Hutton, so, for the price of my linking you with Cary, I want you to pick his brain for any inside information, he might have about what is going on."

"You have a deal," Magda said.

***

Magda was anxious to see Marlene Dietrich performing in the Congo Room of the Sahara. Because of her see-through gown, the press had hailed her as "the world's first topless grandmother."

"If she's a grandmother, then she's the world's most glamorous grandmother," Magda told Cary Grant, who arrived at her suite to escort her to Dietrich's performance.

Back in 1932, Cary Grant had starred with Dietrich in *Blonde Venus,* which had been directed by her mentor, Josef von Sternberg. Privately to her intimates, Dietrich had denied press rumors of an affair with Grant. "I had no romantic feelings for him," she said. "He was a homosexual."

Apparently, Zsa Zsa had flirted with Grant when she'd met him at parties, but her affection led nowhere. Rather cynically, she'd said, "They are trying to show he's a great lover, but they'll never prove it to me."

Armed with these appraisals, Magda was expecting no sexual assault from Grant. But he was a debonair escort, and she found him both charming and amusing.

He told Magda that "Zsa Zsa was wise not to agree to marry Rubirosa. Before the wedding is over, he'll be in the next room bedding someone, who it is is of little importance to him. Forgive me for saying so, but he springs into action whenever he's faced with a hole."

During Dietrich's show, Magda was enthralled. "That's going to be a tough act for my sisters and I, mere mortals, to follow across the street," she told Grant.

After the show, Grant went backstage to renew his friendship with Dietrich, and to introduce her to Magda.

In bathing suits, **Cary Grant** and **Marilyn Monroe** pose for a scene in their film *Monkey Business.*

Both Marilyn and Zsa Zsa seduced a boatload of actors during the course of their careers, but each of these blonde goddesses struck out with Grant.

More sophisticated, Marlene Dietrich didn't even bother to try when she starred with him in *Blonde Venus.*

Instead of treating her coldly, Dietrich was polite, charming, and rather affectionate, even kissing and embracing her.

Grant and Magda were invited back to Dietrich's suite for caviar and champagne, compliments of the Sahara.

They talked until around two in the morning, until Grant excused himself. When he offered to walk Magda back to her nearby hotel, Dietrich intervened. "No dear, I want to talk to Magda some more. We're having such a grand time. We can sleep when morning comes."

Dietrich invited Magda into an alcove off her bedroom, a space with a full-length mirror that functioned as her dressing room. She wanted to show off three gowns that Jean-Louis had designed for her, including one very special creation.

As Steven Bach, Dietrich's biographer, wrote: "It was almost skin-tight black net lined with flesh colored silk below the waist and flesh-colored Marlene above. The transparency was real except for strategically scattered leaf-shaped sequin-and-rhinestone clusters that caressed and riveted attention to her breasts, which were held up and veiled by nothing but black gauze."

"The most glamorous grandmother in the world," **Marlene Dietrich,** was a sensation when she appeared in Las Vegas in a flesh-colored gown.

La Dietrich was intrigued and entranced by Magda's beauty, and there was rumor of a seduction, mostly spread by Zsa Zsa herself.

Dietrich boasted to Magda that she was the most highly paid and most highly publicized nightclub performer in the world.

The draperies were drawn at this point in Magda's life. Zsa Zsa, rather indiscreetly, once claimed that Dietrich seduced her older sister that night. "Magda is about the last person in the world to be considered a lesbian, but I know how overwhelming Dietrich can be when she wants to lure someone to her bed. I'm sure in bed Magda made Dietrich do all the work."

Zsa Zsa admitted that she'd found Greta Garbo more seductive than Dietrich. "If I ever became a lesbian, I'd choose Garbo over Dietrich as my lover."

The following evening, Magda returned to see the show, again with Grant. He'd brought Barbara Hutton's son, Lance Reventlow.

Of all the men Hutton married, Grant had been the only one who ever bonded with Lance. Their intimate relationship continued after the divorce. Magda enjoyed meeting the charming, handsome young boy, and didn't want to listen to rumors that Grant was seducing his former stepson, although this gossip was widespread.

Both Grant and Lance excused themselves to go back to their suite, so Magda went backstage alone to greet Dietrich, who had invited her to a repeat performance.

This time, Dietrich was entertaining Eddie Fisher in her dressing room. "It's worth a trip to Vegas just to hear Eddie singing '*Oh, Mein Papa.*'"

Once again, Magda returned to Dietrich's suite, as did Fisher. She became convinced they were having an affair, and after a glass of champagne, insisted on leaving. But both of these Las Vegas headliners urged her to stay.

Before dawn, Dietrich went into the kitchen to make her famous omelette for Magda and her boyish lover.

Fisher invited Magda to see his show the following night, and she accepted.

To her, he spoke lovingly of his ongoing romantic liaisons with Dietrich, which had existed on and off for a number of years. Later, he wrote about it in his 1999 memoir, *Been There, Done That.*

"To have been seduced by Marlene Dietrich is to have been taught how to make love by an expert," he said. "As a lover, she was incredible. Incredible. Her great skill was making me believe I really knew what I was doing. As much as I loved the sex, just being with her was thrilling."

Fisher told Magda that his male friends accused him of going to bed with a woman too old for him, citing the difference in their ages. "But that makes no difference to me," he said.

Magda told him, "When I reach the age of Miss Dietrich, I hope I can find a young lover as handsome as you."

"Well, when Marlene leaves town, give me a call."

It is not known if Magda ever took him up on that offer.

That night, Fisher was performing a late, late show scheduled for 2am, mostly for the Mafia. After kissing Dietrich and Magda, goodbye, he exited from the suite.

[Eddie Fisher may have flirted with Magda, and even propositioned her, but, according to him, Zsa Zsa didn't fare as well when she was introduced to him.

In his memoir, he wrote: "When I was married to Debbie Reynolds, Zsa Zsa Gabor wouldn't leave me alone."

"Why are you married to her?" she asked him.

In spite of their vast age differences, singer **Eddie Fisher** revealed that he had succumbed to the antique charms of Marlene Dietrich in Las Vegas.

In addition to hookers, he seduced some of the world's legendary women, including Judy Garland and Merle Oberon.

He also claimed that he evaded Zsa Zsa, "who became my chief sexual predator. I ran from her, as I did from Hedy Lamarr, Joan Crawford, and Lucille Ball."

503

"You should be with someone like me, someone who can make you a man."

"Zsa Zsa would come to my show every night and make a big entrance just before I went on," Fisher wrote. "It got to be very embarrassing."

"Come to my bungalow after the show," she told him backstage. "I'll make a man of you." She kept repeating that phrase and promise.

"I just laughed at Zsa Zsa, and I ran," Fisher claimed.

Although he was known to have seduced some of the world's most beautiful women, including his wife, Elizabeth Taylor, he said he fled from such predators as Joan Crawford, who pursued him, as did Hedy Lamarr, who made a pass at him. "Lucille Ball also came on to me, but Lucy Ricardo came on to anything in pants."]

Magda left Dietrich's suite shortly before dawn. Someone in the lobby spotted her, and through the gossipy Las Vegas grapevine, word spread that she'd had a three-way with Dietrich and Fisher.

Apparently, she did have some form of early morning sexual tryst with Dietrich after Fisher had left.

Later, Magda claimed that "All that talk about Eddie Fisher, Dietrich, and I in bed together was pure bullshit. Of course, I might have been tempted just so I could write about it in my memoirs."

Unlike Eva and Zsa Zsa, Magda attempted to write a memoir, but an accident caused her to abandon the project forever.

***

With contracts drawn up, Zsa Zsa and Eva flew to Las Vegas to begin rehearsals at The Last Frontier. The acid-tongued columnist, Louella Parsons, was also in town and came by to visit Zsa Zsa in her dressing room. Parsons had always disliked Zsa Zsa, who favored her rival, Hedda Hopper, over her.

Even so, they air kissed each other, and Zsa Zsa called the dumpy alcoholic *"dahlink,"* welcoming her.

Inevitably, the talk turned to Rubirosa. Parsons was known for lecturing stars on their morality, and had a stern warning for Zsa Zsa: "In spite of your limited acting talent, you've made an impressive debut at MGM. But I've heard that all the major studios are dropping you, mainly because of your notorious affair with Rubirosa, which you are blatantly conducting in spite of being married to the long-suffering George Sanders."

"Yes, *dahlink,* George suffers a lot visiting the bed of Doris Duke, *et al,*" Zsa Zsa claimed.

"There is talk of blacklisting you at the studios, the way they've blacklisted certain artists for being communists. If you go on with Rubirosa, you'll not

504

work for the big studios like MGM again. You can work, of course, but you'll find yourself appearing in low-budget pictures or some Italian, French, or Spanish pictures. Eventually, you'll end up in bit parts and in these, you're likely to be uncredited. "

"Louella, *dahlink,* thanks for your encouraging words," Zsa Zsa said. "Come and see my show. You'll see the woman who's set to replace Marlene Dietrich. Those 19th-Century beauties can hold out only so long when they've got to make way for new young girls like me."

"Debbie Reynolds is a new young talent," Parsons said. "You beauties born during World War I are no longer the freshest blooms in the garden. I call the lot of you faded flowers or the last roses of summer."

Impulsively, Zsa Zsa rose from her dressing table and handled Parsons a bottle of brandy resting nearby. "Dear heart, take this bottle and go back to your suite and have a gay old time."

Parsons stormed out of the dressing room, slamming the door behind her.

She got her revenge, writing that "Zsa Zsa Gabor is the most vulgar and disgusting publicity vamp Budapest has ever produced."

To join her daughters, Jolie also flew from New York to Las Vegas, with a case of diamonds for her daughters to wear. Ostensibly, she wanted to be at The Last Frontier in case they needed her assistance, but her real motive involved promoting her jewelry store in Manhattan.

She wanted her daughters to wear her diamonds. Not only that, but she wanted them to tell the truth about where they came from. "No more claiming they were gifts from rich beaux," Jolie announced. She planned to make it clear that her daughters were to wear these diamonds only for the duration of the show, at which point, they had to be relinquished.

Zsa Zsa had not heard from Rubi since that night he'd stormed in rage from her Bel Air manse. But on her third night, he knocked on her dressing room door. "I'm ready to forgive you for your continuing fascination with that monster, Señor Sanders."

She fell into his arms, not knowing that he'd spent the last few days migrating from the bed of Marilyn Monroe to the suite of Queen Soraya of Iran, who was in town for a visit.

That night in Zsa Zsa's suite at the Last Frontier, "We made love all night, *dahlink,"* she told her sisters. But she had continued to protest about having unprotected sex with him. "You are divorced and unmarried, but I'm still married to George. If I got pregnant, it would destroy my career."

He'd previously assured her that his success with women had occurred in part "because I don't wear a rubber. This doctor in Beverly Hills assured me I'm sterile. He used his mouth to suck out my semen and have it tested in a laboratory, but I accused him of swallowing most of it."

"How utterly enchanting," she said sarcastically. "Why do you torture me with such a vulgar story?"

"I wanted you to feel sexual freedom with me, knowing I can't make you pregnant," he said.

For three days and nights, it was sheer bliss for Zsa Zsa. Not only were the rehearsals with Eva and Magda going well, but her lovemaking with Rubi had increased in intensity, if that were possible. The only dim prospect involved his daily urgings for a hastening of divorce proceedings with Sanders so that she could marry him.

Finally, on the fourth day, his hot temper exploded when she refused yet another proposal of marriage. "I want to marry you the very day your divorce comes final."

"I can't marry you now," she said. "I just can't divorce one man and marry another man the next day. It would not be good for my image."

"If that is your decision, I will inform you of my own decision, although I know it will break your heart," he said. "Thank god you're sitting down. My news is sad. My gambling debts have eaten up all my cash, that and my expenses of running a fully staffed townhouse in Paris, my wardrobe, my restaurant and night club bills. In essence, I have been plunged into heavy debt by demanding creditors."

"Barbara is offering me five million dollars, half of it to be paid at the beginning of our marriage, and the other half delivered to me in cash when we break up. She seems to know already that divorce, in our case, is inevitable."

"During my marriage to Barbara, I plan to continue my love affair with you," he told her. "I'll escape from the rich old hag and into your arms every chance I get. But I've got to marry her because I need the money desperately, or else I'm in serious trouble."

Her anger flashing, Zsa Zsa accused him of "being nothing but a male whore, ready to sell that monster of your to the highest bidder."

"A gigolo perhaps, but not a cheap whore," he protested.

She became so furious that she started pounding her fists into his chest. She later claimed, "I can't remember all the vile names I called him."

When he could take it no more, he struck her in the face, pounding her right eye. The punch was so powerful that she fell onto the floor, where he kicked her in the stomach.

"Get out of here," she shouted at him. "You fucking bastard. I don't ever want to see you again."

He kicked her one final time before storming out.

Summoned to her suite, Dr. Edgar Compton later asserted, "Mrs. Sanders' right eye is as black as the ace of spades."

"Rubirosa disfigured me," she sobbed to her doctor.

As soon as he doctor left, she called Jerry Giesler, her attorney in Holly-wood. He listened, writing down all the details. At the end of her rant, he told her that she should sue Rubi for a million dollars. "He's marrying Hutton, and that bitch has millions she hasn't even counted yet. She'll pay it. Rubi's cock is worth it, so I'm told by Joan Crawford."

Even though they were rivals, Marlene Dietrich rushed to Zsa Zsa's dress-ing room, knowing that the Gabor's nightclub act was to open as a preview that very night.

Dietrich appeared heavily made up and wearing a pair of white leather slacks. She examined Zsa Zsa's eye. "Men are such beasts," she told Zsa Zsa. "I've brought along some panstick to cover most of the damage to that eye. It may not do the job completely, however. Rubi must love you very much to strike you like that."

After Dietrich departed with kisses, Birdwell arrived with a black velvet eyepatch. He announced that he had summoned the Las Vegas press to a con-ference in the hotel's ballroom at three o'clock that afternoon. "We can turn this into the publicity break of the century. Your picture will appear in every newspaper in the nation."

At first, she protested about the patch, but it was clear that Dietrich's pan-stick would not adequately cover the bruises around her eye. "With that damn eyepatch, I will look like a lady pirate from the Caribbean, perhaps the leg-endary Ann Bonney."

\   Finally, he prevailed, and she put on the eyepatch, deciding that it conveyed a certain glamour after all. "Maybe if we play this right, I can turn it into a *cause célèbre*. I'll be the first woman in the world who ever turned down a proposition from Rubi."

Before facing the press that afternoon, Zsa Zsa called in her hairdresser and a makeup expert who made up the faces of such other stars as Judy Gar-land.

Reporters began to congregate thirty minutes before her appearance. One hostile journalist told a colleague, "I've already made up my mind to write a bitchy article about the cunt. She's always good copy. I have to hand it to her. All this interest and her only accomplishment in life is fucking famous men."

"But," a fellow reporter said, "she's still the most quotable woman in Amer-ica."

At the appointed time, Zsa Zsa made a stunning entrance wearing a $5,000 Chanel dress with the matching black eyepatch.

She welcomed the reporters and startled them with her announcement. "A black eye was given to me by a woman beater, a blackguard, and a coward. It happened so suddenly, I couldn't tell whether he hit me with an open palm or if he balled up his powerful fist and plowed it into my eye. He hit me because

I refused to marry him."

Hedda Hopper had flown in from Hollywood and stood in the audience with the all-male armada of reporters.

"Zsa Zsa, my dear, please reveal the identity of this spurned beau of your?" Of course, the columnist already knew the answer to her own question.

"It was His Excellency from the Dominican Republic, Mr. Porfirio Rubirosa," she claimed. "He has his nerve. He stopped off in Las Vegas to plead with me to marry him. When I refused, he flew to New York to marry Miss Barbara Hutton. But he still wanted me. I guess Miss Hutton, in lieu of my turn down of Mr. Rubirosa, must settle for my sloppy seconds."

"I can't take treatment like I received from Mr. Rubirosa, however," she said, "and I won't stand for this. I've instructed my attorney to sue Mr. Rubirosa for a million dollars."

"I just received a call from the sheriff here in Las Vegas," she said. "He told me that men of the Old West did not beat up on ladies. He claimed that if Mr. Rubirosa ever crosses into Nevada again, he will have him arrested immediately."

"In Spanish, Rubirosa means 'a red rose,' but, to me, it means a black eye," she said. "Still, I'm the luckiest woman who ever lived. He might have cracked my skull or broken my nose."

"I predict that the marriage of Mr. Rubirosa and Miss Huttom will last no

In the most famous celebrity shot of the year, **Zsa Zsa** holds up a wedding picture of Barbara Hutton at the time of her marriage to Porfirio Rubirosa.

"He attacked me and gave me a black eye when I turned down his proposal," she told the assembled reporters. "He's not used to being rejected by women. He admitted to me that he's marrying Hutton for her money. He needs a rich purse to pay off his gambling debts. The marriage will last as long as an ice cream cone dropped on the street of Las Vegas during a heat wave."

more than ten days," she said. "He's still in love with me, and I predict he'll fly back begging me to forgive him. He's even approached my mother, Jolie Gabor, pleading with her to intervene on his behalf."

In another part of the ballroom, an angry Jolie was accusing Zsa Zsa of turning the upcoming Gabor show at The Last Frontier into "a freak show."

Photographers demanded that Zsa Zsa remove her eyepatch so that her bruised eye could be photographed.

She adamantly refused. "NO WAY! I can't disappoint my fans. My image is one of glamour. No woman looks glamorous with a swollen eye."

She ended her press conference on a catty note: "I still love my husband, George Sanders. Rubi loves me, and Barbara loves Rubi. But who loves Barbara?"

In dozens of newspapers from the East to the West, Zsa Zsa's charges against Rubi generated pictures and headlines. The most amusing appeared in the *New York Daily News: I SAID NO SO PORFY POKED ME, ZSA ZSA.*

In New York, Walter Winchell suggested in his column that "Rubi should have punched Zsa Zsa in the mouth instead of in the eye—anything to shut that big yap."

Although Birdwell had originally proposed the eyepatch press conference, he felt Zsa Zsa was going over the top, milking a story that was getting tons of publicity, but which was seriously damaging her reputation.

He urged her "to call it back," but she refused. A fight erupted and she denounced him.

Birdwell told her "I've had it with you, you bleached blonde bitch."

The Zsa Zsa/Rubi public slugfest became too much for Birdwell. He announced to the press, "If a client of mine doesn't stay in line, I don't play. You can have publicity within reason, but you can also turn yourself into a lurid publicity generating machine. There is a point where bad taste and vulgarity set in seriously damaging the career of an actress. That is what has happened to Zsa Zsa Gabor. I have officially notified her that I have dropped her from my list of clients. I wish her well, but we can just assume that she has thrown away what could have been a serious movie career."

***

As 1953 neared its inglorious end, the wedding ceremony linking Barbara Hutton to Porfirio Rubirosa began to unfold at the luxurious Pierre Hotel in Manhattan. Barbara's son, Lance Reventlow, had kissed Cary Grant goodbye in California and flown to New York to attend the wedding. It would be the debut of the heiress's fourth marriage .

Each of her previous marriages had failed miserably. Her previous husbands, with the exception of Grant, had taken her for millions, beginning with her first marriage to "Prince" Alexis Mdivani, of Russo-Georgian pseudo-royalty and one of the infamous "marrying Mdivani brothers."

Her second husband, Count Kurt Haugwitz-Reventlow, a Danish nobleman, had forced her to give up her U.S. citizenship. He had the disgusting habit of making her sit nude on his lap while he had his bowel movements.

Although hailed in the press as "Cash & Cary," Grant had divorced Hutton with no alimony paid out by her.

Hutton's fourth marriage, to Prince Igor Troubetzkoy, a Lithuanian nobleman, provoked columnist Inez Robb to write: "For Barbara, marriage is like buying something new she'd been admiring for a long time in the shop window. She may love it when she gets it home, but it doesn't always go with everything else in the house."

Troubetzkoy was an expatriate prince of limited means but world renown, which he earned as the driver of the first Ferrari to ever compete in Grand Prix motor racing when he raced in Monaco's Grand Prix. Later, he won the "Targa Florio" prize. He ultimately filed for divorce from Hutton, who attempted suicide, catalyzing headlines around the world.

A playboy who in some ways evoked Rubi, Fred McEvoy, also wanted to marry Hutton. She was repulsed, however, by his insistence on keeping the embalmed corpse of his baby boy on display in the living room of his hacienda in Mexico.

Zsa Zsa had been in Deauville at the races the day Hutton had approached Rubi. Without even acknowledging Zsa Zsa, Hutton had blatantly announced, "Rubi, I'm going to marry you." Throughout the polo match, she'd kept her field glasses trained on the Caribbean stud. From Doris Duke (her friend and rival), she'd learned of Rubi's sexual prowess.

At the time, Zsa Zsa said, "Poor Rubi. He has a choice. A diamond like me, or a junk peddler of nickel and dime trinkets." She was referring, of course, to a fortune (Hutton's) derived from Woolworth stores across the United States.

Before the wedding, Rubi had met with Hutton's lawyers and signed a prenuptial contract, granting him $2.5 million up front.

In a suite at the Pierre Hotel, Rubi joked privately with reporters, knowing they couldn't print what he told them. He confided in Walter Winchell. "Babs is marrying me for only one reason. And that reason is dangling between my legs. I'm different from all of her former beaux and lovers. They wanted to stockpile her money in their own bank accounts. I want to help her spend it."

Rubi also confided that when he stormed out of Zsa Zsa's dressing room in Las Vegas, he had not flown to New York right away. "I caught Lena Horne's show, and later, she invited me back to spend the night. I love her *café au lait* complexion. The following night, I saw Marlene's show. I didn't fuck her. She really preferred to fellate me, but I think I was her biggest deep throat challenge."

Jimmy Donahue, Hutton's flamboyantly gay cousin, also appeared at her wedding. He told her, "Babs, darling, I'm against you marrying this gigolo. So is the rest of your family. But if you go through with it, you must promise to send him over to my bed at least two nights a week."

Rubi disappeared for a long time in the bedroom, while the minister, the press, and the Hutton entourage waited outside.

Hutton tried to put up a brave front for the press. She claimed, "At last, I have found a man who loves me for myself—and not for my money. I know Rubi will make me happy, as I've never known happiness before."

According to reports, Hutton could talk, but she appeared dazed from having taken too many barbiturates. A reporter, Suzanne Oliver, approached Hutton. "How do you feel about Zsa Zsa Gabor?" she asked.

"I'm terribly sorry," Hutton said. "I don't know the lady, so I have no comment."

Earlier, Rubi had told Oliver, "Miss Gabor is merely trying to get free publicity at my expense. It's all a publicity stunt. Everything she does is fabricated."

It was later revealed what Rubi was doing in that bedroom, minutes before his fourth marriage. He was calling Zsa Zsa in Las Vegas with a last minute marriage proposal. He told her that if she would agree to marry him, he would call off his marriage to Hutton.

Once again, Zsa Zsa rejected his offer. "Hutton must be a brave woman to marry a man like you, one with such a violent temper."

From the bedroom within the Pierre, Rubi emerged. During the ceremony, he held a Cuban cigar in one hand and in the other, a brandy. During his previous wedding ceremony to Doris Duke in Paris, he'd smoked only a cigarette.

From New York, columnist Dorothy Kilgallen telephoned Zsa Zsa in Las Vegas, telling her that Hutton had looked very pale and sickly and appeared in a funereal black dress, more appropriate to a wake. As Kilgallen put it, Hutton wore "pregnant hummocks of widow's netting."

Duke herself placed a private call to Hutton. "I can't believe you married Rubi, who still visits me on occasion for stud duties. He's still in love with that Gabor creature."

"Oh, Doris," Hutton said. "It's not really a marriage. I'm purchasing him, a rental of his sexual equip-

In the bridal suite at the Pierre Hotel in Manhattan, **Barbara Hutton** *(left)* is seated with her new husband, **Porfirio Rubirosa** *(center)* as her perplexed son, **Lance Reventlow** *(right)* looks on.

Earlier that day, Rubi, learning for the first time that Lance had homosexual tendencies, called him aside. He whispered to his stepson-to-be, "Go ahead, feel it. Forget about that small dick of Cary Grant. I've got one that stretches to the moon."

Lance declined the offer, flying that night back to California to join Grant, one of his mother's previous husbands.

ment. I'm not buying his heart, for God's sake!"

Zsa Zsa's spies in New York kept her abreast of the Rubi/Hutton scandals. The groom spent his wedding night in a different suite from the one occupied by Hutton. Instead of his bride, he preferred the company of three showgirls from the Latin Quarter.

On the second night of his marriage, Rubi actually went to the boudoir of his new bride. When he emerged nude and erect from the bathroom, Hutton reportedly screamed and ran from her husband. As she did, she tripped and fell, seriously injuring her already brittle right leg.

For their honeymoon, she chartered a private plane to fly her to Palm Beach. But she had to be lifted into the aircraft, as she was confined to a wheelchair. While she was recovering in her bedroom, Rubi responded to the invitations he was bombarded with from Palm Beach socialites.

Zsa Zsa was sent the wedding picture of Rubi marrying Hutton. Without Birdwell to control her, she summoned yet another press conference and was photographed, wearing her eyepatch, and mockingly holding up the wedding portrait.

"See how unhappy they look," Zsa Zsa said to the reporters in Las Vegas. "I give the marriage six months." She'd apparently forgotten that previously, she'd given it ten days.

She told reporters why she'd refused Rubi's proposal of marriage. "I could not marry him. He wanted me to give up my career and come live with him in his townhouse in Paris. I could never give up acting. It is my life."

"Rubi is Miss Hutton's problem now," she said. "I wish her the best of luck. The poor creature is going to need it. The dear soul is aging and a bit of an ugly duckling. She also lacks charm."

"But in cases like that, it's always good for a woman to be able to write checks for unlimited amounts. In addition to a settlement on him before his marriage, I hear she's buying him a converted B-25 bomber as his private plane. He sold a similar plane that Doris Duke gave him."

"She's also purchasing a 400-acre ranch for him in the Dominican Republic. I'm told at several casinos in Las Vegas that she has already paid off enormous gambling debts. No wonder he married the two richest women on the planet. He's an expensive trinket."

Then, she whispered an aside to reporters, knowing they could not print it. "I hear Rubi sells it by the inch to these rich old ladies. I could never marry him, because I can't afford him. My mother, Jolie, taught us Gabor sisters that the man should always pay, not the *voman.*"

***

Hours before their show opened at The Last Frontier, Magda was furious at both Eva and Zsa Zsa. She confronted Zsa Zsa, accusing her of turning their Vegas debut into "a circus act, subjecting all of us to ridicule." Magda also criticized Eva for the seriousness of her performances. "This is a Vegas crowd of drunken gamblers, and you're coming on as if impersonating Sarah Bernhardt."

Despite Magda's misgivings, the show was received with thunderous applause. Forgetting her previous predictions of doom, Magda told reporters, "This has been the most exciting night of my life."

The next day, one reporter asserted that "except for Marlene Dietrich, Las Vegas has never been exposed to such glamour."

Although Zsa Zsa and Eva were cited for their more traditional beauty, Magda's lovely face and figure had never been appraised so effusively. "The pink lights captured the glow of her stunning red hair, and surely she has the most beautiful skin since God created Eve," wrote one reporter.

"She appeared on stage like a glowing flame."

Jolie hosted all of her daughters in her suite at The Last Frontier, ordering buckets of champagne.

The evening ended disastrously, after Zsa Zsa leveled accusations against Magda. "This was your idea to begin with, and it seems you are hogging all the glory for yourself. You tricked us into becoming your chorus girl backup. I feel betrayed."

***

Far more clever in getting press coverage that Magda, Zsa Zsa seized the day and called yet another press conference. Instead of talking about the Gabor Show as it applied to the trio of sisters who had participated, she focused the event, once again, on herself. "I wore a red gown glittering with sequins and a queen's ransom in diamonds."

She still had on her black velvet eyepatch. She said, "I hear I've started a fashion trend across the country. Marlene had all her showgirls come out on stage wearing my black patch. I hear at parties in Hollywood and New York, both men and women are appearing with my eyepatch. Boutiques and shops are rushing to stock them."

She also decided to embarrass both her husband, Sanders, and Rubi.

"I've just received two phone calls, and it appears that the two men in my life consider me most desirable in spite of their liaisons with the two richest women on the planet. Even though George was the first to file for divorce, he's begging me to drop my countersuit and call the whole thing off. But I'm not

513

going to."

"I also received a call from Mr. Rubirosa from Palm Beach," she claimed. "He said he's so sorry that he ever entered into this loveless marriage with Miss Hutton. He told me that if I will agree to marry him, he will immediately file for an annulment. He revealed a secret. He said that when he is forced to fulfill his marital obligations, he imagines the face he is looking down into is not Miss Hutton's, but mine. I did, however, agree to stop the assault-and-battery lawsuit I filed against him."

Two weeks later, Zsa Zsa's publicity blitz backfired on her. By accident, a wire service reversed the photograph of Zsa Zsa with the black eyepatch over her right eye. In the photograph that went out over the wire services worldwide, the patch appeared over her left eye.

When photo editors caught that, they rushed to print with accusations that neither of Zsa Zsa's eyes had ever been blackened by Rubi—and that she'd faked it.

Even though she had been truly injured, not one newspaper seemed to believe her, and she came in for an avalanche of bad publicity for "staging such a stunt."

Horrified, she issued denial after denial, but to no good.

"It was only the marriage of that tramp, Marilyn Monroe, to Joe DiMaggio that rescued me from these horrible attacks in the press," she claimed. "Monroe knocked me off the front pages. That was the only time in my life that I can be grateful to that cheap slut for upstaging me."

CHAPTER ELEVEN
Love Goddesses and their Private Passions

 After the Gabor's Sister Act in Las Vegas, although Eva still dreamed of major stardom in Hollywood and on Broadway, meaty, evocative roles continued to elude her. In lieu of anything better, she signed as co-star with Vincent Price, "The King of Horror," in the 1954 release of *The Mad Magician*. The 3-D craze, where moviegoers would be outfitted with Polaroid glasses, was nearing the end of its novelty, and *The Mad Magician* would be Columbia Pictures' last effort to exploit this medium.

Director John Brahm and producer Bryan Foy wanted Eva in the role of Claire, the wife of "Gallico the Great," the magician played by Vincent Price. His rival in the film, another magician named "The Great Rinaldi," was cast with John Emery, Eva's former lover from New York and the ex-husband of Tallulah Bankhead.

When Eva met Price on the set, she was fascinated by him. "He was as gay as Liberace, but a gifted actor and author as well as an expert on fine art. He was also a gourmet cook, as I discovered the next day when John Emery arrived on the set. Using a kitchen set aside for the staff, Vincent cooked us a lunch that was one of the best meals I've ever had."

That night, Eva resumed her affair with Emery. "By this point in his life, John knew he would never be another John Barrymore, so he was just getting by, taking what jobs he could, even a TV commercial if he could get one."

"We both knew our affair would be just for the duration of the film," she said. "Having heard of John's enormous endowment, Vincent flirted with him shamelessly, but got nowhere."

Emery later told Eva that "Vincent got to see that all those rumors about me were true when he barged into my dressing room when I was coming out of the shower. His timing was perfect."

Before meeting Price, Eva had only seen him on the screen in the classic hit *Laura* (1944), starring Dana Andrews and Gene Tierney, Emery told her some gossip about the cast. "Judith Anderson, a dyke, was chasing after Tierney, and Vincent and Clifton Webb were pursuing Dana."

Emery and Eva soon finished their respective film commitments and departed with a long, passionate kiss. After a night of love-making, their farewell came in the early dawn of a chilly Los Angeles morning when he had to catch a plane back to New York.

For his parting words, he asked her a question. "Have you noticed that actors spend a lot of time telling their lovers goodbye?"

***

Far more than a movie star, although she was occasionally that, Eva was a road show attraction, appearing in plays from Boston to San Francisco, from Southampton on Long Island to Phoenix in Arizona, with a stint every now and then in Los Angeles, perhaps a detour to Chicago.

Once, when Louella Parsons tried to trivialize her, Eva reminded the alcoholic columnist that she was making $5,000 a week touring with plays, whereas movie stars such as Rock Hudson were contracted for only $1,200 a week, with Marilyn Monroe, who was taking home a weekly paycheck of only $900, getting even less, even though she had by now evolved into a box office sensation.

When **Vincent Price** and **Eva Gabor** made *The Mad Musician*, both of them sought the favors of their heavily endowed co-star, John Emery, the ex-husband of Tallulah Bankhead. Eva won out.

"Even though he deserved better, Vincent was a master of the horror genre," Eva said. "In lollipop colors, he appeared on the screen as a camp terror."

Eva instructed her agent to hold out for generous compensations, although he admitted that his requests were rejected by most directors, who laughed at Eva's demand. He heard the same refrain: "Eva Gabor is not big enough of a star to draw that kind of bread." However, an occasional director agreed to her terms, feeling she would be big enough as an attraction in the hinterlands to fill up a theater—and usually, she was.

She attracted a lot of fans, most of them male, and many sent her love letters with nude pictures. Occasionally, she attracted a stalker, including one she falsely identified as "Ted" in her memoirs. He was the most persistent. He even obtained her unlisted phone number.

"Usually, men told me they were rich oil tycoons from Oklahoma or else bigtime Louis B.

516

Mayer types, even though I would surely have know who they were if they ran a major film studio. This Ted told me he was God's gift to women."

Why did you change to Camels, EVA GABOR?

"I had to be sure my cigarette agreed with my throat. So I tried many different brands. I chose Camels for their day-in, day-out mildness and flavor!"

Eva Gabor

Star of Television, Screen and Stage

One night at a dinner party she hosted, she was called to the phone. It was Ted. He told her, "It's been a long, long time, baby, but I'll make it up to you tonight. Wait until you see what I've got hanging. And the balls, too, big as grapefruits. When I come over tonight, I'll give you a night to remember. You'll be talking about it years from now."

She became frightened by this stalker, realizing just how crazy he was. Over the phone, she shouted at him, "I don't want to see you tonight or any other god damn night. Stop writing me. Never call me again. If you ring my doorbell, I'll call the cops. I've saved all your letters. I'll turn them over to the police. I'll sue you for harassing me."

"My image was for sale, and, to be frank, I was ready to advertise almost any product, except sanitary pads," **Eva** said. "I sold glamour to the American public and saved a scrapbook of my endorsements. My only embarrassment involved selling Camels. I should apologize for whatever role I played in giving cancer to Americans."

Although they swore undying devotion to each other as sisters, Eva and Zsa Zsa often compted for the same men, the same roles, and the same advertising gigs. Much to Zsa Zsa's dismay, Eva was often selected to promote consumer products instead of Zsa Zsa.

The reason along Madison Avenue was well known: Eva was more professional and easier to work with. And in the aftermath of Zsa Zsa's Rubirosa scandal, Eva wasn't as "notorious" as her older sister.

She had already received some fifty letters from him, each bearing a postmark from various points between San Diego and Newark, New Jersey.

Three months later, she received a final "goodbye" letter from Ted. It thanked her for a wonderful evening. He complimented her on her beauty and the lovely satin gown she had worn. "You will always occupy a special place in my heart," he wrote.

"He never wrote or called again," she said. "Fortunately, I moved out of his psychotic, erotic fantasies. I spoke to Ava Gardner about this fan one night. She told me she gets letters like that at least once a week. Lauren Bacall even made a movie about it."

Eva was referring to the 1981 film, *The Fan,* with Maureen Stapleton and James Garner. This bloody, distasteful picture was based on the Bob Randall novel about a Broadway actress (as portrayed in the film by Bacall) being stalked by a psychotic admirer. Eva always claimed that the story was based on her "admirer," Ted.

Fortunately for her, and unlike the gruesome events that transpired in *The Fan,* Eva's stalker turned out to be relatively harmless.

***

Another movie offer came in for Eva to co-star in *Artists and Models* (1955), with Dean Martin, Jerry Lewis, Shirley MacLaine, Dorothy Malone, and Anita Ekberg.

(Upper photo) **Eva Gabor** is being fought over by **Jerry Lewis** *(left)* and **Dean Martin** in *Artists and Models.* In the lower photo, the comedians spoof "the artist's life."

Off screen, Martin asked Eva if she'd like "a roll in the hay." She'd never heard that expression before, but she accepted his offer.

Martin had been cast as Rick Todd; Lewis as his roommate, Eugene Fullstack, with Shirley MacLaine in the lead female role, playing a character bizarrely named "Bessie Sparrowbrush." As MacLaine told the crew, "That's brush, dear ones, not *bush.*"

In the plot, Rich uses the erotic dreams of Eugene to launch a successful comic book.

MacLaine was a friend of Martin's and his pal, Frank Sinatra. One day on the set, Martin warned Eva, "Shirley—I love her—but her oars aren't touching the water."

A producer, Martin Rackin, was more vivid in his appraisal. "Shirley MacLaine is a disaster, a fucking ovary with a propeller who leaves a trail of blood wherever she goes. A half-assed chorus girl, a pseudo-intellectual who thinks she knows politics, thinks she knows everything, wears clothes from the ladies of the Good Christ Church Bazaar."

Eva appraised MacLaine herself, claiming, "My great dream would be to look like I still do but to possess her acting talent."

She remembered only one brief chat with MacLaine, wherein they discussed relationships.

"I have mostly used relationships to learn," MacLaine said. "When the learning process is over, so is the relationship."

"That's perhaps good advice for me to follow," Eva said. "Hell, what am I saying? I've al-

518

ready been following that philosophy."

"Incidentally, I have only one vice, "MacLaine said. "Fucking."

"Oh, *dahlink*," Eva said. "I fear that I, too, suffer from that same vice, and what fun it is."

The comedian, Lewis, was a self-confessed "cunt man," but it was Martin who Eva found sexy. She admitted to having had a one-night stand with him. "All the women were after his Italian salami," Eva claimed. "Our night together began pleasantly enough with wine, candlelight, and tortellini."

"But after a great roll in the hay, as the Americans say, he didn't have that much to say to me the next morning. He always told his girlfriends, so I'd heard, that 'if you want to talk, get a priest.'"

"After he showed me a divine time, all I got was a pat on the ass and a 'see you around, kid.'"

"Dean did promise to invite me to a party to meet Sinatra. He predicted, 'Frankie will go for you big time,' and how right he was about that."

"Dean deserted me to return to the beds of Lana Turner, perhaps Marilyn Monroe, whomever. I heard that June Allyson was mad about the boy."

Eva bonded with the talented Dorothy Malone, who told Eva, "Would you believe it? Liberace's mother wants her son to marry me."

Malone also relayed gossip that disturbed her. "I know Ann Miller. We sometimes indulge in 'who's bedding who' chitchat. You already know, of course, that she's dating Zsa Zsa's ex, Conrad Hilton. But I also learned that she was involved with Charles Isaacs before your marriage to him."

"That tap-dancing slut sure gets around," Eva said.

Malone filled her in on yet another piece of gossip, too. It involved the Swedish bombshell, big-busted Anita Ekberg, who had had an affair with the aging heartthrob, Tyrone Power, when she'd appeared in a small role in his *Mississippi Gambler* (1953).

"Oh, hell!" Eva said. "I wanted Tyrone for myself."

"Go after him, dear," Malone advised.

***

When Eva saw the rushes of *Artists and Models,* she thought, "I've never looked more glamorous."

Edith Head had designed a spectacularly campy costume for Eva for a scene where she'd be dressed as "The Bat Lady." Because of budget constraints, the sequence was never filmed, much to Eva's disappointment, but during the time when it was still a viable proposal, her ensemble included a violet-colored crêpe leotard whose bust featured a detailed replica of a bat outlined with rhinestones, sequins and bugle beads. All that came with a sheer sapphire-colored batwing cape, and a violet-colored headpiece that included a face mask and sequin-enhanced antennae.

[In an auction in 2012, Eva's bat costume sold for $875.]

After viewing the final cut of *Artists and Models*, Eva told Malone, "Frankly, I don't know how any man can resist me."

But despite her positive self-assessment, she feared that the movie was best defined as a showcase for its other stars. "I'm going back to try once again to set Broadway on fire. I think Hollywood can get along without me."

"Hollywood can get along without any actress," Malone said. "That's one commodity it's never come up short with."

***

On Broadway in 1956, *Little Glass Clock* was conceived as a comedy written by Hugh Mills and directed by Alan Schneider. Other than Eva, who played Gabrielle, the female lead, the most famous personality associated with the play was Cecil Beaton, who designed both the scenery and the costumes. He would invite his longtime companion, Greta Garbo, to opening night.

The plot centered on a dashing 18th-Century French aristocrat who is ordered off to war on his wedding day. He disguises himself as a priest to escape identification, and hires another man to impersonate him and join the military in his place.

During rehearsals, Eva had a reunion with Reginald Gardiner, with whom she'd worked at Paramount in the 1940s. On screen, he'd previously played various cads, wits, snobs, and fools. Although she found him amusing as a friend, she'd never seen the sex appeal of this actor, even though sultry Hedy Lamarr had gone for him.

The play opened on March 16, 1956 at the Belasco, attracting harsh reviews and sparse audiences. By the end of the month, it had closed. "My return to Broadway was a complete flop," Eva lamented. "It was very humiliating for me. *The New York Times* was wrong when it predicted I'd become a big star back when I appeared in *The Happy Time.*"

The play, or rather Eva herself, did have one devoted fan, a plastic surgeon named John Williams. He showed up every night during the short, aborted run of *Little Glass Clock.* "He was fairly good looking and intelligent, but I was just not attracted to him," she recalled. "He was the most persistent man, and asked me out every night. Finally, I gave in and went to Sardi's with him for dinner. He clearly found me mesmerizing, and I was fascinated with his fascination for me."

By the end of the play's run, John was asking me to marry him," she said. "There was no way in hell that I was going to marry him. And I was not going to change my mind, regardless of how much he pursued me."

She became even firmer in her commitment one night when she was introduced to "the man of my dreams, Tyrone Power."

***

During his honeymoon in Palm Beach, Rubirosa called Zsa Zsa in Hollywood five or six times a day. His new bride, Barbara Hutton, who had injured her leg, stayed locked away in her bedroom with a young girl attending to her needs. For $10,000 a month, she'd rented the lavish vacation home of the Maharajah of Baroda.

Although on his honeymoon, Rubi assured Zsa Zsa that he loved only her and had never actually consummated his marriage with his new bride, "It is impossible, *ma chérie,*" he assured her. "Besides, she is a very sick woman and drugged day and night. She lies in her bed ordering her staff around. I make an appearance every morning at ten o'clock, when she wakes up, and I bring her a dozen red roses. We talk briefly and then I am dismissed, and I'm free for the rest of the day to play golf." He paused. "Or whatever."

Although she conducted various affairs, Zsa Zsa kept returning to the company of former husbands, most notably, George Sanders, who often indulged in "sleepovers" at her Bel Air manse. On occasion, she was seen having a luncheon at a Hilton Hotel with Conrad Hilton before he succumbed to illness. In Ankara, Burhan Belge still kept in touch, writing her ever so often from his office in his capacity as a member of the Turkish Senate.

Before heading for Arizona to appear on stage in Noël Coward's *Blithe Spirit,* Zsa Zsa threw a lavish costume ball for *tout* Hollywood. Her guests were instructed to dress as their favorite historic or theatrical characters.

Marion Davies showed up as General Douglas MacArthur, and James Mason didn't quite fill out his Superman costume. Pamela Mason appeared as "Zsa Zsa Gabor," wearing a gold wig, a bright red *négligée,* and lots of diamonds. Zsa Zsa herself dressed as Jane Avril, the character she'd played in *Moulin Rouge.*

Her date for the night was Franchot Tone, who came dressed as his former wife, Joan Crawford, as she'd appeared in *Mildred Pierce.*

Tone spent the night with Zsa Zsa. The next morning, during her ritual telephone call with Pamela Mason, Zsa Zsa said, "My God, it's not as long as Rubi's, but it's just as thick. I've missed him, and I bet Crawford does, too, when it's a rainy night."

The following night, Zsa Zsa attended a party at the home of the still glamorous Merle Oberon. The hostess told Zsa Zsa, "Let me introduce you to a very

521

wealthy man who has the most divinely beautiful blue eyes."

"Lead the way," Zsa Zsa said. Within a minute, she was standing in front of Cornelius Vanderbilt Whitney, the scion of both the Whitney and the Vanderbilt families. He'd inherited a large fortune from each of the two branches.

"I saw nothing remarkable about his blue eyes," Zsa Zsa later said, "Although he had other credentials."

Whitney was a businessman, banker, corporate investor, film producer, writer, philanthropist, and polo player. He owned one of the leading stables in America for thoroughbred racehorses. Around the time Zsa Zsa met him, he'd hired John Ford to direct *The Searchers* (1956), starring John Wayne and Natalie Wood, a film that was, years after its release, critically acclaimed as one of the best Westerns ever made.

"He *[Whitney]* obviously wasn't intimidated by Rubi's reputation, and he made an immediate play for me," Zsa Zsa said. "The following night, he was eating a baked ham at my home with Eva and Anne Baxter."

It was a curious evening, since Eva appeared on the arm of John Hodiak, who had previously been married to Baxter. As her date, Baxter showed up with actor Scott Brady.

"After all my guests but one left," Zsa Zsa said, "I invited Cornelius to sleep over. He eagerly accepted. He must have fallen madly in love with me that night, because from then on, he became my stalker, showing up wherever I appeared."

When she flew to Las Vegas to appear at the Riviera, Whitney booked the best table at every show. After that, he flew with her to Phoenix when she appeared there in *Blithe Spirit*. "He sat in the first row every night," she said.

Zsa Zsa never expressed any regrets for not becoming the heiress to the Vanderbilt and Whitney fortunes. **Cornelius Vanderbilt Whitney** *(top photo)* stalked her for weeks.

In the lower photo, he's pictured rowing in his Yale cap.

"He proposed marriage, but frankly, *dahlink*, I never found him all that appealing."

"There was talk of marriage, and he bizarrely insisted that if I married him, he would insist on washing his own underwear every night. He got no argument from me on that."

In Arizona, Zsa Zsa reunited with a close friend of hers, Mary Lou Hosford, who was building a home nearby.

One night, Hosford asked Zsa Zsa if she could dine with Whitney, claiming he must be "bored sitting through the Coward comedy every night. He's learned every line in the play."

Zsa Zsa thought that would be a splendid idea. Whitney might have become bored with the play, but Zsa Zsa was getting bored with his persistency as a suitor.

"After their dinner, I didn't see either of them for two weeks," Zsa Zsa said. "They must have fallen madly in love." Hosford and Whitney were married in 1958, a union that lasted until his death in 1992, when the Associated Press informed America that he'd expired in Saratoga Springs, New York.

"And that, *dahlink*, explains why I never became the heiress to the Whitney and Vanderbilt millions," Zsa Zsa facetiously claimed.

***

Once again, Zsa Zsa flew to Arizona, this time to make a film *Three Ring Circus* (1954), starring the comedy team of Jerry Lewis and Dean Martin.

In addition to Zsa Zsa, the Hal B. Wallis film, directed by Joseph Pevney, had a strong supporting cast featuring Joanne Dru, Wallace Ford, and Elsa Lanchester. Shot in VistaVision, the movie was only a so-so Martin and Lewis comedy, which had them playing discharged servicemen up to trouble in a circus. Lewis was improbably cast as a lion tamer.

Eva, too, had made a film with Martin and Lewis, and she warned Zsa Zsa that both actors were likely to make a play for her. Neither member of the comedy team particularly appealed to Zsa Zsa, especially Lewis. "I might have been tempted by Dean, but his approach was so vulgar he turned me off. He told me 'I've already had Eva, and you're next.' After that, there was no way I was going to succumb to his charm, and he did possess a certain charm. I could understand why women were so attracted to him, unlike Lewis. I couldn't imagine Lewis appealing to any woman…even one with two heads and three vaginas."

In an unlikely role, Zsa Zsa was cast as Saadia, "The Queen of the Trapeze," a character who is egotistical and greedy. "Type casting, *dahlink*," she said. Martin, as Pete Nelson, becomes Saadia's personal assistant. On screen, the bare-chested Pete impresses Saadia, who ends up kissing him and making a play for him. "Dean and I were strictly acting," she said.

Martin later recalled, "None of us had much fun making this damn flick except Zsa Zsa. Porfirio arrived on the set, and when she didn't have to appear on camera, she was getting plowed by his monster dick, which I heard was even bigger than Frankie's" *[a reference, of course, to Sinatra]*.

Zsa Zsa talked to Elsa Lanchester, who played a bearded lady. The veteran actress told her, "I have nothing to say about my role in this movie or about that dreadful Martin and Lewis."

"I was shocked one evening at the Arizona Biltmore in Phoenix," Zsa Zsa said. "Martin and his wife came into the bar, where Lewis and his wife were already seated. Martin and his wife walked right past their table and didn't speak. I don't predict a long future as a screen team for these comedy boys."

The next day, Lewis came up to Zsa Zsa. "I was shocked. He seemed on the verge of tears."

He asked her, "How in hell can I go on making movies with Dean when he doesn't even speak to me?"

***

After only two months of marriage to Barbara Hutton, Rubi discreetly flew to Phoenix aboard his "flying palace," the B-25 bomber that Barbara Hutton had presented him as a gift. "It was the scene of countless airborne fucks," he told his friends.

Zsa Zsa was registered at the Jokake Inn, in Scottsdale, a beautiful Spanish-style hacienda with a red tile roof, where she was staying with her friend, Mary Lou Hosford.

"Not even the richest woman in the world can hold onto my man," Zsa Zsa boasted to Hosford. "Rubi's flying to me…only me, to be with me."

Hosford's role involved concealing Rubi's arrival from the press. She booked a suite for him at the inn under his much-used pseudonym, "William Perkins." Hosford had already given advice to Zsa Zsa about the press. "Tell them everything…but don't tell them anything."

A sharp-eyed reporter from Phoenix had spotted Rubi's arrival, and other reporters and photographers were alerted. The hotel manager claimed that the switchboard there was overwhelmed with calls from journalists. Outside the entrance to the hotel, Zsa Zsa was spotted entering the Jokake Inn. When asked if Rubi were in town, she attacked them, appearing outraged. "How dare you!" she shouted at the press. "Mr. Rubirosa is happily married to Barbara Hutton. What would he be doing here?"

The press was well aware of what Rubi would be doing after hooking up with Zsa Zsa.

He had hidden in the bushes in the Inn's garden, where he was later drenched with the hotel's sprinkler system.

The hotel manager slipped Rubi out the rear of the hotel and drove him to a hideaway in the hills owned by a friend of his. Rubi had been hauled off in the hotel's laundry van.

An hour later, Zsa Zsa slipped out of the Jokake Inn and was driven by a member of the hotel staff to Rubi's secret hideaway, where he was impatiently waiting for her.

"Under the beautiful Arizona sky, a starry night, the hours I spent with Rubi were among the most blissful of my life," she recalled. "We would never know such peace followed by passion followed by peace again. He had to fly out in the morning and I wept. It wasn't goodbye, but a farewell, with the understanding that we'd meet again."

"Rubi told me had had to return to his jailer, a reference to Hutton, of course," Zsa Zsa said.

On the set the next day, the script called for her to appear in black tights with long black stockings. "I have too voluptuous a figure for such attire, especially to go about in front of scores of men whistling at me," she said. "After a night with Rubi, I didn't want any other man to even look at me."

Hal Wallis had learned that Rubi was in town, and he wanted to exploit his reunion with Zsa Zsa for publicity purposes. He asked her if Rubi would pose with her against the backdrop of his B-25 bomber.

"I've already written a final line for Rubi," Wallis said. "He says to you, 'How about hopping in my plane and taking a ride with me, baby?'"

She had to tell a disappointed Wallis that Rubi had already flown back to Palm Beach.

When he was reunited with Hutton, Rubi lied to her, telling her he'd flown to his ranch in the Dominican Republic. But by then, news of his flight to Phoenix had made it into the nation's press.

Hutton filed for divorce after only seventy-two days of "wedded bliss."

"He immediately called Zsa Zsa, telling her the news. "I'm a free man. I'm flying to your arms right away, as soon as Hutton authorizes the final payment of our divorce settlement."

***

Rubi's final divorce decree from Hutton was handed down on July 30, 1955. There were rumors in the press that he'd soon wed Zsa Zsa. For the next eighteen months, the "world's most romantic couple" popped up on the international party circuit that stretched from New York to Hollywood, from London to Paris and the Riviera. He even flew her to the Dominican Republic, where she dined with that country's notorious dictator, Generalíssimo Raphael Leonidas Trujillo. Later, she was taken to meet the Rubirosa family, which convinced her that Porfirio would soon propose marriage.

If she had a film to make in Europe, or a TV appearance, he was her escort, warning her not to even look at another attractive male. She also followed him to rugby games, polo matches, tennis competitions, and car or yacht races, later frequenting casinos, night clubs, and *luxe* restaurants.

Wherever they went, reporters and photographers followed them. Once, trapped in Jolie's apartment in Manhattan, Rubi dressed up in drag and put on her fur coat, escaping from the building undetected. Zsa Zsa later wrote that he was so secure in his masculinity that he "could dare wear women's clothes to escape the wolf pack outside our door."

Everybody had an opinion about the affair, even the fabled English poet and eccentric, Edith Sitwell. She defined Rubi as "Porfirio the Persecuted," asserting that he was a most charming man. "He reminds me of Lord Byron as a figure of unwarranted public rebuke."

At her Bel Air mansion, Rubi and Zsa Zsa entertained like a married couple, "hosting the Humphrey Bogarts, the James Masons, and the Gary Coopers."

In hopes of getting cast in a Western movie, Rubi appeared at one of her parties in cowboy drag, greeting Cooper with a "Howdy, partner!"

Taken aback, Cooper responded, "Why you ol' ornery buzzard!"

Rubi gave Cooper a peashooter, and the duel was on.

"For the next hour, these two grown men ran around my house trying to ambush each other," Zsa Zsa said. "You would have thought each of them were ten years old, not the studs and lady killers of the Western Hemisphere."

"Our life became a whirlwind," Zsa Zsa said. "We were always flying somewhere, going somewhere. I loved every minute of it."

They were not inseparable and sometimes, because of conflicting schedules, they could not be together. At these times, both of them had brief, fleeting, and secret affairs on the side. Just because they were "madly in love" with each other did not mean they were going to alter their lifestyles completely.

***

Rubi accompanied Zsa Zsa to Spain, where she'd been cast as Marilene in a Spanish/French drama called *Love in a Hot Climate.* She was cast opposite the French heartthrob Daniel Gélin, who played her lover, a Spanish bullfighter, in the movie.

Footage for two distinctly different versions of this film was shot, one in Spanish (*Sangre y luces),* in which she wore high-necked dresses, and another (*Sang et lumière)* for more sophisticated French audiences, where she appeared in dresses with plunging *décolletage.*

Born in the Loire Valley of France *[an area of that country known—at least back then— for producing the purest forms of French diction],* Gélin was a handsome charmer, who had been expelled from college for his "uncouthness." His first job was in a shop selling canned salted cod to housewives.

Eventually, he broke into French films, making 150 of them in his lifetime. One of his most famous screen appearances was opposite Jean Gabin and his lover, Marlene Dietrich, in Max Ophüls *La Ronde* (1950).

During Marlon Brando's sojourn in Paris at the beginning of his career, he and Gélin had been both roommates and lovers.

Almost daily, Rubi came to the set to watch Zsa Zsa emote on camera. One afternoon, she was scheduled to film a violent love scene with Gélin on camera. When, clad in a black lace *négligée,* she resisted him, he attacked her, ripping and tearing at her nightgown. He got so carried away at one point that he turned the scene into a true-life "bodice ripper." Her breasts were accidentally exposed.

Screaming in rage, Rubi exploded, denouncing Gélin in Spanish before attacking him. He became such a wild man that the director, Georges Rouquier, had to call security to have Rubi tossed out of the studio.

"Throughout our long-enduring affair, Rubi could never control his jealous rages," Zsa Zsa said. "He wanted to possess me totally, and no man could do that, not even Rubi."

Two days after he was evicted from the studio, Rubi ran off for a night with an attractive script girl from Paris. "I decided to get even with him, and I slept with Daniel," Zsa Zsa said. "The next time I see Marlon in Hollywood, I'm going to compliment him on his good taste in men."

[Ironically, Gélin eventually had an affair with a French model, Marie Christine Schneider. Their union produced a daughter, Maria Schneider. Maria would go on to appear opposite Marlon Brando in Last Tango in Paris *(1972). Gélin refused to acknowledge that Maria was his daughter until she was in her teens.]*

While abroad in Europe, Zsa Zsa shot another film, a musical called *Ball der Nationen,* directed by Karl Ritter and written by Paul Beyer. Released in the United States as *Ball of the Nations,* the film didn't attract an audience. Later on, Zsa Zsa could hardly remember it. "I think I played a revue star, Vera van Loon. An ice queen type beauty. An American journalist, Percy Buck, falls in love with me, but I reject him, as I've rejected so many men in my life, including Dean Martin and Frank Sinatra. Of course, some of these jerks don't take no for an answer. Even if a woman rejects them. Do you want me to name these rapists?"

When **Zsa Zsa** made love on screen with the French heartthrob **Daniel Gélin**, their kisses were so passionate that onlooker Rubirosa flew into a rage, interrupted the filming. As vividly reported by the tabloid press, he was evicted from the set.

"Daniel was a great kisser," Zsa Zsa later said. "I understand why Marlon Brando found him such a hot lover."

527

One night back in Bel Air, Zsa Zsa wanted Rubi to go to work. She told him what he wanted to hear. "You could be a movie star, a Latin version of Clark Gable."

He was intrigued by the idea, even though he was already in his 40s, getting a late start on the screen.

The next day, Zsa Zsa called a friend of hers, Andrew ("Bundy") Solt, a successful scriptwriter with links to pre-war Budapest, who had a string of script credits which included Humphrey Bogart's *In a Lonely Place.* She sold him on the idea of creating a script that would feature Rubirosa as a Latino cowboy star.

Having just finished a script, Solt was eager for a new project. The script concept he conceived to this end was tentatively entitled *A Western Affair.* It would be set in "Deadwood Gulch," South Dakota. Solt's idea was to write a satirical "Hollywood Western farce," with Rubi playing Don Castillo—an elegant gambler and the owner of a successful, rough-and-tumble saloon—who falls in love with a French countess (Zsa Zsa, of course). As a means of accommodating Rubirosa's accent, Solt defined the saloon keeper as Spanish. As for Zsa Zsa's involvement in this already dubious plot, Solt described her as a "dizzy but sexy cowgirl with claims to French nobility."

During the next five months, Rubi buckled down and took the project seriously. "I'd never known him to be so dedicated to any project in his life, except for chasing after women."

He even hired Michael Chekhov—a nephew of the great Anton Pavlovich Chekhov, the Russian dramatist—to teach Rubi how to act. He already knew how to shoot a gun and ride a horse.

Republic Pictures agreed to release the picture, and Zsa Zsa, to help finance it, promised to put up some of her own money.

There remained a major hurdle. Rubi would need a work permit, and for it, he applied for one with the U.S. Immigration Service. After six weeks, his request was denied. "I'd never seen him so crestfallen," she said. "He blamed J. Edgar Hoover at the F.B.I. for his turndown."

"He's voyeuristically investigated me for years. He assigned an agent to get a nude picture of me when I was undressing after a polo match," Rubi told her. "That closeted old fart is a known size queen."

After his turndown by the immigration bureau, he also attacked the American press, claiming to Zsa Zsa, "Those guys have been after me ever since I met you. Now, the government is directly insulting me by refusing to approve such a small common courtesy for something that would have paid only $1,500 a week."

"To escape his depression, Rubi returned to his old ways," Zsa Zsa said. "The late nights, the pursuit of women, the drunken orgies, the ridiculous spending, the dangerous risk when he drove a car or played polo, his shady South American friends who were no better than they should be. In the weeks ahead, he was rarely sober."

"I didn't want to admit it, but our tumultuous affair was heading toward its end, tabloid frenzy and all. The only thing that remained for us was to bury it. That would be painful and humiliating for the both of us. But it was time to move on to other lovers."

***

"There is no doubt about it," Zsa Zsa later recalled. "Tony Gallucci was the only man Magda ever loved. Too bad their lives had to end so tragically."

Their romance was like a roller-coaster ride with its ups and downs, mostly descents.

Previously, he'd placed an engagement ring on her finger and went out for a walk with her poodle, Coco. Two days later, she learned he'd gotten drunk and married another woman.

Gallucci, a brusque, darkly handsome Italian, was the president of one of the oldest building contracting concerns in the United States, and a multi-millionaire.

"He was both amorous and tempestuous," Magda described him to Eva, who had yet to meet him. "Each new day brought something new to do with him: a scenic plane ride over the wilds of Western Maine; a yachting race off the Florida Coast; a flight to Cuba with its gambling casinos and first-rate shows, where he introduced me to Frank Sinatra."

Sometimes, he took her on a tour of his factories, which produced plumbing components.

His initial desertion of her had "bruised her beyond belief," Jolie reported. "On several occasions, she threatened suicide. She was moping about like a doomed heroine, yet turning down offers of dates from some of the most eligible men in America. I finally convinced her to go out."

At that point, Magda was known for dressing only in black and white," Jolie claimed. "When she put on her diamonds, and with that Titian red hair and porcelain skin, she was a spectacular beauty."

Franchot Tone, who occasionally dated Zsa Zsa, pursued Magda while he was in New York. "You're more beautiful than my former wife ever was," Tone told her, a reference to Joan Crawford, of course. "And you're far easier to get along with."

Yul Brynner, when freed from the bed of Marlene Dietrich, took Magda out on three or four dates and taught her to smoke opium in his private apartment. "He was not only handsome, but exceedingly sensual," she confessed. "But he didn't ring the bell like Tony could do."

Johnny Carson dated her twice, but she claimed he was "too oversexed" for her. Such was her complaint against Sammy Davis, Jr., whom she claimed "had the stamina of a bull."

Throughout the course of Gallucci's marriage to the Italian woman, Magda dated, but found no man to interest her for very long.

Often, Jolie rushed to Magda's side, finding her "with a painful barbiturate hangover. She had a great, great love for Tony," Jolie told her friends, "and it won't go away."

Her mother lectured her. "You're one of the most beautiful women in New York, and you're still young, with your life ahead of you. Why throw it away on some Long Island plumber? You're also talented and clever. At many society parties, you're still introduced as a countess, and Americans are impressed with titles. Why, even Tony married his current heifer because she claimed to be an Italian *marquesa.*"

"I was prepared to dislike Tony," Jolie said. "That is, until I met him. He was a real darling, in spite of his low-rent background. I could be dining with someone at a restaurant, and when I requested the bill, the *maître d'* often told me, 'Madam, Mr. Gallucci has taken care of it.' How did Tony even know where I was dining?"

At long last, **Magda** found love when she married **Tony Gallucci**, "America's richest plumber."

She later asserted, "He was the love of my life, in spite of his tendency for wenching and alcohol."

Regrettably, their marriage would end in disaster.

"Then it happened suddenly," Jolie said. "Tony's divorce from that Italian thing came through, and he was proposing marriage to Magda once again. This time, I hoped he wouldn't be a runaway groom like before."

The daffodils were in bloom in Central Park and the sun was shining brightly on April 1, 1956, when Magda became Mrs. Arthur Gallucci.

Their honeymoon night was spent in his luxurious Manhattan penthouse, one of the most glamorous in a city of *luxe* penthouses. That weekend, he drove her to Long Island in his Rolls-Royce that he claimed had recently been owned by

Prince Philip.

She arrived at his mansion in Southampton. "I began to realize just how rich Tony was," Magda told Jolie. "Call him a plumber if you wish. Better married to a multi-millionaire plumber than to an impoverished Polish count living in a castle where the roof leaks."

Within weeks of her marriage, Magda became one of the most dazzling hostesses in Southampton. At one point, Vice President Richard Nixon appeared at one of her events with his best friend, Bebe Rebozo. Apparently, the two men were raising campaign funds from rich donors for a potential run for the presidency in 1960.

It all sounded like a dream," Eva said when she flew to New York and joined the couple for a holiday in the swanky Hamptons, which attracted the elite of New York. "Tony had never conquered his drinking habit. He literally started with Bloody Marys at ten in the morning, bottles of wine at lunch, slept most of the afternoon, and began cocktail hour laden with martinis at five o'clock. He kept promising Magda to give up the booze, but he never did, although his doctors warned him that if he kept drinking and smoking three packages of Camels a day, he'd end up with a heart attack."

Often, when Magda was in Southampton, Gallucci claimed he had business in Manhattan. On several occasions, Jolie's friends reported back to her that her son-in-law was seen "wenching around New York, with a decided preference for leggy showgirls."

Jolie claimed that after one of Gallucci's adulterous affairs, he'd return to Magda in Southampton with either a diamond bracelet or a mink coat. "After a big fight, she always forgave him before he took her off to her boudoir. She claimed he was terrific in bed. She said that only one other man had given her such orgasms—and that was Prince Aly Khan. The others never came close."

Jolie hated seeing her daughter moping about the Southampton mansion waiting for her husband's return, so she tried to get her to resume her theatrical career, such as it was.

Gallucci was adamantly opposed to her return to the stage, but she defied him and went ahead anyway, signing a contract to appear in what even she called "hokum." The play was *This Thing Called Love,* configured as summer entertainment at a theater on Coney Island.

Actor **Charles Martin** and **Magda** played romantic scenes together onstage in *This Thing Called Love.*

Roaring onto the stage from his seat in the audience, Tony Gallucci, overcome with jealous fury, physically attacked both Martin and Magda, bringing the play to a halt.

531

On opening night, Gallucci sat on a folding chair to watch the play unfold. He seemed furious, but exploded when the handsome leading man, Charles Martin, took Magda in his arms and began to kiss her passionately. He picked up his folding chair and adjusted the seat before tossing it at the actor on stage. He then jumped up on the stage and attempted to slap Magda until two stage-hands pulled him off. The police were called and after a fifteen-minute intermission, the play resumed.

***

In Southampton, Magda once expressed a wish for a swimming pool. As a means of apologizing for his outrageous behavior, Gallucci purchased ten expensive acres of adjoining property for the installation of a pool and a row of ten elegantly furnished dressing rooms for their newly acquired friends.

In addition, he erected a small castle on the grounds, where he and Magda could comfortably entertain some 300 guests at any of their lavish parties.

Their daily lives continued. In Southampton, they were known as "the Battling Gallucci Duo." Sometimes at a restaurant, their arguments erupted into a food fight. Gallucci was always willing to settle damages the next day with the owners.

Magda had once beaten Gallucci with a horsewhip. In Southampton, on occasion, she continued to beat him up.

"They fought bitterly and loved each other mightily," Jolie said. "Often in front of me. I was out there one summer night when they attacked each other so viciously, I thought murder would result. These fights would always end in the same way, though. He picked her up in his strong arms and carried her upstairs to their bedroom. I could hear her screams. But she was crying out in passion, not in pain. She told me that he could pound her for an entire hour and that once he had continued for two full hours, if she is to be believed."

"Even Vilmos never made it beyond twelve minutes. That Tony! He was a *roué* but Magda loved him with all her heart. She practically could not utter five sentences without mentioning him two or three times."

During one of her visits to New York, Zsa Zsa dined with Gallucci and Magda. "From what I heard, he was one plumber who always arrived with the right tool."

One night, George Sanders met Gallucci and claimed that he understood his appeal. "There was something about him. A man's man, as it is called. He was rich, successful, and obviously virile. He worked hard and played hard. When he saw something he wanted, as in the case of Magda, he went after it. I think he enjoyed his battles with her. He was a man made for women. He could be thoughtful and considerate one minute, very attentive, and then beat hell out of a woman the next minute."

"He consumed half the liquor supply of the Northeast, but held it well. One night at the Stork Club, Magda was invited to dance by an aging Clark Gable. In the middle of their dance, Tony had the waiter deliver her a note that said simply, 'Miss you.' Apparently, women go for touches like that."

"When he was with Magda, she was the only woman in the world ...and the most beautiful. Back at that moment, I would never have believed that I would one day replace Tony as Magda's next husband."

***

"It was the six most enchanting months of my life," Eva later claimed. "Tyrone Power became my greatest love. I was never so crazy for a man, including past and future lovers—and most definitely my husbands."

It all began one night when her "stalker," Dr. John Williams, called and invited her on a date. It was during the spring of 1955, and she needed an escort to take her to a play, *The Dark Is Light Enough,* by Christopher Fry, a "Winter Comedy" set within the context of the Hungarian Revolution of 1848.

The original Broadway cast at the ANTA Playhouse in Manhattan included Katharine Cornell as Countess Rosmarin Ostenburg. She vied with Helen Hayes as the First Lady of the American Theater. In the role of Richard Gettner was Tyrone Power, appearing as the dashing and morally complex male lead.

In the audience, on opening night at the ANTA, Eva was swept up within an array of celebrities who, to her astonishment, included Eleanor Roosevelt. "I bowed before her, treating her like a queen to pay homage to her for her defense of Jews during World War II. She took me by the arm and raised me to an upright position."

"In America, we don't have to bow to anyone," the former First Lady told Eva.

In the opening night audience, Eva chatted with Marlene Dietrich and Raymond Massey "and a "flotsam and jetsam of Vanderbilts."

Backstage, Power seemed enchanted with Eva, which aroused jealously from Williams. He introduced Eva to Miss Cornell and her husband, Guthrie McClintic, the theater director who had married her in 1921.

[Later, Power told Eva "Katharine's appeal is slipping at the box office. I was teamed with her because Guthrie felt that a big-time movie star would be good for box office. He felt audiences would come to see a movie star but leave the theater singing the praises of Katharine."]

In the play, Power interpreted the role of a cowardly army deserter, while

Cornell played a noble countess, his former mother-in-law. Eva found him "morbidly depressed by this complex and thankless role." *[Later, he was devastated when Brooks Atkinson in The New York Times wrote that "Tyrone Power in his role is unredeemed by wit, brilliance, or cleverness."]*

The star invited her, with Williams, to an after-the-show party, where the cast and select friends waited for the reviews, especially critiques from *The New York Times*.

As the cast party moved into the pre-dawn hours, Eva made an impulsive decision: She dumped Williams and left the party with Power, returning with him to his hotel suite.

"We made love," she later confessed to her longtime companion, Camyl Sosa Belanger. "Actually, he needed support more than passionate, intense lovemaking. Although I found him beautiful and highly desirable as a lover, he also brought out the maternal instinct in me."

During the first week of their relationship, Eva suspected that Power was also seeing someone else on the side, although she had no direct evidence. He would suddenly become unavailable.

She assumed that her competition was another beautiful woman. Years later, she learned that a former boyfriend of Power's had come back into his life. In his biography of Power, author Hector Arce identified the handsome young

man as Tyrone Culhane, an interior designer. The two men, each nicknamed "Ty," met at Garson Kanin's townhouse in Manhattan's Turtle Bay neighborhood, which Power had leased.

To complicate his life even more, Power was in the process of divorcing Linda Christian.

For the most part, Eva's relationship with Power slipped under the radar screen, not attracting the attention of the press. In later years, Zsa Zsa said, "It was a far deeper love affair than nearly anyone knew."

(Upper photo) In one of the few pictures ever taken of **Eva** and **Tyrone Power** together, both of them are beaming with love.

George Sanders had nicknamed Power "Miss Roundheels" *[a British expression implying promiscuity, with the implication that the girl or guy in question tips backwards easily for sex]* after hearing Power say, "Why frustrate people? If I'm feeling horny at the time and I like them, I'll oblige them."

Their affair did not go completely undetected. The public first learned of it on May 26, 1953, when Power visited Eva in her dressing room at NBC, where she was appearing in an episode of the TV series, *Justice*. She starred in two different episodes—"The Blackmailer " and another called "The Intruder." Both of these broadcasts were live. A photographer for *The New York Post* was visiting NBC that day, and he managed to capture a picture of Eva in Power's manly arms, sitting on a sofa. For all he knew, it was just a friendly embrace.

It was columnist Earl Wilson, on October 26, 1955, who came up with the scoop. He was making his usual rounds of the celebrity haunted Metro Club in Manhattan when he spotted Eva on a date with Power. At first, they tried to conceal it, but Wilson was too sharp for that.

Belanger told Eva that she considered Power "a gorgeous hunk of man. Darn. How was he in bed?"

"Not that good," Eva claimed. "But it was fun waking up to those beautiful long lashes. When he opened his eyes, they were so big, he became even more gorgeous."

Belanger later wrote about Eva's assessment of Power's sexual prowess, "She was the kind of person who told it like it is. She was no phony."

"I'm sure that Ty was a far greater lover when he was younger," Eva confided. "But when I met him, he was recovering from infectious hepatitis and was so listless and lacking vitality. He assured me that he was no longer infectious, but he was still weak. To compound matters, he was drinking heavily, but that didn't seem to do much for his unsteady nervous condition."

The American press remained relatively unaware of Eva's affair with Power because most of their relationship was conducted in London, where she'd flown to join him. He was appearing in the West End in the role of Dick Dudgeon, the irreligious son in the revival of George Bernard Shaw's *The Devil's Disciple.*

"Ty had scored a great hit in London when he had appeared there on stage starring in *Mister Roberts,*" she said. "He was hoping to repeat that acclaim. He also wanted to take the play to Dublin where his father, Tyrone Power, Sr., had scored such success as an actor."

In London, early in 1956, Eva met and dined with many of Power's closest friends, including actors Lilli Palmer and Jack Hawkins. They entertained those guests in his suite at the Connaught Hotel as a means of avoiding the press. Eva renewed her friendship with Kurt Kasznar, who had appeared on stage with her in *The Happy Time.* It turned out that Kasznar was practically Power's best friend. "Poor Kurt," Eva confided to Palmer. "He has such a crush on Power that his tongue practically hangs out when he's around his idol."

"A lot of gay men in the theater were attracted to my darling Rex Harrison," Palmer said. "It didn't do them a lot of good. Unrequited love is such a terrible bore."

In London, Power seriously discussed marriage with Eva. "He wanted to buy a manor house in his beloved Ireland and restore it," she said. "There was another reason. He claimed his tax burden in the United States was more than he could stand."

"In Ireland, I could actually save most of the money I make," he told her. "There's another reason. I'm getting older and I'd rather grow old and gray in Ireland than face the cruel cameras of Hollywood."

Jolie flew into London for a reunion with her daughter. She was on her way to St. Moritz for her winter vacation. Once there, she would be reunited with her friend, Greta Keller, who had an extended singing engagement in St. Moritz at Badrutt's Palace Hotel.

"I finally found out why Eva loved London so much," Jolie recalled. "Ty Power was there, and she was madly in love with him."

"I issued dire warnings and told her that Power had a fickle heart," Jolie said. "I mentioned how shamelessly he'd dumped Lana Turner. I also told her that he was a bisexual and had often been seen at Hollywood parties with known homosexuals. I had heard that his indiscretions never made it into the press because so many people in Hollywood like him. He was a nice guy."

Over the years, Power had been linked to a string of both male and female lovers, including screen queens Joan Crawford, Marlene Dietrich, Judy Garland, Janet Gaynor, Betty Grable, Sonja Henie, and Loretta Young. Once, when he was in Buenos Aires, he'd even seduced Evita Perón.

His list of male lovers was also impressive, including Howard Hughes, Errol Flynn, Noël Coward, Rock Hudson, Robert Taylor, and Cesar Romero.

"Finally, at Jolie's urging, I left London and resumed my own life in America," Eva said. "Ty and I promised to link up together upon his return to Hollywood. But that never happened. He moved on to other loves, and I lost him forever."

Jolie claimed, "Ty was her big, big love. Oh, they were very much in love, and she tore her heart out over him."

Jolie later asserted, "Eva's failed affair with Ty Power began a decade of personal unhappiness for her."

[In Madrid, it was a cold, windy morning. The date was November 15, 1958. Tyrone Power was there shooting a swashbuckling film entitled Solomon and Sheba, *co-starring Zsa Zsa's former husband, George Sanders, and the Italian bombshell, Gina Lollobrigida, who was trying to take over some of the movie terrain occupied by Sophia Loren.*

In the film, Sanders, though an intimate personal friend of Power, was cast as his hostile brother. The director, King Vidor, called for a dueling scene, one of the most difficult and taxing shots in the picture.

After two hours, an exhausted Power called out, "Stop the action!" He went and sat down nearby, asking someone to bring him a Camel cigarette. "I've got to quit," he told the director. "I don't feel well. I have these terrible pains in my chest and abdomen."

He was taken to his dressing room, where he was placed on a cot and given a glass of strong Spanish brandy. After downing the brandy, he gasped and fell into an unconscious state.

Placed in Lollobrigida's Mercedes, Power was heading for the Ruber Sanitorium Clinic. Three minutes into the trip, the still-unconscious actor stopped breathing. He was dead on arrival at the medical facility.

News of his tragic death at the age of 44 was flashed around the world. In Hollywood, Eva collapsed after hearing the news.

Her maid and a Mexican gardener carried her upstairs to her bedroom. When she regained consciousness, she began sobbing. "Death was so cruel to take him so early. As long as he was alive, I had this hope...maybe. But it's not to be."

Smitty Hanson, Power's longtime lover, made a comment to the press. "Ty was never as way out and kinky sexually as he was rumored to be. He was linked to many disgusting sexual practices. If those rumors were true, I certainly would have been aware of that. I believed that Ty was basically a homosexual who married girls from time to time."

The producers of Solomon and Sheba scrambled to find a replacement for Power, offering the role to Gary Cooper, William Holden, Charlton Heston, and Robert Taylor, all of whom turned it town. Yul Brynner, however, agreed to take over the role "as a memorial to Ty."

Actually, money may have made up his mind for him. It was agreed that he would get twice the amount that Power had been offered. Ultimately, Brynner received $700,000 plus 15% of the gross over nine million.

Eva stayed in her bedroom for three days and nights, mourning Power's death.

For the rest of her life, she always referred to him as "The Man Who Got Away."]

After his death in 1958, **Tyrone Power** was hailed as "the most beautiful man who ever appeared on the screen," according to The Hollywood Reporter.

Post mortem, newspapers and magazines ran pictures of him in his heyday (the late 1930s) when he posed bare-chested for this photo.

That publicity renewed his status as a pinup favorite of young girls and gay men across the nation.

***

One night in 1964, at a Hollywood premiere, a young man approached Eva. "I understand that you were once in love with Tyrone Power."

"I hardly see why that is your business?" she said icily.

"Please, look in my eyes," he said. "I have Tyrone Power's eyes."

"They don't look like Ty's eyes at all," she said.

"Well, they are," he said. "When he died in 1958, he willed his eyes to the Estelle Doheny Eye Foundation. I was blind at the time. I am the beneficiary of a transplant from him. Tyrone's eyes that once gazed upon you are gazing upon you tonight."

Bursting into tears, Eva ran away from the man.

Entertainers We Remember
Tyrone Power
1914-1958

***

After her breakup with Tyrone Power, Eva launched into an affair she labeled "A Brief Interlude." She had an admirer named Dennison Slater. Without giving any details, Jolie wrote of the encounter in a memoir, claiming that "Denny was crazy for her, and she was crazy for him. Denny helped her recover from her broken romance with Ty."

The affair wilted quickly. One weekend, Slater was to fly Eva to New York, but he failed to show up. He telephoned later, confessing that he'd developed "this little crush on a French singer. It's not a big love, and I'm sure that in time it will pass."

Whether it did or not, she didn't know. She never saw him again. Jolie claimed that her daughter "shed many tears over this Dennis fellow."

Almost in desperation, Eva turned to her constant pursuer, Dr. John Williams, the plastic surgeon.

Shortly afterward, Eva, in Hollywood, phoned Jolie in New York. "John has asked me to marry him," Eva said.

"Are you in love with this doctor?" Jolie asked. "Of course, with all the Gabor gals needing face-lifts, it would be good to have a plastic surgeon in the family."

"I'm not insane with desire for him, the way I was with Ty Power. I don't hate John either, or even dislike him. I'm very lonely, and he fills a gap. Even though he's a plastic surgeon, he's not making a lot of money now. Sometimes, it's hard for him to pay his office rent."

"Don't you have any other richer prospects?" Jolie asked.

"There is this millionaire playboy who wants to marry me," Eva said. "But he's a little too old and far too ugly. I don't think I could stand to go to bed with him."

"Maybe you shouldn't marry either of these candidates," Jolie said. "After all, I didn't mandate that my daughters marry only millionaires."

"*Nuci,*" you never told us we had to do that," Eva said. "Only marry kings."

Before ringing off, Eva asked Jolie to come to Hollywood to bestow her stamp of approval, or her disapproval, on Dr. Williams.

Four days later, Jolie arrived in Hollywood where she found them living in a $450-a-month rented home once reportedly owned by "The Cobra Woman," actress Maria Montez. There were nude sculptures of Montez still standing in the living room, which had a swimming pool that began in one corner and extended outdoors onto an open-air garden terrace. "If someone wanted to break into your house, it would be an easy job if he knew how to swim."

Jolie was shocked at how courtly her prospective son-in-law was. "He was handsome and had wonderful manners. He took me to a romantic candlelit dinner, and then invited me to the movies. At the movies, he held my hand. Later that night, after a champagne cocktail, he gave me a passionate kiss to wish me good night. I had to remind him that it was Eva, not me, he wanted to marry. All that attention heaped on me from such a dashing beau made me feel like a young girl again. I adored him."

The next morning, Jolie urged Eva to marry him. "In the movie house, when he held my hand, it was warm and dry. Had it been cold and sweaty, I would have opposed the marriage. But he passed the hand-holding test."

In Beverly Hills, days later, on April 8, 1956, Williams married Eva in the drawing room of her home. The week before, Magda had married the construction firm owner, Tony Gallucci, in New York.

Then, with her new husband, Eva flew from Los Angeles to New York and drove to Jolie's country house in Southampton. In anticipation of her visit, Jolie had driven there and stocked it with champagne, decorated it with flowers, and even sprinkled rose petals on their honeymoon bed. She doubled the wage of her housekeeper, urging her to take special care of the newlyweds.

After the wedding, a full week passed before Jolie heard from Eva, who telephoned her with an invitation. It was scheduled for that upcoming Saturday afternoon, but Eva claimed that the visit could last only from six until eight o'clock that evening.

"I arrived with fresh fruit baskets, Beluga caviar, and *kolbász,* as well as champagne," Jolie said. "I was dismissed at eight from my own house and had to drive all the way back to Manhattan."

Eva later confided, "Driving to Jolie's country home, I realized I'd made a mistake and should not have gotten married. But it was too late now. All that was left of this hasty marriage was divorce."

Back in Hollywood, after only three months of marriage, Eva telephoned Jolie in New York, telling her, "I'm divorcing John. I need you. You must come to Hollywood."

Ever the dutiful mother, Jolie arrived at Eva's rented home to find that Williams was no longer there. When she inquired as to his whereabouts, Eva confessed she didn't know.

"How did you get rid of him?" Jolie asked.

"Thank god for Marlene Dietrich," Eva said. "I didn't have the courage to kick John out, so I called Marlene. You know how good these Krauts are at displacing people. John had to face a formidable woman who had stood up to Goebbels and Hitler. She even helped him pack his suitcases. At the door she gave him a kick in the butt. 'Good riddance to swine,' she'd screamed at him."

"Poor John," Jolie said, facing a determined Prussian powerhouse and a Hungarian battleaxe," Jolie said. "I hope you gals didn't cut off his testicles."

That night at dinner, Eva poured out what she called a series of abuses. "One night I came home from a television shoot," she said. "After all, I was paying the bills, not his practice. I asked him for a vitamin shot. The bastard refused. He complained that he took care of patients all day and was too exhausted at night to tend to my needs."

Weeks later, Williams called Eva. There would be no alimony, but he wanted half of all their wedding presents. She protested, claiming that all the gifts had come from friends of hers.

At the time of the divorce, Eva gave an indiscreet press conference. "I'm alone and better off for it. Dr. Williams even wanted me to sell my five-story brownstone on Fifth Avenue in Manhattan and reinvest it in property in California where there's a community property law when one gets a divorce."

***

[In the late 1960s, Jolie learned that Williams had gone through many other wives and was making $10,000 a year as a plastic surgeon.

In 1968, Eva got onto an elevator at Century City, going up to meet a television executive. She became only vaguely aware of a man standing next to her. "How are you, Eva?" he asked. "You're looking wonderful after all these years."

She turned and looked at him. "Do I know you?"

"Of course, you do, as David knew Bathsheba," he said. "I'm John Williams. In case you lost count, your third husband."

"Oh, John, you divine thing," she said. "You've gotten even handsomer."

"How about a date tonight?" he asked. "For old time's sake."

"Oh, dear me," she said. "You know you can't go home again." When the

elevator came to a stop on her floor, she fled.

Two weeks later, Williams encountered Zsa Zsa dining at Chasens with an old flame, Douglas Fairbanks, Jr. The doctor approached her table and complimented her on how well she was looking.

"We've met somewhere," Zsa Zsa said. "You look familiar. Were you one of my lovers?"

"I should have been," he said. "I was married to Eva. John Williams. I worked on your nose. Surely you remember that?"

"Oh yes, dahlink," she said. "but let's keep that our little secret."]

***

When she was in Paris, Zsa Zsa received a call from Rubirosa inviting her to watch him play in a polo match in the seaside resort of Deauville, in Normandy. She accepted with some apprehension, as she'd just spent the last three nights in the arms of Baron Elie de Rothschild, who was also heading for Deauville. But she knew the baron was known for his discretion.

Her affair with Rubi was winding down, and both of them knew that, although they had not acknowledged it to each other. In fact, only recently, a reporter had asked Rubi when he was going to marry Zsa Zsa, and the Dominican playboy had answered, "When the lady consents."

Journeying to the northern French coastline in a Rothschild limousine, Zsa Zsa arrived in Deauville. Once there, she found that Rubi had reserved a suite for her separate from his own.

It was August of 1955, the peak of the social season, punctuated with polo games. Brigitte Bardot was spotted, along with Elsa Maxwell, Prince Aly Khan, and Doris Duke, among an array of other "dubious tabloid fodder," as a local paper expressed it.

Rubi socialized with Zsa Zsa and friends until it was time to excuse himself to go to the locker room. After he'd gone, a striking figure of a man came up to Zsa Zsa and introduced himself as Derek Goodman. The name was familiar to her, because Derek often appeared in the same gossip columns as herself.

She knew that he and his twin brother were the sons of a wealthy gold-mining family in South Africa. Derek, like Rubi, was also an avid sportsman—in fact, he was ranked as one of the world's greatest polo players. A globe trotter, he inhabited three continents.

As he stood before her, bowing to kiss her hand, she remembered him as "a handsome peacock of a man, standing six feet, four. He was blonde with lake-blue eyes and a thin mustache popularized by Ronald Colman on the

541

screen."

"Miss Gabor, a long-delayed pleasure," he said. "Do you know why I'm here?"

"Perhaps," she said. "I overheard you inviting Rubi to come to South Africa to play against your team."

"Merely a Machiavellian ruse on my part to disguise the true intent of my visit," he said. "I have a more devious plan in showing up, and that is to propose marriage to you."

"Since I've known you for only two minutes, would you give me an hour to mull over your offer?" she said?

Throughout the polo match, Zsa Zsa didn't watch Rubi on the field, but chatted, laughed, joked, and flirted with Derek, who was the most exciting man she'd met since Rubi.

Rubi played hard and rough, but his team lost. He was furious when he emerged from the locker room and headed for the bar in Deauville's casino.

By the time Zsa Zsa finally caught up with him, he'd gone to the casino, where the manager approached her, warning her that Rubi was drunk and had already gambled away $25,000.

She came to rescue him, finding him in a belligerent mood. He pushed her, ordering her to "get out of my sight."

Humiliated, she joined Derek in the dining room, where he was entertaining the Maharajah of Cooch Behar. "Everybody noticed I was not with Rubi that night," Zsa Zsa said. "Deauville can be a very small village. Derek and I, if I do say so myself, made the most dazzling couple at the casino, me in my black embroidered Pierre Balmain gown and Derek in his well-tailored red velvet tuxedo."

Leaving Rubi to sulk in the casino, she accepted Derek's invitation to go with him to Casanova's, the chic night club rendezvous of Deauville. She later claimed, "I knew by then that Rubi's Caribbean voodoo spell over me had worn off. I was dating another man."

"We spent the night in the company of friends, including Baron de Rothschild, who had switched partners and was dating that international tramp, Pamela Churchill. Henri, the Count of Montbrison, was there along with Prince Aly Khan and Lise Bourdin *[aka Bettina]*, his French mannequin. Even Danny Kaye was there, acting very, very gay. He'd just left London and the bed of Laurence Olivier, or so I'd heard. Call it "Hamlet and the Court Jester." *[She was referring to Kaye's latest movie.]*

The next morning, Rubi called her suite, asking her to go to Paris with him to retrieve $30,000 as a means of paying for his gambling loss the previous night. She rejected his offer, preferring to spend the day horseback riding along the windy French coast with Derek instead. "He was a better horseman than

Rubi," she later said. "It was a romantic day, ending in a candlelight dinner on a terrace overlooking the water."

A problem arose when an irate Martha Robson flew in from Johannesburg to reclaim Derek. Instead of being threatened, Zsa Zsa was intrigued all the more with her new beau, who obviously was so desirable that a woman would fly that far to be with him.

Before she left Deauville, Zsa Zsa and Derek became lovers, as he obviously preferred her over Robson.

As one Parisian reporter noted, "Zsa Zsa Gabor is in the headlines again, being chased around the globe by the handsome, debonair, super wealthy Derek Goodman, a world polo great who is better looking than he should be."

As the days passed, Zsa Zsa, at least temporarily, fell under Derek's spell. "He was fascinating, like a character out of a Harold Robbins' novel," she later said.

[Actually, it was Rubirosa who made his way into the pages of a Robbins novel, the bestselling The Adventurers, *first published in 1966, starring the fictional character of "Dax Xenos." The novel's hero had bedded countless women and had once married the richest woman in the world. The Robbins saga depicted a world of wealth, depravity, and unlimited sex, a mass-market pulp sensation turned into a megabuck movie in 1970. Bekim Fehmiu, a Yugoslav heartthrob, was cast as Rubi. One critic described Fehmiu as a cross between Jean-Paul Belmondo and Ringo Starr.]*

As she came to know Derek, she learned he was on a first-name basis with royalty, including Prince Philip, a fellow polo player. Zsa Zsa and Derek were seen yachting along the French Riviera and hanging out with billionaires such as Aristotle Onassis.

"Derek was a delightful companion," she said, "and filled with exploits from his past. A volunteer in World War II, he'd been a tank driver and had come close to many near-death experiences. He loved driving fast along the Riviera in his Lamborghini. He was the *bon vivant* of his generation, living life in a grand style, with fast sports cars, polo ponies, lovely ladies, champagne, and Beluga caviar."

Derek arranged for Zsa Zsa to visit South Africa, where she was contracted to appear on the stage in "The Hole Wood Cavalcade Revue" He booked her into the Royal Suite of the Carleton Hotel in Johannesburg.

In an open-top limousine, she was driven along Eloff Street, as thousands of fans waved and shouted *ZSA ZSA ZSA ZSA*. From inside her suite, she waved at her adoring public from the balcony of her terrace.

Later, Derek introduced her to his rich family before taking her on a drive through Kruger National Park.

Both Zsa Zsa and Derek were hailed in the press as the most glamorous

couple in all of Africa. He was always by her side, horseback riding with her, lunching with her, shopping with her, and night clubbing with her. He announced to the press that he was flying back with her to Paris.

As it turned out, that didn't happen. She told him that "the party's over" and flew alone to Paris. That night, her first in Paris, she spent in the arms of Prince Aly Khan. The next morning, he introduced her to his vacationing father, the super rich and very fat Aga Khan III.

In Paris, the press hounded Zsa Zsa, who refused to answer questions about her relationship with Rubi.

She'd heard that he was dating Ava Gardner, who was in Europe, and he had also been seen with Gregg Sherwood Dodge, a former pinup cutie who was married to the heir to the U.S. automobile dynasty.

When questioned about Derek, Zsa Zsa said, "It was called a fling, *dahlink*. An interlude. I have contracted to do several movies, and I am returning to Hollywood."

In South Africa, Derek told the press, "It was good while it lasted, but I think Zsa Zsa decided I wasn't quite rich enough for her."

Before she departed from France, Rubi had told Zsa Zsa that he planned to never marry, ever again. But he was never known as a man of his word.

***

By the spring of 1956, Zsa Zsa had grown bored with constant partying, and she returned to Hollywood to pump new energy into an abandoned acting career.

Directors warned that her "wooden acting" would confine her to perhaps a few starring roles in low-budget quickies, and recommended that she might make cameo appearances in films requiring a personality as vivid as hers.

As one reporter claimed, "Her drop-dead gorgeous looks, larger-than-life personality, and talent at self-promotion would allow her to continue in the spotlight, unlike some of her peers languishing like Norma Desmond in a decaying mansion on Sunset Boulevard."

She admitted, "My greatest role is that of Zsa Zsa Gabor. If some producer wanted to make a story of my life, he will find that none of today's actresses are strong enough to play me. Hollywood used to have actresses with personalities as strong as mine. Bette Davis comes to mind. So do Garbo, Marlene Dietrich, Katharine Hepburn, and Joan Crawford. But look what we have today."

Back to work again, and over a two-year period, she racked up an impressive array of appearances in some fifty television shows on both sides of the Atlantic.

America's leading comedians discovered her, and she appeared with Red Skelton, Bob Hope, and Milton Berle, among others.

She became a regular on *The Tonight Show* hosted by Johnny Carson. Her most notorious appearance occurred one night when she came out holding a Persian cat. At one point in the show, she asked Carson, "Would you like to pet my pussy?"

Mugging for just a second, Carson delivered the punch line: "I'd love to, if you'd remove that damn cat!"

She took almost any television drama offered and starred in productions of the Ford Television Theater, General Electric Theater, Playhouse 90, and Lux Playhouse. Over an eighteen-month period, from late 1956 to early 1958, her image was splashed across the covers of some 100 magazines in both Europe and the United States. With virtually no credentials, she was covered like she was an international super star, which she wasn't.

After all that globe-trotting with Rubi, she returned to the screen in the 1956 *Death of a Scoundrel,* a fictionalized adaptation of the life and mysterious death of the international scam artist, Serge Rubinstein

Her co-stars were George Sanders and his brother, Tom Conway. *[The film marked the second joint appearance of the two brothers. In 1942, they'd co-starred together in* The Falcon's Brother.*]* Zsa Zsa's female co-stars included Yvonne De Carlo, Nancy Gates, and Coleen Gray.

The director, Charles Martin, told Zsa Zsa that Sanders, cast as Clementi Sabourin, was a cad who controlled women with his money, power, and sexual allure, while holding them in utter contempt and emotional isolation.

"Oh, *dahlink,*" she said. "You've just described George himself."

Death of a Scoundrel was based on the unsolved, January 27, 1955 murder of a multi-millionaire, Serge Rubinstein, whose pajama-clad body was found in his Fifth Avenue mansion in Manhattan. His hands and feet were tied with a cord, his mouth sealed with a wide band of adhesive tape. He'd been strangled. A woman's white dress glove and handbag were found nearby.

Rubinstein had so many enemies, he filled six thick notebooks with their names and details. A womanizing stock manipulator, he was the son of a financial adviser to that maniacal monk, Grigori Rasputin, in Czarist Russia.

"We had too many suspects, notebooks full of them," a police chief said. "He was a cad only a mother could love, and for a short time, we even suspected her. She lived a floor above."

The murder was never solved.

The first day of shooting, Zsa Zsa received a surprise from Rubi, who contacted her from Paris. "*Chérie*, if you work with George Sanders in this film, I will never see you again."

Despite this ultimatum, she refused to bow out of the picture, and told him so even if it meant losing him. She'd later say, "I never really had Rubi in the first place. I wanted to make this delicious *film noir*, and I wasn't going to let him block me. Rubi was so unfair in wanting me to abandon my acting career, which meant so much to me."

On the set, a reporter asked Zsa Zsa which of Sanders' abilities she admired the most. "His acting, *dahlink*," she responded. She and Sanders got along more than harmoniously. At night, they were seen driving off together. "We became lovers once again," she claimed.

In the *film noir, Death of a Scoundrel*, **Zsa Zsa** starred with her former husband, **George Sanders**, who is depicted lighting her cigarette above. His brother, Tom Conway, was also in the film.

Zsa Zsa found herself in dilemma, caught between intensely competitive siblings: Sanders resumed his former conjugal rights, and Conway proposed marriage to her.

Most of the tension on set was the result of friction between Sanders and his brother, Tom Conway. Conway had become a total alcoholic, and Sanders constantly warned his older brother that he was destroying not only his career, but himself. All these lectures fell on deaf ears. Conway continued to drink heavily.

"I was surprised late one afternoon when Conway came to my dressing room," Zsa Zsa said. "He begged me to marry him, claiming that I could save him. There was no way I was going to marry Tom. I didn't love him, and I was back with his brother at the time."

Death of a Scoundrel was not one of Sanders' best efforts, though his acting got relatively good reviews, one report claiming that he played it "urbane, elegant, and deft," noting that "he'd made a profession of portraying a wide cross-section of heels."

Sanders escorted Zsa Zsa to the film's premiere in Hollywood, the first time they'd been seen as a couple in public since their divorce. There were rumors that they would remarry.

The next morning, Zsa Zsa got only one good

review, and she carried it around in her purse for months to come. The critic for the *Los Angeles Examiner* wrote: "Zsa Zsa Gabor is not only good but wonderful—a personality grown to the status of an actress!"

Her upcoming films, however, would not justify such praise.

***

"If God did create Adam, as rumor has it, and a director wanted to make a film about the guy, Lex Barker would be my top choice to play the world's first man. Lex was living proof that all men aren't created equal. He was the greatest physical specimen, and that's coming from me, *dahlink*, the best judge of male flesh."

So raved Zsa Zsa after only one week of working with her handsome and dashing co-star, Lex Barker, a former movie Tarzan, on *The Girl in the Kremlin (1957)*.

In addition to his work as a publicist, Russell Birdwell, during the course of his long involvement in Hollywood, also directed five films, *The Girl from the Kremlin* being his swan song. There was a certain irony in his hiring of Zsa Zsa as one of its characters. When he'd been her publicist, he'd "fired" her as a client because of her outrageous behavior.

But Birdwell and Zsa Zsa made up, at least for the duration of the filming of this American thriller. The film's plot asked the audience to believe that Josef Stalin (as interpreted by Maurice Manson) faked his own death in 1953. The movie finds him living in Greece, hoarding and spending a fortune stolen from the Soviet treasury.

Zsa Zsa was cast as twins in a dual role. One of the (improbable) characters she played was that of Greta Grisenko, Stalin's nurse and lover; the other portrayed Greta's less malevolent twin sister, Lili. Lili hires an O.S.S. agent (as played by Barker) to find her sister.

In her dual role, Zsa Zsa, as Lili, dresses in a form-fitting black ensemble, complete with beret. She sounds, to modern-day viewers, like Ariana Huffington.

"Lex was a man after my own heart," Zsa Zsa said. "I set out to learn everything I could about him."

"I was expecting to meet some Tarzan beefcake, but I encountered a cultured, refined man who came from a society background in New York and had gone to Princeton."

In 1941, Barker had enrolled in the U.S. Army months before the attack on Pearl Harbor. A gay soldier, who had a crush on him, remembered him "as the star attraction in the shower room."

Lex Barker

By 1949, Barker had drifted to Hollywood, where he became the tenth actor to portray Tarzan. He was the handsomest of his Ape Man predecessors, with blonde hair and a muscled, 6'4" frame. "That's not all he had," said Zsa Zsa.

At the time she met him, Barker's Hollywood career had faded, and he'd moved to Europe to make pictures. (He spoke four languages, including German.)

He'd been married to screen goddess Arlene Dahl, known for her Titian red hair, evocative of Magda's. He'd married Dahl in 1951, but had divorced her the following year. From 1953 to 1957, he was married to another screen goddess, this one a blonde, Lana Turner. She divorced him when she discovered that he'd been molesting her young daughter, Cheryl Crane.

Barker assured Zsa Zsa that Crane's charges of molestation "were a pack of God damn lies."

She told him, "If I were a thirteen-year-old girl, I would love to have been molested by you. What a way to break into love-making."

[At times, Zsa Zsa could show a lack of sensitivity to delicate issues.]

Zsa Zsa once said, "Lana sometimes had the same taste in men as Eva and I, not only Richard Burton, Sean Connery, Conrad Hilton, Clark Gable, Howard Hughes, John Hodiak, John F. Kennedy, Peter Lawford, Dean Martin, Tyrone Power, Frank Sinatra, and Robert Taylor, but Lex Barker and even that adorable gangster, Johnny Stompanato."

Marilyn Monroe once declared in a statement loaded with innuendo that "Lex Barker has a third leg."

"I almost never agree with this Monroe creature about anything," Zsa Zsa said. "But at least when it comes to Lex, she got it right."

Virtually all of the footage for *The Girl in the Kremlin* was shot in just ten days during February of 1957 on a budget of $287,300. In movie annals, it would be listed as one of the worst films ever made, standing alongside *They Saved Hitler's Brain,* released in 1963.

The Girl in the Kremlin flopped and was attacked by both viewers and critics, the reviewer for *The San Francisco Chronicle* defining it as "Unquestionably, the most absurd motion picture of the year."

Variety headlined its review: *IF JOE STALIN DIDN'T DIE, THE GIRL IN THE KREMLIN SHOULD.*

The six-minute scene that caused the most comment involved the revelation of Stalin's secret sexual fetish. In one scene, he forces actress Natalie Darryl, who looked like Jean Simmons, to experience the humiliation of having her head shaved, while Stalin looks on, sexually exited, "getting his jollies," as one reviewer said. For her part, Darryl was given a $300 bonus for allowing a barber to shave her head.

Depending on your point of view, Universal Studios (either wisely or foolishly) has kept *The Girl in the Kremlin* locked up in its vaults for decades, refusing to re-release it.

Years later, after their too brief affair, Barker was in Berlin making German films. In time, he'd make thirteen German-language movies based on the novels of German author Karl May (1842-1912), playing such famous May characters as Kara Ben Nemsi, Dr. Sternau, and Old Shatterhand. He'd even had success singing in German, recording songs based on the soundtracks of May movies. He shipped recordings of two of them to Zsa Zsa—*Ich bin morgen auf dem Weg zu fir* ("I'll Be on the Way to You Tomorrow") and *Mädchen in Samt und Seide* ("Girl in Silk and Velvet").

The Girl in the Kremlin, a creepy, campy, absurd, and fascinating Cold War thriller, maintained the premise that Josef Stalin had faked his own death in 1953 and then moved to Greece with an embezzled fortune in Soviet currency.

In it, **Zsa Zsa** played a dual role, playing twins—one of them Greta Grisenki, Stalin's muse and lover. Her other role was that of Grisenki's sister, an alluring sexpot who emerges from behind the Iron Curtain, hiring Lex Barker, cast as an O.S.S. agent, to locate her.

These became sentimental favorites of hers. "On many a lonely night, they always brought a tear to my eye as I remembered my *dahlink* Lex as the man who got away. Eva cited Tyrone Power as her man who away. For me, it was Lex Barker."

***

The husband-and-wife producing team of Herbert Wilcox and his wife, actress Anna Neagle, offered Zsa

In one of the most controversial scenes in the movie, **Maurice Manson**, cast as Josef Stalin *(right)*, becomes sexually aroused as **Natalie Darryl,** playing a dissident beauty, endures the disgrace of forcibly having her head shaved.

Zsa Zsa defined **Lex Barker** as "the most perfect specimen of manhood God ever created—and I know my manflesh."

"I don't know how Lana Turner could ever let this hunk go, even if she did catch him molesting her daughter."

Zsa a starring role in a movie scheduled for filming outside London. Zsa Zsa readily accepted. She wasn't certain how long she'd be abroad, and she made it clear that if she were offered another film role in Europe after that, she might extend her time away for several additional months.

In the interest of economy, she decided to rent her Bel Air manse at a high price tag. A real estate agent advertised her property, and three young men dressed in dark suits showed up at her doorstep. She found one of them, Johnny Stompanato, "very attractive," as she admitted in her memoirs. She relayed only some superficial details about her relationship with him in print. But she soon learned that the men were part of Mickey Cohen's mob entourage.

She wrote that the following day, "I ran into Johnny at a bakery on Wilshire." She claimed he invited her for coffee. Actually, before he'd left her home the previous evening, he and she had defined the logistics of a rendezvous for the following day.

She later said, "After all, I was now a bachelor gal, and I'd heard that Johnny was one of the town's most exciting lovers, the American equivalent of Rubirosa. Before he'd left Bel Air the previous evening, he had whispered something to her. "Oscar and I have something in common."

She was very hip, and realized at once that he was providing her with information about the length and size of his legendary penis.

After coffee and a croissant, she invited him for dinner that night at her home. "That way," she said, "you can better acquaint yourself with the house."

It was during dinner that he revealed to her that "Lana Turner is pursuing me."

In truth, it was the other way around. Years later, Zsa Zsa said that "Johnny was shopping around to see which rich Hollywood beauty he wanted to honor with his favors. He'd already had affairs with a young Janet Leigh, Ava Gardner, Elizabeth Taylor, and, inevitably, Marilyn Monroe, among countless others."

All these beauties contributed to his reputation as a lady killer.

He asked Zsa Zsa's advice about whether he should go with Turner. "Frankly," he told her, "I can take Lana or leave her."

Zsa Zsa revealed his exact quotation in a memoir.

She claimed that she gave him bad advice in urging him to accept Turner's generous offer.

"If I had really wanted Johnny at the time, I virtually could have had him on a permanent basis," she later recalled. "But I still had Rubi hanging loosely in the wind; I was back, sort of, with George; I was coming down from my affair with Lex Barker; and Vivien Leigh told me that my leading man in my next picture, Anthony Quayle, might not be the handsomest man in England, but made up for it with his skill in bed. I was in a quandary. That's why I gave

Johnny advice that led to his murder."

"But I was determined not to let this handsome hunk of manhood escape without sampling his love-making for at least one night, and maybe again in the future," Zsa Zsa later revealed.

"As a lover, he lived up to his star billing," she claimed to her girl friends. "He did not exaggerate the size of his equipment, and he was a skilled swordsman. After all, he'd had a lot of practice. He had a marvelous physique, flashing brown eyes, black wavy hair, and courtly manners. George Raft was correct in calling him 'the most cunning and cocksure man in Hollywood.'"

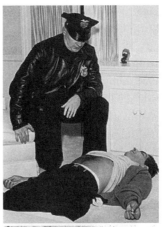

"I succumbed to his charm, even though I knew he was a high-priced gigolo."

Zsa Zsa had read that Mickey Cohen, Johnny's boss, had defined Johnny as the most handsome man he'd ever known. "He is an athlete and all man," Cohen had claimed. "There is no queerness about him."

Zsa Zsa wasn't so sure about that. She'd heard from others that Johnny sometimes hustled Holly-

LANA TURNER'S GIRL KILLS MOTHER'S SUITOR

A police officer, summoned to Lana Turner's home, inspects the lifeless body of the stabbed-to-death gangster, **Johnny Stompanato.**

But did *The National Enquirer* compose its headline correctly? Many of those involved in the drama have insisted that it was Lana herself who knifed him, and that the version she told the police and in court represented her greatest role as an actress.

wood's gay community, some members of whom were eager to sample his hidden assets. Johnny had once bragged that Rock Hudson had given him two-hundred dollars, but that Liberace, in Las Vegas, had presented him with a newly minted thousand dollar bill.

"I found Johnny very, very tempting, but I turned down his offer to come to London with me," she said. "He went with his second choice, which was Lana Turner. I later regretted urging him to go with her."

As she claimed in print, "I liked Johnny a great deal." She was later horrified to hear that he'd been murdered in Lana's home.

In happier times, two bathing beauties, **Johnny Stompanato** and **Lana Turner** strut their stuff.

Many of his fans and followers claimed that Stompanato concealed his greatest weapon in his bathing trunks.

Zsa Zsa later claimed, "He only took up with Lana because I turned him down."

It was announced that Cheryl Crane, Lana's teenaged daughter, had stabbed him when he was threatening to carve up the movie star's beautiful face.

"I had my doubts," Zsa Zsa said. "Frank Sinatra told me that he'd heard from Lana herself that she'd stabbed Johnny and that Crane took the blame. Had Lana confessed to the murder, it would have destroyed her career. She might have ended up in jail if Jerry Giesler didn't fight the ultimate fight. Crane would get off with a much easier sentence if she could be portrayed as a heroine defending her mother against a knife attack."

Johnny Stompanato died in a pool of his own blood in Lana Turner's house on April 4, 1958. "A lot of lonely ladies in Hollywood lost their best friend," Zsa Zsa said, a comment that might have been her own peculiar tribute to the slain stud.

***

After her flight landed at London, Zsa Zsa was mobbed by photographers. In a limousine, she was driven to The Connaught, where a suite had been reserved for her.

That morning, Henry Wilcox, the British film producer and director, had told the tabloids, "Zsa Zsa is one of the intriguing personalities at mid-century, and that's why I cast her in my latest film, *The Man Who Wouldn't Talk.*"

[A courtroom drama, set against the backdrop of the Cold War, its plot focuses on an American scientist charged for murder by the British police for his supposed role in the death of an East European defector.]

Zsa Zsa was delighted, as Wilcox had impressive credentials. In time, he would produce one hundred films, fifty of which he would direct.

That evening, he invited her to dine with him and his actress wife, Anna Neagle, who had been cast as the film's lead, the role of Mary Randall.

For twenty-five years, this beauty would be a top box office attraction in England, her roles ranging from a 17th-century prostitute, *Nell Gwynne*, in a movie of the same name (1934), to Queen Victoria in *Victoria the Great (1937)*. Almost all of her films were produced and directed by Wilcox, whom she'd married back in 1943.

"Anna was a real *dahlink*," Zsa Zsa recalled years later. "I adored her." But Zsa Zsa, being true to herself, couldn't resist a put-down. "Of course, there was a difference in our ages as vast as the Grand Canyon. When Anna was a little girl growing up in East Anglia, her mother used to chastise her when she came home from school. 'Anna, wipe the dinosaur shit off your feet.'"

[Neagle was born in 1904.]

A catered dinner for Zsa Zsa was hosted by the Wilcoxes in their luxurious apartment in Alford House overlooking Park Lane. Before dinner, Michael

Wilding dropped in for a drink, with the understanding that he couldn't stay for dinner.

[Wilding had previously appeared in such films with Neagle as The Court-neys of Curzon Street (1947)*, an "upstairs-downstairs" drama that's cited as one of the most-seen British movies of all time.]*

Zsa Zsa had a thousand questions she wanted to ask him about his marriage to Elizabeth Taylor, but he didn't want to talk about it. She later said, "I'd already had one of Elizabeth's husbands, my beloved Nicky *[Hilton],* and I'd eventually enjoy another husband of hers *[Richard Burton].* That night, I thought Wilding might ask me out on a date, but it didn't happen."

"I was dying to ask Anna about her 1954 appearance with Errol Flynn in *Lilacs in the Spring,* but she didn't have much to say in front of her jealous husband."

"My romantic life began to improve the next morning, when Wilcox introduced me to my co-star, Anthony Quayle," Zsa Zsa said.

His gift to her was a novel he'd written, *On Such a Night,* based on his World War II experiences when he'd served as an *aide-de-camp* to the government of Gibraltar, when that little British colony had bravely held out against a Nazi invasion.

Over lunch, they talked about their respective roles in the upcoming film. Zsa Zsa had been cast as a secret agent, Eve Trent, and Quayle would play a scientist, Dr. Frank Smith.

"Before I met Tony, I used to think all British stage actors were snobbish," Zsa Zsa said. "Take Laurence Olivier, for example. Tony and Larry had performed in Shakespeare plays together, and done a lot more, or so I heard through the grapevine. He was far more down to earth and ingratiating than Larry, however." In her memoirs, she defined Quayle as "a wonderful man."

He shared many memories of working with both Olivier and Vivien Leigh. Once, they'd flown to Denmark to perform in *Hamlet* within the historic Kronberg Castle. "I remember how beautiful Vivien looked," he said, "and I also recalled how far her talent fell short of her beauty."

The Lancashire-born actor also shared his philosophy of life with Zsa Zsa. He told her that, "if one doesn't have that little bit of danger in life, you'd better create it."

"And so I have, *dahlink,*" she answered. She invited him for a private dinner in her suite that night, where they not only became intimate, but friends for life.

Back in Hollywood, not known for keeping a secret, Zsa Zsa told Pamela Mason and others that Quayle as a lover was proficient but not overly passionate. "He was no bodice ripper, but a gentleman who took off his clothes— and mine, too—and hung them up so they would not get wrinkled. He was a

good kisser, but, for my taste, he could have remained a bit longer in the saddle."

In her memoirs, she recalled his "sardonic sense of humor." At one point during filming, he told her, "You are a big star, I a mere actor."

"I guess that's your subtle way of telling me I can't act," she said. "But you said it in such an adorable way, unlike that super prick John Huston. You may be right. I suspect that unlike Vivien, I will never be asked to play Ophelia."

"By the time I encountered that adorable **Anthony Quayle** [depicted in both photos above], both Vivien Leigh and Larry Olivier had lured the poor lad into their beds," **Zsa Zsa** claimed after wrapping a movie with him, The Man Who Wouldn't Talk.

"Tony talked plenty to me, whispering sweet nothings into my ear—and doing a hell of a lot more, too."

At the end of the shoot, in anticipation of her return to America, he drove her to the London airport, where photographers had been tipped off about her departure. As she kissed him goodbye, she whispered to him, "I adore British men. Their bodies are intact, the way nature made them, not surgically altered like many American men today."

[Although she saw little of Quayle during the years to come, they always remained in touch. In 1989, the BBC in London presented the British version of This Is Your Life, *focusing one of its episodes on Zsa Zsa. Unknown to her, Quayle had been asked to recall his experience of working with her during the filming of* The Man Who Wouldn't Talk, *more than thirty years before.*

"I was shocked when I saw him on the screen," she said. "He was sixty-eight years old, but looked like he was ninety. He was emaciated, so very ill. My heart went out to him. I felt so sorry for him."

Three days after the telecast of This Is Your Life, *Quayle died of liver cancer. The date was October 20, 1989.]*

***

In the late 1950s, after what she called "flop after flop in my private life," Eva threw herself into her work again, both in films and on the stage.

Men came and went rather quickly in her personal life in the wake of her loss of Tyrone Power. She referred to these romantic involvements as "flings" or as "brief interludes."

Eva's longtime companion, Camyl Sosa Belanger, expressed

554

a different point of view in her memoir, *Eva Gabor, An Amazing Woman,* writing that her employer was a "horny toad" during this period. Eva admitted to her friend that "only Cary Grant and Merv Griffin eluded my boudoir."

Eva signed with Universal Studios for the 1957 release of the romantic comedy, *My Man Godfrey,* co- starring June Allyson (a zany heiress who hires as a butler a man she thinks is homeless and then falls in love with him) and David Niven (who's actually a debonair millionaire who plays along for the comedic affects).

Director Henry Koster wanted Eva to join a supporting cast that included Jessie Royce Landis and Robert Keith.

The 92-minute film was an unnecessary remake of Gregory La Cava's 1936 screwball comedy of the same name that had starred William Powell and Carole Lombard. The 1957 remake was shallow compared to the original. Marlene Dietrich, who sat through both versions, defined the Allyson/Niven vehicle as "*veak lemonade.*"

Eva's interchanges with Niven and Allyson on the set of this film were much more interesting than the plot that unfolded on the screen.

Famously married to Dick Powell (she had stolen him from Joan Blondell), Allyson had married him in 1945 and remained wed to him until his death from cancer in 1963. "But she was never faithful to her husband," Eva told some of her friends. "In Hollywood, June was known as a nymphomaniac. She was seen on occasion taking a well-muscled grip on the set of one of her pictures to her dressing room for love in the afternoon."

Allyson also ended up sleeping with some of her leading men, including Peter Lawford, her co-star in *Good News (1947).*

Allyson had also made three pictures with James Stewart, beginning with *The Stratton Story* in 1949. "It just happened between Jimmy and me," Allyson told Eva. "We were thrown together so often. Jimmy stammered and stuttered on screen, but off screen, he was dynamite in bed. That guy knew how to hit the spot."

Two years before that, also within the context of her marriage to Powell, Allyson had fallen in love with Alan Ladd, her co-star in the 1955 picture, *The McConnell Story.* Ladd had been married at the time to his agent and manager, Sue Carol. In 1950, Ladd and Allyson were voted "America's Favorite Actor and Favorite Actress."

"Alan wanted to remain married to Sue, and I wanted to stay married to Richard *[Powell],* but we just couldn't help ourselves," Allyson told Eva. "We fell in love, and we're still in love, but have agreed to separate. My heart is broken into so many pieces."

"Did your husband learn about this?" Eva asked Allyson.

"Carol learned about our affair and called Richard," Allyson said. "She told him, 'My husband is madly in love with your wife.' Richard listened politely before saying, 'Who isn't?' Then he hung up and has never chastised me for straying."

Eva later asserted, "I also never chastised June for her adultery….not with my romantic record. In some ways, June was like me. I knew what a broken heart was—Tyrone Power, for example. I also knew it was possible to fall in love with more than one man at the same time. At my peak in the mid-1950s, 'Naughty Eva' had five or six beaux on the string at the same time."

***

On the set of *My Man Godfrey,* Eva also bonded once again with veteran actor David Niven. She had had a brief fling with him when she first arrived in Hollywood during the war years, in some mysterious capacity associated with the defense of his native England.

The young military officer she'd met back then was very different from the mature, veteran actor he had become. He was still suave, debonair, and filled with an understated charm, but he was also deeply troubled—and trapped in an unhappy marriage to a former Miss Sweden, Hjördis *[pronounced YER-diss]* Tersmeden Niven.

Niven told Eva that his wife had become a hopeless and very abusive alcoholic.

A fellow actor, Roger Moore, one of Niven's best friends, had already claimed that "Hjördis was a bitch to him. David was a dear, dear friend of mine, who did nothing but try to please her. In return, she showed him nothing but disdain."

There were rumors circulating around Hollywood at the time, and years later, headline stories in the press, that at one point, Niven had become so miserable with his wife that he even thought of having her murdered.

Eva Gabor signed on as a supporting member of the cast in *My Man Godfrey,* which contained a scene where the too-short **June Allyson** *(left)* tried to kiss her butler, **David Niven.**

Eva accused June of being sex crazed, and warned her that she planned to resume her wartime fling with Niven "at least for the duration of the shoot. So back off, June!"

Eva was very frank with him. "David, there's such a thing as divorce."

His objection to divorce didn't quite convince her. "I want to be the only man in Hollywood who never divorced."

He admitted that he was still in love with his first wife from the 1940s, Primrose ("Primmie")

Rollo, a former British military officer who had died one night during a party at Tyrone Power's house.

Power's guests had been playing a game ("Sardines") of hide-and-seek . The lights had been switched off and guests rushed to hide. In the dark, Primmie had mistakenly opened a door she thought led to the powder room, but she'd fallen down a steep flight of stairs into the cellar. She'd died of a fractured skull and brain lacerations. She had arrived in Hollywood just six weeks before her death at the age of twenty-eight.

"After Primmie's death, I found myself alone with two young sons to raise, David, Jr., five, and Jamie, two," Niven told Eva.

He confided to Eva that he had considered suicide in the wake of his wife's death, but realized how wrong that would be to leave his two sons with neither a mother nor a father.

By 1948, he'd adjusted to life without his "Primmie" and was even considering marriage again. But to whom?

One day, he was introduced to Hjördis and become entranced by her beauty. Or, as he expressed it, "I had champagne in my knees. She was tall, slim, and had auburn hair, an uplifted nose, a lovely mouth, and gray eyes so large it would have provoked envy in Joan Crawford. She had grown up in the Swedish town of Kiruna, which lies north of the ice-bound Arctic Circle. I think on my honeymoon, I came to realize that Hjördis still had Arctic ice in her veins. Before the honeymoon was over, I realized I'd made the biggest mistake of my life."

Without announcing her arrival, Hjördis appeared one day at the studio, unexpectedly walking in to discover her husband lunching with Eva in the commissary. Eva noticed that she appeared to be drunk. "Although still a beautiful woman, she evoked the Madwoman of Chaillot that day."

She had appeared in a *cheongsam [a long dress with a high collar and slit skirt]* which she'd purchased in Hong Kong when she'd gone around the world with Niven, accompanied by Shirley MacLaine.

At the luncheon, Eva took a dislike to Hjördis. "She was filled with anger, and she seemed to resent her husband's celebrity and success. Frankly, I think she

David Niven's marriage to **Hjördis Tersmeden** was so unhappy that he confessed very privately to some friends that he once considered murdering her. Eva recommended divorce instead.

During the filming of *My Man Godfrey*, Hjördis arrived, hostile and unexpected, hoping to catch her husband with his latest "blonde bimbo," a reference to Eva.

557

was jealous. Being Mrs. David Niven was not enough for her. She obviously wanted stardom for herself, but I was told by David that she had no acting talent."

"Whenever David told a story, she interrupted him," Eva claimed.

"David lies and exaggerates everything," Hjördis charged. "He always embellishes even the simplest incident and never reports it right. Instead of an actor, he should have been a scriptwriter."

Hjördis didn't exactly endear herself when she told Eva goodbye. She'd downed four gin martinis at lunch. Niven had been called to the set, but he'd asked one of the studio grips to drive his wife home because she might run over a pedestrian if she were behind the wheel herself.

He asked Eva to escort her back to her car. As Eva helped her into the back seat, Hjördis turned to Eva. "Are you David's latest blonde bimbo? He's come down in the world. He usually fucks blondes with more class—take Marlene Dietrich, for example. You're certainly not in the league of Grace Kelly. I hear all of you Gabor sisters are international tramps."

Eva almost caught Hjördis' foot in the car door as she slammed it, ordering the driver to take her home.

After that ill-fated luncheon, Eva invited Niven to her home for dinner that night.

His son, David, Jr., understood his father's dilemma. "My father told me how unhappy he was," the boy said, years later. "He didn't exactly keep his knees together all the time. But when you're not receiving love and affection at your home, you seek it elsewhere."

Elsewhere, in this case, meant a brief affair with Eva.

"He had such an urbane sense of humor and an easy charm," Eva recalled. "I could easily have fallen in love with David, but I knew I shouldn't. My romance with Ty Power had wounded me, and I wasn't ready to love again."

Eva eased into her affair with Niven during their filming of *My Man Godfrey.* "I found him desperately in need of love and respect. I gave that to him. If things had been different, I wish he'd married me in 1948 instead of that monster."

Niven told Eva that he and Hjördis no longer slept together, but occupied different bedrooms. "I'm discreet about my affairs," he confided to Eva, "but I don't pretend to be faithful. It's true I'd had other involvements—some of which are well known, such as my fling with Grace Kelly. Other more sensational ones, such as my affair with Princess Margaret, have fallen under the radar screen."

"But unlike me, Hjördis flaunts her affairs to me," he claimed. "Two months ago, I arrived home from the studio and she told me she'd just seen a doctor that day. He discovered that she had contracted a sexually transmitted disease—she didn't identify it—but she told me where she'd picked it up. From that priapic senator from Massachusetts, John F. Kennedy."

By the time Eva had encountered Hjördis, she'd already been dissected by Niven's family, by his close friends, and by the Hollywood community in general.

In the autumn of 1951, Hjördis had joined Niven and two of his male friends on a hunting expedition. She was shot, suffering a few non-fatal flesh wounds, in the face, neck, and chest by one of the hunters. Although the incident was officially defined as an accident, rumors spread quickly that Niven had gotten one of his friends to attempt to kill her, claiming afterward that it was a hunting accident.

Eva didn't believe such a rumor. "David was too kind and gentle for that." But one night he did reveal that he'd once had murderous feelings about Hjördis.

"I came home early from the studio and found her drunk in the bathtub, too drunk to even get out of the tub. I thought she would have drowned if I had not come home. It's a dreadful thing to admit, but I actually thought about pushing her down into the water. I could have gotten away with it, particularly when her blood alcohol was tested. Oh, God, I wanted her to die."

Before filming *My Man Godfrey,* Niven had starred in Michael Todd's blockbuster, *Around the World in Eighty Days,* which had won the Oscar for Best Picture of 1956. Niven had been cast as Jules Verne's regimented hero, Phileas Fogg, the punctual, stoic Englishman who loosens up on his global voyage. Todd's movie would become Niven's most famous screen credit. During the course of the film, Niven and Todd had formed a close friendship.

Married at the time to Elizabeth Taylor, Todd had visited the set of *My Man Godfrey* on two separate occasions for lunch with Niven and Eva. She was charmed by his aggressive, macho personality, and she understood Elizabeth's attraction to "this robust bundle of uncontrolled energy," as Eva characterized Todd.

"You should see the ring he gave Elizabeth," Niven told Eva. "He's also bought a twin-engined plane he named 'Lucky Liz.'"

It was a Friday afternoon, and Niven wanted to fly to Las Vegas. He invited both Eva and Todd to accompany him. Todd had another commitment, and didn't want to be separated from Elizabeth, but Eva was eager to go.

Whereas in his memoir, *The Moon's a Balloon,* Niven claimed he went to Las Vegas with Hjördis, but it was actually Eva who accompanied him there. The general manager of the Sands personally checked them into their suite.

On his first night there, Niven was approached at the Black Jack table, a waiter telling him he was wanted on the phone. He picked up the receiver to hear Todd's voice, "Why don't you guys get your asses down here to Palm

Springs?" he asked. "Liz and I would love it."

He talked Niven into it only after Todd promised to send his private plane to Las Vegas to pick them up.

The next morning, Eva and Niven flew to Palm Springs. Two hours after arriving, they joined Elizabeth and Todd in bathing suits for a lunch around the pool of what Todd called "our Palm Springs pad," a luxurious and elegantly furnished home.

Eva and Niven had each known Elizabeth for years, and welcomed the chance to spend some time with her. "She was annoyed that she had to stay in California working on *Cat on a Hot Tin Roof* and that she could not accompany Todd to a testimonial dinner at the Waldorf-Astoria in Manhattan.

After their weekend together, Todd flew Elizabeth, Eva, and Niven back to Los Angeles, where Elizabeth reported back to work at MGM. The director of *My Man Godfrey,* Henry Koster, told Niven and Eva that they weren't needed for retakes after all.

When he learned they were free, Todd invited them to fly with him to New York aboard *The Lucky Liz.* But both Niven and Eva wanted to be alone with each other. Todd then came up with an alternate plan: He'd have his chauffeur drive them back to Palm Springs, where he'd made his vacation home available to them. They gratefully accepted that offer.

Once installed in Palm Springs, Niven received a final call from Todd right before he took off for the long eastbound trip to New York. "We heard the weather was bad, but Todd did not seem overly concerned," Eva recalled. Four hours later, *The Lucky Liz,* with Todd aboard, crashed into the Zuni Mountains of New Mexico. The date was March 21, 1958.

During their transit back to Hollywood, both Eva and Niven wept in the back seat of Todd's limousine. He asked the chauffeur to go to Todd's home, where a stricken Elizabeth was in mourning. To Eva's surprise, she saw Greta Garbo leaving the premises. Garbo rushed past without speaking to Eva.

When they went inside, Elizabeth's butler refused to allow Niven and Eva to go upstairs to comfort her.

Back at home that night, Eva called the Gabors. "David Niven, Elizabeth, and I might well have been on *The Lucky Liz* that crashed and killed Michael Todd. I feel I've escaped from the jaws of death."

CHAPTER TWELVE
The Hunters and the Hunted

When director Muriel Box approached Eva to play a supporting role in a 1957 British comedy, *The Truth About Women,* she was eager to sign, even though she'd be playing the fifth lead.

She was pleased to be working with Laurence Harvey, who had remained Zsa Zsa's friend. He was cast as Sir Humphrey Tavistock, who regales his son-in-law with decades-old anecdotes about "found lovers and lost loves."

Eva was cast in a glamorous role as the sophisticated "Louise Tiere," a diplomat's wife. The female lead went to veteran actress Julie Harris, whose talent Eva envied. She lost enthusiasm for the project when she learned that the Swedish actress, Mai Zetterling, had been cast in the fourth lead, with billing over hers.

Eva arrived sobbing at the dressing room of Harvey. "The Swedish cow stole Ty Power from me," Eva lamented. "He's now living with that low-rent bitch. I don't know how she schemed her way into his heart. I heard she got her start in 1944, fucking Ingmar Bergman in Stockholm. The press calls her a sex symbol. She's about as sexy as fried liver left out in the desert sun for two days. *Dahlink,* I'm the sex symbol, not this Zetterling creature."

When the director, Box, introduced Eva to Zetterling, Eva slapped her face. "Never in my life have I ever behaved so unprofessionally, and I've often worked with both men and women I detested," Eva later confided to Harvey. "But I completely lost control when I came face to face with the woman who took Ty from me. Perhaps there's something about a woman scorned that rings true. I should apologize, but I never will. I truly hate her."

At one point, Eva was so exasperated about Zetterling having been cast that she approached Box, telling him that the Swedish actress was a "card-carrying communist." The director dismissed her charge as a "wild and reckless accusation, based on Eva's jealousy"

Eva's charge was actually very serious. It had been levied during the 1950s, a decade that began with a communist witch hunt among working people in

Hollywood. Senator Joseph McCarthy and FBI director J. Edgar Hoover, sometimes with dubious evidence, had rooted suspected communists out of the film industry. Many of those accused were subsequently blacklisted, their careers and livelihood destroyed.

However, *The Truth About Women* was a British production, and that country had no such blacklist.

Although Eva's accusation was dismissed, she knew more than the rest of the cast. How she obtained such personal information about Zetterling's politics is not known.

During the early part of the 21st Century, the National Archives in London released a lot of previously top secret information.

Zetterling's name appeared on a list of suspects closely watched by British security agents. Records revealed that they had labeled and defined her as "a known communist and possibly a spy."

In 1994, when Eva read of Zetterling's death, she told friends, "There is a certain joy in outliving rivals."

Eva herself only had months to live.

On the set of *The Truth About Women*, Eva got into a catfight with the Swedish beauty, **Mai Zetterling** *(depicted above)*

"I gave the bitch the slap of her life," Eva later said. "She not only stole Ty Power from me, but she adopted my dress, my hairstyle, and my makeup."

"That's not all. The cretin was also a communist spy."

***

In 1957, actor Ben Gazzara was at the low point of his career, even after a run of three hit plays. One of them had included his long-running interpretation of the homosexual football hero, Brick, in Tennessee Williams' *Cat on a Hot Tin Roof*. Gazzara's 1951 marriage to radio actress Louise Erickson was all but over.

The son of Italian immigrants from Sicily, Gazzara admitted that his discovery of his love for acting saved him from a life of crime.

He often spoke of his childhood, where he slept outside on a fire escape in summer, listening on occasion to the screams coming from the nearby Bellevue psychiatric hospital.

Rough, virile, and unconventionally handsome, Gazzara admitted, "I was a babe magnet, also attracting a lot of interest among the gays."

One night at his favorite Manhattan hangout, Harold's Show Spot, a rendezvous for out-of-work actors and writers, along with a train wreck of Broadway sharpies, he'd had a bit too much to drink. Nevertheless, he pulled himself together and attended a chic cocktail party on the Upper East Side, which was attended by three of the co-stars from *All About Eve*—Bette Davis, Anne Baxter, and Celeste Holm. Eva had gone to the party because she'd heard that her former lover, Hugh Marlowe, would be there, but he had failed to show up.

At the party, Gazzara was sitting alone in the corner when, in his words, "A vision of blonde loveliness approached."

In a Hungarian accent, Eva said, "I've seen all of your work, *dahlink*. You are *vonderful.*"

He looked up at her. "I know you. You're one of the Gabor sisters. The youngest and prettiest."

What an acute observer you are, *dahlink*," she said, sitting down beside him. "Those *All About Eve* broads are dominating this party. Let's skip out and go dancing."

"You're on, babe," he said to her.

"I thought I was having a wet dream," Gazzara later recalled. "Dinner, dancing, with the lady picking up the tab. I had only $200 in the bank at the time, having gone through all my Broadway earnings. Later, she put me in a perfumed bubble bath in her apartment in the annex of the Plaza Hotel. As I bathed, she fed me one grape at a time. I was almost tempted to say, 'Beulah, peel me a grape,' borrowing a Mae West line. The grapes were very succulent, and so was Eva that night. She seemed to enjoy the sex as much as I did, maybe more so."

For the next few weeks, Gazzara, at least temporarily, made Eva forget her earlier lovers. At the Stork Club, they chatted with Joan Crawford and Walter Winchell. One night, Gregory Peck stopped by their table. Gazzara told him, "If I had your looks, and retained my talent, I could be the biggest star in the world." Eva told Peck, "I'd settle for your body even without the talent."

Most evenings ended at Chez Vito, where Eva asked the serenading Hungarian violinists to play a song from her youth in Budapest. "It makes me want to cry," she told Gazzara. "Someday, I want to take you to Budapest."

"With no money, I was living the playboy's life and loving it," Gazzara said. "Of course, I kept hoping every day that some producer or director would start thinking about casting me in something. Eva kept up my spirits most of the time by constantly reassuring me that I was terrific in bed."

Gazzara, hanging out at Harold's, told playwright Tennessee Williams, "Eva Gabor sure likes to pay homage to my Sicilian salami."

Williams responded, "And who among us can resist it?"

"I loved Ben, but on occasions, he'd go into the deepest, darkest moods, a wall of depression enveloping him," Eva recalled. "He resented Marlon Brando forging ahead, with him sitting around waiting for a producer to call. He lamented his own mistakes in turning down several offers for films a few months back. He told me, 'I didn't think I was ready. Hell with that! I should have accepted those roles, and I might be a big film star today like Brando.'"

"With so little money, I was grateful for all those dinners I had at the Gabors," he said. "Most of them took place in a townhouse owned by Magda and her husband, Tony Gallucci. At most of the dinners, Jolie was an honored guest. She always wet-lipped me and gave me a bear hug, welcoming me to the family. However, Eva and I had never talked about marriage. The Gabors were great hosts, the sisters were supposed to be jealous of each other, but I never saw any of that."

"During my short affair with Eva, I really bonded with Gallucci," Gazzara said. "He was a low-rent WOP like myself. He often cried in my arms, and I mean that literally. Nothing sexual, just a deeply troubled man who saw in me a kindred spirit. One night, he'd cry about his dead mother. On another night, he'd cry about his dead father. On yet another evening, his sex addiction would bring him to tears. He was madly in love with Magda, but couldn't stop cheating on her. He even cried at his success at making all those millions in plumbing. I listened patiently, thinking I had only $89.31 left in the bank."

"You never knew who would turn up at one of the Gabor family dinners," Gazzara said. "Those lavish meals kept me from starvation. One night, George Sanders showed up and was still treated like one of the family, even though he was no longer married to Zsa Zsa. I was expecting the witty, debonair Addison DeWitt from *All About Eve*. What I got was a sad, lonely man who ate little and said even less. Rumor had it he was deeply troubled about his latent homosexuality."

Actor **Ben Gazzara**, star of the Broadway version of Tennessee Williams' *Cat on a Hot Tin Roof*, admitted, in a rare instance of name-dropping, to "being a babe magnet."

"Marilyn Monroe went after me, and Audrey Hepburn fell in love with me, too," he claimed. "At the Actors Studio, Marlon Brando and James Dean chased after me. And Eva Gabor fell for me, until I ditched her one night for that glittering antique, Marlene Dietrich."

One night, Marlene Dietrich was a guest, and she and I got off on the wrong foot," Gazzara claimed. "I attacked narcissism in actors. She scolded me, claiming, 'Everyone in this world needs a good dose of narcissism to survive, especially if you're an actor.' She said that rather icily, but a few nights later, she warmed to me...and how!"

"I finally got up enough nerve to invite Eva to my dingy local dive, Harold's," Gazzara said. "Our host put on the dog for her, even bringing up a free bottle of *Dom*

564

Pérignon. They boys at the bar crowded around Eva, treating her like royalty. With her stunning beauty, and dressed in diamonds and mink, she sure lit up that place. Not a lot of women patronized the joint, except a few aging prostitutes still plying their trade to tourists on Times Square."

That night, Harold christened Eva 'The Goulash,' a rather unglamorous name for such a glittery star. After that night, Eva sometimes insisted on dropping in to Harold's, joining the bums of Broadway for a night cap. She was very democratic."

Eva was cast at the time in an off-Broadway play, Franz Wedekind's *Lulu,* and she invited Gazzara to attend her opening night performance. Before the curtain went up, he went backstage to her dressing room. "I kissed her, careful not to ruin her makeup. Kneeling at her feet was some wardrobe mistress fiddling with the hem of her gown. When she rose up, it wasn't some old hag at all, but Marlene herself. She wet kissed me like Jolie always did."

"She was a hell of a lot friendlier that night than when we'd first met at Magda's place," Gazzara said. "As we watched Eva from the wings, Marlene did not hide her attraction for me. My god, this screen diva was actually feeling me up and getting me excited, even though she must have been a contemporary of Goethe."

"Before the night ended, Marlene asked me to visit her some night," Gazzara said. "She gave me her unlisted number. 'You must call me,' she urged. Here I was, a greasy Italian kid who grew up in Kips Bay, being pawed over by a Hungarian bombshell and a Prussian goddess who had once brought a tingle to Hitler's sole testicle."

Before flying to Hollywood the next day, Gazzara spent his final night with Eva at her apartment. "He made love to me all night," Eva later told her confidants. "I made breakfast and coffee for him in the morning, and he kissed me goodbye as he headed out the door. He promised to call the next day. He never did."

***

Back again at Metro-Goldwyn-Mayer, Eva signed to appear as Deborah Aldrich, a supporting role in the 1957 comedy *Don't Go Near the Water.* The film also starred Glenn Ford, Gia Scala, Anne Francis, and Keenan Wynn. After the success of *Teahouse of the August Moon (1956),* in which Ford and Brando became mortal enemies off screen, this was the first of several comedies in which Ford would be cast.

For Eva, the most memorable experience working on the film did not involve anything to do with her role, but with her exposure to Glenn Ford, upon whom she'd always had a crush, especially when she saw him in *Gilda,* playing opposite Rita Hayworth *[who became his lover at the time.]*

The film's gay director, Charles Walters, liked Eva, and she often sat with him when he was helming other actors in their scenes. He'd just finished *The Tender Trap (1955)* and *High Society* (1956), both starring Frank Sinatra. She was amused to learn how Bing Crosby and Sinatra had vied for the attentions of Grace Kelly during the filming of *High Society,* a remake of Katharine Hepburn's *The Philadelphia Story.*

"I always like to be directed by a man who's gay," Eva later said. "Such directors always saw that I was photographed looking my most beautiful, and that I appeared in a flattering gown."

The plot of *Don't Go Near the Water* involved a U.S. Navy public relations unit stationed on an island in the Pacific during World War II.

When Eva first met Ford, she, along with the rest of Hollywood, knew that he was an adulterous married man. The list of beautiful actresses he'd seduced had become legendary. Women such as Joan Crawford, Rita Hayworth, Margaret Sullavan, and Barbara Stanwyck had fallen for him.

Not bad for a former stableboy who used to shovel horseshit for that homespun comedian Will Rogers. "He fired me when he came into his stable one afternoon and stepped in a stallion's big, smelly dump," Ford claimed.

Walters told Eva that "Ford approaches his role like a temperamental little boy, going at his own slow pace, regardless of how he's directed. If he were mine, I would make him take off his pants and drop his underwear for a bare-butt spanking."

Eva had been immensely attracted to Ford but found him an enigma she could not solve. She often asked other people about him. One night at a party, Clifford Odets, the playwright and screenwriter, told her, "It is an easily won bet that in a few years Glenn will get just like the other movie people—bored, sprawling, careless, an overly relaxed fallen angel—they are all affable boys out here, almost tramps."

That murky assessment confused her all the more.

She set out to unlock the enigma on her own. Ford had flirted with her since filming on the movie began. She told Walters, "I signaled to him that I was not only available, but panting."

By the time Eva got involved with Ford, his 1943 marriage to dancer/actress Eleanor Powell was nearing its end. Their divorce came in 1959 when Eva co-starred in yet another picture with Ford, *It Started With a Kiss.*

"He was one of my greatest lovers," she said. "In bed, he wasn't a hard-driving demon stud, but had the tender qualities of a late teenager eager to please. He was so endearing. He had this wonderful masculine aroma that was intoxicating. When he got up to leave for work, I longed for him to stay in bed with me all day."

"He was very free with his magnificent body, allowing me to roam at will, exploring each nook and cranny. He was also a great kisser."

Shortly after her first night with Ford, Eva told Walters, "Glenn is the first man I've met who could help me get over Ty Power."

Each day she learned more about Ford and began to understand his unique screen presence. "We were both ideal for the Eisenhower era," she said. "I represented the fake glamour of that time, and Glenn represented all the strong qualities most admired in a man—that is, the man who appeared on the screen, not the little devil in his private life."

"I think I know why Glenn eventually drifted off," Eva said. "One night in Palm Springs, I was so turned on by him, I wanted it four times over a twenty-four hour period. We were in this rented villa, lying around the pool nude. The more I saw that magnificent Canadian stud, the more I wanted him."

Ford's sympathetic good looks made him an ideal leading man for both weepies and romances, and he brought a genial and relaxed sincerity to the screen. Eva agreed with one critic who wrote that Ford "could be a brooding menace, heroic, taciturn, wise, foolish, amiable, dull, or sardonic."

At the time Eva met Ford, he was at the peak of his career, appearing on *Quigley's Annual List of Top Ten Box Office Champions,* rising to Number One in 1958.

Peter Ford, Glenn's son, wrote a 2011 memoir, *Glenn Ford: A Life.* In it, he accurately claimed that Eva was the woman his father "almost married."

"Glenn often talked of marrying me when his divorce from Powell came through," Eva said. "He held out dreams for me that we could star in a series of romantic comedies in the 1960s, perhaps becoming popular like Rock Hudson and Doris Day, who were all the rage at the box office. But it was a dream only to be dreamed."

"During the course of our love affair, I saved on repair work done around the house," Eva claimed. "Glenn knew all about plumbing and wiring, even air conditioning. When there was a leak in my roof, he climbed the ladder and repaired it. One time, a burglar broke plate glass in my windows and robbed my house when I was at the studio. When I called Glenn, he rushed over, inspected the

Eva Gabor made two movies with **Glenn Ford**, *Don't Go Near the Water* and *It Started With a Kiss.*

Eva got her man offscreen during the filming of both movies, and later claimed, "Glenn was the second greatest love of my life after Ty. He instructed a woman as to what he liked. The first time we made love, he told me, 'My hot spots begin with my ears and end with my big toe. Don't miss any of them!'"

"In America, *dahlink*, that's known as an 'Around the World.'"

damage, and returned from the hardware store with new glass to repair the window. He installed the glass himself. Then he took me upstairs and made mad love to me. What's not to love about a man like that?"

"One night Glenn and I spent with his friend, Ronald Reagan, whose career was in great decline," Eva said. "Reagan spent the night discussing politics, which I find boring. In spite of that, he possessed a certain charm, and he was still reasonably good looking, but not like his 1940s screen image."

"After Reagan left, I spoke to Glenn about him. I told him that in spite of his gab, I heard that when Reagan stopped talking, he was a hit with the ladies. I wondered if he were great in bed."

"How in hell would I know?" Glenn asked her. "Unlike you, he's never sucked my dick. All I know is what his former wife, Jane Wyman, told me. 'Ronnie is as good in bed as he is on the screen.' You figure that one out for yourself."

[Although a Democrat when she'd met him, Ford later switched parties, supporting Reagan in both his 1980 and 1984 bids for the presidency.]

"There came a night when I first realized that Glenn was not going to marry me," Eva said. "He'd made a date to pick me up for drinks and dinner at seven that night. In addition to Reagan, William Holden was a close friend, very close. These two good-looking guys had bonded ever since they'd made the movie *Texas* in 1941."

"I looked ravishing that night when I answered the doorbell," she said. "I was shocked when I opened the door. Staring back at me was not Glenn, but a gorgeous Bill Holden, who looked absolutely adorable and ever so sexy."

"What woman in her right mind would turn down a date with Bill Holden?" she asked. "Of course, *dahlink*, I spent the night with him and would have married him if he'd asked me. I later learned that Bill and Glenn were known for exchanging women they considered hot."

"I realized what a fool I'd been to think that Glenn ever had any intention of marrying me. Bill Holden was a great consolation prize. Any woman would have considered him a delight. Just ask Audrey Hepburn, Grace Kelly, Barbara Stanwyck, and—are you ready?—both Lucille Ball and Jackie Kennedy."

When Zsa Zsa heard of Eva's affair with Ford, she told her sister, "At last you've found a man in

Eva said, "I got the surprise of my life when handsome **William Holden** showed up on my doorstep one night. I had dressed for a date with Glenn Ford, but he sent his best friend instead."

"I was heartbroken, of course, because it signaled that Glenn was not going to marry me, but Bill, at least, was a fabulous consolation prize."

Hollywood who hasn't fucked Marilyn Monroe."

[Zsa Zsa was wrong. On October 4, 2008, Peter Ford auctioned off the sofa where his father "screwed Marilyn," the couch selling for $1,750.

Ford had met Marilyn in 1962, the year she was murdered. Both of them were attending a party in Hollywood for Abraham Ribicoff, who was John F. Kennedy's secretary of Health, Education, and Welfare. Ford remembered how Monroe at his home "drank an entire bottle of champagne in about two seconds."

A seduction followed.]

"After *Don't Go Near the Water* was wrapped, and before we made another movie, I saw Glenn perhaps two or three times a month," Eva said. "I recall spending many a rainy night in Los Angeles with him. Funny, he always seemed to show up when it rained."

"I never really cracked the enigma that was Glenn," Eva said, "although I tried. I have no regrets, however. At least I got to enjoy the most romantic sex of my life as opposed to the most passionate. You figure out the difference, *dahlink.*"

***

"A glamour puss has to be found to play Joana in *Present Laughter* with me," Noël Coward said in January of 1958. He thought Eva would be ideal in the stage role, for which he wanted her to appear for a month's engagement in San Francisco and for two weeks in Los Angeles.

Coward's play had been written in 1939 and first staged in London in 1942. The play's title was inspired by a line from Shakespeare's *Twelfth Night.* ("Present mirth hath present laughter").

The plot spins around a comedy actor, Garry Essendine, who is set to tour Africa. Before his departure, he faces a series of farcical events involving women who want to seduce him.

In his first call to Eva, Coward told her his play, in which he'd also star, was "a series of semi-autobiographical pyrotechnics about an actor facing an impending midlife crisis."

Coward had starred as Garry Essendine in the original production. *Present Laughter* had been revived many times with such actors as Nigel Patrick, Albert Finney, Peter O'Toole, Simon Callow, and Ian McKellen playing the leads.

Eva found Coward in a foul mood, denouncing his fellow cast members as "silly asses," and accusing them of "raising hell and clamoring for more money. In general, they made beasts of themselves."

But he praised Eva for raising the spirits of the demoralized cast by her

569

mere appearance.

"She was an adorable darling," he said, "and I was enchanted by her, both on and off the stage."

However, at a dress rehearsal, they had their first artistic disagreement. She appeared in a stunning dress of orange chiffon. He looked her up and down and said, "You're not going to wear that thing, are you?

"What's the matter with it?" she asked. "I look absolutely gorgeous."

"If you wear that, no one in the audience will look at me."

Finally, they agreed she could wear the chiffon number, but only if it were redesigned and remade in muted tones of champagne.

As Coward's biographer, Cole Lesley, wrote, "During the run of the play, Noël would hang his felt hat on one of Eva's beautiful breasts for his quick change at the side of the stage. As he explained it, 'There's no time for messing about.'"

During the course of his long career in show-biz, **Noël Coward** had accumulated an impressive roster of A-list seductions: James Cagney, Louis Hayward, Stewart Granger, Peter Lawford, Cary Grant, Laurence Olivier, Tyrone Power, Michael Redgrave, Michael Wilding, plus such royal figures as Prince George, the ill-fated Duke of Kent.

He once confessed that he'd lost his virginity (at age 13, and aboard a train) to actress Gertrude Lawrence.

Eva Gabor claimed, "I was the only known woman who seduced Noël when he was an adult."

Years later, Eva admitted to her companion and biographer, Camyl Belanger, "I seduced Noël in San Francisco. "He told me that I was the only woman in his entire life who turned him on and that he could not resist me. Of course, we were both a little tipsy on champagne that night."

In response, Belanger told Eva, "I think you probably changed him," referring, of course, to his sexual preference. "Eva had that power, a seductive power that made her a sex vixen. She was very attractive and so feminine."

In spite of Eva's qualities as a sex vixen, she hardly changed Coward's sexual nature.

In fact, after the seduction, he made many indiscreet remarks to personal friends such as Laurence Olivier and Rex Harrison. "A bloody awful experience that I wouldn't want to repeat, my dears."

He also claimed that , "All that open plumbing absolutely revolts me. Being in bed with a woman is like feeling the skin of a snake. God preserve me in my future from female stars!"

When Harrison heard this, he said, "That Noël is a terrible cunt in many ways. If he and Eva made it, as he alleges, they at least had one thing in common: Tyrone Power had already fucked both of them."

In reviews of *Present Laughter* in San Francisco, Eva was cited for her glamour instead of her acting. The play was reviewed as "a wittily impudent and neatly invented burlesque of a French farce," and Coward was praised for his "mockery of the vain, posturing, and yet self-scrutinizing and self-amused matinee idol."

[In 1976, in Chicago, Coward arranged a reunion with Eva and Zsa Zsa when he took his long-time companion, Graham Payn to see them, horribly miscast, in a production of Arsenic and Old Lace.

"They looked like innocent schoolgirls as the two murderesses," Coward said. "We stayed up until two in the morning with Eva, laughing about the times gone by. 'He took all my lovers from me,' Eva said to Graham about me."]

***

At long last, Eva was cast in a movie, *Gigi,* that walked away with a Best Picture Oscar at the annual Academy Award ceremonies in Los Angeles in 1959.

The year before, director Vincente Minnelli had cast Eva in the glamorous role of "Liane d'Exelmans" in this romantic musical comedy staged in *Belle Époque* Paris.

Regrettably, the film's biggest spotlights did not shine on Eva, but to the French *gamine,* Leslie Caron, who played the precocious and carefree Gilberte (aka Gigi). The role was originally intended for Audrey Hepburn.

Cast as the film's wealthy young *bon vivant* (Gaston Lachaille) was Louis Jourdan, once labeled "the handsomest man in the world." The role had originally been offered to the British actor, Dirk Bogarde, a heartthrob who was the current king of British cinema.

Co-starring in the lead character roles were the scene-stealers of the geriatric set, Maurice Chevalier, as Honoré Lachaille, an aging *boulevardier* and Gaston's uncle. As Madame Alvarez, Hermione Gingold, in Eva's words, "ate up the scenery."

Eva was pleased to be reunited with the French Basque actor, Jacques Bergerac, cast as Sandomir, upon whom she'd had such a crush in the early 1950s. "He was in better form than ever," Eva said, "having survived a marriage to

After Audrey Hepburn turned down the role of *Gigi*, it went to the French actress **Leslie Caron**, who used it as the vehicle for her greatest stardom.

Eva desperately wanted to play Gigi, but the producers and directors decided that her Hungarian accent made it almost impossible for her to even be considered. They eventually relented and awarded her a supporting role instead.

Jacques Bergerac *(left)* famous for his marriage to Ginger Rogers, also had a supporting role in *Gigi.* In the photo above, he courts **Eva** in one of the film's subplots.

"He was absolutely adorable," Eva said. "Why is it that Basque men have such sex appeal?"

Ginger Rogers. He was still handsome, in great shape, and more appealingly virile than ever. Yummy, yummy, buy me some of that, Papa."

"Vincente went around the set with his tongue hanging out, panting for Louis, and I went about lusting for Jacques," Eva facetiously claimed.

"One day I lunched with Vincente, and I told him that I would have adored being cast as Gigi," Eva said.

"But Gigi is very, very French," Minnelli said. "With your Hungarian accent, Colette's *novella* would not have worked."

Minnelli told her that originally, the movie was to be entitled *The Parisians,* "but that seemed *déjà entendue.* We figured that Caron had been in too many movies like *Lili* and *Gaby* with cute Gallic nicknames. But *Gigi,* as a title, won out."

The film was a blockbuster, in spite of sometimes critical reviews. *Time Out New York* said it was "like eating a meal consisting of cheesecake. The cast tries to be more French than French, especially Chevalier who redeems himself in singing 'Thank Heaven for Little Girls.'"

TV Guide defined *Gigi* as "overbaked but enjoyable, a feast for the eyes, thanks to Cecil Beaton's sets and costumes. Ten minutes into the movie, you've resolved the plot and are left to wallow in the lovely *frou-frou."*

Even so, *Gigi* was a record breaker (at the time), winning nine Academy Award nominations.

In London, veteran actor John Gielgud saw the movie three times. He told his gay friends, "In one scene those trousers worn by Louis Jourdan were so tight that you could see that this well-hung gentleman possesses enough meat for the poor."

***

In 1959, Eva was "so very pleased, really happy" to be reunited with her lover, Glenn Ford, in a romantic comedy, *It Started With a Kiss."* Debbie Reynolds had the female lead, with Eva in third position, playing the glamorous "Marquesa Marion de la Rey."

"When I returned to Hollywood, Glenn Ford, my fickle lover, was waiting for me," Eva claimed. "Within one day, especially in one night, this handsome hunk was back in both my bed and my good graces. Of course, *dahlink*, I forgave him. Who could look into those adorable eyes of his and not forgive him for anything? If the worst thing he did was to send over that living doll, Bill Holden, to fuck me, how could I hold a grudge about that? I should have gotten down on bent nylon and thanked Glenn for the gift of love."

Debbie Reynolds, a close friend of Ford's, once noted that he was 'hot to trot," even though married to the fabulous dancer and actress, Eleanor Powell. "He couldn't resist looking at and patting a woman," Reynolds said. "Ford loved women, loved to look at them, play with them, touch them. I think he flirted with every woman he ever worked with. He always wanted to have his cake and eat it, too."

Parts of *It Started With a Kiss* would be shot in Spain. It was during the filming of this movie that Reynolds became one of Ford's lifelong friends.

At first, Reynolds seemed unaware that Eva and Ford were on again, off again lovers. "Glenn often spoke about the breakup of his marriage to Eleanor Powell," Reynolds recalled. She'd already experienced losing her own husband, Eddie Fisher, to Elizabeth Taylor .

Years later, Reynolds wrote, "And then, Glenn started making eyes at Eva." Actually he was making more than eyes. Reynolds also claimed that Eva had a boyfriend who would be arriving any minute, "and she wasn't really that interested in Glenn anyway."

"Debbie was wrong," Eva later said. "I was madly in love with Glenn. I would have dropped any of my casual *beaux* at the time for Glenn."

It was during the making of *It Started With a Kiss* that Reynolds realized she could do the best imitation of Zsa Zsa and Eva of any other entertainer.

"I found Zsa Zsa's accent fascinating," Reynolds wrote in a memoir. "There isn't much she won't say or ask."

Ford later said, "Debbie could do every *veddy,* every *zounding, funnee, dooo, izzat, zing, un-uzjo-wull, chuss, lakh, zink,* and *knooo."*

When Eva heard Reynolds impersonating her, she told Ford, "Debbie sounds more like Zsa Zsa."

Eva also shared her worldly wisdom with Reynolds. "*Dahlink*, pearls *muss alvays* fall between the bosoms. The skin *vill* make them *varm* and lustrous."

"When it came to men and lovemaking, Eva was very European, very open, very candid, and funny," Reynolds later wrote in a memoir.

"Glenn often didn't spend the night with me, but stayed out drinking with his favorite director, George Marshall," Eva said. "If that weren't bad enough, I think he was also falling in love with Debbie."

To make Ford jealous, Eva deliberately set out to date other beaux. At a cocktail party in Madrid, she met a handsome young Wall Street broker, Richard Brown. She later said, "Mama knows best. She told me the best way to get rid of an old lover is with a new lover."

Within two days, Brown had moved into her suite in the Spanish capital. Once he was installed, Eva rushed down the hall to the suite occupied by Reynolds. She grabbed the actress's arm. *"Dahlink,"* Eva exclaimed. "My new fiancé is here, and you must meet him."

She practically dragged Reynolds down the hallway and into her suite. Not finding Brown in her living room, she directed Reynolds into the bedroom and from there, pulled her into the bathroom. Brown was discovered sitting in a tub of water without bubbles.

"You can clearly see, *dahlink,* why I'm attracted to him," Eva said.

"That's rather obvious," Reynolds said.

After three weeks of filming in Spain, the cast and crew were flown back to the United States for the interior shots at the MGM lot. As Eva admitted, "My relationship with Glenn was in a state of total confusion. He told me he was still sharing a house with Eleanor Powell, although they didn't speak to each other. Their poor son, Peter, was acting as a go-between for the two different warring camps."

Powell filed for divorce on May 1, 1959, on Ford's forty-third birthday.

"I waited and waited, thinking a marriage proposal might come," Eva said. "But nothing happened. I feared that I might lose Glenn to Debbie when they signed to do another picture, *The Gazebo,* without me."

Debbie told me that Glenn often came by to discuss his failed marriages," Eva said, "their pain and frustration."

In her memoir, Reynolds wrote, "Glenn began to think perhaps he was in love with me." The problem was, she wasn't in love with him, although she did reveal that Ford later asked her to marry him.

"I didn't want to fall in love with anyone at the time," Reynolds said.

"At least Debbie got a marriage proposal out of Glenn," Eva said. "I didn't get that, but his love-making left me with some wonderful memories."

"When Glenn left me for good, I didn't cry over him like I had done when Ty deserted me," Eva said. "By the time *It Started With a Kiss* was released, I had already fallen in love with another man and had even gotten him to marry me."

***

When Eva had a long-delayed reunion with Susan Hayward, she told her friend, "My greatest dream would be to have both Bill Holden and Glenn in bed with me, making love to me all night."

"I've already had Bill, and what fun it was," Hayward said. "We co-starred together in *The Young and Willing (1943).* I was both young and willing. Unlike you, I also bedded Glenn's other best friend, Ronald Reagan."

Eva later wrote, "In my life, I have been the hunter and the hunted, and what depresses me is that in either role, I'm usually the one who gets hurt."

***

Whereas Eva was the most distant of Jolie's three daughters, Magda and Zsa Zsa had a long talk with their mother every other day, some of these conversations lasting for more than an hour.

Eva had not shown up for Jolie's wedding to a much younger man, Edmund de Szigethy, on March 3, 1957. For Jolie, he was husband number three.

He was a war refugee, originally from Transylvania "where Dracula comes from."

In her memoir, Jolie claimed, "Edmund escaped from Eastern Europe after all his lands and property had been confiscated by the communists. He fled to the West with only two suits, wearing one on top of the other. When I first met him, he had $27 left, of which he spent $25 on roses for me."

Eva was not pleased, having warned Jolie—"at your age, *dahlink*, you should have married for money."

In Palm Springs society, where Jolie had a home, as did each of her daughters, she wanted friends to refer to her new husband as a count. "That will make me a countess, like Magda," Jolie proclaimed.

At her wedding, Jolie had managed to "take at least twenty years off my face," having suffered through her fifth "surgical renaissance." She'd advised Eva, along with Magda and Zsa Zsa, to get a face lift—as many as needed. "If a woman doesn't have a good nose, a good chin, then for God's sake, have once carved by one of the beauty butchers."

Magda, too, had had "everything lifted, including those little wrinkles under the eyes."

When Eva finally came to Palm Springs to greet the newlyweds, in-

Jolie *(right figure in the quartet above)*, after a series of face-lifts, found additional rejuvenation when she married a much younger man, **Edmund de Szigethy**. At their wedding, on March 3, 1957, Jolie was hailed by society columnists as "The Bride of the Year."

After the wedding, **Zsa Zsa** *(left)* and **Magda** *(center)* kissed the groom with Jolie's "reconfigured" face looking on approvingly.

Jolie later said, "I would die without my Fairy Prince." She obviously didn't mean it *that* way.

cluding her latest stepfather, she, too, had had everything lifted. She appeared at the desert resort at a gala for Vincente Minnelli. Allene Arthur, society editor of *The Palm Springs Desert Sun,* later wrote: "I inspected Eva's face up close. It was dazzling. She looked no more than a day over thirty."

Unlike Eva, Magda, and Jolie, Zsa Zsa became testy whenever the subject of cosmetic surgery came up. She told Eva that she wanted to publicize her offer of $10,000 to anyone who had definite proof that she'd had a face-lift. "I'm a timeless wonder*, dahlink,*" Zsa Zsa claimed.

In Palm Springs, Eva introduced Jolie to her young stockbroker, *"Nuci,* meet the man who is on the way to becoming *husband number four* for me. Richard Brown."

Jolie later wrote that she found Brown "dark and handsome." Privately, she told her society friends in Palm Springs, "I have been assured that he is very, very, sexy, just like my Edmund."

In the weeks leading up to her marriage to Brown, Eva found herself on the front pages of newspapers that stretched from the New York Islands to the San Francisco Bay.

On April 10, 1959, police in New York found the body of a beautiful model, Venita Ratcliffe. Wrapped in a red silk robe, she was discovered on her bed, having committed suicide by swallowing a bottle of sleeping pills.

A note was discovered near her body: "Dick, my love, I understand now that I would only continue to be a pest in your life. But, Dick, I love you more than life itself. Without you, there is no meaning for me, no reason to go on living."

Her phone records revealed that she had called Brown only an hour before killing herself.

Venita was only twenty six years old, Brown thirty-seven. His love letters to her were also found. He called her "Mommie," and she referred to him as "Daddie."

The suicide launched a month-long feeding frenzy within the tabloids.

A headline in *The New York Post* proclaimed—*EVA GABOR LOVE PIRATE, JILTED MODEL TAKES HER LIFE.* It became known as "The Case of the Heartbroken Model." In San Francisco, a headline described Ratcliffe and Brown as *STAR-CROSSED LOVERS.*

In Hollywood, Eva issued a statement to the press. "I am very, very sorry that this beautiful girl took her life. But I am only an innocent bystander in all of this. The romance between Richard and me began long after he left Venita."

Louella Parsons warned the publicity department at MGM to "defuse this bomb as soon as possible." MGM was about to release *It Started With a Kiss,* co-starring Eva with Glenn Ford and Debbie Reynolds.

"Before we were married," Eva told the press in Hollywood, "a model was in love with him, and she could not face the fact that Richard and I were getting married. Stupidly, she ended her life and people were then talking and all the newspapers were saying that I was a home wrecker, a barracuda, taking every man away from their wives. This is so unfair, so untrue."

The Love Pirate story just wouldn't go away. In desperation, Eva called the Associated Press. "I do not go around taking anyone's man. I am much too spoiled for one thing, and there are so many attractive men around these days. I am not a love pirate. Remember, if a man is truly in love, the most beautiful woman in the world couldn't take him away. Maybe for a few days, but not forever."

After the headlines died down, Eva in Las Vegas went ahead anyway and married Brown. She did not invite the other Gabors. Red Buttons was the best man, and his wife, Helayne, matron of honor.

Jolie later claimed that Eva was not a good daughter during her marriage to Brown. "Often, both of them were in New York and didn't even call me. Brown turned Eva against her family. Even when Eva and Brown were in Palm Springs, and I was spending the winter there, they never came by to visit."

Like her mother, **Eva**, too, thought she'd found the man of her dreams when she wed **Richard Brown**. But from the beginning, the marriage provoked lurid headlines when a model, Venita Ratcliffe, committed suicide.

Ratcliffe had been deserted by Brown, who had subsequently taken up with Eva.

In the aftermath of her death, the youngest of the Gabor siblings endured her worst headlines, some defining her as a home wrecker, "a shark who steals other women's men," and "a love pirate."

Eva told her longtime assistant, Caryl Sosa Belanger, that Brown was "the best husband I've ever had." Belanger thought Eva was much in love with the dashing young man.

After years of rocky marriages and romances, Eva proclaimed, "At long last I've found the man of my dreams."

***

In Miami, Eva stayed with Brown in the exclusive North Bay Village Racquet Club. In its golden heyday, the club had attracted the likes of Woolworth heiress Barbara Hutton and silent screen vamp Gloria Swanson.

The club had always been known for its security and had never experienced a robbery until the first week of January, 1964.

Downstairs, on January 4 of that year, Eva had grown bored with a party that she dismissed as "insurance salesmen from the Middle West with their wives in feedsack dresses." She decided to return to her suite with Brown for a supper of caviar and champagne.

Brown was pulling off his shirt as he came into the bedroom. As he was undressing, he suddenly noticed "a blonde Viking kind of man emerging from the closet with a revolver pointed at my head." A red bandana obscured his face.

"Get the fuck out of here," Brown said to the burglar. "Do you know who we are?"

It was precisely because the bandit knew that he was in Eva Gabor's suite that he was there in the first place. He'd read about all the jewelry she wore.

From the living room came the sounds of Eva's screams. In spite of the gun pointed at him, Brown rushed into the living room to confront another tall, burly man who held Eva in his grip. As he did, Brown tripped and fell over the leg of a piece of furniture. The booted foot of the blonde landed in his stomach.

"Get the fuck up, you dumb son of a bitch," the blonde demanded.

As Brown stood up, he noticed that Eva had been pistol whipped; her face was bloody.

"They're going to kill us," Eva shouted at Brown, who was powerless to help her. The blonde put his revolver into Brown's mouth, pointing it upward toward his brain.

"Make a false move, and I'll blow your brains out," the blonde threatened. "The jewelry! Where does the cunt keep it?"

Eva answered for her husband. "It's locked up in the hotel's safe downstairs. There's nothing here."

As both of them were held at gunpoint, Eva and Brown stood by as the blonde tore apart their suite, searching every drawer. He located her jewel box, but it contained only a valuable wrist watch and a tangle of pearls which were actually fake, a gift from Jolie's shop in Manhattan.

"Where in the fuck are the diamonds?" the blonde demanded to know.

"I told you," Eva said. "In the safe downstairs. You'll have to rob it."

The darker man ordered Brown to get dressed and go downstairs and bring the jewelry back to the suite. "I've got a pocket knife," he said. "If you tip off security, I'll carve up the face of your bitch."

Obeying his orders, Brown dressed quickly and descended into the lobby, where he removed the jewelry. Eva had not traveled with a lot of her gems. The most valuable item was a twenty-carat diamond ring.

Back in the suite, Brown handed the gems to the blonde. When he saw how small the stash was, he kicked Brown in the groin. Bunched up in pain, Brown lay in agony on the carpet. The blonde did not believe he'd brought back "all those diamonds."

He stood over Brown. "You asshole, he shouted at him. "Listen, pretty boy, I'm tempted to plow your asshole. Burst that rosebud and leave it raw and bleeding."

The phone rang and it went unanswered. Fearing that Brown had tipped off security, both men tied Eva and Brown up, putting tape over their mouths. An hour later, a maid discovered and untied them.

Eva rushed down to the lobby, screaming, "Call the police! We were robbed!" Her face was still covered with blood.

An ambulance was called, and, with its red dome flashing, Eva was rushed to the Francis Hospital in Miami. Brown stayed by her side. Fortunately, her injuries were only superficial, but she stayed for two days in the hospital, her doctor fearing that she might have suffered a concussion.

Outside the hospital, after her release, she told reporters, "I don't want to see another diamond as long as I live. I thought those men were going to kill Dick and me."

The burglars were later caught and arrested, turning out to be Jack Murphy (known as "Murph the Surf") and Alan Dale Kuhn, the two most notorious jewel thieves in America. The pair had previously stolen the famous Star of India sapphire. They were arrested, tried, convicted, and sentenced to jail terms.

In Hollywood, Zsa Zsa commented on Eva's robbery. "*[It's]* the curse of being a Gabor, but we'll continue to wear our diamonds. After, all, *dahlinks*, it is our trademark."

***

[Alas, Eva's marriage to Brown did not last, even though it was successful in the beginning.

During its eleven-year run, Eva was most enthusiastic at the marriage's debut. She praised Brown in the press, defining him as "my anchor—both lover and best friend. I am completely dependent on him. When he flies away to New York on business, my heart dies. I don't even leave the house unless I have to. At home, I don't put on a gown to go out with him without first getting his approval. He is a real *man."*

When Brown's career as a Wall Street stockbroker began to wane, Eva used her new clout at CBS—a result of the success of her hit TV series, Green Acres, *to get Brown a position as an executive producer at the studio.*

But it was her success—not his—that afforded them the good life. She became the president of an interior decorating business and chairwoman of the board of a wig manufacturing company. They lived in a beautiful mansion in Beverly Hills filled with valuable paintings and antiques, a real showplace. She and Brown employed four servants and a male secretary, driving around Hol-

lywood in two matching Rolls-Royces.

As the years stretched on, Eva learned that her errant husband was having affairs with other women. This time she turned to Jolie for comfort and advice. Her mother told her, "Women are stupid when they throw out their man for having a little sex on the side with another woman. Personally, I don't cheat on Edmund, but only because no man asks me to."

During the course of her marriage to him, Eva had remained faithful to Brown. She never had sex with another man, except for one night when she was raped. (Details to be revealed later.)

To her chagrin, however, she discovered that in lieu of a random extra-marital affair, Brown had conducted a prolonged sexual tryst with his secretary at CBS. "This was no longer a fling or a passing fancy, but a long, drawn-out affair," Eva claimed. "I think he loved her. I could not tolerate this."

In 1972, she filed for divorce. Mimicking a song from the musical, South Pacific, *she claimed, "I'm going to wash that man right out of my hair."*

Promising to be faithful in the future, Brown vowed to break off his affair. He begged to come home again.

"It's over, Dick," she told him. "Kaput!"

Eva lost little time mourning the loss of Brown. She set out immediately to find a new lover who was husband material. "After all, dahlink, *I'm not as dewy fresh as I used to be, although I still look gorgeous, of course."]*

***

Zsa Zsa still missed Rubirosa and almost nightly longed for him to hold her in his arms again. To her close friends, such as Helen Greco Jones, she confided that she spent many a lonely night wandering around her Bel Air manse, dreaming about her beloved Rubi. "I miss him terribly," she told Jones. "I miss his love-making. He is without equal."

Jones often spent the night at her house, listening to Zsa Zsa's lament about Rubi and her complaints about the constant demands made on her "in my career of just being Zsa Zsa."

She cited the pressure of always having to appear filled with gaiety and looking glamorous before photographers; the constant rehearsing, the long sessions with hairdressers and makeup people—and just polishing my diamonds."

One rainy night in Bel Air—"Why is it always a rainy night?" she asked—a call came in from Paris. Jones picked up the receiver to hear Rubi's voice on the other end. He wanted to speak to Zsa Zsa. Only that night at dinner, Zsa Zsa had asked Jones, "Where will I ever find a man who loves me as much as Rubi does?"

580

As she went to the phone, she whispered to Jones. "Rubi is thinking of me tonight the way I was dreaming about him."

But a very different Rubi confronted her on the phone. He was not so romantic, but rather business-like. "*Ma chérie,* I want you to be the first to know," he said. "I don't want you to have to read it in the newspapers tomorrow. Although in my heart, I still love you, I'm getting married tomorrow to a young model, Odile Rodin. She loves me very much and is willing to give up her career for me."

"You once asked me to give up my career," Zsa Zsa said. "Perhaps if I had, you would still be mine."

"Perhaps," he said. "But in romance, one should never look back to what might have been."

"Oh, *dahlink*, what can I say, but to wish you and your teenage maiden all the happiness in the world," she said. She'd already read about his romance with Rodin in the gossip columns. She felt she was about to burst into tears, and she wanted to get off the phone. She didn't want him to hear her crying. "I will always love you." Then she put down the phone and ran sobbing to her bedroom.

Rubi had met the 17-year-old Odile Rodin in Paris in 1956 when the aspiring actress had graced the cover of *Paris Match.* "I fell in love with her the first time I saw her," Rubi later confessed. "There was a 31-year difference in our ages, but it didn't matter. She was so young, so fresh, so beautiful, and there was a certain mystery about her."

As Rubi expressed a growing interest in Rodin, her mother had been horrified. She warned her daughter that "this Rubirosa is a dangerous man."

Rodin didn't listen. She fell in love with the man who was old enough to be her father.

Kahil Heche, a close friend of Rubi, claimed, "He played Pygmalion to his young bride's Galatea when they got married in October of 1956. He wanted her to dress very conservatively, more like Grace Kelly, the opposite of Zsa Zsa. She got around his dress code by wearing no underwear."

***

At this point in her life, Zsa Zsa began to commit a number of irrational acts, a habit that would continue for decades and in time would land her in jail. Some of her barbs at fellow actresses would lead to libel suits, such as the one threatened (and settled out of court) by Corinne Calvet.

Zsa Zsa feuded with columnist Earl Wilson. She spread the story that he had been broke in Paris, and she gained permission from Rubirosa to feed and house him at his townhouse. Actually, Wilson and his family had rented a suite at the

Between marriages, Zsa Zsa sometimes dated the aging actor **Franchot Tone**, the former husband of Joan Crawford.

"But I dumped him one night when he did not defend my honor. He let a man at a nearby table get away with claiming that I was older than Marlene Dietrich."

No one, *dahlink*, is older than Dietrich. Not even God."

Ritz, and were far from destitute.

One night in Beverly Hills, publicist Warren Cowan invited Zsa Zsa to dine at Prince Mike Romanoff's Restaurant. Wilson, who was seated at a nearby table, walked over and confronted Zsa Zsa "about the lies you've been spreading."

"Right in front of Cowan, Zsa Zsa claimed that what she had been telling was absolutely true," Wilson said. "She sat there on her fat ass with her big lie. On that trip to Paris, I never saw her or Rubirosa."

Two weeks later at the Stork Club in Manhattan, Zsa Zsa was once again dating actor Franchot Tone, the ex-husband of Joan Crawford. She often resumed her ongoing affair with him "between marriages."

At a nearby table, a drunken detective in a loud voice could be heard making unflattering remarks about her. "She's older than Marlene Dietrich, and the Kraut is older than sin," the detective charged. "She's had too much goulash and is fat as a Hungarian goose. Not only that, but she's a slut."

Zsa Zsa burst into a rage, demanding that a drunken Tone get up "and defend my honor."

"Darling, I see no point," Tone told her. "Someone on the staff will kick him out. Besides, he's twice my size."

She picked up an open bottle of champagne from an ice bucket on their table and poured it over Tone's head, drenching his hair and his tuxedo.

It was his last date with her.

***

The 1950s were coming to an end as Zsa Zsa made several attempts to revive a stalled movie career. "On the big screen, the pickings were lean, and I decided I'd do better on television. But a few things turned up for me in movies."

One bizarre offer involved her starring role in *Country Music Holiday (1958),* playing herself—"I do Zsa Zsa better than anyone, even Debbie Reynolds."

The 80-minute quickie, directed by Alvin Ganzer, was a Paramount release starring "gangsters, prizefighters such as Rocky Graziano, and rockabilly tunes." Graziano later told a reporter, "I signed on only because I heard I might get to fuck Zsa Zsa. People said she put out. But she snubbed me."

Inspired by the rise of Elvis Presley, the plot, such as it was, concerned a hillbilly singer's rise to fame. Felrin Husky, cast as "Verne Brand," plays an ex-G.I. from Tennessee with a good singing voice. The movie also starred June Carter before she married Johnny Cash.

Critics labeled *Country Music Holiday* as a "curio," wondering what Zsa Zsa was doing in it, and suggesting that Jayne Mansfield would have been a better choice.

***

One night at her Bel Air manse, a call came in from Orson Welles, asking Zsa Zsa if she would appear in a cameo in his new drama. *[It was later entitled* Touch of Evil, *a crime thriller released in 1958.]* She had always wanted to work with the former boy genius, and he told her he was hoping this offbeat film would "put me back on the top again in Hollywood."

Unexpectedly one day, **Zsa Zsa** *(left)* announced to friends, *"Dahlinks*, I'm starring in a hillbilly musical. You know, *dahlinks*, redneck bubbas."

In *Country Music Holiday*, an oddity for her, she was cast as herself opposite **Rocky Graziano** *(seated)*, one of the greatest knockout artists in boxing history, and character actor **Jesse White** *(standing)*.

Graziano said he signed to do the picture "only because I was hoping to give Zsa Zsa a knock-out punch, if you get my drift."

He'd written the screen play, and was also going to star in and direct the film. Its plot centered around the investigation by an American narcotics detective in the small border town of Los Robles. It evolved into one of the last *films noir* of a cinematic movement *[motivated by the European existentialists]* that had burst onto Hollywood's movie making scene in the 1940s.

Zsa Zsa's brief appearance was as the impresario of a strip club. "Do I have to show the money-maker?" Zsa Zsa asked facetiously.

"You'll be fully clothed," Welles answered.

Her appearance would be only a two-minute segment at the beginning of the movie, which otherwise starred Charlton Heston and Janet Leigh.

Welles came by Zsa Zsa's mansion the following night to discuss her brief appearance in his upcoming film. She was particularly concerned with her wardrobe.

Since his marriage to Rita Hayworth, Welles was no longer as handsome as he once had been, but she found him charming and persuasive. She later admitted to friends that, "I entertained the boy genius in my bedroom later that evening. He was an ardent lover, but a bit too heavy. Naturally, in his condition, he preferred the woman on top." At the time, Welles was only forty-one, but looked much older.

Later, friends of Zsa Zsa's challenged her choice of Welles as a lover. Pamela Mason asked her, "How could you sleep with that pile of whale blubber?"

Zsa Zsa defended her choice of lover for the night by insisting that Welles in the flesh looked far better than his appearances on the screen.

Days after she had completed the filming associated with her involvement in the movie, Zsa Zsa was shocked to hear that Marlene Dietrich, almost at the last minute, had agreed to don a wig discarded by Elizabeth Taylor and interpret the role of "Tanya," a tarot card reader and madam of the local whorehouse. After consulting the tarot cards, she tells the character played by Welles (Captain Hank Quinlan), "Your future's all used up." *[In the film, it is Dietrich, as Tanya, who addresses Welles' grotesquely dissipated character with the line, "You're a mess, honey."]*

"The picture was doomed from the beginning," Zsa Zsa later recalled. "Orson told me he was not allowed any involvement with the final cut and it was badly edited. I was very angry that he did not offer me the role of Tanya. It was a far better cameo than mine. Dietrich stole the show."

Cast as Tanya in *Touch of Evil*, **Marlene Dietrich** had only a small role in this cult classic and *film noir*, but the way she handled her part propelled it into one of the most enduring screen characterizations in the history of film.

On the left is **Orson Welles**, who had himself made up to look as debauched and grotesque as possible.

Zsa Zsa also noted that her photograph was not included on movie posters distributed throughout America. "But because I was so popular in Europe, the studio ran my picture in the European publicity along with photos of the rest of the cast."

When it was released, *Touch of Evil* was viewed as a B-picture running as half of a double-bill. The other half consisted of Hedy Lamarr's A-list picture, *The Female Animal,* her swan song to Hollywood.

In time, a re-edited version of *Touch of Evil* was re-released. It developed a cult following around the world.

[The bitter end of whatever traces of aimiable charity might have existed between Dietrich and Zsa Zsa occurred in Cannes in 1964 when Zsa Zsa attended a

performance of Dietrich's one-woman show. In the middle of her act, Zsa Zsa's personal photographer stood up from a position adjacent to Zsa Zsa and, with flash bulb popping, snapped a picture of Dietrich in the middle of her show and against house rules. The diva stopped her show and shouted at security to remove the photographer from the theater, and to confiscate his camera.

Zsa Zsa rose to her feet. "So he will give you the film, dahlink?" she shouted, addressing Dietrich on the stage but also playing to the audience. "Anyway, he couldn't sell your picture for a penny."

After that hot night in Cannes on the Côte d'Azur, Zsa Zsa's relationship with Dietrich forever after remained north of the Arctic Circle.]

***

Zsa Zsa faced ridicule in the press when she signed for one of her last movies in the 1950s, *Queen of Outer Space*. Without seeing the film, most critics thought she had been cast as a sci-fi queen in the film's title role.

[Queen Ylana (as interpreted by Laurie Mitchell) was a shapely looking but perpetually masked woman who had banished all men from her planet. The reason she was masked was because her face, as the plot revealed, had been disfigured by radiation.]

Zsa Zsa, cast as Talleah, a scientist, longs for the love of men and wants to remove the evil queen from her throne. Zsa Zsa's most famous line from the movie, "I hate *that* queen," brought howls from her gay fans in the audience."

Cast as her leading man, a Californian, Eric Fleming, played astronaut Captain Patterson. Eva and Zsa Zsa had become known for often seducing their leading men. A former U.S. Navy veteran

"My friends mocked me when I played a scientist in a science fiction film called *Queen of Outer Space*," **Zsa Zsa** said.

"I did it to remain a fixture in the movies, and it was the only script offered to me at the time."

"Of course, *dahlink*, I did not expect an Oscar for my role. But my fans loved it, and as it happened, it evolved into high camp for later generations."

"Most people thought that I, Zsa Zsa, interpreted the role of the Queen of Outer Space. But **Laurie Mitchell** played that role, disguised throughout most of the filming with a mask, supposedly because her face had been disfigured by radiation."

"I, of course, *dahlink,* would never play such a role."

"In real life, **Eric Fleming**, the film's male star, actually had his face disfigured during the War," Zsa Zsa said, "but the beauty butchers gave him a new one."

"I found him appealing, and I left the key under the doormat, so to speak, but he never came knocking. I thought his death was tragic."

from World War II, and standing 6 feet, 4 inches, he and Zsa Zsa had no chemistry either on or off the screen. He'd received extensive facial plastic surgeries following injuries to his face during the war.

Right after the completion of the film, he signed to star with Clint Eastwood in the top-rated TV Western series, *Rawhide,* that ran from 1959 to 1966.

"I think Eric might have been gay," Zsa Zsa asserted to Pamela Mason. "I looked gorgeous when I made the film, and he never even made a pass at me. He seemed more entranced with Eastwood on *Rawhide* than with me."

The film's producer, Walter Wanger, had gone to prison for shooting the actors' agent Jennings Lang in the groin for having an affair with his wife, Joan Bennett. After that scandal, and after his release from prison, Wanger could find work only at Allied Artists, the outfit that had purchased Ben Hecht's sci-fi script. It was Wanger who talked with Zsa Zsa about starring in it.

For such a low-budget quickie, the director, Edwards Bernds, famed for his movies with The Three Stooges and with The Bowery Boys, secured Edith Head to design Zsa Zsa's wardrobe, at the cost of $15,000 per outfit.

In later years, Zsa Zsa said, "I had the last laugh. A lot of people made fun of me for starring in science fiction. But *Queen of Outer Space* later became a classic."

In September of 1966, at the end of his *Rawhide* series, Zsa Zsa over her morning coffee was shocked to read about what had happened to Eric Fleming. He had signed for a role in *High Jungle* (1966), an MGM action/adventure film shot in the rain forests of Peru. During the final stages of shooting, his dugout canoe overturned in the rapids of the Huallaga River, and the actor was swept to his death by the strong currents.

***

Zsa Zsa's last major movie role of the 1950s came when she was signed by the director Rudolph Maté for the filming of *For the First Time,* released in 1959 as Mario Lanza's last and final movie. The film told the sentimental story of an operatic tenor, Tony Costa (as interpreted by Lanza), who falls in love for the first time with a young German woman (played by Johana von Koczian) who is deaf. With her friend Kurt Kasznar, Zsa Zsa led the supporting cast. MGM released the film in the dying days of 1959.

Even before there was any discussion about Zsa Zsa appearing in a movie with Lanza, the singer called her late one night at her home in Bel Air. Because he was such a world-famous figure, she took the call out of curiosity.

As she told Pamela Mason the following morning, his phone call shocked her. "Basically, he claimed that if I let him come over, he'd give me the fuck of my life," Zsa Zsa revealed. "He said he'd do that even though he was aware that I'd been royally screwed by Porfirio Rubirosa."

"Size is not everything," Lanza told her. "It's important that a man has the stamina of a bull."

To illustrate, he revealed details to her about the time he was stationed at the Texas Air Base in Marfa, Texas. This was the little Texas town where Elizabeth Taylor, Rock Hudson, and James Dean had filmed *Giant (1956).*

"My buddies made a bet with me that I could not have sex with a dozen women," Lanza confided to Zsa Zsa. "In this local garage, they lined up twelve Mexican prostitutes for me in a circle. While they were cheering me on, I satisfied every one of the *putas*, bringing each of them to climax."

"That is a very impressive record, but, even so, I must refuse your gracious offer," Zsa Zsa told Lanza by phone.

Before ringing off, he said, "Judy Garland went wild over me. If given a chance, I could transport you to heaven. It's your loss, lady."

Baffled and disturbed by the call, Zsa Zsa phoned Kathryn Grayson the next day. She knew that the singer had appeared with Lanza in pictures, beginning with *That Midnight Kiss* back in 1949.

Grayson wasn't at all surprised by Lanza's outrageous request. "The first day on the set, he

An overweight **Mario Lanza** signed to co-star with Zsa Zsa in what would be his last film, *For the First Time,* shot in Rome.

Lanza, as Zsa Zsa already knew, had a gargantuan appetite for food and sex, in that order.

told me, 'You've got to be more sexy. Push up to me. Let me feel your pussy next to my big cock.' When he made his first movie with me, he kept ramming his tongue down my throat. It was the crudest thing I'd ever been exposed to. I didn't welcome his advances, but he kept on Frenching me until I became disgusted."

"He kept it up the next day and the day after," Grayson said. "I went to Helen Rose, my cosume designer, because I wanted to retaliate. I had her sew brass knuckles into all my costumes. When Mario tried to French me again, I fisted him right in the balls—and he's got a big pair of them. He squealed like a pig and never tried to kiss me like that again. He accused me of trying to make a *castrato* out of him."

Before she flew to Rome for the film, Zsa Zsa made a final call to Hedda Hopper, who knew Lanza. The columnist delivered a harsh judgment: "Mario recognizes no authority. He has no discipline. In his behavior, there are no frontiers, except his own gigantic appetite for food, drink,…and sex, of course."

When she first faced reporters at the Teatro dell'Opera (The Opera House) in Rome, Zsa Zsa was asked, "I hear that Mr. Lanza uses dirty language with women. Is that true?"

"I've never heard it," she claimed, obviously shielding him from unfavorable publicity.

On Zsa Zsa's third night in Rome, Lanza invited her for dinner at his rented villa, a building once occupied by Benito Mussolini.

"I met Betty Hicks, Mario's wife, along with his four children, three of whom would die tragically and far too young. I wandered about, trying not to bump into Mussolini's marble furniture."

On the first day of their shoot together, **Zsa Zsa** *(left)* hauled out a bottle of champagne to celebrate with **Lanza**, not knowing he was nearing the end of his life.

She always asserted that he was murdered.

Two nights later, she invited Lanza to dine privately with her at her hotel suite. "During the course of the dinner, I noticed he had a constant problem in consuming far too much wine and pasta."

"Don't you ever worry about being unfaithful to your wife?" Zsa Zsa asked.

"Hell, no! The more I lay other women, the better I am as a husband."

"After dinner," as she'd later confide to Pamela Mason in Hollywood, "the inevitable happened. I gave in to him. He overcame my resistance, which wasn't all that strong to begin with. He was the most persistent suitor I'd ever had. He just wouldn't take no for an answer."

Then she delivered a shocking revelation. "Like the movie title, it was my first time," she told Pamela. "Before making love to me, he sang 'Be My Love' to my vagina."

The next day on the set, Rudolph Maté, the director, asked Zsa Zsa to do him a favor in association with Lanza's big musical numbers within the film. *[They included "Vesti la Giubbia" from* Pagliacci, *and the death scene from* Otello.] "He is very neurotic," Maté asserted. "He needs constant praise. Please keep flattering him. After each number, go up to him and assure him about how wonderful he is."

Once, after one of his arias was filmed, he told Zsa Zsa, "It's all sex when I'm singing. That's me. It comes right out of my balls."

In another incident, she dared to visit him in his dressing room. "He was opening mail from his starstruck fans," Zsa Zsa recalled. "He was receiving very suggestive letters from women all over the world. Many pictures were of young girls in very pornographic poses. Many of these women wrote about what they wanted Mario to do to them."

At the end of filming for the movie, she told reporters, "Mario has a smile as big as his voice. He is absolutely charming, a pleasure to work with. However, he has the habits of a tiger cub. Impossible to housebreak." She'd stolen those lines about Lanza from Hedda Hopper.

***

After Zsa Zsa had flown back to Hollywood, she learned that Lanza, still in Rome, was facing his final curtain.

Lucky Luciano, a Sicilian-born American mobster, was boss of the Genovese crime syndicate, which controlled the nation's heroin traffic.

In Rome, after he was deported from the United States, he visited Lanza. The singer hated the mob and didn't want to make any deal with the crime boss, who had proposed that Lanza appear in Naples and sing for free at a big charity event he had organized.

In retaliation, the gangster at first sent a threat to Lanza that he was going to order the kidnapping of his children. When Lanza still didn't acquiesce to his wishes, Luciano reportedly ordered the singer's murder.

On October 7, 1959, Lanza was rushed to the Valle Giulia Clinic in Rome. There were rumors he'd suffered a heart attack. Lanza's chauffeur accompanied him to the hospital, and slept there in an adjoining room. Late that afternoon, the nurse on duty told the chauffeur she was sending in a substitute nurse because she felt ill. Subsequently, a red-haired woman in a nurse's uniform came into Lanza's private room to administer an intravenous feeding.

Two hours later, when the chauffeur went to check on Lanza, he found his boss dead. The intravenous needle was still plugged into his arm, but there was no fluid in the jar. Only bubbles were entering Lanza's bloodstream. He was dead.

Both Grayson and Zsa Zsa concluded from what they'd heard that Lanza had been murdered.

"I was shattered by his death," Zsa Zsa later wrote. "He was outrageous when I first met him. I suspect that Enrico Caruso was equally outrageous, if not more so. I'm sure Leonardo da Vinci was not a piece of cake. Great men, I'm convinced, behave extravagantly. I came to adore Mario for his extravagances."

Headlines screamed the death of Mario Lanza, at 38 years old, hailing him as "the world's most famous tenor."

***

After Rubirosa married his teenage bride, Odile Rodin, in Paris, Zsa Zsa thought she'd seen and heard the last of him, except for what she continued to read in the gossip columns.

But two months after his marriage, she received a letter from Rubi, which was odd in itself, since, in the past, he had always telephoned her.

"Ma chérie,
For the sake of our wonderful times gone by—recall the happy memories.
I can't think of them as they still make me sad and blue. Please grant me a
favor. My President's son and my dearest friend, Ramfis Trujillo, is study-
ing in Kansas. He wants to visit Hollywood to meet American film stars.
Please, when he comes, introduce him to movie society.
Love, Rubi.

She had first met Ramfis at Manhattan's Colony Restaurant during her torrid affair with Rubirosa, when one Dominican playboy, Rubi, had introduced her to the other leading playboy of the Caribbean. Ramfis had once been Rubi's brother-in-law during Rubi's marriage to his sister, Flor de Oro, daughter of Generalíssimo Rafael Trujillo, the autocratic ruler of the Dominican Republic.

Ramfis' formal name was Rafael Trujillo, Jr., but his friends and the international press called him Ramfis as inspired by the name of the high priest in Verdi's opera, *Aïda*. His closest friends, including Rubi, nicknamed him "Ram."

When Ramfis telephoned her, they agreed to meet not in Hollywood, but in the city of New Orleans, where she was to make a personal appearance at Mardi Gras. He would sail in for the event aboard his yacht.

Ramfis Trujillo, the son of Rafael Trujillo, Dictator of the Dominican Republic, modeled his life on the way Rubirosa led his.

In pursuit of Hollywood movie stars like Zsa Zsa and Kim Novak, he was a *debauché*, recklessly spending money on extravagant gifts for the current lady of his choice.

Known for wild variations in his behavior and moods, some of which led to the whimsical execution of some of his countrymen, he was later commited to a sanatorium in Belgium for electroshock therapy

The *Angelita* was the largest yacht in the world, having once been owned by the super-rich Mrs. Joseph E. Davies, wife of the former U.S. ambassador to Russia.

Outfitted in Nassau, the luxurious yacht was a virtual floating palace.

At the time Zsa Zsa reunited with Ramfis, he was twelve years her junior, but basically they looked the same age.

When he had been four years old, his father, the Generalíssimo, had made him a general in the Dominican Air Force. At the U.S. Army General Staff College in Fort Leavenworth, Texas, Ramfis had operated with the protection and status of a lieutenant colonel.

Zsa Zsa flew to New Orleans where Ramfis had arranged for a limousine to pick her up at the airport and deliver her directly to his yacht, anchored in the harbor.

She interpreted her arrival aboard Ramfis' yacht as the most memorable of her life. "I was a vision in white, even my wide-brimmed white hat and white mink. It was a night of champagne and caviar. I was fascinated by Ramfis, his beauty, his mammoth yacht, his entourage of wealthy friends bowing before me, his gorgeous male servants in their tailored tuxedos. At one point, I was surrounded by six of them, each of whom looked like he'd been fathered by Rubirosa."

Ramfis Trujillo is seen here on a date with **Zsa Zsa**.

"Kim [Novak] and I shared him, *dahlink*," Zsa Zsa claimed.

"I felt I was betraying Rubi, his best friend, by sleeping with Ramfis, but what the hell? We can't remain virgins forever."

That night in New Orleans during her reunion with Ramfis, he was an impressive attraction in his jacket laden with tassels and gold braid, covering a broad chest that led to a slender waist. Silver buttons and "colored ribbons of honor" also added to the jacket's allure. His long, tall legs tapered off to a pair of spit-polished cavalry boots.

"Before we went out that night, I luxuriated in

my suite furnished in Louis Quinze, with a pink marble bathroom," she said. "I poured almost a bottle of Chanel No. 5 into the pink marble bathtub and lounged in the water."

"After a night of dancing at the Roosevelt Hotel's Blue Room in New Orleans, Ramfis brought me back to his yacht. "It was like a romance novel taking place in the rosy dawn of a Southern morning. He held me in his arms and kissed me passionately. But he was more Ashley Wilkes than Rhett Butler. He turned down my invitation to spend the early morning hours in my suite, making love to me."

Zsa Zsa became lost in Ramfis' world, which she characterized as belonging to medieval times, with Ramfis her heroic prince charming, and she his beautiful princess. "This glorious man and I were not of the 20th Century, but belonged to the Age of Chivalry. Think one of those Robert Taylor movies in the '50s—*Ivanhoe*, which he made with George, or *Knight of the Round Table* and especially *Quentin Durward.*"

The next day, Ramfis stood by as Mayor Chet Morrison presented Zsa Zsa with the key to the city. That evening, she was crowned Queen of the Mardi Gras at the Hermes Carnival Ball, the climax of the riotous annual celebration.

The highlight of the ball was preceded by the blare of trumpets. Ramfis, the mayor, and the Grand Marshal appeared carrying a mammoth bouquet of rainbow-hued orchids for Zsa Zsa.

She accepted it as photographers snapped her in her flaming red chiffon designer gown, the most dazzling sold at Martha's along Palm Beach's Worth Avenue. "I was bathed in pink spots," she recalled. "It was a glorious night. No man ever put me on a throne like Jolie wanted for me, but I sat there on a *faux* throne and ruled the night."

After New Orleans, Ramfis flew Zsa Zsa in his private jet back to Los Angeles. Along the way, they were entertained by his personal guitarist, Humberto Diaz. Along for the ride was Ramfis' beloved German shepherd, his most faithful companion, since the women in his life came and went.

"Back in Hollywood, I learned things about Ramfis that wouldn't make him a good prospect for marriage," Zsa Zsa said. "I heard he was already married to Octavia Ricart, who bore him six children."

She had also heard that Ramfis was not the biological son of Rafael Trujillo, but that his father had been Rafael Domincis, a light-skinned Cuban, which explained why Ramfis's physical features were more Caucasian than those of the *Generalíssimo*, who had some African ancestors.

Armed with that evidence, Zsa Zsa ruled Ramfis out as a possible suitor. But she learned that he had a crush on one of her friends, Kim Novak. Novak had just broken up with Sammy Davis, Jr., after he'd received death threats. Novak's studio boss at Columbia, Harry Cohn, had taken drastic strps to end that black-on-white liaison.

At her Bel Air manse, Zsa Zsa agreed to throw a lavish party to introduce Ramfis to Hollywood. His date for that event would be Novak herself. Novak had been previously linked to such names as Cary Grant, heavy-hung John Ireland, Prince Aly Khan, Peter Lawford, Frank Sinatra, and Zsa Zsa's own beloved Rubirosa.

The 200 members of Zsa Zsa's guest list were strictly the elite of Hollywood—Robert Taylor, Robert Mitchum, Kirk Douglas, James and Pamela Mason, Jeanne Crain, Beatrice Lillie, Ginger Rogers, Kathryn Grayson, David O. Selznick and Jennifer Jones, Conrad Hilton, Sr. with Ann Miller, Natalie Wood and Robert Wagner, Rhonda Fleming, who showed up with a surprise date, John F. Kennedy, Shirley MacLaine with Dean Martin, and Maureen O'Hara with John Ford.

To her shock, Rubirosa had flown in from Biarritz with his bride, Odile Rodin. He placed a possessive arm around Rodin when he intro-duced her to Zsa Zsa.

"Rubi, *dahlink*, how nice of you to drop in unannounced, and to bring this charming crea-ture, Odette,"

"It's Odine," the young model said.

Standing with her in his capacity as co-host of the event, George Sanders told her, "*Cokiline,* this is the party to end all parties."

Zsa Zsa later claimed that Rubi spent the entire evening gazing at her instead of at Rodin.

Selznick came up to her, telling her, "You're the only woman alive who could

"After seducing every single woman who ever lived, **Rubirosa** *(right)* fi-nally settled down with a schoolgirl," Zsa Zsa with contempt in her voice. "Her name was **Odile Rodin** *(left)*. Jackie Kennedy and I hated her. That was about the only thing Jackie and I ever agreed on."

"She is so young, so fresh, so pretty," Rubi told an aging Zsa Zsa, a statement that only inflamed her jealousy.

A journalist noted Rodin's "wide smile, almond eyes, freckles, volup-tuous curves, and mod hairdo," la-beling her "a chic Parisian from the city's Left Bank."

At long last, at a party in Zsa Zsa's Bel Air manse, **LA GABOR** contronted **Odile Rodin**, not-ing **Rubirosa's** arm possessively wrapped around her slim waist. To the left of Zsa Zsa, partly hidden, stands **Kim Novak** and, to Zsa Zsa's left, Novak's date for the evening, **Ramfis Tru-jillo**.

Zsa Zsa asked Rodin, "Do you enjoy Rubi's beatings as much as I used to?"

bring two of your ex-husbands, George and Conrad, together at the same party with your most notorious lover, Rubirosa."

"I presided over my gala like an empress," Zsa Zsa recalled. "My ladies-in-waiting were Jolie and Eva. Even *Life* magazine covered it."

For the gala, Zsa Zsa hired two orchestras and three dozen wine stewards, dressing them in red velvet livery with blue satin sashes.

At the time Zsa Zsa arranged a date between Ramfis and Kim Novak, Novak was filming *Bell, Book and Candle* with James Stewart. Ramfis agreed to escort her to Zsa Zsa's party. Novak, as a lavender blonde, arrived at the party looking stunning in black mink and a midnight blue gown designed by Jean Louis.

Both columnists, Louella Parsons and Hedda Hopper, were introduced to Ramfis at Zsa Zsa's party. Parsons cited him as "the ideal heartthrob for Kim." Hopper expressed her belief that Ramfis "looked a little bit like Tyrone Power, but in those skin-tight black trousers he wore, he would give every male except Rubirosa a case of penis envy. George Sanders observed that Ramfis "evoked a captain in an operetta."

Eva observed that Ramfis looked like "Valentino come back from the grave."

Kim Novak was the lavender blonde goddess at Columbia Studios.

Although her gruff boss, Harry Cohn, liked to remind her that "You're nothing but a piece of meat in a butcher shop," to the world at large, she was an icon of desirablity and soft femininity.

Eva's former lover, Tyrone Power, referred to her as "a bitch and a spoiled brat" after filming *The Eddy Duchin Story* with her in 1956.

The morning after the party, Zsa Zsa received an urgent phone call from Novak, who complained that Ramfis didn't ask her to go to bed with him.

Zsa Zsa advised her friend to be patient, claiming that Ramfis was a courtly Spanish gentleman. "He didn't want to rip your clothes off and rape you the first night, *dahlink.* Be patient. Wait until tonight."

Two days later, Zsa Zsa received a call from the most expensive furrier in Beverly Hills, asking her to come by for a fitting at her convenience. She protested, "I didn't order a fur. I have all the mink coats my wardrobe will allow."

"This is a gift from an admirer," the manager told her. She knew at once that it was a gift from Ramfis.

Within a week, she was seen around town wearing a $17,000 floor-length chinchilla coat. Along with the fur came a $3,500 diamond-and-pearl ring. That's not all. In her driveway, the next morning,, she found parked a $11,500 red Mercedes roadster 220S, with a gigantic red ribbon tied around it.

"After telling Ramfis, 'You shouldn't have,' I put the red Mercedes roadster in my garage, with my other expensive chariots."

Although Ramfis offered to pick up the tab for Zsa Zsa's party for him, she refused his offer, paying out the $10,000 herself, which would be the equivalent of about $100,000 in today's currency.

When the press in New York confronted Jolie with news of Ramfis' gifts, she asked a question. "What would a man give a pampered woman like Zsa Zsa? A box of Whitman's chocolates?"

After her party for Ramfis, Rubi wrote yet another note to Zsa Zsa, thanking her. He'd talked to Ramfis and reported that his friend had fallen madly in love with Novak. "They remind me of the time when you and I were in love," he wrote. "Ram wants to marry Kim."

Reportedly, Novak told Zsa Zsa, "Let Grace Kelly have that chubby Prince Rainier. I'll take my handsome, dashing Prince of the Caribbean."

***

For the next few weeks, Ramfis and Novak were seen everywhere together, ordering asparagus omelettes at the Farmers Market or downing "sunset cocktails" at a tavern overlooking the beach at Malibu.

Ramfis gave Novak a lavender Mercedes, priced at $14,000, even more expensive than the one presented to Zsa Zsa. When the gift aroused the ire of congressmen in Washington, D.C. Novak came out to greet reporters on her front lawn. She told the men, "I already have a car. I was only keeping the vehicle for Mr. Trujillo, who is a friend of mine."

At one point during the scandal, a bumper sticker appeared on the cars of young women in Los Angeles—*THIS CAR WAS NOT A GIFT FROM RAMFIS TRUJILLO.*

On one occasion, Ramfis was accused of spending $40,000 for a private plane to fly Novak and himself to Las Vegas to hear Frank Sinatra.

"All this lavish spending from Ramfis invariably attracted press attention. A hawk-eyed reporter

Ramfis Trujillo is seen here with **Kim Novak**,

He became (momentarily) infatuated with her, showering her with presents which included a $14,000 Mercedes (painted lavender, like her hair) and showering her with expensive presents.

His reckless spending of money that officials in Washington, D.C., defined as "U.S. charity to the Dominican Republic," resulted in loud denunciations of both Zsa Zsa and Novak from the floor of the U.S. Congress.

595

for the Associated Press began adding up the price tags of the gifts to Zsa Zsa and Novak. Ramfis had rented a mansion in Holmby Hills (near Bel Air), whose rental was priced at $3,000 a month. He also maintained a staff of twelve servants, including two chauffeurs, day and night. His food and liquor bills came to $25,000 a month. Those figures incited outrage when they were transmitted over the wire services.

In Washington, President Dwight Eisenhower was enraged to read about Ramfis, Novak, and Zsa Zsa, since the United States had recently given $1.3 million to the impoverished Caribbean nation in emergency Federal aid. Ramfis, through connections, had even arranged for the U.S. military to pay for his tuition at Fort Leavenworth, even though the *Generalíssimo* gave him an "allowance" of one million dollars a year.

Congressman Wayne Hays of Ohio demanded an investigation. "Much of our country's aid to the Dominican Republic is going into the personal pockets of the playboy, Ramfis Trujillo, and into the jewel boxes of those blonde Hollywood hussies, Kim Novak and Zsa Zsa Gabor, who is the ultimate gold-digger, still counting the millions from her divorce settlement from Conrad Hilton."

His remarks were greeted with a standing ovation from his fellow Congressmen, with a few dissenters who remained glued to their seats.

In an outrageous display, Hays unfurled a seductive picture of Zsa Zsa as she'd appeared in the film *Lili*. "If this scarlet woman continues her devious tricks with this Caribbean playboy of hers, foreign aid as we know it will come tumbling down. The American taxpayers are subsidizing the lifestyle of a reckless playboy and his concubines.'

"Zsa Zsa Gabor is the most expensive courtesan since the days of Madame de Pompadour," Hays charged, "and that one nearly bankrupted the treasury of France. American aid, sent to the Dominican Republic to relieve poverty, is being sent right back to our shores to pay for mink coats, diamond rings, and custom-designed automobiles for Miss Gabor to add to her fleet of existing luxury automobiles."

Speaking to *The Washington Post* and to reporters from CBS and NBC, Congressman Charles O. Porter of Oregon suggested that Federal aid to the Dominican Republic "might be placed directly into the bank accounts of Kim Novak and Zsa Zsa Gabor. That would save a lot of paperwork in transferring the money from Ciudad Trujillo to Hollywood. That way, the United States could get a return on its money by taxing the bloated income of these two pampered stars."

From his sickbed at the Santa Monica Hospital, where he was suffering from pneumonia, Ramfis spoke to a reporter. "Please tell me what is wrong in giving two ladies a little gift from time to time, especially to repay them for their hospitality and generosity to me?"

At the Santa Monica Hospital, Ramfis had to undergo a sinus operation.

Ramfis' press agent claimed that his client was one of the wealthiest young men in the world. "There is no connection between the money he spends on his personal life and funds granted by the United States to the Dominican Republic."

Just as this was happening, *Life* magazine was delivered to newsstands across the country, with a six-page spread on Zsa Zsa's lavish party for him in Bel Air.

The most damaging part of the *Life* magazine feature was a photograph of Ramfis' wife, Octavia Ricart, and their six children. In the aftermath, many members of the American public came to view Zsa Zsa as a homewrecker.

Stories about Zsa Zsa and Ramfis created a feeding frenzy for the tabloids. *The New York Daily News* headlined its feature—*ZSA ZSA GABOR, THE TIN SOLDIER, AND HIS HONOR FROM OHIO.*

Then the American Legion denounced Zsa Zsa as "a wanton gold-digger."

In Hollywood, after hearing a broadcast of Hays' remarks, Zsa Zsa confronted reporters at her front door. "If Mr. Hays ever comes out from behind his congressional wall of immunity and repeats those slanderous statements, I will sue. *And I will win!"*

To protect Novak's career in movies, her bosses at Columbia Studios, including Harry Cohn, told her to return the jewelry and the Mercedes. To save her flourishing movie career, she was ordered never to see Ramfis again.

Bowing to studio pressure, Novak gave back her expensive gifts to Ramfis. Zsa Zsa, however, in her chinchilla, was seen driving around Beverly Hills in her red Mercedes roadster.

Years later, Zsa Zsa read with glee that Hays had become embroiled in a sex scandal in Washington, as part of events spinning around his secretary, Elizabeth Ray.

"Vengeance is sweet," said Zsa Zsa. "His Karma caught up with him."

***

Ramfis had ordered the crew of his yacht, *Angelita,* to sail to Los Angeles, coming to anchor at a yacht slip in Santa Monica Harbor. This berth would make it convenient for Zsa Zsa to visit Ramfis in the wake of his failed romance with Novak.

After Ramfis had promised Zsa Zsa that he'd seek a divorce, she re-evaluated, more favorably his suitability as a potential lover and husband.

His yacht had been staked out by reporters. At two o'clock on foggy morning, a "blonde with a scarf covering her head and wearing large sunglasses" was seen going aboard the *Angelita*. No one saw her depart from the yacht during a period of three full days and nights. At first, it was speculated that Novak had been "the blonde in the fog."

But months later, Zsa Zsa admitted, "I was that blonde."

Before he sailed back to the Caribbean, Ramfis proposed marriage to Zsa Zsa. His previous pursuits of Novak, and later, of Joan Collins, had each gone astray.

He informed Zsa Zsa that eventually, when his father either died or surrendered control, he would become the dictator of the Dominican Republic. He also unveiled a spectacular plan to establish a "United States of the Caribbean," with himself installed as president of this newly formed federation.

Each night, he dazzled her with plans for their future, even promising to make her the "Queen of the Caribbean."

She succumbed to this dream, fancying herself as an "Evita Perón of the West Indies."

After a final long and passionate sojourn, Ramfis sailed away to his island in the sun. After he left, she began to reconsider her decision to accept his proposal of marriage.

"My marriage to Ramfis would have been the worst mistake of my life, considering what eventually happened to that man."

***

In New York, Jolie summed up the dilemma facing Zsa Zsa. "There aren't enough men around who can feel secure around Zsa Zsa. Women are supposed to be soft, feminine, and helpless, all the things Zsa Zsa isn't. She is one of the most famous, most ravishingly beautiful, most successful, women on earth. She is also rich. She's too beautiful, too demanding, too witty, too everything. She can't even keep servants. Men are afraid of her. She's too busy conquering the world to be a little woman sitting at home adoring a man."

Zsa Zsa virtually wrote her own epitaph when she said, "Who knows, in this life of ours, what is really true and what is enchanting make-believe?"

Congressman **Wayne Hays,** a Deomocrat from Ohio, led the attack on the floor of Congress against Zsa Zsa, at one point calling her "a gold-digging harlot."

He was protected from libel by congressional immunity; otherwise, as she announced, "I would sue the bastard liar."

In 1976, Hays was forced to resign from Congress after a bitter and much-publicized sex scandal of his own.

CHAPTER THIRTEEN
When Roses No Longer Bloomed in May
WHATEVER HAPPENED TO MAGDA?

Magda

"At long last, one of my daughters has a happy marriage," Jolie stated to a reporter. "There are problems, of course, but Magda seems content with Tony Gallucci. At least they are rich, and that always helps a marriage."

But tragedy lurked.

At their mansion in Southampton, Magda and Gallucci had entertained guests on a Thursday evening. In the middle of the night, at around 2am, Magda woke up feeling dehydrated and wanted some orange juice from the kitchen downstairs.

Her French poodle had long ago died, and she'd replaced her with a much bigger dog named Maxim. The dog always slept at the foot of an elaborate spiral staircase Gallucci had imported from Italy. Magda always warned guests not to trip over Maxim when descending the stairs at night. On this particular pre-dawn morning, she didn't heed her own warning and tripped over Maxim. She took a bad fall, hitting her head on a piece of furniture.

She summoned the maid in her downstairs bedroom, who woke up and brought her cold compresses for her head.

Magda complained of a severe headache, but assured the maid she would be all right in the morning.

Thinking that his wife had suffered only a minor bump, Gallucci left for a game of golf late that morning. By three o'clock on Friday afternoon, Magda's headache grew worse, but she had not called a doctor. She did telephone Jolie, who was staying in their guest cottage.

"*Nuci,* he's just ignoring me," Magda said. "Here I am lying in bed dying, and he's downstairs with his butler watching a baseball game on TV."

Jolie didn't realize the gravity of the situation. She told Magda to keep applying those cold compresses and that the swelling would go down. "A bump on the head, nothing serious. Quit angering yourself over Tony and get some rest."

Magda was feeling better Friday night. Gallucci had not only come to her bed, but had made passionate love to her.

By Saturday afternoon, when she'd called Jolie, she assured her mother that she was feeling wonderful and was getting dressed to attend the gala Horse Show Ball that would bring out *tout* Southampton.

Magda was photographed in full regalia astride an Arabian show horse, which had once been owned by Rubirosa.

An urgent call from Gallucci came in at ten that morning. "Jolie, come at once. Magda can't talk. Not a word."

Within fifteen minutes, Jolie was in the Gallucci mansion, racing up the steps to Magda's bedroom. There, she discovered her stricken daughter.

When Magda opened her eyes, she stared blankly at the ceiling. Jolie feared that the entire right side of her body was paralyzed.

Gallucci was on the phone summoning an ambulance. Within five minutes, its siren could be heard as two attendants with a stretcher pulled up in front of their manse.

With her daughter rushed to the emergency room at the hospital, Jolie placed a call to Zsa Zsa, who was in Manhattan attending the premiere of a film. She asked Zsa Zsa to use her influence and contact Dr. Andrew Bernath.

Jolie explained to Zsa Zsa that Dr. Bernath had treated Magda once before, after she and Jolie had had a bitter quarrel. That had occurred five years before. "Magda suffered this little spell, and she lost her speech for a little while. But she recovered quickly."

Zsa Zsa located the physician and persuaded him to travel the one hundred miles to Southampton to treat Magda once again.

After only a cursory examination, Dr. Bernath concluded that Magda had suffered a massive stroke and had to be rushed to Mount Sinai Hospital in Manhattan.

Jolie rode beside her stricken daughter to the hospital, holding onto her limp right hand and at times cradling her head in her lap. She refused to leave Magda's side when the night nurse called a curfew for visitors at nine that evening.

Promising to leave, Jolie acted impulsively after the nurse left. She slid under the covers of Magda's bed, using her mink coat as a blanket, her purse for a cushion. She spent the night beside Magda, listening to her moans and holding back her own tears.

By 5am, Jolie was in the bathroom, applying more makeup and arranging her hair so she would look presentable when two physicians came in to examine Magda at 6am that morning.

During Magda's stay at the hospital, Jolie maintained a constant vigil, with Gallucci joining her at night.

As Magda began to recover physically, she still had not regained her speech. With money no object, Gallucci summoned the best speech therapists in New York, including a team from the Rusk Center in Manhattan.

Finally, both Gallucci and Jolie were told, "Magda will never speak again. It's hopeless. There's nothing more we can do for her."

"I refuse to accept that," Jolie told the therapists. "You wait and see. Miracles do happen when backed up by a formidable human resolve."

When Eva heard the news, she flew from Palm Beach to New York and took a taxi all the way to Southampton to join Magda, who by now had been released from the Manhattan specialists and was back in her home.

Jolie later said, "Magda knew all of us, including Tony, Zsa Zsa, and Eva, and she knew what was happening. But she couldn't utter one word."

Jolie's young husband, Edmund de Szigethy, had a cousin, Dr. Julien Rosenthal, who was a brain surgeon. He was consulted and he examined Magda intensely. He told Jolie and Gallucci, "If I operate, Magda has only a fifty percent chance of living. If I don't operate, she can live a long and peaceful life, but without all her facilities."

Jolie burst into tears. "My darling once spoke eleven languages."

That night, Jolie met with Zsa Zsa and Eva. All three Gabors agreed not to operate, afraid to take the chance with such odds against Magda.

During the weeks ahead, Magda struggled to get just one word out, but to no avail. One night, Jolie was sitting with her. Magda was shedding bitter tears. That day, she'd been told that Gallucci had terminal cancer. Forcing herself, she managed to utter three words—"No speech...die!"

Jolie grabbed her and hugged her. "No, no, if you die, I die."

Magda tried to comfort Gallucci as she watched him suffer from the cancer eating away at his body during the six months before he died.

Just before his burial, wearing a heavy black veil, she stood in front of his casket. As she leaned in to kiss the casket, she formed words on her lips, but no sound came out.

In her weakened condition, and as a widow, she had to handle a nightmarish galaxy of lawsuits from members of the Gallucci family for control of her husband's mammoth estate.

"Magda never regained her speech, although in

Although her speech patterns were greatly impaired, **Magda** *(right)* maintained her position in society in Palm Springs. Here, she dressed up in costume to attend a costume ball thrown by **Jolie** *(center)* in 1974.

Eva *(left)* claimed, "I didn't want to look like Dale Evans. I refused to dress up like a cowgirl."

some way we could understand her a bit," Jolie said. "She was very brave."

***

In the wake of her husband's death, Magda spent many a sleepless night agonizing over the upcoming legal battles for the Gallucci millions. She read law books, and she made clever business decisions, even though she couldn't speak.

She even managed to entertain guests in her Palm Springs home. In trying to tell Jolie about the guests the following morning, she often managed to utter the word "couple" without being able to identify her guests to Jolie.

She urged her lawyers to "Fight! Fight!" for her late husband's millions. In the end, she prevailed, winning control of most of Gallucci's estate, which made her the richest of all the Gabors.

As Zsa Zsa quipped, "Those sewer pipes pay rich dividends, *dahlink.*"

After the estate was settled, she made yet another smart business decision. She sold all her interests in her late husband's plumbing-supply business just before the Gallucci industries failed. She ended up getting all her money out of the companies. The Gallucci family was eventually left with nearly worthless stock.

Although she retained ownership of her house in Southampton, to an increasing degree, she spent time in Palm Springs, where she lived in luxury in a mansion whose kitchen was the size of a dormitory. For nearly a year during its construction she directed workers with her limited vocabulary.

Eventually, Magda evolved into one of the leading hostesses of Palm Springs. As journalist Allene Arthur noted, "The Gabors are to Palm Springs what fancy desserts are to a good meal."

During the years to come, Magda was often seen at the Palm Springs jewelry store Jolie had opened. "You might see her with Mamie Eisenhower or with Governor Pat Brown," Jolie said. "She made herself understood as best she could."

Many famous guests, including Ann Miller, visited Magda's Palm Springs home, which stood atop a hill up a winding road. "You got the idea that Magda liked red—the den, the powder room, the bedrooms, even a red grandfather clock," Miller said. "For her parties, a red invitation went out. The flowers were red, the upholstery red, and the table linens red."

"In spite of her speech problem, Magda always appeared beautifully gowned, made up, manicured, coiffed, and bejeweled," said Frank Sinatra. "She owned enough pearls to stretch to Hungary."

As Arthur noted in an article, Magda "keeps the allure going as if it were a sacred duty."

Of all the many marriages of the Gabor sisters, none came as quite the surprise of Magda's sudden marriage to George Sanders, Zsa Zsa's former husband. Although she later altered her story, Zsa Zsa for years claimed that she was responsible for that quickie marriage.

She "confessed" to Brian Aherne, one of Sanders' best friends, what had happened.

"George stayed with me for weeks in Bel Air, begging me to marry him, but I had no intention of doing that. I had moved on to other beaux and to other husbands."

"One afternoon, I told George to marry Magda," Zsa Zsa said. "I reminded him that Magda was a rich and lonely widow."

In Richard Vanderbeets' biography of Sanders, he wrote: "The idea of marrying Magda took a firm hold in Sanders' head. He charges straight down to Magda's house in Palm Springs and confronts her with the announcement that they were getting married that afternoon, and that is what they did, believe it or not!"

On very short notice, Magda's efficient secretary, Mitzi Meyer, with her connections, arranged for the marriage license and even found a judge to perform the marriage ceremony.

After proposing to Magda, Sanders then visited Jolie, who approved. She later told the press, "It's always nice when you recapture a son-in-law."

Magda took Sanders as her fifth husband on December 4, 1970, at Indio, a town outside Palm Springs. Sanders told a stray reporter, "Marrying Magda was not my idea. It was Zsa Zsa's doing."

Until she actually tried to speak, **Magda** hardly looked like a lady with a speech impairment.

Zsa Zsa later changed her story, suggesting that she had been merely joking when she told Sanders to marry Magda. With bitterness, she later said, "I thought I was going to go insane, and I realized that George married Magda because he wanted to hurt me, because I had wounded his pride in turning him down, and because he had finally accepted the fact that we had no future together."

She evolved into a beloved hostess in Palm Springs, enjoying her role as a social butterfly and a patron of the arts.

Sanders asked Jolie to go with him to purchase a wedding band for Magda, leading her to a junk shop, where he discovered a gold-colored pair of earrings,

Old friends came to call, including David Niven. "Somehow, people managed to understand what she was trying to say."

costing $1.90. "George was such a cheap bastard that day," Jolie recalled. "He haggled with the shopkeeper, claiming he needed only one earring, the owner says that he would sell the earrings only as a pair. I saved the day by offering to spend 95 cents to purchase the other earring."

According to Jolie, Magda's marriage to Sanders was never consummated. Almost from the first, the couple seemed to realize that their marriage, conceived in a moment of impetuosity, was not one of their brighter ideas.

When he called Aherne, he said, "Age is a ghastly phenomenon. I am now an irascible old fart, deaf, and intractable. It seems, as I looked around, that all my friends are either dead or dying. It really *is* the last mile for all of us."

During the brief time Sanders lived in Magda's home, occupying a separate bedroom, he constantly referred to her as Zsa Zsa.

"Calling her Zsa Zsa really hurt Magda," Jolie said.

"George was still mine—no matter how many wives he has," Zsa Zsa later told Magda, which hurt her even more. "I advised Magda to have the marriage annulled, and she complied with my wishes,"

Jolie later said, "There was no alimony, of course. But Magda did get some trinket from the marriage. She kept the Oscar he won for his performance in *All About Eve*. She placed it in her bar, which was painted red, of course."

***

Both **Magda** and **George Sanders** made an impetuous error when they got married in 1970.

The marriage lasted only six weeks before both parties agreed to seek an annulment.

Even though her speech remained impaired, Magda attracted suitors. She was still beautiful, and very, very rich. She learned to put on wigs, makeup, and false eyelashes with the use of her left hand, as her right arm remained useless. She even had a fiancé, actor Gary Moore.

Magda ended her affair with Moore when she came to believe his passion for golf was greater than his love for her.

At one point, Magda had two princely squires in pursuit of her, including Prince Umberto de Poliolo who lived in La Jolla and operated an art emporium, Gallery de Poliolo, in Palm Springs.

Her other suitor was Prince Alfonso de Bourbon, who proposed marriage to Magda. The four Gabors met to consider the offer, and after some discussion, advised Magda to turn him down, even though he was a scion of a famous noble family in Europe, the Bourbons.

604

Over a period of years, Magda also dated the artist, John Morris. He later said, "Magda and I would always be engaged in between her husbands and various beaux."

Even with her affliction, Magda never lost her sense of humor. Once a reporter asked her which of the Gabors was the oldest. "Mother!" she blurted out.

The author, Norma Lee Browning, recalled attending a lavish engagement party at Magda's home to announce her upcoming marriage to "Count Somebody." She didn't remember his name, but recalled that the count had "extravagant manners and wore a diamond earring."

"By midnight, the count had vanished and no announcement came," Browning said. "So we assumed the engagement was broken. But the gypsy fiddler played and Jolie sang 'Never on Sunday.' All of us had a wonderful time."

In spite of her speech impairment, Magda, on August 5, 1972, at the age of fifty-seven, made one final attempt at marriage. In Southampton, she wed Tibor R. Heltai, an economic consultant who later became a real-estate broker. Of all the Gabor marriages, this wedding was the least publicized.

In her memoirs, Jolie suggested that it might not have been a marriage at all.

Jolie claimed that Magda was no longer interested in sex, so the reason for her marriage to Heltai was never known. As Jolie wrote in her memoir, "Magda closed the bedroom door when the last husband, Tibor Heltai, wanted to come in. She shuddered. I don't know whether it was the thought of sex or the thought of Tibor, but I only know she shuddered."

The marriage ended almost before it had begun, although Magda did not file for divorce until 1975. That was the year Jolie published her memoirs, ghost written by the popular author and columnist for *The New York Post,* Cindy Adams.

The book was a fascinating read, not only about Jolie but about her era and her views on the lives of her daughters and their many marriages.

Sometimes, Magda joined the three other Gabors, including making a spectacular entrance when they were honorees at the annual Americana Ball at the Hilton Riviera in Palm Springs in 1980. They came onto the red carpet, with husband Edmund escorting Jolie; artist John Morris with Magda on his arm; escort Glen Bohannan accompanying Zsa Zsa, and Eva arriving with TV host, Merv Griffin, with whom she enjoyed a platonic relationship toward the end of her life.

That night, Griffin was the master of ceremonies, telling the audience, "The Gabors came here poor, without friends, and couldn't speak the language. Now they are successful, rich, and famous. And they still can't speak the language. Eva is now in the hairpiece business, and Zsa Zsa is in the cassette business. They are marketing *vigs* and *wideos*. Jolie swears that Zsa Zsa's first words were "I do."

Madga's longtime secretary, Mitzi Meyer, characterized the Gabors as "holdovers from the Moulin Rouge era, the 1800s world of the artist, Toulouse-Lautrec." That conjured up an image of Zsa Zsa as Jane Avril in her 1952 film, *Moulin Rouge.*

"The Gabors lived in a world of caviar and champagne," Meyer said, "of designer gowns with plunging *décolletage,* of night life with cabaret gaiety, lavish dinners, countless parties and countless husbands and beaux—not to forget the diamonds and mink coats. They represented old world glamour, and they fought their relentless enemy, time, which went marching on as it inevitably does, doing all of us in eventually."

In many ways, Magda remained Jolie's most loyal daughter. She once wrote that her mother in her nineties had "the endurance of the Danube." She stood by Jolie when she cancelled her fifth facelift to have her second hip replacement surgery instead.

All the Gabors, spearheaded by Magda, gathered at the Eisenhower Medical Center until they learned that their matriarch had come through like a German Panzer invading Poland in 1939.

During her final years, Magda often spent hours alone with her wheelchair-bound mother, whose eyesight and hearing were mostly gone. Jolie wanted people to remember her glittering image, so she no longer made appearances.

As journalist Allene Arthur wrote: "She made fashion a religion and man-trapping an art," becoming the role model for Magda and her other two daughters. Arthur claimed, "Jolie fought for a life of spun gold and violins. And won. She has enjoyed 19 sons-in-law and a trillion party invitations."

Magda always liked her stepfather, Edmund de Szigethy, whom Jolie had married in 1957. Her mother told her, "Edmund is a moneymaker. He takes care of me, he takes care of my business, my three homes in Florida, New York, and Connecticut. When I married him, he looked younger than me, but now, he looks older."

Death came to Edmund in 1989.

Eva died in 1995, and Zsa Zsa made a decision not to tell Jolie about the death of her youngest daughter. Born in 1896, Jolie died on April 1, 1997, at the age of 101.

Two months after Jolie's death, Magda herself died on June 6, 1997, from renal failure. She was buried in Desert Memorial Park in Cathedral City, California.

This heroine of World War II was eighty-one years old at the hour of her death. Zsa Zsa mourned her passing.

Of the four fabulous Gabors, Zsa Zsa was left as the sole survivor.

CHAPTER FOURTEEN
Green Acres Deep in December
WHATEVER HAPPENED TO EVA?

Eva had long abandoned hopes of a career as a movie star, although for a 1963 release, *A New Kind of Love,* a role was offered to her. The film starred the husband and wife team of Paul Newman and Joanne Woodward, with Eva cast with veteran character actress Thelma Ritter as the leading supporting players. Maurice Chevalier appeared as himself in this Paramount release.

The comedy concerned a journalist who mistakes a woman for a prostitute. While he tries to interview her about her job, he falls in love with her.

Eva was thrilled to be working with Newman. She told her friends, "I think he has divine looks, and I hear he's an errant husband who sleeps around. I should be so lucky."

On meeting Newman, Eva learned that he didn't really want to do the script. He told her, "I'm appearing in it as a favor to Joanne. After making *The Stripper,* she thinks she's Marilyn Monroe, and she gets to wear some expensive French lingerie in this film."

Eva's own wardrobe was designed by Edith Head who had dressed stars from Mae West to Bette Davis.

As Ritter reported, "It was obvious that Eva was making a play for Paul. She came raving to me one day when she'd heard that he had Hungarian blood flowing through his veins. 'That's why I'm so attracted to him,' she told me."

Reportedly, Woodward had to warn Eva that, "Mr. Newman is taken. In case you didn't know, I'm his wife."

Behind Woodward's back, Eva told Melville Shavelson, the director, producer, and scriptwriter, "Paul is divine but that Woodward creature is a bitch! Also*, dahlink*, you should have let me design that blonde wig of hers. It's hideous on the poor creature."

Years later, at a dinner party thrown by Merv Griffin for twenty-four guests,

Paul Newman and **Joanne Wood-ward** were husband and wife in real life and they co-starred together in *A New Kind of Love*. Eva Gabor was cast in a glamorous role as a supporting player.

She told her fellow co-star, Thelma Ritter, "Any woman married to a handsome hunk like Paul Newman must expect that he'll be faced with endless temptation to stray."

"I don't want to sound immodest," Eva said, "but Paul Newman and I brought beauty to *A New Kind of Love*.

The cast included *(left to right)* **Joanne Woodward, Thelma Ritter, George Tobias**, and **Eva** herself.

Eva was asked if she'd managed to seduce Newman while making that film.

"Of course, I did, *dahlink*," she said. "You didn't think that Woodward could safeguard a handsome hunk like that twenty-four hours a day?"

She whispered to Griffin, "I got him drunk on beer and then raped him."

"I'm very experienced," she told the assembled guests, sounding more like Zsa Zsa than herself. "I've been seducing other women's husbands for years."

A somewhat skeptical Zsa Zsa asked her, "Did you really seduce Newman, or are you just claiming that?"

"Let me put it this way," Eva said. "If I didn't seduce him, I would claim him as my conquest anyway. After all, *dahlink,* I've got a reputation to maintain. So have you, Sister Dear."

Later, Eva claimed, "Paul Newman was a prize, a male body for the ages. Truly a Greek God, except perhaps his legs, which were a bit on the skinny side."

***

Since the early 1950s, Eva had been consistently mistaken for her more famous sister, Zsa Zsa. On a first-class flight to Sydney, Australia, two teenage girls approached her, "Zsa Zsa, may we have your autograph?" one of the girls asked. Concealing her exasperation, Eva replied, "*Dahlinks*, I'm Eva Gabor. But I'd be honored to sign my name in your autograph book. In case anyone asks, I'm the pretty one."

Gossip columnist Joyce Haber defended Eva as "the least boring of the Gabor sisters."

Sometimes, Eva used the public's confusion to escape embarrassment. One June evening after midnight, she was caught swimming nude in the pool at the Beverly Hills Hotel.

Two men shouted, "LOOK, IT'S EVA GABOR!"

Emerging dripping wet from the pool, Eva rushed for one of the hotel's huge bath towels. "No, *dahlinks*," she said. "It's Zsa Zsa."

In addition to sideline commercial enterprises, such as hawking wigs, Eva continued to pursue a career on Broadway, although the prospect grew dimmer and dimmer with each passing year.

In October of 1963, she signed to appear in *Tovarich* in the role of Tatiana on Broadway, replacing Vivien Leigh in the role. Eva's engagement would only last until November of that year.

Leigh had opened in the play in March, attracting a large audience, many of whom came "to see Scarlett O'Hara." Although Leigh later won a Tony Award, she was too weak and too emotionally unstable to appear month after month in the demanding role.

She was assisted and emotionally reinforced, to some degree, by her male co-star, Jean Pierre Aumont, with whom she'd once conducted a love affair.

When Leigh announced she had to leave the role, the producers searched for a big name star to replace her as a draw within the mammoth Winter Garden Theater. Marlene Dietrich was approached, but she turned down the offer.

When Eva was asked, she accepted. She enjoyed working with Aumont, and she formed a close alliance with him. She was aware of the affair the handsome French actor had had with Zsa Zsa when they'd appeared together in the Leslie Caron film, *Lili*.

In his memoirs, *Sun and Shade*, Aumont wrote, "Eva was charming, although she didn't have Vivien's royal bearing. The play wavered a little—Instead of the story of a grand duchess who is transformed into a maid, it became the story of a lovely young thing who disguises herself as a grand duchess. Throughout the play, Eva communicated in a spontaneous and chirping Hungarian twitter which I didn't always understand."

Aumont told the director of the play, Peter Glenville, that "Eva and I made love four or five times. I forgot the exact number. She is far better in bed than she is on the stage."

Eva had a different point of view, confiding in Glenville that once, during sexual

Vivien Leigh and French actor **Jean-Pierre Aumont** had briefly been lovers when they were much younger. They were reunited on Broadway in the play *Tovarich*.

Leigh was neither physically nor mentally able to handle her grueling role. After struggling for several months, she was replaced by Eva Gabor.

climax, Aumont had yelled out, "Grace!"

"The poor boy is still in love with Grace Kelly, and I cannot be her," Eva said.

Right before *Tovarich* closed on Broadway, Aumont received a call backstage from his friend, Porfirio Rubirosa. He invited him to a midnight party at the home of "a certain Mrs. Smith," as Aumont relayed in his memoirs. At first, Aumont, who was tired, didn't want to attend, but Rubi made the party sound so enticing, he changed his mind.

Rubi called back, requesting that "a real VIP at the party wanted to meet Eva, so please bring her along."

Always ready to party, Eva accepted, thinking she was going to meet a big-time movie star and admirer of hers.

At the door to a Park Avenue apartment, they were greeted by "Mrs. Smith," who turned out to be Jean Kennedy Smith, the eighth of the nine children born to Joseph and Rose Kennedy, and the last surviving child by the year 2013.

The moment she got there, Eva excused herself and disappeared into the powder room "to make myself camera ready."

In the meantime, Mrs. Smith introduced Aumont to some of her other guests. "Jack, this is Jean Pierre; Jean Pierre, Jack."

Aumont was awed to have come face-to-face with John F. Kennedy, the President of the United States. The date was November 15, 1963. The president would soon be flying with Jackie to Dallas.

Seated across from JFK were Robert and Ted Kennedy, his brothers. In his memoir, Aumont remembered JFK as "warm, friendly, and witty. I was fascinated by Bobby, but I was under the spell of the president. Some interior fire consumed JFK, some concentrated mission. One moment, he would seem

Smiles before tragedy: *(left to right)* **John, Robert,** and **Ted Kennedy.** Eva later admitted that she and the President had a one night stand at the Hotel Carlyle on November 15, 1963. "I was following in Zsa Zsa's footsteps, *dahlink,*" she told Aumont.

A few days later, JFK was assassinated in Dallas. "It may have been the last affair Jack Kennedy had before his death," Eva told Aumont.

austere, and then a dreamy expression would pass over him. He was a surprising mixture of vigor and timidity."

He admitted that once Eva emerged from the powder room, "none of the Kennedy men, especially Jack, seemed too interested in me. I think she could have gone to bed with all three of them that night."

"Eva was well aware of Zsa Zsa's affair with JFK, and I'm sure she wanted to get one up on her older sister," Aumont said.

The actor said that in the early morning hours, through the nearly deserted streets of Manhattan, he delivered Eva in a limousine to the Hotel Carlyle. She'd been told that JFK was on his way. She was very excited. I kissed her good night, but she had little interest in me. The following night at the theater, I wanted a blow-by-blow description, but didn't get it."

Eva confided only what didn't happen to Aumont: "I wanted to ask the president which Gabor sister was better in bed—Zsa Zsa or me, but I didn't dare."

When Aumont announced he was publishing his memoirs *[they were released in 1977]* he received a surprising telephone call from Eva. "She asked me to respect her privacy and not reveal that she'd had a brief fling with the president. She felt the American people would be outraged to know she'd seduced JFK days before his assassination."

"I would get all the blame, because Jackie was clearly the heroine of that horrible November," Eva told him. "I would look like some devouring monster, a cheap back alley whore slipping around."

Aumont agreed to respect her wishes. "I understand Eva's reluctance to let the world know she'd fucked JFK right before his assassination. So I left out her episode in American history. But I certainly wrote about my own encounter with the President before he was gunned down."

***

Along with Jean Pierre Aumont, Eva was to meet another sitting U.S. President, Lyndon B. Johnson. The occasion came about in Washington, D.C., when both stars were appearing in *Tovarich* after it had closed on Broadway. The president's wife, Lady Bird Johnson, had attended a gala performance of *Tovarich*, and in its aftermath, she invited Aumont and Eva to the White house for tea.

At the tea, Eva was visibly disappointed that President Johnson wasn't there. "I once met President Kennedy, and now I want to meet President Johnson," she protested to Lady Bird.

With perfect manners, the First Lady told Eva that Johnson was in a cabinet meeting discussing urgent matters pertaining to the war in Vietnam.

One afternoon, when Eva was invited for tea at the White House by the First Lady, she rudely demanded to see the President, even if it meant interrupting his cabinet meeting devoted to the Vietnam war.

In the photo above, **Lady Bird Johnson** is dancing with her husband, **Lyndon B. Johnson**, at a White House gala.

After two cups of tea, Eva once again confronted Lady Bird. "I came to the White House to meet President Johnson. Would you please tell him I'm here. I'm sure he'd love to meet me."

In his memoir, Aumont quoted Eva's exact words: *"We're playing this evenink and ve can't wait."*

Finally, Lady Bird left and went into the room where Johnson was presiding over his cabinet.

She presented Eva's demands to the president. In a surprise move, Johnson interrupted the cabinet meeting and excused himself. "To hell with Vietnam. I've got to go out there and meet one of the Gabor sisters. Frankly, I can't tell one from the other. I just hope it's not the fat mama."

Ushered into the room by Lady Bird, Johnson came face to face with Eva. "*Dahlink,* you are exactly like me," she told him.

He seemed amused at that remark, as he gazed down into her plunging neckline. "Well, little darling, I'd say there are a few differences."

"No," she said. "I don't mean it that way. What I mean is you're so much better looking in person than you are on TV. Just like me. Promise me never again to appear on TV."

"Well, little darling, as President of the United States, I can't exactly make that promise. I've got to go, but it was nice meeting you. Now that Lady Bird had to run to the john, I'll make it up to you by giving you a sloppy wet one." He carried through on his promise.

After he'd kissed her, she said, "I'll never wash my lips again."

With a final goodbye, Johnson rushed back to his Cabinet meeting. Lady Bird returned to briefly congratulate Aumont and Eva on *Tovarich* and then quickly disappeared back into her private chambers.

***

Eva was offered the role of Fannie Price in the film adaptation of *Youngblood Hawke* (1964), based on a novel by Herman Wouk. It was a story about the rise and fall of a young writer, inspired by the life of Thomas Wolfe. Warner Brothers cast the handsome actor, James Franciscus, as Youngblood Hawke.

Other members of the cast included Mary Astor, Suzanne Pleshette, Genevieve Page, Lew Bowman, Don Porter, Kent Smith, and Mildred Dunnock.

After the film's release, most critics suggested that the film was "*clichéd* but somewhat compelling trash."

Eva found the star, Missouri-born Franciscus, who'd attended Yale, mesmerizing. Years later, the actor's preppy good looks enabled him to portray JFK in the 1980 TV movie, *Jacqueline Bouvier Kennedy.* The year before, he'd also played the president in *The Greek Tycoon,* based on the Jackie Kennedy/Ari Onassis story.

Actor **James Franciscus**, both because of his talent and his looks, was cast as John F. Kennedy twice onscreen.

"I'd had the real Jack Kennedy, so why not the lookalike?" Eva asked when she appeared with him in *Youngblood Hawke.*

At the time Eva met him, Franciscus was married to Kathlene ("Kitty") Wellman, the daughter of the film director, William Wellman.

Eva never let something like a marriage stand in her way when she wanted a man. She went after Franciscus. He became significant in her life because it marked the last time she succumbed to the "disease of *Leadingman-itis.*" With Franciscus, her predilection for seducing the leading man of whatever play or movie she was in came to an end.

Franciscus shared stories of his life with her, and she got to know him extremely well as he relayed details about his Tom Sawyer-ish boyhood spent fishing, building rafts, and even hunting skunks. "What a stinking job," she said.

He had been nicknamed "Goey*" [pronounced as "Gooey"]* since childhood, and he let Eva call him that, too. When he was a boy, he told her, he almost died when he fell down on a lightening rod that pierced his stomach. He even showed her the scar that remained. "When I saw that, I wanted to see more of his body—and I *did, dahlink.*"

In the photo above, a young **James Franciscus** appears on the French Riviera with his then-lover, **Jane Fonda**,

He'd lost his father, an army pilot, during World War II, and had been brought up by his mother. He'd made his acting debut at an all boy prep school playing a girl.

"I don't know how anyone could mistake him

for a girl," Eva said.

He told her that 200 actors had auditioned for the role of Youngblood Hawke before the part was given to him.

Eva was surprised to learn that Franciscus had been Jane Fonda's first love. In 1957, he even went to Europe one summer with the Fondas, staying at their villa in Villefranche along the French Riviera.

In her memoirs, *My Life So Far,* Fonda claimed that the young actor gave her her first swoon. "My body swooned against him, my knees buckled, and he had to hold me to keep me from falling. When our lips parted, everything was swirling, the sea, the sky. Hemingway's line, 'And the earth moved,' came to me. This is what he meant? The earth moved. Goey caused it."

"The earth didn't exactly move for me," but James rang all my bells," Eva said. "After our first night together, I would have married him if he weren't already taken. He was everything a man should be…and gorgeous to boot. God had certainly been good to him. James was built to give infinite pleasure to a mere mortal woman like myself."

***

Exit James Franciscus. Enter the flamboyant Hungarian aristocrat, Sepy Dobronyi, who was known as "The Hugh Hefner of Miami."

Touring with a play in Miami, Eva met Sepy at a party. "We were enchanted with each other that first night," she said. "It was all so romantic—*Moon Over Miami*…stuff like that."

At the time she met Sepy, he'd just ended a brief fling with Tallulah Bankhead, who was appearing in Coconut Grove in a play by Tennessee Williams.

As Eva remembered Sepy, he was wearing a snakeskin vest, snakeskin pants, and snakeskin boots. "I prefer only rattlesnake skin," he told her. "I like that particular snake because its venom brings a quick death." He made that astonishing statement to her in his native Hungarian language.

His full name was Baron Joseph de Bicske Dobronyi. Born in Budapest, he was a sculptor, royal crown jeweler, art collector, world traveler, movie maker, pilot, wine collector, sportsman, playboy, and *bon vivant.* The raffish expatriate often entertained at home, wearing an ascot and a silk smoking jacket. He told Eva, "I devote my life to hedonism and beautiful women."

The Baron was renowned for his bronze-and-gold sculptures of famous celebrities, including a controversial 42-inch tall statue of movie goddess Anita Ekberg, who had posed for him. "The Ekberg Bronze" had been featured in the August, 1956 issue of *Playboy.*

He radiated Continental charm, and often hung out with celebrities, even seducing them. His list of conquests was impressive, including such screen goddesses as Joan Crawford, Ava Gardner, Rita Hayworth, Brigitte Bardot, and Carmen Miranda.

He often bragged about his seductions. "One night after I fucked Linda Christian, she told me that her husband, Tyrone Power, would love it if I did that to him." Eva didn't like hearing that story about the "love of my life."

Sepy also claimed that he'd screwed another matinee idol, Errol Flynn, in Port Antonio, Jamaica. In Cuba, he'd been friends with Ernest Hemingway and had also supplied blonde-haired American showgirls to the Cuban dictator Fulgencio Batista, before he was overthrown by Fidel Castro's guerrilla army.

Sepy referred to Hugh Hefner as "my best friend," and he was also politically well connected. In 1964, Barry Goldwater had once attended a Republican Party fundraiser at Sepy's mansion in Coconut Grove.

During his first evening with Eva, he enthralled her with stories about his adventures with the Hungarian Air Force during World War II, telling her amazing tales of a flaming parachute jump and a death-defying post-war escape from the communists.

When Eva met Sepy, he was married to Amy Green Brown, the New York heiress, but she was nowhere to be seen. Eva accepted Sepy's invitation to drive her, after her evening performance back to his home in Coconut Grove. She got into the front seat of his Rolls Royce Corniche, which sported a representation of a nude female torso painted on the outside of the passenger door.

"When I came into his living room, I thought I was wandering into the home of Ernest Hemingway," Eva later said. "Sepy had gone on safaris in Africa with Hemingway, and his walls were lined with the heads of wild beasts he'd bagged. He told me, 'I'm known for my African adventures, my New Guinea tribal war wounds, my Swedish marriages, and my Mexican divorces.'"

She was awed by some of his trophies, including 120-pound elephant tusks, two Nepalese temple lion statues, and six Tibetan yak-wool rugs.

He took her on a tour of his fabled wine cellar. "Some of the trophies included what he called the world's largest collection of hotel room keys," she said. "It was a bizarre sight, but some of the wine bottles were adorned with women's underpants."

Later that night, he invited her upstairs to his bedroom, which was centered around a carved bed styled like the replica of a Viking ship. "Please, lie down in this bed, where so many goddesses have lain before you, including Lana Turner, who said she experienced the thrill of her life here."

It was an invitation Eva could not resist.

"Lena Horne and Jayne Mansfield echoed Lana's rave reviews," Sepy said.

"You left out Marilyn Monroe," Eva said.

"She eluded me, but I got the French love goddess, Brigitte Bardot, as compensation. "Frank Sinatra, with me, often fucked the same girl in this bed at the same time."

Weeks later, Eva recalled her first time with Sepy. "Perhaps he exaggerated his sexual prowess, but after only one night with him, sailing away in that Viking ship, I was transported to Nirvana."

After the run of her play, Eva had to leave Miami. Sepy later maintained that "she begged me to marry her, and when I turned her down, she attempted suicide."

There is no record to suggest that that charge was true.

[In 1972, Sepy allowed the Mafia-backed producers of the epic porn flick, Deep Throat, *to film scenes in his trophy-filled home. He seduced Linda Lovelace, the star of the movie, and was later furious at her for "extolling my physical properties in print."*

Years later, Eva recalled "the most bizarre exhibit Sepy displayed to me was a pair of Queen Elizabeth's underpanties that were at least 40 years old...and rather stained."

That undergarment appeared to have been authentic. It was acquired by a friend of Sepy's when the Queen accidentally left them on a private plane she disembarked.

Shortly after Sepy's death of liver cancer on May 29, 2010, The Miami Herald *wrote about the royal underpanties as part of its description of an estate sale of Sepy's possessions engineered by Louis F. Cruz. The owner of the panties today is unknown.]*

***

Eva's greatest exposure to the American public came with the TV debut of *Green Acres.* In the wake of the success of a sister show, *Petticoat Junction, Green Acres* was first broadcast on CBS on September 15, 1965. The series continued until April 27, 1971.

It received solid ratings during its six-year run and exposed Eva to households across rural America whose inhabitants had never seen her perform before.

Green Acres made Eva a multi-millionaire and brought her international recognition, even though she'd been cast as a last-minute choice. The role had originally been written for blonde-haired Martha Hyer, who usually played snobby rich girl roles as she did in *Some Came Running* (1958) with Frank Sinatra. CBS executives were very disappointed when the deal with Hyer fell through. A total of twenty-six actresses were auditioned. Finally, in desperation, CBS settled on Eva, despite their fears that rural American TV viewers would not understand her accent.

Hyer had been one of the supporting players in the 1957 film *My Man Godfrey,* in which Eva also had a supporting role. When Eva learned that CBS had originally wanted Hyer to star in the series, she cattily remarked, "She is an innocuous and singularly unspectacular talent. You didn't know I could use such big English words like that, did you, *dahlink?"*

In the series, Eva was cast opposite Eddie Albert, an easy-going actor with a comfortable manner, who had gotten his start in Hollywood in 1938, appearing with Ronald Reagan in *Brother Rat.* In *Green Acres,* he was cast as the constantly befuddled city-slicker-turned-farmer, Oliver Douglas. In New York, before escaping from urban life, he'd been a lawyer.

His glamorous Hungarian wife—who as the series' theme song defined and explained, "preferred Park Avenue to the farm"—was played by Eva, cast as Lisa Douglas. Their supporting player was a pig named Arnold Ziffel.

Eva, as Lisa, a former Manhattan socialite, became known for dressing in diaphanous gowns and fabulous *négligées,* and for uttering such lines as *"I gad allergic smalling hay."*

Before signing on, Eva cemented an agreement with the producer of the show, Paul Henning, that she would always appear in Jean Louis designer frocks, even while feeding her two favorite chickens, "Henrietta" and "Alice." *Green Acres* was set in Hooterville, the same backdrop for *Petticoat Junction* (1963-1970).

In the most inappropriate wardrobe in the history of television, Eva drifted through chicken coops and hogpens in outfits that included marabou *négligées,* always overdressed, always looking ready to attend a ball at the Waldorf Astoria. She pulled off this stunt through 120 episodes, and the public loved her charm and style. "My character was inane, but popular," she said. "I was more Marie Antoinette than Lisa Douglas, but who's counting?"

"I was supposed to be a complete idiot in some scenes," Eva recalled.

One critic asserted: "Lisa's skewed world view and domestic ignorance provides fertile ground for recurring gags. Much of her early life was lived in Hungary, where she grew up as a diva of her time, which explains

"Gothic America" never looked this good, when **Eddie Albert** (as Oliver Douglas) and his Hungarian wife (**Eva Gabor**) moved to Hooterville to startle the local hayseeds with their ideas about how to manage a farm.

Eva slopped the hogs in a Jean Louis frock and became a household word to the American public, most of whom had never seen any of her screen or stage appearances.

her lack of education and her ignorance of normal household chores. Her waterless coffee oozes from the pot in a thick, tarlike sludge; her hotcakes are inedible, so tough that Oliver makes head gaskets for his truck and tractor using her recipe. Her sandwiches included such epicurean delights as liverwurst and jelly."

"I was a dazzler in my silk, organza, and chiffon, along with my ostrich feathers, sequins, and rhinestones," Eva said. "On some episodes, I appeared in seven different outfits."

"Every morning, I had to get up before dawn and go to the studio in a chauffeur-driven limousine to face my hairdresser. My hair was teased and tormented. My character of Lisa preferred a skyscraper hairdo on top of my head."

"I virtually had to give up my life," she claimed, "to maintain this 4:30am to 9pm regime five days a week. No more partying for me. I almost never went out. During part of the run, I flew to New York to be with Richard Brown, to whom I was married at the time. He was a stockbroker on Wall Street. Things eased up a bit when I got him a job with CBS in Hollywood."

Albert defined the series as "all slapstick, silliness, and *schtick,*" and Eva agreed.

"Eddie was a dear man," she said, "and very kind to me. He was a tireless conservationist, crusading for healthy food, endangered species, and against polluting the bay at Santa Monica."

"In later years, there were some women who have come forth alleging that he'd raped them," she said, "but I saw no sign of such violence during all my years of working with him."

"Eddie jogged every day, and was proud of the way he kept his body trimmed," Eva said. "One morning on the set, after jogging, "He whipped off his robe to show off his physique. He was clad in a pair of jockey shorts that were almost transparent. He might as well have been nude."

"Eat your heart out," he said.

"That was as close as we ever came to having sex," Eva said.

During the first season of *Green Acres,* Eva was voted the most popular woman actress on television. "I was written up as an overnight sensation, but it took me twenty-five years to really make it at a time when I was dangerously close to forty. The Hollywood Hills are filled with talented actresses who were never offered a job after they turned thirty-five."

During its first four seasons, *Green Acres,* along with *The Beverly Hillbillies,* remained among the top twenty TV shows. The series was canceled by CBS, however, in 1971 during that network's famous "rural purge," inaugurated as a result of its hopes of attracting a younger viewer demographic. Most viewers of *Green Acres* at the time were at least 40 years old.

After that, although one final husband lay in Eva's future, *Green Acres* would represent the highlight of her show-biz career. "With a little gig here and there, and some voiceovers, it would mainly be *Here's Lucy, The Flintstones,* and frequent appearances on *The Merv Griffin Show* for me," Eva said. "Oh, yes, lest I forget, there were several appearances as a panelist on *Match Game* between 1973 and 1982. And of all things, *Tales of the Klondike* in that 1981 miniseries. But in other words, after *Green Acres,* Eva Gabor, as an actress, was on the road to nowhere."

***

One of Eva's worst episodes with a male movie star was so traumatic she revealed it to no one outside her family, with the single exception of celebrity seer, John Cohan, author of the book, *Catch a Falling Star: The Untold Story of Celebrity Secrets,* published in 2008. Over the years, many of his celebrity clients, including Elizabeth Taylor, told their most intimate secrets to this sensitive, loyal, and deeply intuitive man.

Cohan has been a celebrity psychic to the stars for more than three decades, offering insights to such stars as Natalie Wood, Merv Griffin, River Phoenix, and Elvis Presley. Nicole Brown Simpson was a friend of his, as was "the love of my life," Sandra Dee, former wife of Bobby Darin. Eva Gabor numbered among his friends and clients.

At one point, she shared a dark secret with him: One which involved her brutalization and rape by actor Lawrence Tierney.

That fateful evening began at the recently re-named Cocoanut Grove Night club at the Ambassador Hotel in Los Angeles. Eva had wanted to attend Sammy Davis, Jr.'s appearance at the Club. Because he was one of the investors, the club had been temporarily renamed, at his instigation, with the trendier label, "The Now Grove." Previously, Eva's close friend, Merv Griffin, had appeared for several singing engagements at the club.

The Celebrity Seer and psychic advisor to the Hollywood stars, **John Cohan,** learned shocking secrets from, and offered advice to, clients and friends who included Eva Gabor, Elizabeth Taylor, and dozens of others.

Eva knew who Tierney was, but was not that familiar with his career, having seen him in only one movie, *Dillinger,* the 1945 gangster film, a tale of "blood, bullets, and blondes."

Eva revealed to him the ugly details of one of the most traumatic experiences she ever suffered.

She was aware of his reputation as one of the "Bad Boys" of Hollywood, but viewed him as rather harmless, except for his heavy drinking.

Griffin was supposed to have been Eva's escort for the evening, but at the last minute, he had taken ill. Through some change of plans, it was arranged for the actor Lawrence Tierney (brother of movie star Scott Brady) to escort her instead.

Eva knew that Tierney had been involved in a number of drunken brawls, which had landed him in jail on occasion. In just seven years between 1944 and 1951, Tierney was arrested twelve times for drunk and disorderly conduct, often as part of violently public fistfights.

The Brooklyn-born actor was Eva's same age, and had been a star athlete in school, and for a brief period, had modeled tight-fitting jockey shorts for Sears Roebuck & Co.

He'd lost that job when the editor of the Sears catalogue decided that Tierney looked obscene in his panties. "We don't want to give our less endowed customers a case of penis envy," the Sears executive had said.

When they were introduced, Eva found Tierney "rather handsome and very masculine. He had quite a lot of sex appeal. Over drinks, we bonded in talks about our stalled film careers."

"I resent having to play all those bold, bad killers," he told her. "I never thought of myself as that kind of guy. I'm really a nice guy who wouldn't do such rotten things."

Not all of Eva Gabor's experiences with Hollywood leading men were romantic.

Her worst encounter was with **Lawrence Tierney,** seen in this picture as if stripping down for sex.

The brutal attack on her from "Hollywood's most dangerously sociopathic bad boy" traumatized Eva for years.

She later claimed that she felt "Lawrence was speaking from the heart."

He admitted that in the 1960s, movie roles had been scarce. When he returned to New York, hoping to find stage work, he'd been forced to take odd jobs, working as a bartender, construction worker, and even driving tourists in a horse-drawn carriage through Central Park.

Before Eva confided details of her night of terror to Cohan, with the clear understanding that "I've never been a nun." She insisted that she enjoyed sex when it was within the context of meaningful encounters with men she liked. "Touches of interpersonal warmth and humor from a man are requisites to whether I will consent or refuse a suitor," she claimed.

"My sexual experience with Tierney was horrible, brutalizing, and terrifying," she told Cohan.

At the night club when not listening to Davis sing, "Tierney manipulated me with his tales of woe. At the end of the act, he feigned illness, shutting his eyes. He said he needed to lie down."

She admitted escorting him to the bedroom that had been arranged for her use, thanks to the patronage she enjoyed through Griffin and his long-standing relationship with the Ambassador Hotel.

Once inside the room, Tierney recovered quickly from his so-called illness and changed into Mr. Hyde, Eva charged. "Like a lady, I refused his offer of sex, because at this point, he turned me off. I first tried to tease him when he felt my breasts. I pushed him away. 'Don't be a naughty boy,' I told him. But he was very persistent. When he saw that I was going to resist his advances, he slapped me real hard. He shoved me back onto the sofa and ripped off my gown."

"He was very strong, and had once done some boxing, so he quickly overpowered me. I was afraid he'd injure me or harm my face, unless I gave in to him. He told me, 'You'll love it, bitch. All the sluts in Hollywood go for my big dick.'"

"He forced himself into me, a brutal penetration. It seemed like he was deliberately causing me pain as a means of showing off what a big man he was."

"It seemed like an hour, but was probably much shorter," she recalled. "I wanted it over with. I was afraid he might harm me."

"Finally, he pulled out of me, but was no less threatening," she said. He told me 'If you tell anyone about this, I'll come after you.' I felt terrorized by him."

"I suffered from that attack for years," she said. "For a long time, I felt a fear of intimacy until I remarried. I had once been carefree, but he traumatized to me the danger of living the life of a celebrity."

"The movie tough guy could really be tough beating up on a woman," Eva said, bitterly.

A few years later, after her rape from Tierney, she read that he'd been arrested and questioned by the New York City police in connection with the death of his 24-year-old girlfriend. She'd plunged from the window of her apartment to her death below. Tierney was in the apartment at the time. He claimed she'd jumped in a suicidal leap.

Eva told Merv Griffin, "I have my doubts. I think he pushed her to her death. It could have happened to me had I not given in to him."

***

In 1972 Frank Sinatra began to pursue Eva Gabor.

Before TV talk show host Merv Griffin became more intimately linked with Eva, he often referred to Zsa Zsa and Eva as "my favorite and most amusing guests on TV," the "Gorgeous Gabors" and "The World's Greatest Sister Act."

Nine years after the assassination of JFK, in advance of the presidential elections of 1972, Frank was no longer supporting the Democrats, and had switched his allegiance to Richard Nixon and Spiro Agnew. The world learned that Frank was dating Eva when he showed up with her at several Republican Party events at the invitation of Agnew, who had become his close friend.

Because of her unpleasant experiences with Frank in the late 1950s, Zsa Zsa warned Eva about Frank.

"My *dah-ling* Zsa Zsa, all men are dangerous," Eva responded. "I would think a woman of your age had learned that by now."

On their fourth date, Frank decided it was time to seduce Eva, and she seemed most willing. But disaster occurred later that evening. Eva had had lovers before, including Tyrone Power and Glenn Ford, but none with a penis the size of Frank's.

Although known as a gentle lover, he apparently got carried away that night and plunged too deeply into Eva. As she later told her mother, Jolie Gabor, "He split me in two. Something ripped inside me." She had to be rushed to the hospital that night in an ambulance, as she was bleeding.

One would think that was enough to turn her off Frank. But in three weeks they were back together again. But this time they had an agreement. He was not to plunge all the way in.

Instead of being ashamed for harming Eva, Frank seemed elated. He bragged about it to his fellow Rat Packers. He wanted the story to get back to Rubi. "Zsa Zsa could easily take Rubi, but I sent Eva to the hospital," Frank bragged.

In her memoirs, Eva's long-time companion, Camyl Sosa Belanger, wrote about Eva and Frank in her biography, *Eva Gabor: An Amazing Woman*, published in 2005.

Belanger claimed that "Eva and Frank were in love, wild about each other, and they were eager to be married." Their hot romance lasted for six months until it cooled down. Eva was between husbands at the time, and Frank was on a rebound after Mia Farrow.

Eva had divorced her fourth husband, stockbroker Richard Brown, and had not yet married her fifth spouse, Frank Jameson, Vice President of North American Rockwell.

Eva later said that her romance with Frank was "the most passionate I ever had, far more than all my husbands combined. We were both on the rebound, but the right age, and each in the peak of our prime."

"Since we were on the rebound, our only healer was sex," she claimed. "We could not wait to go into the bedroom. We made love on the carpet of my living room, in the shower, on the kitchen table, and everywhere else, even out by the pool."

"One night he was in my kitchen making spaghetti, but couldn't find the oregano," Eva said. "Since he couldn't make the sauce without the oregano, we did the next best thing and ended up making out on the kitchen floor."

"They were very hot for each other," Belanger claimed in her memoirs. "Eva was that hot sexy type, and so ardent that she did not hide it and whoever escaped Eva it was their loss."

English, of course, was Belanger's second language.

Frank later told Peter Lawford, "I had to go slow and break Eva in, but now that she's used to my size, she can't get enough of me. After I finish with her, I will have ruined her for all other men."

"My passion for Frank Sinatra was just too intense," confessed Eva Gabor to her longtime companion, Merv Griffin.

"It was just destined to burn itself out. He was at that age when men start looking around for a very young girl—in this case, Mia Farrow. We glamour queens of yesterday had lost some of our glow. He really enjoyed me in the beginning, perhaps too much so. But I watched his roving eye night after night—in restaurants, clubs, and bars. Slowly, ever so slowly, he began to lose interest in me."

Eva's first sexual encounter with **Frank Sinatra** sent her to the hospital. But she came back for more, and they developed a hot and torrid ongoing romance. Both were on the rebound from failed relationships.

"Eva got romance from Sinatra," protested Zsa Zsa, "but all he did for me was to rape me."

"I tried to hold on, but I could see it was a hopeless cause. If he had married me, I would have been very European about his other women. As long as the diamonds and the money kept rolling in, I could forgive an occasional dalliance from a husband."

***

The date was September 21, 1973, and the organist played "More Than the Greatest Love." Eva married her fifth and final husband in a double ring ceremony. Zsa Zsa caught the bouquet, although Eva had aimed it at Tina Sinatra.

Her husband was Frank Gard Jameson, vice president of the manufacturing and electronics giant, North American Rockwell.

[After a series of mergers, spinoffs, and acquisitions, it later changed its name to Rockwell International.]

Jameson lived in Beverly Hills. Jolie, in her memoirs, said "He's not tremendously rich, but he's among the industry barons of the world. He is tall

Eva Gabor's last and final husband was **Frank Jameson**, a Los Angeles "Old Guard socialite" and aeronautical millionaire. The marriage, inaugurated in 1973, would last a decade.

For many years, it was viewed as the perfect match. But as Eva said herself, *"Dahlink*, things are not always what they seem to be."

and very good-looking."

Cindy Adams, the columnist for *The New York Post,* facetiously suggested that "Eva was marrying her 44th husband."

At the party to announce her engagement, Eva appeared in a gown that Adams described as "very *décolleté.* Between the flesh hills of Eva was a cross larger than St. Peter's Basilica. The Gabors were Jewish, so I asked Jolie, 'What's with the goddamn cross?' Jolie said, 'Eva's about-to-be husband hates the Jews, so when you write my memoirs you make us Catholic.'"

In Ms. Adams summation, "The Gabors have always lived with no reality. There was never any truth to anything."

After her honeymoon, Eva went to live in a baronial manse in Beverly Hills, filled with costly antiques, silk upholsteries, and satin curtains. Jameson's hobby involved raising orchids in a mammoth greenhouse.

He noted that most of Eva's day was spent beautifying herself, keeping her body in shape on his tennis courts, in his Olympic-size swimming pool, and in his private gym. "She had developed keeping young to a science," he once remarked to her friend, Merv Griffin. At Eva's request, the gym was equipped with huge mirrors on all its walls.

When Griffin invaded her home with his TV cameras for his talk show, she spoke about how to remain "forever young."

"It's sheer torture," Eva said. "I have to be up with the chickens every day and go to work on my body. First comes the stretching, then the weights. I hate it, but I suffer through it. I've been training to be an actress since I was four. At age five, I began to take beauty sleeps."

She went on: "I'm acting when I'm a hostess, acting when I run my wig business. I was born to act, and life itself is the greatest role. Acting to me isn't just a TV series, a talk show, or a play. I'm a workaholic."

She concluded that she had "come a long way since I arrived in Hollywood. One time, I had only thirty cents in my purse and a husband to support."

"Like Scarlett O'Hara in *Gone With the Wind,* I vowed I'd never go hungry again," she claimed.

By the time of her final marriage, Eva knew most of the major stars in Hollywood, including Cary Grant, James Stewart, and David Niven.

Suddenly, as Mrs. Jameson, she was entertaining a whole new set of friends from the world of politics. They included Richard and Pat Nixon, Ronald and Nancy Reagan, and Spiro Agnew, who once made a pass at Eva, or so she later claimed.

It wasn't clear whether she was a Republican, because she once hosted a "Democrats for Nixon" bash that was hailed as one of the legendary gatherings in Hollywood. For the occasion, Eva rented the Malibu mansion belonging to the former Mrs. Paul Getty.

When Reagan swept into the White House in 1980, Eva continued to entertain the President and his First Lady at parties in Beverly Hills, New York, Palm Beach, and Washington, D.C.

"I had two careers," she told Griffin, "each a 24-hour-a-day job. One was just being Eva Gabor, the other was being the wife of Frank Jameson and entertaining the movers and shakers of the world."

"Just the other day, I got a call from Frank, warning me that he had invited 250 guests over for Sunday buffet. 'Of course, *dahlink,*' I told him. 'That was *vonderful.*'"

"In addition to everything else, there's my wig-and-dress business, which is another 24-hour-a-day job. As a sideline, hawking my lightweight wigs for around $25 each, I take in half a million dollars a year…at least."

As Jolie put it, "My daughter is very very rich. All my daughters are rich!"

[Perhaps Eva didn't have time for marriage after all. It all became too much. She and Jameson divorced in 1983. She would never marry again.]

***

It was 1988, a balmy night in Southern California. All heads turned as Merv Griffin made his way across the floor of L'Escoffier—"the most exclusive restaurant in the world"—on the eighth floor of the Beverly Hilton. And well they should. He not only owned the hotel but was the chief honcho of a multibillion empire. The *maître d'* rushed toward him to usher him to the best table in the house. In fact, legend had it that Merv had bought the hotel to make sure he always had his favorite table.

Leading the march across the elegant room, with its panoramic views, was the Hungarian beauty, Eva Gabor, who'd become his permanent "arm candy." He'd never seen her look more stunning in her taupe gown and what she called "my Cinderella slippers." Around her swan-like neck was a diamond-and-ruby necklace he'd presented to her only that afternoon. He told her that it had once belonged to Marie Antoinette, knowing that she didn't really believe that but would loudly advertise it as fact.

She loved the necklace but had really wanted an engagement ring to solidify their relationship. He knew, however, that wasn't going to happen. There would be no other Mrs. Merv Griffin. It had taken him three years to untangle himself from his one and only marriage. He had no interest—certainly no sexual interest—in entering into another permanent bond with a woman.

Earlier in the evening he and Eva had stopped off at the hotel bar, making the rounds and encountering Steven Spielberg, Harrison Ford, and Nancy Sinatra. She told him that she'd come just to sample the egg rolls at Trader Vic's that night.

He also ran into a deeply suntanned George Hamilton, who said, "Look around you. There are at least five or six big-time movie stars here with their off-the-record girlfriends. But it's so God damn dark you can't make out anybody. Thank God there are two entrances. If a wife walks in one, the waiter can hustle the mistress out the other door."

In spite of the sad news he'd learned earlier in the day, Merv had a light step as he made his way through the restaurant greeting guests. He'd long ago learned to disguise his true feelings. He was still "every mother's favorite son-in-law," although getting a bit long in the tooth for that appellation.

He always felt more of a man when he had a beautiful woman like Eva on his arm, even though she was an expensive adornment. Hollywood was nothing if not public images. It was a city where truth didn't matter. Only the method you chose to deceive the public. All his life he'd believed in playing by the rules, not changing the game.

He didn't want to die like his best male friend, Liberace, did in disgrace, succumbing to AIDS and having his reputation destroyed. If Merv could control events, there would be no notoriety to surround his death the way it had in the case of Rock Hudson, his former lover in the 1950s.

Unlike Rock and Liberace, Merv knew how to protect himself. No virus would get to him. As he candidly told Eva, his most trusted confidante, who knew all his secrets, "I plan to die of natural causes. Not some disease I picked up from an overnight trick."

Seated at table in L'Escoffier, and looking like a Hungarian princess, Eva didn't have to request her drink of the evening. Her champagne was already chilling. "Could you imagine a Gabor drinking any-

Eva Gabor and **Merv Griffin** appear as a happy couple.

The TV talk show host loved her deeply during the course of his platonic relationship with her. He provided a luxurious lifestyle for her, and she was willingly used as "arm candy" to deflect rumors about his homosexuality.

thing else?" she had once asked him. Indeed he couldn't.

But there was one big change on her menu for the night. She'd abandoned her usual caviar for a treat the chef had secured for her. The best salami from Budapest had been flown in.

Eva would give up anything for salami. "It is a delicacy created by the Gods," she told him.

To take the "curse" off such a lowly cold cut, Merv had ordered the most beautiful orchids placed on their table. Eva said that when she consumed salami, she always wanted to be wearing diamonds and surrounded by orchids. In fact, she'd entitled her tell-nothing memoir, *Orchids & Salami*.

Tonight in familiar, swanky surroundings, Eva was in what she called "my gay mood"—she still used the word in its old-fashioned sense. Skilled as a courtesan and arguably trained at the role since birth, she knew that her job was to entertain Merv.

On this particular night, Griffin did not seem amused by either her wit or her charm.

"What is it, *dahlink*?" she asked, sympathetically taking his hand. "You look so sad, so blue." Usually he was jolly and fun, filled with amusing anecdotes. After all, he'd interviewed or else had known practically every celebrity in the world from Marilyn Monroe to Marlon Brando. "It's Nancy," he said, looking depressed and dejected.

During his good moods or bad ones, he could always count on Eva to listen patiently to his troubles. Like a good courtesan, she was always reassuring. "You succeeded beyond your wildest fantasies," she told him. "You became not only rich, but the wealthiest man on the planet."

"I wouldn't go that far," he cautioned her.

"Rich and adorable, an irresistible combination," she said. "Zsa Zsa and I have found that rich men are all bastards. You're a marvelous exception to that rule. Who on Earth doesn't adore Merv Griffin?"

Eva knew that Nancy Davis Reagan was his best friend. He'd canceled many an engagement with Eva to escort Nancy to some function. Once when Eva had an argument with him, she accused him of plotting to marry Nancy after her husband, Ronald Reagan, died. "That would be the ultimate triumph for you," she charged. "Marrying the woman who presides over the Free World. You could get a lot of publicity marrying the First Lady. Aristotle Onassis did. Did you know he proposed marriage to me before he asked for the hand of Ms. Jacqueline Kennedy?"

"In your dreams," he said.

Eva had stormed out of his living room, but the next morning they made up at breakfast. It seemed that every night they had some silly argument, yet in most ways, she, not Nancy, was his best friend. He privately told his confidants that "Nancy is best friend, Eva first mistress." He always laughed at his own joke, and so did his staff, although no one seriously believed that he'd ever gone to bed with Eva.

"You still haven't told me why you're so sad," she said.

"You've got to keep this a secret," he said. "Nancy will break it to the world when the time comes. No one must know."

"What is it?" she asked, genuinely interested.

"Nancy called me this afternoon from Washington with the bad news. She's just found out: Even Ronnie doesn't know yet. But the President has been diagnosed as having Alzheimer's disease."

"Oh, my God!" she gasped. "No one must find this out. The Stock Market would crash. There could be calls for his impeachment."

"That's why you're going to keep this news under that pretty blonde wig of yours."

After fifteen minutes of trying to console Merv, she said, "You need some serious distraction. You need some fun and games, and I know you've got something planned later in the evening to take your mind off the Reagans. Your mother knows about such things."

"You're so understanding," he said.

"But you're such a cad. You could have planned some fun and games for little ol' Eva. Perhaps that handsome lifeguard you hired two weeks ago. Don't tell me you've not had him already."

"You know too much," he said. "Fortunately, you're not in a habit of calling the *National Enquirer.*" After dinner, Merv ostentatiously escorted Eva to her suite. Passers-by in the hall saw him as he disappeared inside with her, an indiscretion he wanted them to publicize. But he was going only for a nightcap.

She poured him a drink and gave him a feather-light kiss on the mouth before heading into her boudoir and dressing room to begin her nightly beauty treatments designed to keep her, in her own words, "forever young."

During her long relationship with Merv Griffin, Eva sometimes entertained close friends of his, **President Ronald Reagan** and his wife, **Nancy**, *(depicted above).* "Even at their age, Ronnie and Nancy were still passionate with each other," Eva said.

Eva considered herself Griffin's best friend, and resented it when he informed people that "Nancy is my best friend."

***

Griffin had met Eva when both of them had been cast in a TV show entitled *The Wonderful World of Toys*.

Before this meeting with her in the early 1960s, he'd seen her hilarious appearances with Jack Paar on his talk show. At the time Merv met her, she was deep into her fourth marriage to Richard Brown.

Years later, Merv recalled his first luncheon with Eva. He found her witty, charming, and beautiful. As a gay man, he was not sexually attracted to her, but found her desirable as an amusing companion. As he recalled, "Eva and I parted as potential friends. She gave me a light kiss on the lips."

"Someday, when we're both older," she predicted, "we'll be friends. We Hungarians are like gypsies. We know of such things. But, right now, both of us have too much living to do."

He was amused at their keen ability to deliver one-line zingers. Zsa Zsa was the best at fast quips.

On his show, Eva sometimes gave beauty tips, especially if it concerned the wigs she was promoting. "A girl likes to look her best, even if she cheats a bit, or especially if she cheats a bit. All women have to deceive the world, especially about their age."

Sometimes, Zsa Zsa became angry at Eva's on-air remarks, as when she said, "I was the first actress in the family, and I am still the *only* actress in the family. I shouldn't be saying that. It just slipped out."

Merv was often asked if Eva was like the character she played on *Green Acres*.

"She was a smart business woman, but sometimes she could be just like her character," he said. "I remember once when I invited Eddie Albert and her to stay at my ranch. That morning Eva came down the stairs in a feather boa. Eddie is a big animal rights guy, and he was outraged. 'Eva, don't you know where those feathers come from?' he yelled at her. She screwed up her face, very quizzical, and said, 'Pillows?'"

One of Merv's fondest memories of Eva as a guest on his talk show involved the episode when she appeared with Eddie Albert, her *Green Acres* co-star, alongside the then-most-powerful TV critic in the industry, Cleveland Amory. "He'd panned their show," Merv said, "And on-camera, both Eddie and Eva attacked him. He might have been the nation's number one television critic, but he left that show really scathed. I learned from that broadcast that you never wanted to get on the bad side of Eva."

Merv once claimed that "Eva was born to appear on TV talk shows." In 1951 she'd been a guest of Steve Allen on his first talk show for CBS. Allen, in fact, did even more than Merv to introduce the Gabor Sisters to American television. "The glamour and humor of the Gabors came into family living rooms across the nation," Merv said, "And Zsa Zsa was even better at the *double en-*

tendre than Eva."

Sometimes, especially when Merv had been drinking, he privately asked Eva outrageous questions. "Is it true that when you worked on *Artists and Models* with Jerry Lewis and Dean Martin, you slept with both men? And is it true that Jerry has three inches, Martin ten?"

"No woman should ever reveal a man's most closely guarded secret, even to his enemies," Eva diplomatically responded.

She would say things whimsical, gracious, and charming, such as "All any girl needs at any time in history is simple velvet and diamonds." On the other hand, Zsa Zsa would utter something funnier. "I wasn't born, *dahlink*, I was ordered from room service."

After watching so many appearances by both Eva and Zsa Zsa "on the couch" on TV talk shows, author Anthony Turtu said, "Eva's turns were always glamorous, witty, and serene—unlike appearances by her unpredictable sister, who could always be counted on for her brand of fireworks."

Merv called Zsa Zsa, Magda, and Eva "*Vonderful Vimmen*. They conquered kings, princes, playboys, movie stars, and millionaires, broke hearts while amassing fortunes, and became adored by the world at the same time. Of course, all women held tightly on to their husbands when one of them walked into the room. They were the Budapest Bombshells."

***

On an impulse in 1979, Eva called Merv and asked him to join her vacation party on their upcoming tour of Asia. In dire need of a long holiday, he told Eva, "What the hell? You only live once." So he arranged for several shows to be pre-taped in advance of his time away, and agreed to join Eva and her then-husband, Frank Jameson, on the tour, with the understanding that it would include stops in South Korea, Hong Kong, Taiwan, and the Philippines.

They were guests of William Rockwell, Jr., the CEO of Rockwell International (a manufacturer of advanced weapons systems), and his wife, Constance. For Rockwell, this was a major showcasing of the company's products. For others in the party, including Eva and Merv, it was just a bit of vacation fun. Rockwell and his entourage were flown aboard a converted 727. Preoccupied with the serious business of PR, corporate politics, and weapons sales, Jameson "tolerated" Merv. Eva, however, adored him. It was the first time she'd ever spent a great deal of time with him.

"You really know how to enliven a boring party," Eva told him, looking directly at her husband as she said that.

Rockwell's converted 727 had scheduled a stop on Midway Island, famed for a role during World War II as a battleground between the naval forces of the

U.S. and the Empire of Japan.

When Merv landed there, he discovered that several hundred Navy personnel and their wives followed a daily routine which involved watching *The Merv Griffin Show* on a communal wide screen TV. During the broadcast, business in the Midways virtually came to a halt. "It was an important ritual for them in those remote islands," he wrote in his second autobiography. "It was one of the ways they maintained a connection to home."

When Merv, Eva, and members of the Rockwell contingent walked in, with fanfare, at the end of one of the broadcasts, it caused pandemonium.

After Eva's divorce from Jameson in 1983, she turned to Merv for comfort. "Despite the many husbands she'd had, Eva was crushed by the final divorce," he claimed. "In her way, she really loved Frank and hated losing him."

He invited her to visit his ranch in the cool mountain air over the Carmel Valley. "She came to heal herself, and we grew close," he said. He generously offered her long-term use of one of the half dozen guest cottages on site. "Stay here forever," he told her. "You're most welcome."

Like the protagonist in the play, *The Man Who Came to Dinner*, Eva moved in, interpreting as a literal fact his invitation to stay forever. It cemented the long-enduring friendship that would last almost until her death.

He recalled that at the ranch she'd get up early every day. "I'd get up an hour later and walk down to the stable. By then, every horse in the pasture would have red lipstick on it."

In the next few months, Eva became his "arm candy," going on trips with him and appearing with him at premieres and public events.

"Eva had a love for Merv, but at his age and at his weight it was not sexual," Jolie confided to friends. "Every day of my life I tried to get Merv to marry my daughter. I knew if she married Merv, she would be secure for life and never worry about having to sell wigs or appear in some dumb TV sitcom."

As Merv revealed in his second autobiography, he and Eva often passed the day to-

In 1984, **Merv** and **Eva** came up with an idea for a TV series that included both Eva and Zsa Zsa. He even hired scriptwriters, who concocted the story of *Two Hungarian Maids*.

"These maids would be more like queens," Merv said. "The most hilarious duo of house servants history has ever known. Regrettably, the networks turned it down."

"Just as well," Zsa Zsa said. "Who would ever believe that Eva and I could be maids?"

gether lying on sofas in his living room. "I'd get on one couch, Eva on the other," he said. "We'd lie there for days at a time—laughing, sleeping, laughing, watching television, laughing, eating, and laughing some more. We almost never argued except when we watched *Wheel of Fortune*. She'd get furious because I knew all the answers in advance."

Zsa Zsa knew the full details of the "arrangement" between Merv and Eva, but in her second autobiography, *One Lifetime Is Not Enough*, she chose to be discreet. "She is happily involved with Merv Griffin and has a marvelous life with him," Zsa Zsa claimed. "I like Merv a great deal, did hundreds of shows with him, and am glad that Eva is now so happy."

Behind the scenes, Zsa Zsa, like her mother, was constantly urging Merv to marry Eva and "make an honest woman out of her. There are many marriages without sex. It's an old Hungarian custom. Men marry, have children with their wives, and then stash them away so they can spend the rest of their lives with various mistresses."

Merv got a taste of Zsa Zsa's famous temper in 1989 after she'd been thrown in jail for slapping the policeman who stopped her for a traffic violation. "All my friends came to support me in court," Zsa Zsa told Merv. "But not you—and not Eva." She took particular exception to a quote by Eva that appeared in the press. The item quoted Eva as saying, "Mrs. Kirk Douglas and I just had lunch, and we agreed that if Zsa Zsa hadn't talked so much, this stupid thing would never have happened."

Before slamming down the phone, Zsa Zsa told Merv, "I'll never speak to the bitch ever again."

But in a few days, he succeeded as peacemaker, bringing the two warring sisters together for dinner. Over wine, with tears, both Eva and Zsa Zsa poured out their "undying love" for each other.

***

In 1991, Eva stood by Merv during what she called his darkest hour. "If ever he needed a friend, it was during that awful year."

Double jeopardy came for Merv at the age of sixty-five, when he was slapped with both a palimony suit and a sexual harassment suit. Filing the complaint was a handsome thirty-seven-year-old former employee, Brent Plott. He had previously been Merv's "secretary/driver/horse trainer/and bodyguard." In his complaint, Plott stated that in addition to the duties cited, he'd been Merv's lover.

He also charged that he'd been Merv's business consultant and was entitled to a share of the Griffin fortune. As an example, Plott maintained that he'd played a big role in the creation of *Wheel of Fortune,* and he also took credit for personally selecting Vanna White as hostess of the show.

The lawsuit sought in excess of $200 million, according to Miami attorney Ellis Rubin, who filed the claim with Los Angeles attorney Stephen Kolodny.

Plott had left Merv's employment in 1985, moving to Florida. It is not known why he waited until 1991 to file the lawsuit.

Rolling Stone, in a piece written about Merv, analyzed the issues associated with Plott's palimony suit and the subsequent sexual harassment suit.

"Merv does not refute the underlying implication in both cases: that he is gay," the magazine claimed. "Nor does he admit to it. Instead, he mentions the high-profile relationship that he began with actress Eva Gabor at the time of his legal troubles. They were photographed everywhere: Atlantic City, La Quinta, Hollywood premieres. Merv says that they discussed marriage, and he parries any direct questions about his sexual orientation. 'You're asking an eighty-year-old man about his sexuality right now!' he cries. 'Get a life!'"

Plott had alleged that Merv's relationship with Eva was a cover-up. "Every picture she's in, I am there too," he claimed. "She went where Merv and I went. The editors crop me out."

The most insiderish look into Eva's relationship with both Merv and Brent was published by Camyl Sosa Belanger in her memoir, *Eva Gabor: An Amazing Woman*, in 2005. Camyl had worked as a personal assistant to Eva for some twenty years.

In February of 1991, Belanger recalled that she had been at Eva's home when Merv and Eva returned together from a trip to Palm Springs.

"*Dahlink*, can I tell Camyl?" Eva asked.

"Sure, why not?" Merv said.

"Merv and I are getting married," Eva told her friend.

Belanger had been urging the marriage for years—"a better catch, forget it." Her book makes it obvious that she knew that it would be a marriage based on financial security, not romance. The next day Eva told her that Merv was insisting on a prenuptial agreement.

After Plott filed his palimony suit in April of 1991, Belanger said "All hell broke loose." Merv called Eva, because he wanted her to know what had happened before it appeared in the news media.

After the call from Merv, Eva turned to Belanger. "Remember Brent?"

Belanger said that, of course, she remembered him. "Is he back?"

Merv Griffin only proposed marriage to Eva after **Brent Plott** *(above)* brought a $200 million palimony suit against him.

When the case was dropped, so was Merv's proposal of marriage.

At one point Eva admitted that "the kid deserves all the money he's asking for. It is no peanuts. He wants millions. No wonder Merv asked me to marry him. He knew all along that Brent was planning to sue him."

Belanger later asserted that news of the lawsuit did not come as a shock to Eva because she knew about "the close relationship" between the two men right from the beginning.

Eva called her friends, including Zsa Zsa, and Eva's voice was filled with remorse. "We've known for decades that Merv was a homosexual. Now the public will know. The whole world will know. The secret is finally out in the open."

Belanger wrote about Eva's tolerance, about her acceptance of Merv's homosexuality, and specifically about his love affair with Plott. "Eva was at the time really annoyed and humiliated because, after all, Eva loved and respected her friend, and seeing him like a wounded soul was no joy to Eva. Eva knew it all along, and she lived with them, and they went out to places together and to long trips on the road and to Europe, so Eva was used to that kind of life and she did not care."

Belanger wrote that Eva enjoyed "traveling like a queen and with expenses paid."

Many of Eva's friends later admitted that "she's one of the most gay-friendly women in Hollywood, where the competition for that title is keen."

Belanger herself was saddened by the lawsuit, because she too had seen the relationship between the two men first hand. "How can anyone destroy many years of happiness and drag each other in the mud when there was so much love during the young fresh years when one had eyes only for each other? From what I had seen during the fresh years, it was love and equality and eating from the same table."

In the days and weeks ahead, Eva was hounded by the national media for an articulation of her reaction to the lawsuit. *The Star*, *The Globe*, and *The National Enquirer* were virtually harassing her day and night. Belanger claimed that both Plott and Merv had treated Eva with "love and kindness like a little sister, especially after her last divorce." It was obvious to Eva's friends that her loyalties were tested. In the end, of course, she sided with Merv.

Putting up a brave public front, Eva told the press, "I've been with Merv for nine years, and I can tell you, this is ridiculous." Privately to her friends, Eva had maintained all along that Merv was gay and that her relationship with him was platonic.

In an outrageous statement on *The Joan Rivers Show*, Zsa Zsa suggested that it was Eva who should be suing for palimony. "After all, she lived with Merv for nine years."

In November of 1991, Plott's case against Merv came before Judge Diane

Wayne of the Los Angeles Superior Court. She dismissed it "with prejudice," meaning that the case could not be refiled. The court also fined Plott two thousand dollars for bringing the case against Merv. A spokesman for Merv claimed, "This was a totally baseless suit from a guy trying to make a quick buck."

Many observers disagreed with that opinion, thinking the case "had a lot of legs." Others were surprised at the quick dismissal.

When news reached Eva that the lawsuit against Merv had been dismissed, Belanger asked Eva about the status of Merv's marriage proposal.

Eva's answer was somewhat enigmatic. "Come on, *dahlink*, don't play dumb. It is out in the air and that is all—and there is nothing to worry now."

***

In the spring of 1998, Merv granted an interview to Matt Tyrnauer of *Vanity Fair*. During their time together, Merv discussed Eva, who had died three years before. "Those years had great ups and downs," he said. "We really loved each other a lot, but sometimes we would leave each other and go to different people. She would go to someone else, and I would go to—say, Princess Elizabeth of Yugoslavia. We had broken up just before her death, but when we were together we traveled everywhere: Morocco, all the islands."

The Pulitzer Prize-winning columnist Herb Caen of *The San Francisco Chronicle*, once said, "If Merv and Eva ever stopped laughing, they'd get married."

"Now everyone says, 'God, we really miss the two of you,'" Merv said. "We were like another version of Lucy and Desi."

He refused to tell Tyrnauer the reason he split from Eva, although he did confess that they'd planned to be married, with Nancy Reagan serving as the matron of honor. "There was a pre-marital agreement," he said. "But we could never agree which house we'd live in, and I couldn't agree which of her staff she would bring with her and that really drove us apart. It's awful, because there is so much more I can't tell. It was a monstrous problem and it wasn't mine—but I will never drag Eva's name through the mud."

The "monstrous" problem that he referred to was Eva's demand that he settle fifty million dollars on her for all the years she'd been his companion. If he didn't come across with the money, Eva was threatening to file a palimony suit against him, like his former companion Brent Plott had done.

After learning of her intentions, he could not forgive her, and ordered her from La Quinta and all of his other properties. When she'd returned to her own home and recovered from her immediate anger, Eva told her friends, "I don't know what got into me. My Hungarian temper, I suppose. I would never have sued Merv, but he should have made some financial settlement on me."

The unresolved marriage—or money—issues between them bubbled over "when he fell madly in love with a young hustler and wanted to spend all his evenings with the handsome little stud—and no more evenings with me," Eva said.

In June of 1995, after her split from Merv, Eva journeyed to Baja, Mexico, where she had a home. Bitterly disappointed over the failure of her relationship, she claimed she was in desperate need of a vacation.

On June 2, she "ate a bad piece of fruit" in her words and contracted viral pneumonia. As her condition weakened, she refused to seek help from Mexican doctors, having no faith in them. In her disoriented state, she collapsed on a staircase in her house, falling about ten steps to her foyer. Her hip was broken.

Eva's housekeeper placed a call to Merv, who claimed he was "devastated" to hear of Eva's injury. He immediately called for a private jet to transport Eva from Baja to the Cedars Sinai Medical Center in Los Angeles.

When Eva was admitted there on June 21, doctors discovered fluid in her lungs and a blood clot. She was also running a dangerous fever. Put on a respirator, she was given the injectable anticoagulant drug Heparin for the clotting and antibiotics for the pneumonia.

Experts have speculated that Eva may not have died of viral pneumonia, but of pneumococcal pneumonia, a horrible bug that can kill within twenty-four hours.

Under heavy medication and with her condition worsening by the hour, she slipped into a coma. Death came at 10:05 on Tuesday, July 4, 1995. Presumably, Eva was seventy-six years old, although some have disputed that.

The increasingly senile Jolie wasn't immediately informed of her daughter's death, but Zsa Zsa and Magda, her older sisters, attended a 7pm memorial service at the Good Shepherd Catholic Church in Beverly Hills. Eva had been cremated.

Paying his last respects was her faithful co-star of *Green Acres*, Eddie Albert. He embraced Merv, who also greeted fellow mourners Rosie O'Donnell, Johnny Mathis, and Mitzi Gaynor. The matriarch of the Gabor clan, Jolie, and Eva's older sister, Magda, would each survive another two years.

From aboard his yacht, *The Griff*, Merv had heard about Eva's death and went into shock before flying back for the funeral. "Only because we'd had an argument, and we hadn't settled the argument yet, and I was mad, and I was off on my boat, and she died while I was gone. That was rough."

Reportedly, his final words to Eva before they departed forever were, "I've loved a thousand times, but never been in love."

CHAPTER FIFTEEN
As Long as Memory Lasts
WHATEVER BECAME OF ZSA ZSA?

As Rubirosa moved into the final years of his too-short life, Zsa Zsa continued to follow his every move. Rafael Trujillo, the ruthless dictator of the Dominican Republic, appointed Rubi ambassador to Cuba. That made his wife, Odile Rodin, the youngest ambassadress in the world at age nineteen. Guerilla fighter Fidel Castro had seen pictures of Rodin, and he once told a reporter, "When I install myself in Havana, I'm going to make this girl my mistress."

However, when Batista forces fled from Castro's guerillas, Rubi and Rodin also left Havana. Rubi's greatest concern involved arranging for his polo ponies to be safely transported back to the Dominican Republic.

Even though he professed love for Rodin, Rubi wasn't always faithful to her. On a trip to visit his friend, John F. Kennedy, on a summer yachting trip in Hyannis Port, he managed to seduce Patricia Kennedy Lawford.

After the President's assassination in November of 1963, Rubi even made overtures to his widow, Jackie Kennedy. She turned him down

At one point, Rubi had gone through all the money given to him by his two former wives, Doris Duke and Barbara Hutton. In one year alone, he'd wasted two million dollars. When she read this, Zsa Zsa said, "Rubi is going to have to learn to live like a poor person again." He was forced to sell his elegant townhouse in Paris, and all the antiques Duke had presented to him.

With Rodin, he moved to a small village outside Paris, Marnes-la-Coquette, where Maurice Chevalier was their neighbor.

His friend, designer Oleg Cassini, said, "To live without money was torture for Rubi. At one point, he told me he might divorce Rodin and marry Patricia Kennedy Lawford when her divorce from Peter Lawford came through."

"He had many schemes to make money," Cassini said, "none of them successful. Sometimes I paid his bills. He tried to launch a perfume called 'Rubi,' in ruby-colored glass. He attempted to market a Caribbean aphrodisiac made from herbs and tree bark. It was the first liquid Viagra. To capitalize off the reputation of his legendary penis, he also made the outrageous claim that the essence would cause a man's penis to increase in length by three inches."

The Greek shipowner, Stavros Niarchos, claimed that aboard his three-masted schooner, *Creole*, Rubi even shot his own version of *Goldfinger*, casting himself as James Bond and Rodin as Pussy Galore.

In the early morning hours of July 5, 1965, Rubi's team won *La Coupe de France* polo tournament, defeating Brazil. He had celebrated the night away at Jimmy's, the chic nightclub. In the pre-dawn hours, he left the club, intoxicated, driving his own Ferrari.

As he was cutting through the Bois de Boulogne, on the western periphery of Paris, he lost control of his car and rammed it into a chestnut tree. In the crash, he was pinned to the ground under the wreckage. A fellow motorist saw the car wreck and called the police. An ambulance was rushed to the scene to take Rubi to the hospital, where he died shortly after admission.

It was Eva who was up early, listening to the news over the radio. She was the first to call Zsa Zsa in Bel Air. A witness reported that Rubi's last words were "Zsa Zsa."

In a memoir years later, Zsa Zsa wrote, "I cried for him, I cried for his charm, for his passion, for his verve, for our love, our romance."

[In 1967, on a trip to Paris, she visited Rubi's grave at Père Lachaise Cemetery. She had a difficult time finding it, searching through the tombstones of dead celebrities who included Colette and Oscar Wilde. When she finally located Rubi's grave, she was shocked to see it unattended.

That very afternoon, she ordered red roses in honor of his name ("Rubirosa"), and placed them in two black marble urns she'd purchased. She also arranged with the caretaker for perpetual maintenance of the grave and a weekly delivery of fresh red roses.

Months later, Zsa Zsa was notified that the two black marble urns had been stolen—presumably by souvenir-hunting fans of the Dominican—and that Rodin had prohibited the caretaker from maintaining Rubi's gravesite and the placement upon it of fresh red roses.

In the years to come, whenever journalists wrote about Rubi, Zsa Zsa's name was forever linked to his legend.]

***

In 1960, Zsa Zsa starred in an Italian film, *La Contessa Azzurra (The Blue Countess),* filmed in Italy, mostly in Rome and Naples. In her second memoir, she devoted almost no space to her role in this movie. Today, it basks in obscurity.

What she recalled more vividly was that one of her former beaux, William Randolph Hearst, Jr., began another "hot pursuit" of her, as she defined it.

Even before she'd married George Sanders, the second son of the press baron, William Randolph Hearst, Sr., had chased after Zsa Zsa, proposing marriage, an invitation she turned down, although their friendship had remained intact. "He was a decade older than her, and she remembered him as "sweet, charming, and clever. He once won a Pulitzer Prize."

[She was referring to his 1955 prize for an interview he'd conducted with the Soviet leader, Nikita Khrushchev.]

"I had divorced George, and my love affair with Rubirosa was over," Zsa Zsa said. "In Rome, Bill and I had separate suites at the Excelsior, but the *paparazzi* was hot on our trail. They had been tipped off by the bribed hotel staff. Bill told me that he'd never stopped loving me, and he was so very, very rich that Jolie would have been pleased to have him as a son-in-law. Although we made love, and it was most satisfactory, I was not in love with him. I later regretted not marrying him."

His father's longtime mistress, screen actress Marion Davies, had been a friend of Zsa Zsa's. At the lavish castle, San Simeon, which Davies shared with the elder Hearst, she often facetiously introduced Zsa Zsa to party guests, informing them, "Here is my bastard daughter, Zsa Zsa Gabor. Her father was Calvin Coolidge."

Bill Jr. amused Zsa Zsa with stories of how he secretly slipped liquor to Davies, who was an alcoholic. "I put booze in Coke bottles," he said, "and we stored bottles of gin in the water tanks of toilets."

After the senior Hearst died in 1951, and after Davies married Captain Horace Brown in the wake of Hearst's death, Zsa Zsa gave a party for the newlyweds. At that time, she resumed her affair with Bill, Jr.

The life story of mining heir and newspaper mogul **William Randolph Hearst** *(far right)* was the inspiration for the lead character in Orson Welles' film, *Citizen Kane*, often hailed by critics as the greatest movie ever made.

He is seen here with his long-suffering wife, **Millicent Veronica Willson**. Between them stands one of their five sons, **John Randolph Hearst**. To the far left is **William Randolph Hearst, Jr.**, who had a love affair with Zsa Zsa and proposed marriage.

"He wanted me as his wife, so bad that he was willing to turn his back on his family, or whatever," Zsa Zsa said. "It was so hard to continue to say no to him. I must give him credit, though. He was the most persistent man I ever knew. Imagine pursuing one woman for decades."

Hearst accompanied Zsa Zsa to Naples, where she had to appear on screen as an old-fashioned vamp styled after the silent screen star, Theda Bara. "I emerged overdressed, with two cougars on the leash. My secretary had brought my little Yorkie to the set that day, and held her in her arms while I filmed the scene."

"The cougars picked up the scent of the Yorkie, and went after her," Zsa Zsa claimed. "My Yorkie jumped out of the secretary's arms and the race was on."

Neapolitans still remember Zsa Zsa outfitted in an elaborate period costume, chasing the cougars along the waterfront of Naples, screaming, "They're going to eat my dog."

Fortunately, stevedores on the dock rescued the Yorkie, and brought the cougars under control.

Back in Rome, Bill, Jr. confronted Zsa Zsa one more time before his plane left for New York.

"Will you marry me?"

"You're the dearest man I know," she said, "but the answer remains no. I love you, but I'm not in love with you."

"Okay, Zsa Zsa," he said, "That was your last chance, I'll never propose again. Goodbye, my dear. A final kiss for what might have been."

Later that night in her suite, "I cried over losing him and was disappointed in myself for not marrying him. Let's face it: I made a lot of bad decisions in selecting husbands. Bill might have been the ideal man for me. Oh, to hell with it."

***

Back in California, Zsa Zsa's theatrical agents at the William Morris agency were receiving all sorts of offers for her services, including continuing proposals of marriage from around the world. "Bill Hearst wasn't the only man, it seemed, who wanted to put a wedding band on my finger," she said. She became one of the first celebrities who actually was paid to attend a party, something that in the 21st Century would be widely practiced by a distant "relative," Paris Hilton, who had a weak link with Zsa Zsa through her former marriage to Conrad Hilton, Sr.

A letter was received from the Teamster boss, the notorious Jimmy Hoffa, who was willing to pay $10,000 if Zsa Zsa would appear in Miami at his wife's upcoming birthday party. He'd married Josephine Poszywak (1918–1980) in 1936.

Zsa Zsa had heard that the labor boss had links to organized crime, but this connection didn't bother her. She told friends, "Frank Sinatra has links to organized crime. It didn't hurt him. If anything, it helped his career."

"I was attacked for flying to Miami to hang out with this truck driver," Zsa Zsa said. "Actually, Jimmy told me that he'd never worked as a truck driver, even though he was head of the Teamsters. He spent a good part of the evening talking about his hatred of Robert Kennedy, who was the Attorney General going after him."

She later claimed that she found Hoffa and his Polish wife "charming and intelligent."

His wife, perhaps on signal, retired early, leaving Zsa Zsa alone with Hoffa in her hotel suite. "I thought they might have an open marriage, and that this was a set-up for me to get seduced by Hoffa. Frankly, I would not have minded, as I was attracted to his raw masculinity."

"But within a half hour after being alone with the labor leader, I became suspicious of his intent, he might have wanted to seduce me, but he had another goal on his mind."

"Hoffa was battling the Kennedys," she said. "I'd heard rumors that he was collecting data on Jack Kennedy and Marilyn Monroe, and he was also interested in other women Jack had slept with. It was a long list. I knew some of the women, notably Joan Crawford, Marlene Dietrich, June Allyson, Susan Hayward, Jayne Mansfield, Kim Novak, Jean Simmons, Lana Turner, and Sonja Henie. Hoffa was aware that I also had been one of Jack's conquests."

"He wanted to know not only about my affair with the President, but what I knew about his other relationships with women. Frankly, my affair with Jack was widely known in Hollywood…. I didn't want to be coy. He was, after all, paying me $10,000. In addition to that, he gave me a $20,000 diamond-and-ruby bracelet that was stunningly beautiful. We Gabors know the price of our diamonds. I admitted to my affair with Jack and supplied him with some details. After all, he was charming with me, and the man was fighting for his life. He didn't want to rot in jail."

"In the coming years, I felt some guilt about having been so frank during my talk with Hoffa," Zsa Zsa said. "Perhaps I should have kept my luscious lips zipped. But everybody knew about Jack's affairs in Hollywood, especially with Marilyn Monroe. So I don't think I revealed anything that was a great secret. Besides, I was

Teamsters' boss **Jimmy Hoffa** was caught giving the finger to Robert F. Kennedy during an investigation into his labor union activities.

Zsa Zsa was paid handsomely for her participation in Miami in a fact-gathering mission Hoffa was conducting. He was seeking information from actresses with whom JFK had had affairs.

amply rewarded. Whenever I have a slight guilt feeling, I try on that bracelet, which makes me forgive myself. Besides, Jack was betraying Jackie by sleeping with all those women. Don't you think so, *dahlink?"*

[In 1964, long after his brief involvement with Zsa Zsa, Hoffa was convicted of jury tampering, attempted bribery, and fraud. After he exhausted the appeals process, he was sentenced to 13 years in jail. As part of a pardon agreement with President Richard Nixon, he was released from prison in 1971. On the night of July 30, 1975, Hoffa was last seen leaving the Machus Red Fox Restaurant in suburban Detroit. His whereabouts became unknown and, on that same date in 1982, he was ruled dead in absentia.

His body has never been found.]

***

It was 7am on a windy morning in Bel Air. Still wearing her diamond earrings, Zsa Zsa was asleep. She had no engagement at any studio that day, and no airplane to catch, so she was furious at this interruption of her beauty sleep.

"Louella Parsons is on the phone," the maid said.

Zsa Zsa did not like Parsons, but was afraid not to take her call. After she picked up the receiver, Parsons wasted no time with preliminaries. "What is your reaction to George Sanders becoming engaged to Benita Colman?"

At first, Zsa Zsa could not believe her ears. For years, Zsa Zsa and Sanders had socialized with Ronald Colman, the English actor, and his wife Benita, a British former actress. Ronald had died in May of 1958. At no time during his friendship with the Colmans had Sanders shown the slightest interest in Benita. Obviously, their romance had developed in secret.

In front of her enemy, Parsons, Zsa Zsa did not want to appear overly concerned. "Yes, I've known about this," she lied. "I've already wished them all the happiness in the world." Then she quickly put down the receiver.

That afternoon, a cable arrived from Sanders:

"Cokiline,

Don't be unhappy. I am really much too old for you. You need someone closer to your own age, someone who can respond to your admirable effervescence, someone who can identify with your goals, someone who has a little more vitality.

I shall always love you, and yield to no one in my admiration of your many qualities.

A big kiss for Francesca, a hug for you.
George"

Before her marriage to Ronald, Benita had been an actress, making her British screen debut at nineteen. One of her films had been Alexander Korda's *The Private Life of Don Juan* (1934), where she co-starred opposite Douglas Fairbanks, Sr.

Her wedding to Sanders took place at the British Consulate in Madrid on February 10, 1959.

Right after his marriage, Sanders wrote Zsa Zsa: "After twenty-two years of uninterrupted residence in America, Benita remains uncontrovertibly English. I think we have a good chance to be happy. Ronald never liked me very much, but Benita does. Benita's experiences parallel mine. We think alike on all subjects and our values are the same. Living in England, we miss the Brian Ahernes, the Joseph Cottens, the Charles Boyers, and the Ronald Reagans."

Quite by coincidence, weeks later, Zsa Zsa was dining in London with the producer Jimmy Woolf and his lover, Laurence Harvey. Alec Guinness had also joined the party.

Afterwards, they opted to appear, collectively, at Annabel's, the very posh and most sought-after nightlife venue in London at the time. As it happened, Benita was there, dining with Lady Sylvia Ashley, known as the former Mrs. Clark Gable.

At one point, Benita approached Zsa Zsa's table, and in a reference to Sanders, said, "Dear heart," she said, "I'm going to take good care of the old boy."

Benita complimented Zsa Zsa on her looks, but all Zsa Zsa could do in return was to tell Benita how stylish her hat was. It was only after Benita left their table that Guinness told Zsa Zsa, "Benita was not wearing a hat."

In time, Zsa Zsa forgave both Sanders and Benita for marrying each other, and finally admitted that Benita was a good wife to her former spouse. At dinners with Zsa Zsa, Benita always referred to Sanders as "our husband."

Sanders and Benita eventually left Hollywood and went to live on the farm in Kent, England, she'd purchased with Ronald during better days.

As the 60s tragically moved on, Sanders wrote Zsa Zsa that Benita was "desperately ill. She's eaten up with

George Sanders and **Benita Colman**, Ronald Colman's ex-wife, pose as a happily married couple in Lausanne in 1963, four years after their wedding. At first, Zsa Zsa was shocked, but she retained her friendship with the couple.

With great good humor, Benita jokingly advised Sanders, "We should adopt Zsa Zsa as our beloved daughter."

cancer and has become a skeleton. I cannot go into her bedroom to face her. The shock I could not conceal on my face would tell her I knew there was no hope, and it is by the smallest margin of hope that she hangs on to life, each painful, tedious day."

***

Zsa Zsa always made the claim that Frank Sinatra pursued her because he wanted to prove that he was a greater lover than his friend, Porfirio Rubirosa. "Rubi's affairs with women put Frank to shame," Zsa Zsa said. "Although he liked Rubi, Frank was also very jealous of him, even more so because these two men often messed around, as it's called, with the same women, notably Marilyn Monroe."

Both Rubi and Sinatra had also seduced Joan Crawford, Lana Turner, Eartha Kitt, Jayne Mansfield, Kim Novak, Marlene Dietrich, and Judy Garland.

Sinatra was aware that all of these beauties could, from memory, compare the size of his penis and boudoir skills with those of the legendary Rubirosa's. Sinatra didn't like that at all, telling Sammy Davis, Jr., "I'm the great lover of the western world—not Rubirosa!"

Frank's friendship with Rubi was severely tested when he read in the gossip columns that Rubi had shacked up with Ava Gardner before Frank's marriage to her in 1951. But both Rubi and Frank survived Ava, and their friendship continued over the years.

Frank decided to pursue Zsa Zsa, although she'd previously gone on record for not preferring Latin men. Obviously, Rubi had been an exception to her dating rule. "Maybe this was because, along with his Latin blood, he had a mixture of other kinds of plasma in him, the way they do in the West Indies," Zsa Zsa said.

"Also he was quite a bit French, since he was brought up and went to school mostly in France. This made for a wonderful combination. I've always said that in animals I prefer purebreds . . . but not in men! Think of that wonderful Prince Philip, who is Greek and German, and I don't know what else. I seriously considered, for a time, becoming the Royal Mistress of Buckingham Palace. I'm sure Queen Elizabeth would not have minded. But back to Rubi. Talk about mixed bloods! Think of all those American men, the result of a great melting pot. Such men as these mixed breeds are the best of everything. Regrettably, only Italian blood flowed through Sinatra's veins. Italian men, of course, have their charms, but also their flaws . . . many flaws."

In 1955, Zsa Zsa Gabor was thirty-eight years old . . . at least. She'd already survived three divorces—the Turkish diplomat, Burhan Belge; the hotelier Con-

644

rad Hilton, and actor George Sanders who later married—briefly—her older sister, Magda.

In Frank's opinion, "Zsa Zsa was ripe for plucking and also . . . rhymes with plucking."

It's true that Frank seduced two of the Gabors, both Eva and Zsa Zsa, but his experiences with each of the glamorous sisters were remarkably different.

He first encountered Zsa Zsa in the late 1950s after she'd divorced actor George Sanders. Over the years she'd seen him at various Hollywood parties, but she had never been alone with him.

When she received a party invitation from Mrs. Delmer Davies, the wife of a producer, she was told that Frank wanted to escort her there.

Frank arrived on time at Zsa Zsa's house in Bel Air and even met her daughter, Francesca Hilton. Francesca seemingly adored Frank and was very impressed that her mother was "dating such a heartthrob."

"I really turn on the eight-year-olds," Frank said jokingly as he drove to the party with Zsa Zsa.

The evening began with dinner at La Rue Restaurant on Sunset Boulevard, where Frank kept his hat on throughout the entire meal. "To hide his bald spot, *dahlink*," Zsa Zsa later claimed.

Whenever anyone made revelations about him to the press, **Frank Sinatra** *(as in the photo above)* never managed to conceal his anger.

Although Eva had enjoyed her affair with Frank, Zsa Zsa had not. She always claimed that he'd raped her.

"He wanted to prove to me that he was a better lover than Rubirosa, which he was not," Zsa Zsa said.

Later, at the party, Zsa Zsa and Frank created a "sensation" with their joint appearance. Then he drove her home. "A little kiss with tongue I anticipated," she recalled. "But he pushed by me and forced his way inside."

In her entrance vestibule, he told her, "When I take a woman out to dinner and a party, I always make love to her before the evening is over. With you, I have no intention of putting a blot on my record."

"I am not one of your statistics," she shot back at him.

"He just wouldn't move," she recalled. "It was a Mexican standoff. When he pleaded that he had a migraine from hell, I told my maid, Maria, to show him to the guest room."

With Frank out of the way, Zsa Zsa rushed up the stairs and locked herself in her own bedroom. Two hours later he was banging on her door, demanding to be let inside. She adamantly refused and ordered him to go home.

Later, she fell asleep. When she didn't hear any more from him, she assumed that he'd let himself out and that he'd driven himself home in his gold Cadillac.

But when she arose the next morning to see Francesca off to school, she found Frank's car was still there in her driveway.

She knocked on the guestroom door and he told her to come in. He was walking around in the nude. He grabbed her and allegedly told her, "I'm not leaving until you make love to me."

There are various stories about what happened next. Eva once claimed that Zsa Zsa told her that Frank raped her. "I told Zsa Zsa to send word to Frank that he could rape me any night he wanted to," Eva said.

"Since he wouldn't leave, I made love to him," Zsa Zsa wrote in her memoirs, not defining the experience as rape. "I made love to Sinatra so that he would leave, and from then on, I hated him. And Frank knew it."

Initially Zsa Zsa claimed that she didn't want her daughter to leave for school and see Frank's Cadillac still in the driveway. "I didn't want her to think less of her mother."

Zsa Zsa later claimed that Frank wreaked his revenge upon her, especially in Las Vegas. He'd arranged for her to be a guest star on one of his TV series. "He kept me waiting and never showed up," she claimed. On another occasion, she was appearing in a show at the Riviera and Frank in a competing show at the Sands. He asked her to come on with him for ten minutes at the Sands, and he would return the favor and appear with her at the Riviera the following night. "I didn't fear rape that night because Frank was being sexually satisfied by Dinah Shore."

As part of his act at the Sands, he introduced her as "Zsa Zsa Grabber. Oh boy, would I like to grab her."

The next night, Frank never showed up at the Riviera, where Zsa Zsa was getting $35,000 a week. "My bosses were furious that I'd appeared at the Sands for free. I was embarrassed and humiliated and knew that this was Frank's revenge on me."

Even though Zsa Zsa made it clear she didn't want to have sex with him again, there was yet another unwanted encounter when he was married to Mia Farrow. She accepted an invitation to a screening of his latest movie at Frank's home on Mulholland Drive. In the middle of the film, Zsa Zsa got up to go to the toilet. She was surprised to find no lock on the door of what she called "the powder room."

Once she was inside, Frank walked in on her without knocking. He bluntly told her, "I want to make love to you again." He grabbed her breasts and began to undo the buttons on her black silk blouse. She pushed him away. "I'm leaving your home—never to return," she told him. "Don't you ever put your hands on me again."

On the way home that night, Zsa Zsa came to realize that Frank wanted to seduce her because of the reputation of Rubi. "Frank's persistent attempts to make love to me had been prompted by his burning desire to prove that he was as great a lover as Rubi."

There was also the battle of the penises: Which of them had the larger organ? Frank wanted to use Zsa Zsa to prove that he—not Rubi—was the better hung.

Zsa Zsa later admitted, "Had Frank not come on to me like a bull in the china shop, I might have been charmed by him—he did have charm. I might have gone to bed with him. We might even have been happy together and embarked on an affair."

***

With Sanders settled down into contentment with Benita Colman, Zsa Zsa looked elsewhere for a beau, eventually settling on Hal Hays, a multi-millionaire building contractor. "He was good looking and wholesome," she said. "Hal and I sometimes double dated with Jolie and Liberace—yes, Liberace. For a brief time, he kept proposing to Jolie, even though she was happily married. Obviously, Liberace wanted to conceal his deepest secret behind the façade of marriage. Jolie knew that Liberace was seeking a lavender marriage."

After meeting Zsa Zsa, Hays pursued her every day, presenting her with a 25-carat diamond engagement ring after only two weeks. It cost him $250,000, although it would be worth $3 million today. "I couldn't return a ring that valuable," she said,. "So I agreed to marry him." She later claimed that the ring weighed *Forty Carats,* which was the name of a Broadway play in which she appeared in 1969.

During the time she was dating Hays, Zsa Zsa made a scandal that was featured in newspapers across the country. She engaged in a catfight with the aging actress Merle Oberon, who had invited her to her home in Beverly Hills for a party she was hosting for Mr. and Mrs. Henry Ford II. Zsa Zsa asked Hays to escort her to the party, not knowing that he had once been Oberon's lover. After he dumped her, Oberon had been bitter.

At her party, Oberon greeted Zsa Zsa but didn't speak to Hays. Within thirty minutes, Oberon had cornered Zsa Zsa, telling her that she could stay for dinner, but that Hays would have to leave her home after finishing his cocktail.

Zsa Zsa was stunned, later telling the press, "Miss Oberon must know that I am not in the habit of going to parties alone. I always arrive with an escort. I just assumed Miss Oberon's invitation included my escort."

With Hays at her side, Zsa Zsa bolted from Oberon's party to face a dozen reporters and photographers outside. They had been covering the arrival of all the A-list visitors who were there to honor the Fords.

Playing to her audience, Zsa Zsa sobbed, "It was such a shock to me that

Miss Oberon would treat me in such a way. She kicked out my *fiancé*. I thought she'd learned how to behave at parties. Perhaps she's been living in Acapulco too long. I think the Mexican sun has poached her brain."

"Come along, Zsa Zsa," Hays said, taking her arm. In the limousine *en route* home, he admitted that he had been Oberon's lover. "I walked out on her, and she's never forgiven me. When she saw me with you tonight, she went into a jealous rage."

After the debacle at Oberon's party, Zsa Zsa staged her own dinner party, tipping off the press. At the Cocoanut Grove nightclub in the Ambassador Hotel, she invited "the ten most eligible bachelors in Los Angeles," including Hays. She was the lone female.

The picture that made the papers was of an architect, John Lindsay *[no relation to the New York City mayor]*, pointing a water pistol at Hays, warning him to keep away from Zsa Zsa.

"All the men at my party were millionaire businessmen—not one actor among them," she said. "Before the night had ended, I danced twice with each of them."

Zsa Zsa went to live with Hays in his seven-floor house built alongside a mountain overlooking Sunset Strip. Torn from the pages of Architectural Digest, it was one of the most dramatic residences in the Greater Los Angeles area.

Hays' previous lover, actress Joan Blondell, had lived in the house with Hays before his involvement with Zsa Zsa.

Businessman Hal Hays specialized in lucrative government contracts for the construction of cheap, prefabricated houses. He also specialized in glamorous movie stars. His former lovers had included **Merle Oberon** *(top photo, left)* and sexy **Joan Blondell** *(top photo, right)*.

"Hal and I used to throw parties for 200 to 300 guests," Blondell said. "It was the swankiest bachelor pad in Los Angeles, complete with an artificial beach and an orchid grotto. Guests parked on street tracks cantilevered out past retaining walls."

"A live oak tree grew out of the living room floor, and a real brook filled with coral fish ran through, right under a twenty-foot waterfall in the foyer."

His dramatic home *(lower photo)* rose seven floors alongside a mountain overlooking Sunset Strip. It was accessorized with a fortified bomb shelter in the event of a nuclear attack. After Zsa Zsa's departure, the house was briefly occupied by Mike Todd and Elizabeth Taylor.

"The most luxurious touch were the gold faucets pouring forth the best Scotch, bourbon, and vintage champagne. Hal called them booze faucets."

"Some of the parties were raucous," Blondell claimed. "Guests stripped down in the living room, beside a swimming pool whose waters flowed out under the walls and into the garden."

"Hal was also afraid of a nuclear attack from the Soviets. He built an underground tunnel that led to a fortified and hermetically sealed underground cave with oxygen tanks and enough provisions to last a year."

When Jolie visited the mountain-hugging house, she said it was a good thing that Zsa Zsa never married Hays. "The place was huge, but there would not have been room for their respective wardrobes. My God, the man had racks of tailor-made suits, sports jackets, and tuxedos, all from Savile Row in London. He owned at least a hundred pairs of shoes, many of them made from the skins of endangered species."

"Hal and Zsa Zsa did not have a true love affair," Jolie claimed. "She was just filling in between marriages. Unlike George Sanders, Hal was not stingy with Zsa Zsa, and he was richer than the kings of most small countries."

Another scandal erupted when Zsa Zsa was living with Hays. Using low-interest loans from the government, he had become famous for the construction of cheap housing on U.S. military bases, supervising a construction empire that boasted that it could erect a home, assembled from prefabricated components, in thirty-four minutes.

The press began publishing breathless reports about the massive diamond that Hays had presented to Zsa Zsa. Newspapers reported its size at forty-five carats. Officials in the government wondered how Hays was able to afford such a valuable ring when he was tardy in his loan repayments to the government. An investigation was called, in which Zsa Zsa's name was frequently mentioned.

After being fined, Hays slipped away quietly to exile in Mexico. For years after his departure, his legendary seven-story home continued to attract a celebrity clientele. At one point it was briefly occupied by Elizabeth Taylor and Mike Todd.

After biting off Evander Holyfield's ear, boxer Mike Tyson reportedly wanted to buy the house. One of its most famous recent tenants was (the musician formerly known as) Prince who rented it from the owner Carlos Boozer (yes, that's right), the Utah jazz player. He sued Prince for painting the house in purple stripes.

A devotee of movie stars, multi-millionare **Hal Hays** escorts **Zsa Zsa** to dinner where she cuddles up to him, perhaps in appreciation for his gift of a mammoth diamond ring—"The kind I adore, *dahlink*."

***

With Hays living in exile and departed from her life, Zsa Zsa was offered a small role in the 1962 film *Boys' Night Out,* starring Kim Novak. The movie was about three married men, as played by Tony Randall, Howard Duff, and Howard Morris, who are looking to meet needs not satisfied at home with their wives. They share the rent on a love nest apartment with their divorced friend (James Garner). Zsa Zsa was assigned the unnamed role of "Boss's Girlfriend."

On the set, she had a reunion with Novak, whom she hadn't seen since the headlines about their involvement with Ramfis Trujillo. Novak brought Zsa Zsa up to date on the tragedies he had endured since she'd seen him last.

After his scandal-soaked involvements with Novak and Zsa Zsa, Ramfis had returned to his island home, where his wife, Octavia Ricart, filed for divorce. He also fell out with his father, Dominican dictator Generalíssimo Rafael Trujillo, who had heard stories about his son's participation in gang rapes and his "frivolous" calls for the murders of local citizens who displeased him.

Ramfis had been sent to a sanatorium in Belgium, where the staff diagnosed him with severe psychological problems, which led to his receiving electroshock treatments. He would undergo these severe treatments until the end of his life.

On May 31, 1961, Generalíssimo Rafael Trujillo was assassinated, ending his iron-fisted, thirty-one year dictatorship of the Dominican Republic. Ramfis returned to the Caribbean island and ordered the murders of many of the suspects implicated in the death of "The Goat," as Trujillo had been mockingly nicknamed by his enemies.

Ramfis, too, had many enemies, and later, in 1961, he was forced into exile, fleeing to France aboard his luxury yacht, *Angelita,* where he had previously made love to Zsa Zsa. On board he had stashed $4 million in cash and jewelry.

In 1962, Ramfis settled in Spain under the protection of another notorious and much-loathed dictator, Generalíssimo Francisco Franco.

In a fate similar to that of his friend, Rubirosa, Ramfis was the driver of a car that, on the outskirts of Madrid, sustained a head-on collision with a car driven by Beltran de Lis, the Duchess of Albuquerque, killing her instantly. He lingered for a few days in a hospital before dying on December 27, 1969.

Neither Zsa Zsa nor Novak attended the funeral.

***

650

Before her next marriage, Zsa Zsa managed to seduce three of the leading sex symbols of the world, each an actor: Richard Burton, Richard Harris, and Sean Connery. "I always preferred British men over others in the world, although there were many, many exceptions to my rule. I was merely stating a preference, not a practice."

As Jolie once remarked, "Frank Sinatra may have ended up on Zsa Zsa's list of most despised men, but not Richard Burton. Zsa Zsa knew him so very well before he flew off to find comfort in the arms of Liz Taylor, or whatever it was he found, *dahlink.*"

It was New Year's Eve, 1961. Producer Jimmy Woolf (without Laurence Harvey) had invited Zsa Zsa to a party. He arrived at her Bel Air home in a tuxedo to pick her up. She was surprised to see that his "date" for the evening was Richard Burton.

She invited both men in for a drink. Burton accepted, claiming, "I've been known to indulge." Woolf excused himself to go into the library to place a phone call to Harvey, who was in London.

"Seated opposite me, Richard wasted no time in idle chit-chat," Zsa Zsa later said. "Those gorgeous blue eyes of his seemed to have radar vision. I just happened to be wearing a Dior gown of red velvet with a plunging *décollétage*. He could see all the way to Honolulu."

"Let's skip the fucking party, ducky," he said. "Let's head up the stairs to your bedroom, where I want to make mad, passionate love to you all night."

"In spite of his pockmarked skin, I was overwhelmed by this man," she said. "I had enough smooth skin to make up for the both of us. Like a common tramp, I accepted his invitation. Of course, that meant we had to ditch Jimmy, and he was such a *dahlink*. He'd have to go to the party without us, where I knew he'd meet a lot of beautiful young men who wanted to get cast in his next picture. After Richard and I kissed Jimmy goodbye, we were off for a night of dancing at the Cocoanut Grove."

"On the dance floor, Richard held me so tightly, I thought he'd smother me," she said. "I could feel something growing down below. He became so excited I warned him to save it for later. When he wasn't whispering sweet nothings into my ear, he was

"The Prince of Players, **Richard Burton**, performed brilliantly in my bedroom," Zsa Zsa later proclaimed to her friends.

"Shortly after our affair, and when he made *Cleopatra* with Elizabeth Taylor, Richard became defined in the press by his personal life—not for his uncanny ability to act."

"His story was never really told—take the time he was caught in a bordello with Errol Flynn or the night he and Frank Sinatra got into a fist fight. He indeed had some wild nights in Hollywood and London."

tonguing it. I decided right there and then that there was a god in heaven after all."

Back at Bel Air, she told him that they were alone in the house. Francesca was away, and Zsa Zsa had given the staff a three-day holiday because of the New Year.

"I will always remember that night and our subsequent days alone together," she said. "We'd already sung *Auld Lang Syne* at the Cocoanut Grove. Now it was time for other maneuvers. He couldn't even wait to go upstairs. Before I knew what was happening, he had all my clothes off, and we were lying nude on a white fur rug in front of my fireplace."

"His love-making was unrelenting and divinely satisfying," she said. "He was an animal, violently attacking me, and I adored this style of working man seduction from the coal mines of Wales. As he seduced me, he never stopped talking, even reciting a Shakespeare sonnet in that erotic, romantic voice of his. When he called me his bitch and tore into me, I was enthralled. Not since Rubirosa had I ever experienced such a lover."

"We slept until noon on New Year's Day, and when he woke up, I served him champagne, caviar, smoked salmon, and Hungarian salami. Even though he was married, I decided he should get a divorce and wed me."

"We made love twice that afternoon, once in my swimming pool," she said. "The day was a bit chilly, but the pool was heated. He even took me on the tiles on my kitchen floor."

"He talked a lot about his former life, his goals, his hopes and dreams," she said. "He even spoke of his previous love life. Most men didn't do that. I wasn't jealous of all those other women like Lana Turner and Ava Gardner. He was here with me now...and mine. Claire Bloom, eat your heart out!"

"Either on top of me or else just talking, he exuded virility. He even spoke of his homosexual past when, as a young actor in London, he'd succumbed to the advances of such stars as Laurence Olivier and John Gielgud."

"But he found he preferred women," she said. "His style was to take a woman by the sheer force of his personality. There was a certain roughness and lack of grooming to him, but that seemed to make him more enticing. He literally devoured a woman. He seemed enraptured by my beauty. He told me that Elizabeth Taylor, whom he'd met, and myself were the two most beautiful *femmes fatales* of the 20th Century."

"Once, in the middle of the act, he asked me if his 'mighty mallet' was hitting all the right spots. I assured him that it was."

"He consumed a lot of liquor during his stay with me, but it didn't seem to slow him down sexually," she said.

"He told me that when he was a young man growing up in Wales, his chums called him 'Beer Burton'"

"I could down two pints of beer in just ten seconds," he told her. "One night, a student spiked my beer with wood alcohol, and I crashed down a flight of stairs and nearly broke my neck and spine. Drinking can be hazardous. So can heavy wenching, when you get caught *in flagrante delicto* with some irate husband's wife."

He was also very casual about nudity. Since they were in the house alone, he virtually didn't get dressed during his entire three-day stay. He told her that he was unable to appear n *Women in Love,* based on the D.H. Lawrence novel, so consequently, the two lead roles went to Oliver Reed and Alan Bates, who appeared in a full frontal nude wrestling scene. "I had another commitment; otherwise millions of fans around the world would have gotten to see what Burton uses to whack off."

"With Richard, I increased my English vocabulary" she said. "He called the imperfections on his skin 'grog blossoms,' from too much grog consumption. He also taught me another word he'd picked up as a boy in Wales: Shagging. He defined it as 'knocking off' everyone in sight."

"I've picked up women in pubs, at the cinema, even going to shop for supplies," he told her. "When I married Sybil, I made love to our hotel maid within hours of saying my marriage vows. I was born with the devil in me, hell bent on going on a sexual rampage through life. God put me on this earth to raise sheer hell. I drank hard. I played hard, and, with a woman, I rule the roost."

"I should have been like Marilyn Monroe and kept a diary," Zsa Zsa said. "I adored his quotes."

"I like my reputation," he told her. "That of a spoiled genius from the Welsh gutter."

"When I was young and randy, I used to drop my trousers in a pub to show off my 'wand of lust.'"

"When I made *The Ice Palace* in 1960, I told the crew, 'If there's a dame on this set I can't screw, my name's not Richard Burton,' I think I lived up to that boast."

"I was in a state of absolute rapture during those three days and nights I lived with Richard Burton," she said. "To hell with tomorrow. Unfortunately, tomorrow eventually came."

Burton had to leave to make a film on location, and he passionately told Zsa Zsa goodbye after a night of love-making. They would never be lovers again, although they would sometimes encounter each other in the years to come.

"We remained friends, although I wished he'd proposed to me," she said. "Elizabeth Taylor finally got the prize. Richard was not the only time Elizabeth and I pursued the same man, beginning with Nicky Hilton when he was just a teenage boy."

***

[When Richard Burton returned to Hollywood after his appearance in The Longest Day, *he arrived at Zsa Zsa's mansion. He didn't have her phone number, so he just showed up at her doorstep.*

Zsa Zsa was out on a date that evening. But Eva was visiting Zsa Zsa after having flown in from New York.

Since Zsa Zsa wasn't at home, Burton took advantage by seducing her younger sister instead.

"People have even written in biographies that Richard and I never made love to each other," Eva said. "How would they know? Damn it, we did make love. How dare some moron write that we did not?"

"I found Richard an absolute charm," Eva said. "Irresistible, in fact. He had pockmarks all over his face and back—very bad skin—and stood no more than five feet six. But he made up for it in every other way, with his powerful torso, rugged features, hypnotic blue eyes, and that compelling voice of his."

"Of course, I'm just trying to set the record straight," Eva said. "No need to tell Zsa Zsa, dahlink. That will teach her to stay at home."]

***

Another British actor, Richard Harris, had a very different, more combative relationship with Zsa Zsa. Since she was going to be in Europe making a film for an extended period of time, she decided to rent her home in Bel Air to Harris.

Richard Harris and **Vanessa Redgrave** as they appeared in the film version of *Camelot* (1967).

A boisterously drunken Harris had sung "If Ever I Would Leave You," on the lawn of Zsa Zsa's Bel Air manse.

The following day, after apologizing, he performed other stunts for her, too.

As a "Welcome to Bel Air" gesture, she decided to introduce him to the neighbors at a party. As she recorded in a memoir, he showed up intoxicated. Burton had told her, "Harris makes even me look sober."

Wearing an Indian headband, he brought his own butler and even his housekeeper, who spoon-fed him because he was too drunk to eat by himself.

Zsa Zsa claimed that in front of gossip columnist Rona Barrett, Harris told her, "I'm not going to leave this house tonight until I fuck you!"

She ordered him out the door, where

654

he collapsed on her lawn, singing, "If Ever I Would Leave You," from *Camelot.*

Zsa falsely claimed in a memoir that she had to call the Bel Air Patrol to haul him off. Actually, however, as witnessed by her butler, she put him into a rented car and had his own butler drive him back to his bungalow at the Beverly Hills Hotel.

[The night Harris sang "If Ever I Would Leave You" on Zsa Zsa's lawn, he might have rather bizarrely interpreted it as an early rehearsal for his role of King Arthur. He would star in the 1967 film version of Camelot *with Vanessa Redgrave. Like Zsa Zsa, she, too, would have an outrageous story to tell about Harris.*

One day he came onto the set proudly displaying his erection to the cast. He told director Joshua Logan, "I wanted something handmade for my queen."]

The next day, Harris showed up on Zsa Zsa's doorstep with two dozen red roses. He was sober and contrite, asking to be shown around the house to learn its eccentricities before moving in. "I promise I won't attack you, although you are so beautiful any bloke should be forgiven for raping you."

"He was such a rogue, but he had a lot of male flash and charm," Zsa Zsa said. "When he flashed that famous smile of his, all was forgiven."

She invited him for lunch. Out on her terrace he settled for only one beer. He even tried to explain his reckless behavior. "Ever since I was a boy, I was a horny bastard. I had this one picture of Merle Oberon, and for about three years when I was growing up, I used to masturbate to that damn picture. Guess what? Since coming to Hollywood, I've had the pleasure of having the real thing, Merle herself."

"She invited me into her bedroom, where she later appeared in this see-through *négligée* with nothing on underneath. I could see these fabulous tits and a gorgeous black bush. Sadly, my fantasy as a teenage boy was better than the real thing. Fantasies always are."

At the time Zsa Zsa met Harris, he was married to Elizabeth Rees-Williams, the daughter of David Rees-Williams, 1st Baron Ogmore. She didn't ask about his wife, and Harris didn't mention her name.

As the afternoon lengthened, he told her about his early life and how he'd wanted to be a rugby star until his career was cut short when he came down with tuberculosis.

He related how he put all his savings into the Clifford Odets play, *Winter Journey,* a script eventually turned into *The Country Girl* before Grace Kelly starred in its film version. In 1954, she won the Oscar because of it. "My play was a critical success, but nobody came to see it," he told her. "I ended up homeless, sleeping in a coal cellar with the rats for six weeks."

Zsa Zsa had seen only one of his films, *This Sporting Life* (1963), where he'd played a bitter young coal miner who became an acclaimed rugby league player. The role earned him an Oscar. She praised his extraordinary talent, and he seemed flattered by the attention.

"I've always been searching for the right woman, a woman to haunt me, a woman to tear my insides out. At least that's how I feel sometimes. At other times, my ideal woman is a beautiful, mute nymphomaniac who runs the local boozer. I can't tell you how disheartened I'd be if a love affair didn't end tragically. I've no idea who I am. I'm five people, and each of them is fighting the other four. When I'm in trouble, I'm an Irishman. When I turn in a good performance, I'm an Englishman."

"What eventually won Zsa Zsa over was when Harris sat at her piano and played the Jimmy Webb song, "MacArthur Park." Although she found the wording strange, the sound was very moving. "He sang it like a little boy lost, looking for a woman to cradle him in her breasts."

[In 1968, Harris would release a recording of "MacArthur Park," which shot to the top ten list of hits in both the U.S. and Britain.]

In spite of warning bells going off, she found Harris a compelling and fascinating personality. Before the afternoon ended, she had agreed to let him move into her house in advance of the official debut of his lease so he wouldn't have to pay the high rent for the bungalow which had only recently been vacated by Howard Hughes. "He could afford it, and I can't."

As she became more intrigued with him, she found he had a sensitive nature. He'd even written an ode to her, which he read to her. He'd entitled it "Zsa Zsa in the Rosy Glow of Dawn."

[For whatever reason, it was not included in his 1973 book of poetry, I, In the Membership of My Days.*]*

Zsa Zsa admitted to her friends that, "What really won me over to Richard was when he kneeled before me and kissed my hand ever so gallantly. With those beautiful eyes, he looked up at me. 'All I need to straighten me out is the right woman to love me. I need love. Oh, so desperately I need someone to love me and see through all this bluster of mine to the poor wounded Irish soul who lurks beneath my skin.'"

"After that, *dahlink,* what could I do but take this divine man to bed with me? We both knew it would be a momentary pleasure, and we'd each move on with our lives. But, for once, dear heart, there was a Camelot in my life."

***

When Sean Connery met Zsa Zsa in a London studio, he must have been impressed with her because she claimed he began to call her five times a day. However, three months would go by before they hooked up with each other in

Hollywood.

"I'm in town, and I must see you at once," he told her.

She was on the way out the door for the fitting of a satin gown at the studio of designer Rubin Parnis. She suggested Connery could meet her at the shop on Melrose Avenue.

She remembered him showing up in jogging clothes, which made all the salesgirls practically swoon. She found him "sizzlingly handsome, rippling with masculinity and virility."

In her memoir, she was rapturous about him. "He had an amazingly beautiful body, one of the most beautiful bodies I had ever seen. His skin feels as soft as velvet, as sensuous as silk. He was more romantic than passionate, but a great lover."

The handsome Scottish actor was thirteen years younger than Zsa Zsa. He soon added her to a list of conquests which included Ursula Andress, his co-star in *Dr. No (1962);* Lana Turner, his co-star in *Another Time, Another Place* (1958); and Shelley Winters.

Before arriving at Zsa Zsa's Bel Air manse, Connery's reputation had preceded him. Most actors sung his praise, but journalist Pete Hamill claimed "Sean Connery is a great, big, conceited, untalented, wooden-headed ninny."

In contrast, Steven Spielberg called him, "One of the five genuine movie stars in the world. He's also a classy guy, and you don't come across many of those in this business."

Terence Young, director of three of the James Bond films, claimed, "Sean could become the biggest movie star since Gable, but he doesn't give a damn about the ancillary assets of being a star."

"I know actors don't like to be compared to other actors, " Zsa Zsa said, giving her own evaluation. "But I found Sean the closest that any other actor came to Clark Gable, who was a friend of mine. Sean had the same mix of mustache and twinkle. He looked world weary before his time."

Movie critic Davis Thomson found Connery "glossy, supercilious, rather cruel, close to absurdly attractive, and as hard and abstract as the wig he wore."

Honor Blackman, who had interpreted the role of Pussy Galore during her 1964

"Sean Connery was gorgeous, sexy, charismatic—a dashing hunk of Scottish manhood" proclaimed Zsa Zsa. "No wonder Lana Turner and Shelley Winters couldn't get their fill of him."

"I think he was put on this Earth for two reasons: To play the James Bond character, and to make love to beautiful women."

appearance with him in *Goldfinger*, also sounded his praise. "I find Sean attractive and sexy. I think he's got a pair of the best eyes that have ever been seen on the screen, apart from anything else he might have—and there's plenty of *that.*"

"I invited him for dinner, and he wanted to drive me to the Farmers Market to pick out the ingredients," Zsa Zsa said. "He selected a leg of lamb along with some 'weird' English veggies like Brussels sprouts and parsnips. Apparently, the English ate these root vegetable in the Middle Ages."

In the opulent surroundings of her Bel Air home, Connery spoke of growing up poor in Scotland. "My father was a lorry driver, and my mum a char. I went to work at the age of nine, delivering milk. Once I worked for a local butcher, hauling out the guts of animals he'd cut open."

"He had a voice that could make you melt," Zsa Zsa said. "He confided to me that he really wanted to be a singing star. In fact, he sang 'Pretty Irish Girl' to me. He'd done that in a movie he'd made in 1959 called *Darby O'Gill and the Little People.* With a title like that, no wonder moviegoers stayed away."

"He'd had such a success with the James Bond pictures appearing in *Dr. No* and others," she said. "But he told me he hated the role."

"I think the movie was glitzy, mannered, and dangerous," he claimed. "There is so much speculation about my image these days, whether I'm really like Bond, rude and aggressive. What am I supposed to do about it? Go around wearing a sign saying I have played the classics on stage and read books—the whole of Ibsen, Pirandello, Shakespeare, and as much of Proust as I could wade through?"

Now, everybody wants me to star in something, but it wasn't always that easy," he told her. "When Michael Winner was casting a film called *West Eleven,* he called Oliver Reed and me strictly B-picture actors. He thought Julie Christie was a useless blonde bimbo, and James Mason a has-been."

At one point the subject of women-beating came up, and she confessed that she'd been beaten by both George Sanders and Rubirosa.

"I don't think there's anything wrong in hitting a woman," he said. "Although I don't go around recommending it, an open-handed slap is all right if a wench gets out of line. If a woman is a bitch, or hysterical, or bloody-minded continually, then I'd do it."

"You can rough me up any time, *dahlink*," Zsa Zsa said.

As the night lengthened, he told her, "If you proposition, me, you'll find that I have a weak will. I discovered that when I was fourteen, walking along a London street in my military uniform. An older woman approached me and took me back to her flat. There, she demanded that I rape her. I'd never had a woman before."

In her boudoir, Zsa Zsa was enthralled when he stripped down for her.

658

"He was a magnificent specimen, a great physical beauty. He'd been praised for his 'satanic sensuousness,' whatever in the hell that meant. He was a real gentleman, aiming to please a lady, and he did so splendidly. I wish he'd kidnapped me and made me his forever, but alas, he had other fish and chips to fry. For him, I would have made the greatest sacrifice and eaten Brussels sprouts."

"In my exploration of his body, I discovered that he had two tattoos which dated from 1946, when he was sixteen and a member of the Royal Navy. One was a bird with a scroll in its mouth that said 'Mum and Dad,' the other a heart with a dagger through it proclaiming 'Scotland forever.'"

"Other than the obvious, the greatest treat in his lovemaking was his full-on Scots burr whispered into my ear," she claimed.

Before he left the next morning, he presented Zsa Zsa with a nude sketch of himself dating from his young days when he'd posed in a classroom at the Edinburgh School of Art. "The girls always wanted to sketch me up close. It was embarrassing. The girl who did this charcoal drawing of me flattered me. She said I lacked nothing 'down there.' In fact, she claimed I was the biggest she'd ever seen. I was given fifteen shillings for posing for a one-hour session."

"I hated to see Sean depart," Zsa Zsa said. "I knew I could not hold onto him on any ongoing basis. I just wish I'd known him when I was a teenager. He was the man I would have chosen to lose my virginity to."

***

Drifting from lover to lover, Zsa Zsa, early in 1962, attended a fund-raising banquet at the Plaza Hotel in Manhattan, raising money for St. Jude's Hospital. Sitting next to her was a multi-millionaire businessman, Herbert Hutner, who had gray hair and a courtly manner. His date for the evening was a beautiful princess from India.

Hutner, a graduate of Columbia, had been an attorney before turning to commerce, making millions as a Wall Street financier.

He called Zsa Zsa the following morning, as she'd discreetly hinted that she was staying at the Plaza in a suite.

She accepted his invitation to the Stork Club for that evening. Within three dates, a twenty-three carat blue-and-white diamond was delivered to her suite. Along with the ring came a marriage proposal.

In 1982, on F. Lee Bailey's televised *Lie Detector Show*, she would claim, "I married all of my husbands for love. There was only one man I married for his fortune, and that was Herbert Hutner."

After knowing Hutner for only two weeks, Zsa Zsa married him. Jolie attended the wedding, but intoned later, "It was no big deal."

Zsa Zsa learned only after marrying him that he was chairman of the board at Struthers Wells Corporation. As Eva saw it, "Herbert lent dignity and old line money to Zsa Zsa."

"He was deliriously happy to be married to me," Zsa Zsa later said. "I was his arm candy, and he liked to show me off everywhere. But I felt trapped. He didn't want me to continue my career. When an offer came in for $100,000 for me to appear in a movie, he offered me $200,000 if I would not make the film."

On two separate occasions, Hutner relented and allowed Zsa Zsa to return to the screen. Bert Gordon, the director, called her and explained his dilemma. Hedy Lamarr, in what was to be her last picture, had been arrested for shoplifting and was being removed from any participation in the film *Picture Mommy Dead* (1966).

At the last minute, Zsa Zsa was asked to take over the third-billed role (formerly assigned to Lamarr) in a horror film starring Don Ameche and Martha Hyer. The blonde actress would be the first one asked to portray Lisa Douglas in TV's *Green Acres,* a role that eventually went to Eva.

Also starring in *Picture Mommy Dead* was Signe Hasso, the actress who had been one of Erik Drimmer's lovers when he was married to Eva during the 1940s.

"It was hokey—I'd learned that English word—melodrama—but it was good to be working again, although Hedy got really furious at me for taking over her role." Zsa Zsa said. "Frankly, Hedy didn't miss out on all that much."

Herbert also agreed to go to Cannes with Zsa Zsa when she was offered one

"Of all my husbands, I loved **Herbert Hutner's** money more than I did the man," **Zsa Zsa** once candidly confessed.

of the leads in *Arrivederci Baby!* (1966). *[Later, its title was changed to* Drop Dead Darling.*]*

Tony Curtis was cast as the male lead, a gigolo who goes around marrying wealthy women and then murdering them. "Tony was a Hungarian and we got on very well...very well indeed, especially when the unit flew to London. Tony and I shot our love scenes at Shepperton Studios, and the director, Ken Hughes, had to keep calling *CUT! CUT! CUT!"*

In his memoirs, *American Prince,* Curtis admitted that of his four leading ladies, he wondered which one he might seduce. He found Nancy Kwan a sensitive beauty, but involved in another relationship. He didn't get along with Anna Quayle. An Italian actress, Rosanna Schiaffino, seemed well guarded by her sister and her husband. That left Zsa Zsa.

As Curtis wrote: "When it came to men, Zsa

Zsa knew exactly what she was doing. She knew exactly which guy she was going to bed, and how, and when. She was quite a bit older than I was, though, so I was lucky."

When she was later asked if Curtis' legendary smooth charm worked on her, Zsa Zsa said, "The smallest equipment but the fastest action."

"As for my movie role, I'm seen dedicating a new space capsule where I get locked into the satellite and launched into orbit," she said. "That movie didn't launch my career into orbit. From then on, the roller coaster ride that was my screen career was racing downhill…and how."

***

"Back in Hollywood, Herbert put me on a pedestal," Zsa Zsa said. "I was his Venus de Milo to be worshipped. For me, it was a marriage without passion."

"He became close friends with Judy Garland, whom we'd met at the home of Humphrey Bogart and Lauren Bacall. The next night, we invited Judy to our house. Betty—that's Bacall's real name—warned me to 'watch out for Judy. She'll swallow every pill in your medicine cabinet.'"

Judy and Hutner became fast friends, not lovers." Zsa Zsa said. "They'd sit at my piano, and she'd sing to him song after song, always concluding the night with *Over the Rainbow.*"

"Age was advancing on Judy at a terrible pace, and she looked at least twenty years older than her years," Zsa Zsa said. "She wasn't able to cope. 'All I have to do is look in the mirror, and I cry,' she once told me. She also couldn't face the end of her superstardom. It was a very sad sight."

During the course of her marriage to Hutner, a California wildfire swept over Zsa Zsa's Bel Air manse, leaving it an ashen shell, along with others in the vicinity. She was in London at the time, but flew back with Hutner to survey the damage at 1001 Bellagio Road.

"The fire had played hopscotch with our homes, leveling

Although her new husband didn't want **Zsa Zsa** to appear in any more films, she couldn't resist an offer to co-star with **Tony Curtis** in *Arrivederci Baby!* (also entitled *Drop Dead Darling*). In a memoir, Curtis confessed that of the four leading ladies in the film, "I got lucky only with Zsa Zsa."

The Christian Dior gown that she wore during the filming of a scene in the movie was later recycled at her wedding to Joshua Cosden, Jr.

mine and the home of Burt Lancaster, but skipping over Kim Novak's residence. I lost my jewelry, my furs, my gowns, my antiques, my paintings, and my memorabilia."

After the fire, looters descended on the ruins. They'd combed through the ashes, removing anything of value, later offering to sell some of Zsa Zsa's possessions back to her.

***

In 1966, Hedda Hopper accurately predicted, "If Herbert Hutner lets Zsa Zsa go for one day of his life, he will never see her again."

The columnist was commenting on how Hutner followed Zsa Zsa around, even at parties. He seemed afraid she would meet another man.

"Fate intervened," Zsa Zsa said. "Herbert fell and broke his leg just as we were preparing to fly to Fort Worth, where I was scheduled to appear at this charity benefit as the guest of honor. I went without him."

In Texas, Zsa Zsa's hostess learned that she was traveling alone and arranged a blind date for her, promising that "he's charming and divorced."

She dressed in a mint-green Guy Laroche gown decorated with bugle beads, and put on long white gloves and a floor-length white mink.

"As I was putting on a diamond necklace—"talk to me Harry Winston, tell me all about it"—the doorbell rang. Elizabeth Keleman, my traveling companion, went to the door and came back into my dressing room."

"Zsa Zsa, your next husband has arrived. He's waiting in the drawing room for you."

"I had been expecting some Texas oil millionaire who looked like a broken down Lyndon Johnson, who had once made a play for me."

Standing in the living room was a tall, slim man with graying hair and sky blue eyes. "He looked like Jimmy Stewart used to look. I was introduced to the 'Prince of Texas.'" I knew it was all over between Herbert and me. I had met my next husband."

"His name was Joshua Cosden, Jr."

***

It took a lot of courage, and I postponed it as long as I could, but finally, on a plane ride from Los Angeles to New York, I delivered the bad news to Herbert Hutner," Zsa Zsa said.

"I told him I wanted a divorce from him so I could marry Joshua Cosden, Jr."

"We were seated in the first row of the first class cabin," she said. "The plane turned out to be the wrong venue for him to receive this news. Herbert cried like a baby, and I felt horrible. Even the stewardess tried to comfort him. It was all so embarrassing."

"But by the time we landed in New York, he had recovered his composure," she said. "In our suite at the Plaza, he gave me permission to marry Joshua. Herbert was not the prettiest of the men I married, but he was the kindest. The day we parted, he told me that I was the love of his life and he'd never get over me. Of course, I'd heard that line before, *dahlink*, but perhaps he meant it. Anyway, I quickly got over Herbert in the arms of my darling Josh."

Eva opted to accompany Zsa Zsa aboard a flight to Juarez, Mezico, where she obtained her divorce from Hutner. A few days later, on March 9, 1966, she married Cosden in Los Angeles. She was forty-three years old and he was fifty-one. He gave her a sapphire-and-diamond ring.

"I'm wildly in love with Joshua," she told the press. "It was love at first sight. I met him in Texas on a blind date."

"Who is he, *dahlink*?" she answered reporters. "He's a Texas oilman, the only kind to marry from the Lone Star State. I've married a Texan before. If I remember correctly, he owned some hotels."

At her wedding, Conrad Hilton (Senior) showed up, as did her close friend, Kathryn Grayson, along with such luminaries as Gregory Peck and his wife, Véronique. Other guests included Charlton Heston, who had been her friend since they'd made *Touch of Evil* for Orson Welles.

Her marriage to Cosden was not a happy occasion, because he was suffering from cancer. Privately, his doctor told her, "He may not live for very long."

Shortly before their marriage ceremony, he'd had a seizure and was rushed to the hospital. Once there, and after a series of tests, he had one lung removed in a dangerous operation. Throughout the ordeal, Zsa Zsa had camped out at the hospital to be by his side.

At her wedding ceremony, Zsa Zsa, in her snow white Christian Dior gown intertwined with lilies of the valley, looked in the peak of health. Even though he'd undergone a painful and debilitating operation, Cosden appeared reasonably well. No member of the press knew at the time about his cancer.

"Okay, so I wasn't a virgin any more," Zsa Zsa said. "Hell with tradition. I wanted to be married in white."

From the beginning, the marriage seemed disastrous.

At the Bistro Gardens Restaurant in Los Angeles, Cosden accompanied her to a dinner party hosted by Kathryn Grayson. But after surveying the room, Cosden told her, "There are too many Jews here. I'm leaving."

"What in hell are you saying?" she asked. "Don't you know I'm a Jew? Nearly all my friends are Jews."

"It meant a lot to Joshua to be in the Social Register," Zsa Zsa said. "When we returned home, he got the shock of his life. The Register had dropped him because of his marriage to an actress. Poor Joshua. He was mortally wounded."

More problems were on the way. Two weeks before, Cosden came to his new wife with a business proposal. "A great opportunity has come up for me. I can buy the Four Star TV Studio in Houston and compete with Lady Bird Johnson for television viewers."

"What's the asking price?" she asked.

"Just four million dollars. I'm sure you can spare that. You must have millions you haven't counted."

"You're wrong," she said. "I don't even have four million dollars."

He was crestfallen and shocked.

"Our marriage would never be the same again," she said.

Their clash over values continued. Two weeks later, he sat down with her to watch *The Sammy Davis, Jr. Show* in which she had made a guest appearance. At the end of the show, the ever-effusive Davis kissed Zsa Zsa.

Before storming out of the room, Cosden said. "God damn it! I'll never be able to go back to Texas. I bet everybody there saw my wife being kissed by a nigger."

With the insurance money paid in the aftermath of the fire in her burned-out home, Zsa Zsa purchased a Regency-style house on St. Pierre Road in Bel Air, which had been decorated by her old friend, Lady Elsie Mendl. The original owner had been Mervyn LeRoy, who had directed her in her film debut at MGM in *Lovely to Look At.*

In Texas, **Zsa Zsa** was snapped by a photographer as she dined with her oil-man husband, **Joshua Cosden, Jr.** Within the year, she would be divorced.

Although Cosden didn't look ill at the time, he was dying from the cancer eating away at his once robust body.

Although she had viewed it as her dream house, she decided not to move in when she arrived to find that inside, a bird had died of starvation. It had become trapped when the workmen had finished their labors and shut the doors.

"I lost thousands," she later said, "but I sold the house before living there. I thought the dead bird was a bad omen."

She realized that a divorce was inevitable. "We were just too different," she said. "I detested his world, and he had little regard for mine, which was peopled by black persons, Jews, homosexuals, former prostitutes who were now movie stars, and former dishwashers who were millionaires living in Beverly Hills."

"I flew back to Juarez in Mexico, and

I was greeted with a banner that read—*WELCOME BACK ZSA ZSA*."

Her divorce was granted on October 18, 1967. "I'm free at last," she told reporters. "Stay tuned for husband number six, number seven, and so forth."

***

For the most part, George Sanders remained alienated from his brother, Tom Conway, seeing him only on rare occasions. At those times, Sanders argued with Conway over his alcoholism. Zsa Zsa was more supportive, and was saddened to see her former brother-in-law sink deeper and deeper into depression and excessive drinking.

Early in 1965, Conway had undergone cataract surgery. Later that year, he made unwanted headlines when a reporter discovered him living in a $2-a-night flophouse in Venice, south of Los Angeles. For a while, Conway's former fans sent him money, which helped him pay his hospital bills and rent. But in just a few weeks, those contributions had dried up, and the actor, the former "Falcon" in those 1940s detective movies, was broke again. He was seen panhandling along the beach in Venice (California) trying to raise money to buy more liquor.

At one point, a doctor told Conway that he had only months to live. In desperation, he telephoned Zsa Zsa, urging her to put him in touch with his brother. In an appeal to her former husband, she got him to agree to drive with her to Venice. In a flophouse, they discovered Conway "at death's door," in Zsa Zsa's words.

Sanders made a deal with him, thinking his brother had only a short time to live. "Before coming here, I had my bank issue a cashier's check for $40,000. I want you to take this money and go to Capri to live out your final days."

Conway agreed to this generous offer and did indeed fly to Rome, where he hired a driver to deliver him to Naples. There, he boarded a ferry to Capri, where he resumed his heavy drinking.

On Capri, he had some mysterious encounter with a German scientist, who claimed he had a risky cure for alcoholism. He asked Conway to volunteer as a guinea pig. "You're going to die anyway, so why not take a chance you can be cured?"

The facts are murky at this point, but the serum seemed to have worked. Conway was temporarily cured of alcoholism. With all his money spent, he returned to the flophouse in Venice, where he urged both Zsa Zsa and Sanders to continue their financial aid.

At one point, Conway was hospitalized.

Upon hearing this, Zsa Zsa drove down the coast to visit him. She found him shaking nervously and looking emaciated. She was greatly saddened by his gaunt appearance, remembering how strong and virile he'd once looked. His doctor told her that Conway was suffering from a severe case of cirrhosis of the liver, with his weight dropping drastically.

Before leaving that day, she gave him $200, telling him, "Tip the nurses a little bit so that they will be good to you."

After she left, Conway got dressed and fled from the hospital. Once outside, he spent the $200 on liquor and headed to the house of a former girlfriend, where he drank excessively. He became gravely sick and died in her bed on April 22, 1967, at the age of sixty-two.

Both Sanders and Zsa Zsa decided not to attend his memorial service in London.

***

For reasons even Zsa Zsa herself didn't understand, she was still in love with Sanders. After his marriage to Magda had been annulled, he moved in with Zsa Zsa again. He'd finally given up on asking her to remarry him.

"When we got married," he told her, "I was the star. You were waiting in the wings. Now you're on the phone talking with agents and producers, and I'm just lying about, waiting for something to happen."

She later claimed that he talked frequently about committing suicide, but she never took him seriously. A psychiatrist had told her that people who frequently threaten to commit suicide rarely carry through with that fatal act of desperation. She was about to realize how wrong that observation was, at least as it related to Sanders.

During the last three years of his life, Sanders' health began to fail, and he suffered a minor stroke. He also suffered from dementia. In Majorca, he even lost his ability to play the piano. He dragged the piano outside his door and smashed it into pieces with an axe.

At the time, he was living with a girlfriend he'd picked up in Mexico. She was thirty years younger than him. She urged him to sell his beloved home in Majorca, which he regretted till the end of his life. When the sale was concluded, he took only his clothes from the house, leaving all his personal letters and memorabilia behind.

Released in the year of his death (1972), his last three pictures had titles that ironically seemed to mirror his own life—*Doomwatch, Endless Night,* and *Psychomania.*

At this point in her life, Zsa Zsa knew all of Sanders' weaknesses, including his darkest ones. There has always been speculation that she was unaware of his closeted homosexuality, a form of sexuality he rarely indulged in America. Reportedly, he reserved such pleasures for his visits to such countries as

666

Italy, Spain, and Greece, showing a particular fondness for teenaged Mediterranean boys. He was also seen in Tangiers on the north coast of Morocco, visiting the boy brothels there.

The only "name actors" he was ever rumored to have gotten involved with emotionally and sexually were Tyrone Power and the closeted homosexual French actor, Charles Boyer.

Boyer lived for a time with Sanders at his house in Majorca, where they indulged in sexual liaisons with a number of island youths, paying each of them with a ten dollar bill.

One night, at a party in Paris, Zsa Zsa had apparently had a fight with Sanders and was angry at him. In front of columnist Earl Wilson, she said, "*Dahlinks,* George Sanders is the only man I vill ever love, but he is queer for little boys."

According to the journalistic standards of his day, Wilson did not report that comment in his newspaper column. However, he did include it in his 1974 memoir, *Show Business Laid Bare.*

Zsa Zsa signed to do a British comedy, *Up the Front* (1972), co-starring with the comedian Frankie Howerd. Sanders was in London at the time, and she called him and arranged for a dinner.

Before she saw Zsa Zsa, Sanders visited his sister, Margaret Sanders, at her home in Horsham. She later said, "I was completely shocked at the change in him. He had had some sort of serious emotional collapse—too many pills and too much vodka. He talked about suicide. He was in a state of deep emotional agony."

Zsa Zsa's final dinner with Sanders occurred in London in April of 1972. She had been in England playing Mata Hari in *Up the Front.*

Sanders told her, "Apparently, you take any shitty film offered. Why? You don't need the money. You're cast only because the producers and directors want to make fun of your outrageousness. What you do is not acting. It's making public appearances in a film!"

Even after that insult, she went with him to

The closeted French actor, **Charles Boyer** *(photo above)*, was an intimate friend of George Sanders. "As a young man, I made every effort not to fall in love. I was selfish enough to avoid it." At age thirty-four, he entered a 44-year marriage to British actress Pat Paterson, but often traveled with Sanders.

Boyer committed suicide in Arizona in 1978, two days after his wife's funeral, following in the footsteps of Sanders, who had killed himself on the Costa Brava in 1972. His only child, a son, had committed suicide in 1965 at the age of 21.

the airport to see him off. He was flying to Barcelona, where he would be driven to the Hotel Rey Don Jaime in Castelldefels, which lay ten miles north of Barcelona along the windswept Costa Brava.

His final words to Zsa Zsa at the airport were, "You know, every day I think of that dear man, Tyrone Power, who died in his forty-fifth year when we were making that dreadful movie in Spain. He died in possession of all his faculties and in the full bloom of manhood. That is the way to go, *Cokiline.* Who the gods love die young." Then he kissed her goodbye for the final time.

When her work on *Up the Front* was completed, Zsa Zsa flew back to California to prepare for her upcoming special with Bob Hope.

She was checking her wardrobe when the call came in from Spain. A local radio station had broadcast the news that Sanders had been found dead in his hotel room, having consumed sixty capsules of Nembutal. His suicide note read:

"Dear World,
I am leaving because I am bored. I feel I have lived long enough. I am leaving you with your worries in this sweet cesspool. Good luck."

Zsa Zsa began an uncontrollable sobbing that she could not stop. A doctor was summoned to her home in Bel Air, where he sedated her.

She later said, "I'll never get over George...or his death."

In mourning, Zsa Zsa said. "I should have listened more closely. One night George told me that he had no intention of growing old, ill, and decrepit. The mere thought that one day he might be incapacitated and in a wheelchair drove him into the deepest depression. Once Bette Davis, his co-star in *All About Eve,* had told him, "Old age is not for sissies."

Death came on April 25, 1972. Sanders was sixty-five years old. His body was flown back to London for funeral services, after which it was cremated, his ashes scattered across the English Channel.

***

It would be years before Zsa Zsa would take another husband. In the meantime, she'd enjoy affairs with a number of men, some of whom were already married.

Many of her high-profile sexual liaisons with famous men never made the press.

When producer David Merrick had called to ask her to replace Julie Harris on Broadway in *Forty Carats,* Zsa Zsa was understandably nervous. Harris had been hailed as one of the finest actresses on Broadway, and Zsa Zsa was none too anxious to follow in her footsteps.

But she forged ahead, learned the role, and *tout* New York turned out for her opening night. She brought an entirely new interpretation to the role, making it more frivolous, but she managed to fill the house most evenings until the play closed. Thousands of her gay fans flocked to see her, hoping to witness a performance of high camp. For the road show version of that play, Lana Turner, sometimes co-starring with the handsome and talented Peter Coffield, signed on as the lead.

One of her most ardent admirers, and this came as a shock to her, was John Vliet Lindsay, the mayor of New York City, who was four years younger than she was. In 1972, he would launch a brief, unsuccessful bid for the 1972 Democratic nomination for President of the United States.

In 1949, he'd married Mary Harrison, a descendant of President William Henry Harrison and Benjamin Harrison. During their long marriage, which lasted until Lindsay's death in 2002, he managed to work in a few discreet affairs.

Zsa Zsa's rendezvous with Lindsay came about through a robbery. While performing in *Forty Carats,* she was installed in the Waldorf Towers with all her diamonds, furs, and gowns.

One weekend, President Richard Nixon arrived to stay in the presidential suite. The Waldorf was swimming in Secret Servicemen.

"I felt very safe and secure wearing my diamonds," she later said. "I stepped into the elevator late one night to go upstairs and didn't pay much attention to two elegant men dressed in tuxedos."

Midway in ascension, one of the men pressed the halt button. Suddenly, both men pointed guns at her. One of them demanded, "Give me your diamond ring."

"I had to hand over my $3 million diamond ring, a gift from Herbert Hutner, and even my diamond earrings," Zsa Zsa said. Fearing for her life, she also surrendered to them her blue turquoise and diamond ring as well.

The gunmen managed to escape, brushing past the Secret Servicemen guarding Nixon. Zsa Zsa called the police before heading to the 51st Street Precinct to face a bevy of reporters. News of this daring multi-million robbery, so close to the presidential suite occupied at the time by a sitting president, went out on wire services around the world.

Merrick was delighted when he heard the news. "Some people are saying it was a publicity stunt. Our play is *Forty Carats,* and your ring is forty carats. What a coincidence. How great for the show! It will extend the run."

"I'd lost millions by coming to New York, and he was paying me only $2,500 a week," Zsa Zsa lamented.

The gunmen were never apprehended, and Zsa Zsa's jewelry was never recovered.

Mayor Lindsay was horrified at the "black eye" that crime-ridden New York was getting in the press. Not only was the robbery within one of the city's finest hotels, but it took place a few feet from where the President of the United States was installed.

As a consolation prize to Zsa Zsa, he offered to take her to dinner at a restaurant of her choice. She chose one owned by Merv Griffin, where the lavish banquet with champagne was complimentary.

After dinner, she invited Lindsay back to her suite for a night cap, and was somewhat surprised that he accepted.

She'd later relate to Merv Griffin and to others the details of what happened that evening: "At one o'clock, John was still in my suite, but making no moves. He was so god damn polite. I had to take the bull by the horns...or whatever, *dahlink*."

"I lured him into the bedroom, and we got out of our clothes. What can I say? I agreed with other women who have gone to bed with him over the years and written about their experiences."

"It was a polite fuck, carefully controlled, well mannered, but lacking in passion. The thrill of going to bed with His Lordship was having that good-looking movie star face of his looking down into your eyes. His eyes were more seductive than his nether regions. I liked him a lot and admired his politics."

"I even invited him back for a repeat performance, but he was too busy running the city. He was involved in all sorts of racial conflicts at the time—blacks against Jews, all sorts of things."

"He was a fine and decent man, and he smelled nicer than any other man who ever took me to bed."

"Before he left, he thanked me. There was a sad look in his eyes as he departed. His final words to me were, 'I feel like an exile in my own city. Every group is against me, or so it seems.'"

At the Waldorf-Astoria, where she was staying, and in spite of high security, Zsa Zsa was robbed of her jewelry. In the aftermath, New York City mayor **John Lindsay** *(top photo)* visited her to apologize for the robbery. "Then he stayed around for other things, *dahlink*." Zsa Zsa later claimed.

The lower photo shows Hizzoner **John Lindsay**, mayor of New York, politicking.

***

"I would never have to pay another grocery bill in my life," Zsa Zsa claimed. "The catch was, I would have to marry Huntington Hartford, and he was rather too eccentric for my appetite."

When she met him at a cocktail party in Manhattan in the early 1970s, his supermarket empire was at its peak. There were 16,000 A&P stores in the United States, making it the largest retail empire in the world.

Hartford was fresh from a divorce from his third wife, Diane Brown. His mother, Henrietta Guerard Pollitzer, had wanted her son to marry tobacco heiress Doris Duke, whom Zsa Zsa's George Sanders had once wanted to wed, but struck out.

Hartford's first wife, Mary Lee Eppling, had once been married to Douglas Fairbanks, Jr., one of the Zsa Zsa's lovers when she had landed in Hollywood straight from Hungary.

Hartford was dazzled by Zsa Zsa's beauty, and she was dazzled by his vast wealth. He wasn't just a businessman, but a philanthropist, filmmaker, and art collector. She called him "a Renaissance man."

"When he invited me to come up and see his etchings, it was an entire museum," she claimed.

She was referring to his vast collection of 19th and 20th century art, housed in the "lollipop building," the Gallery of Modern Art at Columbus Circle in Manhattan. Looking at his works by Toulouse-Lautrec brought back memories of her early film role as Jane Avril in *Moulin Rouge.*

"On one of our first dates, he flew me in a private plane to Nassau," she said. Once there, they journeyed across the water to Hog Island, which he'd renamed Paradise Island. He described his lavish plans to turn it into another Monte Carlo.

"He was America's most eligible bachelor, but I could not keep up with his race car mind," she said. He came up with an earth-shaking idea every minute."

"I was fascinated by his theatrical ambitions," she said. "He wrote *The Master of Thornfield* based on Charlotte Brontë's *Jane Eyre.* He cast Errol Flynn in the lead. He also discovered a then unknown actor, Al Pacino, and starred him in a Broadway play called *Does a Tiger Wear a Necktie?"*

"He even suggested that we call on Mae West in Hollywood and secure the rights to her *Diamond Lil,* and adapt it for me to tour America," she said. "He promised me that I would be

Huntington Hartford, the A&P heir, might have been cited as the most eligible bachelor in America, but Zsa Zsa turned down his generous offer of marriage, even though she wasn't getting any younger.

"There was much about him that was dazzling, but there were also dark pockets I didn't want to reach into."

a sensation and make millions."

When it came time for him to propose marriage to her, she turned him down but never publicly said why.

To her closest friends, she confessed, "In the boudoir, he wanted us to perform unspeakable acts."

***

At a party in London's Mayfair district, Noël Coward introduced Zsa Zsa to Randolph Churchill. "He was so very English," she recalled. "So very randy, as the Brits say. He looked at me with that gleam in his eye, and I knew what he had on his mind."

Randolph, of course, was the son of the British Prime Minister, Sir Winston Churchill and his wife Clementine, who never wanted to have much to do with her son after giving birth to him. In contrast, Sir Winston spoiled him and constantly agreed to pay off his gambling debts.

Zsa Zsa later admitted that her main interest in Randolph was not just his name, but that she viewed a seduction of him as "payback time" for Pamela Churchill Harriman, who had been married to Randolph during the war years. Zsa Zsa and Pamela had vied for the affections of Baron Elie de Rothschild, and in some perverse way, Zsa Zsa seemed to regard an affair with Randolph as a script for a revenge fuck.

In the days and weeks ahead, she got to know him during the time he had sobered up enough. "Talk about heavy drinking. The English call men like Randolph a lager lout, but in his case, his poison was Scotch."

"Even as kid, I was an uncontrollable bully," he told her. "But my father viewed my rebellion as showing an independent spirit."

She found him intelligent but conceited.

"At Oxford, my classmates didn't like me and used to chase me around campus to debag me," he said.

"I don't know what that means," she said.

"Removing my trousers to humiliate me," he said.

He told her he'd been in Houston, where he'd met Conrad Hilton. "I also journeyed to Oklahoma, where a one-night encounter led to me becoming the father of a bastard daughter. I'm definitely the black sheep of the Churchills."

At the time she met him, he was trying to sober up as a means of fulfilling a contract obligation. Randolph had signed a deal with Robert F. Kennedy, wherein he'd write a book about RFK's slain brother. "I'm just beginning to work on it. Bobby gave me access to the Kennedy archives."

Randolph's book on the life and accomplishments of JFK would never be written. Ironically, Randolph would die of a heart attack at age 57 on the same day (June 6, 1968) that RFK himself was murdered in the kitchens of the Ambassador Hotel in Los Angeles.

On her first night outside London with Randolph, he drove her to a remote inn "somewhere in Buckinghamshire."

"We stayed two nights and ran up a big bill," she said. "When it came time to settle the tab on Monday morning, Randolph got into a big fight with the manager, accusing him of vastly inflating our charges. He struck the manager, who called the police."

When the bobbies arrived, one of them asked Zsa Zsa for her autograph. The other policeman negotiated peace between Randolph and the manager, who let him go.

As one policeman told Zsa Zsa, "After all, his father kept us from becoming slaves of the bloody Nazis, so I guess we owe the son this one favor."

As the days went by, Zsa Zsa grew more and more disenchanted with Randolph. As biographer Sally Bedell Smith wrote, "He chased women, gambled, drank prodigiously, and insulted his hosts at dinner parties. Years of dissipation had begun to show after all those decades of drunkenly crashing through the drawing rooms of London, Paris, and New York."

Zsa Zsa never expected him to propose and when he did, she discussed the proposal with Noël Coward.

"Randolph lives beyond his means," Coward said. "You would end up paying off his debts. His gray eyes have become milky gray these days and his belly has become Pickwickian. Don't accept his proposal of marriage. He's not looking for a wife...more a nanny with a fat bank account."

On her final night with Randolph, he told her, "If you marry me, I can mold you into the woman you were destined to become. You've got wit and intelligence. I would start you off having you read Gibbon's *The Decline and Fall of the Roman Empire.* Then I'd put you onto my father's works. As a husband, I could give you both cerebral pleasure in the library and sensual pleasure in the boudoir."

Randolph Churchill *(above)* was a disappointment to his father, Sir Winston. He was a gambler, a lout, and a womanizer.

"I like red-headed tarts," Randolph said. "If one isn't available, a bottle blonde will always do in a pinch."

"I finally turned down his proposal of marriage, although at first I had been flattered by it," Zsa Zsa said. "When I met him, he was already too deep into alcoholism to be a fit husband for any woman. In my opinion, he suffered from being compared all his life to his illustrious father. Like his dad, Randolph tried for a political career, but he didn't go far with that."

"How in bloody hell can I, a mere mortal man, measure up to a towering figure like Sir Winston Churchill?" he asked her one night. "After all, he's listed as one of the ten greatest men who ever lived. He was the leader of the Free World in 1940, its darkest hour, when he stood up to Nazi tyranny. As for me, I'll go down as a footnote in history as the errant son who kept the distilleries of Scotland in business."

***

Perhaps not wanting to make herself appear as an opportunistic gold-digger, Zsa Zsa, in a memoir, claimed she never flew to Texas at the invitation of H. L. Hunt.

Born in Illinois in 1889, Haroldson Lafayette Hunt, Jr., held one of the world's largest fortunes. He was the chief inspiration for the character of J. R. Ewing in the popular TV series, *Dallas.*

She was curious to meet Hunt, as he was the stuff on which legends were based. People had told her he was "a mean son of a bitch," and the fact that he had fifteen children by three wives also did not impress her. But when such a powerful man in world finance sends his private plane, she thought she'd better heed his call.

Even before he met her, he had his pilot deliver her a note. The message was clear: *I WANT TO MARRY YOU!*

She'd read profiles of him, It was said that when he was broke, at the age of 32, he played a game of five-car stud in the Arkansas boomtown of El Dorado. In the game, he won his first oil well. With that meager beginning, he'd pyramided his poker windfall into a global oil empire that had made him one of the world's half-dozen wealthiest men. At the time of his death in 1974, he was worth about $5 billion.

His fortune had been based on his securing title to a massive oil field in Deep East Texas. This title of his controlled what was then the largest known oil deposit in the world. He'd paid only a million dollars for it.

"He was an awesome thing to see," Zsa Zsa said. "His ego was as big as the size of Texas. I was intimidated by him until he told me I could call him 'Popsie.'"

"Over a drink, he liked to put his 'cards on the table,' as he expressed it," she said. "He told me that if I married him, I'd live in a style that would have put Cleopatra to shame—all the servants, jewelry, clothing, furs, automobiles, your little heart desires."

"His revelations frightened me," she said. "He told me that his son from his first wife—H. L. Hunt III, *[nicknamed 'Hassie']*—had been the co-owner of Hunt Petroleum. 'He got that god damn idea of succeeding me in the family business,' he said. 'I had the kid lobotomized. He was diagnosed with schizophrenia.'"

"Our first dinner together was not a romantic evening," she said. "Everything was about business and his sons, after telling me what a grand lifestyle I could enjoy with him."

"I was shown around the Hunt mansion before dinner," she said. "It was an oversized replica of George Washington's Mount Vernon, but outside Dallas. I discovered he was an arch-conservative, perhaps about ten miles to the right of Himmler, Hitler, Göring, and Goebbels."

"He asked me to join him in a yoga class, which I did, putting on a lavender colored sweat suit. During yoga, I pulled something in my back."

"At dinner, I expected a big, juicy Texas steak, but I got alfalfa sprouts, blueberries, raw celery stalks, and marinated celery sticks. I learned he was a health food faddist—none of my goulash for him."

"The next morning I discovered him crawling around his mansion on his hands and knees. He told me that this was the best exercise in the world, and invited me to join him. I demurred."

"He had to go to his office, but arranged to meet me for dinner," she said. "I was shocked to see him leaving the house. His chef had packed his lunch in a brown paper bag. Before he left, he gave me four credit cards to the most expensive and elegant designer shops in town. I didn't want to take advantage, but I admit to spending some $50,000 before the end of the afternoon. With temptation like that, what's a girl to do? I'm weak willed when it comes to shopping with another man's money."

"It was announced that "Peaches' was going to entertain us before dinner," she said. "Peaches turned out to be June Hunt, one of his daughters. She was a budding gospel singer who had a recording contract with Stax Records, and she also hosted a daily religious radio show, *Hope for the Heart.*"

"It was a horrible concert—not my thing at all—but I sat through it,"

Posing for a photograph, **H. L. Hunt** *(upper photo)* of Texas was one of the world's richest men. One morning, he woke up with a desire to marry Zsa Zsa, and sent his private plane to fly her to his home .

If Zsa Zsa had married Hunt, she'd have been the mistress of an oversized replica *(lower photo)* of George Washington's Mount Vernon, an outpost of what one of her friends defined as "a Bible-thumping Americana Hell on steroids."

she said.

"Her recital was followed by a family singalong of religious songs, none of which I'd ever heard before, including something called 'Gimme That Ol' Time Religion.'"

"I met some of his other sons and daughters—what a large family. The one that impressed me the most was Nelson Bunker Hunt, who was only nine years younger than me. He was very ruddy faced, very aggressive, and rambunctious. His father had made him his chief executive at Hunt Oil."

What most impressed her about Nelson Hunt was his reputation as a horse breeder. He owned 400 thoroughbred racehorses, which was undoubtedly a world record. She was taken on a tour of the stables and later went riding.

[In later years, Nelson would make world headlines when he bought $200 million worth of silver bullion, trying to corner the world market. He also managed to stave off nationalization of Hunt Oil interests in Libya for two years after the holdings of other companies had been expropriated by the brutal dictator of Libya, Colonel Muhammad al-Gadhafi.]

Zsa Zsa told Hunt she'd give him her answer to his marriage proposal once she returned to Los Angeles and thought it over. In two weeks, she wrote him a polite but firm no, rejecting his offer.

"I could have kicked myself," she later said. "Once again, I made a stupid mistake. By the time Popsie divorced his wife, Ruth Ray, and married me, he would already have been at death's door. He left his stock in Hunt Oil to Ruth. By the time we would have gotten married, he would probably have been in the hospital. I might not ever have had to sleep with him, and I would have become the Oil Queen of Texas. Black gold, *dahlink*. But, alas, in my stupidity, I didn't have the Machiavellian instincts to pull this one off. Hell, I could have stood right beside him and led those harmonious family singalongs before dinner. How many would there have been before Hunt's death? Maybe only three or four. For those Texas oil millions, I surely could have endured 'Shall We Gather at the River?'"

***

Beginning in the late 1960s and the early '70s, Zsa Zsa began to show signs of a nervous breakdown, and her erratic behavior generated headlines. "She's always good copy, even if she's not important," said the editor of *The New York Post*.

In London, in 1968, she'd summoned a press conference, in which she claimed that an assassin had been hired to kill her and also to murder Jolie.

She did not immediately accuse him, but left the impression that it was Conrad Hilton, Sr., who had organized the plot.

Her second husband would die in 1979, but not before he had told friends and associates that Francesca was not his daughter, but the daughter of his son, Nicky Hilton, with whom his then-wife had had a long affair. If the senior Hilton believed that, it would explain why the hotelier left Francesca only $100,000, while he designated his surviving son, Barron, a billionaire today.

[Nicky Hilton had died of a heart attack in 1969, two months before his 43rd birthday.]

Zsa Zsa had always insisted that Francesca was the biological daughter of Conrad, Sr., but she was deeply disturbed that her former husband was claiming otherwise. Of course, Zsa Zsa might not have been certain of the paternity, because she was sleeping with both father and son at the moment of conception.

Beginning at that 1968 press event in London, during a period of about eighteen months, Zsa Zsa sounded off on the charge that she was a target for assassination. She told a reporter from London's *Daily Mail,* "I'm sure that one morning, a maid will come in and find that I've been murdered overnight in my bed, perhaps in this very suite."

One night, she granted an interview to a reporter for the BBC. Londoners were shocked to hear her say, "They're going to kill me before the month is over, and I don't even know why they are going after me."

The reporter suggested she should go to Scotland Yard immediately.

As if the idea had never occurred to her, she promised she'd go the next morning.

She did, showing up in a simple black Chanel suit with no jewelry.

A Scotland Yard detective pressed her for what she might know about this conspiracy against her life.

All she could do was present him with a series of news clippings about troubles she had encountered in Italy, London, Portugal, and Spain. "The plot against me is perhaps international," she said.

She had left a trail of unpaid bills across Europe. She'd checked out of hotels without paying the bill; she'd bought expensive items in boutiques in Paris, London, and Rome, but never paid for them.

She was constantly accused of attacking defenseless personnel in various establishments, as when she'd slapped the face of a young bellboy at the Ritz Hotel in London. She'd claimed that he'd brought her laundered towels, not newly purchased ones. "Zsa Zsa Gabor does not accept towels used by a hundred filthy guests before her."

In September of 1968, she'd had a hysterical spat with employees of the Palacio Hotel in Estoril, outside Lisbon. The manager had refused to accept her $500 check as payment. Word had spread that Zsa Zsa often wrote legitimate checks but stopped payment on them before they could be cashed.

In Estoril, she accused the manager of wanting to hold her jewelry, worth a million dollars, until he was assured that the payment would be honored by her bank.

"I was humiliated because they opened my suitcases in the lobby and found that I had wrapped my chinchilla coat in several hotel towels. I told them that the maid had given me permission."

She called a press conference in the lobby in front of embarrassed hotel staff. She sobbed before reporters, claiming that she was suing management for "manhandling me and dislocating my arm."

A compromise was reached, as Zsa Zsa agreed to return the towels and pay $200 in cash, which was all the money she had on her. The hotel reluctantly accepted a check for $300. It later bounced.

From Lisbon, she'd flow to Barcelona and onto the island of Majorca, where she created more scandals. The staff at the Hotel Son Vida complained that she was abusing them, screaming vile insults at them. She stormed out of the hairdressing salon because she said the woman's body smelled of garlic.

She visited the most expensive boutique in Palma de Mallorca and ordered two dozens of their most expensive dresses. She also purchased eight evening gowns and a dozen hats, along with several hundred dollars worth of accessories. The manager later said, "She practically emptied our store. She promised to send over payment before leaving the island. But the money never arrived, and the boutique's owner called the police."

When the policeman came aboard the aircraft to arrest her, she saw that he was very tall. She had to stand up on her seat to give him a really hard slap. That led to her arrest.

"I was treated like a common criminal and hauled off the plane," Zsa Zsa claimed. "I was thrown in the back of a police car and mauled. At the jailhouse, I was roughed up and thrown into a squalid cell with no toilet. I was denied food and water, and the temperature that night was more than 100° F. It was the worst night of my life. When I had to relieve myself, two guards brought this horrid chamberpot and wouldn't take their eyes off me."

"Later, they beat me with a rubber hose. I screamed, but there was no one to come to my aid."

After payment was made to the boutique, she was released. She called a nurse, who bandaged her before she appeared again at the airport for her flight back to Barcelona and on to New York.

Before she walked up the ramp leading to the first class compartment, she spat on the ground. "I'm leaving this wretched island, never to return. These people are savages."

Jolie admitted that Zsa Zsa had behaved badly in Majorca. "She came into a bar in the middle of the afternoon and decided to lie down across three bar stools. She abused people. She told everybody off. She was literally crazy about

George, who was in Majorca in a house he shared with Charles Boyer. All she wanted was George, and he didn't want her."

In New York, she denounced the police in Majorca, claiming "their justice system is from the Middle Ages. At one point, I thought they were going to burn me at the stake. It was the Spanish Inquisition all over again. Americans should avoid spending their vacation money in Spain. An international boycott is needed to wreck their tourist industry. Maybe then they will show more regard for their visitors."

George Sanders came to her defense, as he still had a home on the island. "Her treatment was barbaric. They are still a bit uncivilized on this island."

As she traveled about, she generated headlines wherever she went. Landing in London, she faced a customs inspector who ferreted out a very high strung terrier she was trying to smuggle in within the folds of her fur coat. He reminded her that England maintained a strictly enforced quarantine on the importation of animals, including dogs.

She fought back, denouncing him. "When he suggested she wait for the arrival of his superior officer, she shouted, "Zsa Zsa Gabor waits for no one. And take off your fucking hat when you fucking talk to a lady." Then she knocked his hat off his head.

The police hauled her before a magistrate's court, where the judge charged her $24 for using profane language, and levied a $96 fine for having attempted to bring a dog illegally into Britain.

Once in London, she launched a spectacular spending spree, even purchasing a townhouse in Belgravia. She charged nearly a million pounds during the purchase of antiques, including a small mirror priced at $25,000. At London's Ritz Hotel one evening, she gave a million dollar diamond necklace to some woman she'd just met, evoking a similar stunt Barbara Hutton had once pulled in Venice. Impulsively, she ordered all the contents of her Bel Air home to be shipped to London.

When she heard of this spree, Jolie flew at once from New York to London, where she had Zsa Zsa committed to the Priory Nursing Home on Upper Richmond Road. She entered the clinic two days after Christmas of 1968, where it was announced that she was undergoing "psychological treatment" as well a getting a much needed rest.

Abe Greenberg in his "Voice of Hollywood" column wrote that "Zsa Zsa Gabor is more to be pitied than scorned—the girl needs air."

Within moments of her arrival in London, Jolie went into damage control. She retrieved the diamond necklace after a bitter fight, and she blocked shipment of Zsa Zsa's Bel Air possessions to London. She also returned all the merchandise, including the antiques that Zsa Zsa had purchased, and she cancelled the townhouse buy before the deal had gone into the final contract. "There were penalties to be paid," Jolie said, "and I had to settle as best I could, using my own money."

***

Back in Hollywood, Zsa Zsa called Jolie. "You're not going to believe this, but I've got a call from J. Paul Getty. He wants me to fly to London."

"Isn't he richer than H. L. Hunt?" Jolie asked."

"By a few billion, I believe," Zsa Zsa said.

"So dump the shit-kicker and go with Getty Oil."

"Good thinking," Zsa Zsa said. "As you know, I always take my mother's advice…sometimes."

Fortune magazine had named the Anglo-American industrialist, J. Paul Getty, the world's richest living American, and the most recent *Guinness Book of Records* had cited him as the world's richest private citizen. In today's currency, his fortune would amount to $8.5 billion dollars.

Getty had pursued Zsa Zsa more than twenty years before, when she'd been in London shooting scenes from *Moulin Rouge (1952)*. "But I was too much in love with George Sanders at the time, so I didn't return his calls."

But in 1973, he invited her to appear at a benefit for Bangladesh at the swanky Grosvenor House Hotel in London, and she agreed to fly there for this charity benefit.

It took three fashion experts and makeup men in Zsa Zsa's suite to prepare her for her entrance into the Grosvenor House ballroom. Her appearance was dazzling. She wore a white gown—"laden with diamonds and rubies, *dahlink."* Getty himself introduced her to the other guests, much to the annoyance of Margaret, Duchess of Argyll, who was chasing after the Getty millions at the time. Margaret obviously didn't welcome this stunningly beautiful competition.

After the benefit, Zsa Zsa was driven in a chauffeured limousine to Getty's legendary 72-room Tudor-era palace, Sutton Place, for a house party. Built in 1525, and Getty's home for the final 17 years of his life, it was located twenty-three miles from London in the country town of Guildford in Surrey. Its former owner had been the much marrying type, Henry VIII.

Zsa Zsa had once attended a party at Getty's home in the Los Angeles. Lying on Wilshire Boulevard, it had been used as the setting for Norma Desmond's home in the 1950 movie *Sunset Blvd.,* starring Gloria Swanson. But Getty had not been there at the time.

When the aging Getty turned his sky blue eyes onto Zsa Zsa—she referred to his eyes as magnetic—she found him perfectly tailored from Savile Row and still possessing vitality. He, of course, was no longer the wildcatter working in his father's oil fields in Oklahoma. But for a man born right before Christmas in 1892, he appeared in remarkably fine condition.

When she came to stay with Getty, she learned that he'd been married and divorced five times, and had five sons. But he was free at last. He told the press, "A lasting relationship with a woman is only possible if you're a business failure." That, he was not.

Her first night at Sutton Place had been troubled, and Zsa Zsa had gotten little sleep. She claimed she was haunted by the ghost of Anne Boleyn, a previous occupant of the bedchamber she was in. After imprisonment in the tower of London in 1536, the second wife of Henry VIII was beheaded, her reign as Queen of England having lasted only three years.

Over a breakfast that featured grilled kidneys, a dish she found revolting, Zsa Zsa began to meet Getty's fellow guests, including three visiting oil-rich Sheiks from the Middle East. She was surprised to hear Getty speak Arabic. The basis of his fortune came from a 60-year-old concession he had purchased for a tract of barren land near the border of Saudi Arabia and Kuwait.

After she turned down H. L. Hunt, another oilman, **J. Paul Getty**, the richest private citizen in the world at the time, also sought Zsa Zsa's hand in marriage.

"When I met him, he had aged and was facing the end of his life. Had I been the gold-digger I was supposed to be, I'd be in charge of Getty Oil today."

During the course of her first morning at Sutton Place, she discovered that she was not alone in her status as a woman being considered for the role of Getty's sixth wife. In addition to the Duchess of Argyll, there was a so-called princess from the Loire Valley of France, plus a Prussian countess from Leipzig.

Some reporter learned of Zsa Zsa's short visit to Guildford and sent word to the BBC. In an evening broadcast, a newscaster claimed that "Zsa Zsa Gabor, the American actress, and industrialist J. Paul Getty are engaged to be married."

"We were never engaged, *dahlink,* but we did discuss marriage," Zsa Zsa claimed. "I chose not to consider his age. It was apparent to me, however, that if I married him, and only three or so years went by, I would be a widow in charge of Getty Oil and the president of 200 other businesses."

That afternoon, Getty took her into his library, where he displayed all 122 of the works of historical fiction—all first editions—from the vast repertoire of G.A. Henty (1832-1902). He told her that these books, which he'd been reading since he was a boy, told him all he needed to know about how to make money. He gave her a copy of his favorite novel, *The Dragon and the Raven* (1866) for her to read in bed.

That night, he screened Greta Garbo's *Queen Christina,* which he'd seen at least thirty-six times since its initial release in 1933.

Zsa Zsa jokingly suggested that, "It's Garbo you should be considering for marriage—not me."

"I would," he told her, "if only she liked men."

Before she departed from Sutton Place, Zsa Zsa was invited into Getty's private drawing room. She suspected that he was about to demand either a "yes" or "no" about his marriage proposal.

"I encountered a defeated and broken man," she recalled. "All the life seemed to have been drained from him. He was not the vigorous man who had greeted me when I arrived at his place. He gave me the bad news. His son, George Franklin Getty II, born to his first wife, Jeanette Demont, had committed suicide at the age of forty-nine."

"There was no further talk of marriage," she said.

The great industrialist died on June 6, 1976, three years after Zsa Zsa's visit to Sutton Place. But one night when she was appearing in *Forty Carats* in Boston, an elderly British man in a Homburg appeared at the stage door. He asked to present her with a jewel case. "Paul wanted you to have this," he said, without introducing himself. He quickly departed.

She opened the jewel case to find "the most beautiful pair of diamond earrings I had ever seen, and I've seen plenty."

"It was a posthumous gift for the marriage that was never meant to be," she lamented.

***

Jack Ryan, the multimillionaire industrial designer, and Zsa Zsa lived in neighboring mansions in Bel Air and had known each other for a decade. During that time, she was busy with other marriages. But, suddenly free of husbands, she decided to pursue him. After being relatively indifferent to him, she suddenly focused all her attention on him.

He was noted for hosting parties that became noisy. Zsa Zsa on many an occasion had called the Bel Air Patrol with complaints. Entertainment and diversion at these parties was usually provided by, among others, go-go dancers and/or minstrel singers, rock-and-roll bands, and Swiss yodelers, along with young prostitutes of both genders.

"Once I'd forgiven her for all those complaints she'd lodged against me, I fell in love with her," Ryan said.

Ryan claimed that Zsa Zsa went after him with marriage on her mind. "Night after night, she invited me to her house. Elegant candlelit dinners, a hostess not only beautiful but irresistible. I cancelled a thousand engagements to come to one or another of her candlelit suppers that had other benefits. One night in her bedroom, I took in the golden vision before me. I thought to myself, 'Holy hell! I'm going to bed with Zsa Zsa Gabor!'"

Having sex with her is like getting caught in an avalanche of eroticism," Ryan said. "She's the heroine of the greatest romance novel ever written."

"I think Rubirosa taught her a lot about sex, and I benefitted from it. She once told me that Rubi was a 'walking encyclopedia of sex.'"

In a scene evoking Norma Desmond (Gloria Swanson) in the 1950 movie *Sunset Blvd.,* Zsa Zsa showed Ryan her films of the 1950s on a huge television screen. "She was romantic and sensual, especially as Jane Avril in *Moulin Rouge."* He had never seen these movies before.

Jack Ryan, millionaire inventor of weaponry mass produced by Raytheon for the U.S. Military, and of the Barbie Doll, whose look was marketed to millions of American adolescents as their role model of the perfect American girl. Here, he's shown with **Zsa Zsa.**

Even after their marriage, he never officially moved from his mansion into hers, and she never "officially" visited the S&M dungeon he allegedly maintained within his cellars.

After watching her on the screen, he defined her appearances as an aphrodisiac to him, which led to other intimacies, night after sensual night.

An eccentric, Ryan lived in a Tudor-styled mansion known as "Ryan's Castle." It consisted of forty rooms into which he'd installed his inventions and creations. "I think every bedroom had a mechanical sex doll," Zsa Zsa said.

He'd built a treehouse large enough to accommodate a dinner party for twelve seated diners. He had the main house equipped with 140 telephones. Each phone had a different ring tone, the sound evoking a particular bird, be it crow or whippoorwill. He even installed an electronic system from a surplus Navy destroyer which had been active during World War II. He'd sit at its console, controlling hundreds of lights and gadgets, even opening distant doors in the far corners of the house.

Ryan's Barbie Doll had become the best-selling doll of all time, and he'd also designed the mechanics of the "Chatty Cathy Doll." He designed dozens of toys for Mattel, Inc., one of the nation's largest toy manufacturers. He also had a "space-age savvy." As an engineer at Raytheon, Inc., he designed the prototypes for what later evolved into the Sparrow and Hawk missiles. He applied that same knowledge to toy engines that simulated motorcycle engine sounds and to the V-RROMM! X-15 "velocipede" (a revved-up version of a motorized tricycle) of the 1960s.

He finally proposed to Zsa Zsa, presenting her with a $12,000 engagement ring as part of the pitch. When she announced her engagement, Zsa Zsa told reporters, "*Dahlinks*, I've never married an Ivy Leaguer before." *[Ryan had graduated from Yale University.]*

Renting the bridal suite at Caesars Palace in Las Vegas, Ryan married Zsa Zsa on October 6, 1975. She claimed on her marriage certificate that she was fifty-five. Ryan was forty eight. Actually, she was within a sneeze of turning sixty.

"I had doubts about this big Irish lug," she said. The press claimed the next day that Ryan had married a true-to-life Barbie Doll. In fact, he proposed manufacturing a "Zsa Zsa doll," but never did.

During her marriage ceremony, she wore a Bob Mackie accordion-pleated chiffon gown. "Once again, *dahlinks,* I wore virginal white at my wedding, perhaps fooling no one. We gals of a certain age can still pretend to possess our cherries."

At her wedding, she hired the catering facilities at the Las Vegas Hilton in honor of her former marriage to Conrad Hilton.

Jolie referred to her new son-in-law as "The biggest catch in the whole world. He's good looking, and she adores him."

After her honeymoon night, she phoned Jolie. "I didn't dream I'd own such a man. I'm the happiest woman in the whole world."

Depicted above is the "Pink Diamond" model of **the Barbie Doll**, a design from which Ryan earned millions.

It was suggested at the time of her wedding that he re-tool his designs for production of a "Zsa Zsa doll," but it never came to fruition.

Within eight months, all parties concerned had begun to view the marriage as a mistake.

For their honeymoon, Ryan flew Zsa Zsa to Tokyo, where he met with toy manufacturers. He hired a guide for her. Zsa Zsa found him "handsome, young, and very charming."

Her tour guide drove her to an elegant inn and fed her caviar and wild duck. After the meal, he said, "Mr. Ryan said I must now take you to bed."

She was horrified, realizing that her new husband was a 1970s swinger—cocaine parties, husband-and-wife swapping, the works. She turned down the young man, but became aware of the kind of lifestyle Ryan had planned for her.

After a few weeks of what both of them described as bliss, their marital fights began. "She was a very stubborn and determined woman with her own agenda. She seemed to forget that I ran a business and had to meet demands and deadlines. I could not drop everything I was doing to run off with her on a moment's notice."

"For the first weeks of marriage, she makes you feel like you're the greatest lover in the world. But things go downhill. You end up feeling like a dud in bed."

"She was the devil on wheels at times," he claimed. "If her orange juice didn't arrive at the right temperature on her breakfast tray, there was hell to pay."

"She wanted a consort more than a husband, and I ushered her into galas in Beverly Hills, parties in Palm Springs, and jet set gatherings among the *nouveau riche* in Palm Beach," he said.

"I should have listened to the advice of George Sanders," Ryan said. "He told me that being married to Zsa Zsa was 'like drinking the nectar of the gods. It's very sweet at first, but it becomes too sweet and then sickens the stomach.'"

Instead of taking money from her, Ryan was a shrewd businessman. He negotiated a series of department store appearances that netted her $250,000. He never revealed the extent of her fortune, claiming she was "rich by an ordinary lady's standards."

Throughout the course of his marriage to Zsa Zsa, Ryan lodged and employed a dozen male students from UCLA whom he dressed in police uniforms, presumably for their assistance at his many parties and charity events. "They were very studly boys," Zsa Zsa said, "each one very good looking, and very sexy. I never asked Jack exactly what duties these boys performed for him—I didn't dare. One night he asked me if I'd like to take all of them on at once. But I turned him down."

Some nights when she was at Ryan's home, she heard screams coming from the basement. One of the UCLA boys told her, "That's Jack's torture chambers. It has all this shit used in the Middle Ages. Everything is painted in black. The walls are covered with black fox fur."

She turned down his invitation to go downstairs to "watch the show," where Ryan was dressed in a black leather jockstrap—and nothing else.

"Jack never sold his adjoining house to move in with me," Zsa Zsa said. "Nor did he abandon his mistresses and a secretary called Linda, whom he'd hired when she was sixteen. Anytime we had an argument, he announced, 'You'll find me next door with my mistresses.'"

After seven months of marriage, Zsa Zsa had had it with Ryan. He also wanted to divorce her. He didn't want to tell her directly, so he wrote her a note. He carried it around for two months before he presented it to her. In it, he declared, "I feel that I'm unqualified to continue in the role of consort—and even if I had all the qualities in the world, I cannot continue."

He'd leave the marriage with two projects uncompleted: He'd only half finished building a Moulin Rouge-style structure on the top floor of her house, and he had disassembled her Rolls-Royce, planning to accessorize and improve it with a series of revolutionary new features. He left the marriage with the automotive parts disassembled, its components scattered in a difficult-to-decipher mess.

He left to Zsa Zsa the task of announcing their upcoming divorce to the world, knowing how much she relished the spotlight. She told reporters, "*Dahlinks*, he cared more for his Barbie dolls than he did for me. And who wants to play second fiddle to a plastic doll? I'm a real woman, not a toy."

When asked about his divorce, a motion that was finalized in 1976, Ryan told a reporter from the Associated Press, "The thing I'll miss the most is the electricity she generated in bed."

The last time Ryan saw Zsa Zsa was at a gala dinner party she'd throw for him on the evening of October 6, 1983, a half-dozen years after their divorce. Zsa Zsa was inaugurating a lavish ballroom that he'd built onto her mansion and paid for, even though they were divorced. "It was a fabulous night and I was the guest of honor," Ryan said. "Eva was there, so was Merv Griffin. I sat next to Fred Astaire. The guests were various nobility—you know, barons and dukes—a flotsam of billionaires and an Indian maharaja or two."

"It was a magical night," he said, "and my last with her. I've got to hand it to her. She improves, like a vintage wine, with age."

At the age of sixty-five, after a life of dissipation, Ryan died on August 13, 1991. For the last two years of his life, he'd been confined to bed after suffering the debilitation of a stroke. The last words he ever said about Zsa Zsa were, "She dwells in a perpetual fairyland that never was."

***

Zsa Zsa's life had dipped into caricature, which would haunt her for the rest of her life. The mere mention of her name conjured up ridicule. Bob Hope and Johnny Carson, among others, mocked her while having her as a guest on their shows.

What was remarkable was that although Zsa Zsa had entered a dangerous stage for most actresses in Hollywood, she continued her role as a media event without the film credits to back up such publicity and acclaim. Most of her contemporaries, especially actresses like her in their late 50s going into their early 60s, had become relatively forgotten by the 1970s. They were replaced with newer, fresher faces, and most of them had retired from both the screen and from any (obvious) romantic entanglements.

Where were Jean Arthur, Mary Astor, Lynn Bari, Ella Raines, Hedy Lamarr, Myrna Loy, Norma Shearer, Sylvia Sidney, or Claire Trevor?

In marked contrast, Zsa Zsa was still around, even though movie role were

686

few and far between. She still appeared frequently on television and invariably on the front page with some new scandal. Unlike many other actresses, such as Janet Leigh, Zsa Zsa had retained her youthful vibrance and her beauty. She could still attract men—in some cases they were decades younger than herself. She did not look her age, and she kept moving her birth date forward from 1917 until she was "born practically the same year as Marilyn Monroe *[i.e., 1926]*," Jolie said.

A turning point in her life came when she walked into the office of her new divorce lawyer. Her former lawyer, Bentley Ryan, who had served her well, had died of a heart attack. Michael O'Hara was suggested as the attorney to handle her divorce from Jack Ryan.

When she entered his office, Zsa Zsa admitted that she was "enthralled by him—he was six feet four with green eyes and a suntan—beautiful, sexy, and the epitome of masculinity."

She invited him to dinner that night, and by midnight, he was sharing her bed.

"Love at first sight is not a new emotion for Zsa Zsa," Jack Ryan had claimed.

O'Hara might have been ten or twelve years younger than Zsa Zsa. As one friend of hers said, "He looked like a once-upon-a-time fullback for the USC team who had traded in his uniform for bespoke suits that made him appear to be a banker."

"When I first saw Michael, I thought I was staring into the face of James Garner, whom I'd always considered one of the handsomest men on the screen," Zsa Zsa said. "I was impressed by his appearance. I later learned his hair was cut by Jon Peters—you know, of Barbra Streisand notoriety. Michael was breathtaking in a suit that must have cost $750. I decided after talking to him for five minutes that he would become my next husband—after I dumped Jack Ryan, of course, *dahlink.*"

Right before the wedding, she received a phone call from her sometimes friend, Merle Oberon, who had forgiven Zsa Zsa "for your outrageous behavior at my party. But a working girl of a certain age like you has to keep her name in the paper."

"Never marry an attorney, my dear," Oberon warned. "They'll end up costing you plenty."

Sound advice, but Zsa Zsa was so mesmerized by O'Hara that she didn't take it.

At first, she thought that with a name like O'Hara, she was getting another Irishman. That is, until she learned he was a Yugoslav—a descendant of the once ruling family of Serbia, the Karageorgevics.

"He wasn't Atatürk, *dahlink,*" she told Oberon after her honeymoon. "But

I adore him. He's a fantastic lover. There are problems, though. He sometimes goes into these dark, black moods."

In 1976, three days after the finalization of her divorce from Ryan, she married O'Hara in the same Las Vegas chapel where she'd wed Ryan the previous year. The minister winked at her, "Back again so soon?"

As she was leaving the chapel with O'Hara, the minister called after her. "Miss Gabor, see you soon."

The marriage started with O'Hara making love to Zsa Zsa every night, or so she said. By 1982, each of them was living in separate parts of her Bel Air home.

In her memoirs and to her friends, Zsa Zsa, a normally talkative woman, chose not to share the private pain she experienced during her long marriage to O'Hara. He had long ago left the marriage bed before his divorce from her in 1982. During that time, she engaged in a number of high profile affairs, often with world famous figures, but she had to keep these liaisons concealed because revelations would have led to various scandals based on the fact that she as well as some of her famous conquests were trapped in wedlock.

The best insight into the bizarre private lives of the O'Haras was provided by British journalist David Gerrie, who published his revelations in London's *Daily Mail.*

Zsa Zsa's 1976 marriage to her divorce attorney, **Michael O'Hara**, eventually became a nightmare for her.

They began living in different parts of her Bel Air manse long before her divorce from him in 1982. "Merle Oberon warned me not to marry a lawyer, and I should have listened to her advice."

"I stayed on friendly terms with all of my other husbands after our divorces. But once divorced, Michael and I never spoke to each other again."

He described Zsa Zsa's "overriding narcissistic ego, her outrageous temper, and a vindictive love of making defenseless people suffer."

George Sanders had likened life with Zsa Zsa as a "swim in vintage bubbly," but Gerrie found it was "more cyanide than champagne."

While married to O'Hara, Zsa Zsa hired Gerrie as her personal assistant. After months of servitude under Zsa Zsa, he would later assert, "She was a monster beside whom Joan Crawford would look like one of Jack Ryan's Barbie dolls."

Gerrie was awed not by his new employers, but by the house in which they lived. He compared it to a movie set. Originally, it was constructed by Howard Hughes, and in time, it was inhabited by Elvis Presley and his Memphis Mafia.

In 2013, it doubled as the *faux* home of the flamboyant entertainer, Liberace, as a setting for the movie *Behind the Candelabra* which had starred Michael Douglas as the gay pianist and Matt Damon as his lover, Scott Thorson.

Because of her failing health, Zsa Zsa may not even have known that a film crew was using her home to film the intimate domestic life of the actors portraying Liberace and Thorson.

On his first day on the job, O'Hara told him Gerrie he could take anything he wanted from the refrigerator. But when it came time for lunch, he discovered only an open can of dog food and a half-empty bottle of Dom Pérignon.

As Jolie herself admitted, Zsa Zsa went through housekeepers, cooks, and maids faster than any other star in Hollywood.

After five weeks on the job, Gerrie became embroiled in a fight between Zsa Zsa and her black maid, who had displeased her boss by putting her undergarments in the wrong drawer.

Zsa Zsa stormed into Gerrie's office. "Go tell that fucking nigger bitch she's fired!"

In the living room, as Zsa Zsa continued her rant, the maid could take the racial slurs no more. She charged toward Zsa Zsa's head with a massive glass ashtray. Gerrie stepped in and knocked the ashtray from the maid's hand, preventing possible massive destruction to Zsa Zsa's face.

During Gerrie's employment, Zsa Zsa got only one major film role in which she was the star. *Every Girl Should Have One* was a 1978 independent *"whodunit"* film formatted as a (low-budget) 35mm film. It was billed as a "14 Karat Caper."

Directed and written by Robert Hyatt, it ran for only eighty minutes, with a supporting cast which included John Lazar, Sandra Yacey, and Robert Alda.

In a bizarre bit of casting, Alice Faye, in a minor role, made one of her last appearances on the screen. Older fans remembered Faye as the reigning star of 20th Century Fox during the late 1930s, before Betty Grable replaced her during World War II.

As Faye told Zsa Zsa, "I got bored sitting around with Phil Harris *[Faye's' husband]* and decided to appear in this piece of shit. Oh, for those pre-war days when Tyrone Power made love to me on screen. I chased after the handsome hunk, but he eluded me."

Gerrie characterized Zsa Zsa's marriage to O'Hara as an "emotional vacuum."

"They had not only separate bedrooms, but led separate lives."

He remembered O'Hara coming home, working out in the gym, then disappearing into his section of the house. Like Zsa Zsa, he had a fierce temper.

Gerrie helped Zsa Zsa with her check writing. She'd sometimes write a check but stop payment on it after it had been mailed. Gerrie got used to the command from Zsa Zsa to members of her staff. "Just tell her *[or him]* to fuck off. She's fired."

After a few months of "living in hell," Gerrie decided he could take it no more. That occurred at the time Zsa Zsa wanted him to accompany her to Alaska, where she was slated to appear in a television commercial.

Jobless, he went to the public relations firm which had arranged for his employment with Zsa Zsa. There, he asked the secretary to try to intervene to get his final check from Zsa Zsa.

He was shocked to learn that payment was not forthcoming. Zsa Zsa had telephoned the agency, claiming that Gerrie had stolen some of her jewelry, which was not true.

She also added a bizarre aftertaste, telling the agency that Gerrie had misrepresented himself. "He's actually a Jew. His name is Gittelson, not Gerrie."

That, too, was a lie. Gerrie was not a Jew and not misrepresenting himself as someone he wasn't.

Gerrie's experience at the Gabor household was the nightmare of his life. "The only satisfaction I draw from all this is that if you ask people to name more than one film Zsa Zsa Gabor starred in, you'll be met with a blank stare."

Although Zsa Zsa appeared to be in love with O'Hara in the beginning, she ended up calling him more vile names than any of her other husbands. Of all her former spouses, he would be the one she would never speak to again. As she was quoted, "I thought I was marrying some big-shot successful lawyer, but I wound up footing all the bills, just like Merle Oberon had warned me."

After their divorce in 1982, O'Hara made no comment, referring to his experience with Zsa Zsa as "a closed book."

***

A single woman again, Zsa Zsa once again launched her decades-long search for the man of her dreams. Each day, her secretary, an Ohio-born girl named Betsy, delivered the latest offers for a rendezvous, or even a marriage.

She was back in Las Vegas, appearing at the Flamingo, "where all the broken down whores from Hollywood turn out not to see me perform, but to sit down front to see how I'm aging."

She made disparaging references to fading Hollywood beauties who had attended her shows. Lana Turner was chief among them, along with Marlene Dietrich, Hedy Lamarr, former child star Margaret O'Brien, Jeanne Crain, and the once beautiful Rita Hayworth.

One night a messenger arrived at the Flamingo with a special invitation. It was from Elvis Presley, who was also appearing in town. He wanted to meet Zsa Zsa in his dressing room after his late show.

To Betsy, she disdainfully dismissed Presley as "that sleazy little singer," She had never been impressed with him, and had little desire to meet him. She knew little of Presley, his private life, or his career, categorizing him as "a hill-billy from Tennessee—not my kind of man." Besides, she'd heard that he preferred only teenage girls.

But as it turned out, Betsy was one of Presley's greatest fans, and she urged Zsa Zsa to accept the invitation.

Zsa Zsa was delivered to the singer's dressing room backstage about fifteen minutes before the conclusion of his act, which was playing to the frenzied applause of a "standing room only" audience.

She recalled in her memoirs that when the door was thrown open to his dressing room and Presley himself appeared in the flesh, she found him "one of the most gorgeous, sexy men I've ever seen in my life, a cross between a gentleman and a big black sexy snake. Elvis radiated sexuality."

Although she indicated that Presley propositioned her with a whisper in the dressing room, she claimed she was in love with someone else at the time and refused his offer of love.

In a contradictory statement in her memoir, she had just admitted that when she met the popular singer, she was single and looking for love.

Merle Oberon claimed that Zsa Zsa called her when she got back from Las Vegas. "She was practically foaming at the mouth," Oberon said, "'Elvis Presley made love to me in Las Vegas,' Zsa Zsa shouted into my ear. At first, I didn't believe it, although I later heard from other sources that it was true."

"I always heard that **Elvis Presley** only went after young girls, so I was surprised when he viewed me as a sex symbol" Zsa Zsa said.

"Zsa Zsa filled me in on enough bizarre details about Elvis in the boudoir that I finally came to believe her," Oberon said. "The more I thought about it, I said, 'Why not?' After all, practically every twenty-year old beach boy in Acapulco pursued me."

"It was very flattering. I had never thought much about him until I actually met him in person in Las Vegas"

Zsa Zsa claimed that before Elvis seduced her, he wanted to know if she'd ever had a child. "I can't stand going to bed with a woman who's borne a child," he told her. "It's a complete turnoff for me."

"As we made love, an early recording of his ('Baby, Let's Play House') was playing the background."

Since Presley had obviously not heard of her daughter Francesca, Zsa Zsa lied to him, telling him that she'd never given birth. "None of the Gabor sisters ever had a child."

"What do you mean by 'sisters'" he asked. "I thought there was only one of you."

"The other two were born ugly," she said, "and our mother keeps them hidden."

"I see," he said. "My twin brother died when Gladys gave birth to the both of us. If he had lived, he might be out there tonight competing with me for the babes in Vegas."

"Sisters can be very competitive," she said, "often going after the same man."

Zsa Zsa told Oberon, who took delight in repeating the story at parties, that Presley was hot and sweaty after the show, but didn't want to take a full bath. He headed for the bathroom, where Zsa Zsa heard the faucets running.

He called back to her. "I've got this hillbilly pecker *[A reference to the fact that he was uncircumsized]* and I'm washing it clean before I come to bed."

Zsa Zsa claimed that as a young girl and later as a woman growing up in Eastern Europe, she was well acquainted with the uncircumsized penis. "None of my husbands was cut," she assured Presley.

"That's the way it used to be in this country," he told her. "Now any young girl born after the war insists that her man be cut. They won't sleep with you otherwise. Take Streisand, for instance. One time, maybe. After that, she insists you call her Jewish doctor in the morning."

When Zsa Zsa flew into New York and met with Earl Wilson at "21," the columnist confirmed that she told him she'd had a one-night stand with Presley in Las Vegas.

"What Zsa Zsa wrote in print and what she said in her private life were two different animals," Wilson recalled. "She practically salivated in talking about Elvis. But I think it was an ego trip for her. My God, the woman must have been sixty if a day. I'd heard it from all of Elvis's gals—Jayne Mansfield, Nancy Sinatra, Tuesday Weld, Natalie Wood, that he was a lousy lay."

"What turned Zsa Zsa on to this hot little firecracker, who was born in 1935, was that he came on to her, a woman born in the dying days of the Austro-Hungarian empire. He was a man who could have any woman in the world, or so it seemed, a man who had seduced everybody from Doris Duke to Marilyn Monroe. I think Elvis made Zsa Zsa feel young and alive again."

During their rendezvous, Zsa Zsa got confidential with Wilson, knowing that he could not print a word of her revelations, but that he'd tell his friends, including Frank Sinatra, that Elvis Presley had seduced her.

"Elvis came out of the bathroom jaybird naked, as Southerners say. I made one request before he hopped into bed. I asked Elvis to shake, rattle, and roll in his birthday suit."

He looked at her and said, "Lady, you're on!"

***

[Zsa Zsa was flattered by Elvis Presley's momentary interest in her. She dined out on the story. It proved so popular she began to relate another story about how she'd spent a night with the Beatles in the late 60s. She'd been invited to London to perform briefly before introducing them on stage in "Night of the 100 Stars," an annual charity event.

Backstage, she was introduced to John Lennon, Ringo Starr, Paul McCartney, and George Harrison. She had not listened to their music and was not a fan. However, meeting them for the first time, she bonded with them, and the Beatles seemed to like her Hungarian accent, her beauty, and charm.

"I didn't know what to expect, but I found them very amusing," she later said. "They liked my Hungarian accent and I went for their Liverpudlian accents, whatever in the hell that meant."

"After the show, I invited them for late night drinks at my suite at the London Hilton overlooking Park Lane," she said. "To my amazement, all four of these beetle bugs agreed to come over."

In her memoirs, she wrote of the Beatles, although denying any romantic link to them, in spite of rumors appearing in the British tabloids. She did confirm that Harrison was her favorite Beatle, defining him as "the quiet one," and suggesting that "George is very different from the other Beatles."

At the time of her meeting with Harrison, he was twenty-six years her junior.

Years had gone by when Zsa Zsa spoke of her one night with the Beatles at a dinner Merv Griffin had hosted for her in Palm Springs, with Eva functioning as the hostess.

"I loved hearing Zsa Zsa tell her tall tales," Griffin later said. "But I had to sift through them carefully, because she exaggerated so much. Yet every one of her stories contained a

Beatlemania: Here, **Zsa Zsa** is seen rehearsing for "A Night of a Thousand Stars" at the London Palladium. From *left to right* are Paul McCartney, George Harrison, Ringo Starr, and John Lennon.

Of the four, Harrison was clearly her favorite. She claimed she seduced him.

693

grain of truth. The trick was in picking out the one or two kernels."

She told Griffin, Eva, and the other dinner guests of that evening about the night the Beatles came to her suite for drinks. "I loved the humor of these boys, their irreverence about institutions which most of the Western world viewed as sacred. They seduced me one at a time. Ringo went first, followed by Paul Mc-Cartney, and then John Lennon. George was the last, and he was the best of the lot."

After Zsa Zsa left Griffin's party that night, Eva told Griffin that she doubted very seriously if Zsa Zsa went to bed with all four of them. "But there was something between George and Zsa Zsa. From what I heard, he spent the night in her suite and was seen leaving at nine o'clock the following morning."

"The boys seemed to really love each other, and I don't mean that in a sexual way," Zsa Zsa told Eva and Griffin. "They seemed to belong to each other, and it was sad that they eventually broke up. I'd never seen four people relate to each other like that before in such a caring way. George seemed to look upon John as something of a father figure, a disciple perhaps. But he would also challenge John when he said something way out of line."

"George seemed to be the baby of the group—In fact, Paul called him baby brother at one point. Yet George told me that Paul often 'pissed' him off. In time, the boys would take radically different paths, but it was exciting to be in their vibrant presence, if only for a short time. I felt connected with young people for a change."

"Of course, dahlinks, if George and I had become friends, even lovers, we, too, would have had our conflicts," she said. "I could not tolerate his hang-ups on Hinduism and all those gurus and yoga. He also hung out with those Hare Krishna guys, you know, the types who assault you in airports. Instead of being bled dry by these Swamis, he could have better spent his fortune on buying diamonds for me."

After Zsa Zzsa left the dinner party, Griffin concluded that, "We'll never know what really happened that night with Zsa Zsa and the Beatles. It should have been filmed. I doubt very seriously if she seduced all the Beatles, as she claimed, unless they had an orgy. That was possible. After all, I read the Albert Goldman book , The Lives of John Lennon. In it, Goldman wrote: 'Their sex life can be summed up in one word: Orgy.' Eva and I agreed that it was likely Zsa Zsa took George to bed in what Michael Jackson would later refer to as 'a sleepover.'"

In a final comment on her experiences with the Beatles, Zsa Zsa said, "I've always had a tremendous weakness for all types of Englishmen."

***

"Zsa Zsa was on a roll, and I always looked forward to an invitation to one of her dinner parties in Bel Air," Merv Griffin said. "She often entertained Eva and me with 'tawdry tidbits' from her scandalous past."

"For years I'd heard rumors that she and Prince Philip had had an ongoing affair over a period of time, although that's not what she wrote in her memoirs. But I think she wanted to spare the feelings of Queen Elizabeth."

"Perhaps Zsa Zsa drank too much of her own champagne one night," Griffin claimed. "She was in a confessional mood. It went something like this… 'Would you believe that in 1952, Prince Philip seduced me?' That was the year Princess Elizabeth ascended to the throne."

Way back when Zsa Zsa was filming *Moulin Rouge* in London in 1952, she'd hired the veteran actress and one of the grandest of the *grandes dames* of the British Theatre, Constance Collier as her vocal coach. Collier was intimately associated with Katharine Hepburn. "Constance and I were seen about London together so much that the press hinted at an affair, like the one she'd had with Katharine Hepburn," Zsa Zsa said. "Nothing could be farther from the truth."

Collier had been born in 1875, and by the time Zsa Zsa met her, she was in her final months. *[The noted luminary of the British stage died in April of 1955.]* "She was beyond such things as sex by then, but was a fascinating tour guide to London," Zsa Zsa said. "She was one of the haughtiest icons of the British theater, and had been a friend of Queen Mary."

Her proudest possession, prominently displayed in her living room, was a photograph of Queen Mary holding her granddaughter, little Princess Elizabeth.

"One afternoon, as Zsa Zsa related, she arrived for her voice lesson, only to find Collier in a state of extreme nervousness. "I received a call from Buckingham Palace this morning. Prince Philip has requested the pleasure of your company."

"Have I been included on the guest list of the Queen and Prince Philip for some gala event?" Zsa Zsa asked. "I'd better start polishing my diamonds."

"I'm afraid, my dear, you don't understand," Collier said. "You never impressed me as being naïve."

"I truly don't know what you're trying to tell me," Zsa Zsa said.

"His Majesty wants to arrange a private rendezvous…just the two of you," Collier said."

"Of course, we must be very discreet about this. You're to go alone to the address he will provide to you. The Queen will not be there. No one must know of this intimate meeting."

In her memoir, Zsa Zsa claimed that she rejected Prince Philip's invitation for romance, even after he called three more times, each time asking for an appointment to see her in private.

She also claimed that she refused the offer from the Prince out of respect for the Queen.

What she didn't write was what Collier had to say: "My dear, Her Majesty expects loyalty from her prince—not fidelity. He's known for his…shall we say *'involvements?'* with other women."

"I'll see him whenever Huston doesn't need me on *Moulin Rouge,* she promised.

"Remember, my dear, discretion is the word," Collier warned her.

"Armies could not drag it from me," Zsa Zsa said.

To her credit, she kept quiet about it for many years.

A gossip monger, Griffin was delighted that Zsa Zsa was finally revealing her long-kept secret. He had so many questions to ask. "I hear Philip's enemies in England call him a 'cantankerous old sod.'"

"When he's serving as the Queen's royal consort, Philip is, of course, stiff and formal," she responded. "But when the lights are dimmed, and he feels in comfortable, safe surroundings, he's a hell of a lot of fun, with a wicked sense of humor. You should hear him tell stories about his visit with President Jimmy Carter. No two men were so different. And you should have heard what Philip had to say about Rosalynn Carter, that Georgia peach."

"A lot of people don't understand Philip's sense of humor," Zsa Zsa said. "Elizabeth Taylor did. She told me about the night Philip attended the premiere of *Elephant Walk* in London. She said she wore a very low-cut gown that looked like she had two pillows in there. Before Philip approached her, she heard him tell his aide, 'Hop in, old boy.'"

Perhaps Zsa Zsa decided to reveal the details of her affair with Prince Philip, conducted over a number of years, because of her ongoing jealous rivalry with Merle Oberon. The Mexican press had written about Prince Philip's visits to their country, documenting his visits to Oberon's sumptuous villa in Acapulco, her palace in Cuernavaca, and her estate in Mexico City.

Oberon entertained Prince Philip so frequently that David Patrick Columbia, the New York society columnist, had the audacity to print, "The Queen's husband is Merle's boy. He's her big social ticket."

When Zsa Zsa visited Oberon at her home in Beverly Hills, she noticed that she kept several pictures of Prince Philip encased in gold frames, spread throughout her house, including one next to her bed. One of the photographs depicted Philip playing polo.

In front of Griffin, Zsa Zsa mocked Oberon. "It's a constant chatter of 'Philip loved my place in Cuernavaca. He adores my villa in Acapulco.' It's 'Philip this, Philip that.' She drives me crazy with all this 'Philip' name dropping."

"Prince Philip has fucked me repeatedly, but, unlike Merle, I don't take out ads in newspapers."

In *The Royals,* biographer Kitty Kelley wrote that Oberon provided Philip with "cashmere blankets, silk sheets, a French chef, and vintage wines. Although married to the world's richest woman, he did not live sumptuously. His wife was frugal and accustomed to scratchy tweeds and sensible shoes. Her palaces were cold and drafty, and required electric space heaters in every corner. Merle had heated marble floors, heated towel racks, and gold leafed beds swagged with silk tassels."

Griffin kept pressing Zsa Zsa for more details, wanting her to confirm the rumor that Philip maintained a bachelor apartment near Berkeley Square in London.

Zsa Zsa recalled the last time she'd seen Philip, which was at Windsor when he played polo in front of the Queen and the Queen Mother. After the game, she said that Philip "was sweet and friendly to me, and we chatted a lot about animals."

As she later wrote, "In an impatient move, the Queen interrupted us, asking 'What are you two jabbering about?' She reclaimed Philip from my clutches."

"Philip was showing his age, but when I first knew him, he was a classic male beauty, with a great body," Zsa Zsa said. "And he had something the Duke of Windsor wished he'd had."

"And what might that be, my dear?" Griffin asked impishly. "I'm all ears."

"You know exactly what I mean, you size queen," Zsa Zsa answered. "It belonged not on a mere prince, but perhaps on a king or even an emperor."

***

On another night, dining with Griffin and Eva, Zsa Zsa revealed yet another episode from her scandal soaked past. It had also transpired in 1952, in London, during the filming of *Moulin Rouge.*

It was with Louis Mountbatten, 1st Earl Mountbatten of Burma. Zsa Zsa claimed that he'd been "handsome and distinguished" when she met him at the premiere of a play in London's West End. She also claimed that she was wearing a green satin gown with plunging *décolletage* that "kept His Lordship's eyes glued in only one place. He was so intrigued, he could hardly lift his eyes to look into mine."

At the time she met Mountbatten, he was fifty-two years old, but looked much younger "with a body that was ready for military maneuvers."

He was the uncle of Prince Philip—"and just as dashing," Zsa Zsa said.

She'd heard many rumors about him. In 1922, he'd married Edwina Cynthia Annette Ashley, and they'd had two daughters. His Lordship once frankly

697

admitted that he and Edwina "spent all our married lives getting into other people's beds." Like Prince Philip, he could be amazingly indiscreet in revealing very personal details to those with whom he enjoyed intimacy.

In his autobiography, Britain's Labour MP Tom Driberg claimed that "Lord Mountbatten, like myself, had a sex preference for men."

Mountbatten was said to have seduced countless handsome young men in the British Armed Forces. Kitty Kelley in her book, *The Royals,* reported that "he also adored glamorous movie stars."

"My god, *dahlinks,*" Zsa Zsa once said. "I'd heard that His Lordship once went to bed with that sleazy blonde, Diana Dors." *[i.e., Britain's sex symbol of the 1950s and that country's answer to Marilyn Monroe.]*

Zsa Zsa was never one to allow rumors to get in the way of a possible romance. "All of us, *dahlinks*, have skeletons in our past," she said. "Nobody is perfect."

In her memoirs, Zsa Zsa revealed that "Dickie," as Lord Mountbatten was called, phoned her the day after their meeting for permission to visit her on the set of *Moulin Rouge,* where John Huston was directing her. She did admit that "I was bowled over by Dickie, and he kissed me and wanted to make love to me."

But then, in a memoir, she claimed that Huston called her to the set, and "I never did consummate our relationship."

So she claimed in print.

To Eva and Griffin, however, she told a different story with a radically different ending.

That weekend, he drove her to Broadlands, his estate in Hampshire, where Prince Philip and Princess Elizabeth had spent part of their honeymoon.

Trapped between two Royals, **Zsa Zsa** *(center)* found herself being romanced by both **Prince Philip** *(left)* and **Lord Mountbatten** *(right).*

"Each of them made me feel like Queen for a Day," she told her friend, Merv Griffin.

She claimed that "the dirty deed" took place not in his bedroom, but in Lady Mountbatten's suite, which was better decorated and more comfortable.

"It was here in this bed that Philip deflowered his new bride," Lord Mountbatten said to Zsa Zsa, pointing to a magnificent four-poster Henry VIII type of bed.

"I gazed upon Salvador Dalí paintings on the wall as I found myself nude, lying on shocking pink satin sheets and being made love to by one of the military legends of Britain."

In the afterglow, as Lord Mountbatten lay in bed with Zsa Zsa, he revealed more than he perhaps should have: "After his first night in this bed, Philip told me that his new bride wanted sex constantly. 'I can't get her out of bed,' he lamented to me. 'She's insatiable. She's always there wanting to be serviced. She's driving me mad.'"

He also revealed to Zsa Zsa that Philip's marriage to the princess had been arranged. "He's not in love with her, but he respects her."

Back in Hollywood, Zsa Zsa encountered Cary Grant at a party in Beverly Hills. "I hear you and Dickie have become intimate friends," Grant said to her. "But, sweetcheeks, get this: I had him long before you did, and I've got pictures to prove it."

Shortly before he died in 1993, John Baratt, Lord Mountbatten's private secretary for a period that lasted more than twenty years, claimed that his boss "had a brief affair with the American actress and socialite, Zsa Zsa Gabor. She was involved with both Prince Philip and His Lordship. They sometimes passed women between them."

An underground paper in London published a (previously secret) list of movie stars that Lord Mountbatten and Prince Philip had enjoyed. It included some minor British stars, but some surprising Hollywood names were on the list too. Although everyone had expected Merle Oberon's name to appear *[and it did]*, the public was surprised to see Zsa Zsa's name on the list too. What came as an even bigger surprise to Londoners were the names of both Jane Russell and Shirley MacLaine. One newspaper editor at *The Daily Mail,* feigning indignation, referred to that revelation as "mind boggling."

***

Since virtually the debut of her arrival in America, Zsa Zsa had been a Republican. "Conrad Hilton told me that was the party to belong to, so I went along. I once made a headline in 1970 when I told a radio interviewer in Denver, "I think Richard Nixon is the sexiest man in politics—lucky Pat Nixon!"

"Someone on his staff must have alerted the President, because he sent me a thank you note. 'I'm usually called a son of a bitch by my enemies. It's good to know that I have a fan—and a beautiful one at that.'"

Appearing with Merv Griffin on one of his talk show one night *[it was taped at Caesars Palace in Las Vegas]* Zsa Zsa made a claim that elicited boos and catcalls from his audience. "I think Richard Nixon is the greatest president of modern times. He opened up Red China for us. He opened up the Soviet Union. The guy deserves a break instead of all this criticism."

Her right-wing politics drew her into the social and political orbit of Ronald and Nancy Reagan, who became her friends, meeting her at parties and at an occasional dinner.

When Nixon ran for a second term in 1972, Zsa Zsa joined other right-wing actors, John Wayne and James Stewart, in a nationwide campaign to get him re-elected. "At this point in their careers, neither man looked very appetizing to me, so I let them alone in their beds at night," she confessed to Griffin.

She proved popular with Republican audiences, especially one night when she appeared with Nelson Rockefeller and Ronald Reagan. The audiences shouted—*ZSA ZSA FOR PRESIDENT!*

"If I'd gone on the ticket for president that year, I would have had to compete with another candidate, Linda Lovelace, that *Deep Throat* slut."

After his successful election in 1972, Richard Nixon placed an hour-long call to her, even though it unfolded in the middle of a dinner party she was hosting in her Bel Air manse. He quizzed her about Turkey and Hungary, and was very interested in anything she had to say about Atatürk and his points of view about the United States.

Zsa Zsa viewed **President Richard Nixon** as the sexiest man in politics.

She is the only known woman who went to bed with both Elvis Presley and Richard Nixon. "But not at the same time, *dahlink.*"

At the end of their telephone dialogue, as her dinner guests waited for news about what had been said, Nixon said to her, "It's about time we got together. I'll have someone on my staff send you the details, but I'll be in San Francisco attending this state dinner. I want you to be there as my hostess. Pat's staying in Washington."

Before the State dinner in San Francisco, Nixon held her hand and kissed her on both cheeks, which was not customary for him. She had wanted to be seated beside him, but she found herself positioned between "a German prince of some sort and a short, dumpy man."

During her chat with "the toad," she discovered that he had a brilliant mind in spite of his looks. "I didn't appreciate his hand on my knee.

700

If he expected me to go to bed with him, he had another thought coming."

At the end of the dinner, she learned that the toad was actually Henry Kissinger, the U. S. Secretary of State, who had gone out with some famous actresses before her.

Although Kissinger had shown an interest in her, she sought bigger game that night. "I could always save Henry for another day, *dahlink*," she later told friends.

Only to her intimates, who included Jolie and Eva, did Zsa Zsa even suggest that she'd spent the night in Nixon's presidential suite in San Francisco. Word leaked out over the years, however, even as late as 2010.

In a profile for *Marie Claire* magazine entitled *Zsa Zsa Gabor: The Original Fame Seeker,* reporter Helen Gent wrote: "Gabor had affairs with everyone from Richard Burton and Sean Connery to Richard Nixon."

As far as it is known, Nixon never had sex outside his marriage except for his encounter with Zsa Zsa and with what one reporter defined as "a modern day Chinese Mata Hari."

[In Hong Kong in 1958, Nixon, then Vice President under Eisenhower, met Marianna Liv, his tour guide. She was only eighteen (he was forty-five) and very beautiful. When not escorting VIPs on tours, she worked as a hostess in The Opium Den, a swank cocktail bar in the Hong Kong Hilton.

Unknown to Nixon, Hoover's FBI was watching the couple, documenting their activities with secret photographs.

Nixon met Liv again in 1964, 1965, and 1967 during subsequent visits to Hong Kong as a private citizen. When Nixon wasn't in town, Liv was said to fraternize with U.S. Navy officers.

Liv showed up in Washington to attend one of the balls associated with Nixon's second inauguration.]

Zsa Zsa later referred to Nixon's seduction of her as "very professional, very competent, but no one would ever call him a great lover."

"He was very stiff around women," she recalled. "Forgive the pun, *dahlink*."

"Even in bed, he insisted on being called Mr. President, although 'Dick' might have been more appropriate," Zsa Zsa said.

"There was much that we didn't agree on politically," she said, "especially about gays. He told me that in San Francisco, everyone was 'so faggy that I'm afraid to shake their hands. You know, don't you, that it was homosexuals that destroyed ancient Greece—Aristotle and Socrates were both fags.'"

Nixon always refused to comment on any of his extramarital affairs. Once, however, at a dinner for the Walter Annenbergs, in front of Pat Nixon, he began to talk about the beauty of Chinese women and how they were much more beautiful than women of the West.

President Gerald Ford and **Zsa Zsa** could have danced all night together at a White House gala, but First Lady Betty Ford had other plans for her husband and broke up "those dancing fools."

"I wept when Nixon was forced out of office by those raving jackals," Zsa Zsa said. "It was so silly. Some little breakin. There wasn't any jewelry stolen. Talk about robberies. I've had thefts where diamonds were looted. I've lost millions, and the world overthrows a great president because of a robbery he didn't commit himself."

"I was also a supporter of Gerald Ford when he became president," she said. "The Fords invited me to a White House dinner. I sat on the left of the President, although he had warned me not to sit too close because there were photographers. He was afraid he'd drop his baked Alaska in my lap and that the pictures that emerged from its aftereffects would make every frontpage in the country."

"After dinner, when he danced with me, he told me that there were two women in the world that he wanted to go to bed with—Ann-Margret and me."

"That night, he danced with me so much that Betty Ford came up to us and chided him. 'Mr. President, must I remind you? There are other guests here tonight—not just Miss Zsa Zsa Gabor.'"

The New York Post ran a picture of Ford dancing with Zsa Zsa under the caption: *ZSA ZSA DANCES WITH GUESS WHO?*

"During the course of my lifetime, I flirted with Ronald Reagan, I flirted with Ford. I bedded Jack Kennedy, and I bedded Richard Nixon. It is certain that I could have easily become the mistress of any one of them, but I chose not to. Jack Kennedy at one point offered to fly Air Force One to pick me up. But I didn't want to play Number Two to their wives. I've always preferred being a wife and not a mistress."

***

In San Francisco, Zsa Zsa had been ushered out of Nixon's suite at five o'clock "the morning after" by two Secret Servicemen. Back in her own suite, she went to bed and was awakened by a phone call at around ten o'clock that morning. It was from the White House. She was informed that Mrs. Richard Nixon was on the other end of the phone line.

At first, she went into panic, fearing that Pat Nixon had some spy secretly working for her within the Secret Service. With apprehension, on the phone, she greeted the First Lady only to learn that she was calling to ask her to date Henry Kissinger.

"Mrs. Nixon," Zsa Zsa said. "I had no idea you were a matchmaker like Dolly in that musical *Hello, Dolly.*"

"From time to time I do that," she answered. "I think you and Henry would be terrific together. You've dated ugly men before, I'm sure. Dick used to be better looking. Now one side of his face is larger than the other."

Before ringing off, Mrs. Nixon suggested that if they were ever in New York at the same time, that they should make a date to go to the theater together. "I like shows like the *Hello, Dolly!* we mentioned...perhaps *My Fair Lady.* I feel there's enough seriousness in the world without having to watch some mentally disturbed poor Southern woman get raped by Marlon Brando, who is a leftie."

Mrs. Nixon must have telephoned Kissinger, informing him that Zsa Zsa was willing to go out with him. Later, after Zsa Zsa had flown back to Los Angeles, and Kissinger happened to be there, too, he called her and invited her to dinner at the Bistro Gardens Restaurant in Beverly Hills. She accepted.

Before their rendezvous, she researched the key details of his life and career, learning that he had been born in 1923 during the brief heyday of the Weimar Republic to a family of German Jews. In 1938, he fled from Nazi Germany, settling briefly in London before going on to New York. He became a naturalized U.S. citizen in 1943.

In spite of his looks, she'd read that he had a reputation as a ladies' man, although he mocked that label. "I'm not really a secret swinger. Power is the ultimate aphrodisiac."

After dinner and back at her Bel Air manse, Zsa Zsa claimed in a memoir that "Henry showed signs of making an amorous approach" when his beeper suddenly sounded. It was Nixon ordering him to drive immediately to his home at San Clemente.

Kissing Zsa Zsa goodbye, Kissinger set off, but crashed into her electronic gates when they malfunctioned. She ran out to help him, discovering that his car had been badly dented. "He was in a tizzy. It turned out that he had wrecked Nixon's car."

"That date didn't come off, but when I was in Boston, appearing on stage in Noël Coward's *Blithe Spirit,* he phoned from the

LA GABOR *(center)* is torn between two admirers, **Richard Nixon** *(left)* and **Henry Kissinger** *(right)*.

In San Francisco, Zsa Zsa slipped away to entertain the President in his suite, and even fielded a phone call from an unsuspecting Patricia Nixon about an unrelated matter early the next morning.

But after a romantic dinner with Kissinger, when boudoir issues were raised, he was interrupted by the President, who summoned him on his beeper.

White House. He volunteered to fly to Boston to take me out. But a day later, I received another urgent call from him cancelling our date. I demanded to know why."

"Zsa Zsa, you're the only person who knows this, outside the White House, but I'm telling you the real reason I can't make it. Tomorrow morning, the United States is going to invade Cambodia."

"To be frank, *dahlink*, I thought he'd call me for future dates," Zsa Zsa said. "But after a long silence, when I dined in Manhattan at '21' with Dick and Pat Nixon, I told them that her attempt at matchmaking didn't work out, and I was so sorry. 'If it's not Cambodia, it's something else,' I said."

Pat Nixon shot right back. "That may be so, but forget I ever suggested that you date him. He seems to find time in his busy schedule to date Liv Ullmann and Jill St. John."

Then she turned to her husband. "Henry is so unlike my beloved husband, who has such a busy schedule he hasn't had time to visit my bedroom in the past five years."

***

In Palm Beach, Zsa Zsa met Felipe de Alba at a polo match, finding him "handsome, gallant, and chic." She really didn't know who he was, but he was intriguing, and she asked about him. It turned out that he was a Mexican attorney, seven years her junior. He'd also appeared in a number of movies in the 1940s and 50s, his most famous being a role in *Robinson Crusoe* (1954), directed by the legendary Luís Buñuel, wherein both Spanish and English-language versions were shot simultaneously in Mexico.

She forgot all about De Alba in the months ahead, until she read about him in the gossip columns. He became involved with the very rich Estée Lauder and other wealthy women in Palm Beach. She assumed he was a playboy who made a profession of being the boyfriend of rich women.

Around 1983, she made several trips to Palm Beach, where she had a villa at the Palm Beach Polo Club. There, she began to run into De'Alba so frequently, she thought he might be stalking her.

One day, as she emerged from a chic boutique on Worth Avenue, he was parked in front of the store in a Rolls-Royce. She accepted his invitation to drive her home.

Zsa Zsa claimed that she was still emotionally bruised from the breakup of her marriage to Michael O'Hara and that she wasn't ready to rush into another romance so soon.

Her friends differed in their opinions about De Alba, some urging her to drop him, calling him "just a gigolo." But in contrast, her friend, Liz Whitney, urged her to marry the attorney, asserting that he had been educated in Switzerland, that he was a real gentleman, and that he spoke six languages.

Eva was still married at the time to Frank Jameson, and Zsa Zsa accepted an invitation to join them aboard their yacht, *Laura,* which was temporarily berthed in Puerto Vallarta, Mexico. She was surprised to find John Huston at the port. He'd fallen in love with the Mexican town in 1964, when he'd shot and directed Tennessee Williams' *The Night of the Iguana* there with Ava Gardner and Richard Burton. Trailing Burton to Mexico, Elizabeth Taylor had also "adored" Puerto Vallarta and had purchased a villa there.

On April 13, 1983, Eva and Jameson decided to throw a dinner party aboard the *Laura,* to which they invited Huston. A twenty-four piece mariachi band was hired for the event.

Zsa Zsa checked out the vision she projected in her salmon-colored, floor-length Oscar de la Renta gown made of velvet. "As my former movie title had it, I was *Lovely to Look At,"* she said.

She was shocked to see that one of her sister's dinner guests was Felipe de Alba, who had returned to his native Mexico.

Perhaps it was the champagne, perhaps it was the charming Mexican, but several hours into the events of that evening, Zsa Zsa told Eva, "I fell madly in love with Felipe that night. Not only that, but I wanted to marry him that very evening."

Responding to the giddy excitement generated by Zsa Zsa and amplified by his wife, Eva, Jameson ordered the captain of his *Laura* to sail away from the port for the immediate execution of a marriage at sea ceremony, which the captain was legally authorized to organize and make official, but only if the *Laura* were a minimum of 12.3 miles offshore.

Unknown to Zsa Zsa, Jameson ordered that the marriage ceremony be performed, but in a location only eight miles offshore from the coast. That way, he told Eva, "If Zsa Zsa sobers up tomorrow and decides Felipe wasn't all that good in bed, she can get out of the marriage without any legal complications."

Eva agreed what a clever fox her husband was.

It was the shortest marriage in Hollywood history after **Zsa Zsa Gabor**, at sea, married the Mexican attorney **Felipe de Alba**.

She later defined him as "a professional gigolo. We never had time to go to bed together—that's how short the marriage was."

"Felipe is the second of my husbands who I never slept with."

She was no doubt also referring to her first husband, Burhan Belge.

By the time she woke up the next day, Zsa Zsa had reconsidered the marriage. She called her lawyer in Beverly Hills, who informed her that she couldn't have remarried either at sea or on land, because her divorce papers from Michael O'Hara had not become final.

She later claimed that the marriage had not been consummated aboard the yacht. "We were too drunk, *dahlink*," she later told Huston. "The marriage is going to last only a day."

Huston quipped, "I didn't give it that long."

With De Alba beside her, Zsa Zsa told Jameson and Eva goodbye as she flew with De Alba to Los Angeles.

"At that point, we hadn't even kissed properly," she later claimed.

To her astonishment, upon her arrival at Bel Air, some hundred guests had assembled to welcome her eighth husband and to celebrate their marriage.

Greatly embarrassed, she had to tell the guests, "It is the marriage that never was."

After some complicated dialogues and negotiations with De Alba, she convinced him to move to New York, alone, using a ticket she paid for, along with $10,000 in cash.

It was Michael O'Hara, husband no. 7, who drove De Alba, husband no. 8, to the Los Angeles airport for his flight to New York.

De Alba relocated in New York and faded from the radar screen, though dining out for years on the fact he'd once been married to Zsa Zsa.

He appeared in a 2002 film, *Real Women Have Curves.* He died in November of 2005 in New York. His marriage to Zsa Zsa had long ago been annulled.

***

Zsa Zsa had one final fling before she bowed out and settled down with her ninth and final husband. Little is known about her last romantic encounter, and even less about her suitor.

In her memoirs, Zsa Zsa admitted that after her "folie" with De Alba, she took up with a man she identified only as "King Rechad."

About the only thing they had in common was that he spoke Hungarian, her native tongue.

Although much younger than her, he proposed marriage to her and continued to pursue her even after she became engaged to Frédéric Prinz von Anhalt.

Jolie wanted to put a stop to her romance with Rechad. She told her daughter, "You can't begin your marriages with a Turk and wind up with a Tunisian Arab."

"King Rechad's" actual name was Prince Rechad al-Mahdi al-Hussaini.

706

He was a pretender to the throne—because of his links to the Husainid Dynasty (1705-1957)—of the abolished Kingdom of Tunisia.

[Tunisia, which had been a French protectorate since 1881, achieved independence from France in 1956 in a movement spearheaded by Habib Bourguiba, who maintained his grip on power until 1987 as the leader of one of the most repressive regimes in the Arab World.

The last "bey" (i.e., "king") of Tunisia was Muhammad VIII al-Amin, who died in 1962. He ruled from 1943 to 1956, when he was deposed and placed under house arrest without ever formally abdicating his rights to the throne.

The Husainid Dynasty, with its political origins inextricably linked with the Ottoman Turks, and, more embarrassingly, with the stigma of functioning for years as puppets of the colonial French, has almost certainly entered the dustbin of history, with virtually no chance of its restoration within the context of events which have transpired in Tunisia since the Arab Spring of 2013.]

As a child, **Zsa Zsa** had dreamed of becoming the Queen of England. She never completely abandoned her fantasy of sitting on some throne.

Her last desperate attempt to fulfill that dream came with the man she called **"King Rechad,"** a pretender to the throne of Tunisia.

Her vision wasn't really taken seriously. The restoration of the Husainid Dynasty as rulers of Tunisia, with Zsa Zsa as its titular Queen, would be viewed by most modern-day Tunisians as either ridiculous or insulting, or both.

Rechad was not one of the king's sons. He was nonetheless a member of the extended Hussaini family, and he became a controversial claimant, many Tunisians disputing his right to the non-existent throne. However, *Burkes World Peerage* was convinced for many years of the validity of his claim.

To begin with, Rechad was not a king—nor would he ever be. Zsa Zsa told her friends that she might become the "Queen of Tunisia," because Rechad had convinced her that the monarchy of this North African country would eventually be restored.

At some point, perhaps through the intervention of Jolie, Zsa Zsa came to the realization that she would never occupy the throne of Tunisia.

Nonetheless, after the departure of Rechad from her life, she continued to be impressed with royal, or dubiously royal, associations in her search for an appropriate new husband.

***

Zsa Zsa continued to pursue her career, mainly in television, after she broke up with Rechad, whom she continually referred to as "His Majesty."

She continued her role as a familiar figure on both *The Merv Griffin Show* and on Johnny Carson's *Tonight Show*. The public seemed to devour her brand of *risqué* humor.

One evening on *The Tonight Show,* she met Marlon Brando, and later claimed she was powerfully attracted to him. At the time, she was wearing an extremely low-cut Oscar de la Renta gown.

On the air, Brando told the audience, "I don't know why Zsa Zsa needs to talk so much. With her boobs, she really doesn't have to say anything."

In a shocking move, Brando looked first at Zsa Zsa and then at Carson. "Do you know what I want to do with that girl, Johnny? I want to fuck her." Then he turned to Zsa Zsa. "A man can only do one thing with you: Throw you down and fuck you!"

Brando's "fuck" words were, of course, bleeped, but audiences at home seemed to know what he was saying anyway.

Jolie phoned her later that night, chastising her daughter for appearing on TV with "a truck driver." She seemed unaware of Brando's status as a cult icon and Oscar-winning actor.

Surprisingly, Zsa Zsa was not offended. At her age, she was flattered that a hot actor like Brando was so entranced by her ample breasts. She confessed later—and in print—that she wished she'd had an affair with him.

The other actor she wanted to bed was Sylvester Stallone, whom she found most attractive and sexy, referring to him as, "wild and intelligent." However, she was turned off by Warren Beatty, when she was introduced to him at Chasen's by producer Jimmy Woolf.

Before the night ended, Beatty asked if he could go to bed with her. Even though she admitted that she found him "beautiful and full of life," she turned him down, or so she claimed, because he was "too obvious," whatever that meant.

In between dating, having her last affair and venturing into another marriage, she returned to the screen.

It was the 1980s, and pickings were slim. Along came an offer from director Myron J. Gold for her appearance in *Frankenstein's Great Aunt Tillie* (1984). Set in Transylvania, and weakly configured as an unfunny comedy, it starred Donald Pleasence as Old Baron Frankenstein and Yvonne Furneaux as Matilda ("Tillie") Frankenstein. Aldo Ray, winding down his career as an actor, was cast as the Bürgermeister. Zsa Zsa's role as "Clara" was miniscule.

Two years later, based on reasons that may never be fully understood, she agreed to appear in the disastrous *Charlie Barnett's Terms of Enrollment* (1986). Directed by Laurie Frank, it starred the *über*-hip actor and comedian, Charlie

Barnett, who got little support from other cast members, including Zsa Zsa, who was cast in the role of "A Star Hungry Celebrity."

[Charlie Barnett, who died of AIDS in 1996 based on complications from heroin abuse, first made a name for himself in the early 1980s, performing raunchy comedy at outdoor parks in New York City. Barnett, who lost out on an important role on Saturday Night Live *because he was illiterate and could not read his lines, went on to appear on television and in film, often competing for roles with Eddie Murphy. In the 1983 comedy,* D.C. Cab, *Barnett played the role of Tyrone. He had a recurring role on the hit 1980s TV series* Miami Vice.]

On the set, Zsa Zsa met fellow cast members who included the famous psychiatrist and advice guru, Dr. Joyce Brothers. Other players included the earthy comedian Andrew Dice Clay and singer Cathy Lee Crosby.

The film more or less killed Barnett's career, and certainly didn't do anything for Zsa Zsa's standing in the film community either.

As Zsa Zsa entered the twilight of her screen career, she made the mistake of appearing in *Smart Alec* (1986). Its director and producer, Jim Wilson, cast her in a small role in this low-budget film about a man's attempt to raise money for a movie. In his search for a sponsor for his intended movie, Alec Carroll (Ben Glass) is introduced to Zsa Zsa, who plays herself.

The film died along with her fading film career, which was belaboring its way to a final whimper and gasp, prolonged only by her occasional appearances as herself in various cameos or in some cases, with voice-overs that showcased the campy aspects of her voice and persona.

Zsa Zsa's farewell to the big screen was marked by the 1992 comedy, *The Naked Truth Trip,* starring Robert Caso and Ken Schon. One reviewer noted that the film also featured some "C-List celebrities," including Zsa Zsa Gabor, Yvonne De Carlo, and Little Richard. The movie was a take-off on Marilyn Monroe's *Some Like It Hot.* The plot involves two men who witness a murder, dress up like women, and escape, winding up hiding in the house of a drug dealer.

She continued to work into the 1990s, appearing very briefly in a French quasi-documentary , *Est & Ouest: Les paradis perdus (East & West, Paradise Lost)* in 1993. Greeted with a lukewarm reception in both France and the U.S., it examined the unhappiness of the modern age, based on the premise that both "the American Dream" and the Russian concept of the Soviet Union as a "Worker's Paradise" had failed.

Even her TV appearances faded after she played herself in a sketch in 1994 on *The Late Night Show with David Letterman.*

***

Her beauty fading, Zsa Zsa entered the final chapter of her life. One afternoon, along came her Prince Charming. But it would not be the typical Cinderella story—far from it. His name was Frédéric Prinz von Anhalt.

She met him through a German photographer working for a magazine published in Berlin. In an ironic twist, the photographer had been assigned to photograph Frédéric for a picture layout. The photographer's schedule also called for a completely separate photo shoot, later, for a magazine article featuring Zsa Zsa.

At the home of "this German royal," the photographer discovered that Frédéric had filled his living room with glamorous pictures of Zsa Zsa. "Do you know her?" the photographer asked.

"No, but I plan to marry her." When the photographer informed Frédéric that his next assignment involved photographing Zsa Zsa, the prince offered him $5,000 if he'd arrange an introduction.

With Frédéric accompanying him, the photographer arrived at his appointed rendezvous with Zsa Zsa at a horse show where she was riding her beautiful stallion, "Silver Fox."

At first, Zsa Zsa was indifferent to the prince. But she said she fell in love with him when she saw him giving her horse champagne from a paper cup.

That night, he joined Zsa Zsa and the photographer for dinner at Le Restaurant in Los Angeles. A reserve naval officer in Germany, Frédéric arrived in his formal "naval whites" with braid. Two or three tables filled with Jewish diners whispered loudly, "Look at that Nazi."

One of them yelled, "Didn't you get the news, buddy? You lost the fucking war!"

Zsa Zsa later recalled that these unfair attacks made her sympathetic to the prince, since she felt he was being treated like an underdog, and she was always sympathetic to underdogs.

Every day for the next three weeks, Frédéric spent $500 on sending her ninety-six pink (her favorite color) roses mixed with orchids.

When Zsa Zsa flew to Munich to appear in *Circus of the Stars*, Frédéric showed up, too, escorting her around in a rented Rolls Royce, which he hoped would impress her. Before his arrival, he'd sent her some two dozen love letters.

When she returned home to appear in the 1983 production of *Forty Carats* in Philadelphia, he, too, journeyed to Philadelphia to escort her back to her hotel suite at night. "One night I invited him to lie with me in my bed, because I was feeling depressed. He comforted me, but we did not make love."

Tragedy struck before 1983 ended when Frédéric learned of the death of his adoptive mother, Princess Marie-Auguste von Anhalt, the former daughter-in-law of the German Emperor Wilhelm II. He now had the claim to the title of

"Crown Prince of Germany," although that was interpreted by "Royalty Watchers" throughout Germany and Europe as a dubious claim.

Frédéric had to leave Zsa Zsa for six entire months, as he flew east to settle the princess's estate, battling with members of the Von Anhalt family over the inheritance.

While he was away in Germany, she took time to learn more about this potential husband:

Born Hans Robert Lichtenberg, he was one of five children, each the offspring of the chief of police in Frankfurt. He'd been born in the summer of 1943, as the war against his native then-Nazi Germany raged on both the eastern and western fronts. That made him twenty-six years younger than her.

In an amazing turn of events, Lichtenberg was adopted when he was thirty-six years old by Princess Marie-August von Anhalt (1893-1983), the daughter-in-law of Kaiser Wilhelm II, the German emperor. Marie-Auguste's first husband had been Prince Joachim of Prussia, the youngest son of Wilhelm II. After four years of marriage, in 1920, Prince Joachim had committed suicide.

After his adoption, Lichtenberg's name was legally and officially changed to "Frédéric Prinz von Anhalt." After Marie Auguste's death in 1983, he assumed the German-language title of Duke of Saxony *[Herzog zu Sachsen und Westfahlen, Graf von Askanien]*

Although adopted, Frédéric was not recognized by the ducal family Von Anhalt, whose other members did not consider him as part of their prestigious lineage. Actually, titles of nobility were meaningless in Germany, having been abolished in 1918 at the end of World War I.

[In an astonishing assertion, Zsa Zsa, after her marriage to Frédéric, perhaps as part of an attempt to bolster her new husband's claim to some (or any) royal lineage, stated "I came close to arranging for Frédéric's adoption by an unnamed member of the British Royal Family."]

It was during his stay in Germany that Frédéric wrote to Zsa Zsa proposing marriage, and she more or less accepted. When he returned home, he presented her with some of Marie-Auguste's jewelry, including a diamond bracelet which had once belonged to Catherine the Great of Russia. He

In poses befitting royalty (or at least Hollywood versions of it), **Frédéric Prinz von Anhalt** and **Zsa Zsa**—a veteran of dozens of roles which plunked her into one *faux* court or another—pose as claimants to the much-disputed titles of "Duke" and "Duchess" of Saxony.

711

also gave her a $350,000 diamond-and-emerald tiara.

He then delivered a bombshell that he wanted her to know before it broke in Germany's tabloid press: he claimed that while he was away, he'd had an affair with a seventeen-year-old Andrea Molnhar, who had been proclaimed Miss Hungary, a title that many writers still asserted had once been held by Zsa Zsa herself.

What turned the affair into a scandal was when the pageant winner flew to Cairo after Frédéric broke off their affair. Once there, she purchased snake poison and used it to kill herself, evoking to some degree the suicide of Cleopatra.

He also told her that he'd been married and divorced six times, "All of them were beautiful blondes like you," he claimed.

Zsa Zsa was used to errant husbands and lovers, and she quickly forgave Frédéric. "Besides, *dahlink*," she said. "We have never gone to bed together. I decided to marry Frédéric, since I'd abandoned my plan to become the Queen of Tunisia. Perhaps I still stood a chance to become Queen of Germany—Jolie would love that—if those fools ever restored the monarchy and quit putting people into power like that Hitler creature."

At her flower-filled Bel Air manse, Zsa Zsa Gabor married Frédéric Prinz von Anhalt on August 14, 1986. He later told the press, "We didn't marry for love. It was a friendship, but when you're with someone over a certain time, you fall in love."

Zsa Zsa had a slightly different response. "A girl must marry for love, and keep on marrying until she finds it."

After the ceremony, Zsa Zsa confronted reporters waiting outside, telling them that unlike her other marriages, "This one is for life."

Reporters later discovered that she'd listed her birth date as 1930 on her marriage certificate. That would have made her seven years old when she married her first husband, Burhan Belge, the Turkish ambassador.

Zsa Zsa even had stationery printed, referring to herself as "Princess von Anhalt, Duchess of Saxony," although the legitimacy of that title was being aggressively questioned by royal genealogists.

She did admit that her own marriage was "volatile and completely unconventional." She told reporters that Frédéric was the heir to the throne of Germany, overlooking, at least for the moment, that there was no throne of Germany.

When an offer for Zsa Zsa came in to make a film in East Germany, she accepted. Frédéric went along with her, as their time abroad was conceived as a honeymoon in which all their expenses would be paid.

Her last serious film role was in *Der König ohne Krone (Johann Strauss, The King Without a Crown)* released in 1987. It starred Oliver Tobias as Johann Strauss. Zsa Zsa interpreted the role of "Aunt Amalie."

In the former German capital of Weimar, near Berlin, Zsa Zsa and Frédéric checked into the Elephant Hotel, whose famous visitors in the past had included both Bach and Tolstoy. Thomas Mann had used the hotel as a partial setting for his novel, *Lotte in Weimar (The Beloved Returns)*.

The hotel's manager, who spoke only German, greeted her, telling her that her visit was the greatest honor since the *Führer* had slept here. He was offering her Hitler's former suite, the finest in Weimar.

"Fuck you!" she said to him.

Since he didn't understand any English, he misinterpreted her remark, shouting in response, "*Sieg Heil!*"

"We had to sleep in Hitler's bed, since it was the only room available," she said. "The next morning, this old bedbug, which had probably once bitten the *Führer*, crawled out of the mattress and sunk his fangs into me. The bug was probably anti-Semitic and couldn't stand the taste of Jewish blood in Hitler's bed."

Soon, one hundred fans had assembled in front of The Elephant. After she'd dressed and made herself up, Zsa Zsa appeared on the balcony overlooking the street. It was the same balcony where Hitler once had proclaimed the extermination of the Jews—"The Final Solution."

After they left Germany, during their transfer back to Los Angeles, she stopped over in New York. The next morning, she received a call from Donald Trump, who kept her on the phone for an hour. "He was clearly flirting with me, telling me that he adored European women," she said. "I already had Frédéric or else I might have shared my charms with Donald. I don't think he was deprived, not with all that money."

"I had just one regret," she said. "Had I not met Frédéric, I might have taken up with Donald before he met Ivana. Alas, one lifetime is not enough."

Later, Zsa Zsa had lunch with Ivana, where she later criticized almost everything about her—her dress ("which was all wrong"), her yellow "peroxide hair," her barking orders at her staff. "I think she was just showing off. I didn't want to remind her that when I was only seventeen, I had been mistress of the Plaza when Connie ran the place."

All of Zsa Zsa's dubious film achievements were acknowledged on October 26, 2004, when she was inducted into the B-movie Hall of Fame, a website celebrating the art of low-budget film-making.

One hot day, June 14, 1989, Zsa Zsa put on a stunning black dress with red and purple roses and adorned herself with diamonds. She set out, driving herself in her $110,000 Rolls-Royce Corniche to keep a luncheon date with a woman friend.

As she was driving along La Cienega, she heard a policeman's siren, signaling her to pull over.

Within minutes, she was confronted with the six feet four, 38-year-old Paul Kramer, a highway patrolman. She found him "handsome, looking like Tom Selleck, a dominant, macho male."

He told her that her license plate had expired, and he demanded to see her driver's license. He discovered that it, too, had expired. She asked him to give her a ticket, claiming that she would miss her appointment. Instead of describing her destination as a luncheon date, she said it was for emergency work at her dentist.

When she told Kramer to "get the lead out" (an American expression she'd picked up), she later claimed that he told her to "Fuck off!"

She would later allege that she had lived in England for a long time. She went on to say, "To the British, 'Fuck off' means to leave." Without checking with Kramer, she drove off, leaving him in the dust.

He gave chase and forced her to the side of the road again. "Get out of that damn car," he allegedly said. "Who in the fuck do you think you are?"

She'd later claim that Kramer threatened to break her arm, but no one believed that he'd actually done that.

Noticing the gun in his holster, Zsa Zsa told police that she feared Kramer was going to shoot her. Again, this exaggeration was not believed.

Outside the car, Kramer alleged that Zsa Zsa slapped him... "really hard." She did admit to having a Hungarian temper, but denied the slap.

Kramer later told *People* magazine, "You should have seen the hatred in her eyes."

She later charged that Kramer ordered her to bend over the trunk of the Rolls, where he slapped handcuffs on her. That's not all. She alleged that Kramer kicked her in the thigh, another unlikely charge. "I was forced to crouch down in the sun. My diamond brooch became unfastened."

By this time, her screams had attracted onlookers.

The crowd was favorable to Zsa Zsa. After all, she still amused them on TV. To the onlookers, it appeared that a super macho policeman was abusing an elderly lady, who was calling for help. The crowd screamed obscenities at Kramer, some of them calling him a pig. Many in the crowd alleged police brutality.

As Zsa Zsa continued to scream for help, three reinforcement policemen arrived on the scene, rescuing her from Kramer. He reported his latest discovery to these reinforcements: an open bottle of Jack Daniels was found within her Rolls.

She was hauled off in a squad car to face charges at the police station.

The policeman who checked her in was, in her words, "a gracious Mexican who called me '*Bonita Señora*.'" She was forced to pose for mug shots and fingerprinted.

She would later say, "I felt I was in Nazi Germany. Kramer could definitely play an SS officer. I always believe that America was the Land of the Free."

Before that afternoon ended, she was rescued by her doctor, Deborah Judelson, who successfully managed to maneuver her return to the comfort of her home in Bel Air. She was told she'd be tried on various charges, not only the auto-related violations, but for resisting arrest and for "assaulting" a police officer. Frédéric was outraged at the way she'd been treated.

Her arrest became a national news event. In some broadcasts, she led off the evening news. On July 27, 1990, she was forced to appear before Judge Charles Rubin.

Frédéric was at Zsa Zsa's side, telling the judge, "The rich and famous should be judged differently. This city couldn't live without the tax money paid by the rich, not the paltry sums the little people pay in taxes."

Rubin countered, "The same law applies to everybody, rich or poor."

Kramer appeared in court to testify against her, denying her more outrageous charges of what he did or said.

Rubin sentenced Zsa Zsa to seventy-two hours in jail and a fine of $13,000 for court costs. That sentencing made even more headlines, including one in *The Los Angeles Times*—*PAPRIKA PRINCESS JAILED.*

She was sent to El Segundo City Jail, a seventeen-room facility outside Los Angeles. When she was shown the first cell, she protested that she'd smother in the eight-by-ten "box."

Her attorney, Harrison Bull, arranged for her to be locked up in a larger cell. Once she was locked away, she immediately

Police officer Paul Kramer had no respect for royalty.

The 38-year-old "Tom Selleck looka-like" responded to **Zsa Zsa's** assault—"the slap heard around the world"—by shackling her with handcuffs and hauling her to a police station. There, she posed for **mugshots** and was finger-printed "like a common criminal, dahlink."

She later made the outrageous claim that inmates in a Nazi concentration camp were treated better than she was.

During her 72-hour incarceration, she became the most celebrated prisoner in any American jail.

715

sprayed the cell with the contents of a bottle of Chanel No. 5 she'd brought with her in her handbag, which had been searched.

Before being jailed, she'd been stripped nude by what she called "lesbian vultures who probed every inch of my body, including my vagina."

That night, she was served what she called "the worst meal in the history of the world." No sleep came to her, as she was kept awake "by the cries of drunken prostitutes."

"Throughout my ordeal in that squalid hellhole, I was treated like an ax murderer or else a crazed drug dealer who had just gunned down thirty children in a schoolyard."

"I feared for my life," she said. "I knew that Kramer, the Hun, had friends on the force," she said. "I was afraid that they would stage some sort of 'accident,' which would lead to my death."

At long last, her seventy-two "agonizing hours" in jail came to an end. She knew the nation's press was waiting outside. Her jailer had refused her request to have her hairdresser brought in, but she was able to cover her hair with a cowboy hat. From her makeup kit, she made her own emergency repairs.

Outside, she told a reporter, "It's like an escape from Buchenwald. You cannot imagine the humiliation and brutality I've endured. One of my jailers threatened to beat me with a rubber hose if I didn't stop complaining. All I did was ask for a glass of water so I could swallow my pills. I was even refused that."

A few days after **Zsa Zsa** was released from "my concentration camp," she associated not with "drunken prostitutes," but with the President of the United States (**Ronald Reagan**) and his chicly dressed First Lady (**Nancy Reagan**).

A claimant to the anachronistic title "Duke of Saxony," **Frédéric Prinz von Anhalt** *(far right)* joined in this powerful company.

"I should have sought a presidential pardon," Zsa Zsa later lamented.

"No Jew sent to a concentration camp received such inhumane treatment I endured," she claimed. "I lived in fear of getting raped by the savage jailers, including the butch lesbian numbers."

Judge Rubin also ordered her to undergo nine sessions of psychiatric evaluation. She attended the sessions, for which she paid $150 per hour. "At all those sessions, neither the doctor nor I said anything."

At the final session, he spoke up: "I want to divorce my wife. "You've been through many divorces. Based on your extensive experience, what advice would you give me?"

716

Her so-called psychiatric evaluation was followed by 150 hours o
munity service. She was assigned to work in a shelter for homeless n
and abandoned children. She found the plight of these people appalling and asserted that they lived in squalid conditions.

When she reported back to Judge Rubin, he told her that he'd heard she
had not completed all 150 hours of service. Consequently, he sentenced her to
another 160 hours of community service.

This time, she was sent to the McBride Special Education Center in West
Los Angeles, a public school (kindergarten through 12th grade) where she encountered children who had been "raped, abused, drugged, infected with AIDS,
and those who were unable to walk, talk, or find anyone to love them."

"My heart went out to these unfortunate children," she said. "I was particularly touched by a little blind girl dying of pancreatic cancer. The judge refused
my request to bring presents to the children."

Even after she'd completed her hours of service, Zsa Zsa continued to visit
the McBride School. This time, as a private citizen, she brought whatever presents she wanted to. When the children saw her coming, they rushed toward her,
even if they had to reach her in wheelchairs. Even without presents, the children adored her and crowded around her. Some of them even called her "Jar
Jar."

After being set free, she capitalized on the incident of her arrest by making appearances on TV, beginning with *The Naked Gun 2 ½: The Smell of Fear*
(1991). In the movie, she is pulled over by a police car at the end of the opening credits. She gets out of her car and slaps a red light, then walks away, mut-
tering, "*Ach,* this happens every time I go shopping."

She also spoofed the incident in the 1993 film, *The Beverly Hillbillies. [A
parody of her traffic incident was referred to as a "drive-by slapping"]*, and in
A Very Brady Sequel (1993), and in an episode of *The Fresh Prince of Bel Air.*

She also discussed the incident on *The Howard Stern Show,* thereby becoming the oldest celebrity ever to appear on the "shock jock's" program.

Stern asked her about homosexual rumors associated with George Sanders.
Although fully aware of the actor's preference for young Mediterranean boys,
she denied such rumors as unfounded.

***

In 1993, Zsa Zsa faced a disaster far greater than a jail term. It came like a
thunderbolt from Elke Sommer, a Berlin-born actress and a sex symbol who
had originally been discovered by film director Vittorio De Sica in Italy.

Sommer had moved to Hollywood in the early 1960s, where she became a
popular pin-up girl, even posing for *Playboy* in 1964 and 1967. She appeared

717

Zsa Zsa faced financial ruin when the Berlin-born actress and sex symbol, **Elke Sommer,** filed a multi-million dollar libel suit against her and Von Anhalt.

In its aftermath, Sommer won the largest libel judgment in history.

in a number of films, including *A Shot In the Dark* (1964) with Peter Sellers. She also starred in both comedies and dramas with actors who included James Garner, Stephen Boyd, Paul Newman, Bob Hope, and Dean Martin.

Zsa Zsa's feud with Sommer had actually begun in 1984 when both of them had appeared as part of a charity event, *Circus of the Stars.* By 1993, their feud would escalate into a multi-million dollar libel suit.

Allegedly, the feud began when Zsa Zsa heard that Sommer had made a disparaging comment about her "big butt."

In 1990, Zsa Zsa and Frédéric attacked Sommer in three different articles, one in a women's magazine, *Freizeit-Revue,* and two in the German newspaper *Bild.* In one article, Zsa Zsa claimed that Sommer "hung out in sleazy bars and supported herself by selling hand-knitted sweaters for $150 apiece."

"The woman is broke," Zsa Zsa said. "She had to sell her house in Hollywood and is now living in the worst section of town."

The *Bild* article quoted Frédéric, who accused Sommer of lying about her age He maintained that she claimed to be 49, but actually was 62. He also suggested that she had almost no hair left on her head, "and looked 100 years old."

Sommer filed a defamation of character and libel suit, seeking $10 million on the grounds that these false statements caused her great emotional distress and hurt her career.

The jury ordered Zsa Zsa and Frédéric to pay Sommer $3.3 million in damages "for describing her as a haggard Hollywood has-been."

This was the largest libel judgment ever recorded till then.

Reportedly, the judgment brought Zsa Zsa to the brink of financial disaster, from which she's been trying to recover ever since.

***

In the 90s, Zsa Zsa's career both in films and on television was coming to an end. During a career which had witnessed eight interludes as an entertainer in Las Vegas, she made the last of her appearances there in 1991 on New Year's Eve. She was delighted to hear that tickets to her show outsold those of Frank

Sinatra and Julio Iglesias

In a bizarre twist, Frédéric reportedly adopted several men, including Marcus Prinz von Anhalt, who was formerly known as Marcus Eberhardt. Today, he refers to himself as "Prince Germany."

He and Zsa Zsa officially adopted another man. Oliver Bendig became known as Oliver Prinz von Anhalt, and Michael Killer (yes, that's right) became known as Michael Prinz von Anhalt.

Newspapers in Berlin speculated that Frédéric may have sold his name to his adopted "sons." Under German law such an adoption would be invalid, and—as filtered through some interpretations—a criminal offence as well.

It was also reported in some publications that Frédéric sold some 58 "knighthoods" for $50,000 each.

On November 9, 2000, Frédéric sued the makers of Viagra, claiming he'd become addicted to the drug. The 59-year-old said that after taking the infamous blue pills, he found that he was impotent without the assistance of the medication. "At first, I took the pills to increase my desire. Now, nothing happens at all without Viagra. My addiction to Viagra has harmed the nerves of my wife, Zsa Zsa Gabor, who has even had to go to a clinic. After all, she also has her needs, which should be satisfied."

The case went nowhere.

On November 2, 2002, Zsa Zsa was involved in an automobile accident. At the age of eighty-five, she was riding as a passenger with her male hairdresser, who was driving a red Corvette. The car went out of control and crashed into a light pole in West Hollywood. Police sergeant Bruce Thomas later reported that Zsa Zsa had not fastened her safety belt.

At first, it was reported that she was in a coma, but she was conscious when a medical team in an ambulance arrived on the scene. The driver suffered only minor injuries.

She was flown to Cedars Sinai Medical Center by helicopter and put on a respirator.

Zsa Zsa suffered broken bones and received stitches to close wounds to her head, hands, arms, and legs.

At the hospital, she learned she might never walk again. In despair, she said, "I don't have the courage to face life anymore."

She was released in January of 2003, but was placed in a wheelchair and was bedridden because of partial paralysis. She had to undergo intensive physical therapy at the Motion Picture and Television Hospital, a retirement community and health facility for aging members of the entertainment industry in Woodland Hills, a short distance west of Beverly Hills.

At Woodland Hills, she celebrated her 86th birthday in a luxury suite. She announced that for her birthday, "Frédéric is going to surprise me with something. I hope it's something very, very shiny."

One disaster followed another. On July 7, 2005, Zsa Zsa suffered a massive stroke at her Bel Air home, and was rushed to the hospital for emergency surgery to clear a blocked artery.

Frédéric told the press, "Doctors said the artery was completely closed. Zsa Zsa would have suffered a major stroke and would have died unless she was operated on at once. She underwent a near death experience."

Despite dire predictions, she made a miraculous recovery by July 15, and was returned to her home in Bel Air. But in early September of 2007, at the age of ninety, she was back in the hospital again, having to undergo more surgery to deal with the after-effects of her previous stroke.

She faced more surgeries, one of them to treat a leg infection which had developed as a result of her immobility.

In 2007, Frédéric was making salacious headlines on his own. On February 9, he faced the press, revealing that he had conducted a decades-long affair with that blonde bombshell, Anna Nicole Smith. He said that he was the father of her infant daughter, Dannielynn.

He also admitted that Zsa Zsa was devastated by claims of his affair. "I was told that if I bring the baby home, it's over between us. If my wife wants to divorce me, then it's up to her."

However, by March of that year, tests showed that Dannielynn's father was actually Smith's ex-boyfriend, Larry Birkhead.

January of 2009 got off to a bad start when the Associated Press reported that attorney Chris Fields claimed that Zsa Zsa may have lost $10 million that had been invested with swindler Bernard Madoff, possibly through a third-party money manager, Marcus Prinz von Anhalt, a German nightclub owner and the adopted son of Frédéric.

On July 30, 2009, Frédéric was back in the headlines, following a bizarre claim that he'd been stripped and robbed at gunpoint by "three hot lesbians." Even though his hands were strapped to the steering wheel of his Rolls-Royce, he said that he managed, through a feat not explained, to place an emergency call to 911, which summoned the police to the scene. They untied his hands, but not before taking a picture of him. At the time, with his hands strapped to the steering wheel, he was nude.

He told police that he was tricked into letting three female "tourists" into his car when they told him they wanted to take a group photograph. Why such a photo would be snapped inside and not outside the car was never explained.

Once inside the car, one of the lesbians pointed a gun at his head. He was forced to surrender $1,800 in cash, along with his car keys and a platinum-and-diamond watch. The lesbians then, according to Frédéric, tied his hands to the steering wheel and escaped with their loot in a Chrysler convertible.

On February 16, 2010, Frédéric called a press conference, announcing that he'd be running in the upcoming elections as a candidate for office of Governor of California. As part of his platform, he called for the legalization of prostitution in a format similar to what was allowed in his neighboring state of Nevada. "All the money spent on men driving to Nevada to seek out prostitutes would stay right here in California."

On July 17, 2010, Zsa Zsa was watching her favorite TV program, *Jeopardy,* when she fell out of the bed and injured herself.

Discovering her, Frédéric called an ambulance and rode with her to the Ronald Reagan UCLA Medical Center. He told the press, "She's not young any more. She has broken bones, including her hip, and a concussion."

While in the hospital on July 24, 2010, she underwent hip replacement surgery. The doctor reported that after the operation, "her eyes are open, but she isn't communicating." The fear was that she'd suffered a stroke.

The outlook was bleak, but her publicist, John Blanchette, put a better spin on it. "Zsa Zsa's body is fragile, but her mind is strong. She's a fighter, and we're hopeful that things will work out well."

On August 10, Zsa Zsa was returned to her Bel Air home. Frédéric told reporters, "She is smiling and flirting with the guys who brought her home in an ambulance. That's a good sign. When she's able to flirt, she's in good shape. I feel she is strong, and can go on for a number of years."

After that optimistic forecast, she collapsed four nights later and had to be rushed back to the hospital to remove two blood clots from her upper body, one of them dangerously close to her heart. The surgery took five hours. There was talk of performing some surgery on her liver, but she was given only a 50-50 chance of surviving it, so it was called off.

Blanchette appeared before the press again, claiming that Zsa Zsa, at her request, had been given last rites. "She was conscious during the ceremony, but could not speak. Her husband was by her side. They celebrated their 24th anniversary in the hospital.

Frédéric took the occasion to withdraw from the governor's race, citing Zsa Zsa's ill health.

By August 19, Frédéric himself collapsed at their home, claiming he felt dizzy and that he had blacked out. A source said he was not able to use his right arm and was suffering from exhaustion. To complicate matters, Zsa Zsa suffered complications from hip surgery and was returned to the hospital on August 31.

On September 2, Frédéric had recovered and told a German newspaper that he wanted to "plastinate Zsa Zsa's body when she dies" and perhaps exhibit her. "I want to preserve her so her beauty will last forever. She's always dreamed that her beauty would be immortal. Perhaps I could exhibit her in a setting from *Moulin Rouge* where she played Jane Avril."

He knew of Gunther von Hagens, the German anatomist, who was celebrated for his exhibitions showing plastinated bodies, a process restricted to specimen preserved, in theory at least, for medical illustration and anatomical instruction.

By October 10, Frédéric was rushed to the hospital after he swallowed a bee which then stung the inside of his throat.

There was yet another emergency in 2010, three days before Christmas. Frédéric was again rushed to the hospital after gluing his eye shut with fingernail glue. Apparently, he had picked up a bottle of nail glue imagining that the bottle contained eyedrops. At the hospital, he underwent surgery to unglue his eye and was then given painkillers.

Zsa Zsa ended her horrible year (2010) with two round-the-clock nurses taking care of her. She was treated with intravenous antibiotics and also was taking oral medication for a separate (i.e., unrelated) blood infection.

Ironically, on December 12, the Health and Retirement Fund Division of the American Federation of Television and Radio Artists cancelled her pension benefits because the staff there thought she had died.

Zsa Zsa launched 2011 by being rushed to the Ronald Reagan UCLA Emergency Ward. After examining her, doctors concluded that they might have to amputate part of her right leg below the knee because of the onset of gangrene. "The lesion is very deep," the doctor told Frédéric. "I'm afraid it may extend into the bone. But before taking the drastic measure of amputation, we want to give her some powerful antibiotics."

It was soon discovered that during a period of two months, the lesion had grown from about an inch in length to almost a foot.

Even so, Zsa Zsa "yelled and screamed," not wanting to submit to the surgery until she celebrated New Year's Eve at her manse with champagne and caviar.

The operation could not be postponed any longer, and on January 14, three-quarters of her right leg was amputated. Had it been postponed any longer, her doctors insisted that gangrene would have taken her life.

Zsa Zsa was under such heavy sedation she did not know her leg had been amputated and would not discover that until many months later.

With money dwindling, and with medical bills mounting, Frédéric announced on February 11 that he had gone to Julien's of Beverly Hills *[a firm specializing in estate auctions and sales of Hollywood memorabilia]* where he was consigning Zsa Zsa's clothing, furs, jewelry, and even some of her antiques for auction. "It doesn't make sense to keep them," he said, "because she will never use them again, and we're paying storage bills."

The designer, floral-patterned dress she had worn when she slapped Officer Kramer was sold at auction. Other possessions consigned to the block included a sculpture of a horse, purchased for $150,000 in the 1960s by her then husband Herbert Hutner.

Frédéric's next move, on April 14, shocked Zsa Zsa's fans. Daughter Francesca called it "weird." He wanted Zsa Zsa to become a mother again by using an egg donor, artificial insemination, and a surrogate mother. "I've gone through the initial steps of donor matching," he told the press, "along with blood work. The next week the donation process will begin. I've been working with Dr. Mark Surrey of the Southern California Reproductive Center in Beverly Hills."

In June of 2011, Zsa Zsa was back in the hospital again, recovering from a bout of pneumonia. She was also suffering an infection at the site of her feeding tube. While she recovered in the hospital, her Bel Air manse, once inhabited by Howard Hughes and later by Elvis Presley, was put on the market.

The original asking price was $28 million, but in a bad real estate market, the asking price was trimmed to $15 million. Frédéric claimed that he and Zsa Zsa lived in only four of the rooms, and that both of them would prefer to move into a high rise near a hospital, or else into a gated community.

Some unusual (some observers called them "deal-killing") conditions were attached which a potential buyer would have to agree to. Zsa Zsa wanted a guarantee that she could live in the house for another three years, plus she also wanted to be paid an annual stipend of $325,000.

By June 11, Zsa Zsa, within her home, was photographed in a white and black robe as she was propped up in bed. She was seen toasting her husband with a glass of champagne on his 68th birthday. "She doesn't want to suffer any more, and I don't want her to suffer any more," he said. "She is happier now."

Francesca was angered when Frédéric released a picture of her mother to Reuters News Agency. The for-

This picture of a bed-ridden and heavily medicated **Zsa Zsa** being supplied with champagne by **Frédéric Prinz von Anhalt** on the occasion of his 68th birthday (June 11, 2011) went around the world.

Zsa Zsa's daughter, Francesca Hilton, was enraged that Frédéric was giving her alcohol, and friends who included Debbie Reynolds complained, "There's no way in hell that Zsa Zsa would ever have consented to allow a picture of her without makeup to go out over the wire services."

mer siren was photographed without benefit of makeup and a hairdresser. Her friend, Debbie Reynolds, claimed, "Zsa Zsa would have died a thousand deaths before she'd allow such an unflattering picture of herself to go out across America."

Francesca said, "Perfect grooming was always vital to my mother. Von Anhalt is giving her alcohol, which could be detrimental to her condition, since she is on numerous medications. It's disgusting, and no one is doing anything about it."

The press continued to report on the ongoing feud between Francesca and Frédéric over Zsa Zsa's care, security, and health. The daughter had accused Frédéric of not allowing her visitation rights, and for keeping her friends away.

In 2005, Frédéric had attempted to sue Francesca, claiming she'd taken out a $2 million loan against Zsa Zsa's house without her permission or approval. Zsa Zsa, however, refused to sign the papers allowing the case to go forward, and the court eventually dismissed it.

On July 26, Frédéric came up with an idea to celebrate their 25th wedding anniversary. He paid $68,000 for a month's lease of a giant billboard on Sunset Boulevard, depicting their original wedding picture with the caption: *PRINCE FRÉDÉRIC AND PRINCESS ZSA ZSA—25 YEARS AND COUNTING*.

He later said, "I wanted to do something special. She can see the billboard on television. It's worth the cost. To be married to her for this long is priceless."

"She loved the billboard. She still loves show business so much. Ben Affleck was in the house with George Clooney. Ben was shooting a scene for his film *Argo*. If Zsa Zsa had been told that Clooney was here, she would have jumped out of bed on one leg."

For their anniversary party, Frédéric hired the makeup artist and Beverly Hills hairdresser, Guiseppe Franco, to come by and do both her hair and makeup. Raju Rasiah, a jeweler based on Rodeo Drive in Beverly Hills, lent her a ruby-and-sapphire necklace for the party. An array of media and Hollywood stars saw Zsa Zsa lying in her bed, wearing a pink dress with silver star shapes all over it.

She was greeted by Kirk Douglas, Nancy Reagan, Angie Dickinson, Sylvester Stallone, Laine Kazan, Larry King, and Quincy Jones. The famous chef, Wolfgang Puck, designed the anniversary cake. Also showing up at the party was Phyllis Diller, one of Zsa Zsa's oldest friends. "Diller died within a year, but I didn't tell Zsa Zsa because I didn't want to upset her," Frédéric said.

A surprise guest was actor Robert Blake, the star of the TV series *Baretta*. In 2005, he'd been tried and acquitted of the 2001 murder of his second wife, Bonnie Lee Bakley. "Zsa Zsa made a lot of strange friendships over the years,"

Frédéric claimed.

Zsa Zsa ended 2011 by being rushed to the Ronald Reagan UCLA Medical Center again after losing consciousness. A feeding tube had become dislodged from her stomach, which caused internal bleeding and a high fever. Surgery was performed.

In 2013, Zsa Zsa was still clinging to life, with the lights growing dimmer month by month.

Frédéric said, "She's the only thing I have. If she dies, I don't have anybody else to live for. She does not want to be left alone. I sleep in a couch with my feet dangling, but that's okay. We made promises that we would take care of each other until the end."

Shortly before his own death in 2007, Merv Griffin arranged to bring one of his best friends, Nancy Reagan, to Zsa Zsa's home, where the building's owner appeared chipper and articulate, although she faded before the end of their visit.

"She seemed to be having some sort of review of the way she'd spent her life," Griffin later recalled.

"I've managed to crowd nine lives into one, but even that was not enough," Zsa Zsa said. "I've had so many adventures. It's truly amazing, the men and the one woman who have loved me: presidents of the United States, kings, princes, Rubirosa, Greta Garbo."

"I blazed through the century making headline after headline. Not bad for a little girl from Budapest who launched her love life by kissing the coalman and getting soot all over my white dress. Men have been 'blackening' me ever since. I don't regret the men who seduced me, only those who didn't get around to it."

"There's an axiom in Hollywood," Zsa Zsa told them. "Actors get older, but actresses grow old. My life goes on, although I don't know for how long. It's shocking to have been called the most beautiful woman on earth and have to confront my mirror in the morning. Most of my lovers or husbands are long gone, except for my dear Prince. The grim reaper is at my door, but I've lived a great life. I was brought into intimate contact with some of the luminaries of my age. I met everyone from Adolf Hitler to Jack Kennedy. I've loved a few but been loved by countless others."

***

Vanity Fair summed up Zsa Zsa's present realities: "Is the *ersatz* princess, otherwise known as Zsa Zsa Gabor, being held prisoner by an *ersatz* prince in her gilded aerie, a decaying Bel Air mansion that once hosted Hollywood's most dazzling luminaries but now brings to mind an ominous scene out of *Sun-*

set Blvd.?"

Griffin said, "To borrow a line from Frank Sinatra, Zsa Zsa's former rapist, she did it *Her Way*. It is not likely the world will ever see the likes of her again."

"Zsa Zsa is unique. She's a woman from the court of Louis XV who has somehow managed to reappear in the 20th Century. All the Gabors were glamour personified. They burst onto the society pages and into the gossip columns so suddenly—and with such force—it was as if they'd been dropped out of the sky, which they probably were."

Then he added: "Of all the roles she ever played, her greatest performance was as Zsa Zsa Gabor."

"One Lifetime Is Not Enough"

In Memorium and In Honor of
Miss Zsa Zsa Gabor

ACKNOWLEDGMENTS

My greatest gratitude goes to the Austrian cabaret entertainer, Greta Keller, who once shared a house with me over a period of three years. Overflowing with anecdotes about the social protocols of the Weimar Republic, Old Vienna, and pre-communist Budapest, and the counter-cultural scandals of Hollywood during its so called "Golden Years," she was the unofficial godmother of the Gabor sisters. For many of the insights into the early years of the Gabor sisters, I drew upon our unpublished manuscript describing Greta's turbulent life.

Greta's longtime friend was Jolie Gabor, who was a frequent visitor, gossiping with Greta and churning out Austro-Hungarian meals in my kitchen. What Zsa Zsa, Magda, and Eva didn't tell, Jolie did. A sometimes cantankerous font of ever-flowing information, she could be honest about the foibles and shortcomings of her famous daughters. She loved each of them dearly. Zsa Zsa was her favorite.

The advertising executive, Stanley Mills Haggart, worked on various commercial endorsements with both Zsa Zsa and Eva, and told wonderful stories about each of them. Much material for this book was drawn from his unpublished memoirs, which are especially rich in Gabor anecdotes from the late 1940s and throughout the 50s.

He didn't want to be listed as a source, but a famous Anglo-American actor on the island of Majorca granted me an audience ("I don't have anything else to do") when I was researching the Balearic Islands for *Frommer's Guide to Spain*. He knew more about the Gabors than most men. He should, because he married two of them.

Many famous people, and hundreds not so famous, contributed over the decades. Special thanks to Tamara Geva and Tallulah Bankhead (the former wives of actor John Emery), Susan Hayward, Merv Griffin, Ben Gazzara, Lana Turner, Jack Paar, John Huston, Howard Keel, Jimmy Donahue, Merle Oberon, Jack Ryan (Zsa Zsa's former husband), José Luís de Vilallonga, and to my friend, Helga de Bordes, the late and long-time social director and duenna of the *Techniker-Cercle Ball der Industrie und Technik* (one of the Vienna Opera Balls), who befriended me during my research in Budapest and Vienna for anecdotes associated with the Gabors during their formative years in those glittering and endlessly fascinating cities.

Endless thanks go to all the people in various European and American cities who knew, loved, or were critical of the Gabors. I massed previously unknown information about them while researching such books as *Frommer's Los Angeles, Frommer's Budapest, Frommer's Vienna, Frommer's Austria & Hungary, Frommer's San Francisco, Frommer's Italy, Frommer's France, Frommer's Madrid, Frommer's Lisbon, Frommer's London, Frommer's Rome, Frommer's French Riviera, Frommer's Paris, Frommer's Switzerland, Frommer's Jamaica, and Frommer's Dominican Republic.*

In Santo Domingo, I met two Spanish filmmakers who wanted to raise money for a film about Zsa Zsa's most famous lover, Porfirio Rubirosa. They were willing to share boxes of the material they'd compiled from the local and international press.

In essence, Zsa Zsa and Eva—and to a much lesser extent, Magda—wrote the story of their own lives.

Their favorite subject was the Gabors, and they constantly spoke of their social and romantic adventures around the world, at dinner parties, to friends, on talk shows, and to their legion of spouses and lovers. Their critics also had a lot to say as well. The roundup took only half a century.

Everyone who came into contact with the Gabors had a story or revelations to tell. It could be something they said about themselves, or something they said about a third party. Invariably, their statements were piquant and, in many cases, fascinating.

The difficulty involved organizing this vast array of material into some form of coherent order. The Herculean task was made more difficult because Eva and Zsa Zsa would often deny something during one decade and, with the passage of time, reveal in another decade that the tale had been true after all.

Dozens of TV and movie crews, who worked behind the scenes with Eva and Zsa Zsa, relayed the details of revealing incidents. The British theatrical and film producer, Jimmy Woolf, was particularly helpful, as was comedian Phyllis Diller, who visited Zsa Zsa right before her own death.

I also owe a large debt to the greatest of the Gabor fans, Herbert Jacobson, originally a native and long-time resident of Brooklyn who retired to Miami. Over the course of his lifetime, he collected four large trunks of Gaborabilia in both English and other languages. In the 1970s, based on my role as the Key West Bureau Chief and Entertainment Columnist of *The Miami Herald*, he allowed me to wade through his trove of treasures.

When I learned of his death in 1979, I journeyed to Miami to purchase the ephemera from his estate.

To my regret, I discovered that his heir was a young man who obviously did not share Herbert's fascination for the Gabors, and who didn't realize what a (historically) valuable collection of memorabilia he'd inherited. He had consigned the dust-covered collection of clippings to the dustbin.

Fortunately, I had already gleaned tons of useful information before the collection was destroyed as garbage.

Although I've painted a portrait of the Gabors that is both flattering and horrific, it is, nonetheless, a tribute to these *vonderful vimmen* who in some strange way enriched our lives by sharing the planet with us.

Darwin Porter
New York City, July 2013

TWO ARDENT DEVOTEES OF THE GABORS COLLABORATED IN THE PRODUCTION OF THIS BOOK:

Darwin Porter

As an intense and precocious nine-year-old, **Darwin Porter** began meeting movie stars, TV personalities, politicians, and singers through his vivacious and attractive mother, Hazel, a somewhat eccentric Southern girl who had lost her husband in World War II. Migrating from the depression-ravaged valleys of western North Carolina to Miami Beach during its most ebullient heyday, Hazel became a stylist, wardrobe mistress, and personal assistant to the vaudeville comedienne Sophie Tucker, the bawdy and irrepressible "Last of the Red Hot Mamas."

Virtually every show-biz celebrity who visited Miami Beach paid a call on "Miss Sophie," and Darwin as a pre-teen loosely and indulgently supervised by his mother, was regularly dazzled by the likes of Judy Garland, Dinah Shore, Veronica Lake, Linda Darnell, Martha Raye, and Ronald Reagan, who arrived to pay his respects to Miss Sophie with a young blonde starlet on the rise—Marilyn Monroe.

Hazel's work for Sophie Tucker did not preclude an active dating life: Her *beaux* included Richard Widmark, Victor Mature, Frank Sinatra (who "tipped" teenaged Darwin the then-astronomical sum of ten dollars for getting out of the way), and that alltime "second lead," Wendell Corey, when he wasn't emoting with Barbara Stanwyck and Joan Crawford.

As a late teenager, Darwin edited *The Miami Hurricane* at the University of Miami, where he interviewed Eleanor Roosevelt, Tab Hunter, Lucille Ball, and Adlai Stevenson. He also worked for Florida's then-Senator George Smathers, one of John F. Kennedy's best friends, establishing an ongoing pattern of picking up "Jack and Jackie" lore while still a student.

After graduation, as a journalist, he was commissioned with the opening of a bureau of *The Miami Herald* in Key West (Florida), where he took frequent morning walks with retired U.S. president Harry S Truman during his vacations in what had functioned as his "Winter White House." He also got to know, sometimes very well, various celebrities "slumming" their way through off-the-record holidays in the orbit of then-resident Tennessee Williams. Celebrities hanging out in the permissive arts environment of Key West during those days included Tallulah Bankhead, Cary Grant, Tony Curtis, the stepfather of Richard Burton, a gaggle of show-biz and publishing moguls, and the once-notorious stripper, Bettie Page.

For about a decade in New York, Darwin worked in television journalism and advertising with his long-time partner, the journalist, art director, and distinguished arts-industry socialite Stanley Mills Haggart. Jointly, they produced TV commercials starring such high-powered stars as Joan Crawford (then feverishly promoting Pepsi-Cola), Ronald Reagan (General Electric), and Debbie Reynolds (selling Singer Sewing Machines), along with such other entertainers as Louis Armstrong, Lena Horne, Arlene Dahl, and countless other show-biz personalities hawking commercial products.

During his youth, Stanley had flourished as an insider in early Hollywood as a "leg man" and source of information for Hedda Hopper, the fabled gossip columnist. When Stanley wasn't dishing newsy revelations with Hedda, he had worked as a Powers model; a romantic lead opposite Silent-era film star Mae Murray; the intimate companion of superstar Randolph Scott before Scott became emotionally involved with Cary Grant; and a man-about-town who archived gossip from everybody who mattered back when the movie colony was small, accessible, and confident that details about their tribal rites would absolutely never be reported in the press. Over the years, Stanley's vast cornucopia of inside Hollywood information was passed on to Darwin, who amplified it with copious interviews and research of his own.

After Stanley's death in 1980, Darwin inherited a treasure trove of memoirs, notes, and interviews detailing Stanley's early adventures in Hollywood, including in-depth recitations of scandals that even Hopper during her heyday was afraid to publish. Most legal and journalistic standards back then interpreted those oral histories as "unprintable." Times, of course, changed.

Beginning in the early 1960s, Darwin joined forces with the then-fledgling Arthur Frommer organization, playing a key role in researching and writing more than 50 titles and defining the style and values that later emerged as the world's leading travel accessories, The Frommer Guides, with particular emphasis on Europe, California, New England, and the Caribbean. Between the creation and updating of hundreds of editions of detailed travel guides to England, France, Italy, Spain, Portugal, Austria, Germany, California, and Switzerland, he continued to interview and discuss the triumphs, feuds, and frustrations of celebrities, many by then reclusive, whom he either sought out or encountered randomly as part of his extensive travels. Ava Gardner and Lana Turner were particularly insightful.

One day when Darwin lived in Tangier, he walked into an opium den to discover Marlene Dietrich sitting alone in the corner.

Darwin has also written several novels, including the best-selling cult classic *Butterflies in Heat* (which was later made into a film, *Tropic of Desire,* starring Eartha Kitt), *Venus* (inspired by the life of the fabled eroticist and diarist, Anaïs Nin), and *Midnight in Savannah,* a satirical overview of the sexual eccentricities of the Deep South inspired by Savannah's most notorious celebrity murder. He also transformed into literary format the details which he and Stanley Haggart had compiled about the relatively underpublicized scandals of the Silent Screen, releasing them in 2001 as *Hollywood's Silent Closet,* "an uncensored, underground history of Pre-Code Hollywood, loaded with facts and rumors from generations past." A few years later, he did the same for the country-west-

731

ern music industry when he issued *Rhinestone Country.*

Since then, Darwin has penned more than a dozen uncensored Hollywood biographies, many of them award-winners, on subjects who have included Marlon Brando, Merv Griffin, Katharine Hepburn, Howard Hughes, Humphrey Bogart, Michael Jackson, Paul Newman, Steve McQueen, Marilyn Monroe, Elizabeth Taylor, Frank Sinatra, John F. Kennedy, Vivien Leigh, Laurence Olivier, and the well known porn star, Linda Lovelace.

As a departure from his usual repertoire, Darwin also wrote the controversial *J. Edgar Hoover & Clyde Tolson: Investigating the Sexual Secrets of America's Most Famous Men and Women,* a book about celebrity, voyeurism, political and sexual repression, and blackmail within the highest circles of the U.S. government.

He has also co-authored, in league with Danforth Prince, four *Hollywood Babylon* anthologies, plus four separate volumes of film critiques, reviews, and commentary.

His biographies, over the years, have won more than 30 First Prize or runner-up awards at literary festivals in cities which include Boston, New York, Los Angeles, San Francisco, and Paris.

Darwin can be heard at regular intervals as a radio commentator (and occasionally on television), "dissing" celebrities, pop culture, politics, and scandal.

A resident of New York City, Darwin is currently at work on his latest biography: *Pink Triangle, The Feuds and Private Lives of Tennessee Williams, Gore Vidal, Truman Capote, and Famous Members of their Entourages.*

Danforth Prince

The publisher and production manager of this biography, **Danforth Prince** is one of the "Young Turks" of the post-millennium publishing industry. Today, he's president of Blood Moon Productions, a firm devoted to the research, compilation and marketing of "tell-all" celebrity biographies, most of whose subjects are associated with the Golden Years of Hollywood.

Prince has celebrated Zsa Zsa since his adolescence in a suburb of Chicago. "In an uncharacteristic nod to pop culture, my parents named our spaniel 'Zsa Zsa' in honor of LA GABOR's notoriety as the mistress of Porfirio Rubirosa. I didn't understand what the customers along my delivery route for the *[now defunct] Chicago Daily News* found so amusing as I yelled for 'Zsa Zsa' as she trotted and panted, following me as I delivered papers on my bike."

"Later, my mother's most notorious dress (a low-cut rhinestone-studded cocktail wrap) was selected purely on its merits as 'The Zsa Zsa look,' during one of her rare (and well-deserved) moments of escapist whimsy."

"Because of this," Prince said, "my 'Gabor quotient' and my role as a sometimes unwitting publicist for Zsa Zsa has been part of my consciousness virtually since birth. I confess with pride that I adore her, always and forever."

One of Prince's famous predecessors, the late Lyle Stuart (self-described as "the last publisher in America with guts") once defined Prince as "one of my natural successors." In 1956, that then-novice maverick launched himself with $8,000 he'd won in a libel judgment against gossip columnist Walter Winchell. It was Stuart who published Linda Lovelace's two authentic memoirs—*Ordeal* and *Out of Bondage.*

"I like to see someone following in my footsteps in the 21st Century," Stuart told Prince. "You publish scandalous biographies. I did, too. My books on J. Edgar Hoover, Jacqueline Kennedy Onassis, and Barbara Hutton stirred up the natives. You do, too."

Prince launched his career in journalism in the 1970s at the Paris Bureau of *The New York Times.* In the early '80s, he resigned to join Darwin Porter in researching, developing and publishing various titles within *The Frommer Guides*, jointly reviewing the travel scenes of more than 50 nations for Simon

& Schuster. Authoritative and comprehensive, they were perceived as best-selling "travel bibles" for millions of readers, with recommendations and travel advice about the major nations of Western Europe, the Caribbean, Bermuda, The Bahamas, Georgia and the Carolinas, and California.

Prince, along with Porter, is also the co-author of several award-winning celebrity biographies, each configured as a title within Blood Moon's Babylon series. These have included *Hollywood Babylon—It's Back!; Hollywood Babylon Strikes Again; The Kennedys: All the Gossip Unfit to Print;* and *Frank Sinatra, The Boudoir Singer.* Their most recent joint authorship venture was *Elizabeth Taylor: There Is Nothing Like a Dame.* Prince, with Porter, have also co-authored four separate books of film criticism.

Prince is the president and founder (in 1996) of the Georgia Literary Association, and of the Porter and Prince Corporation, founded in 1983, which has produced dozens of titles for both Prentice Hall and John Wiley & Sons. In 2011, he was named "Publisher of the Year" by a consortium of literary critics and marketers spearheaded by the J.M. Northern Media Group.

According to Prince, "Indeed, there are drudge aspects associated with any attempt to create a body of published work. But Blood Moon provides the luxurious illusion that a reader is a perpetual guest at some gossippy dinner party populated with brilliant but occasionally self-delusional figures from bygone eras of The American Experience. Blood Moon's success at salvaging, documenting, and articulating the (till now) orally transmitted histories of the Entertainment Industry, in ways that have never been seen before, is one of the most distinctive aspects of our backlist."

Publishing in collaboration with the National Book Network (www.NBN-Books.com), he has electronically documented some of the controversies associated with his stewardship of Blood Moon in more than 40 videotaped documentaries, book trailers, public speeches, and TV or radio interviews. Any of these can be watched, without charge, by performing a search for "Danforth Prince" on **YouTube.com**, checking him out on **Facebook** (either "Danforth Prince" or "Blood Moon Productions), on **Twitter** (#BloodyandLunar) or by clicking on **BloodMoonProductions.com**.

During the rare moments when he isn't writing, editing, neurosing about, or promoting Blood Moon, he works out at a New York City gym, rescues stray animals, talks to strangers, and regularly attends Episcopal Mass every Sunday.

INDEX

737

739

740

744

747

750

751

Walters, Charles 479, 566
Wanger, Walter 412, 586
Warner, Harry 359
Warren, Sidney 404, 405, 409
Warsaw Flying Club 92
Washington Post, The 235
Watson, Peter 139
Wayne, John 700
Wayne, Judge Diane 635
We're Not Married 457, 459
Webb, Clifton 152
Wedekind, Franz 565
Weissmuller, Johnny 190, 433
Wellcome, Henry 141
Welles, Orson 242, 388, 583, 584
Wellman, Kathlene ("Kitty") 613
Wellman, William 613
Wells, Carole 420
Wells, H.G. 93, 96, 97
Werner, Karl 27
West Eleven 658
West, Mae 137, 147, 215, 424, 671
Western Affair, A 528
Wheel of Fortune 632
"When You Make Love to Me, Don't Make
    Believe" 156
White Cargo 182
White, Vanna 633
Whitestone, Annabelle 155
Whitney, Cornelius Vanderbilt 522, 523
Whitney, Elizabeth 378
Whitney, Jock 390
Whitney, Liz 704
Why England Slept 354
Wiener Zeitung 37
Wife of Monte Cristo, The (1946) 322, 323
Wilcox, Herbert 549, 552
Wilde, Cornel 357
Wilde, Oscar 221
Wilding, Michael 423, 477, 478, 553
Wiles, Gordon 143, 144
Wilhelm II, Emperor of Germany 710
Williams, Dr. John 533, 538, 539, 540, 541
Williams, Esther 479
Williams, Tennessee 563, 614
Wilson, Earl 285, 535, 667, 692
Wilson, Jim 709
Winchell, Walter 331, 361, 451, 494, 509,
    510, 563
Winner, Michael 658
Winston, Harry 82, 234, 443
Winter 390
Winter Garden Theater (NYC) 609
Winter Journey 655
Winters, Shelley 657
Winwood, Estelle 391
Witney, William 146

Wolfe, Elsie de (aka Lady Mendl) 132, 133,
    134, 151, 199, 201, 220
Wolfe, Thomas 612
Women in Love 653
Women, The 474
Wood, Natalie 619
Woodward, Joanne 607
Woolf, James 468, 472, 728
Woolf, John 468
Wright, Frank Lloyd 313, 316
Wyman, Jane 124, 163, 197, 277, 568
Wynn, Evie 291
Wynn, Keenan 291, 565
Yaban (Stranger) 48
Yacey, Sandra 689
Yankovich, Paul (aka "Ferenc") 52, 56
You'll Never Get Rich 163
"You're the Top" 163
Young and the Willing, The 574
Young, Loretta 264, 265
Young, Terence 657
Youngblood Hawke (1964) 612
Zalábondy, André 18, 324, 328, 336
Zambona, Jutta 176
Zanuck, Darryl F. 110, 189, 191, 192, 205,
    206, 255, 285, 286, 393
Zanuck, Virginia Fox 286
Zender, Gladys 419
Zerbe, Jerome 493
Zetterling, Mai 561
"Ziffel, Arnold" 617
Zog, King of Albania 64, 160
"Zsa Zsa Gabor: The Original Fame Seeker"
    701
"Zsa Zsa in the Rosy Glow of Dawn" 656
Zugsmith, Albert 434

752

BLOOD MOON PRODUCTIONS

Entertainment About How America Interprets Its Celebrities

Blood Moon Productions is a New York-based publishing enterprise dedicated to researching, salvaging, and indexing the oral histories of America's entertainment industry.

Reorganized with its present name in 2004, Blood Moon originated in 1997 as the Georgia Literary Association, a vehicle for the promotion of obscure writers from America's Deep South. For many years, Blood Moon was a key player in the writing, research, and editorial functions of THE FROMMER GUIDES, the most respected name in travel publishing.

Blood Moon maintains a back list of 30 critically acclaimed biographies, film guides, and novels. Its titles are distributed within North America and Australia by the National Book Network (www.NBNBooks.com), within the U.K. by Turnaround (www.Turnaround-uk.com), and through secondary wholesalers and online retailers everywhere.

Since 2004, Blood Moon has been awarded dozens of nationally recognized literary prizes. They've included both silver and bronze medals from the IPPY (Independent Publishers Assn.) Awards; four nominations and two Honorable Mentions for BOOK OF THE YEAR from Foreword Reviews; nominations from The Ben Franklin Awards; and Awards and Honorable Mentions from the New England, the Los Angeles, the Paris, the New York, the San Francisco, and the Hollywood Book Festivals. Two of its titles have been Grand Prize Winners for Best Summer Reading, as defined by The Beach Book Awards.

For more about us, including access to a growing number of videotaped book trailers and public addresses, each accessible via **YouTube.com.** (Search for key words "Danforth Prince" or "Blood Moon Productions.")

Or click on **WWW.BLOODMOONPRODUCTIONS.COM;** visit our page on Facebook; subscribe to us on Twitter (#BloodyandLunar); or refer to the pages which immediately follow.

Thanks for your interest, best wishes, and happy reading.

Danforth Prince, President
Blood Moon Productions, Ltd.
July, 2013

PINK TRIANGLE

The Feuds and Private Lives of Tennessee Williams,
Gore Vidal, Truman Capote,
and Famous Members of their Entourages

Darwin Porter

Available in November of 2013
Softcover, 528 pages, with photos   ISBN 978-1-936003-37-2
Also available for e-readers

The *enfants terribles* of America at mid-20th century challenged the sexual censors of their day while indulging in "bitchfests" for love, glory, and boyfriends.

This book exposes their literary slugfests and offers an intimate look at their relationships with the glitterati—Jaqueline Onassis, MM, Brando, the Paleys, a gaggle of other movie stars and millionaires, and dozens of others.

This is for anyone who's interested in the formerly concealed scandals of Hollywood and Broadway, and the values and pretentions of both the literary world and the entertainment industry.

Within its pages, celebrity biographer Darwin Porter takes Myra Breckinridge on a rocky, Cold-Blooded ride on A Streetcar Named Desire.

ABOUT THE AUTHOR:

Darwin Porter, himself an unrepentant *enfant terrible*, moved through the entourages of this Pink Triangle with impunity for several decades of their heyday. In November of 2013, he'll release a book about it.

"Every literate person in America has strong ideas about The Pink Triangle. This *exposé* of its members' feuds, vanities, and idiosyncracies will be required reading if you're interested in the literary climate of 'The American Century.'"

—Danforth Prince

INSIDE LINDA LOVELACE'S DEEP THROAT

DEGRADATION, PORNO CHIC, AND THE RISE OF FEMINISM

DARWIN PORTER

A Bronx-born brunette, the notorious Linda Lovelace was the starry-eyed Catholic daughter in the 1950s of a local cop who called her "Miss Holy Holy." Twenty years later, she became the most notorious actress of the 20th century.

She'd fallen in love with a tough ex-Marine, Chuck Traynor, and eventually married him, only to learn that she had become his meal ticket. He forced her at gunpoint into a role as a player within hardcore porn, including a 1971 bestiality film entitled *Dogarama.*

Her next film, shot for $20,000, was released in 1972 as *Deep Throat.* It became the largest grossing XXX-rated flick of all time, earning an estimated $750 million and still being screened all over the world. The fee she was paid was $1,200, which her husband confiscated. The sexy 70s went wild for the film. Porno chic was born, with Linda as its centerpiece.

Traynor, a sadist, pimped his wife to celebrities, charging them $2,000 per session, It became a status symbol to commission an "individualized" film clip of Linda performing her specialty. Clients included Elvis Presley, Frank Sinatra, Milton Berle, Desi Arnaz, Marlon Brando, William Holden, Peter Lawford, and Burt Lancaster. The Mafia had found its most lucrative business—pornography—since Prohibition.

After a decade of being assaulted, beaten, and humiliated, Linda, in 1980, underwent a "Born Again" transformation. She launched her own feminist anti-pornography movement, attracting such activists as Gloria Steinem, and scores of other sex industry professionals who refuted their earlier careers.

Critics claimed that Linda's *Deep Throat* changed America's sexual attitudes more than anything since the first Kinsey report in 1948, that she super-charged the feminist movement, and that to some degree, she re-defined the nation's views on obscenity.

The tragic saga of Linda Lovelace is now a major motion picture. This book tells you what the movie doesn't.

Darwin Porter, *author of more than a dozen critically acclaimed celebrity exposés of behind-the-scenes intrigue in the entertainment industry, was deeply involved in the Linda Lovelace saga as it unfolded in the 70s, interviewing many of the players, and raising money for the legal defense of the film's co-star, Harry Reems. In this book, he brings inside information and a never-before-published revelation on almost every page.*

The Most Comprehensive Biography of an Adult Entertainment Star Ever Written
Softcover, 640 pages, 6"x9", with hundreds of photos. ISBN 978-1-936003-33-4

How the FBI and its G-Men Investigated Hollywood

Darwin Porter's saga of power and corruption has a revelation on every page—cross dressing, gay parties, sexual indiscretions, hustlers for sale, alliances with the Mafia, and criminal activity by the nation's chief law enforcer.

It's all here, with chilling details about the abuse of power on the dark side of the American saga. But mostly it's the decades-long love story of America's two most powerful men who could tell presidents "how to skip rope." (Hoover's words.)

Winner of 2012 literary awards from the **Los Angeles** and the **Hollywood Book Festivals**

"**EVERYONE'S DREDGING UP J. EDGAR HOOVER.** Leonardo DiCaprio just immortalized him, and now comes Darwin Porter's paperback, *J. Edgar Hoover & Clyde Tolson: Investigating the Sexual Secrets of America's Most Famous Men and Women.*

It shovels Hoover's darkest secrets dragged kicking and screaming from the closet. It's filth on every VIP who's safely dead and some who are still above ground."

—**Cindy Adams, The New York Post**

"This book is important, because it destroys what's left of Hoover's reputation. Did you know he had intel on the bombing of Pearl Harbor, but he sat on it, making him more or less responsible for thousands of deaths? Or that he had almost nothing to do with the arrests or killings of any of the 1930s gangsters that he took credit for catching?

"A lot of people are angry with its author, Darwin Porter. They say that his outing of celebrities is just cheap gossip about dead people who can't defend themselves. I suppose it's because Porter is destroying carefully constructed myths that are comforting to most people. As gay men, we benefit the most from Porter's work, because we know that except for AIDS, the closet was the most terrible thing about the 20th century. If the closet never existed, neither would Hoover. The fact that he got away with such duplicity under eight presidents makes you think that every one of them was a complete fool for tolerating it."

—**Paul Bellini, FAB Magazine (Toronto)**

J. Edgar Hoover and Clyde Tolson

Investigating the Sexual Secrets of America's Most Famous Men and Women
Darwin Porter
Softcover, 564 pages, with photos   ISBN 978-1-936003-25-9.   Also available for E-Readers

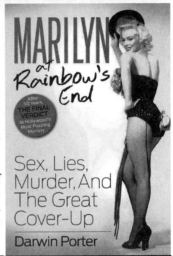

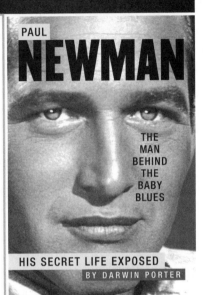